Non-executive Director's Handbook

Non-executive Director's Handbook

Glynis D. Morris, BA, FCA

and

Professor Patrick Dunne, BSc, MBA

Amsterdam • Boston • Heidelberg • London • New York • Oxford
Paris • San Diego • San Francisco • Singapore • Sydney • Tokyo
CIMA Publishing is an imprint of Elsevier

CIMA Publishing is an imprint of Elsevier
Linacre House, Jordan Hill, Oxford OX2 8DP, UK
30 Corporate Drive, Suite 400, Burlington, MA 01803, USA

First edition 2003; Second edition 2008

British Library Cataloguing-in-Publication Data
A catalogue record for this book is available from the British Library

Library of Congress Cataloging-in-Publication Data
A catalog record for this book is available from the Library of Congress

ISBN: 978-0-7506-8419-4

For information on all CIMA publications
visit our Web site at www.books.elsevier.com

Typeset by Charon Tec Ltd (A Macmillan Company), Chennai, India
www.charontec.com

Working together to grow
libraries in developing countries

www.elsevier.com | www.bookaid.org | www.sabre.org

ELSEVIER   BOOK AID
International   Sabre Foundation

Contents

Foreword

I was delighted to be asked to write the foreword for this second edition of the Non-executive Director's Handbook. In the foreword to the first edition, which was published in 2003, I commented that:

> 'The expectations of investors, the media, regulators and the demands of code-writers have risen sharply. As a consequence the need for those taking on the role to be fully informed as to best practice has never been greater.'

That comment is even more to the point today. Expectations continue to rise and the pressures on directors have increased, most evidently in the USA but also in the UK.

The success of the first edition of this book was no surprise. It filled a gap in the literature and its layout, practical approach and plain language in dealing with complex issues contrasted with much that had previously been written on the subject.

I have had the pleasure to work with some excellent non-executives in a broad range of businesses, from fledgling start-ups to FTSE 100 worldwide market leaders. As Chairman of 3i Group I have also witnessed the tremendous value that high quality Chairmen and Directors can add to small and mid-sized businesses. Our focus at 3i is on maximising the potential of businesses whether they are in a start up, growth or buy-out phase and on helping these businesses achieve their ambitions in a responsible way.

When reflecting in 2003 on the common characteristics of the best directors I had known I said that it had become clear to me that their defining qualities related to their 'knowledge, judgment and influencing skills'. Today I would add 'energy and engagement', as the commitment required of non-executives has never been greater. But that, perhaps, is what continues to make the role interesting and professionally rewarding.

The speed of change in the regulatory environment makes this second edition a welcome update to what has become a classic, and will undoubtedly prove as useful as the first.

Baroness Hogg
Chairman 3i Group plc

About the Authors

Glynis D Morris BA, FCA

After taking an Honours degree in German Language and Literature at the University of Manchester, Glynis Morris trained with KPMG in Leeds and qualified as a chartered accountant in 1979. She spent 20 years with the firm, working in their offices in Leeds, London and Cambridge and gaining wide experience of both listed companies and groups and smaller private businesses. She specialised in technical and research work for a number of years, developing technical material for internal use and also for distribution to clients, and speaking regularly at conferences on accounting and company law issues. She became a partner in the firm in 1991, with a particular expertise in work in the education and charity sectors.

She left KPMG to set up her own practice near Cambridge in January 1996, providing accounting, audit and tax services to range of local clients as well as writing and lecturing extensively on accounting, auditing, company law and corporate governance issues. She relocated to mid-Wales in 2006 and now operates her practice from there.

She is the author of 'Finance Director's Handbook', 'Tolley's Manual of Accounting', 'UK Accounting Practice' and 'An Accountant's Guide to Risk Management'. She also contributes to a number of other company law publications and writes regularly for professional websites, newsletters and magazines.

Professor Patrick Dunne BSc, MBA

Patrick is Communications Director for 3i Group plc, a world leader in private equity and venture capital. 3i is an FTSE100 company, invests across Europe, Asia and the USA and has been a pioneer in board practice in the private equity industry.

He joined 3i in 1985 and his career has also involved making and managing investments and, building up 3i's unique people programmes for chairman, chief executives and non-executive directors. These programmes have been responsible for several thousand appointments to boards across the world. Today he is responsible for 3i's external and internal communications globally including investor relations.

Patrick is a regular speaker and commentator on boardroom issues internationally and was a member of the Higgs review group in the UK and has written several books on the subject. These include 'Running Board Meetings' first published in 1997 and now in its third edition and 'Directors Dilemmas' first published in 2000.

He is a member of the General Council of Warwick University, a Visiting Professor at Cranfield School of Management, an associate fellow at Warwick business School, a Visiting Fellow of Kingston University and a member of the CBI's London Council. Patrick is also Chairman of the charity LEAP – Confronting Conflict, the UK's leading organisation in the field of helping young adults to deal with conflict.

Disclaimer

Whilst every care has been taken to ensure the accuracy of the contents of this work, no responsibility for any loss occasioned to any person acting or refraining from action as a result of any statement or examples in it can be accepted by any of the authors or the publisher.

Preface

As Baroness Hogg has said in her foreword, the role of the non-executive has become ever more demanding and a quick scan through our list of contents bears this out. To be an effective non-executive requires a high level of judgement and skill and an increasing amount of knowledge. The aim of this book is to provide a comprehensive reference point for non-executives no matter how experienced they are.

Throughout the book we will refer to the simple model of board effectiveness below.

This model was developed by one of the authors as a process for increasing effectiveness in underperforming boards.

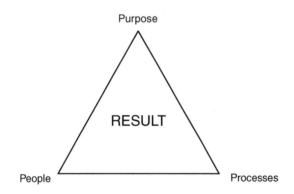

The premise of the model is that any board can increase its effectiveness by considering these three fundamental aspects. In high performing boards all members are clear on what the purpose of the board is, the membership of the board fits that purpose and the board has good processes in place to ensure it has the right strategy, the right resources and the right governance.

It is a good challenge for any prospective non-executive to question the current state of the board they are considering joining and also how they may be able to contribute in enhancing the performance of the board as well as the company.

We have researched widely to discover latest best practice drawing on the many surveys on the role of non-executives as well as the excellent guidance notes available from organisations such as the Institute of Chartered Secretaries and the National Association of Pension Funds.

The first edition of this book was published in the wake of Sir Derek Higgs' review of the role and effectiveness of non-executives in 2003. At the time there was much speculation about what the long-term effects of this review would be. The debate in the press fuelled by a number of naive zealots on the subject and some high profile autocratic chairman, who felt that some of the suggestions were the thin end of the wedge, was heated.

However, the reality has been that the Higgs review was a good evolutionary contribution to effective governance. Almost all of his recommendations have been adopted without causing unnecessary bureaucracy, and the UK's 'principles and comply or explain' philosophy has proven to be far more effective than the more legalistic and rules-based philosophy adopted in the USA. Indeed in a Korn Ferry survey in 2005, 58% of the US directors surveyed felt Sarbanes Oxley should be repealed or overhauled.

Whilst the book has been written with UK directors principally in mind we believe the principles covered are applicable internationally. However we have also included a brief summary of the major differences in the way that boards operate in different countries.

The Appointment Process for Non-executives

1.1 Introduction

1 The Appointment Process for Non-executives

1.1 Introduction

> **At a Glance**
> * The role of non-executive director must be clear and agreed before inviting candidates to apply.
> * The new non-executive needs to be prepared for the workload that awaits them, and should consider any training and development opportunities available.
> * The board should follow a standard process for recruiting a non-executive, and be rigorous in their assessment.
> * Hiring a non-executive should be followed up by a thorough induction and review process.

The appointment process of any new board member must be considered in the context of the board as a whole and take into account the specifics of the particular organisation involved. It also needs to be considered from the perspectives of the company, the non-executive, other board members and shareholders.

From the company's point of view the process is usually:

* agreement of the role;
* commitment to a selection and appointment process and
* execution of that process up to and including the induction of the new board member.

From the prospective non-executive's perspective the process is:

* response to an approach from a company or a company's adviser;
* initial familiarisation and agreement to take part in the selection process;
* if selected, detailed due diligence;
* formal appointment and
* induction.

For shareholders in public companies who aren't on the board the process has traditionally been very straightforward and limited to formally agreeing to the resolution to appoint the person.

In order to comply with the Combined Code the boards of listed companies must ensure that the process is 'formal and transparent'. However the reality has been that shareholders, other than those who are directors, have had little or no input to the appointment process, other than in situations of crisis. Indeed, research conducted for the Higgs Review (see **CHAPTER 6**) led to the view that 'a high degree of informality surrounds the process of appointing non-executive directors. Almost half of the non-executive directors surveyed for the Review were recruited to their role through personal contacts or friendships. Only 4% had a formal interview, and 1% had obtained their job through answering an advertisement'.

Quite the opposite is true for private equity and venture capital businesses where the investors traditionally play an active role in the directors. In other private companies the key shareholders are normally involved as described above for the company.

At this stage matters will be kept simple by considering the issues with regard to a single appointment in a public company and going through the process comprehensively from the company's point of view.

Issues relating to multiple appointments at the same time are dealt with in **PARAGRAPH 1.3.3**. Private companies can easily adapt the process described omitting the obvious steps which a public company must take simply because it is listed. Looking at the process from the company's point of view is beneficial to the non-executive, especially if they also sit on a nominations committee, but some issues for prospective non-executives and candidates for specific appointments have also been added at the end.

If there is an effective nominations committee (see **CHAPTER 16**) then it is this group which is likely to be delegated to undertake or lead all of the above tasks. The remainder of the board then simply needs to endorse or refine their recommendations and support the process.

If there isn't a nominations committee of the board then it is well worth considering forming one on a temporary basis for the particular appointment. The principles of a good nominations committee are easily adapted to small companies.

1.2   Agreeing the Role

If the role of the board is clear then defining the role of the non-executive becomes a relatively straightforward task. A good place to start, if the basic description of the role of the board are accepted as being:

- Right strategy:
  To ensure that there is the right strategy for the ownership as well as the business, that it is being implemented and monitored and that there is a good process for formulating and adapting it.
- Right resources:
  To ensure that the organisation has the right resources in place to meet the agreed strategy for the business and its ownership. The most important of these resources relate to people and money.
- Right governance:
  To ensure appropriate corporate governance.

is to consider what role it is intended that the non-executive should play in each of the above. The Higgs Review came up with a broadly similar definition which was incorporated into Section A of the Combined Code.

> **The Role of the Board**
> The board is collectively responsible for promoting the success of the company by directing and supervising the company's affairs.
> The board's role is to provide entrepreneurial leadership of the company within a framework of prudent and effective controls which enable risk to be assessed and managed.
> The board should set the company's strategic aims, ensure that the necessary financial and human resources are in place for the company to meet its objectives, and review management performance.
> The board should set the company's values and standards and ensure that its obligations to its shareholders and others are understood and met.

They will need to fit the strategy for the business, the strategy for the ownership and of course with the board you have or are in the process of building.

They will also need to share or be able to work with the board's belief in whom they are working for. Reference is made in **CHAPTER 3** to Prof. Jay Lorsch's book *Pawns and Potentates* which has a very good description of the range of beliefs that directors have on this subject. For example, some believe absolutely in shareholder primacy whilst others subscribe to the model which is very common in continental Europe, that is, co-determination.

In practice the non-executive role is a complex one in which different aspects come to the fore at different times. The chart below is a summary of what one highly experienced non-executive believes he actually does.

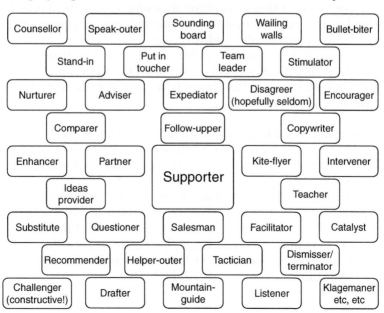

The reason *Supporter* is given such prominence is that the individual believed very strongly that unless he was seen as such by the CEO and executive directors of the company he would be unable to have sufficient influence when restraint was required.

What is clearly required is an approach which takes into account the generic qualities one might look for in a non-executive as well as the specific knowledge, skills, behaviours and potential pertaining to the particular circumstance.

1.3 Defining the Role and Developing the Candidate Specification

Clarity about the role of the board makes it easier to clarify the role of the chairman or non-executive you are seeking. With this description it is then possible to develop a set of requisite competencies and experiences which candidates should have. All of which makes it easier to conduct a search and manage the process.

In CHAPTER 3 the generic role of the chairman is defined as follows:

1.3.1 Role of Chairman

- To organise the composition, business and efficiency of the board.
- To lead the board in the determination of its strategy and in the achievement of its objectives.
- To ensure that the board has accurate and clear visibility of results and likely future trends.
- To ensure that board committees are properly established, composed and operated.
- To ensure effective relationships are maintained with all major stakeholders in the business, that is, customers, shareholders, employees, suppliers, government, local community, industry, etc.
- To enhance the company's public standing and reputation.
- To develop a strong working relationship with the chief executive/managing director and ensure that there is a clear definition and agreement of the division of responsibilities.

All of which is underpinned with good judgement of people and commercial situations and the possession of strong influencing interpersonal skills. Again this description is consistent with that proposed by the Higgs Review for listed companies.

The importance of a clear definition and agreement of the division of responsibilities between the chairman and the chief executive cannot be understated and this is dealt with in more detail in CHAPTER 3.

It is now uncommon in large plcs for the roles to be combined, with the exception of a temporary period where the chairman has fired the chief executive and is fulfilling the role on an interim basis.

The percentage of FTSE 100 companies with separate chairman and chief executives has been over 90% for many years and there is also a trend for the role to be split in the US. However there is still a marked difference. For example, Russell Reynolds 2006 survey on the subject showed that the percentage in S&P 500 companies although increasing was still only 29%. The proportion in NASDAQ companies was higher at 45%, possibly because more of these companies had been venture capital or private equity backed prior to flotation. The survey also showed that the Eurtop100 was closer to the UK with the role split in 79% of companies.

Research conducted for the Higgs Review found that only five FTSE 100 companies, and 11% of companies outside the FTSE 350 has a joint chairman/ chief executive.

1.3.2 Role of Non-executive

In **CHAPTER 3** the role has been split into two components 'Ensuring' and 'Adding Value'. It is believed that the non-executive who adds significant value has much greater influence with the other directors and is therefore much more likely to bring that influence to bear in ensuring that there is good governance.

The role of non-executive director includes ensuring that:

- there is a robust strategy for the ownership and development of the business, that it is regularly monitored and adapted as required;
- the company has the appropriate resources in place to meet its strategy. The two most important being human and financial and
- there is appropriate corporate governance and a high standard of investor relations;

and adding value by:

- being a confidential sounding board to the directors;
- bringing an independent and broad view to the board and
- helping the executive to achieve their business plans in whatever form is relevant given their experience and network.

It goes without saying that everything under 'Ensuring' adds value. This description is again consistent with that conceived in the Higgs Review.

A survey of 3i-backed CEOs across Europe in 2002 showed that what they wanted most from their non-executives was the following. We doubt much has changed since.

At this stage it is also helpful to consider the board team as a whole. An analysis of the current board members in terms of knowledge, skills and behaviours can be helpful in clarifying requirements. If you are going to do this it needs to be done in the context of matching the board against the intended strategy and the succession plans for existing members.

'In your company, in which of the following areas are
non-executive directors principally expected to perform a role?'

Area	Percentage
Strategy of the business	78%
Board appointments	62%
Remuneration policy	56%
Investor relations	50%
Strategy of the ownership	46%
Financial strategy	46%
Financial controls	45%
Coaching the executives	34%
Fund raising	30%
Risk management	28%
Human Resources policy	13%
Finding new customers	12%
Technical input	11%
Other	5%

One approach to developing a candidate specification is to take the role and then consider what core competencies and experiences someone would have to have in order to fit this role in the specific situation concerned.

The core competencies can typically be grouped under the following headings:

- Personal
- Professional and managerial and
- Entrepreneurial.

It should then be a fairly straightforward task to come up with a list of specific questions to ask at interview and in referencing to ascertain whether the candidates possess the requisite competencies. We make the assumption that the reader is a competent interviewer of senior business people but explores some of the differences between interviewing executives and non-executives in **PARAGRAPH 1.11.**

Some examples of competencies and characteristics which might be included within the three headings above are listed below.

1.3.3 *Personal Qualities*

An interviewer will want to know that the candidates possess not just the personal qualities of a good non-executive director but that they will also work well with the team.

Here are some of the key qualities:

- Integrity
- Judgement
- Leadership
- Motivation
- Resilience
- Communicating and influencing style
- Interpersonal sensitivity
- Listening skills
- Intelligence
- Cultural flexibility
- Sense of responsibility
- Independence.

If an interviewer is looking at candidates as potential future successors for the current chairman or for the role of senior independent non-executive then they may also seek more depth in certain of these qualities.

Motivation and capacity are not strictly competencies. Motivation has been included not just because the role has become demanding to execute well but also because the authors believe that an effective non-executive needs to be highly motivated to become sufficiently knowledgeable about the company's business and marketplace. Moreover a significant commitment is required to be sufficiently vigilant in terms of corporate governance.

Capacity is important because to be effective the non-executive has to commit sufficient time to the role, be available at short notice and not be distracted when involved. In the 2007 Independent Remuneration Solutions ('IRS') survey of independent chairman and non-executive directors who held 835 appointments between them the average number of appointments held individually was two and a half. The typical time commitment was two days a month for non-executive roles and three for chairman though there was clearly considerable variance with many chairman spending a day a week.

Independence has become a particularly hot topic in the post Enron, Worldcom and Marconi era. Why? Because of the sensitivities around remuneration, accuracy of financial disclosure and consequences of flawed strategic decisions. The challenges to US investment banks with regard to the way they managed conflicts of interest in the late 1990s bull market added further fuel to fire.

How do people define independence? One widely used definition is:

'Capable of exercising objective judgement'.

This definition is used by a number of leading institutional investors including CALPERS. The UK's NAPF has a more detailed definition which we have included in the APPENDICES and according to their survey 82% of the top 400 UK listed companies met this definition. It is based on describing what doesn't constitute independence, for example, if the individual was formerly an executive or is paid by the company in any capacity other than as a non-executive director.

The Higgs Report to the government in January 2003 defined independence as follows.

Independence

A non-executive director is considered independent when the board determines that the director is independent in character and judgement and there are no relationships or circumstances which could affect, or appear to affect, the director's judgement.

Such relationships or circumstances would include where the director:

- is a former employee of the company or group until five years after employment (or any other material connection) has ended;
- has, or has had within the last three years, a material business relationship with the company either directly, or as a partner, shareholder, director or senior employee of a body that has such a relationship with the company;
- has received or receives additional remuneration from the company apart from a director's fee, participates in the company's share option or a performance-related pay scheme, or is a member of the company's pension scheme;
- has close family ties with any of the company's advisers, directors or senior employees;
- holds cross-directorships or has significant links with other directors through involvement in other companies or bodies;
- represents a significant shareholder or
- has served on the board for more than 10 years.

The board should identify in its annual report the non-executive directors it determines to be independent. The board should state its reasons if a director is considered to be independent notwithstanding the existence of relationships or circumstances which may appear relevant to its determination.

1.3.4 *Professional and Managerial Qualities*

In order to fulfil the role well the candidate will need to be professionally competent, knowledgeable and experienced in a number of obvious areas, such as:

- strategy;
- technical;
- organisational;
- analytical;
- problem solving;
- chairing and
- committee membership.

At 3i there is a strong preference for independent directors to be experienced chairmen, CEOs or finance directors so that they have encountered the professional and commercial situations that the executives are likely to encounter.

Technical knowledge means the knowledge of issues relating to being a director, for example, in the accounting and legal area, as well as a current knowledge of best business practice. In addition if the business is of a highly technical nature itself then the non-executive may require specific professional experience to be able to make informed judgements and communicate effectively with the rest of the board.

1.3.5 *Entrepreneurial Qualities*

Entrepreneurialism is a much used word but seldom defined. For the purposes of this handbook it will be defined as being about 'capturing the value associated with a commercial opportunity'.

Entrepreneurialism is usually associated with people who enjoy making money and are strongly profit motivated. So what are entrepreneurial competencies?

- *Vision*: Seeing the opportunity.
- *Judgement*: Deciding whether the opportunity has significant value potential.
- *Conviction*: Preparedness to listen, but also not to be swayed by every opinion. To have a point of view and be prepared to stand up for it but also to take advice.
- *Decisiveness*: Being prepared to seize opportunities, and prepared to recognise and act on mistakes.
- *Commercial acumen*: Especially in terms of understanding value and timing.

In the authors' view these competencies or characteristics are relevant whatever the context of the business.

Interestingly a survey of the CEOs of 3i-backed businesses in the autumn of 2002 produced the following response to the question:

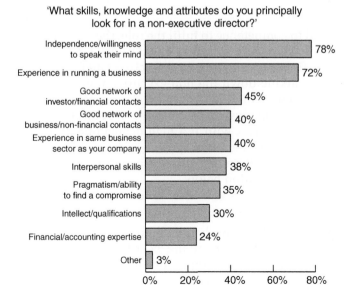

'What skills, knowledge and attributes do you principally look for in a non-executive director?'

Independence/willingness to speak their mind	78%
Experience in running a business	72%
Good network of investor/financial contacts	45%
Good network of business/non-financial contacts	40%
Experience in same business sector as your company	40%
Interpersonal skills	38%
Pragmatism/ability to find a compromise	35%
Intellect/qualifications	30%
Financial/accounting expertise	24%
Other	3%

In summary, by going through the process of considering the context of the business and the core competencies and characteristics sought, a detailed candidate specification is straightforward to prepare.

1.4 Issues for Prospective Non-executives or Candidates for Appointments

Firstly, standing back from particular situation, it is worth anyone considering embarking upon a career as a non-executive addressing some basic questions such as these:

- Why do you want to take on these types of roles?
- Do you have the basic competencies to be effective?
- What will be your general approach and attitude to the role?
- What additional training do you require?
- Do you understand the risks involved?
- What sort of companies would be most appropriate?
- Can you organise the logistics and manage to fulfil other existing roles?
- Have you considered the financial and tax issues involved?
- If you are an executive in an existing business what will the likely reaction be amongst your existing colleagues, shareholders and press?
- How will you put yourself in the position to be considered for suitable positions?

Motivations vary but usually comprise one or all of the following:

- To learn through different roles or different types of business.
- For the retiring senior executive to keep involved in business.
- For those planning to retire in the medium term a non-executive role is a good step towards that transition.
- For the active executive, personal development.
- Prestige.
- Compensation.

With regard to competence to fulfil the role, the generic competencies and characteristics have been covered at **PARAGRAPHS 1.3.1–1.3.4**. There are however some specific issues relating to the active chief executive or other full-time director embarking down the non-executive route for the first time, for example, time commitment. The CEO role today especially in a public company is a very demanding one logistically. Degree of control is another issue. The chief executive's role carries with it a high degree of authority and status within a company. The non-executive's power is derived more from influence. Some CEOs find this transition difficult or frustrating. We cover some general observations on role transition below.

A number of factors will determine a candidate's approach and attitude to the role and these are:

- the experience they have had with non-executives in other situations;
- their views on the role of the board and in particular who they think they are working, for example, do they believe in shareholder primacy or

co-determination? This is discussed in greater detail at the beginning of CHAPTER 3;

- the stance they adopt with the executive, for example, oversight, control or collaborator;
- the influence of external perception for example the press and
- their personality.

For a particular appointment what due diligence should a candidate undertake before accepting an offer to join the board?

PARAGRAPH 1.18 provides a good list of basic information candidates will need. Other things that need to be understood are:

- the owner's agenda;
- the strategy;
- how comfortable candidates are with the people;
- the financial position of the company and the key systems and controls;
- the quality of board processes; and
- the reality of joining a board and an awareness that not everything may be up to the expected standards.

For some public company boards have become less attractive to join than they used to be. The main challenge from those no longer attracted to plc positions relates to the balance between risk and reward. This may arise from a combination of greater actual risk but also greater awareness of the risks following Higgs.

Why were venture capital and private equity businesses so popular? Possibly because the VC and private equity firms are more realistic in their expectations, the rewards through having an equity interest are greater and the shareholders' objectives are clearer.

For those preparing for their first non-executive role it is well worth considering the chart below from a piece of work by Chris Parker and Ralph Lewis at Cranfield over 20 years ago. It was called '*Moving up... How to handle transitions to senior levels successfully*'. Although written clearly for executive transitions it is just as relevant for those moving into a non-executive role for the first time. Parker and Lewis came up with what they called the *transition curve* (see below).

The transition rollercoaster

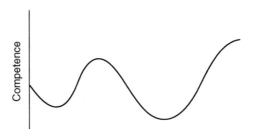

Competence

Time ⟶

Interestingly whenever 3i has conducted research into what happens to managers involved in management buy outs through the buyout process it follows a similar pattern. This has been labelled *'the emotional rollercoaster'*.

Parker and Lewis describe eight stages to the transition for those that get through it. We have adapted these for the non-executive.

Rosy positive picture	*'It's going to be fantastic'.* This stage is usually before you start. The position has been oversold. You may have had less time for due diligence than you would have ideally liked.
Immobilisation	*'This isn't the job they told me it would be'.* Natural feelings of shock. You become overwhelmed. There has been a serious mismatch between expectations and reality.
Disbelief	*'I'm not having this, they'll have to sort it out'.* Temporary retreat. It's someone else's responsibility to help me. False competence. I'll just carry on doing what I'm good at. Better explain why so 'In my last company we …'
Incompetence	*'Now everything is going wrong, it could be me'.* Awareness of the need to change. Frustration at not knowing what to do. Sink or swim time.
Accept reality	*'Forget what's happened. I've got to sort this out'.* Let go of the past. I can see where I am going wrong. I need to find the solution.
Testing	*'I think this might work'.* High energy. Determination to find the way out. Anger at the fact you have to and for all the false starts. Wonder if this is the way we should do it?
Search for meaning	*'Hey it's working'.* Understanding how it all fits together. Figuring out what works. Post-rationalising a little experimental success.
Integration	*'Everyone else thinks so as well'.* Getting your act together. Gaining credibility. Doing it naturally with people. Understanding why.

For situations where there are multiple new appointments simultaneously several people could be experiencing this at the same time. What happens if they all reach the valley of incompetence together? The rollercoaster doesn't fit everything but the basic principles are interesting. Just by thinking about this beforehand helps.

For executives taking on their first non-executive role this could be particularly appropriate. As could considering some of the training and development options described in **CHAPTER 19**.

Where there are multiple appointments being made at the same time a number of other factors need to be taken into account. Namely that there will obviously be a bigger impact on the team dynamic. Care will be needed to ensure that the different candidate specifications are compatible and induction processes will need adapting.

1.5 Commitment to a Process

In order to gain commitment to a process from the board as a whole there needs to be agreement about what needs doing, who needs to do it and how they are going to do it. A rigorous process inevitably involves a significant time commitment from those involved.

1.6 What Needs Doing?

Normally, the following:

- Developing the role and candidate specifications.
- Agreeing a sourcing and selection process for candidates.
- If relevant selecting a search firm.
- Sourcing, assessing and selecting candidates.
- Offering and agreeing the terms of the appointment.
- Formal approval of new board member.
- Induction and review.

Agreeing the role and developing a candidate specification has been covered above at **PARAGRAPHS 1.2** and **1.3**.

1.7 Agreeing a Sourcing and Selection Process for Candidates

Once the board has a clear idea of the sort of person it is looking for, the next decision concerns the approach it is going to take to sourcing and selecting candidates. The basic approaches to sourcing are one or a mix of the following:

- Using its own network.
- Recommendations from its professional advisers or financial backers.
- Using a professional search firm.

PLCs will almost invariably use a search firm even if they intend using their own networks, advisers or advertising, for the following reasons:

- They need to be able to demonstrate to shareholders that the selection process has been carried out rigorously and objectively.
- A search firm will have access to a wider pool of candidates.
- A search firm should be able to add value in terms of its selection processes.

The 2007 IRS survey of independent chairman and non-executives stated that there had been a significant increase in the use of professional search firms. In larger quoted companies (over £500 million revenue) this had more than doubled to over 90% over approximately the four-year period since the Higgs. However in smaller private companies personal contacts and the company's lawyers and accountants are still the dominant source.

1.8 *Selecting a Search Firm, Sourcing, Assessing and Selecting Candidates*

If a search firm is used they will need to be carefully selected. It may be that the company has an established relationship with a firm who knows the board well and this can be an advantage. However this isn't always the case as the relationship may be too cosy, their skills are in recruiting executives rather than non-executives or they may not have access to the sorts of candidates the company is looking to attract. In any event it is always useful to benchmark them against an alternative.

Let us assume that a company is in the position where it also has to select a search firm, agree their role in the process and how they will be managed. If we're conducting a selection process we will need some criteria for selection and to conduct a beauty parade of potential suppliers.

These are the normal criteria for selection in these circumstances:

- Track record of the firm in the non-executive area relevant to your company.
- Track record of the individual leading the assignment and their research assistant.
- Quality of their processes.
- Ability to deliver within the timeframe you have agreed.
- International capability if relevant.
- Knowledge on compensation issues.
- Strength of their assessment and referencing techniques.
- Fit with your type of business.
- Cost.

The company will also need to know from them who their off-limits clients are. This is usually less of an issue than it is in the executive area.

In terms of conducting a beauty parade there are a number of factors to consider:

- Who from the nominations committee will take part in the selection?
- The board will need to select a small number of appropriate firms, three is usually enough.
- Consideration needs to be given as to how they are going to be paid – fixed fee or success related. For non-executive appointments it is normal for the fee to be fixed and not linked to package as is customary for executive roles.
- Good search consultants will want to be sure that the specification is right so a company should be prepared to be challenged on it and worry about those who don't.

Some good beauty parade questions are:

- What experience do you have of similar appointments?
- Can you give me the names of company chairmen and the non-executives you have found for them and would you be happy for me to call them?

- How is your candidate database organised?
- Would it be possible for one of our staff to visit your offices and see your database?
- What core competencies do you think a non-executive for our business should have?
- What will your role in the process be?
- Can I interview the researcher who will be helping you with this assignment?
- Could you describe your candidate referencing process in detail?
- How attractive a role do you think this will be?
- How will you describe our company to potential candidates?
- How will you describe the role to potential candidates?
- Is this a role you think you will need to advertise for?
- If so what is your process for doing this and what will the associated costs be?
- With regard to cost will it be on a retained or contingent basis?
- Will the cost be linked to the successful candidate's package and if so which elements?
- Will there be compensation if the candidate proves unsuccessful within the first year?

The firm should also be referenced and not just with the referees they provide.

Careful consideration needs to be given to the issue of whether to undertake a discrete targeted search or a more open approach involving advertising for candidates. There has been an increase in the number of companies doing both. Traditionally if search firms were used at all it was for a discrete search and advertising was unusual. Here are some of the issues involved in considering using an advertised approach.

1.9 Advertising

- May take longer because it involves a bigger processing job.
- Is usually done in addition to search so may be more expensive.
- Reaches a broader audience so may attract candidates you would never had access to.
- Is another means of advertising your company and showing you recruit in a professional way.

Once a search firm has been selected for the assignment they will need careful management. The best way to ensure this occurs is to agree a timetable at the outset together with a process for approving expenses and then insist on weekly status reports. The first response from them should include the following:

- Detailed candidate specification.
- Summary of the process to be adopted for fulfilling the assignment.
- Terms and conditions of the search firm for this specific assignment.

An example of a letter from a leading search firm to a new client following a verbal briefing is contained in **APPENDICES**.

1.10   The Gender Issue

According to the 2006 Female FTSE report from Cranfield School of Management women are achieving non-executive positions at a slow but steady pace but are still underrepresented in the boardroom in relation to the percentage of women in the workforce (46%). Of the FTSE 100 companies, only 53 companies have women on their executive committee (the senior team chaired by the CEO), 30 have all male committees and the rest do not reveal their senior executive team.

The report also showed that the total number of female-held directorships was down from 121 in 2005 to 117 in 2006. In the Female FTSE Index, companies with the highest percentage of female board directors include first place Astra-Zeneca (four female NEDS) and second place British Airways (3 NEDS). Lloyds TSB had two female executive directors and two female non-executive directors. Reuters joined Lloyds TSB at the top of the executive committee index with its 33% female executive committee, as well as having two female NEDS.

3i Group remained the only FTSE 100 company with a female chairman.

As part of the research conducted in 2002 for the Higgs Review a census was taken of listed company directors. At the time only 4% of executive director posts and 6% of non-executive posts were held by women. In his published review Sir Derek recommended a widening of the selection pool as a way of making faster progress. It would seem that despite the best intentions progress has been much slower than it should have been despite the fact that the Tyson review set up following Higgs made similar recommendations and generated further momentum for the issue.

As there has been a trend for less executive directors to serve on boards, it is the authors' view that one way in which faster progress could be made is for chairman of nomination committees to consider more women serving on executive committees in addition to those serving on main boards.

1.11   Interviewing Candidates

In this section, comments will focus on the areas of main difference between interviewing executives and non-executives. The authors make the assumption that the reader is an experienced and competent interviewer of the former. The authors make the further assumption that the interviewing process will involve a number of candidates. In their view choice is essential.

The interviewing process is typically defined by:

- Who is doing it?
- How they do it?
- How they interpret what they learn?

With regard to who is doing it for non-executive appointments, where a search firm is involved the process would normally be interviews with:

- the search consultant;
- the chairman of the nominations committee and/or someone delegated by them to undertake the first interview on behalf of the company;
- a series of second interviews with the chairman and chief executive and
- meetings for the purposes of endorsement with as many of the other executives or non-executives as appropriate in the circumstances.

The balance of buying and selling between the company and the applicant may differ significantly in this context and it might well be the case that the candidate requires to meet all of the directors before he is prepared to accept a seat on the board. Clearly then there is a significant time commitment required from both sides. It is therefore important to communicate well with candidates throughout the process and for candidates not chosen to be told as quickly and sensitively as possible.

In terms of the approach taken to interviewing it is recommended that a competency-based approach be adopted that takes into account the seniority of the candidate. The fundamental principles behind a competency-based approach are that it involves structured interviews, significant preparation beforehand, and a focus on evaluating whether the candidate has the knowledge skills and behaviours to undertake the role.

In the authors' experience very senior people have few problems with a rigorous approach being adopted as long as it is respectful and handled in a non-mechanistic way. At this stage in the relationship the approach taken to the interviewing process will be providing the candidate with a view of how seriously the company takes the role and the professionalism with which it approaches senior appointments. Moreover highly successful chief executives or senior executives don't always make good non-executives due to their dominant personalities and egos. If the candidate is not prepared to go through a more rigorous process it should be understood why.

The SAE method of interview is also relevant in this context. The objective of this approach is to find the evidence to demonstrate a competency. Put simply the interviewer asks the candidate to describe a **Situation** which they think may be appropriate, discovers the **Actions** taken by the candidate and then follow through by finding out what the **Effect** was. It makes the referencing process later much easier. Grateful thanks go to Carmel Siverosa from Oxford Consulting Group who first introduced this to one of the authors.

Using actual strategic issues that the company has to explore the likely contribution the prospective non-executive can make is a good way of gathering evidence as to their judgement and influencing style. It may not be appropriate at this stage of the discussions to share the most sensitive issues the company is facing so hypothetical situations may need to suffice.

It is also important to determine the relevance of a candidate's experience and skills to the company. In addition the board will want to test for a compatible belief system about what a board is about, test for potential conflicts of interest and ensure there are no logistical issues which might inhibit performance.

1.12 *Referencing*

Referencing is undertaken principally to calibrate the views derived from the interviewing process and confirm that there is a good fit in terms of competence and compatibility. At the same time it is to ensure that the individual's integrity and reputation meet the required standard.

A referencing process is defined by the following:

- When it is done?
- Who is doing it?
- Who they seek references from?
- What they ask?
- How they ask it?
- How they interpret what they learn?

With regard to who undertakes the referencing this is usually a mix of the chairman of the nominations committee, the company secretary and if relevant the search firm. The chairman of the board as a whole may also want to make his own enquiries.

Most candidates will have provided a list of people they would be willing for the board to contact. The obvious issue if the exercise is confined to these people is that they are inevitably likely to be positive. Most search firms have a database of contacts and the facility to select from that people who worked with, in, or served on the boards of, the same companies as the candidate.

In terms of what to ask, the following provides a useful framework for questions for establishing both competencies to fulfil the role and fit with the team:

- Establish how well the referee really knows the candidate, in what context, how objective the referee is and how qualified the referee is to express a view on non-executive competence.
- Gain information relating to key competencies sought, motivation, capacity, style and weaknesses.
- Probe situational effectiveness of candidate.
- Confirm track record, integrity and reputation.
- Finally always ask the open 'is there anything else you feel I need to know about them' question.

The 'how?' is normally telephone or letter. The phone is much more powerful. Whatever the method good preparation is the key and it is always advisable to prepare a question plan and a sheet to record views under the key headings.

In addition to the above it is now normal for qualification and credit checks to be performed. The search firm will generally undertake this as part of their referencing process. One thing it is very important to remember when recording personal information is the requirements of the *Data Protection Act 1998*.

The decision as to when you undertake referencing in reality is down to the specific circumstances. Typically a degree of informal referencing will take place before candidates are met with the more formal and rigorous elements taking place later in the process.

Finally it is important to remember to get back properly to unsuccessful candidates, they could still be very useful contacts for the business or your next non-executive director.

1.13 *Who Needs to Do What?*

The chairman of the nominations committee should be leading the process and ensuring that the board is well informed and appropriately involved. The operation of nominations committees is covered in CHAPTER 16. One interesting aspect is the role of the chairman of the board and the CEO. The quality of the chairman and CEO and their attitude to the appointment has a significant influence on its attractiveness to candidates.

1.14 *Offering and Agreeing the Terms of the Appointment*

An appointment will typically be offered subject to formal approval by the board (see below).

According to the 2007 IRS survey of independent chairman and non-executives 80% of those surveyed signed three-year agreements compared to just over 50% in 2002.

CHAPTER 9 covers remuneration and benefits in more detail but some summary comments are made here.

1.15 Compensation

We will confine ourselves here simply to the process of determining what will be the appropriate remuneration for the non-executive. CHAPTER 9 contains comprehensive data on current rates for particular profiles of situation.

The nominations committee and the remuneration committee should already have an agreed package for the non-executives with details on all the components of the package. These will normally include:

- A basic fee based on an assumed time commitment.
- An additional fee payable for membership of board committees.
- An agreed basis of payment for circumstances where the director's time commitment is significantly greater than originally envisaged, for example, during a takeover, initial public offering, etc.
- A description of allowable expenses and the process for claiming them.
- Clarity over directors' and officers' liability insurance, that is, whether it is paid for by the company or the individual and the details of the cover provided. According to the 2007 IRS survey such cover was provided in 93% of appointments. However it was only considered adequate in 85% of appointments. It is also worth noting that the Combined Code states that 'The company should arrange appropriate insurance cover in respect of legal action against its directors'. See CHAPTER 13 for more information relating to directors' and officers' liability insurance.

- A proposal regarding obtaining equity in the company where relevant for example in venture capital or private equity backed businesses.
- Services provided by the company to enable the director to carry out his duties (e.g. access to legal advice).

If they do and this has been recently reviewed then this should be the starting point of a proposal to the candidate. If they don't then **CHAPTER 9** covers how to develop a remuneration scheme for non-executives.

It is important to be clear and realistic about the time commitment expected of the non-executive and have arrangements in place for circumstances when there may well be significantly more input required.

Number of days – Company turnover (£m)	<10	11–30	31–100	101–500	501–1000	1000+
Independent directors						
Formal meetings						
Board	7	8	9	9	9	9
Strategy, budget, other	1	3	2	3	3	3
Preparation and contact	3	4	4	4	4	5
Sub-committees						
Audit	2	3	3	3	4	4
Remuneration	1	2	3	3	3	3
Nominations	0	1	1	1	2	3
Co-visits and research	1	1	1	2	2	2
Total	15	20	20	22	25	27
Chairman						
Additional days	3	4	4	6	7	9
Preparation and contact	1	4	4	5	6	8
Total	19	28	28	33	38	44

Once it has been decided what will be paid and how, the next thing to decide is whether this is discussed directly or through the search firm. Usually this will all have been agreed at the beginning of the process, the search firm will have clear parameters in which to operate and the package will have been communicated to candidates at the start of the process.

For most sizeable businesses remuneration consultants will have been consulted to ensure that executive and non-executive remuneration is comparable to similar organisations. For smaller organisations there are a number of surveys which can be used as reference points including the annual 3i Independent Remuneration Solutions Independent Chairman and Non-Executive Director Survey. The company's lawyers, accountants and, if it has them, venture backers should also be able to provide guidance.

1.16 *Formal Approval of New Board Member*

If the board has a nomination committee, the process for the particular appointment is likely to have been approved at an earlier board meeting. It is also normal for the recruitment process to include interviews of the prospective new board member by the chairman, chief executive and other members of the board. Good non-executives often won't accept the offer to join the board until they have met the entire board. Therefore at the point the nominations committee is making its recommendation to the board as a whole, the candidate is likely to have been met by most or all of the board. Approval is therefore likely to be a formality.

Other issues to consider at this stage are notifications which it will be necessary to make, for example, stock exchange, bank and the press. In venture capital and private equity backed situation the investors are normally actively involved in the process and, if on the board, likely to be a member of the nominations committee.

1.17   *Induction Process*

One of the major challenges any new non-executive faces is how to gain sufficient familiarity with the business and its markets to make informed judgements. The quality of the induction process will have a significant influence on their success in meeting this challenge. So what are the objectives of a good induction process, what should the non-executive gain familiarity with first and how should the process be organised?

1.18   Objectives of a Good Induction Process

There are two key objectives and these are:

- to gain sufficient knowledge to make well-informed judgements and
- to build relationships with the key players to gain the influence to bring those judgements to bear.

In the authors' view the induction process should be planned and agreed before the appointment is formalised and then summarised in the appointment letter (see **APPENDICES**). The following is an extract of the relevant section from such a letter. As can be seen this involves a considerable volume of material to read and absorb.

1.19   How will the Non-executive Director Will Gain Familiarity with the Business?

Obviously you will have already been provided with extensive information in order for you to make an informed decision in accepting our offer to join the board. However for ease of reference and completeness we are delighted to include the enclosed pack which includes the following:

- Summary of key shareholders.
- Description of our key business activities with strategy and business model summaries for each.
- Board agendas, papers and minutes for the last 12 months.

- Schedule of matters reserved for the board.
- Board calendar for the next 12 months together with a list of key dates.
- Copies of the last five years' audited accounts, together with the management letters from our auditors.
- Summary of our key profit recognition policies.
- Our budget document for the current year.
- Management accounts and commentary for the year to date.
- A selection of our latest promotional literature for the key parts of the business.
- Copies for the last year's staff magazines.
- Press cuttings for the last (relevant period).
- Our latest strategic plan document including the detailed plans for our major business units.
- A summary list of all of our subsidiary companies and a brief statement of their purpose and current financial and legal position.
- An organisational chart together with CVs and contact details for the members of the board.
- Investor relations strategy paper.
- A summary list of our key banking arrangements including the key covenants.
- Copies of the investment agreements between the company and our venture capital backers.
- (If public company) copies of our brokers' reports for the last two years.
- A list of the company's key advisers and their contact details. Incidentally we will write to them all notifying them of your appointment once it has been formalised.
- Memorandum and Articles of Association.
- Description of the review process for our non-executives.

We are delighted to let you know that we have now arranged the following induction schedule for you:

- Meetings with key business unit leaders.
- Meeting with chairman and chief executive to agree objectives for the year ahead.
- Meetings with company's key advisers.
- Attendance at company's sales conference in Harrogate on 1 December.
- Attendance at board's strategy away day on 15 December.

1.20   *Review Process*

The simplest way to review the performance of a new director is to ensure that they become part of the board's overall performance management system. The key elements of this for an individual director in most systems are:

- objectives set at appointment and reviewed annually with the chairman;
- a formal review after the first three months;

- feedback gathered by the chairman from the directors and other parties as relevant;
- that the non-executive is expected to give 360 degree feedback on other board members including the chairman and
- an annual review meeting is held with the chairman. This is a two-way meeting enabling the chairman to give feedback on performance, the non-executive and the chairman to set objectives for coming year and for the non-executive to give feedback to chairman.

The execution of this process is described in more detail in **APPENDICES**.

'Some guidance on how to do this in practice is contained in the Performance Evaluation Guidance' section of **APPENDICES**. Essentially the Combined Code for listed companies states that:

> 'The Board should undertake a formal and rigorous annual evaluation of its own performance and that of its committees and individual directors'.

Companies have adopted a variety of methods when conducting these evaluations and the majority in the UK have preferred to do this for themselves rather than use independent advisers. ICSA's Review of 2006 Annual Reports of UK Listed Companies, on Board Performance Evaluation, stated that less than a quarter of the biggest 200 UK listed companies used external advisers when performing board performance evaluations in 2005 and 2006. However of the companies surveyed, all but four were undertaking some kind of board evaluation in line with Principle A6 of the Combined Code.

The board also needs to set time aside each year to review its own operation.

Audit Matters

2 Audit Matters

2.1 Audit Committees

At a Glance
* A well-constituted and well-run audit committee can bring considerable benefits.
* The Smith Guidance sets out additional recommendations on the role and activities of an audit committee.
* The audit committee should be formally constituted and should have written terms of reference.
* The Combined Code includes specific provisions on the membership of the audit committee.
* Appointments to the audit committee should be by recommendation of the nomination committee and should be for a fixed term.
* Audit committee members must disclose any potential conflicts of interest.
* The company should provide an induction programme and ongoing training and support for audit committee members.
* Management must provide the audit committee with all the information that it needs to discharge its responsibilities.
* The precise role of the audit committee should be tailored to the circumstances of the company.
* The audit committee should review all financial reporting documents before publication.
* The audit committee should monitor the company's internal control and risk management systems, and the procedures for whistle-blowing.
* The audit committee should monitor and review the activities of the internal audit function.
* The audit committee has primary responsibility for making a recommendation to the shareholders on the appointment, reappointment or removal of the external auditors.
* The audit committee should approve the terms of engagement and remuneration of the external auditor.

* The audit committee should assess the independence and objectivity of the external auditors each year.
* The audit committee should agree with the board the company's policy on:
  ○ the employment of former partners and employees of the audit firm and
  ○ the provision of non-audit services by the auditors.
* The audit committee should agree the scope of external audit work each year.
* The audit committee should review the results of the external audit in conjunction with the annual report and accounts.
* The audit committee should consider the auditor's report to management, together with management's response to the points raised.
* At the end of the audit cycle, the audit committee should assess the effectiveness of the external audit process.
* The audit committee should meet sufficiently often to be able to review and monitor major issues, and at least three times each year.
* Only audit committee members are entitled to be present at meetings, but other individuals may attend by invitation.
* The audit committee chairman should report regularly to the main board.
* The annual report should include a separate section each year describing the role and responsibilities of the audit committee and the actions taken to discharge those responsibilities.
* The effectiveness of the audit committee should be reviewed annually by both the committee and the main board.
* The Institute of Chartered Accountants in England and Wales (ICAEW) has published a series of guidance booklets to help non-executive directors meet their responsibilities as members of an audit committee.

2.2　Benefits of an Audit Committee

Audit committees have become an important aspect of corporate governance in recent years, partly as a result of the recommendations set out in the Combined Code but also because companies have begun to appreciate the benefits that an effective audit committee can bring in terms of providing additional assurance on the adequacy of the company's system of internal control and on the quality of its financial information (for both internal and external use) and of its financial decision-making. Although the Combined Code applies primarily to listed companies, the principles underlying the recommendations apply to every company and all directors are therefore encouraged to follow them. The recommendations are equally relevant for not-for-profit organisations, particularly where there is a high degree of public interest in their activities, for instance charities and public sector bodies. The potential benefits of an audit committee include:

• improved quality of financial reporting and increased public confidence in the credibility and objectivity of financial statements;

- the creation of a climate of discipline and control, which can help to reduce the opportunity for fraud;
- the opportunity for non-executive directors to contribute their independent judgement and play a positive role within the company;
- the provision of a forum for the financial director to raise issues of concern;
- the provision of a strong channel of communication between the external auditors and the board, enabling the auditors to raise issues of concern and to assert their independence in the event of a dispute with management and
- the strengthening of the internal audit function, by increasing its independence from management.

Reports issued as part of the UK post-Enron initiative identified the work of an audit committee as being central to the restoration of confidence in the capital markets, and audit committees continue to be widely regarded as playing a key role in maintaining that confidence.

The EC Statutory Audit Directive (see **PARAGRAPH 2.50**) includes a new requirement for public interest entities to have an audit committee. Whilst this is currently recommended under the Combined Code, stricter enforcement will be needed in future in order to meet the requirements of the Directive.

2.3 Potential Drawbacks

However, there are some potential difficulties that companies need to be aware of when establishing and operating audit committees:

- The existence of an audit committee can result in the main board abdicating its collective responsibilities in respect of the audit and the review and approval of the annual accounts.
- The audit committee can become a barrier between the external auditors and the executive directors of the company.
- The audit committee will not function effectively if it lacks the necessary understanding to deal with the accounting and auditing issues that will be brought to its attention.

Careful planning can prevent these becoming real issues in practice.

2.4 The Smith Guidance

As part of the UK Government's response to the collapse of Enron, a small working group was appointed by Financial Reporting Council (FRC), under the chairmanship of Sir Robert Smith, to develop further the initial guidance on audit committees included in the original Combined Code. The resulting report 'Audit Committees: Combined Code Guidance', commonly referred to as the Smith Report, was published in January 2003. The report noted that the audit committee has a particular role, acting independently from the executive, in ensuring that the interests of shareholders in relation to financial reporting and internal control are properly protected. However, this was in no way intended to create a departure from the UK principle of the unitary board – all directors continue to have the same legal responsibility for the company's affairs and any disagreements must be resolved at board level. The report included the draft of a revised section of the Combined Code on audit committees, together with supplementary guidance intended to assist boards in establishing and operating an audit committee and also to assist directors who serve as members of an audit committee. Certain essential requirements for audit committees were set out in bold text in the guidance, which noted that compliance with these was considered necessary in order to achieve compliance with the Combined Code. The revised Combined Code, published by the FRC in July 2003, changed this approach slightly. In addition to the provisions on the role, responsibilities and membership of the audit committee, four of the previous 'bold text' items from the Smith Report became Combined Code provisions – these cover the audit committee's work in relation to:

- reviewing the company's whistle-blowing procedures;
- reviewing the effectiveness of internal audit (or the need for an internal audit function where the company does not have one);
- the appointment of external auditors and
- the provision of non-audit services by the external auditors.

For accounting periods beginning on or after 1 November 2003, listed companies are required to confirm their compliance with these provisions or explain any departures. Other aspects of the Smith Report originally highlighted as being essential simply became part of the supplementary guidance, published as an appendix to the Combined Code along with the Turnbull Guidance and other recommendations on good practice. An updated version of the Combined Code was published in June 2006 and applies for reporting years beginning on or after 1 November 2006. Only a small number of amendments were made, none of them affecting the recommendations in respect of the audit committee. However, this version of the Code no longer includes Appendices setting out the Turnbull Guidance on internal control, the Smith Guidance and the Higgs good practice recommendations. The Turnbull Guidance was the subject of a separate review in 2006 and is available separately from the FRC's website at http://www.frc.org.uk/corporate/internalcontrol.cfm. The FRC also continues to make the Smith Guidance and the Higgs good practice recommendations available on its website at http://www.frc.org.uk/corporate/combinedcode.cfm but emphasises that, whilst companies may find them helpful, these guidance documents have no formal status and companies are not required to follow them when applying the Combined Code. Nevertheless, relevant issues from the Smith Guidance are discussed in the following sections.

2.5 Constitution and Terms of Reference

The Combined Code recommends that an audit committee is constituted formally as a sub-committee of the main board, to ensure that there is a clear relationship between the two. The audit committee should report regularly to the main board and be answerable to it. The Combined Code also recommends that the board should provide written terms of reference for the audit committee and make them publicly available (e.g. by publication on the company's website), and that the annual report should include a separate section describing the work of the audit committee in discharging its responsibilities during the year (see 2.32). The Smith Report included an example terms of reference under the following headings (although this has not been reproduced in the Smith Guidance attached to the revised Combined Code):

- constitution;
- membership;
- attendance at meetings;
- frequency of meetings;
- authority;
- responsibilities and
- reporting procedures.

A further example, based on that in the Smith Report, is given in **APPENDIX 2** to this chapter. However, this is not intended to be prescriptive and companies are encouraged to develop and tailor it to suit their own circumstances. In particular, the example is drafted from the perspective of an individual company and will need adapting to cover the specific circumstances of a group. Terms of reference should be realistic and should give the committee sufficient resources and authority to perform its role effectively. The Smith Guidance recommends that the audit committee should carry out an annual review of its terms of reference and recommend to the board any changes that are considered necessary.

2.6 Membership of the Audit Committee

Membership of the audit committee is a critical issue – any committee can only be as good as the people that serve on it. In particular, the effectiveness of the audit committee often depends on a strong, independent chairman who has the confidence of both the board and the external auditors, and on the quality of the non-executive directors. The size and complexity of the company, and the size of the board of directors, will usually have a direct bearing on the size and membership of the audit committee. The Combined Code recommends that:

- the audit committee should have at least three members, all of whom should be independent non-executive directors (see **PARAGRAPH 6.17**) and
- at least one member of the audit committee should have significant recent and relevant financial experience (the Smith Report suggested that this might be as an auditor or a finance director of a listed company) and the Smith Guidance notes that this member should preferably hold a professional accountancy qualification.

At present, the chairman of the company should not be a member of the audit committee. However, the FRC announced in October 2007 that it intends to begin a consultation in November 2007 on two proposed amendments to the present Code, one of which would allow the chairman of a smaller listed company to be a member of the audit committee provided that he/she was considered to be independent on appointment. If agreed, this change is expected to come into effect from June 2008. The members of the audit committee should be identified in the annual report.

2.7 Skills and Attributes

There should normally be wide consultation before recommending that an individual is appointed as a member of the committee. The Smith Guidance suggests that appointments should be by recommendation of the nomination committee (where there is one), in consultation with the audit committee chairman. Qualities that will commonly be taken into account in assessing an individual's suitability for membership of the audit committee will include:

- breadth of general business experience;
- knowledge of the company's operations, finances and accounting;
- understanding of the roles of external and internal auditors and familiarity with the main concepts of auditing standards;
- knowledge and understanding of the key aspects of financial reporting;
- personal qualities and
- commitment (including the amount of time that the individual can make available).

The audit committee will usually function as a team and it may therefore be appropriate to consider the balance of experience and abilities across the membership as a whole. The nature of the audit committee's activities makes it particularly important for the committee as a whole to have an adequate understanding of the management of business risk, accounting and financial reporting and internal control. Additional relevant skills may be needed, depending on the nature of the company's activities – for instance, where it is involved in specialised financial activities. Members of the company's executive management team should not be appointed to the audit committee as their attendance at every meeting could inhibit others from raising sensitive issues. However, their input to audit committee discussions may be needed from time to time and there should a facility for them to attend audit committee meetings by invitation (see **PARAGRAPH 2.29**).

2.8 Appointing a Chairman

The Cadbury Committee emphasised the importance of the chairman in ensuring the effective operation of the audit committee and the Smith Report highlighted the need for a frank and open relationship, and a high level of mutual trust, between the audit committee chairman and the board chairman, chief executive and finance director. The chairman of the audit committee will usually be appointed by the board as a whole. Particular qualities that will need to be assessed in appointing a chairman include:

- strength of personality;
- experience of the role of chairman;
- attitude to business risk management and control, and related ethical issues;
- attitude towards the audit function (both external and internal) and
- commitment (including the amount of time that he/she can make available).

2.9 Length of Appointment to Audit Committee

The long-term nature of the activities of the audit committee mean that a certain degree of continuity of membership is helpful. However, this needs to be balanced against the need for fresh input and a new outlook from time to time. The Smith Guidance recommends that appointments should be for a period of up to three years, extendable by no more than two additional periods of three years, provided that the individual continues to be sufficiently independent. From a practical point of view, it is often helpful for the appointment periods of the individual members to end in different years so that the company is not faced with a loss of significant audit committee experience by two or three members retiring at the same time.

2.10 Avoiding Conflicts of Interest

Individuals recommended for appointment to the audit committee should be required to confirm their independence at the time of appointment. Once appointed they are responsible for ensuring that their entry in the register of directors' interests is kept up to date and for declaring any potential conflict of interest in respect of agenda items at meetings of the audit committee. They should not vote on any item in respect of which they have a potential conflict of interest.

2.11 Training and Support for Audit Committee Members

The Smith Guidance recommends that an induction programme is provided for each new audit committee member, covering:

- the role of the audit committee and its terms of reference;
- the expected time commitment and
- an overview of the company's business, including the main business and financial dynamics and risks.

It may also be helpful to provide new members with summaries of the issues raised in recent reports from both external and internal auditors. Ongoing training should be provided to all audit committee members to enable them to keep up to date with issues relevant to their role. This training might cover:

- principles and developments in financial reporting and related company law;

- understanding financial statements, applicable accounting standards and recommended accounting practice;
- the regulatory framework for the company's business;
- the role of external and internal audit and
- risk management.

The Smith Guidance notes that both induction programmes and ongoing training might take a variety of forms, including attendance at formal courses and conferences, internal seminars and briefing sessions led by external advisers. The audit committee should also be given the facility, and the funding, to obtain independent legal, accounting or other advice where it considers this to be necessary.

2.12   Information Provided to Audit Committee

The Smith Guidance emphasises that management has an obligation to ensure that the audit committee is kept properly informed and to provide the information that it needs to fulfil its role. Management is expected to take the initiative in providing information to the committee, rather than waiting to be asked for it, and to make clear to all directors and employees that they must co-operate with the audit committee and provide any information requested.

2.13   Role and Activities of the Audit Committee

The role of audit committees has become increasingly diverse as they have become more common. The detailed role and activities of the audit committee must be tailored to the needs of the individual company, but the principal role of the audit committee is summarised as providing assurance that the board's collective responsibility for financial matters and internal control is rigorously discharged. The Smith Guidance summarises the role and responsibilities of the audit committee under the following headings:

- Financial reporting.
- Internal financial controls and risk management systems.
- Whistle-blowing.
- The internal audit process.
- The external audit process:
  - appointment,
  - terms and remuneration,
  - independence and the provision of non-audit services and
  - the annual audit cycle.

In the case of a group of companies, the parent board should ensure that there is adequate co-operation within the group, and with the external and internal auditors of each company within the group, to enable the audit committee to discharge its responsibilities. The Smith Guidance also emphasises that the work of the audit committee is wide-ranging, time-consuming and sometimes intensive – it is therefore important that members of the committee are able to make the appropriate amount of time available for the task and that they receive appropriate recompense for this.

2.14   Financial Reporting

The audit committee's responsibilities in relation to financial reporting cover:

- the half-yearly report;
- the preliminary announcement;
- the company's financial statements;
- the operating and financial review (OFR);
- the company's corporate governance statements and
- the summary financial statement (where one is prepared).

Wherever practical, the audit committee should also review other statements containing financial information which require board approval prior to publication – for instance, the release of price sensitive information, or financial reports to regulators. Management are responsible for preparing accounts which show a true and fair view, and for meeting relevant accounting and disclosure requirements, and the audit committee's review should focus in particular on:

- comparisons with the previous year and the explanations for any significant variances;
- any changes in accounting policies and their disclosure in the accounts;
- any significant issues involving a high degree of judgement;
- any adjustments necessary as a result of the work carried out by the external auditors;
- going concern;
- disclosure of any significant commitments or contingent liabilities;
- impact of any significant events since the balance sheet date;
- compliance with accounting standards and other reporting requirements (including, where appropriate, those laid down by the Financial Services Authority (FSA));
- the clarity and completeness of the disclosures, and whether they are set properly in context and
- the results of the external audit.

In particular, management should explain the accounting treatment of any significant or unusual transactions, particularly where the treatment is open to different approaches, and the committee should consider whether the approach adopted is appropriate. Following their review, the audit committee should submit the relevant financial statements to the board with their recommendations on approval. If it is not satisfied with any aspect of the company's financial reporting, the audit committee should report its views to the board.

Audit Matters

2.15   Internal Financial Controls and Risk Management Systems

The audit committee should monitor the integrity of the company's internal financial controls and, in the absence of other arrangements (for instance, the establishment of a separate risk committee) should assess the scope and effectiveness of the company's systems for assessing, managing and monitoring financial and other risks. Management should report to the committee on the effectiveness of the systems that they have established and, in particular, the results of any testing carried out by the internal and external auditors. Following their assessment, the audit committee should review the directors' statements in the annual report in respect of internal control and the management of risk (see **CHAPTER 14**).

2.16   Whistle-Blowing

The audit committee should also review the company's procedures to enable staff to raise, in confidence, concerns about possible improprieties in respect of financial reporting or other issues, and should consider whether these provide for proportionate, independent investigation and follow-up of the matters raised (see **CHAPTER 11**).

2.17   The Internal Audit Process

Where the company has an internal audit function, the audit committee should monitor and review internal audit activities. This should normally include the following:

- Reviewing and approving the remit of the internal audit function.
- Confirming that there is appropriate liaison between external and internal auditors, to prevent duplication of work and make the most effective use of the available resources.
- Confirming that the head of internal audit has direct access to the board chairman and to the audit committee, and is accountable to the audit committee.
- Ensuring that the internal audit function is adequately resourced, maintains a suitable degree of independence from other functions within the company, has appropriate standing within the company and is given access to the information that it needs in order to fulfil its remit.
- Reviewing the proposed annual programme of internal audit work before this is submitted to the board for approval.
- Monitoring progress against the plan during the year.
- Reviewing the results of internal audit work, together with management's response to the points raised.
- Monitoring and assessing the role and effectiveness of the internal audit function in the context of the company's risk management system.

The Smith Guidance also notes that the audit committee should approve the appointment, or termination of appointment, of the head of internal audit. Where the company does not have an internal audit function, the Combined Code recommends that the audit committee should consider annually whether there is a need to establish one and should make a recommendation to the board on this. Where an internal audit function is not considered necessary, the audit committee should explain the reasoning behind this decision in the relevant section of the annual report. The annual review of the need for an internal audit function was initially covered in the Turnbull guidance on internal control, but has been removed from the latest version now that responsibility for the review rests with the audit committee. The original guidance recommended that the review should take into account:

- Whether the board has other means of obtaining sufficient and objective assurance on the effectiveness of the company's system on internal control.
- Whether there are any trends or current factors in the company's internal environment, markets or other aspects of its external environment that have increased, or are expected to increase, the risks faced by the company – for instance:
  - changes in organisational structure, reporting processes or information systems;
  - changes in key risks as a result of changes in products or services, entry into new markets, or changes in regulatory requirements;
  - adverse trends apparent from the monitoring of the internal control system or
  - increased incidence of unexpected or unacceptable results.

2.18   Appointment of External Auditors

The Smith Guidance notes that the audit committee is responsible for overseeing the company's relationship with the external auditors, and for overseeing the selection process where the appointment of new auditors is being considered. Technically, the annual appointment of the external auditors is a matter for the shareholders, but the board of directors will usually put forward recommendations for the shareholders to consider. Under the Combined Code, the audit committee should have primary responsibility for making a recommendation on the appointment, reappointment or removal of the external auditors. The recommendation should be made initially to the board, and then to the company's shareholders. If the board does not accept the recommendation of the audit committee, the directors' report must include a statement from the audit committee explaining its recommendation and why the board has taken a different view. The audit committee's recommendation each year should be based on an assessment of the qualifications, expertise, resources, effectiveness and independence of the external auditors. The assessment should cover all aspects of the audit service and, as part of their review, the audit committee should obtain a report on the audit firm's own internal quality control procedures. If the external auditor resigns, the audit committee should investigate any issues giving rise to the resignation and consider whether any further action is required.

In June 2007, the Professional Oversight Board (POB) issued a consultation document on proposals to change the arrangements for reporting on the results of quality reviews carried out by the Audit Inspection Unit (AIU). The AIU inspects firms who audit listed companies, and an earlier POB consultation and subsequent discussions with interested parties identified a clear need for greater transparency in reporting the results of the AIU's work. In particular, the benefits arising from the publication of more detailed information on audit firms are felt to include the provision of useful information for audit committees, the promotion of greater choice in the audit market, and an enhancement of audit quality. However, the reports prepared by the AIU for regulatory purposes are not considered suitable for wider publication. The POB therefore proposes that the AIU should also prepare a high-level report on the findings of each full inspection carried out for general publication. The POB proposes that the new arrangements should apply to all inspections commencing on or after 1 April 2007, with the first publication date likely to be in the first half of 2008.

The POB also proposes that the AIU should prepare a similar high-level report on each individual audit engagement reviewed and that audit firms should share these high-level reports with the audit client concerned. The POB notes that it expects audit firms to advise the client when an audit engagement has been selected for review by the AIU and to adopt a policy of sharing high-level reports as a matter of course. However, the POB also intends to publish an annual list of the audits reviewed by the AIU to help encourage an appropriate level of transparency.

2.19   Terms and Remuneration of External Auditors

The audit committee should approve the terms of engagement and the remuneration to be paid to the external auditor in respect of audit services. The committee should review the audit engagement letter at the start of each audit and confirm that it has been updated to deal with any new issues or requirements and any other changes in circumstances since the previous year. Where the audit committee considers the scope of the audit to be inadequate, it should arrange for additional work to be undertaken. The committee should also satisfy itself that:

- the remuneration payable is appropriate for the service provided and
- an effective audit can be carried out for that fee.

Under Section 493 of the Companies Act 2006 (CA 2006), the Secretary of State has the power to make regulations requiring the disclosure of the terms of on which a company auditor is appointed, remunerated or performs his duties. Regulations made under this section will be able to:

- require disclosure of a copy of any written terms or a written memorandum of any terms that are not in writing;
- specify the time and place of such disclosure;
- require the place and means of disclosure to be stated in the notes to the accounts, the directors' report or the auditors' report.

However, the Department of Trade and Industry (DTI) consultation document Implementation of CA 2006' published in February 2007 suggests that there is no intention to exercise this power in the near future.

2.20   Independence

The audit committee should have procedures to assess the independence and objectivity of the external auditors each year, taking into account relevant professional and regulatory requirements. The assessment should cover all relationships between the company and the audit firm, including the provision of non-audit services. In the case of listed companies, professional auditing standards require the auditors to make certain disclosures in respect of their independence each year (see PARAGRAPH 2.40) and the Smith Guidance also recommends that the audit committee seek annual information from the audit firm on the policies and processes that it adopts to maintain independence and monitor compliance with relevant professional requirements, including the requirement under Auditing Practices Board (APB) Ethical Standards (ES) for the appointment of the audit engagement partner to be rotated at least every five years and that of other key audit partners to be rotated at least every seven years and current UK guidance on fee dependency. Factors to consider when assessing independence are covered in more detail in PARAGRAPHS 2.38–2.43.

2.21   Employment of Auditor's Former Employees

The Smith Guidance recommends that the audit committee should agree with the board the company's policy on the employment of former partners and employees of the audit firm, especially any who were part of the audit team and moved directly to the company. The committee should then monitor the application of the policy and should consider in particular the number of such individuals currently employed in senior positions within the company and whether this could impair, or be perceived to impair, the independence of the audit firm. Detailed requirements and guidance on this issue are set out in APB Ethical Standard for Auditors 2 (ES2) 'Financial, business, employment and personal relationships' which includes consideration of the following situations:

- A partner or employee of the audit firm working for an audit client on a temporary or 'loan' basis.
- A partner joining an audit client.
- Another member of the audit engagement team joining an audit client.
- A close family member of a partner and or other senior individual within the audit firm joining an audit client.
- A director or senior employee of the audit client joining the audit firm.

The EC Statutory Audit Directive (see PARAGRAPH 2.50) also prohibits key audit partners from taking up a key management position in an audited entity for two years after they have ceased to be auditor. The DTI consultation document 'Implementation of Directive 2006/43/EC on Statutory Audits of Annual and Consolidated Accounts' published in March 2007 notes that this requirements could be dealt with either as a new offence created under the CA 2006 or through the rules of the recognised supervisory bodies.

2.22   Provision of Non-audit Services

The audit committee should develop and recommend to the board the company's policy on the provision of non-audit services by the audit firm, the objective being to ensure that the provision of such services does not impair the independence or objectivity of the auditor. Issues to be considered by the audit committee include:

- whether the audit firm is a suitable supplier of the services – for instance, as a result of its skills and experience;
- whether appropriate safeguards are in place to prevent any threat to independence or objectivity in the conduct of the external audit;
- the nature of the non-audit services and the related fee levels, individually and in aggregate, relative to the audit fee and
- the criteria which govern the compensation of the individuals performing the audit.

Other issues to consider in the context of the provision of non-audit services are summarised in **PARAGRAPHS 2.41–2.42**. The company's formal policy should specify the types of work for which the external auditors can be engaged without formal approval, those from which the external auditors should be excluded, and those which require formal referral to the audit committee for a decision. The committee may also wish to set fee limits in general or for specific classes of work. In principle, the audit committee should not agree to the auditors providing non-audit services which:

- result in the external auditor auditing the work of its own firm;
- result in the external auditor making management decisions for the company;
- create a mutuality of interest between the external auditor and the company or
- put the external auditor into the position of advocate for the company.

The Combined Code recommends that the annual report to shareholders explains how the company's policy provides appropriate protection of auditor independence and objectivity. For accounting periods beginning on or after 1 October 2005, more stringent requirements have been introduced on the disclosure of non-audit services provided by the auditors and their associates, and the related remuneration received (see **PARAGRAPH 2.78**).

2.23   Agreeing the Scope of the External Audit

Before the detailed audit work commences each year, the audit committee should discuss and agree with the auditors the scope of their work and the overall work plan, including planned materiality levels and proposed resources to carry out the plan. In the case of a group with a complex structure or overseas interests, more than one firm of auditors may be involved, and the audit committee will need to be satisfied that proper co-ordination between the various auditors can be achieved. This meeting with the auditors will also provide a suitable opportunity to consider recent changes in accounting standards and reporting requirements and the potential impact for the company. Where additional information needs to be prepared or collated as a result of these changes, early consideration of the issues should help to ensure that the company has sufficient time to put the necessary procedures in place. It will also be important to consider any changes that have taken place within the business, or are planned for the near future, and their impact for the annual accounts and the audit (for instance, new business activities or potential closures). The aim should be to identify any likely problem areas at this stage, so that solutions can be identified in good time. If the company has an internal audit function, it will be important to ensure that there is good liaison between the internal and external auditors, to avoid any potential duplication of work and make the most effective use of all the available resources. In the case of listed companies, the auditors will often have additional reporting responsibilities in respect of the half-yearly report and corporate governance issues, and the nature and scope of their work in these areas also needs to be considered and agreed.

2.24   Reviewing the Results of the External Audit

The results of the external audit should be reviewed in conjunction with the annual report and accounts as the two are inextricably linked. In particular the audit committee should:

- discuss with the auditors any issues identified during the course of their work, distinguishing those that have been resolved and any that remain unresolved, and any reservations that the external auditors have in respect of the annual report and accounts;
- review the key accounting and audit judgements and
- review the level of errors identified during the audit and obtain explanations from management and the auditors for any that remain unadjusted.

The audit committee should also review the audit representation letter before it is signed by management, and consider whether the information given is complete and appropriate, based on the committee's own knowledge. In particular, the committee should explore any non-standard issues raised in the representation letter. Other issues that may need to be considered at this stage include:

- adequacy of the company's accounting records and systems of internal control;
- any breakdowns in systems and controls identified during the audit;
- any other irregularities identified during the course of the audit and
- where relevant, the auditors' opinion on the company's statement of compliance with the Combined Code and the consistency of the company's statements on going concern and internal control with the knowledge gained by the external auditors during the course of their work.

This will usually be an appropriate time for the audit committee to discuss the actual audit costs with the auditors and to begin thinking about any changes to the audit approach that may be needed for the following year – planning for the next year will usually be most effective when the successes and difficulties of the current year are fresh in the mind.

2.25   Reviewing the Auditors' Report to Management

At the conclusion of the audit, the auditors will usually issue a formal written report on:

- any significant weaknesses in the accounting or internal control systems that have come to their attention during the audit, together with their recommendations for improvements;
- any significant business issues that have come to their attention during the audit, together with their advice (for instance, potential economies or improvements in efficiency) and
- any significant errors identified during the audit and comments on any individual accounting policies or practices that they consider need to be drawn to the attention of the directors or senior management.

The audit committee should consider this report, together with management's response to the points raised. This is considered in more detail in **PARAGRAPH 2.68**.

2.26   Assessing the Effectiveness of External Audit

At the end of the audit cycle, the audit committee should assess the effectiveness of the external audit process and review:

- any significant changes from the original audit plan and the reasons for these;
- the robustness and perceptiveness of the auditors in handling the key accounting and auditing judgements identified and in responding to questions from the audit committee;
- feedback from key individuals (e.g. finance director, head of internal audit) on the conduct of the external audit and
- the content of the management letter and any commentary on the systems of internal control, to assess whether these demonstrate a good understanding of the business and whether any recommendations have been acted upon.

2.27   Frequency and Timing of Audit Committee Meetings

In practice, most audit committees meet between two and four times a year, depending on the complexity of the company's activities. The Smith Guidance recommends that there should be no fewer than three meetings each year, to coincide with key dates within the financial reporting cycle, although it also notes that most committees will need to meet more often than this. The important point is for the committee to meet sufficiently often to be able to review and monitor major issues. The terms of reference may provide for additional meetings to be held in emergencies (for instance, where a prompt decision is needed) or for specific purposes. It is also important to consider the timing of the audit committee's meetings in relation to:

- the scheduled meetings of the main board, so that the audit committee can report and put forward its recommendations in a timely manner and

- the company's financial timetable – in the case of quoted companies, this will need to take into account the publication of the interim report, preliminary announcement and annual report and accounts so that the audit committee can make its input at the appropriate point.

Sufficient time should be allowed between audit committee and main board meetings to enable issues requiring further work to be properly followed up and reported to the board where appropriate. Meetings should be planned well in advance to encourage a good attendance by committee members and so that finance staff, external auditors and internal auditors have plenty of notice of when information will need to be presented. In larger organisations, it may be appropriate for the location of the meetings to be varied, to give audit committee members the opportunity to visit key operational sites. The Smith Guidance also notes that the audit committee chairman, and to a lesser extent, other committee members, will usually want to keep in touch on a continuing basis with key individuals within the company and with the external audit lead partner.

2.28   Agendas

The annual accounts production and audit schedules will often provide a useful starting point when scheduling meetings of the audit committee and agreeing agendas. A suitable schedule of meetings for a quoted company might be as follows:

Timing	Main agenda items
Approximately five months into the financial year	(i) Consideration of the scope of the external auditors' work on the half-yearly report. (ii) Consideration of report from the Head of Internal Audit, covering: ○ progress with planned work programme; ○ issues arising since the last report; ○ follow-up of significant points raised in previous report. (iii) Self-assessment of the committee's effectiveness and review of terms of reference for the committee to confirm these are still appropriate or to identify changes to be put to the board for consideration.
Approximately seven months into the financial year	(i) Consideration of recent or imminent developments in financial reporting and their impact for the company. (ii) Review of the half-yearly report prior to its release. (iii) Consideration of the results of the external auditors' work on the half-yearly report. (iv) Discussion with the external auditors on the proposed audit approach and the audit plan. (v) Consideration of proposed external audit fee.

Audit Matters

Timing	Main agenda items

Approximately 10 months into the financial year	(i) Consideration of report from the Head of Internal Audit, covering:
	  ○ progress with planned work programme;
	  ○ issues arising since the last report;
	  ○ follow-up of significant points raised in previous report.
	(ii) Consideration of the scope of internal audit work for the next financial year.

Prior to the publication of the annual report and accounts	(i) Consideration of the annual report and accounts.
	(ii) Review of the results and effectiveness of the external audit.
	(iii) Review of external audit costs.
	(iv) Review of the service provided by the external auditors and their independence, and recommendation on appointment (or reappointment) of auditors.
	(v) Consideration of annual report from the Head of Internal Audit, covering:
	  ○ summary of work completed for the previous financial year and comparison with planned work programme;
	  ○ issues arising since the last report;
	  ○ follow-up of significant points raised in previous report.
	  ○ progress on work planned for the current financial year.

Where the company has an internal audit function, the review of reports from this department may be dealt with as a separate agenda item at the meetings dealing with external audit issues (as suggested above), or may be covered in separate meetings. For instance, in the case of an unquoted company, there will not usually be a half-yearly report and it may therefore be appropriate to schedule four audit committee meetings during the year to deal alternately with internal audit and external audit issues.

2.29   Other Attendees

The Combined Code states categorically that no one other than the relevant committee chairman and members is entitled to be present at meetings of the main board committees (i.e. the audit, nomination and remuneration committees) and the Smith Guidance reinforces this point in relation to the audit committee. However, other individuals may attend by invitation of the committee and the finance director, the head of internal audit and the external auditors will usually be invited to attend meetings of the audit committee. Depending on the circumstances, they may only need to attend for part of the meeting. It is recommended that the audit committee should meet at least once each year with the external and internal auditors without management present to ensure that the auditors have an opportunity to raise any issues of concern. In practice, this can usually be arranged to take place at the conclusion of one of the regular audit committee meetings.

2.30   Attendance Records

It is good practice to keep detailed attendance records for audit committee meetings and for the board of directors to review these on an annual basis to confirm that each member is making an appropriate contribution to the work of the committee. Attendance information will also need to be retained for inclusion in the annual report on the committee's activities (see **PARAGRAPH 2.32**).

2.31   Reporting to the Main Board

The agendas for meetings of the main board should include a report from the chairman of the audit committee as a regular item. This enables the audit committee to report to the board on the main points arising from its discussions with both external and internal auditors and also to put recommendations to the board when appropriate. The board has collective responsibility for the annual accounts and for internal control within the company, but will usually look to the audit committee for advice on issues relating to financial reporting, internal controls and the financial aspects of corporate governance. The audit committee will also have responsibility for making recommendations to the board on the appointment or reappointment of auditors and the agreement of the external audit fee. Minutes of the meetings of the audit committee will usually be circulated to all board members for information. The Smith Guidance notes that, where there is disagreement between the audit committee and the board, adequate time should be made available for discussion, and hopefully resolution, of the issue. If the matter cannot be resolved, the audit committee should have the right to report the issue to the shareholders within the annual report on its activities.

2.32   Reporting to Shareholders

The Combined Code recommends that the annual report includes a separate section each year describing the role and responsibilities of the audit committee and the actions taken to discharge those responsibilities. The suggested contents of the report include the following:

- A summary of the main responsibilities of the audit committee.
- The names of all members of the audit committee during the period (with appointment and resignation dates where appropriate) and details of the relevant qualifications, expertise and experience of each member.
- The number of audit committee meetings and the attendance by each member.
- The actions and procedures carried out to:
  - monitor the integrity of the financial statements,
  - review the integrity of the company's internal financial control and risk management systems,

- review the independence of the external auditors, including disclosure of the company's policy on the provision of non-audit services and an explanation of how this protects auditor independence,
- oversee the external audit process, including confirmation that its effectiveness has been assessed.

Other areas that may need to be covered include:

- an explanation of the recommendation to the board on the appointment of the external auditors and, where applicable, the process adopted to select a new auditor;
- confirmation that the plans and work of the internal audit department have been reviewed or, if there is no internal audit function, an explanation of the committee's consideration of the need to establish one;
- details of the remuneration policies for members of the audit committee (or a cross-reference to the directors' remuneration report) and
- details of any dedicated resources available to the committee.

The Smith Report included an outline of such a report, but this is not reproduced in the current version of the Smith Guidance. The audit committee chairman should also be present at the Annual General Meeting (AGM) to answer questions, through the board chairman, on this report and on any other matters that come within the scope of the audit committee's responsibilities.

2.33 Self-assessment and Appraisal

The Combined Code recommends that the board should undertake a formal and rigorous annual evaluation of the effectiveness of each board committee. In the case of the audit committee, this might be done by considering developments generally in the role and activities of audit committees and discussing with the main board the extent to which the audit committee is considered to have fulfilled the various aspects of its terms of reference. Feedback might also be sought from the head of internal audit and the external auditors on these points. Specific issues to consider might include the following:

- Are there appropriate procedures for appointing committee members?
- Does the committee have the appropriate mix of knowledge and skills?
- Is the amount and nature of training and administrative support appropriate?
- Are the committee's terms of reference appropriate?
- Does the committee adequately fulfil its role?
- Is the frequency and timing of committee meetings appropriate?
- Are agendas and appropriate supporting information circulated to committee members in good time?
- How effective are the committee's relationships with management, internal audit and the external auditors?
- Does the committee's workload require a change of emphasis?
- Does the committee need subsidiary committees to deal with significant or overseas business units?

- If subsidiary committees are already in place, are the arrangements working effectively?
- What significant issues does the committee need to address in the coming year?

The appendices to the Combined Code also include a performance evaluation checklist, setting out questions that may be relevant to an assessment of the performance of the board and of individual non-executive directors.

2.34   Additional Guidance

Since the introduction of the revised Combined Code in 2003, the ICAEW has published a series of guidance booklets designed to help directors, and in particular non-executive directors who are members of an audit committee, to meet their responsibilities. The following publications may be of particular interest to finance directors and audit committee members:

- Company Reporting and Audit Requirements (November 2003)
- Working with your Auditors (November 2003)
- Evaluating your Auditors (November 2003)
- Reviewing Auditor Independence (November 2003)
- Monitoring the Integrity of Financial Statements (March 2004)
- Whistle-blowing Arrangements (March 2004)
- The Internal Audit Function (March 2004).

All of the above are available free of charge from the ICAEW website (www.icaew.co.uk). Details of additional publications dealing specifically with internal audit matters can be found in **PARAGRAPH 2.114**.

2.35   Appointment of External Auditors

At a Glance
- Every company is required to appoint auditors, unless audit exemption applies.
- Only certain individuals and firms are eligible for appointment as a company auditor.
- The auditors must be, and must be seen to be, independent of the company.
- In particular, the provision of non-audit services by the auditors may impact on their independence.
- APB ES set out detailed requirements on the regular rotation of audit partners.
- The audit committee should consider periodically whether a change of auditor is required.
- Complex provisions apply under CA 1985 on a change of auditor.
- Professional standards require any new auditor to communicate with the predecessor audit firm.

* Company law grants auditors specific rights to information, and imposes specific duties on them.
* Certain changes will need to be made to current requirements in order to implement the EC Statutory Audit Directive.

2.36   Requirement to Appoint Auditors

Under Section 384(1) of the CA 1985, every company must appoint an auditor or auditors. The only exceptions to this, set out in Section 388A of CA 1985, are for dormant companies and certain small companies, which may be exempt from an annual audit under Sections 249AA and 249A, respectively. The legislation sets out specific procedures for the appointment process, and for the filling of any casual vacancies that arise. The auditors appointed generally hold office from the conclusion of the meeting at which they are appointed until the conclusion of the next general meeting at which accounts are laid. A separate process is set out for the appointment of the first auditors, and separate provisions also apply in the case of a private company which chooses to take advantage of the elective regime to reduce the need for regular formal meetings of the company.

Broadly similar requirements on the appointment of auditors are set out in Sections 485–491 of the CA 2006, although the new legislation sets out separate provisions for private and public companies to reflect the fact that private companies will no longer be required to lay the accounts before the members in general meeting. Most of the audit provisions of CA 2006 are due to be brought into effect from 6 April 2008, but Sections 485–488 (which deal with the appointment and reappointment of auditors by private companies) have been brought into effect from 1 October 2007, together with the new provisions on company meetings and resolutions.

2.37   Eligibility for Appointment As Company Auditor

Under Section 25 of the CA 1989, either an individual or a firm may be appointed as a company auditor, but they will only be eligible for appointment if they are a member of a recognised supervisory body (as defined in Section 30 of CA 1989) and eligible for appointment under the rules of that supervisory body. Specific requirements on recognised supervisory bodies are set out in Schedule 11 to CA 1989. The supervisory bodies currently recognised in relation to the appointment of company auditors are the:

* Institute of Chartered Accountants in England and Wales.
* Institute of Chartered Accountants of Scotland.
* Institute of Chartered Accountants in Ireland.
* Association of Chartered Certified Accountants.
* Association of Authorised Public Accountants.

Special provisions apply to certain individuals who qualified for appointment as a company auditor prior to 1 January 1990 other than by membership of one of these bodies. An auditor who becomes ineligible for appointment during his term of office must vacate office immediately and give written notice to the company. The auditor is also required to make a formal statement of any circumstances connected with his ceasing to hold office (see **PARAGRAPH 2.45**). Where an auditor was ineligible for appointment for any part of the period during which the audit was conducted, the Secretary of State can require the company to engage the services of someone who is eligible for appointment to audit the relevant accounts again or to review the original audit and report on whether a second audit is required.

Similar requirements will continue to apply under CA 2006 once this comes into effect.

2.38   Auditor Independence

Under Section 27 of CA 1989, a person is ineligible for appointment as auditor of a company if he or she is:

- an officer or employee of the company; or
- a partner or employee of such a person, or in a partnership of which such a person is a partner or
- ineligible by virtue of either of the above for appointment as auditor of any associated undertaking of the company – in this context, an associated undertaking is defined as:
  - a parent undertaking of the company,
  - a subsidiary undertaking of the company or
  - a subsidiary undertaking of any parent undertaking of the company.

The rules therefore encompass the widest group of which the company is a member. Section 744(1) of CA 1985 defines an officer of the company as including a director, manager or secretary – an individual or firm therefore cannot act as both auditor to and secretary of the same company. The report of the DTI Co-ordinating Group on Audit and Accounting Issues (CGAAI) published in January 2003 emphasised the importance of the external auditor being perceived to be independent as well as actually being independent in practice.

2.39   Professional Requirements on Independence

Historically, professional requirements on auditor independence were set by the recognised supervisory bodies. However, the various post-Enron reviews in the UK concluded that responsibility for standards on auditor independence should be transferred to an independent body. In December 2004, the APB published the following five ES for Auditors:

- ES 1 'Integrity, objectivity and independence'
- ES 2 'Financial, business, employment and personal relationships'
- ES 3 'Long associations with the audit engagement'

- ES 4 'Fees, economic dependence, remuneration and evaluation policies, litigation, gifts and hospitality'
- ES 5 'Non-audit service provided to audit clients'

These are available from the APB website at http://www.frc.org.uk/apb/publications/ethical.cfm and are effective for financial periods beginning on or after 15 December 2004 (and, in certain cases, contractual arrangements accepted before 5 October 2004). They generally impose more stringent requirements than the previous professional guidance in the UK. In developing the standards, the APB attempted to comply with both the International Federation of Accountants (IFAC) 'Code of Ethics for Professional Accountants' and the EC Recommendation 'Statutory auditors' independence in the EU: A set of fundamental principles' and, where these two documents took a different approach, adopted the more stringent recommendations. The APB has also imposed its own more stringent requirements where it considers this to be necessary.

Limited exemptions are offered to small companies (as defined in company law) by the ES 'Provisions Available for Small Entities'. The need for additional safeguards must be properly considered and actioned in each situation where the reliefs are applied and the audit report must disclose their adoption.

In July 2007, the APB published the results of recent research into the impact of its ES for Auditors. This was undertaken as part of a more wide-ranging review of the standards and is expected to result in the publication of an exposure draft of proposed revisions to the standards later in 2007. The revisions will also take into account recent statutory developments, including the requirements of the EC Statutory Audit Directive, and practical experience of working with the current standards. Key points highlighted in the APB's research include:

- many listed company finance directors and audit committee chairs thought that threats to auditor independence had decreased, although the majority of unlisted company respondents thought that the position was unchanged;
- a majority of respondents felt that there is now a higher degree of transparency in the relationship between a company and its external auditor;
- a majority of respondents felt that auditor communication on significant issues that could impact on their objectivity and independence was working effectively;
- most respondents with experience of partner rotation felt that this had not affected audit quality, whilst a significant minority thought that audit quality had improved; and
- an analysis of accounts disclosures indicated that non-audit fees paid to company auditors had generally decreased, although many respondents indicated that they had remained the same (or in some cases reported an increase).

The full APB report is available at http://www.frc.org.uk/apb/publications/other.cfm.

2.40 Annual Disclosures on Independence

The auditors of listed companies are required by the UK & Ireland version of International Standard on Auditing 260 (ISA 260) 'Communication of audit matters with those charged with governance' to disclose at least annually in writing to the audit committee all relationships between the auditor firm (and its related entities) and the client (and its related entities) that may reasonably be thought to affect the independence of the audit firm and the objectivity of the audit team, together with the related safeguards that are in place.

The auditors must also confirm in writing to the audit committee each year:

- that, in their professional judgement, the audit firm is independent within the meaning of regulatory and professional requirements and that the objectivity of the audit team is not impaired;
- that the firm has complied with the APB's ES and
- the total amount of fees charged to the client and its affiliates by the auditor and its network firms, analysed into appropriate categories and with separate disclosure of any future services that have been contracted or for which a written proposal has been submitted.

Any concerns over independence and objectivity that are raised in these disclosures should also be discussed with the audit committee. As part of its series of guidance booklets for non-executive directors serving on an audit committee, the ICAEW published 'Reviewing Auditor Independence' in November 2003. This is available free of charge from the ICAEW website at www.icaew.co.uk.

2.41   Post-Enron Developments

Auditor independence was also considered in detail by the DTI as part of the post-Enron review. The CGAAI report made the following points:

- UK requirements should continue to be based on principles rather than detailed, prescriptive rules but there need to be tougher and clearer safeguards, particularly on the provision of non-audit services to an audit client.
- There is a need for improved qualitative guidance for audit firms on economic dependence on a single audit client (which can arise at the level of the firm as whole, an individual office or an individual partner).
- For periods starting on or after 1 January 2003, audit firms with listed and other public interest clients should voluntarily publish an annual report including whole firm financial information, details on their organisational structure and reward systems, information on how quality is achieved and monitored, and their policies and procedures for managing threats to their independence.
- Audit firms with listed and public interest clients should disclose in that annual report any fees representing more than 5% of total fees and should also ensure that the audit committee or board of the relevant audit client is aware of their potential economic dependency on the appointment.
- The responsibility for setting standards on independence should be transferred from the regulatory bodies to an independent body.
- The unit responsible for monitoring the performance of audit firms with listed clients should continue to develop inspection themes (such as auditor independence) and should publish annual information on how it monitors

the independence requirements and aggregate information on the effectiveness of the management of such matters by the major audit firms.

The review decided against the mandatory rotation of audit firms on the grounds that this:

- may have a negative impact on audit quality and effectiveness, particularly in the early years of an audit appointment;
- would create significant additional costs, especially in terms of management time and
- has had no strong positive impact in countries where it has been introduced.

The review group concluded that there were sensible and effective alternatives to mandatory rotation. These include giving the audit committee specific responsibility for periodic consideration of whether a change of external auditors is needed and professional requirements on the rotation of key audit partners on a regular basis (see **PARAGRAPH 2.43**).

2.42   Provision of Non-audit Services

There has been considerable debate in recent years over whether auditor independence is impaired by the provision of additional services (such as taxation services and consultancy advice) to audit clients and the Combined Code now recommends that audit committees should keep the nature and extent of any additional services under review. APB ES 5 deals in detail with the provision of non-audit services to an audit client and sets out comprehensive guidance on what is and is not acceptable in terms of the provision of the following services:

- internal audit;
- the design and implementation of IT systems;
- valuation and actuarial valuation services;
- taxation;
- litigation support and other legal work;
- corporate finance and other transaction-related services and
- accounting assistance.

The Companies (Audit, Investigations and Community Enterprise) Act 2004 also introduced new provisions on the disclosure of other services provided by the auditors and the related remuneration received by them, and new disclosure requirements under these provisions were introduced for accounting periods beginning on or after 1 October 2005 (see **PARAGRAPH 2.78**). The main reason given for the changes was that the provision of non-audit services to an audit client could undermine the auditors' independence, and that shareholders and others need to be given sufficient and appropriate information to be able to assess this potential threat and to make relevant comparisons between companies. Although many companies were already giving more than the previous statutory minimum disclosure, there were continuing concerns that a voluntary approach to disclosure was resulting in a lack of comparability.

2.43   Rotation of Audit Partners

APB ES 3 sets out the latest requirements on the rotation of audit partners. Generally, firms which audit listed companies are expected to have policies and procedures to ensure that:

- no individual acts as audit engagement partner or independent partner for such an engagement for a continuous period of more than five years;
- where the independent partner becomes the audit engagement partner, the combined period of service in those positions does not exceed five years;
- an audit engagement partner or independent partner who has acted in that role, or in a combination of the roles, for a period of five years (either continuously or in aggregate) does not hold any further position of responsibility in relation to the audit until a further period of five years has elapsed;
- no one acts as the key audit partner for a continuous period of more than seven consecutive years;
- where a key audit partner becomes the audit engagement partner, the combined period of service in these roles does not exceed seven years and
- an individual who has acted as a key audit partner for a period of seven years (either continuously or in aggregate) does not hold any further position of responsibility in relation to the audit until a further period of two years has elapsed.

Similar rotation requirements may also need to be applied in certain other cases (e.g. audits of other public interest entities). ES 3 generally applies for accounting periods beginning on or after 15 December 2004 but a limited degree of flexibility was permitted for financial periods beginning on or before 15 December 2006 where rotation might otherwise impair the quality of the audit. The guidance also allows for some flexibility in situations where partner continuity is particularly important (e.g. where the business is undergoing significant management changes or is involved in a takeover). Audit firms are expected to have policies and procedures to monitor the length of time that individuals serve in a senior role on any audit engagement that is not subject to the above rotation requirements, and ES 3 notes that serving as an audit engagement partner for a continuous period of more than 10 years may lead a reasonable and informed third party to conclude that the firm's independence is impaired. Although continuity of audit partner and audit staff can be helpful, companies should therefore expect their auditors to plan for changes over time.

2.44   Regular Review of Audit Arrangements

Changes in audit appointments may come about when auditors resign, do not seek reappointment or are not reappointed by the company. Broadly similar rules apply under CA 1985 whatever the reason for the change. It is normal practice for companies to review their audit arrangements on a regular basis. This may be particularly important as a business develops and expands and its overall needs change. In the case of a listed company, the audit committee is required to carry out an annual assessment of the independence, objectivity and effectiveness of the external audit (see **PARAGRAPH 2.26**), and should consider periodically whether any change of audit firm is needed. Issues to be considered might include the following:

- Do the auditors have the appropriate degree of industry knowledge and experience?
- Is the independence of the auditors still assured?
- Can the auditors provide the necessary geographical coverage?
- How effective has the audit service been in recent years?
- How well do the auditors communicate with company management on significant business issues and any material weaknesses identified in the systems of internal control?
- Does the audit provide value for money?
- Are the auditors able to provide the full range of services that the company requires (subject to professional considerations in respect of independence – see **PARAGRAPH 2.42**)?

From time to time, the company may wish to invite other firms to submit a proposal and fee quote for undertaking the audit. This may result from a positive decision to appoint new auditors (for instance, if the company is not satisfied with the audit service it is currently receiving, or if expansion of the business means that the current auditors are no longer able to provide the level of service that the company requires) or it may be done simply to confirm that the company is receiving value for money under its present arrangements. The process can involve a considerable amount of management time and will therefore not usually be undertaken more regularly than once every three to five years.

2.45   Resignation or Removal of Auditors

Complex provisions apply under CA 1985 when auditors resign from office, do not seek reappointment or are removed during their term of office. These provisions give the auditors certain rights to bring any information they consider necessary to the attention of the members or creditors of the company, and impose certain obligations on the company and its directors to ensure that the information is duly conveyed. Special notice must also be given for any resolution to remove auditors before their term of office has expired and for any resolution to appoint as auditors someone other than the retiring auditor, and there are detailed provisions in the legislation on sending copies to the auditors concerned. In particular, CA 1985 requires any auditor who ceases to hold office, for whatever reason, to deposit at the company's registered office:

- a statement of any circumstances connected with their ceasing to hold office that they consider should be brought to the attention of the members or creditors of the company or
- a statement that there are no such circumstances.

If the auditors' statement details circumstances that they consider should be brought to the attention of members and creditors, the company has 14 days in which to send a copy to every person who is entitled to be sent copies of the accounts or to apply to the court on the grounds that the auditors are using the statement to secure needless publicity.

The EC Statutory Audit Directive (see **PARAGRAPH 2.50**) includes a new requirement that the dismissal of statutory auditors should only be permitted where there are proper grounds. The DTI consultation document 'Implementation of Directive 2006/43/EC on Statutory Audits of Annual and Consolidated Accounts' published in March 2007 identifies three options for enforcement but expresses a preference for treating the dismissal of an auditor without proper grounds as unfair prejudice, so that shareholders can apply to the court for an appropriate remedy under Part 30 of CA 2006.

2.46   New Notification Requirements Under CA 2006

CA 2006 includes similar requirements to those explained in **PARAGRAPH 2.45**, except that:

- In the case of a quoted company it requires the auditors to make a statement of the circumstances connected with their ceasing to hold office.
- In the case of an unquoted company it requires either a statement of the circumstances connected with the auditors ceasing to hold office, or a statement that there are no circumstances that need to be drawn to the attention of the members or creditors of the company.

However, the new legislation also imposes certain additional notification requirements on both the auditors and the company in certain cases. These apply to all major audits (see below), irrespective of why the auditors cease to hold office, and in any other case where auditors cease to hold office before the end of their term of office (i.e. where they have resigned or have been dismissed). In these situations, the auditors must:

- notify the appropriate audit authority that they have ceased to hold office;
- accompany that notification with a copy of the statement of the circumstances connected with their ceasing to hold office that has been made to the company and
- if this statement is to the effect that there are no circumstances that need to be brought to the attention of the members of creditors of the company, provide a statement of the reasons for ceasing to hold office.

A major audit is defined in Section 525 of CA 2006 as a statutory audit of a listed company or of any other entity in which there is a major public interest. The FRC is expected to develop guidance on what constitutes a major public interest in this context.

In the case of a major audit, notification to the appropriate audit authority must be made at the same time as the auditors' statement is deposited at the company's registered office. In other cases, the timing of notification is to be decided by the audit authority but will not be earlier than the depositing of the statement with the company. For major audits, the appropriate audit authority will be the Secretary of State or a body to which functions relating to the supervision of statutory auditors have been delegated (currently the Professional Oversight Board (POB)), and in other cases it will be the relevant supervisory body.

The company must also notify the appropriate audit authority in any case where the auditors cease to hold office before the expiry of their term of office and must provide either:

- a statement by the company of the reasons for the auditors ceasing to hold office or
- where relevant, a copy of the statement by the auditor of the circumstances connected with his ceasing to hold office that need to be brought to the attention of the members or creditors of the company.

This notification must be given no later than 14 days after the date on which the auditors deposit their statement at the company's registered office.

2.47   Professional Requirements on a Change of Auditor

Where a company proposes to appoint new auditors, professional standards require the new auditor to communicate directly with the outgoing auditor before accepting appointment. The new audit firm will usually seek written permission from the company to communicate with the outgoing auditor and will ask the company to give written authority to the outgoing audit firm to discuss the matter freely with the proposed new auditor. If this permission is refused, the proposed new auditor will generally not be able to accept nomination or appointment. If an issue of conflicting viewpoints between the company and the existing auditor is raised in the response, the prospective audit firm is required to discuss the conflict with the company and satisfy themselves either that the company's view is one which they can accept as reasonable, or that the company accepts that the new auditor might have to express a contrary opinion (for instance, that the issue might result in a qualified audit report).

The EC Statutory Audit Directive (see **PARAGRAPH 2.50**) includes a new requirement for an outgoing auditor to provide all relevant information to the incoming auditor. The DTI consultation document 'Implementation of Directive 2006/43/EC on Statutory Audits of Annual and Consolidated Accounts' published in March 2007 proposes that this should be included in the rules of the recognised supervisory bodies.

2.48   Rights of External Auditors

Company law grants external auditors various rights in relation to their appointment. In particular they are:

- entitled to receive all notices of, and other communications relating to, any general meeting of the company which a member of the company is entitled to receive;
- entitled to attend any general meeting of the company and to be heard at any meeting they attend on any part of the business which concerns them as auditors and
- given a right of access at all times to the company's books, accounts and vouchers and entitled to require from the officers of the company the

information and explanations that they consider necessary in order to perform their duties as auditors.

The provisions were updated by the Companies (Audit, Investigations and Community Enterprise) Act 2004, so that the following persons now have a statutory duty to respond to enquiries by the auditors:

- any officer or employee of the company;
- any person accountable for the company's books, accounts or vouchers;
- any subsidiary incorporated in Great Britain, together with its officers, employees, auditors and any persons accountable for its books, accounts or vouchers and
- any persons who fell within one or more of the above categories at the time to which the auditors' enquiries relate.

It is an offence for any of the above to fail to respond, or to delay responding, to the auditors' enquiries. It is also an offence for them to knowingly or recklessly make an oral or written statement to the auditors that is misleading, false or deceptive in any material respect.

Separate provisions apply in respect of a subsidiary undertaking that is not a body corporate incorporated in Great Britain (for instance, a subsidiary incorporated overseas or an unincorporated UK entity, such as a partnership). These give the auditor the right to require the parent to obtain any information or explanations reasonably needed for the purpose of the audit, and create a statutory duty for the parent to take all steps reasonably open to it to obtain the relevant details.

Also, where the company's accounts are subject to audit, Section 234ZA of CA 1985 requires the directors' report to include a formal statement that, at the date on which the report is approved, no director has withheld information from the auditors which he or she knows, or ought to know, would be relevant to the audit. Information is covered by this requirement if:

- a director is aware of the information, or it would be reasonable for him or her to obtain it by making enquiries;
- the director knows, or ought to know, that the auditors are not aware of it and
- the director knows or ought to know that the information is relevant to the audit.

As with similar company law provisions, whether a director ought to know a matter is to be assessed on the basis of whether it would be known by a reasonably diligent person with the knowledge, skill and experience expected of a person carrying out the functions of a director and also the specific knowledge, skill and experience that the individual director has. This disclosure requirement applies for accounting periods beginning on or after 1 April 2005 and ending on or after 6 April 2005.

Similar provisions are retained under CA 2006.

In July 2007, the Audit Quality Forum (AQF) published a booklet in its 'Fundamentals' series dealing with the extent to which third party information and advice is currently disclosed to auditors and the potential impact of this on audit quality (available for download free of charge from http://www.icaew.com/auditquality). In particular, it considers the complex issue of legal professional privilege and its impact on disclosure to auditors. Auditors currently have no statutory right to obtain information from third parties and there may little reason or incentive for the third parties to co-operate in the audit process, unless this has been specifically included in the contract between the company and the third party. In some cases, auditors may be unaware of the involvement of a third party, or of certain aspects of the company's relationships with the third party. The AQF aims to promote debate on whether enough is being done, both in the UK and internationally, to make third party information available to auditors where appropriate and sets out a number of recommendations for change, including:

- the development of detailed guidance for directors on their obligations in respect of the preparation of true and fair accounts and the provision of information to auditors and covering in particular:
  - the requirement for each director to make appropriate enquiries in respect of disclosure to the auditors;
  - the drafting of instructions to third party advisers; and
  - company policy on the conduct of relationships with third parties;
- the development of standards or guidance on the provision of valuations, advice and similar services;
- a public debate on the merit of introducing a criminal offence for third parties who knowingly provide false, misleading or deceptive information to auditors, and on the possibility of introducing a duty for third parties to respond to auditor enquiries;
- revision and extension of the existing guidance on auditor requests to lawyers for information relevant to the audit, together with the development of related guidance for lawyers on responding to such requests; and
- a public debate on the possibility of extending the scope of legal professional privilege to include company auditors, and their professional regulators, where third party advice impacts on financial statements.

2.49 Duties of External Auditors

The duties imposed on external auditors under CA 1985 are:

- To report to the members on all annual accounts of the company that are to be laid before the company in general meeting during their term of office (see **PARAGRAPH 2.51**).
- To report on whether the information given in the directors' report is consistent with the accounts for that financial year.
- To carry out appropriate investigations to enable them to form an opinion on whether:
  - proper accounting records have been kept by the company;
  - proper returns adequate for audit purposes have been received from any branches not visited by them and

- ○ the company's individual accounts are in agreement with the accounting records and returns;
- ○ if the auditors are not satisfied on any of these issues, they must state this fact in their report on the annual accounts;
- If they have not received all the information and explanations they consider necessary in order to perform their audit, to state this fact in their audit report.
- If the accounts do not include all of the required disclosures in respect of directors' emoluments and other benefits, or transactions between the company and its directors or other officers, to include a statement of the missing details in their audit report, so far as they are reasonably able to do so (in the case of listed companies, the FSA also requires the auditors to review certain disclosures in respect of directors' remuneration required by the UK Listing Rules, and to provide details of any missing information in their report, although many of the disclosures required under the Listing Rules now overlap with company law requirements in respect of the directors' remuneration report).
- If the directors have taken advantage of Section 248 of CA 1985, which relieves small- and medium-sized companies from the requirement to prepare group accounts, but in the opinion of the auditors the company is not entitled to this exemption, to state this fact in their report on the company's accounts.

In highly regulated sectors, such as the banking and financial service sectors, auditors may be required to report directly to the regulator on certain matters specified in legislation or by the relevant regulator. They also have a duty to report directly to the regulator information which comes to their attention during the course of their work if there is reasonable cause for them to believe that this information may be of material significance to the regulator in carrying out his functions. A separate section of the UK & Ireland version of ISA 250 'Consideration of Laws and Regulations in an Audit of Financial Statements' sets out detailed guidance on this duty to report.

Auditors also have a duty under the Proceeds of Crime Act 2002 and the Money Laundering Regulations 2003 to report to the Serious Organised Crime Agency (SOCA) knowledge or suspicions of money laundering. This is given a very broad definition encompassing the possession, handling or concealment of the proceeds of any criminal activity. Fraud, tax evasion and the breach of other legislation (e.g. failure to comply with health and safety requirements) potentially come within the reporting requirement and there is no *de minimis* limit, so every offence will need to be considered, regardless of the amount involved.

2.50   Changes Under the EC Statutory Audit Directive

The EC Statutory Audit Directive is wide-ranging and aims to establish basic principles for the conduct and oversight of statutory audits within the EC. Member States are required to implement the requirements of the Directive into national law by June 2008 at the latest. Many of the requirements are already included in the UK framework for statutory audits and the regulation of auditors, although certain changes will need to be made. The DTI consultation document 'Implementation of Directive 2006/43/EC on Statutory Audits of Annual and Consolidated Accounts' published in March 2007 sets out an overview of the new Directive (which replaces the EC Eighth Company Law Directive) and the DTI's proposed approach to implementation. The DTI hopes to implement most of the changes from 6 April 2008 when Part 16 (Audit) of the CA 2006 will generally be brought into effect.

The DTI's proposals for implementation are likely to result in a combination of new regulations, amendments to CA 2006 (some of which will provide statutory underpinning for arrangements that are already in place) and changes to the APB's ES and related guidance.

The most significant changes are likely to result from the following requirements:

- Statutory audit fees must not be influenced by the provision of other services and cannot be based on any form of contingency – the APB is to review its ES in the light of the Directive's requirements.
- New provisions will apply on the documentation of group audits – these are expected to be adequately covered by the UK & Ireland version of ISA 600 (revised) 'The Audit of Group Financial Statements' but transitional arrangements may be needed until this comes into effect.
- The dismissal of statutory auditors will only be permitted where there are proper grounds (see PARAGRAPH 2.45).
- An outgoing auditor will have to provide all relevant information to the incoming auditor (see PARAGRAPH 2.47).
- Auditors of public interest entities will have to publish an annual transparency report about the firm – the POB has already consulted on this and brief details of the latest proposals are given below.
- Public interest entities will be required to have an audit committee (see PARAGRAPH 2.2).
- Key audit partners will be prohibited from taking up a key management position in an audited entity for two years after they have ceased to be auditor (see PARAGRAPH 2.21).

The requirement under the Directive that an audit report should be signed by the senior statutory auditor in his/her own name on behalf of the audit firm is already included in Section CA 2006 (see 2.52).

In May 2007, the POB published a short document summarising the responses to its initial consultation on transparency reporting by auditors and its current plans for implementation of the new requirements. The POB plans to publish draft regulations later in 2007 and to be ready to introduce them from 6 April 2008. This is some three months earlier than the deadline for implementation under the Directive, but the Government is keen to bring all impending accounts and audit changes under CA 2006 and recent EC Directives into effect from a single date. The main proposals are that:

- transparency reporting will be restricted to the auditors of listed companies;
- audit firms will be required to publish transparency reports either as a separate document or as a clearly identifiable part of an audit firm's annual

report, and the POB will provide a link on its website to each available transparency report and

- the regulations will not impose mandatory disclosures over and above those required by the Directive, but firms will be free to provide additional information on a voluntary basis.

The POB also notes that greater transparency on the capabilities of individual audit firms is one of the issues being considered in the FRC project on Choice in the Audit Market and that any recommendations from this project will be taken into account in finalising the requirements on transparency reporting. Additional non-statutory reporting guidance may also be developed in consultation with the professional accountancy bodies.

2.51   Reporting by External Auditors

At a Glance
* The auditors are required to report to the members on all annual accounts of the company.
* Auditors must also express an opinion on whether the directors' report is consistent with the financial statements for the relevant accounting periods.
* Company law and the UK & Ireland version of ISA 700 'The Auditor's Report on Financial Statements' set out detailed requirements on the form and content of auditors' reports.
* A separate audit opinion is required on summary financial statements prepared by a listed company.
* Auditors are also required to express an opinion on any revised accounts or reports issued by the company.
* If the audit report is qualified, the auditors must make a separate report in respect of any proposed distribution by the company.
* CA 1985 requires a formal report from the auditors (or, in some cases, from independent accountants) in certain other circumstances.
* The auditors will usually also report to management on any issues arising from their work.
* In the case of a listed company, the auditors are required to review certain disclosures and statements made by the directors under the Combined Code.
* The auditors may also review and report on any half-yearly report published by the company.

2.52   Report on Annual Accounts

The auditors are required to report to the members on all annual accounts of the company that are to be laid before the company in general meeting during their term of office (or, in the case of a private company that has elected to dispense with the laying of accounts, on all annual accounts sent to the members and others during the auditors' term of office). For accounting periods beginning on or after 1 January 2005, Section 235 of the CA 1985 specifies that the auditors must state whether, in their opinion:

- The annual accounts have been properly prepared in accordance with CA 1985 and, where relevant, with the International Accounting Standards (IAS) Regulation.
- The accounts give a true and fair view in accordance with the relevant financial reporting framework:
  o in the case of an individual balance sheet, of the state of affairs of the company at the end of the financial period;
  o in the case of an individual profit and loss account, of the profit or loss of the company for the financial year and
  o in the case of group accounts, of the state of affairs of the undertakings included in the consolidation as a whole, and of the profit or loss of those undertakings for the financial year, so far as concerns the members of the company.
- For accounting periods beginning on or after 1 April 2005, the information given in the directors' report is consistent with the accounts for the relevant financial year.
- In the case of a quoted company, the auditable part of the directors' remuneration report has been properly prepared in accordance with CA 1985.

The auditors' report must also:

- identify the accounts on which the auditors are reporting and the financial reporting framework under which they have been prepared;
- describe the scope of the audit and identify the auditing standards in accordance with which the audit has been conducted;
- be either qualified or unqualified, and include a reference to any matters to which the auditors wish to draw attention by way of emphasis without qualifying their report.

Most of the above requirements were introduced by the CA 1985 (IAS and Other Accounting Amendments) Regulations 2004 (SI 2004/2947) and the CA 1985 (OFR and Directors Report, etc.) Regulations 2005 (SI 2005/1011). Prior to this, the legislation included similar requirements for the auditors to express an opinion on whether the accounts showed a true and fair view and had been properly prepared in accordance with CA 1985 and for the auditors of quoted companies to report on certain elements of the directors' remuneration report but, in the case of the directors' report, required the auditors to report only on any inconsistency with the accounts. The legislation did not refer in any way to the financial reporting framework used, the audit scope or the auditing standards adopted.

Similar requirements will apply under CA 2006. However, where the auditor is a firm, the new legislation requires the audit report to be signed by the senior statutory auditor in his/her own name, for and on behalf of the audit firm. In other words, the audit engagement partner with overall responsibility for the audit will in future have to sign the audit report in his/her own name as well as that of the firm. This change anticipates a new requirement under the EC Statutory Audit Directive, which must be introduced in all Member States no later than June 2008 (see **PARAGRAPH 2.50**). The DTI consultation document 'Implementation of CA 2006' notes that, in the absence of any EU standards on identification of the senior statutory auditor, the DTI intends to ask the POB to develop appropriate guidance. There are also provisions enabling the name of the auditors and of the senior statutory auditor to be withheld where there are reasonable grounds to indicate that disclosure would create a serious risk of violence or intimidation, provided that certain conditions are met.

CA 2006 also introduces a new criminal offence of knowingly or recklessly causing an auditors' report on a company's annual accounts to:

- include any matter that is misleading, false or deceptive in a material particular or
- omit a statement required by the legislation in respect of:
  - accounts not agreeing with the accounting records and returns,
  - necessary information and explanations not being obtained or
  - the directors of a small company wrongly taking advantage of the exemption from the preparation of group accounts.

The wording of this aspect of the legislation gave rise to considerable debate during the passage of the legislation through Parliament and the accountancy profession raised a number of concerns over the potential implications. The Government maintains that recklessness has a significantly higher threshold than ordinary negligence or carelessness and that, in order to be caught by the offence, an auditor would need to have been aware that acting or, more likely, failing to act would carry certain risks and to have decided to proceed, regardless of this. In other words, an individual cannot be reckless inadvertently. The DTI consultation document 'Implementation of CA 2006' published in February 2007 indicates that the Secretary of State will issue guidance on the prosecution of auditors under the new offences and that the DTI intends prosecution to be used only in the most serious cases.

The audit provisions of CA 2006 are due to be brought into effect from 6 April 2008.

2.53   *The True and Fair View and IAS Accounts*

Following implementation of the IAS Regulation, which requires listed companies to prepare group accounts in accordance with IASs and gives most companies the option of adopting IASs in place of UK accounting standards, the Financial Reporting Review Panel (FRRP) and FRC have published two documents on the true and fair view in the context of IAS accounts:

- A legal opinion by Freshfields Bruckhaus Deringer on the effect of the IAS Regulation on the requirement for accounts to show a true and fair view – this concludes that, for companies preparing IAS accounts, references to the 'true and fair view' in the legislation are references to the requirement under IASs for accounts to achieve a fair presentation.

- A paper entitled 'The implications of new accounting and auditing standards for the true and fair view and auditors' responsibilities', which concludes that the concept of the true and fair view remains a cornerstone of financial reporting and auditing in the UK and that there has been no substantive change in the objectives of an audit and the nature of auditors' responsibilities.

Under Section 393(1) of CA 2006, directors must not approve accounts unless they are satisfied that those accounts give a true and fair view of the assets, liabilities, financial position and profit or loss of the company or the group (as appropriate), and Section 393(2) requires the auditors to have regard to this duty of the directors when carrying out their functions as auditors. This new section will apply to all accounts, irrespective of the financial framework adopted, and so should eliminate any remaining concerns over this issue. The existing requirements on the true and fair view and the true and fair override are retained in the section on Companies Act individual and group accounts. These provisions of CA 2006 are due to be brought into effect from 6 April 2008.

2.54 *Requirements of Auditing Standards*

For accounting periods beginning on or after 15 December 2004, detailed requirements on the form and content of an auditor's report are set out in the UK & Ireland version of ISA 700 'The Auditor's Report on Financial Statements'. This requires an auditor's report to include the following basic elements:

- A title.
- Details of the person(s) to whom the report is addressed.
- An opening or introductory paragraph which:
  - identifies the financial statements that have been audited;
  - explains the respective responsibilities of the entity's management and the auditors in respect of the financial statements.
- A scope paragraph which:
  - refers to the auditing standards in accordance with which the audit has been conducted;
  - describes the work that the auditor has performed.
- An opinion paragraph which:
  - refers to the financial framework used to prepare the financial statements;
  - expresses an opinion on the financial statements;
- The date of the auditor's report.
- The address of the auditors.
- The signature of the auditors.

Although the ISA includes illustrative wording for audit reports, the latest examples of auditors' reports for use in the UK are set out in APB Bulletin 2006/6 *Auditor's Reports on Financial Statements in the United Kingdom*.

2.55   *Financial Framework*

One of the key issues considered in Bulletin 2006/6 is the requirement to refer in the audit report to the financial framework that has been used to prepare the accounts and to state whether the accounts give a true and fair view in accordance with that framework. The example reports describe the financial reporting framework in the paragraph dealing with the directors' responsibilities in respect of the accounts as:

- 'in accordance with applicable law and with International Financial Reporting Standards (IFRSs) as adopted by the European Union' where IFRSs have been adopted and
- 'in accordance with applicable law and with United Kingdom Accounting Standards (United Kingdom Generally Accepted Accounting Practice)' where UK accounting standards have been adopted.

Equivalent wording is also used in the paragraph setting out the auditors' opinion. A similar illustrative audit opinion is given for small companies adopting the Financial Reporting Standard for Smaller Entities (FRSSE), although in this case the auditor's opinion refers to 'United Kingdom Generally Accepted Accounting Practice applicable to Smaller Entities'.

The Bulletin also deals with more complex issues, including requests for the auditor to express a 'true and fair' opinion in relation to full IFRSs as well as IFRSs adopted by the EU, and the difficulties that can arise when a parent company prepares IFRS group accounts but prepares its individual accounts in accordance with UK GAAP, and where advantage is taken of the exemption in Section 230 of the CA 1985 from publication of the parent company's own profit and loss account and certain related information.

2.56   *'Bannerman' Wording*

Following a judgement in the Scottish Court of Sessions (Royal Bank of Scotland v Bannerman Johnstone Maclay and others), the professional accountancy bodies issued a recommendation to their members that the following additional paragraph should be included in an auditor's report as protection against potential exposure to claims by third parties:

> 'This report is made solely to the company's members, as a body, in accordance with Section 235 of the CA 1985. Our audit work has been undertaken so that we might state to the company's members those matters we are required to state to them in an auditor's report and for no other purpose. To the fullest extent permitted by law, we do not accept or assume responsibility to anyone other than the company and the company's members as a body for our audit work, for this report, or for the opinions we have formed.'

It has therefore become normal practice for this to be included in all auditors' reports.

2.57   *Qualified Opinions, Adverse Opinions and Disclaimers*

Under ISA (UK and Ireland) 700 (see **PARAGRAPH 2.54**), auditors are required to express a qualified opinion when:

- they disagree with the treatment or disclosure of an item in the financial statements or
- there has been a limitation on the scope of their work (for instance, where there is inadequate evidence to support a figure in the accounts) and
- in the auditors' opinion, the effect is, or may be, material to the financial statements.

An adverse opinion must be issued when the effect of a disagreement is so material that the auditors conclude that the financial statements are seriously misleading, and a disclaimer of opinion must be expressed when the possible effect of a limitation in scope is so material that the auditors are unable to express an opinion on the financial statements.

In June 2007, the Financial Reporting Panel (FRRP) issued a consultation paper on whether it would be appropriate for registered audit firms to disclose on a voluntary basis to the FRRP any audit report that they issue with a qualified opinion. The disclosure would apply only to entities that come within the remit of the FRRP (i.e. issuers of listed securities, public companies and groups, and private companies and groups that do not qualify as small or medium-sized) and would be designed to facilitate the early identification of accounts that may not comply with company law requirements, so that prompt corrective action can be taken where necessary. Audit reports including an emphasis of matter paragraph (see **PARAGRAPH 2.58**) would not require disclosure under these arrangements. Comments on the proposals were invited by 31 July 2007 and further developments are awaited.

2.58   *Significant Uncertainty*

ISA (UK and Ireland) 700 also considers the situation of a significant uncertainty which is adequately accounted for and disclosed in the financial statements (for instance where the outcome of a significant litigation issue is still unclear, or the negotiation of bank facilities is still in progress). In these circumstances the auditors should consider adding an explanatory paragraph to their report, drawing attention to the uncertainty but making clear that their opinion is not qualified in this respect.

The standard specifically requires such a paragraph should be added to the auditor's report where the significant uncertainty involves a going concern problem.

2.59   Summary Financial Statements

Section 251 of CA 1985 enables companies to issue summary financial statements to their members, rather than copies of the full accounts, provided that certain conditions are properly observed (see **CHAPTER 10**). Summary financial statements must be derived from the annual accounts and directors' report, and must comply with the requirements of Section 251 of CA 1985 as regards their form and content. The summary financial statements are specifically required to include:

- An opinion from the auditors on whether the summary financial statement is consistent with the full accounts and (in the case of a quoted company) with the directors' remuneration report and, where the statement includes information derived from the directors' report, with that report or review.
- An opinion from the auditors on whether the statement complies with Section 251 of CA 1985 and any regulations made under that section.
- A statement on whether the auditors' report on the full accounts and, where relevant, the auditable part of the directors' remuneration report was qualified or unqualified – if it was qualified, the report must be set out in full, together with any additional information needed to understand the qualification (e.g. a particular note to the accounts).
- A statement on whether the auditors' report on the full accounts contained a statement under Section 237(2) of CA 1985 (inadequate accounting records or returns, or accounts not in agreement with the accounting records or returns) or under Section 237(3) of CA 1985 (failure to obtain all information and explanations the auditors considered necessary) – if such a statement was included, the auditors' report on the full accounts must be set out in the summary financial statements.
- A statement on whether the auditors' opinion on consistency between the directors' report and the accounts was qualified or unqualified – where the opinion was qualified, it must be set out in full, together with any additional material needed for the qualification to be understood.

Guidance on the procedures that the auditors should undertake is set out in APB Bulletin 1999/6 *The Auditors' Statement on the Summary Financial Statement* and the latest example of an auditors' report on summary financial statements is set out in APB Bulletin 2007/1 *Example Reports by Auditors under Company Legislation in Great Britain*. The APB is currently consulting on whether Bulletin 1999/6 should be updated to take account of the recent legislative changes in respect of summary financial statements or whether a UK & Ireland version of ISA 800 'The Independent Auditor's Report on Summary Audited Financial Statements' should be adopted in its place.

2.60   Revised Accounts and/or Reports

Where the company issues revised annual accounts under Sections 245 or 245A of CA 1985 and the Companies (Revision of Defective Accounts and Report) Regulations 1990 (SI 1990/2570 as amended by subsequent SIs), the auditors are required to state whether, in their opinion:

- the revised accounts have been properly prepared in accordance with the provisions of CA 1985 as they have effect under the Regulations;

- a true and fair view, seen as at the date on which the original annual accounts were approved, is given by the revised accounts with respect to the matters set out in Section 235(2) of CA 1985 and
- the original annual accounts failed to comply with the requirements of CA 1985 in the respects identified by the directors.

Where a revised directors' report or directors' remuneration report is issued under the same sections and regulations, the auditors are required to state whether, in their opinion, the information given in the revised report is consistent with the annual accounts for the relevant year (which must be stated). Example reports are given in APB Bulletin 2007/1 *Example Reports by Auditors under Company Legislation in Great Britain*. If there has been a change of auditors, the directors can resolve that the report be made by the auditors who reported on the original accounts and directors' report, provided that they are willing to do so and that they would still be eligible for appointment as auditors.

2.61   Distribution Where the Audit Report is Qualified

Where a company intends to make a distribution and the auditors have issued a qualified audit report on the last annual accounts, Section 271(4) of CA 1985 requires the auditors to make a written statement on whether, in their opinion, the matter in respect of which their report is qualified is material for the purpose of determining whether the proposed distribution contravenes the requirements of Sections 263–265 and 270 of CA 1985 on profits available for distribution. The auditors can make this written statement either simultaneously with their report on the annual accounts or at a later date, but it must be laid before the company in general meeting before the distribution is made. An example report is given in APB Bulletin 2007/1 *Example Reports by Auditors under Company Legislation in Great Britain*. The report can only be made by the auditors who qualified their report on the relevant accounts.

2.62   Distribution by Public Company Based on Initial Accounts

Where a company wishes to make a distribution during its first accounting reference period, or before the accounts for that period have been laid before the members or delivered to the registrar, initial accounts must be prepared to support the distribution. In the case of a public company, Section 273 of CA 1985 requires initial accounts to be:

- properly prepared in accordance with the normal accounting requirements of CA 1985;
- approved and signed by the directors and
- delivered to the registrar.

The auditors are required to report whether, in their opinion, the initial accounts have been properly prepared (which is specifically defined as showing a true and fair view of the state of the company's affairs at the balance sheet date and the profit or loss for the relevant period, and complying with the relevant accounting provisions of CA 1985). An example report is given in APB Bulletin 2007/1 *Example Reports by Auditors under Company Legislation in Great Britain*. If the report is qualified, the auditors must also state whether, in their opinion, the matter in respect of which their report is qualified is material for the purpose of determining whether the proposed distribution contravenes the requirements of Sections 263–265 and 270 of CA 1985 on profits available for distribution. The auditors' report (and the statement, where relevant) must be delivered to the Registrar of Companies with the initial accounts before the distribution takes place.

2.63   Reregistration of a Private Company As a Public Company

A private company that wishes to reregister as public must deliver certain documents to the Registrar of Companies, including an audited balance sheet and related notes as at a date not more than seven months before the application to reregister. The auditors are required to make an unqualified written statement that, in their opinion, this balance sheet shows that the amount of the company's net assets (as defined in Section 264(2) of CA 1985) at this balance sheet date was not less than the aggregate of its called up share capital and undistributable reserves. An example report is given in APB Bulletin 2007/1 *Example Reports by Auditors under Company Legislation in Great Britain*. If the company's last audited accounts covered a period ending more than seven months before the application, an updated balance sheet will need to be prepared by the company and audited by the auditors.

2.64   Redemption or Purchase of Own Shares Out of Capital

Where a private company redeems or purchases its own shares wholly or partly out of capital, the directors are required by Section 173 of CA 1985 to make a statutory declaration specifying the amount of the permissible capital payment for the shares in question and setting out their opinion that:

- there are no grounds on which the company could be found unable to pay its debts immediately following the payment out of capital and
- the company will be able to continue to carry on business as a going concern throughout the year immediately following the date of the payment and will be able to pay its debts as they fall due.

The form and content of this declaration, and the issues that the directors must take into account when making it, are specified in the legislation. When the declaration is delivered to the registrar, it must have attached to it a report by the auditors, addressed to the directors, stating that:

- they have enquired into the company's state of affairs;
- in their opinion, the amount specified in the declaration as the permissible capital payment has been properly determined in accordance with Section 171 and 172 of CA 1985 and
- they are not aware of anything to indicate that the opinion expressed by the directors in the declaration is unreasonable in all the circumstances.

An example report is given in APB Bulletin 2007/1 *Example Reports by Auditors under Company Legislation in Great Britain*. The legislation makes no provision for this report to be qualified, so if the auditors are unable to make these statements the redemption or purchase cannot proceed.

2.65   Financial Assistance for the Purchase of Own Shares

Financial assistance for the purchase of own shares can only be given in very specific circumstances. Before the assistance is given, the directors must make a statutory declaration setting out details of the proposed financial assistance and expressing their opinion that:

- there are no grounds on which the company could be found unable to pay its debts immediately following the giving of the financial assistance and either
- the company will be able to pay its debts as they fall due during the year immediately following the giving of the assistance or,
- if it is intended to commence the winding-up of the company within 12 months, the company will be able to pay its debts in full within 12 months of the commencement of the winding-up.

The form and content of this declaration, and the issues that the directors must take into account when making it, are set out in Section 156 of CA 1985. When the declaration is delivered to the registrar, it must have attached to it a report by the auditors, addressed to the directors, stating that:

- they have enquired into the state of affairs of the company and
- they are not aware of anything to indicate that the opinion expressed by the directors in the declaration is unreasonable in all the circumstances.

An example report is given in APB Bulletin 2007/1 *Example Reports by Auditors under Company Legislation in Great Britain*. Once again, the legislation makes no provision for this report to be qualified, so if the auditors are unable to make these statements, the directors cannot proceed with the proposed financial assistance.

CA 2006 makes a number of changes to the current requirements on the purchase of own shares. In particular, it abolishes the prohibition on a private company giving financial assistance for a purchase of its own shares, but retains the prohibition (together with certain exemptions) in the case of public companies. However, the new provisions are not due to be brought into effect until 1 October 2008.

2.66　Allotment of Shares by a Public Company Other than for Cash

Where a public company proposes to allot shares for consideration in a form other than cash, it is usually required by Section 103 of CA 1985 to obtain a report on the value of the assets to be received as consideration for the shares. This report must be obtained in six months before the date of allotment and must be made by independent accountants who may, but need not, be the auditors of the company. If they are not the auditors, they must be qualified to act as auditors (see **PARAGRAPHS 2.37** and **2.38**). Under Section 108 of CA 1985:

- The independent accountants may rely on a valuation made by another specialist who appears to them to have the requisite knowledge and experience, and who is not associated with the company (e.g. as an officer or employee of the company or group) – in practice they will have to follow the detailed guidance in the UK & Ireland version of ISA 620; 'Using the work of an expert' if they wish to adopt this approach.
- Their report must state:
  - the nominal value of the relevant shares;
  - the amount of any premium payable on the shares;
  - a description of the consideration;
  - if they have valued part (or all) of the consideration themselves, a description of that part, the method of valuation and the date of valuation and
  - where all or part of the consideration has been valued by another person, a statement of this fact, the valuer's name, knowledge and experience, a description of the consideration, and the method and date of valuation.
- The report must also contain, or be accompanied by, a note by the independent accountants that:
  - where a valuation has been carried out by another person, it appeared reasonable to them to arrange or accept this;
  - the method of valuation was reasonable in all the circumstances;
  - it appears to them that there has been no material change in the value of the consideration since the valuation and
  - on the basis of the valuation, the value of the consideration together with any cash to be paid is not less than the aggregate of the nominal value of the shares and any premium to be treated as paid up.

An example report is given in APB Bulletin 2007/1 *Example Reports by Auditors under Company Legislation in Great Britain.* The legislation makes no provision for the independent accountants' report to be qualified. Additional requirements apply under Section 108(7) of CA 1985 where the consideration for the transfer of a non-cash asset is only partly satisfied by the allotment of shares.

2.67　Transfer of Non-cash Assets to a Public Company by a Member of the Company

In the first two years following registration or re-registration as a public company, Section 104 of CA 1985 requires a company to obtain approval by an

Audit Matters

ordinary resolution of the company if it wishes to purchase from a subscriber to the company's memorandum a non-cash asset for consideration worth one tenth or more of the nominal value of the company's issued share capital. In addition, a valuation report similar to that required on the allotment of share for non-cash consideration must have been made to the company in the six months immediately preceding the transfer. The report must be made by independent accountants qualified to act as auditors (although they need not be the auditors) and the same rules apply on accepting a valuation carried out by another person as for the allotment of shares by a public company other than for cash (see **PARAGRAPH 2.66**). In addition, under Section 109 of CA 1985, the independent accountants' report must:

- State the consideration to be received and given, describing the assets and specifying any amounts to be paid or received in cash.
- State the method and date of valuation.
- Contain, or be accompanied by, a note by the independent accountants that:
  - where a valuation has been carried out by another person, it appeared reasonable to them to arrange or accept this;
  - the method of valuation was reasonable in all the circumstances;
  - it appears to them that there has been no material change in the value of the consideration since the valuation and
  - on the basis of the valuation, the value of the consideration to be received by the company is not less than the value of the consideration to be given.

The legislation makes no provision for the independent accountants' report to be qualified. Additional requirements apply under Section 109(3) of CA 1985 where the consideration is given only partly for the transfer of a non-cash asset. An example report is given in APB Bulletin 2007/1 *Example Reports by Auditors under Company Legislation in Great Britain.*

2.68   Reporting to Management

During the audit, or at the conclusion of their work, the auditors will usually report formally to the directors or senior management on:

- any significant weaknesses in the accounting or internal control systems that have come to their attention during the audit, together with their recommendations for improvements;
- any significant business issues that have come to their attention during the audit, together with their advice (for instance, potential economies or improvements in efficiency) and
- any significant errors identified during the audit and comments on any individual accounting policies or practices that they consider need to be drawn to the attention of the directors or senior management.

If the company has an audit committee, these issues may be reported to the directors through the audit committee (see **PARAGRAPH 2.25**). Auditing Standards require auditors to report significant weaknesses in accounting and internal control systems to the directors or senior management on a timely basis, unless the weakness has already been identified by the entity and appropriate corrective action taken. The auditors will usually ask directors or senior management to respond to the points raised in their report, indicating the actions to be taken. Less significant issues will usually be discussed at a meeting with the directors or senior management and the points raised documented for future reference, together with any action agreed. It is normal practice for auditors to follow up all the issues that have been reported, usually during their subsequent audit, to confirm that the action agreed in response to the points raised has actually been taken.

2.69   *Scope of Report*

The auditors' work is carried out on a test basis and will normally be concentrated on those areas that present the highest risk of material error or misstatement in the accounts. The nature of the work therefore means that the auditors' report to management cannot be a comprehensive statement of all weaknesses which may exist in the accounting and internal control systems, or of all improvements that could be made. The auditors' formal report will therefore usually emphasise that it covers only those issues that have come to their attention during the course of the audit, and may give an explanation of the audit approach to help the directors understand the scope of the work undertaken.

2.70   *Confidentiality of Reports*

The reports that auditors issue to the directors or senior management are confidential documents and the auditors will therefore usually include in the report a statement that it has been prepared solely for the use of the company's management and should not be disclosed or quoted to another party without the prior written consent of the auditors. Similarly, the auditors will not usually provide a copy of the report to another party without the prior written consent of the directors. However, in certain regulated industries (such as the banking and financial services sectors) and in the public sector, auditors will often have a duty to provide copies of their reports to the relevant regulatory body or funding council.

2.71   Reporting Under the Combined Code

The FSA Listing Rules require the directors of listed companies to make statements in the annual report on compliance with the best practice provisions of the Combined Code and on going concern. These requirements are considered in more detail in **CHAPTER 6**. Where the FSA requires the directors to make such statements, the Listing Rules stipulate that they must also be reviewed by the auditors. In the case of the compliance statement, the auditors' review is only required to cover those aspects of the Code that can be verified objectively. There is no requirement under the Listing Rules for the auditors to prepare a formal report on the results of their review, or for such a report to be published.

The latest APB guidance now requires the extent of the auditors' review of the corporate governance statements to be explained in the section of the audit report that explains the auditors' responsibilities. The latest examples can be found in APB Bulletin 2006/6 *Auditor's Reports on Financial Statements in the United Kingdom*. If the auditors are not satisfied with the adequacy of the corporate governance disclosures and cannot resolve the problems through discussion with the directors, they are required to report their concerns in a separate paragraph as part of their opinion on the financial statements, but this will not constitute a qualification of their report on the annual accounts.

2.72   *Agreement of Scope of Review*

It is important that the respective responsibilities of the directors and the auditors in relation to the corporate governance statements, and the scope of the auditors' work on the statements, are clarified at an early stage to prevent any potential misunderstandings. The intention of the present Listing Rules is to ensure that auditors provide some assurance on the directors' corporate governance disclosures, but to avoid substantial additional audit work and the consequent financial implications that this would have for companies. The scope of the auditors' work in respect of corporate governance statements should be set out in a formal engagement letter between the company and the auditors. This can be dealt with as a stand-alone document or as a separate section of the engagement letter for the statutory audit. APB Bulletin 2004/3 *The Combined Code on corporate governance: Requirements of Auditors under the Listing Rules of the FSA* sets out guidance on the detailed procedures that auditors should normally undertake when reviewing corporate governance statements.

2.73   Reporting on Half-Yearly Reports

Listed companies are required by the FSA Listing Rules to issue a half-yearly report each year, giving details of their results for the first half of the financial year. Certain changes to the requirements have been introduced for accounting periods beginning on or after 20 January 2007 as a result of UK implementation of the EU Transparency Directive (see **PARAGRAPH 10.106**). There is currently no formal requirement for auditors to review or report on interim reports before they are published. For accounting periods ending before 20 September 2007, APB Bulletin 1999/4 *Review of Interim Financial Information* sets out guidance on the procedures that should be undertaken where auditors are asked to review a half-yearly report, although it notes that the directors (or, where relevant, the audit committee) may ask the auditors to carry out specific agreed procedures as an alternative to this. For accounting periods ending on or after 20 September, APB Bulletin 1999/4 is superseded by a UK and Ireland version of International Standard on Review Engagements 2410 (ISRE 2410) *Review of Interim Financial Information Performed by the Independent Auditor of the Entity*. Earlier adoption of this standard is also encouraged. The approach taken in ISRE (UK & Ireland) 2410 is broadly consistent with that previously adopted in Bulletin 1999/4, and the APB considers that the new requirements should not result in a significant increase in the amount of work carried out.

Where a half-yearly report is reviewed in accordance with the APB standard or guidance, the FSA Listing Rules require the auditors' review report to be published as part of the half-yearly report. The Accounting Standards Board (ASB) Statement 'Half-yearly Financial Reports' also recommends disclosure of the extent to which the information given in the half-yearly report has been audited or reviewed. The latest guidance on the wording of the review report can be found in ISRE (UK & Ireland) 2410. Because the recommended review work is limited in scope, and does not constitute an audit, the auditors will normally report in terms of 'negative assurance' – in other words, they report that nothing has come to their attention to indicate that material modification is required to the information presented in the report. Where the scope of the work agreed between the directors and auditors is less than that set out in the APB standard or guidance, the directors should describe the half-yearly report as 'neither audited nor reviewed'.

2.74 Remuneration of External Auditors and Their Associates

At a Glance
* The directors are usually authorised to agree the remuneration of the external auditors.
* The remuneration paid to the auditors for their work as auditors must be disclosed in the notes to the accounts.
* The accounts must also disclose any remuneration paid to the auditors and their associates for non-audit services.
* The ICAEW has issued detailed guidance on the disclosure requirements that apply for accounting periods beginning on or after 1 October 2005.

2.75 Remuneration for Services As Auditors

CA 1985 provides for the remuneration of the auditors to be fixed as follows:

* Where the auditors have been appointed by the company, their remuneration should be fixed by the company in general meeting, or in any other way decided by the company in general meeting (in practice, most companies resolve to give the directors authority to agree the auditors' remuneration).
* Where the auditors have been appointed by the directors, their remuneration should be fixed by the directors.
* Where the auditors have been appointed by the Secretary of State, their remuneration should be fixed by the Secretary of State.

The legislation defines remuneration as including amounts paid in respect of expenses and any benefits in kind, but in practice, professional and ethical guidelines will usually prevent auditors from accepting benefits in kind from the company. In the case of listed companies, the audit committee should be responsible for making recommendations to the board, and thence to the shareholders, on the remuneration of the external auditors (see **PARAGRAPH 2.19**). Similar requirements will continue to apply under CA 2006.

2.76 Disclosure of Remuneration for Services As Auditors

For accounting periods beginning before 1 October 2005, Section 390A of CA 1985 required the remuneration paid to the auditors in respect of their work as auditors to be disclosed in the notes to the annual accounts. For accounting periods beginning on or after 1 October 2005, a revised Section 390B of CA 1985 gives the Secretary of State new powers to make regulations on the disclosure of remuneration received or receivable by the auditors, and detailed requirements are now set out in the Companies (Disclosure of Auditor Remuneration) Regulations 2005 (SI 2005/2417). These supersede the previous regulations on the disclosure of auditor remuneration and cover fees for both audit and non-audit work. However, the changes relate primarily to the disclosure of fees for non-audit work. The requirement to give separate disclosure of the auditors' remuneration as auditors continues to apply to all companies. The amount to be disclosed should include the audit fee, any amounts payable in respect of expenses and the estimated money value of any benefits in kind received by the auditors in respect of their services as auditors. The nature of any benefits in kind should also be disclosed. However, professional and ethical requirements will usually prevent auditors from accepting benefits in kind from the company.

The amount to be disclosed is the remuneration payable in respect of the current year. This will usually be an estimate of the amount to be charged for the audit (including expenses). Minor adjustments to this figure are not usually disclosed but if the audit fee for a particular year has effectively been under/overstated by a material amount, it will usually be appropriate to disclose the adjustment separately in the following year's accounts.

2.77 *Particular Issues in Group Accounts*

The new disclosure requirements make a number of changes to the disclosure of audit fees in group accounts. These are considered in some detail in the guidance prepared by the ICAEW (see **Paragraph 2.82**). In particular:

- the amount to be disclosed is the fee receivable by the auditor of the parent company in relation to the audit of the individual accounts of that company and the audit of the consolidation, including any work carried out by the parent company auditors on consolidation returns prepared by the subsidiaries;
- any fees receivable by the parent company auditors in respect of statutory audit work for one or more of the individual subsidiaries (i.e. separate from

the audit work on the group accounts) do not form part of this disclosure and should instead be included in the first disclosure category for fees for non-audit services (i.e. the auditing of accounts of associates of the company pursuant to legislation), together with any similar fees receivable by the auditors' associates – this represents a significant change from the previous requirements, where audit fees for companies included in the consolidation were aggregated for disclosure in the notes to the group accounts and

- where a subsidiary is audited by a firm that is not associated with the parent company auditors, this audit fee will no longer be included in the group accounts disclosures.

Companies may provide additional information on a voluntary basis if this is considered helpful to users of the accounts, but the disclosures required by the regulations must be clearly and separately identified.

2.78   Remuneration for Non-audit Services

For accounting periods beginning on or after 1 October 2005, a revised Section 390B of CA 1985 empowers the Secretary of State to make provision for disclosure of the nature of any services provided by the auditors, to require the details to be given by a particular class or description, and to require the disclosure of the separate amounts received by the auditors and their associates, or the disclosure of aggregate amounts. Regulations can also specify that disclosure should be given in the notes to the accounts, the directors' report or the auditors' report.

The Companies (Disclosure of Auditor Remuneration) Regulations 2005 (SI 2005/2417) were laid before Parliament in August 2005 and supersede the previous disclosure requirements for accounting periods beginning on or after 1 October 2005. They require companies to give separate disclosure in the notes to the accounts for each type of service specified in Schedule 2 to the regulations and the amount paid to the auditors and their associates for that service, with no *de minimis* exemptions. The following categories are specified for disclosure:

- auditing the accounts of associates of the company pursuant to legislation;
- other services provided under legislation;
- other services relating to taxation;
- services relating to information technology;
- internal audit services;
- valuation and actuarial services;
- services relating to litigation;
- services relating to recruitment and remuneration;
- services relating to corporate finance transactions and
- other services.

Where a service could fall within more than one of the specified categories, it should be treated as falling within the first one listed. As under the previous disclosure requirements, remuneration includes any benefits in kind (although these should be rare in practice) and the nature and estimated money value of such benefits must be separately disclosed. The auditors are also required to provide the directors with any information needed to comply with the disclosure requirements. Where more than one person has acted as auditor during the year, separate disclosure is required for each auditor and their associates.

2.79   *Disclosure Exemptions*

Small- and medium-sized companies and groups continue to be exempt from the detailed disclosures in respect of non-audit services, although they must continue to disclose the remuneration paid to the auditors in respect of the audit of the company's accounts.

However, the DTI consultation document 'Implementation of Directive 2006/43/EC on Statutory Audits of Annual and Consolidated Accounts' (see **PARAGRAPH 2.50**) notes that changes under this Directive include the introduction of a requirement for medium-sized companies to supply additional information on non-audit services provided by their auditors if so requested by the POB. This will require a change to the regulations on the disclosure of auditor remuneration.

There is also no requirement for the disclosures in respect of non-audit services to be given in the individual accounts of a parent company, or of its subsidiaries, when the parent is required to prepare group accounts under CA 1985, provided that the individual accounts state that the relevant disclosures are required to be given in the group accounts.

2.80   *Associates of the Company*

The disclosure requirements cover services provided to the company and its associates. A company's associates include any subsidiary, other than one in respect of which severe long-term restrictions substantially hinder the exercise of the company's rights, and any associated pension scheme, which is defined as a scheme for the provision of pension and similar retirement or death benefits to directors and employees (or former directors and employees) of the company or any subsidiary, where either:

- a majority of trustees are appointed by the company or a subsidiary (or a person acting on their behalf) or
- the company or a subsidiary exercises a dominant influence over the appointment of the auditor to the scheme.

Overseas entities are included within the definition. For each service category identified in **PARAGRAPH 2.78** above, separate details must be given for services provided to the company and its subsidiaries, and services provided to any associated pension schemes.

2.81   *Associates of the Auditors*

Under the new regulations, the following are included within the definition of associates of the auditors:

- any person controlled by the auditors or by an associate of the auditors (unless the control arises solely as a result of an insolvency or receivership appointment);

- any person or group of persons which controls the auditors;
- any person using a common or similar trading name to the auditors, if the auditors intention in using that name is to create the impression of a connection between them;
- any party to an arrangement with the auditors under which costs, profits, quality control, business strategy or significant professional resources are shared and
- any partnership which has a partner in common with the auditors, or any body corporate which has a director in common with the auditors.

The regulations also cover a number of more complex situations involving links and associations with other partnerships and bodies corporate. Overseas entities are also included within the definition of associates. The definitions are comprehensive and will capture a wide-range of individuals and organisations with connections to the auditor. Careful judgement will therefore need to be applied in assessing whether a particular individual, partnership, body corporate or other entity meets the new definition of an associate.

2.82   ICAEW Guidance

In October 2006, the ICAEW published detailed guidance on the practical implications of the new disclosure requirements in TECH 06/06 'Disclosure of Auditor Remuneration' (available from http://www.icaew.co.uk). A updated version of this document, under the same reference and title, was issued in July 2007. This leads the reader through a series of questions on the disclosure requirements that apply for accounting periods beginning on or after 1 October 2005 and provides as an Appendix a comprehensive worked example of how the detailed requirements might be met in practice. Particular issues highlighted in the guidance include:

(i)   significant changes to the way in which information on auditor remuneration should be presented in group accounts;

(ii) the disclosure exemptions for parent and subsidiary companies and the fact that these apply only where the parent is required to prepare group accounts under CA 1985 and

(iii) the practical implications of the revised definitions of associates of the auditors and associates of the company.

There is also guidance on how certain more common work assignments (such as reviews of half-yearly reports, reports relating to government grants, and statutory or regulatory reports on internal controls) should be categorised for disclosure purposes.

2.83   Liability Limitation Agreements

At a Glance
* Auditors have a contractual responsibility to the company.
* Auditors may also be liable in tort to the company if they are negligent in carrying out their duties as auditors.

Audit Matters

> * CA 2006 introduces new provisions on liability limitation agreements for company auditors.
> * The changes are due to be brought into effect from 6 April 2008.
> * Further changes may be implemented as a result of EU requirements.

2.84   Contractual Relationships

Although the auditors are required by company law to report to the shareholders, they are engaged by the company. They consequently have a contractual responsibility to the company, not to the shareholders, and are contractually bound to carry out the terms of the engagement that they have been appointed to fulfil. Professional auditing standards require auditors to summarise the respective rights and responsibilities of the directors and the auditors in relation to the annual accounts and the audit in formal terms of engagement between the company and the auditors. This helps to ensure that each party is clear about the respective responsibilities and should help to prevent any potential misunderstandings. The terms of engagement may be limited to the statutory requirements or may be extended beyond these, depending on the agreement between the two parties. Auditors are liable to the company for any breach of contract under the terms of their engagement with the company.

2.85   Liability in Tort

Auditors are also liable in tort to the company where they are negligent in carrying out their duties as auditors and potentially also to a third party who suffered damage or loss as a result of relying on the auditors' report. However, case law demonstrates that a substantial burden of proof is required in order to demonstrate liability in tort. In Caparo Industries plc v Dickman (1990 2 AC 605), it was held that, in the absence of any contractual or other special relationship with an investor, potential investor or third party, auditors do not owe a duty of care to individual shareholders or to the public in general who may rely on the audited accounts of the company. Auditors are liable only to the company and to the existing shareholders, as a body, in respect of their governance rights – they generally have no liability to shareholders or potential investors who may rely on their audit report when making investment decisions, or to creditors making decisions on whether to extend credit to the company. However, more recent cases, such as ADT Limited v BDO Binder Hamlyn (1996 BCC 808) and Barings plc (in administration) and others v Coopers & Lybrand (a firm) and others (1997 BCC 498), have suggested that auditors may owe a duty of care to a potential acquirer where they are aware of the reliance being placed on their report and that the auditors of a subsidiary may, in certain circumstances, owe an additional duty of care to the holding company. A subsequent case in the Scottish Court of Session, Royal Bank of Scotland v Bannerman Johnstone Maclay and other (unreported, 23 July 2002), also suggested that auditors could owe a duty of care to a company's bank if they know, or ought to know, that the bank will rely on those accounts (see also **PARAGRAPH 2.56**).

2.86 Position Under CA 1985

Section 310(1) of CA 1985 prevents auditors from being exempted from liability or indemnified by the company, or by contract, against liability for negligence, default, breach of duty or breach of trust in relation to the company. However, a company is permitted by Section 310(3) to purchase or maintain for the auditors insurance against such a liability, or to indemnify auditors against any liability incurred by them in successfully defending any civil or criminal proceedings or where the court grants relief from liability under Section 727(1) of CA 1989 on the grounds of honest and reasonable conduct.

2.87 Company Law Review

A DTI consultation document towards the end of 2003 considered the issue of the liability of both company directors and auditors. This explained the background to the significant difficulties surrounding this issue and sought responses to a substantial number of questions in the hope that a consensus would emerge on the best way forward. Existing company law provisions on the limitation of liability were no longer considered adequate or appropriate, given the significant changes in the business environment since they were originally introduced. Directors were particularly concerned that they may face legal action for breach of the duty of skill and care even where they had acted in good faith and in what they considered to be the best interests of the company. This gave rise to further concerns that high-calibre individuals may be reluctant to take on the role of company director, and in particular that of a non-executive director, because of the significant personal risks that this might entail. For auditors, the concerns centred on their current exposure to unlimited liability and the difficulty (and cost) of obtaining appropriate professional indemnity insurance cover.

The Companies (Audit, Investigations and Community Enterprise) Act 2004 made changes to improve the position in respect of directors' liability but did not deal with the issue of auditor liability. However, the Government did express concern at two issues raised by investors and companies in response to the earlier consultation document – a view from some investors that the present audit process may not be serving them well, and a view from some of the largest companies that their choice of auditor was limited – and indicated that it would be willing to consider the introduction of a system that would allow auditors to limit their liability on a proportionate basis by contract with the shareholders if it was clear that this would both improve audit quality and enhance competition.

2.88 Liability Limitation Agreements

Sections 532 of CA 2006 retains the general prohibition against a company exempting or indemnifying its auditors from any liability in connection with negligence, default, breach of duty or breach of trust in respect of the audit of the company's accounts, except as permitted by:

(i)   Section 533 in respect of an indemnity for the costs of successfully defending proceedings or

(ii) Sections 534–538 which set out new provisions in respect of liability limitation agreements.

In particular, Section 533 no longer allows a company to purchase or maintain insurance for its auditors against any relevant liabilities, as is currently permitted by Section 310(3) of CA 1985.

A liability limitation agreement is defined as an agreement that seeks to limit the liability owed to a company by its auditors in relation to the audit of its accounts. The agreement can cover any liability for negligence, default, breach of duty or breach of trust but it cannot cover more than one financial year and so must specify the year to which it relates. The limitation must also be fair and reasonable, taking into account in particular:

(i)   the auditors' responsibilities;

(ii) the nature and purpose of the auditors' contractual obligations to the company and

(iii) the professional standards expected of the auditors.

The legislation does not require the agreement to be framed in any particular way and states specifically that the limit on the amount of the auditors' liability need not be a sum of money, or a formula, specified in the agreement. However, the Secretary of State is empowered to make regulations that require or prevent the inclusion of specified provisions.

The new provisions are due to be brought into effect from 6 April 2008.

2.89   Authorisation Process

A liability limitation agreement must be authorised by the members but can be put into place by an ordinary resolution unless the company's articles require a higher majority (or unanimity). It can also be withdrawn by ordinary resolution at any time before the company enters into the agreement or before the beginning of the financial year to which it relates. In the case of a private company, an agreement may be authorised:

(i)   by the company passing a resolution, before it enters into the agreement, which either waives the need for approval or approves the principal terms of the agreement or

(ii) by the company passing a resolution granting approval of the agreement after it has been entered into.

Similar arrangements apply in the case of a public company, except that the agreement must always be approved by the members (i.e. authorisation cannot be achieved by waiving the need for approval). In the case of advance approval, the principal terms must include the type of act or omission covered, the financial year to which the limitation relates and the limit to which the auditor's liability is subject.

2.90 *Disclosure Requirements*

Section 538 requires the fact that the company has entered into a liability limitation agreement with its auditors to be disclosed as prescribed in regulations to be made by the Secretary of State. These regulations will be able to specify that disclosure should be made in a note to the accounts or in the directors' report. The DTI consultation document 'Implementation of CA 2006' published in February 2007 notes that the DTI intends to require disclosure to be made in a note to the accounts and to include:

(i) the principal terms of the agreement and
(ii) the date of the resolution approving the agreement or, in the case of a private company, waiving the need for shareholder approval.

2.91 European Context

The question of auditor liability is currently under wider consideration within the EU. In common with the earlier UK discussions and consultations, options put forward in the European Commission's consultation on how a limitation on auditor liability might be introduced include:

(i)   a fixed monetary cap;
(ii) a cap based on the size of the company, measured by its market capitalisation;
(iii) a cap based on a multiple of the audit fees charged or
(iv) the introduction of the principle of proportionate liability.

Although the proposals raised correspond closely with those already considered in the UK, there is no guarantee that the solution reached at the EU level will be the same as that introduced by CA 2006.

2.92 Internal Audit

At a Glance
* The primary role of internal audit is to assist in the identification of risk and provide assurance that the internal control system is effective in reducing risk to an acceptable level.
* There are significant differences between the roles of external and internal auditors.
* A strong internal audit function can enable management to demonstrate that they are taking their responsibilities seriously.
* Internal auditors may also carry out special assignments to assist in the achievement of business objectives.

> * An internal audit function can be established in-house or sub-contracted to an appropriate external organisation.
> * Formal terms of reference should be developed for internal audit.
> * The head of internal audit should have appropriate professional expertise and carry the respect, confidence and support of senior management.
> * The internal audit department must have adequate resources to carry out its work.
> * Internal auditors must be genuinely independent of the company's systems and operations.
> * The scope of internal audit work should generally be unrestricted.
> * The first stage in planning internal audit work is to prepare an audit needs assessment and strategic and annual internal audit plans.
> * Internal audit should issue individual reports on each system or operational area covered.
> * The audit committee should review summary reports and an annual report.
> * Good liaison between the internal and external audit can help both to operate more efficiently.

2.93   Role of Internal Audit

The role of internal audit has altered considerably over the years, reflecting the changing needs of business and management. This is especially true in recent years, as corporate governance issues have been given an increasingly high profile. Directors and senior management are much more aware of their responsibilities for the control of business risk and for the establishment of systems and controls to safeguard assets, prevent fraud and irregularity and enhance the efficient operation of the business. The primary role of an internal audit function is to assist management in identifying potential risk and to provide assurance that the company's system of internal control is effective in reducing business risk to an acceptable level. It also acts as a useful source of information for management on what is actually happening in practice within the business, and provides support and advice by identifying needs and recommending policies, procedures and controls to resolve potential problems as they are identified. In the case of a public company, the work of internal audit will usually be a significant factor in enabling the directors to report on internal control as required by the Combined Code. The Code also recommends that companies that do not have an internal audit function should from time to time review the need for one. Under the proposals in the Smith Report, this review will become an annual requirement.

2.94   Distinction between External Audit and Internal Audit

There are significant differences between the roles of external auditors and internal auditors. External auditors are appointed by the shareholders and report to them by expressing an independent opinion on whether the company's annual accounts show a true and fair view of the state of affairs of the company at the balance sheet date and of its profit or loss for the financial year. The work of the external auditors is therefore directed towards identifying any potentially material misstatement in the annual accounts, and confirming that the accounting treatments and disclosures required by the legislation and by accounting standards have been properly dealt with. Internal audit is a service function of the company, focusing its efforts on the effectiveness of the company's systems of internal control and reporting any weaknesses and concerns to management. Companies legislation generally requires every UK company to appoint external auditors (the only exceptions being dormant companies and certain small companies as explained in **PARAGRAPH 2.35**), but management can choose whether or not to establish an internal audit function.

The principal distinctions between external and internal audit can therefore be summarised as follows:

	External auditors	**Internal auditors**
Appointed by	Shareholders	Management
Report to	Shareholders	Management
Role defined by	Statute	Management
Primary function	Independent opinion on the annual accounts	Assisting management with the identification and control of business risk

Although the roles of external auditors and internal auditors are quite distinct, good liaison between the two can help both to operate more efficiently.

2.95   How Not to Use Internal Audit

Historically, there been a considerable degree of confusion over the precise role of internal audit. It is important to recognise that internal auditors are not responsible for designing and implementing systems and procedures, nor are they responsible for the prevention and detection of fraud and irregularity. These are, and must always remain, the responsibility of management. Internal auditors have an important role to play in assisting management to fulfil their responsibilities, and they will frequently recommend changes to systems and procedures, or new controls that should be introduced. However, if they were to become directly involved in designing and implementing systems and procedures, their independence from the operating functions could be seriously impaired. For the same reason, it is essential that internal auditors are not seen as a floating resource who can be used to cover for the unexpected departure or long-term absence of accounting and other staff.

2.96   Benefits of Internal Audit

The heightened profile of corporate governance issues, and public reporting on aspects such as internal control under the Combined Code, has generally increased management's awareness of their responsibilities and encouraged them to reconsider how these responsibilities can best be fulfilled in practice. Internal audit has had a relatively high profile within the public sector for some years, but has generally been slower to develop within the private sector, except in the largest organisations. In the past, internal audit departments tended be given a low status within the organisation, but the benefits of an well-organised and high-calibre internal audit function are now becoming clearer to companies of all sizes. Management always retains the responsibility for identifying business risk and introducing procedures and controls to reduce risk to an acceptable level. However, establishing a strong internal audit function to assist with this can enable management to demonstrate clearly that they have paid due attention to the relevant issues, and that the procedures and controls that have been put in place are being subjected to continual scrutiny. This is particularly important as the business develops – without regular independent scrutiny, the procedures and controls can easily become out of date and fail to provide adequate cover in new areas of operation.

2.97 Areas Usually Covered by Internal Audit

Internal audit will usually provide assurance on:

- safeguarding of the company's assets;
- the completeness and accuracy of the company's accounting and other records;
- the adequacy and effectiveness of measures to prevent fraud and other irregularity;
- the overall efficiency of the operations.

The internal auditors should develop a strong, in-depth knowledge of the company's operating systems, coupled with their own professional expertise, and they are therefore in a good position to advise management on the assessment of risk and the implementation of procedures and controls. If there is no internal audit function, the external auditors will usually need to carry out some review and testing of the company's systems and controls, but as their focus is the material accuracy of the annual accounts, their work will concentrate on financial controls rather than the company's overall system of internal control. The level and extent of their review and testing will also be lower, as the level of assurance needed for external audit purposes will not be as extensive as that required for effective management of the business.

2.98 Special Assignments

As well as assisting with the assessment and control of business risk, internal auditors often carry out special assignments and investigations to assist management in the achievement of business objectives, such as value for money reviews and more extensive investigations of specific business areas (for instance, a review of the effectiveness and efficiency of an individual part of the business operation, or of a particular service function, such as catering or maintenance). The areas selected for review may have been identified by management as needing investigation, or may have been highlighted by the internal auditors during their other work, or by the external auditors.

2.99   Establishing an Internal Audit Function

An internal audit function is a service department within the organisation, assisting management to fulfil its responsibilities. In larger entities, there will usually be a separate internal audit department, its staffing levels being dependent on the size and complexity of the organisation and the level of work required throughout the year. In the case of a group, one internal audit department will normally serve all locations and subsidiaries within the group. In a smaller organisation, there may be insufficient work to justify a fully staffed internal audit department, or it may be that the department would be so small (for instance, requiring only one or two members of staff) that it would be difficult for it to command the necessary authority within the business. However, this does not mean that it is totally impractical for a small company to operate an internal audit function. It should be possible to sub-contract internal audit work to an external organisation with the necessary skills and experience (for instance, a firm of accountants with internal audit expertise). The fact that the function is an internal one does not prevent it being provided from an outside source, although particular care may be needed in defining the terms and scope of the work.

2.100   Terms of Reference

The purpose, authority and scope of work of the internal audit department should be set out in a formal document. This will help to give the internal auditors the high profile within the organisation that is necessary if they are to function effectively. It should also clarify the independence of the internal auditors from the other parts of the business and the remit of internal audit, ensuring in particular that this is not restricted in any way and covers all aspects of the business. Where internal audit work is sub-contracted, these matters will normally be dealt with in an engagement letter between the parties. In all cases, the terms of reference for the internal audit function should be regularly reviewed and updated, usually through the audit committee.

2.101   Head of Internal Audit

It is important that the internal audit function, however it is organised, is headed up by an individual who has the necessary professional expertise and carries the respect, confidence and support of other members of the senior management team. He or she should preferably have an appropriate professional qualification, relevant experience and the personal skills needed to deal with individuals throughout the organisation and to handle potentially difficult and sensitive issues. There needs to be a close working relationship between the head

Audit Matters

of internal audit and the executive directors and also, where relevant, good communication between the head of internal audit and the audit committee. If the internal audit function is a separate department within the organisation, the head of internal audit will be a management appointment. If internal audit work is sub-contracted, the person with overall responsibility for the work (for instance, a partner in a firm of accountants) is in effect the head of internal audit, and it will be important to ensure that the necessary relationships can be put into place quickly and effectively. Where the company has an audit committee, this committee should participate in the appointment. The head of internal audit should have a direct line of communication to the chairman of the audit committee, to enable sensitive issues to be raised and discussed without executive management being present where necessary, and to demonstrate and strengthen the independence of the internal audit function.

2.102   Staffing

If the internal audit department is to achieve the necessary degree of respect and confidence within the organisation, it is essential that it has adequate resources to carry out its work. Wherever possible, internal audit staff should be suitably trained and professionally qualified. This does not necessarily mean that everyone needs to hold the same qualifications. The department should be viewed as a team and the skills and expertise available should be appropriate for the range of work that the department is expected to cover. The skills needed will inevitably vary, depending on the nature and complexity of the business. As well as financial expertise, the internal audit function may need skills in areas such as computing, logistics or environmental issues. On occasions it may be appropriate to second high-calibre staff with particular skills from elsewhere in the organisation to assist with specific internal audit projects. This can be valuable in increasing general awareness and understanding of the internal audit function within the company, and can help to raise the profile of internal audit. It is important to remember that internal audit staff will need to deal with individuals throughout the organisation, and that they may sometimes be required to handle potentially difficult and sensitive situations. All internal audit staff need to have strong interpersonal and communication skills and to be confident in dealing with senior management.

2.103   Independence and Objectivity

Internal auditors must be genuinely independent of the systems and operations that they review and report on. Without a high degree of professional independence and objectivity, the internal audit function will not achieve the status and level of authority necessary for it to become a strong and effective management resource, and it will not command the respect and confidence of management and staff. There is also a risk that internal audit staff will not be able to make genuinely unbiased and impartial judgements if they have a close involvement in the detailed operations. It is essential that the head of internal audit is not given additional executive responsibilities within the organisation and that audit staff are not involved in the day to day operations of other parts of the business. This does not preclude the secondment of staff from other departments to assist with specific internal audit assignments as explained above, but long-term internal audit staff should not have a regular involvement in other departments.

It is particularly important that internal auditors are not seen as a floating resource who can be used to cover for the unexpected departure or long-term absence of key members of staff. The ability of the head of internal audit to communicate directly with the chairman of the audit committee whenever he or she considers necessary helps to demonstrate the independence of the internal audit function from the executive management. The audit committee (or management where there is no audit committee) should satisfy themselves each year that appropriate procedures are operating to safeguard the independence and objectivity of the internal audit function.

2.104   Scope of Internal Audit Work

The scope of the internal auditors' work should generally be unrestricted and should cover the full spectrum of the company's system of internal control. The scope of the work undertaken by the internal auditors will vary depending on the circumstances of the company and should be discussed and agreed by the board. Where appropriate, this will be dealt with initially by the audit committee, who will then submit detailed proposals to the board for consideration and formal approval. The scope of internal audit work will usually include:

- understanding and assessing the key business risks and reviewing the procedures used to identify and manage these;
- reviewing the adequacy and effectiveness of controls over financial and other operational information;
- reviewing the adequacy and effectiveness of the procedures established by management to safeguard the company's assets and resources, and to prevent fraud and irregularity;
- reviewing the adequacy and effectiveness of procedures designed to ensure compliance with law and regulations that are central to the business;
- reviewing the adequacy and effectiveness of procedures designed to ensure that the policies and plans agreed by management are brought into effect and
- reviewing the efficiency and effectiveness of particular aspects of the business.

2.105   Internal Audit Needs Assessment and Strategic Plan

The initial stage in planning internal audit work will usually be to develop an internal audit needs assessment. This will identify all the aspects of the company's operations that will be subject to review by the internal auditors. In most organisations it will not be practical for all areas to be covered by internal audit in one year. It is normal practice for internal auditors to operate on a three- or four-year cycle, ensuring that all systems and operations are covered during the three or four-year period. In some cases, all the work on a particular system or operational area may be carried out in one year – in other cases, work on an individual system or operation may be spread over the full audit period, so that some aspects are covered in each year of the cycle. Where a system or operational area is considered to be particularly critical to the business, it may be deemed necessary for it to be covered by internal audit each year. The overall audit needs assessment must therefore be developed into a strategic audit plan to demonstrate how full coverage will be achieved over the audit cycle (i.e. the three or four-year period). In order to prepare a strategic audit plan, there will need to be some prioritisation of internal audit work over the audit cycle. Areas that are identified as high risk will generally be covered earlier in the audit cycle, and may be covered on more than one occasion during the cycle; areas that are deemed medium or low risk will generally be covered later in the audit cycle. Both the internal audit needs assessment and the strategic audit plan should be developed by the internal auditors in discussion with management and should be formally approved by the board (through the audit committee where appropriate).

2.106   Annual Review

The internal audit needs assessment and strategic audit plan must be reviewed and updated annually. There are very few situations where the needs assessment and strategic plan developed at the beginning of an audit cycle will not need to be adapted during the course of the cycle. Changes may be needed to:

- incorporate new systems and operations as the business develops;
- amend priorities because changes in circumstance have increased or reduced the risk associated with a particular aspect of the business;
- amend priorities on the basis of the results of internal audit work already completed.

Both the internal auditors and management should be involved in the review and update of the internal audit needs assessment and the strategic audit plan, and the revised documents should be approved by the board (through the audit committee where appropriate).

2.107   Detailed Internal Audit Plan

Once the internal audit needs assessment and strategic audit plan have been approved, the internal audit department must develop a detailed audit plan for the current year, setting out the areas to be covered, the proposed timing of the work and the proposed reporting timetable. The plan should include adequate time for following up points raised in the reports on previous audits to confirm that the agreed action has in fact been taken and that the problem originally identified has been resolved as far as is practicable. The detailed audit plan for the year should also be approved by the board (through the audit committee, where appropriate). The head of internal audit should report regularly to management and to the audit committee on the progress of audit work against the plan for the year and explain any significant variations.

2.108   Reports on Individual Systems and Operational Areas

Internal audit will issue individual reports on each system or operational area that has been subject to audit. Their reports will normally draw an overall conclusion in respect of that system or area, and will concentrate on highlighting any potentially serious weaknesses or concerns identified during the audit, along with the internal auditors' recommendations for changes and improvements. The recommendations will normally be discussed with management and the agreed action noted for each item. It is usually helpful to agree a standard structure for internal audit reports – for instance:

- Executive summary.
- The overall conclusions drawn by the auditors.
- The detailed findings and recommendations for improvement, divided into:
  - major weaknesses and concerns and
  - other issues.

It is important that weaknesses and concerns are rigorously followed up by internal audit later in the year (or, where appropriate, later in the audit cycle), to confirm that the agreed action has actually been taken and that the potential problem originally identified has been satisfactorily resolved.

2.109   Summary Reports

Summary reports on the results of the detailed work carried out by internal audit should be presented formally to the audit committee by the head of internal audit on a regular basis during the year. This reporting will normally take place on two or three occasions each year and may be combined with reports on the progress of audit work against the annual audit plan. A specific timetable for this level of reporting should be agreed at the beginning of the year.

2.110   Annual Report

The head of internal audit may also be asked to prepare an annual report summarising the work completed during the financial year and the overall conclusions drawn on the operation of the company's system of internal control. This will be particularly relevant for directors of listed companies who are required under the Combined Code to state in the annual report that they have reviewed the effectiveness of the company's system of internal financial control. An annual report from the head of internal audit will be one source of supporting information that the audit committee and board of directors will usually wish to review when considering the various directors' statements relating to compliance with the Combined Code.

2.111   Liaison with External Auditors

Although the roles of external auditors and internal auditors are quite distinct, good liaison between the two can help both to operate more efficiently and prevent any unnecessary duplication of work. Liaison normally works best when there are regular meetings and continuous dialogue between the two groups of auditors and each has a good understanding of the audit approach adopted by the other. The most crucial aspect is to ensure that there is good communication each year at the planning stages of both internal and external audit work. If the external auditors are consulted when internal audit work is being planned, this may help to increase the usefulness of the results for external audit purposes and enable the external auditors to reduce the extent of their detailed audit testing. This does not mean that the external auditors should in any way decide the scope or nature of the internal audit work – this must remain a management responsibility – but by discussing and agreeing issues such as the timing of the work, the methods of sample selection and the documentation of results, it should be possible to ensure that the work of the internal auditors is of maximum benefit to the external auditors as well as to management. Similarly, when the detailed external audit work is being planned, it will be important for the external auditors to take full account of the extent and results of internal audit work. Where appropriate, the audit committee will usually be responsible for the overall monitoring of liaison between the two groups of auditors.

2.112   *Impact of Internal Audit Work on External Audit Procedures*

The external auditors retain sole responsibility for the independent audit opinion on the annual accounts, for deciding the nature and extent of the audit procedures to be carried out in support of that opinion and for all matters of judgement in relation to the audit opinion. However, as part of their work, the external auditors will need to obtain assurance on the completeness and accuracy of the company's accounting records (which will form the basis for the annual accounts) and the adequacy and effectiveness of the company's internal financial controls. Where the company has an internal audit function, the external auditors may be able to place reliance on the work of the internal auditors to help them achieve the level of assurance they require for external audit purposes, and this in turn may enable them to reduce the extent of some of their detailed audit testing. The external auditors will usually need to be satisfied that the internal audit function is adequately resourced, appropriately staffed and independent of those on whom it is reporting, that the work of the internal auditors is properly planned, supervised and documented, and that the recommendations made by the internal auditors carry appropriate weight within the organisation. Their procedures to assess these issues will usually include reviewing the reports and working papers of the internal audit department.

2.113   *Impact of External Audit Work on Internal Audit Procedures*

There is generally less scope for internal auditors to make detailed use of the work of the external auditors. However, regular feedback on weaknesses and irregularities identified during external audit work can be helpful in directing the work of internal audit to areas of potential business risk. The external auditors may also highlight operational areas where value for money reviews, efficiency reviews or other special investigations may usefully be incorporated in the internal audit work programme.

2.114   Additional Guidance

In November 2003, the Audit and Assurance Faculty (AAF) of the ICAEW published 'Evaluating the Effectiveness of Internal Audit' to help audit committee members monitor the effectiveness of internal audit. The guidance recommends that monitoring is carried out by means of a regular review of internal audit reports during the course of the year and an annual review, which will usually comprise some form of self-assessment by the head of internal audit, together with supporting feedback from management, the external auditors and any other relevant bodies (such as regulators). The guidance also draws attention to the standards developed by the Institute of Internal Auditors, which recommend that an independent review of the internal audit function is carried out at least every five years. The AAF has also published 'The Power of Three: Understanding the Roles and Relationships of Internal and External Auditors' and 'Obtaining Value from Internal Audit'. These booklets are available free of charge to members of the AAF and can be purchased by non-members for £7.50 a copy (www.icaew.co.uk/aafac or 020 7920 8493). Also, as part of its series of guidance booklets for non-executive directors serving on an audit committee (see **PARAGRAPH 2.34**), the ICAEW published 'The Internal Audit Function' in March 2004. This is available free of charge from the ICAEW website at www.icaew.co.uk.

Audit Matters

Appendix 1

Useful Websites on Audit-Related Matters

FRC	www.frc.org.uk
FRRP	www.frc.org.uk/frrp
APB	www.frc.org.uk/apb
POB	www.frc.org.uk/pob
Accountancy and Actuarial Discipline Board	www.frc.org.uk/aadb
Institute of Chartered Accountants in England and Wales	www.icaew.co.uk
ICAEW AAF	www.icaew.co.uk/aafac
Institute of Internal Auditors (UK and Ireland)	www.iia.org.uk

Appendix 2

Specimen Terms of Reference for an Audit Committee

These specimen terms of reference are for guidance only and are based on the example published in the Smith Report (see **PARAGRAPH 2.4**). Terms of reference should be developed and adapted to suit the specific circumstances of the company or group.

1 Constitution

1.1 The Board hereby resolves to establish a committee of the board, to be known as the Audit Committee ('the committee').

2 Membership

2.1 The committee shall be appointed by the board. All members of the committee shall be independent non-executive directors of the company. The committee shall consist of not less than three members. Two members shall comprise a quorum at any meeting of the committee.

2.2 The chairman of the committee shall be appointed by the Board from amongst the independent non-executive directors.

3 Attendance at meetings

3.1 The finance director, the head of internal audit and a representative of the external auditors shall attend meetings at the invitation of the committee.

3.2 The chairman of the board and other board members shall attend meetings if invited by the committee.

3.3 There should be at least one committee meeting, or part of a meeting, each year where the external auditors and internal auditors attend without management present.

3.4 The company secretary shall be the secretary to the committee.

4 Frequency of meetings

4.1 Meetings shall be held not less than three times each year and, where appropriate shall coincide with key dates in the company's financial reporting cycle.

4.2 Additional meetings shall be held as required, and the external auditors or internal auditors may request a meeting if they consider that one is necessary.

5 Authority

5.1 The committee is authorised by the board to:
- investigate any activity within its terms of reference;
- seek any information that it requires from any employee (and all employees are directed to co-operate with any request made by the committee) and
- obtain external legal or other independent professional advice and request advisers to attend meetings as necessary.

6 Responsibilities

6.1 The responsibilities of the committee shall be:
- To consider the appointment of the external auditor and assess the independence of the external auditor, ensuring that key partners are rotated at appropriate intervals.
- To oversee the process for selecting the external auditor and make appropriate recommendations, through the board, to the shareholders for consideration at the AGM.
- To recommend the audit fee to the board and preapprove any fees in respect of non-audit service provided by the external auditor, and to ensure that the provision of non-audit services does not impair the independence or objectivity of the external auditor.
- To discuss with the external auditor, before the audit commences, the nature and scope of the audit, and any additional assurance or reporting that may be required, and to review the auditor's quality control procedures and the steps taken to respond to changes in regulatory and other requirements.
- To consider whether there is appropriate liaison and co-ordination between the internal and external auditors.
- To review the external auditor's management letter and management's response.
- To review the internal audit programme and ensure that the internal audit function is adequately resourced and has appropriate standing within the company.
- To consider management's response to any major internal audit or external audit recommendations.
- To approve the appointment or dismissal of the head of internal audit.
- To review the company's procedures for handling allegations from whistle-blowers.
- To review reports from management and the internal auditors on the effectiveness of the systems for internal financial control, financial reporting and risk management.
- To review, and challenge where necessary, the actions and judgements of management in relation to the interim and annual financial

statements before submission to the Board, paying particular attention to:

- critical accounting policies and practices and any changes in them;
- decisions requiring a major element of judgement;
- the extent to which the financial statements are affected by any unusual transactions in the year, and how they are disclosed;
- the clarity of disclosures;
- significant adjustments resulting from the audit;
- the going concern assumption;
- compliance with accounting standards and
- compliance with stock exchange and other legal requirements.

- To review the company's statements on compliance with the Combined Code, going concern and the review of the effectiveness of the company's system of internal control prior to endorsement by the board, and in particular to review:
  - the policies and processes for identifying and assessing business risks and the management of those risks by the company;
  - the company's policies for ensuring compliance with relevant legal and regulatory requirements;
  - the company's policies for the prevention and detection of fraud;
  - the effectiveness of such policies and procedures in practice.
- To discuss any problems and reservations arising from the external audit and any matters that the external and internal auditors may wish to discuss (in the absence of management where necessary).
- To consider other topics and issues, as defined by the board.

7 Reporting procedures

7.1 The secretary shall circulate the minutes of meetings of the committee to all members of the board.

7.2 The chairman of the committee, or as a minimum another member of the committee, shall attend the board meeting at which the annual accounts and reports are approved.

7.3 The committee's responsibilities and activities during the year shall be disclosed in the annual reports and accounts.

7.4 The chairman of the committee shall attend the AGM and answer questions, through the chairman of the board, on the committee's responsibilities and activities.

8 Terms of reference

8.1 The committee shall conduct an annual review of its terms of reference and make recommendations to the board.

Board Structure and Practice

3.1 Role of the Board

3 Board Structure and Practice

This chapter will start with role of the board and then look at the general principles around structuring an effective board. In this attention will be given to the purpose and the people rather than process and consider the importance of the context in which the board is operating.

3.1 Role of the Board

At a Glance
* The board is responsible for ensuring that the business has the necessary framework within which to function.
* The chairman has the responsibility for co-ordinating the board, it has been advised that this role not be combined with that of CEO.
* A clear majority of large UK firms have a senior independent non-executive (SINE), but there are dangers that the holder of this role could compete with the chairman.
* It is important to be clear which matters are reserved for the board and which are to be delegated to board committees.

It is absolutely critical that the role of the board is not only clear but well understood and agreed by all of its members. What follows is what the authors feel is a good general description of the role of the board.

* Right strategy:
  To ensure that there is the right strategy for the ownership as well as the business, it is being implemented and monitored and that there is a good process for formulating and adapting it.
* Right resources:
  To ensure that the organisation has the right resources in place to meet the agreed strategy for the business and its ownership. The most important of these resources relate to people and money.
* Right governance:
  To ensure appropriate corporate governance.

This description is entirely consistent with that described in the Higgs Review (see **PARAGRAPH 1.2**).

But who is the board working for and to whom does it owe its responsibilities? A useful discussion of the issues around this topic is contained in Professor Jay Lorsch's *Pawns and Potentates* (see **BIBLIOGRAPHY**). Professor Lorsch has been Harvard Business School's board guru for some time and the book is clearly written for a US audience. Nevertheless it is a thought provoking publication for directors in any country.

Professor Lorsch puts forward three basic beliefs that boards or individual directors have. He labels directors as 'Traditionalists', 'Rationalisers' or 'Broad Constructionalists'.

To quote:

The Traditionalists

'These directors adhere to the strict belief in the primacy of the shareholder and decline to recognise that conflicts exist between their traditional legal perspective and that of other constituencies. They are in our experience, a true minority, and if we question the narrowness of their perspective, we question neither the integrity nor the competence they bring to the boardrooms. They have no doubts in the land of the corporation, the shareholder is king.'

The Rationalisers

'These directors see the conflicts and feel the tensions inherent in their responsibilities in an increasingly complex world. However they rationalise them away, implicitly following the view of the Delaware Courts that what's good for the shareholder will be good for the other constituencies, and for the corporation.'

The Broad Constructionalists

'In contrast to the rationalisers, a larger, perhaps more thoughtful, group of directors openly recognises that their responsibilities encompass more than shareholders. If this attitude produces conflicts, they recognise and deal with them, without assuming that every decision must be in the shareholders' interests.'

If we liken directors to Africa's magnificent ostriches, the broad constructionalists would be actively constructing the dangers of life on the sandy plains, while the rationalisers might gaze enviously at the buried heads of the traditionalists.

No secrets for which group of birds Professor Lorsch prefers. From the author's point of view it would seem that the success of a 'broad constructionalist' board or individual director will be down to the quality of their judgement.

In the UK, the USA and many other countries the unitary board is the prevailing system supported by the recognition of corporate social responsibility.

In France, Germany, Holland and other countries a two-tier system is in operation. This book is designed principally for the directors of UK companies. However these companies may have subsidiaries in other countries and indeed the directors themselves may be members of boards operating in a two-tier environment. For these reasons it is worth considering the issues involved.

The most useful book the authors found on the two-tier system is Gregory Francesco Maasen's *An International Comparison of Corporate Governance* first published in 1999 by Spencer Stuart.

In it he includes the following chart based on some work done by Gedajlovic at Concordia University Montreal in 1993. It is designed to show the spectrum of perspectives towards corporate governance.

Shareholder ←—————————————→	Stakeholder
Executives and non-executives are fiduciaries of shareholders	Executives and non-executives are fiduciaries of a variety of claimants
Executives and non-executives should adopt principles consistent with maximisation of shareholder value	Executives and non-executives should balance pluralistic claims
Profitability and economic efficiency are the standards of efficacy	Profitability and economic efficiency are important in addition to survival, long-term growth and stability
The corporation is subordinate to the interests of shareholders	The corporation is seen as a superordinate entity

It is exactly because of these different perspectives that the unitary or two-tier approach is taken. The dominance of the principle of co-determination in Germany and Holland results in a two-tier approach.

3.2 What Are Two-Tier Boards?

The two tiers are usually a supervisory board and a management board. The supervisory board controls broad issues of policy and appoints the management board. The management board is responsible for the day to day control of the organisation. One of the main functions of two-tier boards is to give employees and other stakeholders who may not be shareholders some control over a company.

The principle difference between the unitary and two-tier approach to boards is therefore to do with decision-making. The operation, names and composition of boards operating under the two-tier system vary from country to country.

3.3 Board Context

There are several factors, which will determine the context in which the board operates, namely:

- nature of ownership;
- type of business;
- size of organisation;
- international reach;
- financial position of the company;
- market position of the company;
- reputation of the company;

Board Structure and Practice

- ambition/vision;
- stability of the company and
- legal and regulatory environment.

Each of these factors has an impact on the ideal composition of the board, the specific nature of the board's role and on the key processes which will ensure that the board is effective.

A clear analysis and statement of the above is also a very useful input to board performance reviews and also to the recruitment process for new directors.

3.4 The Key Board Roles and Board Composition

We see six key board roles and these are:

- chairman;
- chief executive officer;
- chief financial officer;
- non-executive;
- executive and
- company secretary.

The authors have also commented on the role of the senior independent director, which came to prominence through the Hampel Committee's work. The focus of this book is on the non-executive; consequently every chapter contains significant detail on the non-executive's role in the relevant subject area. For this reason the authors have kept the description of the non-executive's role at a high level here and focussed on the other roles of chairman, chief executive and finance director.

The detailed roles of each are discussed later. The company secretary is normally differentiated from the others described above in that he or she is not usually a formal member of the board.

With regard to the composition and balance the model adopted by most UK plcs has tended to be for the chairman and the non-executives to be in the majority but only by a couple of board seats. The US model is also for the non-executives, or outside directors as they are known, to comprise the majority. Moreover in the USA there tends only to be two executive directors on the board, the President/CEO and the Chief Financial Officer. Some of the largest UK companies are trending towards this US practice.

For private companies in the UK there is often a majority of executive and just two active non-executives.

The majority of UK plcs have opted to separate the roles of chairman and CEO. This was not the case prior to the seminal Cadbury Report on the Financial Aspects of Corporate Governance in 1992.

In his report Sir Adrian said:

> 'Given the importance and particular nature of the chairman's role, it should in principle be separate from that of the chief executive. If the two roles are combined in one person, it represents a considerable concentration of power. We recommend, therefore, that there should be a clearly accepted division of responsibilities at the head of a company, which

will ensure a balance of power and authority, such that no one individual has unfettered powers of decision. Where the chairman is also the chief executive, it is essential that there should be a strong and independent element on the board.'

In private companies for the roles to be combined. However it is normal in companies with significant venture capital or private equity backing for there to be a separation of roles.

The diversity of the background of board members has become a growing issue in many countries. As part of Derek Higgs Review into the role and effectiveness of non-executive directors in the UK, a census of plc directors was made. This showed the following with respect to the diversity of UK plc boards:

- Only one FTSE 100 had a female chairman (3i Group plc).
- Only two had female chief executives.
- 4% of executive directors are women and 6% non-executives.

As board composition is the responsibility of the chairman it is up to the chairman to ensure that the board is comprised of people from sufficiently diverse backgrounds to meet its objectives.

3.4.1   *Role of Chairman*

We see the role of the chairman as being to:

- organise the composition, business and efficiency of the board;
- lead the board in the determination of its strategy and in the achievement of its objectives;
- ensure that the board has accurate and clear visibility of results and likely future trends;
- ensure that board committees are properly established, composed and operated;
- ensure effective relationships are maintained with all major stakeholders in the business (i.e. customers, shareholders, employees, suppliers, government, local community, industry, etc.);
- enhance the company's public standing and reputation and
- develop a strong working relationship with the chief executive/managing director and ensure that there is a clear definition and agreement of the division of responsibilities.

In summary the chairman is the leader of the board. As such they should be prepared to step into the CEO role for short periods until a successor is appointed if necessary.

We also believe that it is essential for there to be a written description of the role of the chairman and for all directors of the company to be familiar with its contents. The chairman should also be subject to the board's performance review. In larger quoted companies the review of the performance of the chairman is normally led by the senior independent non-executive (SINE) who gathers the views of the other directors and provides the chairman with feedback. In smaller companies or where there isn't a SINE then this is often done by the chief executive.

Organising the composition of the board includes dealing with the succession of the chief executive. This is covered in the next section on the role of the CEO. With respect to organising the composition of the board, clearly the chairman needs to ensure that there is an effective nominations process which the board supports.

There has been some debate as to whether the title 'non-executive chairman' has any validity. Many including the authors subscribe to the view that 'a chairman is a chairman' and believe that the role as described above is quite distinct from that of the non-executive. The responsibilities are exactly the same if there is the word chairman in the title.

Some including Hugh Parker, author of *Letters from a Chairman*, hold strong views on this point:

> 'Any chairman who calls himself – or allows himself to be called – a "non-executive chairman" comes perilously close to being a non-chairman!'

The insertion of 'non-executive' into the chairman's title is often simply to indicate that he or she is part-time.

So what are the core competencies of a chairman? The core competencies and characteristics for non-executives were discussed in **PARAGRAPHS 1.3.2–1.3.5**. These were grouped under three headings:

- Personal
- Professional and managerial
- Entrepreneurial.

Whilst we believe that the lists are just as valid for chairmen as non-executives we would emphasise three things as being especially important for a chairman:

- Integrity
- Judgement
- Leadership.

A chairman is the leader of the board and should take responsibility for the team dynamic and ensuring that the potential of all board members is fulfilled whether they are executives or non-executives. To do this requires strong communication skills as well as significant commitment to the role.

Who organises the succession – the chairman? If the chairman is effective he or she will have considered succession, agreed a process with the board and an orderly succession will take place. Additionally the board will have a contingency plan to cope with the need to suddenly replace the chairman as a result of illness etc. There may or may not be a clearly identified successor appointed as deputy chairman.

The situation that is most difficult is where the chairman is underperforming and there is no agreed process for replacing them. The approach to this difficult situation obviously depends upon the shareholding structure of the company, whether it is a listed company and so on.

Let's look at the larger quoted company situation first. If there is a senior independent director as described below then this person is the focal point for shareholders and other board members to make their views known on the performance of the chairman and their desire for change. If no one has been formally identified as a senior independent director and there is a deputy chairman then he or she will fulfil the role. If there is neither a SINE nor deputy chairman then either one of the non-executives or the chief executive will have to lead the process.

Whoever takes on the role of resolving the situation if they have the unanimous or overwhelming majority support of the rest of the board and the key institutional shareholders then the situation can be resolved fairly straightforwardly. The person simply informs the chairman that he has lost the confidence of his board and the company's key shareholders and gives him the opportunity to resign.

So why are so many situations unlike that described above? Often because:

- there isn't a clearly identified person to resolve the situation;
- the views of the other board members are not unanimous;
- even if they are some may not be prepared to support the chairman's removal;
- the chairman may not share the view that he is underperforming;
- personal interests may be placed ahead of those of the company or
- the chairman may recognise reality but be reluctant to make it easy for his colleagues.

In smaller companies and especially private businesses where the chairman is also the major shareholder it can be much more difficult. An excellent book by Manfred Kets De Vries and Eric van der Loo on family companies, *Family Business*, covers this subject in great detail. In venture capital and private equity-backed businesses where the chairman is appointed by the lead investor, there is usually a mechanism for replacing them, whether the circumstances are a natural succession or removal for underperformance. For many smaller businesses there is no succession but instead a sale of the company. The important thing for any chairman is to have someone they trust and respect who will be able to hold up the mirror and help them decide when the time is right to go. They need not be in the business or on the board to do this. Indeed this is a role many a trusted adviser has fulfilled.

A number of real life situations and some guidance on affecting the removal of directors are contained one of the author's other publications *Directors Dilemmas* published by Kogan Page.

3.4.2   *Role of Chief Executive Officer*

A huge volume of literature is available on the subject of the role of the chief executive. There is even more if you count the autobiographical works of the more prominent CEOs in the USA. This book will limit itself here to a fairly straightforward definition of the role, consider the competencies required of a CEO and then discuss some of the issues for non-executives working with CEOs.

The role of the chief executive officer can be described simply as:

'To execute the plans and policies established by the board.'

In order to do this they will need to possess a wide range of knowledge and skills and the behavioural characteristics required to lead the rest of the company. They must also not just be a good CEO but one relevant to the circumstances of the company.

So what are the core competencies required of a CEO? There is as has been said much already written on this subject. What follows is a distillation of that and the conclusions of some work conducted by the 3i CEO programme to identify the competencies of successful CEOs in venture capital-backed situations. Clearly the competencies required of any CEO are situation-dependent but we feel that the following provide a good generic basis from which to start.

The competencies are grouped under four categories:

- Leadership
- Strategic capability
- Enterprising and commercial
- Problem solving and analytical capability.

We would define these as follows.

A CEO who is a competent leader:

- initiates action and takes responsibility;
- sets objectives for others gain their commitment;
- motivates and empowers others;
- introduces and leads change;
- recruits and develops high calibre people;
- builds a team spirit and inspires loyalty;
- instils a high degree of integrity in the organisation and
- is conscious of the organisation's social responsibilities.

A CEO who has strong strategic competence:

- provides a compelling vision of the organisation's future potential;
- develops and communicates strategies and organisational goals;
- evaluates business options, anticipates trends and consequences;
- demonstrates a broad-based, long-term view of issues, events and activities;
- produces new ideas, approaches or insights and
- is conscious of the overall strategic aims when discussing operational issues.

A CEO who is enterprising and commercial:

- thinks in terms of driving growth and adding value;
- enjoys making money and is strongly profit-oriented;
- demonstrates financial awareness, generating cash and controlling costs;
- understands the commercial drivers of a business;
- identifies new business opportunities for the organisation and
- keeps up to date with competitor activity and market trends.

A CEO who has good problem solving and analytical capability:

- gathers comprehensive information to support decisions;
- probes for greater understanding and challenges assumptions;
- identifies and focuses on key issues;

- makes rational judgements from available information and analysis;
- thinks laterally and considers problems from different perspectives and
- produces workable solutions.

It is hard for a CEO to possess all of the above without the underpinning of a fine sense of judgement, strong interpersonal skills and good antennae to sense issues ahead.

Evaluation of CEO performance is normally led by the chairman within the context of the evaluation of the board's performance as a whole. As with any other position the chairman has to judge whether the board has the right CEO and this may not be as simple as looking at current performance. Potential to implement the plans for the future is just as important.

The power and influence of the CEO changes in different settings. The CEO of a FTSE 100 company is a powerful person but may have less power over his board than the CEO of the company who owns 100% of its equity. A description of the sources of power that non-executives have is contained in **PARAGRAPH 3.5**.

The style of CEOs varies as much as the attitude that they have towards their board. For some, the rest of the board is a necessary inconvenience; for others, a powerful supporter in achieving their objectives. It is important for the non-executive to ascertain what this attitude is before taking the appointment and if the CEO's stance is not the most constructive to influence them to change.

A CEO needs people to calibrate views and keep their feet firmly on the ground. Even for the most wise and sensible chief executive the feelings of invincibility that can emerge following a period of prolonged success can prove highly damaging to them and their companies. The chairman should provide this type of support but non-executive directors can also be helpful.

Jack Welch the legendary former chief executive of General Electric gives a graphic example of the dangers of a chief executive who gets too full of himself and dominates the board in a delightfully named chapter 'Too full of myself' in his autobiography *Jack: Straight from the Gut*:

'For chrissakes, Jack what are you going to do next? Buy McDonalds?'

The remark came from a foursome of guys across the seventh fairway at Augusta as I was teeing off from the third hole in April 1986. Four months after announcing the deal to buy RCA, I had just acquired Kidder, Peabody, one of Wall Street's oldest investment banking firms.

While the guys were only kidding, there were others who really didn't think much of our latest decision. At least three GE board members weren't too keen on it, including two of the most experienced directors in the financial services business Citibank Chairman Walt Wriston and J.P. Morgan President Lew Preston. Along with Andy Sigler, then Chairman of Champion International, they warned that the business was a lot different from our others.

'The talent goes up and down the elevators every day and can go in a heartbeat,' said Wriston. 'All you're buying is the furniture.'

At an April 1986 board meeting in Kansas City, I had argued for it – and unanimously swung the board my way.

> It was a classic case of hubris. Flush with the success of our acquisitions of RCA in 1985 and Employers Reinsurance in 1984, I was on a roll. Frankly, I was just too full of myself. While internally I was still searching for the right feel for the company, on the acquisition front I thought I could make anything work.
>
> Soon I'd realise that I had taken it one step too far.

The best way for the non-executive towards developing a relationship with a CEO, regardless of whether they are taking a constructive attitude or not, is to provide significant added value on issues of importance to the CEO.

We now come to the challenging issue of CEO succession.

3.4.2.1 *CEO Succession*

The selection of a new chief executive is definitely a defining moment in a company's history. Making the right choice is one of the board's most important responsibilities. Getting it wrong risks de-stabilising the board or worse could be disastrous for the company. If the typical period for a non-executive to serve is two three-year terms then CEO succession is something you are likely to encounter.

The situation where a board may find the need to select a new CEO is usually where the current CEO:

- is retiring, leaving a well-resourced and managed business with a clear strategy;
- is retiring, leaving significant issues in terms of strategy, resourcing or governance;
- becomes ill or dies and needs replacing urgently or
- is fired for poor performance, poor conduct or some other reason.

Whether the succession is deemed to be planned and orderly or abrupt due to a crisis the change always generates a high degree of anxiety both within and outside the company. Reactions to the choice the board makes will not only influence the success of chosen CEO but also influence the reputation of the board as a whole.

So how does the board give itself the maximum chance of making the right judgement, managing the process in the most effective way and coming out with a result that is defensible?

The starting point is to consider what approach the board would like to adopt both generally and for specific circumstances. There are a variety of ways. Not all of them will meet the objectives of the Combined Code that the process be 'formal and transparent'.

At one end of the spectrum there is what we would call the 'relaxed' approach. Essentially the board waits until the need arises and picks the best available candidate internally or externally. The relaxed approach is clearly less effort in the short term but carries a greater degree of risk than the approach at the other end of the spectrum, which we would label the 'ultimate control' approach. Here the company has an overall succession plan and progressive management development programmes. There are a number of internal successors benchmarked against the best available outside. A good example of this recently was the very well-publicised transition at General Electric from Jack Welch to Jeffrey Immelt in the USA.

The reality for most boards is an approach somewhere between 'relaxed' and 'ultimate control' and somewhere between 'having a choice' or 'one well-groomed heir apparent'. The important thing is to be clear what approach you are taking and why. If the company is a public one then the approach will need to be justified to shareholders and possibly the media. The risk, time and cost involved are different for each approach.

Before deciding the board should set some objectives, for example you may want to:

- have a formal and transparent process;
- obtain the best successor available internally or externally;
- make the appointment within a certain timeframe and cost;
- minimise the risk of an interregnum or
- achieve maximum buy-in from executive directors.

Does the board have an overall succession plan for other key roles? If not, a non-executive should be suggesting that there is one in place.

Having decided on an approach for the CEO succession, the board needs to decide how it wants to communicate on the issue. Some boards ensure that the process is well understood internally and externally. Others prefer a more discreet approach. If the succession is taking place as a result of an abrupt departure then it is far harder to manage the process behind closed doors.

If it is a retirement then the attitude of the current CEO will have an influence on the process. What should a retiring CEO's role be? At one level they should have had a major influence by producing a number of strong internal candidates. Inevitably they may have a preferred choice and this may be known to the board as a whole or just the chairman. A formal and transparent process may or may not endorse this choice and the chairman who is likely to be leading the process needs to ensure that the CEO doesn't steer the board inappropriately to choosing his preferred candidate. Many CEOs have the envelope in the safe for 'just in case' situations.

Historically CEOs used to pick their own successors, especially in the days of combined chairman and CEO.

When should the succession process start for an orderly transition where the CEO is leaving positively? It is easier if the chairman has a clear understanding of the CEO's intentions and ambitions. In these circumstances many chairmen have a preference for announcing who the new CEO will be at the time of the announcement of the current CEO's plans to retire. Where this is the case the board usually anticipates making an internal appointment.

The alternative is to announce the retirement and declare that a process to find a suitable successor is underway. The board may or may not disclose whether consideration is being given to external candidates.

Here are some of the views people have on whether the internal or external approach is better. Clearly they are not mutually exclusive and an internal candidate who genuinely wins over the best external candidates will have a stronger mandate.

- 'The board will have been seen to have failed in its duty if it hasn't been able to develop a successor who knows the business and is well-respected externally.'
- 'External candidates tend to be favoured where the previous CEO appointment has failed and the company has significant issues.'
- 'There may be less turbulence and risk with an internal candidate.'
- 'You should avoid destructive competitions – businesses need depth of talent. A competition will just result in the disappointed candidates leaving.'
- 'It's so much easier to make an informed choice with internal candidates if you know them well already.'
- 'Don't narrow down to a single choice too soon, the best guys feel better for having won a competition.'
- 'If you've got an interregnum situation and you promote someone into the caretaker role and set an external process going, you'll almost certainly lose your caretaker.'

If the board ends up selecting a candidate who is going to be in the group CEO role for the first time it is important that they understand the differences in the new role and receive appropriate development. The transition rollercoaster referred to in **Paragraph 1.4** is relevant again.

Interregnum situations are often the most difficult, although the UK system of having separate chairmen and chief executives makes it easier than in the USA where the roles are combined.

If the chairman has stepped into the CEO role and the board has granted additional powers to executive directors for a temporary period they need to recognise that it is easier for the chairman to step back once the successor is in place than it is for the executives to give up their recently gained powers.

The final thing to say on CEO succession is that getting it right makes the whole board's job a lot easier so it is well worth the effort in making the right choice.

3.4.3 *Role of Finance Director*

Every non-executive is fundamentally dependent upon the quality of their finance director. Yet how do you ascertain before you join the board whether the FD is appropriate? This is an especially relevant question for non-executives on nominations committees who get involved in the selection of finance directors.

The simple model below is one way of thinking about the key elements of a finance director's capabilities. As you will see at the very base, underpinning everything else is integrity. Integrity means different things to different people. So it is critical for the non-executive to ensure that the FD has the shared sense of integrity.

This was developed for a very popular 3i event for independent directors entitled *How do you know a good FD when you see one?* The event was run in the UK, France, Germany and Italy with attendees coming from a broad range of sectors and sizes of companies. The surprising thing was the level of consistency

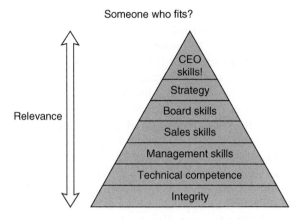

Someone who fits?

across the different countries and company contexts in what independent directors considered to be critical. There was a great deal of consensus around the above hierarchy and the importance of ensuring relevance of fit between the finance director and the company.

There was also consensus on what a finance director is there to do which was split between 'ensuring' and 'adding value'.
Ensuring that:

- financial controls and systems are effective;
- financial resources are appropriate to meet the company's long- and short-term requirements;
- the board is made fully aware of the company's financial position and has good visibility of future financial performance;
- the company has good relationships with providers of finance and
- the finance team is appropriate and highly motivated.

Adding value by:

- being an active and contributing member of the board on issues other than finance;
- communicating well internally on financial matters so that staff have a good appreciation of the company's financial position and the impact on the company's finances of their actions;
- having a high reputation externally and
- providing the board with insightful analysis from which to make key decisions.

The above seems a fairly simplistic description of the enormous range of duties a finance director has. However, a glimpse at the contents list of Tolley's *Finance Director's Handbook* reveals the true depth of the role.

One issue however where there was a lot of debate was over whether you really wanted to have a finance director who was capable of assuming the role of CEO. If the finance director has the capability to take on the duties of a CEO then they probably have a comparatively broad skill set and range of abilities which can be highly beneficial to the company, and they are often seen as an insurance policy if the CEO leaves or fails. The alternative view is that if they have the capability and ambition to become CEO then this may impair their relationship with the current CEO and make them less focussed on their key role. The obvious point to make is that it is important to understand both the capability and ambition of the finance director and whether this is appropriate to the circumstances of the company.

One considerable challenge for finance directors relates to them performing their function as a board member. The nature of their job is that they provide a key service to the board in terms of the provision of information and enablement of compliance with the legal and regulatory framework within which the board operates. It is probably harder for the finance director to escape his functional silo than any other board member. The wise finance director uses his team well to present information to the board saving his own airtime for input as a member of the board as opposed to the head of the finance function.

One way for the finance director to gain experience as a fully contributing board member is by taking a non-executive position elsewhere.

In summary given the criticality of the finance director's role it is important for the non-executive to develop a good working relationship with the finance director.

3.4.4 *Role of Senior Independent Director (SINE)*

The term SINE first really came to prominence in the Hampel Report in 1998 and was intended to apply principally to listed companies.

In his report Sir Ronnie said the following:

> 'Cadbury also recommended that where the roles of chairman and chief executive officer were combined there should be a strong and independent element on the board, with a recognised senior member (Code 1.2). But even where the roles of chairman and CEO are separated, we see a need for vigorously independent non-executive directors. There can, in particular, be occasions when there is a need to convey concerns to the board other than through the chairman or CEO. To cover this eventuality we recommend that a senior independent non-executive director (e.g. a deputy chairman or the chairman of the remuneration committee) should have been identified in the annual report. We do not envisage that this individual would for this purpose need special responsibilities or an independent leadership role, nor do we think that to identify him or her should be divisive.'

In his recommendations therefore he concluded that:

> 'Whether or not the roles of chairman and chief executive officer are combined, a senior non-executive director should be identified in the annual report, to whom concerns can be conveyed.'

The Combined Code says that the SINE should be identified in a company's annual report. According to the Higgs review over 80% of the UK's top 400 companies had identified a SINE in their annual reports. We would expect this to be higher today. But what is the role of a SINE and how does this relate to the role of the deputy chairman?

Hampel's intention was simply that one of the directors accepted the responsibility for acting as a focal point if there was subsequently a lack of confidence in the chairman amongst shareholders or the board. He had no intention of this position driving a wedge between the shareholders and the chairman. To avoid the danger of this many companies select a non-executive who is not a possible candidate to succeed the chairman.

In practice the SINE also tends to be chairman of one or a number of the key board sub-committees (e.g. remuneration or audit).

The two important words in the title are 'senior' and 'independent'. Independence is discussed in **PARAGRAPH 1.3.3**. Given that the SINE position is primarily intended for listed companies the definition of most importance is that of the key shareholders (i.e. the institutions). The NAPF criteria for independence are contained in the **APPENDICES**. Hermes, which has been a leading investor in terms of recognising the importance of good governance and investing resource into research and the development of best practice, produced a job description for the SINE.

The term 'senior' simply means that this is the nominated director to whom any unresolved concerns can be addressed, about the way in which the board operates, the implication being that they will do something about it. In practice it is normal for the institutional shareholders to express concerns they have about the chairman himself. Experience is developing of this role but to date it does seem to have been reserved for these situations.

Of all the issues raised by the Higgs Review the one which generated the most controversy was to do with the role of the SINE, which is ironic given it is one of the briefest sections of his report. By way of introduction he recognises the sensitive area up front:

> 'Responses to consultation contained a range of views on the identification of a senior independent director. Some saw the role as unnecessary or divisive. It was pointed out that shareholders may make use of their own connections with non-executive directors, or contact the chairmen of board committees if they have concerns',

and

> 'Most respondents, however, supported the concept of a senior independent director, noting the importance of sensitivity in the conduct of the role. I agree with them.'

So naturally he then says the following:

> '*I therefore endorse the code provision that a senior independent director be identified.* They should of course meet the test of independence set out in this report (**PARAGRAPH XX**). Unless it is anticipated that they will become chairman, and provided they meet the test of independence, the role could be assumed by the deputy chairman if there is one.'

So far so good. It was the final paragraph in this section which caused some very strong reactions from chairmen, company secretaries, chief executives and finance directors who thought that he had simply gone too far was undermining their authority and creating a considerable extra burden.

> 'I see the role of the senior independent director as important in the relationship between major shareholders and the board as set out in 15.15 and 15.16 (see below). *The senior independent director should be available to shareholders, if they have reason for concern that contact through the normal channels of chairman of chief executive has failed to resolve. The senior independent director should also chair meetings between non-executive directors where the chairman does not attend.*'

Sections 15.15 and 15.16 were as follows:

> 'In addition, I propose that the senior independent director should attend sufficient of the regular meetings of management with a range of major shareholders to develop a balanced understanding of the themes, issues and concerns of shareholders. The senior independent director should communicate these views to the non-executive directors and, as appropriate, to the board as a whole.'
>
> 'Boards should also recognise that non-executive directors may also find it instructive to attend meetings with major investors from time to time and should be able to do so if they choose. Moreover, non-executive directors should expect to attend such meetings if requested by major investors in the company. They should, however, rely on the chairman and the senior independent director to ensure a balanced view is taken of the range of shareholder views.'

There was also strong feedback from some institutional investors that, notwithstanding their feedback in the consultation process that they wanted more contact with non-executives, Higgs proposals if accepted would produce too great a time burden on them.

Such was the strength of feelings on this issue that it is likely that these proposals were adapted before gaining the approval of the Financial Reporting Council.

The role of deputy chairman in UK companies appears to be quite varied. In some they play an active role in promoting the company, are clearly identified as the chairman's successor and are someone who frequently represents the views of the company. At the other end of the spectrum they are respected elder statesman who have the role by dint of their past contribution but have minimal input.

The important thing is for the board and of course the individual to have clarity about what role they are expected to play and for shareholders to be comfortable with what that role is.

3.4.5   *Role of Non-executives*

The focus of this book is on the non-executive; consequently every chapter contains significant detail on the non-executive's role in the relevant subject area. For this reason we have kept the description of the non-executives role at a high level here. PARAGRAPHS 1.3.2–1.3.5 contain details on what core competencies non-executives are expected to have.

The title non-executive is a rather odd one in that it says what the role is not, that is not an executive of the company, but it gives no clue as to what it is. There has been some debate as to whether a more constructive title would be of benefit. A survey conducted by 3i of non-executives in 2002 showed that many people didn't like the title 'non-executive' but that there was a great diversity of view over what would be better. The most popular choice was independent but 'only if there is a workable definition of what Independent means'. The independent review of non-executive directors came to the same conclusion and so it seems unlikely that there will be any change in the foreseeable future.

What the non-executives are expected to do is probably more important than what they are called. In CHAPTER 1 we split the role into two components 'ensuring' and 'adding value'. We believe that non-executives who add significant value have much greater influence with the other directors and are therefore much more likely to bring that influence to bear in ensuring that there is good governance.

Ensuring that:

- there is a robust strategy for the ownership and development of the business, that it is regularly monitored and adapted as required;
- the company has the appropriate resources in place to meet its strategy. The two most important being human and financial and that
- there is appropriate corporate governance and a high standard of investor relations.

Adding value by:

- being a confidential sounding board to the directors;
- bringing an independent and broad view to the board and
- helping the executive to achieve their business plans in whatever form is relevant given their experience and network.

It goes without saying that everything under 'ensuring' adds value.

3.4.6   *Role of Executive Directors*

What is the role of executive directors as board members as distinct from their roles as functional or business unit heads? Firstly it is important that they consider issues from the perspective of the company as a whole and avoid becoming too representative of the interests of their own particular area of activity. The reality is that this is hard to do but that also other board members will take account of this. The good chairman develops the executive in this area and ensures that they are not confined to their functional silos.

Another issue relates to the degree of preparation the executive undertakes before board meetings. Striking the balance between an unhealthy level of rigorous preparation and ensuring that board meetings are not just a show for the non-executives are important.

The best board will involve good constructive contributions from executives and non-executives. It can happen that a chief executive of a major company would put a proposal of significance to the board without having the support of his executive although it is unlikely. Skilful chairmen and non-executives will sense whether this is the case and draw out the concerns if they haven't already been expressed.

The non-executive director needs to develop a good degree of knowledge of the executive and a significantly strong relationship with them so that they are prepared to trust and confide in them. This is especially so for those executive directors who are candidates to succeed the chief executive. Equally it is important for executive directors to take the initiative and make the same effort.

Most major companies will have an executive committee. This will sometimes be a straightforward subset of the board, that is all of the executive directors but more typically it will include the executive directors and a small number of other senior personnel. The company secretary is also likely to be a member.

3.4.7 *Role of Company Secretary*

All companies are legally required to appoint a company secretary. There has been much debate over the years as to what the role of a company secretary should be. The debate centring around whether the role should be confined to the administrative matters relating to the smooth operation of the board and compliance or whether it should be much broader encompassing insurance and other functions. The current view of the Institute of Chartered Secretaries and Administrators (ICSA) is that the role comprises the following responsibilities:

- Ensuring compliance with law, regulation, the organisation's constitution and codes of practice.
- Raising matters which may warrant the attention of the board/trustees, especially legal and governance matters.
- Advising the board/trustees/directors as to their responsibilities to uphold good corporate governance and on constitutional and legal issues.
- Maintaining statutory records and submitting records to relevant regulators/registrars such as Companies House.
- Communicating with shareholders or external stakeholders in the organisation.
- Taking minutes of meetings, preparing agendas and ensuring that the necessary action is taken.
- Managing pensions, contracts, employee benefits, insurance, property, risk or health and safety.

Whatever falls within the company secretary's remit, as decided by the board, the company secretary must know what is going on within the company to be effective. For this reason the relationship the company secretary has with the chairman, the chief executive and the other executive directors and the attitude that they take towards him or her is critical. It is much easier in our view for the company secretary to be effective if they are a member of the executive committee of the board.

As the company secretary plays an important role in servicing the non-executives it is wise for any non-executive to establish good relationship with them. This can be done in all sorts of ways starting with straightforward acknowledgement and demonstration of thanks for the support the company secretary provides.

Another role most company secretaries have is in helping the chairman and chief executive prepare board agendas. The topic of board agendas is covered in more detail on **PARAGRAPH 4.8**. Good ones canvass the non-executives for their views on what they would like on the agenda. This not only saves the chairman time but also can be a useful source of feedback for the chairman on what is really concerning the non-executives.

Company secretaries will normally report to the chief executive with a strong dotted line to the chairman and possibly some aspects of their role reporting through the finance director. The ICSA website www.icsa.org.uk contains some very helpful guidance notes and best practice guides on a whole range of issues relating to the role of the company secretary. It also includes a detailed specimen job description for the corporate governance role of the company secretary.

Finally it is worth noting that Section A.5.3 of the Combined Code contains the following sentence:

> 'Both the appointment and the removal of the company secretary should be a matter for the board as a whole.'

3.5   Sources of Power and Influence for Non-executives

For a non-executive to be effective they have to have influence with their fellow board members and especially the chairman and chief executive. Without influence it is hard to make a genuine contribution no matter how good your judgement or relevant the knowledge that you possess. A well-intentioned non-executive who takes the role seriously will become frustrated if their views are not respected or listened to. Respect is a very important word for non-executives.

Management guru Warren Bennis is reported to have said that:

> 'Power is the ability to convert vision into reality.'

This is a very relevant quote for non-executives, whose power may be more ambiguous than executives.

So where do non-executives derive their power to influence their fellow directors? There are various sources.

One of the most straightforward descriptions of the sources power that people can use in business is contained in a 1995 Harvard Business School paper by Linda Hill entitled *Power Dynamics in Organisations*. Again this is another piece aimed at executives and probably those looking to become executive directors and leaders of businesses but the principles are just as relevant to non-executives.

The thesis is that there are principally two sources of power for managers 'positional' and 'personal'. The components of each are listed below:

Positional power	Personal power
Formal authority	Expertise
Relevance	Track record
Centrality	Attractiveness
Autonomy	Effort
Visibility	

Some are more obvious than others. *Formal Authority* is simply the rights, responsibilities and sanctions you possess by virtue of holding the position. For example the chairman of the remuneration, audit or nominations committee may feel more powerful than a non-executive who doesn't hold a chairmanship.

Relevance relates to how relevant your contribution is to the current priorities of the organisation or in our case board. Following our earlier case at various times the chairman of the different committees will be more or less influential.

Centrality relates to the position the person has in networks, which are important to the committee. A good example of this would be where the non-executive is a highly respected city or industry figure. They are in the position of bestowing patronage or access to resources.

Autonomy is a difficult one for non-executives as on the one hand they have few delegated powers from the board other than those associated with their roles on the various sub-committees. On the other hand they arguably have more freedom to act in the sense of expressing views than their executive colleagues on the board.

Visibility is a relevant one for non-executives. The principle here is that the more visible your performance is, the more widely dispersed and recognised your power will be. Whilst their value to the chairman or chief executive is high, the fact that they are invisible to other executives means that the non-executive's real contribution is frequently underestimated by those other than the chairman and chief executive.

These are the positional power sources. In Hill's paper she contends that the less you rely on the formal powers the more power you have. The authors believe this is a very relevant point for non-executives.

So, looking at the personal power sources:

- *Expertise*: Possibly the most obvious source of power as long as the expertise has relevance to the situation. It is often through using their expertise to support the executives that non-executives increase their influence.
- *Track record*: This is another more obvious source of power. The non-executive who has successfully done what the executive directors are setting out to achieve and is in at least the same peer group as the other non-executives has an obvious advantage. 3i has found it much easier to introduce second time entrepreneurs, that is those who have already completed a successful start-up, buy-out or buy-in as non-executives or chairman than those without this experience.
- *Attractiveness*: This relates to physical and behavioural characteristics that others find attractive. A non-executive relying on physical attractiveness as a source of power would be unusual. Though there is one physical characteristic which, looking at the annual reports of US companies, might anecdotally reinforce Hill's point that height has been shown to help in the USA.

  Although some would argue that physical attractiveness helps, we suspect that attractive behavioural characteristics count for more in the non-executive context. The charismatic and likeable find gaining support for their ideas easier than the grumpy or solemn.
- *Effort*: Individuals who work hard are perceived as being more committed. Since the quality of the non-executive's relationships with other board members are important, effort needs to be put in to build and maintain them. In the post-Enron environment all non-executives are aware of the effort required to ensure that they have sufficient knowledge of the company and the directors.

In another Harvard Business School paper on the same subject, *Exercising Influence*, Hill argues that in order to use your power to exercise influence on a subject you need to consider the following questions:

- Whose co-operation do you need?
- Whose compliance do you need?
- Whose opposition would keep you form accomplishing your objective?

These are very helpful questions.

One other source of power relates to the power received by threatening resignation. This obviously should be reserved for special occasions and carefully used. There are a number of difficulties for a non-executive contemplating resignation and these relate to:

- reputational issues for them and the company;
- leaving the company with a weakened board;
- legal issues and
- financial loss.

A non-executive with a reputation for threatening to resign every time he or she doesn't agree with something will find it hard to gain influence or additional appointments. A non-executive who does resign needs to do so in a very careful way to avoid reputational risk. Shareholders may be sympathetic as to the reasons why but disappointed that the non-executive has left them with a weakened board.

What other sanctions do non-executives have? As has been mentioned earlier, considerably more if they are involved in the audit, nominations or remuneration committees. However withdrawing consent or withholding signature may prove only a temporary source of power.

Finally, the authors believe that there is one other source of power for the non-executive that provides considerable influence and that is the moral high ground which is reached by always acting in the best interests of the company rather than one's own.

3.6 Powers and Responsibilities of the Board and Committees

Confusion between the powers and responsibilities of the board, the committees of the board and individual board members reduces the effectiveness of the board and increases the risk of weak governance. Achieving clarity on the role of the board and the individual directors is the foundation stone of good governance and board effectiveness. However it is also important to be absolutely clear and precise about what decisions should only be decided by the board as a whole ('Matters reserved for the Board'), what decisions should only be decided by nominated committees of the board ('Matters delegated to the sub-committees of the Board') and those to be decided by the executive ('Matters delegated to the executive').

The context of the board should drive the specifics but we have attempted below to look at the key areas to be considered in arriving at a detailed description for a specific business.

3.7 Matters Reserved for the Board

The ICSA has produced an excellent Guidance note which is also available on their website (www.icsa.org.uk) on Matters reserved for the Board. Although this has been produced for public companies it is easy to adapt for the purposes of private ones. A copy is contained in **APPENDICES**.

The key items it covers are:

- companies act requirements;
- stock exchange/financial services authority;
- board membership and board committees;
- management and
- Combined Code recommendations;

as well as a whole series of other items including:

- internal controls;
- health and safety;
- environmental;
- litigation and
- dealing with urgent matters.

The most challenging areas for many boards are included under the ICSA's management heading. Why? Because this covers:

- approval of the long-term objectives and strategy;
- approval of budgets;
- key management appointments and
- changes to the companies' management and control structure.

The board's role in strategy is dealt with in **CHAPTER 7**.

With respect to urgent matters the ICSA guidance note states that:

'In all cases however the procedures should balance the need for urgency with the overriding principle that each director should be given as much information as possible and have an opportunity to requisition an emergency meeting of the board to discuss the matter prior to commitment of the company.'

3.8 Matters Delegated to the Sub-committees of the Board

The first issue is to determine what sub-committees of the board it is appropriate to have.

If the company is a listed one then in order to satisfy the Combined Code there will be the following as a matter of course.

- Audit
- Nominations
- Remuneration.

The nature of business and other contextual factors will then determine the need for additional committees (e.g. environmental, regulatory, risk management).

Sample terms of reference for each of the audit and compliance, nominations and remuneration committees are contained in the **APPENDICES**.

3.9   Board Balance

The Combined Code for listed companies states:

> 'that the board should include a balance of executive and non-executive directors (including independent non-executives) such that no individual or small group of individuals can dominate the board's decision taking.'

In larger companies the trend seems to be for a smaller number of executives to be on the board than was historically the case. As a consequence of this, and the need for there to be sufficient numbers of non-executives to staff board committees, many companies now have a larger majority of non-executives than was traditionally the practice. This though, can be frustrating for Non-executives who don't like to get all of their input from the chief executive or Finance Director. They may feel that no matter how good the Chief Executive or Finance Director are, their knowledge and perspective of the company is limited as a consequence. The evolution of "Management" or "Executive" committees who attend board meetings with members who are not formal board members may provide a solution to this problem and help senior executives appreciate the board more. However it does also present additional challenges for the Chairman in chairing meetings and for the executives who are used to contributing actively in the meetings they attend.

3.10   Board Away Days

CHAPTER 7 covers the board's role in strategy in detail. In this section we provide the following guidance for making away days effective:

- Be clear on the purpose of the away day and what your desired outcomes are (e.g. selection from a number of strategic options).
- Decide whether to use an external facilitator.
- Decide whom to involve who isn't a member of the board (internal or external).
- The chairman or CEO should brief the facilitator about the team dynamics, 'politics' or taboo subjects.
- Hold the away day offsite.
- Don't allow interruptions except in an emergency.
- Don't start with an operational board meeting.
- Participants should be prepared to challenge each other, in particular to surface differences – a key to success is the quality of debate, both content and challenge.
- No one should be allowed to dominate the debate.
- Action points should have an individual(s) assigned to them with delivery deadlines and reporting criteria.
- Consideration should be given during the away day to the personal implications of any decisions taken.
- Ensure critical outputs from the away day get put on the agenda for subsequent board meetings.
- Follow up and review the output of the away day.

Using an external facilitator for such days has a number of advantages. However if you use one they need to be:

- credible with the participants and experienced at the appropriate level;
- prepared and able to challenge participants (collectively and individually);
- able to maintain an objective and neutral approach;
- able to generate an appropriate atmosphere and
- have a clearly defined process for running the day, which is flexible enough to deviate from it when the participants require to do so.

Creating the right atmosphere is essential. A good chairman will ensure that there is the right blend of formality and informality. The social aspect is also important in building relationships, trust and respect between the board members.

We are especially grateful to Murray Steele at Cranfield School of Management for his support in compiling the above.

3.11 Professional Advice for Non-executives

It has become the norm for non-executives to want to have access to independent (from the company) legal and technical advice. However this is an area not without its difficulties. Some of the issues involved are as follows:

- What type of advice is it appropriate and reasonable for a non-executive to request?
- What is the process for agreeing this?
- Which advisers should be used?

With respect to the type of advice that it is appropriate and reasonable for a non-executive to request the Combined Code gives a healthy degree of room for the board to decide.

Section A.5.2 of the Code states that:

> 'The Board should ensure that directors, especially non-executive directors, have access to independent professional advice at the company's expense where they judge it necessary to discharge their responsibilities as directors.'

The majority of advice sought by directors in this context is of a legal nature. However there may be occasions where directors need accounting and regulatory advice from other than the company's advisers. Examples might include mergers, acquisitions, buy-outs or corporate recovery situations.

Clearly the specific situation will determine the most appropriate process. Key determinants will be whether the specific advice required is for all directors, the non-executives as a group or whether the advice is required for just one of the directors.

It would normally be expected that the issue would be discussed with the chairman and the company secretary beforehand and then formalised in writing. This usually takes the form of a letter from the director to the chairman or company secretary. The letter would state the background to the situation, the purpose of the advice, why the advice needs to be taken independently, as well as giving details of the firm to be used to provide the advice as well as an estimate of their costs.

In some circumstances, for example if the issue relates to the chairman, then it might be appropriate for the discussion to take place with senior independent director and he and the company secretary may provide the authority to proceed.

As with any other advice commissioned by the company, the directors will want to ensure that there is a proper process for instructing and monitoring advisers. The chairman, or senior independent director, would be expected to only approve such costs up to clearly stated maximum amount and if the advice was also available to other directors. They would also usually only give such approval subject to receiving progress reports.

The chairman will also usually withhold consent to the company paying for such advice if it relates to the personal interests of the director for example his service contract, shareholdings or if the director was in dispute with the company.

Meetings

4 Meetings

4.1 Introduction

> **At a Glance**
> * A company's Articles of Association often govern many aspects of board meetings, including convening meetings, quora of meetings and delegation of duties to individual directors.
> * While most boards have sub-committees, too much delegation of authority to them is sometimes seen as an abdication of responsibility.
> * A company's accounts, and the directors' interests, shall be laid before the members at an Annual General Meeting (AGM).
> * An alternate director is not an agent, and is not obliged to vote the same way as the absent director.
> * Minutes and post-meeting notification should be checked to ensure that they are accurate and that they fit with directors' recollections of what happened.

This chapter focuses on the formal aspects of the formal meetings that non-executive directors become involved in. These formal meetings are an important opportunity for non-executive directors to fulfil their role through adding value and ensuring good governance. These are not the only opportunity. The informal meetings and telephone conversations that non-executive directors hold with other directors are just as important in building the relationships and knowledge required to influence key decisions.

Two other books by one of the authors, *Running Board Meetings* and *Directors Dilemmas* (see **BIBLIOGRAPHY**) cover the informal aspects in considerable detail.

The main types of formal meetings non-executive directors become involved in are:

* Board meetings.
* Board sub-committee meetings.
* Annual General Meetings.
* Extraordinary General Meetings.
* Meetings for specific classes of shareholder ('class meetings').

The first two being 'meetings of directors' and the others being 'meetings of members' at which the directors attend. Before going into the formalities of each in detail we think that a non-executive should consider the following questions before any meeting.

- What is the purpose of the meeting?
- Who should be there?
- What role should each of the participants play?
- What should be on the agenda?
- What preparatory information is required to make the meeting effective?
- When should this information be circulated?
- How should the meeting be managed?
- What should be their own contribution to the meeting?
- How will decisions taken at the meeting be communicated and then brought into effect?
- Finally what formalities need to be observed?

4.2 Meetings of Directors

There are some general points to be made with regard to meetings of directors and these are as follows:

- The convening and holding of board meetings will normally be governed by the company's Articles of Association.
- Any director and the secretary at the director's request are usually empowered to call a meeting.
- The quorum for a board meeting will normally be fixed by the Articles. The *Companies (Tables A to F) Regulations 1985 (SI 1985/805)* Table A allows a quorum to be fixed by the directors and unless so fixed, shall be two. (More detail on Quorum issues are provided in **PARAGRAPH 4.19**.)
- It is usual for the Articles to require that a quorum be maintained throughout proceedings.
- A director interested in business to be conducted at a meeting must declare his interest. A quorum must be disinterested.
- Decisions of the directors may be recorded by resolution in writing, signed by all the directors.
- The Articles of a company normally permit the delegation of certain powers of the directors to a committee.
- We have ignored sole director and single member situations on the grounds that there won't be a non-executive director involved!

4.3 Board Meetings

Board meetings are the most frequent and generally the most important meetings that a non-executive director attends. These meetings of the executive and non-executive members of the board are where the key decisions are taken with regard to the strategy, resourcing and governance of the company. The chairman has the primary responsibility for managing these meetings and maximising their effectiveness.

4.4 *Notice*

The Articles of Association will normally set out the procedure for convening and holding board meetings. The *Companies (Tables A to F) Regulations 1985 (SI 1985/805)* Table A states that:

> 'A Director may, and the secretary at the request of a director shall, call a meeting of the directors' (*Regulation 88, Table A*).

It also provides that directors may regulate their proceedings as they think fit. There are no statutory provisions relating to the length of notice to be given for a board meeting and so 'reasonable' notice should be given to all directors. For most companies, board meetings are held at regular, predetermined intervals of which due notice is given, but from time to time meetings are called as and when necessary. As mentioned above it is good practice for the company (usually the company secretary) to produce a board calendar for the year ahead.

The notice reasonable for a particular meeting will depend, amongst other things, on the urgency and importance of the business to be discussed and the availability of the directors.

Notice of a board meeting may be given verbally, although it would be usual for written notice to be given. It is now common for companies to have made provision in their Articles to give notice electronically (i.e. by e-mail). Notice of a board meeting need not specify the business to be transacted, although it is good practice to do so.

As well as the agenda, a notice of a meeting will usually include the place, date and time for the meeting and unless directed in the Articles this can be circulated in any manner appropriate to a company, either by letter, fax, e-mail or verbally.

4.5 *Meetings by Telephone*

The Articles may permit directors to hold or participate in meetings by telephone. They require directors to be deemed present to be able to speak and be heard by the other directors at the 'meeting'. Consequently, unless the Articles specifically provide, a series of telephone calls on a one-to-one basis is unlikely to be permitted. Where a meeting is held by telephone/video conference the place of the meeting is taken as the place where the chairman participated from.

4.6 *Frequency*

There are differing views as to how frequently board meetings should be held. Some argue that to be sufficiently well informed, build the board's 'team spirit' and get through the increasing volume of work they should be monthly. Others argue that a monthly frequency tends to make them too operational in content and it is better to have fewer. A survey conducted by Top Pay Research Group and 3i in 2002 of over 400 directors who sat on over 1200 boards from start-ups to multi-billion pound companies showed the pattern below.

'We would expect that current board practice would be similar with most boards meeting 9–12 times a year.'

How many times a year does the board meet?

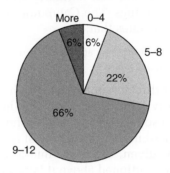

The average was eleven.

Source: Top Pay Research Group/3i survey 2002.

Eighty-nine per cent also met for separate budget or strategy sessions.

4.7   *Length*

With regard to the time a board meeting should take, again there are differences of view. The distribution in the 2002 TPRG survey was as follows.

'We would expect that current board practice would be similar.'

Average time of full board meeting (hours)

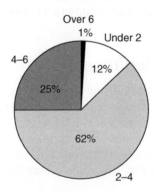

The average was four hours.

Source: Top Pay Research Group/3i survey 2002.

4.8   *Agendas*

Unlike shareholder meetings, which are strictly governed by both the Articles and the Companies Act, directors are free, within fairly broad perimeters, to regulate their affairs as they feel fit. Matters to be discussed at a board meeting will be dependent on the nature of the company's business and the number of directors. Board papers and reports are either circulated with the agenda or tabled at the meeting.

Board meeting agendas are usually developed by the chairman, company secretary and chief executive. It is good practice to plan out the board's time for the year ahead given that there will be certain matters which need to be covered at certain times of the year, for example budgets, accounts, dividends and so on. In the authors view most boards only have five or six really important matters to decide each year and the board should therefore plan these items into the forthcoming agendas so that the proper preparation time is allowed. The company secretary will normally focus on the legal and compliance issues and ensure that the board is spending enough time on these.

How many agenda items?

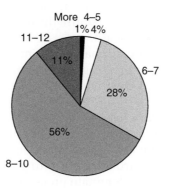

All routine items, for example, approval and signature of minutes of the last board meeting, any general meetings held after the last board meeting and financial statements, should be included in the agenda.

It is good practice, following a board meeting, for the chairman and/or company secretary to gather feedback from those attending and to ask them what items they would like to see on forthcoming agendas.

Reviewing agendas for the previous year is a healthy discipline and one normally performed by the company secretary. It can be fascinating to reflect on what the board actually spends its time on.

In researching *Running Board Meetings*, one of the authors noted that many directors complained that the following relationship occurred all too often.

Meetings

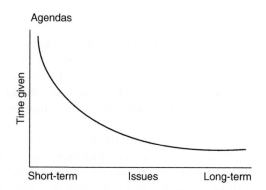

Cutting the number of board meetings is one way of solving this problem. Fewer meetings should lead to more focus on priorities; however this shouldn't be done at the expense of the board's knowledge of the company.

Quorum issues are dealt with below at **PARAGRAPH 4.19**.

4.9 *Conduct of Meetings*

There is no requirement of company law for a company to appoint a chairman. It is not a statutory position. However, the Articles of Association of most companies permit and sometimes require the directors to appoint one of their number to be chairman of the board.

In practice the chairman has the primary responsibility for ensuring the success of a board meeting. Engendering an atmosphere of energy, purpose, seriousness, rigour and trust will be the natural objective for any thoughtful chairman.

They will also work hard to harness the collective knowledge, skills and behaviours of those present to obtain not only the best decisions for the company but the maximum chance of those decisions being brought into effect. A good chairman is in control of the meeting and works hard but doesn't allow himself or anyone else to dominate proceedings.

The skilful chairman manages to achieve the right amount of pressure on the board. Using the analogy of the chart below, too little pressure in the boardroom leads to sloppiness, and too often to hasty and ill-thought through decisions.

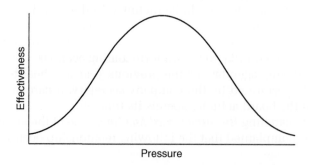

The strength of the chairman's relationships with the board members and the respect with which they are held will influence their ability to achieve the right balance.

It is probably the case in the most effective boards that the views expressed by the directors and their level of engagement will reflect their true position. However, in underperforming boards and even in the best performing boards there may be times when some of the board become 'silent seethers', who are unhappy with the conduct of the meeting yet for some reason not prepared, in the meeting at least, to say what they really think. The good chairman is alive to this and will either draw the person out in the meeting or make sure he follows up after the meeting has closed.

It is said that the best chairmen really do seem to know what is in the thought bubbles above their colleagues' heads. The chairman has a duty to ensure that all directors who wish to speak on a particular topic are given a reasonable opportunity to put forward the point of view. If matters become too heated, the chairman can, at his discretion, adjourn the meeting to enable tempers to cool. Adjournment may be for a few minutes or could, in some circumstances, be until the next board meeting.

The Combined Code for listed companies also says that 'each director should receive the same information concerning the matters to be considered and each director should be given sufficient time in which to consider such information.'

Table A (*SI 1985/805*) confers the following specific powers upon the chairman of a board meeting and of general meetings:

- In the case of an equality of votes, the chairman shall have a second or casting vote (*Regulation 88* for board meetings), and for general meetings. This casting vote is in addition to any other votes that the chairman may have. It is normal practice for the chairman to use this casting vote to maintain the status quo on the grounds that there is no majority in favour of change. However, it is entirely the chairman's discretion how he uses this vote, if at all.
- At a meeting of the directors or of a committee of the directors if a question arises as to the right of a director to vote, the question may, before the conclusion of the meeting, be referred to the chairman and his ruling shall be final and conclusive (*Regulation 98*).

When a director considers that a course of action to be taken by the board is potentially damaging, depending on the nature of the action, he may feel it necessary to make a formal objection to the board. This being the case the formal objection should be minuted. It may also be appropriate for the dissenting director to resign, although this is unlikely to be considered an adequate discharge of his duties where the company is insolvent. The dissenting director must select the appropriate course of action based upon the nature and scale of his dissatisfaction with the affairs of the company.

Managing the contribution from the executive is another important ingredient of success. The artful chairman avoids the situation where the board meeting is simply a show for the non-executives or where the only executive who has a chance to speak is the chief executive. He also brings out the finance director as a fully functioning board member and doesn't confine them simply to the role of provider of information.

What should the non-executive director's contribution to board meetings be? In summary, to be very well prepared and to contribute to the discussions in a way that meets the objectives of their role. In order to do this they will recognise that there is limited airtime in which to make their contributions.

Consequently they are unlikely to squander it on minor points of detail or issues where others may make a stronger contribution. Asking good questions rather than giving good speeches is more likely to achieve this. They will also see themselves as a member of the board team and actively contribute to the team spirit of the board. This does not mean that they have to lose their objectivity.

The best non-executives spend some time after every board meeting reflecting on their performance and are conscious of where they have contributed to most effect and where they did the opposite. The best chairmen will also be providing them with regular and constructive feedback.

If the non-executive director feels that board meetings are not as effective as they should be he should raise this in a constructive manner with the chairman. Ultimately poorly managed board meetings will lead to deterioration in performance. If the chairman isn't able to enhance the effectiveness of board meetings then there is clearly an issue with the chairman (see **PARAGRAPH 1.3.1** for more information).

4.10   Standing Committee Meetings

The board may delegate certain powers to a standing committee. However they cannot do so unless the Articles of Association so provide. The Articles will normally also regulate the proceedings of such committees.

The directors must ensure that the board resolution establishing a committee is carefully drafted so that the committee's status and functions are clearly defined in terms of reference. Also, any limitation of the powers delegated by the board needs to be stated in the terms of reference.

It is useful from time to time to establish *ad hoc* committees of the board to deal with specific matters that cannot be dealt with practicably by the full board or which may require urgent attention between regular board meetings, that is, progressing the acquisition or sale of certain assets, final sign off of accounts, etc.

The Combined Code for listed companies recommends the establishment of standing audit, remuneration and nomination committees.

The most common board sub-committees are:

- audit,
- remuneration and
- nominations and appointments;

and these are covered in detail in chapters 2, 18 and 16 accordingly. There may be others depending on the nature of the business, for example an environmental committee.

Board sub-committees if managed well can save the board as a whole a considerable amount of time by delegating the detailed discussion of technical, time consuming or less strategic complex but vital issues. They also allow for more considered discussion with external advisers. The balance of what is discussed at board meetings and what is discussed in committee meetings needs to be carefully considered. Some directors see the proliferation of committees and the increasing scope of their work as a potentially dangerous abdication of responsibility.

In smaller companies with smaller boards it may seem difficult to adopt this approach. However many smaller companies have adopted and adapted the principles of delegation, specialisation and planning to suit their own requirements and situation.

Non-executive directors should know and understand:

- the terms of reference of all board sub-committees whether they are on them or not;
- the specific powers delegated to that committee by the board as a whole;
- the way in which the work of each sub-committee is to be communicated to the board and should
- expect especially in public companies to be a member of at least one of the board sub-committees.

The selection of people to serve on sub-committees should be done on a rational basis. Whilst it is important that any member of a particular committee needs to be motivated to take part, just occasionally those most keen may not be the best choice.

4.11   Annual General Meetings

An Annual General Meeting must be held once a year and not more than 15 months after the date of the last such meeting (*CA 1985, s 366*). The first Annual General Meeting, however, must be held within 18 months of incorporation.

There are divided views on the benefits of AGMs. Some share the view of the following company secretary:

> 'I do not believe that there is much, if any upside in the way a company conducts an AGM, but there is almost unlimited downside if it is not handled properly.'

Others share the view of a highly experienced chairman who preferred not to be named:

> 'We all know that the people who turn up won't be able to change the decisions at the meeting given the dominance of institutional shareholders these days. So you may say what's the point? What a waste of money and so on. The point is that the process we go through as a board to make sure that we can account well for ourselves on any point is a wonderful discipline.'

The ICSA best practice guide to AGMs (see **BIBLIOGRAPHY**) has the following to say:

> 'Although all companies are required to hold an AGM of their shareholders, the event is not merely a matter of legal form. It provides the principal forum in which directors account to the shareholders for their stewardship of the company. It also gives shareholders an opportunity to raise issues before voting on matters which require approval.'

The directors of a company will normally convene an Annual General Meeting but if the directors default in convening such a meeting within the statutory period, the Department of Trade and Industry may call or direct the calling of a

Meetings

general meeting upon the application of any member (*CA 1985, s 367*). The usual business of an AGM comprises the following:

- consideration of the annual report and accounts;
- declaration of a dividend (if any);
- election or re-election of directors;
- appointment or re-appointment of auditors and
- giving of authority to the directors to determine the auditors' remuneration.

This business is often referred to as 'ordinary' business although it is unusual for Articles of Association to now draw a distinction between ordinary and special business (Table A (*SI 1985/805*) does not).

The following points of practice should be noted with regard to the business of an Annual General Meeting.

- An Annual General Meeting must be held within the statutory time limits even if audited accounts are not available for consideration by the meeting at that time. Unless there is other business to transact it is normal for such meetings to be immediately adjourned, to be reconvened when accounts become available.
- Any business that may be transacted at an Extraordinary General Meeting of the company may also be transacted at an Annual General Meeting (sometimes referred to as 'special' business).
- Except where the members of a private company have approved an elective resolution to dispense with an AGM, directors are obliged to lay audited accounts before the company in a general meeting within 10 months of the end of an accounting period for a private company, and within seven months for a public company (*CA 1985, s 244*). These time limits may be shorter in the case of a first accounting period.
- There is no statutory requirement for the notice convening the meeting or the auditors' report to the accounts to be read at the meeting. It is now common practice for members to be invited to take both as read.
- Attendance sheets should be made available at the meeting for completion by all persons (members and others) attending the meeting.
- The register of directors' interests must be available for inspection at the meeting.
- The members do not approve the audited accounts. The statutory requirement is merely that the accounts be laid before the company (*CA 1985, s241(1)*). The accounts are therefore 'received' or 'adopted'.
- The quorum required for an Annual General Meeting will be set out in the Articles of Association.
- There is no statutory requirement for resolutions to be seconded at meetings of members. It is also unusual for the Articles to require resolutions to be seconded but nevertheless this remains a procedural custom for many companies.
- Resolutions have traditionally been decided on a show of hands. This does not take account of the number of shares held by each member present, nor does it include proxy votes received. Consequently most major public companies will also present to the meeting the proxies cast in favour of each motion. The chairman or a specified number of members are normally authorised to demand a

poll and the Articles should be consulted to ascertain the exact requirements for the calling and conduct of a poll.

- Resolutions for the appointment or reappointment of directors to a public company should be voted upon separately; a single resolution to appoint two or more directors will be void (*CA 1985, s 292*). Although permitted, it is not good practice to present such a composite resolution at the AGM of a private company.

A private company may elect, by elective resolution, to dispense with the holding of Annual General Meetings (*CA 1985, s 366A*). An elective resolution is one approved by all the members entitled to attend and vote at a general meeting (*CA 1985, s 379A*).

An election has effect for the year in which it is made and subsequent years. An election cannot be used, however, to correct a default that has already taken place in failing to hold an AGM.

Where an election is in force and no AGM has been held for a particular year, any member may give notice to a company not later than three months before the end of the year, requiring the holding of an Annual General Meeting in that year. Such notice may be in writing or, with agreement, by electronic communication.

Where an election ceases to have effect (as a result, for example, of the company in general meeting approving an ordinary resolution to that effect), the company is not obliged to hold an AGM in that year if less than three months of the year remain when the election ceases to have effect.

It is usual for an election to dispense with the holding of AGMs to be coupled with elections to dispense with the laying of accounts and reports before a general meeting and to dispense with the obligation to appoint auditors annually.

The Institute of Company Secretaries and Administrators (ICSA) has produced an excellent guide on the subject entitled *A best practice guide to Annual General Meetings*.

4.12 Extraordinary General Meetings

There are three important things to note before we consider Extraordinary General Meetings in more detail and these are that:

- all general meetings other than Annual General Meetings are termed Extraordinary General Meetings;
- notice required for an EGM depends upon the resolution or resolutions to be considered, the Companies Acts and the Articles of Association and
- all the business of an AGM may be considered at an EGM except that the Articles of Association may require directors to stand for re-election only at an AGM.

It normally falls to the directors to convene an Extraordinary General Meeting but *CA 1985, s 368* provides that on a member's requisition the directors of a company shall forthwith proceed to convene an Extraordinary General Meeting (see **PARAGRAPH 4.18**).

Meetings

The following points should also be considered regarding EGMs.

- The period of notice necessary for an Extraordinary General Meeting depends upon the resolution or resolutions to be proposed, the provisions of the Companies Acts and the Articles of Association (see **PARAGRAPH 4.15**).
- Agreement to short notice of an Extraordinary General Meeting requires the approval of those members, who, being entitled to attend and vote at the meeting, hold not less than 95% in nominal value of the shares giving a right to attend and vote at such meeting. In the case of a company not having a share capital, the approval of the members exercising not less than 95% of the total voting rights is required (the members may elect to reduce this percentage in the case of a private company limited by share or by guarantee).
- It is possible for all the business of an Annual General Meeting to be conducted at an Extraordinary General Meeting (with the possible exception of the re-election of directors which may be reserved for an AGM by the Articles of Association (see the *Companies (Tables A to F) Regulations 1985 (SI 1985/805)* Table A). Accordingly, if two sets of audited accounts are to be laid before the shareholders in one year (because, for example, an accounting period has been shortened), it is possible for the second set of accounts to be received by an Extraordinary General Meeting.

4.13   Class Meetings

The rights attaching to a particular class of share, or the provisions of *CA 1985*, may require a separate class meeting of shareholders to be held from time to time to approve a particular matter. Generally, the statutory provisions relating to the holding of general meetings apply equally to class meetings. However, particular provisions relate to a quorum and the giving of short notice (*CA 1985, ss 125(6)* and *369(4)*). All resolutions proposed at a class meeting are extraordinary resolutions.

The statutory provisions for the convening and holding of general meetings and the provisions in the Articles of Association relating to such meetings apply to class meetings with any necessary modifications. However, the quorum at a class meeting shall be two persons holding or representing by proxy at least one-third in nominal value of the issued shares of the particular class, and at an adjourned meeting one person holding shares of the class in question or his proxy (*CA 1985, s 125(6)*). Fourteen days' clear notice of a class meeting must be given to those entitled to receive notice. Agreement to short notice may, however, be given by a majority in number of the holders of the particular class of shares holding not less than 95% in nominal value of the shares (*CA 1985, s 369(4)*).

Resolutions to be proposed at a class meeting are extraordinary resolutions. Such resolutions require approval of three-quarters of the holders of the particular class attending, and entitled to attend and vote, in person or, where proxies are allowed, by proxy at a separate class meeting (see *CA 1985, s 378(1)* and hereafter). A copy of every extraordinary resolution must be filed at Companies House within 15 days of its date.

4.14   Written Resolutions of Private Companies

There are five key points with regard to written resolutions for private companies and these are as follows:

- Any company may approve members' resolutions by Resolution in writing. The Articles of Association will normally set out a procedure to be followed and, in the case of a private company, a statutory procedure is also available (*CA 1985, s 381*).
- Any resolution, whether Special, Extraordinary or Elective, may be approved by written resolution, *except* resolutions for the removal of the director or auditor.
- A written resolution may consist of one document or several documents signed by all the members.
- A copy of every written resolution must be sent to the auditors.
- In the case of certain resolutions, particular documents must be circulated to shareholders at or before the time a resolution is supplied to the member for signature.

It has been generally accepted that where all members demonstrate their consent to a particular matter which a general meeting of the shareholders has authority to approve, the consent will be as binding as a resolution of the shareholders at a general meeting properly convened and held.

Which resolutions can be written? Any resolution whether ordinary, special, extraordinary or elective (for private companies) may be approved by written resolutions, except resolutions for the removal of a director or auditor. In these cases the resolutions must be proposed at a general meeting duly convened and held.

The signatures may appear either on the same document or on several documents in like form. The resolution is dated when the resolution is signed by or on behalf of the last member to sign.

All written resolutions must be entered in a book, in the same way as minutes of proceedings of a general meeting of a company. Any such record, if purporting to be signed by a director of the company or by the secretary, would be evidence of the proceedings in agreeing to the resolution (*CA 1985, s 382A*).

The acceptance of written resolutions has necessitated the introduction of various procedural changes relating to the circulation of documents to shareholders. The company secretary will normally arrange this and will confirm that it has taken place. They principally relate to resolutions concerning:

- pre-emption waivers;
- purchase of own shares either on or off market and
- directors' contracts or expenditure.

Non-executives should consult their company secretary if they have any doubts about whether the correct procedure is being followed with regard to a written resolution.

Meetings

4.15　Notice of General Meetings

Generally, the length of notice to be given for general meetings is as follows.

- AGM: not less than 21 days (*CA 1985, s 369(1)*).
- Special resolution being proposed at a meeting: not less than 21 days' notice must be given, whether or not the meeting is an AGM or other general meeting of the company (*CA 1985, s 378(2)*).
- EGM: not less than 14 days' notice (*CA 1985, s 369(1)*). In the case of an unlimited company, not less than seven days' notice shall be given of a general meeting.

These will be understood to be 'clear days' notice, that is to exclude the day the notice is served and the day of the meeting itself. The ICSA guideline is that notice of an AGM and accompanying documents should be circulated to members not less than 20 working days (excluding weekends and bank holidays) in advance of a meeting. This recommendation is echoed by the Combined Code on Corporate Governance for listed companies.

Meetings of members may be called upon less than the statutory notice if approved by specified majorities of members. *All* members are generally entitled to receive notice of the meeting. The Articles should be consulted. In addition, the auditors and directors of the company should be given notice. Certain details must be set out in a Notice of a meeting, either as a matter of practice or of law. A listed public company must also have regard to stock exchange requirements.

The Articles of a company may not provide for shorter notice periods to be given to members without consent. However, meetings may be called at shorter notice upon the agreement of members as follows:

- *AGM*: by all members entitled to attend and vote.
- *Other general meetings*: by a majority in number of the members having a right to attend and vote at the meeting and holding not less than 95% in nominal value of the shares giving a right to attend and vote at the meeting (*CA 1985, s 369(3)* and *CA 1985, s 378(3)*). The same majority must also consent to short notice of a meeting at which a special resolution is to be proposed (*CA 1985, s 378(3)*).

This 95% in nominal value required for agreement to short notice may, in the case of a private company, be reduced to not less than 90% by elective resolution of the members (*CA 1985, s 369(4)* and *CA 1985, s 378(3)*).

- *Separate class meetings*: the provisions in relation to 'other general meetings' above also apply to separate class meetings.
- *Elective resolutions at general meetings*: agreement to short notice may not be given to any general meeting (or that part of a meeting) at which an elective resolution is to be proposed. An elective resolution may, however, be approved by written resolution, if practicable, thereby circumventing the notice requirements.

As has been said above the Articles will almost invariably provide that 'clear days' notice is required, that is excluding both the day of service of the notice and the day of the meeting. The position may be further complicated by a provision in the Articles stating that notice will be deemed to be given at the expiration of a certain period. For example, *Regulation 115* of *Table A (SI 1985/805)* provides that a notice shall, unless the contrary is proved, be deemed to be given at the expiration of 48 hours after the envelope containing it was posted. It is common for other Articles to provide that service shall be deemed to be given at the expiration of 24 hours.

Great care must, therefore, be taken to ensure that the correct period of notice is given and, in this regard, it is essential that reference be made to the Articles. For example, a company adopting *Companies (Tables A to F) Regulations 1985 (SI 1985/805)* Table A might give notice of an AGM as follows:

Date of notice	1 October
Deemed date of service	3 October
21 days run from	4 October
Expiry of 21 days	24 October
Earliest date for meeting	25 October

Notice of a general meeting may be given to a person electronically either to an address notified by the person to the company for that purpose or where the company and the person have agreed by access to a website (*CA 1985, s 369(4A)(4B)*). Where a notice is displayed on a website the person must be notified, in a manner for the time being agreed for the purpose between him and the company of:

- the publication of the notice on a website;
- the address of that website and
- the place on the website where the notice may be accessed and how it may be accessed.

The notice must be published on the website throughout the period, beginning with the giving of the notification and ending with the conclusion of the meeting (*CA 1985, s 369(4C)*).

The notice displayed on a website must state that it concerns a notice of a company meeting served in accordance with *CA 1985*, must specify the place, date and time of the meeting and state whether the meeting is to be an Annual or Extraordinary Meeting (*CA 1985, s 369(4C)*).

The provisions in *CA 1985* relating to the giving of notice by electronic communication override any provision in a company's Articles of Association to the contrary (*CA 1985, s 369(4E)*). In as far as the Articles of a company do not provide for notices and notifications to be served using electronic communications, the provisions of *Companies (Tables A to F) Regulations 1985 (SI 1985/805)* Table A shall apply (*CA 1985, s 369(4F)*).

The proceedings of a meeting shall not be invalidated if a notice is published on a website for a part but not all of the period mentioned in *CA 1985, s 369(4C)* and this is wholly due to circumstances which it would not be reasonable to have expected the company to prevent or avoid (*CA 1985, s 369(4D)*).

Notice of a meeting must be given to all those persons entitled to receive notice. This includes the following:

- Every member of the company or every member of a particular class in the case of a separate class meeting, except:
  - a holder of shares of a particular class which does not enjoy the right to receive notice of or to attend or vote at general meetings (e.g. non-voting preference shares);

○ a member who has no right to receive notice in terms of the Articles of Association, for example a member resident overseas who has not provided an address within the UK for service of notice (*Regulation 112, Companies (Tables A to F) Regulations 1985 (SI 1985/805)*);
○ in the case of joint holders, where the Articles provide that notice need only be given to the joint holder whose name first appears in the register of members in respect of the joint holding (*Regulation 111, Companies (Tables A to F) Regulations 1985 (SI 1985/805)*).

- The auditors of the company.
- The directors of the company.
- All persons entitled to a share where a member has died or is bankrupt.

An omission to give due notice to any person entitled to receive it invalidates the meeting. However, the Articles normally provide that an accidental omission to give notice, or the non-receipt of notice by a person, should not invalidate the proceedings (*Regulation 39, Table A (SI 1985/805)*).

A notice convening a general meeting must show the following:

- the name of the company;
- the date, place and hour of the meeting and the general nature of the business to be transacted;
- if appropriate, the fact that the meeting is the Annual General Meeting;
- the text of the resolutions to be proposed at the meeting and their type (i.e. ordinary, special, extraordinary or elective);
- a statement that a member entitled to attend and vote may appoint a proxy;
- the name of the director or secretary authorised to sign the notice and their office of director or secretary;
- date of the notice and
- registered office address.

A public company must also have regard to stock exchange requirements. In addition, further ICSA guidelines for best practice for AGMs include a recommendation that where the meeting includes special business, the notice should be accompanied by a letter or circular giving a full explanation of the resolution(s) to be considered.

An example of a notice of an Extraordinary General Meeting is given in APPENDIX 1.

Appendix 1

Notice of Extraordinary General Meeting
Resolutions

PLC

   NOTICE IS HEREBY GIVEN THAT an Extraordinary General Meeting of the Company will be held at..............on.........at.......to consider and if deemed fit to approve the following resolutions namely:

4.16   *Ordinary Resolutions*

1. **THAT** the board be and is hereby generally and unconditionally authorised to exercise all powers of the company to allot relevant securities (within the meaning of *Section 80* of the *Companies Act 1985*) up to an aggregate nominal amount of £10,000,000 provided that this authority shall expire on the date of the next Annual General Meeting after the passing of this resolution save that the company may before such expiry make an offer or agreement which would or might require relevant securities to be allotted after such expiry and the board may allot relevant securities in pursuance of such an offer or agreement as if the authority conferred hereby had not expired. The authority conferred upon the directors by resolution approved on is hereby revoked.

2. **THAT** the employee share option scheme ('the scheme') set out in the draft rules produced to the meeting and signed by the chairman for the purposes of identification be and is hereby approved and that the directors be and are hereby authorised to:
   (a) do all acts and things which they consider necessary or expedient to establish and carry the scheme into effect;
   (b) vote as directors on any matter connected with the scheme, notwithstanding that they may be interested in the same and any prohibition on interested directors voting contained in the Articles of Association of the Company be suspended to that extent, except that no director shall vote on any resolution concerning his own participation in the scheme or be counted in the quorum required for the consideration of any such resolution;
   (c) to issue to participants in the scheme such ordinary shares of each in the Company up to the limit contained in the rules of the scheme in satisfaction of the options exercised in accordance therewith.

3. **THAT** the directors and the company be and hereby are authorised to enter into the contract with..............PLC (the 'Bank') for the subscription by..............the Bank for..........ordinary shares of......................each at a subscription price of pence per share and for the subscription by the Bank for £..............unsecured loan..........stock, further particulars of which are contained in Part 1 of the document of which this notice forms Part 2.

4.17 *Special Resolutions*

4. **THAT** subject to the passing of the previous resolution the board be and is hereby empowered pursuant to *Section 95* of the *Companies Act 1985* to allot equity securities (within the meaning of *Section 94* of the said Act) for cash pursuant to the authority conferred by the previous resolution as if *subsection (1)* of *Section 89* of the said Act did not apply to any such allotment provided that this power shall be limited:

   (a) to the allotment of equity securities in connection with a rights issue in favour of ordinary shareholders where the equity securities respectively attributable to the interests of all ordinary shareholders are proportionate (as nearly as may be) to the respective numbers of ordinary shares held by them;

   (b) to the allotment (otherwise than pursuant to subparagraph (a) above) of equity securities up to an aggregate nominal value of pound.

5. **THAT** the draft regulations produced to the meeting and initialled by the chairman for the purposes of identification be adopted as the Articles of Association of the company in substitution for and to the exclusion of all the existing Articles of Association.

Date:.....................   BY ORDER OF THE BOARD
Registered Office   **Secretary**

A member entitled to attend and vote at the meeting is entitled to appoint a proxy to attend and vote in his place. A proxy need not be a member.

4.18 *Notes*

Resolution 1: Directors cannot allot shares in the company (other than the shares allotted pursuant to an employee share scheme) unless they are authorised to do so by the company in general meeting. This resolution which replaces the previous authority given to directors at the AGM on .... will permit the directors to allot shares up to a maximum nominal value of £10,000,000. This will allow the directors to make the proposed issue of .... Ordinary Shares of .... pence each.

Resolution 2: This resolution seeks approval to the proposed new employee share option scheme. The scheme is intended to be an 'approved' scheme, that is approved by the Inland Revenue in terms of the *Income and Corporation Taxes Act 1988* (as amended) and enjoying the favourable tax treatment conferred upon such schemes. Application has been made to the Inland Revenue for formal approval of the scheme. A copy of the draft rules of the scheme and of the draft option agreement are available for inspection by any member at the Registered Office from the date of this notice until the date of the Extraordinary General Meeting on any weekday (Saturdays, Sundays and public holidays excepted) during normal business hours and at the meeting itself.

Resolution 3: This resolution is included to give shareholders an opportunity to consider the transaction.

Resolution 4: Under *Section 89* of the *Companies Act 1985*, if the directors wish to allot any of the unissued shares for cash (other than pursuant to an employee share scheme) they must in the first instance offer them to existing shareholders in proportion to their holdings. To enable the directors to make the specific allotment of shares to ...., the provisions of *Section 89(1)* of the Act must be waived by resolution of the shareholders. Except in the case of a rights issue, the waiver is limited to shares with an aggregate nominal value of £.............. (the aggregate nominal value of the proposed share issue to ....). The reasons for recommending this application, the amount to be paid by .... and the directors' justification of that amount are set out in the chairman's letter to shareholders accompanying this notice.

Resolution 5: The agreement with .... necessitates changes to the Articles of Association. Details of the main changes are set out in the chairman's letter to shareholders accompanying this notice. A copy of the proposed new Articles of Association is available for inspection by any member from the date of this notice until the date of the Extraordinary General Meeting at the Registered Office on any weekday (Saturdays, Sundays and public holidays excepted) during normal business hours at the meeting itself.

4.19   Requisitions by Members

Members of a Company are empowered by *CA 1985* to requisition the directors to convene an Extraordinary Meeting. However:

- The requisitionists must hold not less than one-tenth of the paid-up voting share capital of the company or if the company does not have a share capital to be able to exercise not less than one-tenth of the total voting rights.
- On receipt of the requisition, the directors must convene an EGM within 21 days of the requisition date for a date not more than 28 days from the date of the notice of meeting. If they do not do so, the meeting may be convened by the requisitionists themselves for a date not more than three months after the date of the deposit of the requisition.
- Members have the right to requisition directors to include a resolution in the notice of an AGM.

On receipt of the requisition, the directors must proceed to convene an Extraordinary General Meeting within 21 days from the date of therequisition or, if they do not do so, the meeting may be convened by the requisitionists or any of them representing more than one-half of the total voting rights of them all. A meeting convened by the requisitionists shall be convened, as nearly as possible, in the same manner as that in which meetings are convened by the directors but no such meeting may be held more than three months after the date of the deposit of the requisition. Directors are deemed not to have duly convened the meeting if they convene a meeting for a date more than 28 days after the date of a notice convening the meeting (*CA 1985, s 368(8)*).

The company is obliged to reimburse the requisitionists for any reasonable expenses incurred by them by reason of the company's failure to convene a meeting, such amount to be retained by the company out of any fees or remuneration due or to become due to the directors in default.

Members also have the right to requisition the directors of a company to include in the notice of the next Annual General Meeting any resolution which may be properly moved and is intended to be moved at that meeting (*CA 1985, s 376* and *CA 1985, s 376(1)(a)*). Such requisitionists must be members representing not less than one-twentieth of the total voting rights of all the members, having, at the date of the requisition, a right to vote at the meeting to which the requisition relates, or not less than 100 members holding shares in the company on which there has been paid-up an average sum, per member, not less than £100.

The requisitionists may also require the company to circulate to members any statement of not more than 1000 words with respect to the matter referred to in any proposed resolution or the business to be dealt with at that meeting (*CA 1985, s 376(1)(a)*). Any requisition to include a resolution and to circulate a statement must be carried out at the expense of the requisitionists. Any requisition must be signed by the requisitionists, deposited at the registered office of the company and, in the case of a requisition requiring notice of a resolution, must be given to the company not less than 6 weeks before the meeting and, in the case of the statement, not less than 1 week before the meeting (*CA 1985, s 377*). There must be deposited or tendered with the requisition a sum reasonably sufficient to meet the company's expenses in giving effect to it.

4.20   Quorums: Some Points to Note

A quorum is defined as:

> 'The minimum number of persons whose presence is required, and who are entitled to vote, at a duly convened meeting.'

In general, no business may be transacted at a meeting at which a quorum is not present or maintained and any resolution passed at a meeting at which there is no quorum will be invalid. However, *Regulation 90* of *Companies (Tables A to F) Regulations 1985 (SI 1985/805)* Table A provides that if the number of directors in office falls below the number necessary for a quorum, those directors may act, but only for the purpose of filling vacancies or for calling a general meeting.

Other points to note are that:

- The quorum for a directors' meeting is usually fixed by the Articles. Table A provides for a quorum of two and it is usual, in the case of a private company, for the Articles to permit a quorum of one.
- *CA 1985* provides that unless the Articles make specific provision, two persons present in person or by proxy will be a quorum at a general meeting.
- It is usual for the Articles to require that a quorum be maintained throughout proceedings.

- The quorum for an adjourned general meeting may differ from that required for the original meeting.
- Where a quorum cannot be raised for a particular reason it may be possible to make application to the court for a declaration that a meeting of the members comprising less than the prescribed quorum may nevertheless conduct the valid business.
- It is normal for a company's Articles of Association to allow for proxies to be counted in the quorum of a meeting.
- A member who is disenfranchised for any reason may not be counted in a quorum.
- *CA 1985, s 125(6)* sets out the quorum necessary for any separate meeting of a particular class of shareholder as two persons holding or representing by proxy at least one-third in nominal value of the issued shares of the class in question and at an adjourned meeting one person holding shares of the class in question or his proxy.
- A quorum must be disinterested. *Regulations 94* and 95 of *Companies (Tables A to F) Regulations 1985 (SI 1985/805)*, for example, provide that, except for certain specified transactions, a director interested in business to be conducted at a meeting may not be counted in the quorum for the particular business to be transacted nor may he vote upon such a matter. Where a quorum cannot be raised for a particular item of business, it may be necessary for the matter to be placed before the company in a general meeting.
- Provision is now made in the Articles of many companies for members to attend electronically (i.e. videoconferencing). For this to be effective the chairman and other board members need to be very mindful of the remote attendee and ensure that they have the same opportunity to engage as those physically present.
- It is common in small private companies for the Articles to relax the provisions of *Regulations 94* and *95* of *Companies (Tables A to F) Regulations 1985 (SI 1985/805)* so that any director who declares an interest in a contract or arrangement made, or proposed to be made, with the company may, having declared such interest, be counted in the quorum of the meeting and be entitled to vote in respect thereof.

4.21   Declarations of Interest

A general notice of interest can be given by a director declaring the nature of his interest. For example a statement that he is a member of another specified company or connected person which is seeking to do business with the Company of which he is a director.

Section 346 of the *Companies Act 1985* should be checked to ascertain who is connected with the director. However, such a notice must be given at a meeting of the directors, or the director must ensure that it is read at the next meeting of the directors after it is given.

Should the interest fall within the remit of *Section 320* of *CA 1985* as a substantial property transaction involving a director acquiring from or transferring to the company a non-cash asset, the approval of members to the transaction by means of an ordinary resolution will be required, unless the value of the transaction is less than £1000, or less than the lower of £100,000 or 10% of the company's net asset value.

In practice interests are often well known and this is a formality. However failure to notify the board of an interest risks seriously undermining trust and respect within the board and can damage reputations very easily. It is important therefore for directors to be diligent in notifying interests.

4.22   Alternate Directors Attending Board Meetings

There may well be occasions when due either to prior commitments or unforeseen circumstances a director is unable to attend a board meeting. Should a director wish his opinion on a particular matter to be heard at a meeting and is unable to attend by telephonic or electronic means, the traditional option available to them is to appoint an alternate director. The *Companies Act 1985* does not contain provisions regarding alternate directors. The Articles of Association will need to be consulted to ensure that the director has the power to appoint an alternate director. If the company has adopted Table A, the provisions concerning alternate directors are contained in *Regulations 65–69 Companies (Tables A to F) Regulations 1985 (SI 1985/805)*.

The appointment of an alternate director will often require the consent of the remaining directors.

The alternate director has the right to receive notice of all meetings of directors and all meetings of committees where the appointor is a member and to attend and vote at such meetings in his appointor's absence.

An alternate director is responsible for his own actions and his mistakes. He is not the agent of the director appointing him.

Under the provisions of *Regulation 88 Companies (Tables A to F) Regulations 1985 (SI 1985/805)*, a director who is also an alternate at a board meeting can be entitled to two votes, one in his own right and the other on behalf of his appointor if they are absent.

If the appointment of the alternate director is only made for one meeting the appointment and the termination of that appointment should be notified at Companies House within the 14-day limit. If the company is fully listed, trading on AIM or has an OFEX dealing facility the appointment of an alternate director should be notified within the time period described under the continuing obligations for each.

4.23   Observers and Advisers

Independent advice and support are increasingly seen as an essential element of an effective board.

A board will often require their professional advisers to make presentations to the directors on specific issues when necessary. These advisers may, if permitted by the meeting, attend the entire meeting or just that part they are concerned with.

The auditors of a company have the statutory right to attend general meetings at which audited accounts are considered. If auditors attend board meetings regularly and advise on non-accounting matters they could be deemed to be a shadow director and thereby a director of the company for all purposes.

If a company has securities quoted on the stock exchange, AIM or on OFEX with a large shareholder base, the company's register of members will be maintained by a share registration agent. Share registration agents deal with all types of share transactions enquiries from shareholders, brokers and members of the public. They will also administer the distribution, receipt, scrutiny and recording of proxies and assist with the running of general meetings, which they would usually attend to process attendees and assist with voting if required.

4.24 Minutes and Post-meeting Notifications

Section 382 of the *Companies Act 1985* requires the directors to maintain minutes of all board meetings. This includes meetings held by telephone or through other electronic media. The statutory requirement is reinforced by *Regulation 100* of *Companies (Tables A to F) Regulations 1985 (SI 1985/805)* (where applicable), which requires a record to be kept of all appointments of officers by the directors and all meetings of members, directors, committees of directors and holders of any class of shares.

The director should ensure that minutes kept are concise, accurate, impartial and unambiguous. All formal resolutions and decisions should be recorded with a short narrative where necessary. All matters of records should also be minuted. This would include declarations of interest, the tabling and consideration of reports and accounts and other documents, and more generally, such matters as members of the board wish to be recorded formally.

It is usual, and best practice, for the secretary to send draft minutes to the chairman for initial comment. The draft agreed by the chairman should then be circulated to those also present at the meeting for their consideration prior to the next meeting. It is important for a non-executive director to read these carefully and ensure that if his recollection differs from what has been recorded he raises it immediately with the company secretary. This is especially important for companies in difficulty or in danger of becoming insolvent.

There is sometimes a debate over whether the minutes should contain a summary of the discussion or just the decisions on a particular point. Views vary over the depth of detail required. In the USA there was a trend (pre-Enron and Worldcom!) to adopt a somewhat sterile and minimalist approach leaving less for lawyers to pick over and find fault with. The danger of this approach though is that it may be hard for the board to subsequently prove that it exercised due care on a particular issue. A variety of approaches are taken in the UK with a consensus on recording the key discussion points or matters taken into account.

Minutes of general meetings and board meetings should be kept separately. Shareholders do not have a right to inspect minutes of meetings of the directors and for this reason such minutes should be maintained separately.

Decisions by the board of a company on dividends, profits and other matters requiring announcement must be notified to the Company Announcement Office without delay and no later than 7.30 a.m. on the next following business day (Listing Rules 9.35).

5

Corporate Ethics

Corporate Ethics

5 Corporate Ethics

5.1 What Are Corporate Ethics?

> **At a Glance**
> * Corporate ethical behaviour is becoming an increasingly high-profile issue.
> * A business that operates in an ethical way will be directly and indirectly sensitive and responsive to the reasonable needs of its various stakeholders.
> * Corporate ethics should focus on internal issues that are within the company's control and over which it can exercise real influence.
> * The specific ethical matters needing consideration, and the potential problem areas, will vary depending on the nature and scale of the company's operations.
> * Ethical behaviour can only be achieved in a corporate culture where honesty and integrity are considered to be paramount.
> * The benefits of ethical conduct may be difficult to measure, especially in the short-term, but high ethical standards are increasingly seen as an asset and unethical behaviour as a liability.
> * Increased bureaucracy and controls are likely to be imposed if companies are not prepared to act voluntarily and demonstrate their commitment to corporate ethics.

5.2 Increase in Ethical Awareness

The issue of corporate ethics has received an increasingly high profile in recent years, especially in the light of the problems at businesses such as Enron and Worldcom. In the past, it may have been tempting for directors to regard business ethics as well-intentioned but as of little practical value in the real world. However, ethical perspectives are coming more and more to the forefront of social thought, and the public – and in particular potential employees, investors and customers – are generally better informed and more ethically conscious than they were even 10 years ago. There is currently a general degree of unease and scepticism about large, multinational corporations in particular. Many people have concluded that a company cannot consistently maintain both high profits and high principles, and that company executives are frequently engaged in the unscrupulous pursuit of profits at considerable cost to the environment and to the health and well-being of their employees and of consumers in general.

5.3   Responsible Action

A business that operates in an ethical way will be directly and indirectly sensitive and responsive to the reasonable needs of its various stakeholders – for instance, employees, customers, suppliers, the local community, the environment and society in general. Even company law recognises that the fiduciary duties and responsibilities of directors extend beyond their responsibility to the shareholders. The statement of duties set out in CA 2006 (and which has been brought into effect from 1 October 2007) requires each director to act in the way that he considers, in good faith, would be most likely to promote the success of the company for the benefit of its members as a whole. In doing so, he must have regard (amongst other matters) to:

- the likely consequences of any decision in the long term;
- the interests of the company's employees;
- the need to foster the company's business relationships with suppliers, customers and others;
- the impact of the company's operations on the community and the environment;
- the desirability of the company maintaining a reputation for high standards of business conduct and
- the need to act fairly as between members of the company.

The duties of directors under company law are considered in more detail in CHAPTER 8.

A business that operates in an ethical manner will devote time and attention to meeting customer requirements, acting in a socially and environmentally responsible way, and making wise use of energy and non-renewable resources.

5.4   Internal or External Focus?

Corporate ethics and corporate social responsibility are sometimes seen as involving an outward-focussed social vision for improvement – for instance, broad ideals set out in corporate codes and mission statements. In fact, they are much more about internal issues that are within the company's control and over which it can exercise real influence. The general public is becoming increasingly sceptical about codes and statements which do not appear to have any noticeable impact on the company's day to day activities and which perhaps represent good intentions rather than an actual commitment to change. Corporate ethics should be based on the broad principles of integrity and fairness, and should focus on issues such as product and service quality, customer satisfaction, fair business dealing, sound employment practices, transparency and accountability, and the responsibilities of the business to the local community and the environment. Acting in an ethically responsibly manner means acting thoughtfully and weighing up the benefits and harm that each particular course of action might bring in the longer term. Unethical conduct is often focussed on short-term advantages without considering the mid- and long-term consequences.

5.5 Complex Issues

Corporate ethics is not a straightforward subject and many of the surrounding issues can be complex. The specific ethical matters needing consideration in any business will vary depending on the nature and scale of its operations, but they might include:

- the sourcing of goods from low-wage countries;
- the use of child labour in developing countries;
- equity in pay and conditions;
- protecting the environment;
- ethical trading, and in particular the acceptability of making 'commission' payments.

Many of these issues will need to be considered in context of local conditions in the country concerned and the impact on the lifestyle of the individuals involved.

5.6 Corporate Culture

Ethical behaviour can only be achieved in a corporate culture where honesty and integrity are considered to be paramount. Recent accounting scandals have raised numerous questions about the adoption of aggressive accounting techniques, the manipulation of profits and the use of off balance sheet financing and other financial engineering techniques to create a more favourable impression of the business. Directors need to give serious consideration to the following questions:

- What kind of organisation do we want this to be?
- Which values really matter to us?
- How do the directors articulate and reinforce these to other managers and staff?
- How do the directors react to the pressures arising from market expectations?
- How does this impact on other managers and staff?

Trust cannot be manufactured, but it is possible to create a climate where people feel that they can trust each other. This will only happen if the individuals at the top of the organisation set the appropriate ethos, targets and expectations and demonstrate these in their own actions, as well as communicating them clearly throughout the workforce and monitoring progress against the objectives.

5.7 Potential Problem Areas

Potential problem areas will also vary depending on the nature and scale of the company's operations, but some of the more common issues include the following:

- *Incentive schemes*: Whilst incentive schemes can be a useful motivation tool, they also bring inherent dangers – it is now well-recognised that the payment of

Corporate Ethics

large executive bonuses, especially in the form of share options or based on profits, can encourage managers to take whatever action they deem necessary to maintain profit levels or keep the share price up. They can also encourage individuals to focus on short-term results rather than longer-term issues such as the company's credibility and reputation. Reward schemes need to be designed around the company's longer-term aims and to reward genuine performance (which may be more difficult to measure) rather than short-term achievements.

- *Market pressures*: Financial analysts tend to be preoccupied with immediate results and steadily rising earnings, but there are very few businesses that can achieve these over an extended period of time. Many executives feel compelled to feed the market's hunger for rapid growth and this can divert their energies away from managing the actual business towards managing the market's expectations of the company. Market demands can also result in over-optimistic predictions of growth and a reluctance to make a public acknowledgement of problems and weaknesses, although it is inevitable that difficulties will be encountered in any business from time to time.

- *Business survival*: Executives will sometimes feel compelled to adopt practices that they would otherwise consider unacceptable because it seems necessary to ensure the survival of the business and/or to protect their own careers – commercial demands therefore prevail over the guidance of their own consciences.

- *Commission payments*: The payment of a bribe is a legal offence in some countries, whilst others permit its deduction as an expense for tax purposes. Demands for 'commission' payments for favours done in business dealings can be a particular problem when dealing with officials and individuals in developing countries. Gaining an unlawful advantage by means of corruption is never legitimate under any circumstances and businesses are generally advised to publicise the fact that they do not tolerate this, even when it might be commercially advantageous and would probably go undetected. However, there may be circumstances where a business sees less of a moral dilemma in making a payment in order to speed up a process that is legal and will be carried out in due course – although this undoubtedly puts those who can afford to pay at an advantage, and could therefore be considered contrary to fair trading. It is for each business to decide what is acceptable and what is not, but once this decision has been made, no compromise of the company's agreed standards should be permitted.

- *Gifts*: Gifts and hospitality from customers, suppliers and other business contacts may also give rise to problems. It is advisable to develop guidelines for both the giving and receiving of such items, usually with a requirement for disclosure of any significant gifts or hospitality offered.

It is also important that mechanisms are in place to allow appropriate consultation and discussion within the company on particular situations where it may be difficult to reach a judgement on whether a particular course of action is ethical or not.

5.8   Investor Confidence

Investor confidence is critical to the successful operation of the economic market. Clarity, transparency, accountability and fairness, supported by a sound system of financial reporting, are all essential if the public as a whole and investors in particular, are to be able to evaluate risk, establish a market value for shares and generally participate in the equity culture.

5.9　Benefits of Ethical Conduct

The benefits of ethical conduct may be difficult to measure, especially in the short-term. The disadvantages, in terms of lost business and additional costs, are likely to be more readily apparent, especially in the early stages. It should also be recognised that a strict ethical policy will invariably lead to loss of market share in some countries. However, commercial success is usually interpreted these days as more than financial results and corporate reputation is now regarded as a valuable asset, albeit one which takes time to build. High ethical standards are increasingly recognised as an asset and unethical behaviour is seen as a liability. A strong corporate image can also bring competitive advantage and can help to attract investors, customers and potential employees. The benefits of high ethical standards include the following:

- Attracting high-quality employees – an ethically sound business is generally seen as a more attractive employer, especially as many employees today look at more than just remuneration when applying for a position.
- Greater job satisfaction for employees – research has shown that there is a direct correlation between ethical conduct and job satisfaction and that employees generally have a greater sense of belonging, and are more committed and innovative, in an environment in which ethical conduct has strong support from senior management.
- Reduced likelihood of friction with campaigners and protest groups – such activities can divert a considerable amount of management time.
- Reduced internal friction – employee morale tends to fall if the company becomes the focus of public criticism or if colleagues are seen, or thought, to be advancing their own careers in an unethical way.
- Good relationships with the local community improve company credibility and reputation and can help to generate valuable public support for company expansion programmes.

Whilst some may have felt in the past that businesses acting in a socially responsible manner would not survive in a cut-throat, competitive, profit-focussed market, research has in fact shown that such companies are usually more profitable in the long term. Although financial costs may be incurred in developing and maintaining ethical awareness programmes, these appear to be significantly outweighed by the subsequent benefits gained.

5.10　Avoiding Further Regulation

Businesses frequently complain about the extent and complexity of laws and regulations and the administrative overload that this can create. However, commercial freedom goes hand in hand with responsibility and the increased public awareness of, and demands for, ethical behaviour is likely to lead to increased

Corporate Ethics

bureaucracy and controls unless companies are prepared to act voluntarily and demonstrate their commitment to corporate ethics. Company directors need to accept the rapidly changing environment and be proactive in championing ethical standards rather than trying to defend positions that may have been acceptable in the past but are no longer considered to be so. Whilst individual corporate action may seem to have only a marginal affect, a positive example set and made plain for all to see may encourage others to follow suit and begin an upward trend. Positive change has to begin somewhere.

5.11   Action Points for Directors

- Set a good example and avoid involvement in anything that could lead employees to conclude that corrupt practices are encouraged or tolerated by the company.
- Develop an ethical code and require employees to confirm in writing each year that they have read, understood and applied these guidelines in their work (see PARAGRAPH 5.12).
- Make clear whether (and to what upper limits) gifts, hospitality and other favours may be accepted from business contacts, and when internal reporting of these is required.
- Require full disclosure from employees in strategic positions of their financial or other connections with suppliers, creditors and other business contacts.
- Develop a regular training programme for employees on ethical issues (see PARAGRAPH 5.18).
- Appoint at least one senior individual to whom employees can turn for advice on ethical issues.
- Appoint one or more senior individuals to whom suspicions of unethical conduct can be reported in confidence (making it clear that such action will have no negative consequences for the reporting employee).
- Where appropriate, introduce procedures and controls that segregate duties and require at least two individuals to be involved in potentially sensitive decisions, and consider adopting a system of job rotation (see also CHAPTER 14).
- Inform all business partners of the company's rules and encourage them to introduce corresponding safeguards if these are not already in place.
- Monitor compliance with the company's ethics code and be prepared to act on any violation that is identified (see PARAGRAPH 5.20).

5.12   Developing and Operating an Ethical Code

> **At a Glance**
> * An ethical code should establish the corporate culture that the board wishes to create and set down the standards of behaviour that the company expects.
> * Every company should examine its corporate culture from time to time and consider whether any change is needed.

* A company's ethical code should reflect its specific circumstances and should not attempt to set standards which cannot reasonably be expected to be applied in practice.
* An independent review can help to ensure that the code takes account of all relevant interests and opinions.
* Ethical issues should incorporate into the company's ongoing training programme.
* Many companies find it helpful to require employees to sign an annual declaration that they have read, understood and applied the company's ethical code in their work.
* Regular checks should be made on compliance with the company's ethical code and stringent action taken in respect of any violations.
* The International Federation of Accountants (IFAC) has published guidance to help companies develop a code of conduct.

5.13   What Is an Ethical Code?

An ethical code should be more than a list of rules or instructions that must be followed – it should establish the corporate culture that the board wishes to create, and set down the standards of behaviour that the company expects when commercial decisions have to be taken under time or financial constraints. In particular, it should make clear that management is not indifferent to the way in which business goals are achieved. Directors might begin by considering the following questions:

* Does every employee understand what is expected of him/her?
* Is every employee encouraged to behave responsibly?
* Does the business have values that should never be sacrificed in pursuit of profit, and are these communicated effectively across the organisation?
* Is there a well-understood framework for making decisions on ethical issues – and does this applies to all levels within the business?
* Are employees encouraged to discuss any ethical dilemmas that they encounter – and is it clear who they should approach in these circumstances?
* How does the company respond in such a situation?
* Is it evident that the company expects and rewards ethical behaviour?

An ethical code can be established and operated in any size of organisation and, once developed and communicated, it should be regarded as binding on all directors and employees.

5.14   Examining and Changing Corporate Culture

Every company has a corporate culture – the unwritten rules that are understood, accepted and followed by everyone and which establish how the company is run on a day to day basis. In some companies, a specific corporate culture will have been created by management, whilst in others the culture may simply have evolved over time, without much attention being paid to whether or not it is right for the business. Every company should therefore examine its corporate culture from time to time and should consider whether any aspects have become out-dated. More traditional, long-established companies may find it more difficult to accept that their corporate culture has become out of step with the views of today's society and that change is needed.

5.15 Contents of an Ethical Code

Ethical codes can cover a broad range of issues, which generally include:

- the legal obligations of employees;
- employee conduct;
- insider dealing;
- honesty and integrity – including the transparency of company policy and actions;
- equity and fairness – including the treatment of stakeholders such as customers, suppliers, employees and their families, the local community and shareholders (especially any minority shareholders);
- stakeholder rights – including the confidentiality of information;
- product or service standards and
- the exercise of corporate and managerial power.

To be effective, the code must reflect the specific circumstances of the company and should not attempt to set standards which cannot reasonably be expected to be applied in practice. It is important that a company's ethical code addresses any issues that are particularly sensitive, or that imply particular vulnerability, in the context of its activities. For instance, a company that has an extensive business involvement in developing countries may be more susceptible to requests for bribes or 'commission' payments and its ethical code must make clear what is and is not considered to be acceptable behaviour. Similarly, the approach to research and experimentation will be highly relevant to some businesses, but of no relevance whatsoever in others. It should also be remembered that a commitment to comply with legal requirements may not be sufficient to achieve ethical conduct when dealing with countries that offer little in the way of legislation on issues such as child labour, child protection, product safety and environmental protection. What is legal will not necessarily be ethical.

5.16 Developing an Ethical Code

The key steps in developing an ethical code are as follows:

- Identify the company's stakeholders and how they are affected by the company's actions.

- Summarise the company's goals and how each employee can make an ethical contribution to achieving them.
- Decide on the company's ethical expectations and present these in the form of easily understandable, measurable and actionable statements.
- Design a training programme to ensure everyone understands how to implement the agreed principles on a daily basis and provide an ongoing facility for dealing with any queries that may arise.
- Incorporate the achievement of ethical goals into the employee appraisal process and reward programme.

Once finalised, the code is usually made available to the public as well as internally.

5.17   Independent Review

Commissioning an independent review of the company's proposed ethical code can help to ensure that it deals with the underlying issues on a broad basis and takes into account all relevant interests and opinions, particularly where complex issues are involved. Whilst the final decision on the content of the code rests with management, an independent review can also help to ensure that any differences of opinion have been fully explored and resolved through sound argument rather than through the use of executive and managerial power.

5.18   Implementation and Training

Effective training and good internal communication are key elements in the process of implementing an ethical code. Encouraging ethical conduct involves developing good habits and it is important that ethical issues are incorporated into the company's ongoing training programme and not considered to be a one-off training matter. This also makes it easier to implement changes to the company's code where necessary. Case studies can be a valuable tool in encouraging a debate on specific ethical problems and can help to emphasise the fact that the underlying issues will often be complex and require careful consideration. Such discussions can also help to develop greater understanding between colleagues and to dispel the attitude that 'everybody does it' – employees might otherwise be tempted to use this to justify potentially unacceptable behaviour, especially if they consider it necessary for their own career development. It is important that the internal communication programme covers all directors and employees, and that at least one individual is identified who can be approached in confidence with queries on ethical issues.

5.19   Annual Employee Sign-Off

Many companies find it helpful to require employees to sign an annual declaration that they have read, understood and applied the company's ethical code in their work. This highlights the importance of the code and helps to keep ethical goals and standards at the forefront of the mind. Similarly, incorporating compliance with the code into the employee appraisal process and reward pro-gramme helps to demonstrate management's commitment to the underlying prin-ciples, although it is not always easy to find appropriate criteria by which to measure or evaluate ethical conduct.

5.20 Violation of the Code

Regular checks should be made on compliance with the company's ethical code. For instance, this might be incorporated into internal audit work or might be dealt with as a separate exercise by the officer with overall responsibility for ethical issues. Any potential violation of the ethical code must be investigated and stringent action taken where appropriate, so that all employees are given the clear message that management considers this to be a serious matter. Directors may also wish to implement whistle-blowing or similar confidential procedures to ensure that potential violations are highlighted at an early stage.

5.21 IFAC Guidance

In June 2007, the IFAC published 'Defining and Developing a Code of Conduct' (available at http://www.ifac.org/). This has been developed by the IFAC Professional Accountants in Business Committee and sets out guidance to help companies develop a code of conduct. The document forms the first in a series of principles-based good practice pronouncements. It is intended to be equally relevant to those who are developing a code for the first time and to those who wish to review and improve an existing code.

The document sets out the business case for developing a code a conduct and notes that such a code can be particularly helpful to decision-making in widely spread operational units where formal supervision may be more diffi-cult. The main part of the document looks at the nature of a code of conduct, sets out the key principles for the development of a code and provides detailed guidance on applying those principles in practice. The Appendices include an illustrative example of a code of conduct for a corporate entity and additional guidance on the development of codes of conduct within the public sector.

5.22 Reporting on Business Ethics

At a Glance
* There is an increasing interest in the approach of individual companies to business ethics and to corporate social responsibility in particular.
* Companies should consider developing a formal policy on corporate social responsibility issues.

* The Association of British Insurers (ABI) has issued disclosure guidelines to encourage companies to discuss corporate social responsibility matters in the annual report.
* The Department for Environment, Food and Rural Affairs (DEFRA) has published detailed guidance on reporting on environmental issues.
* The Global Reporting Initiative (GRI) has also developed guidelines on sustainability reporting.
* The Government has set up a website to highlight the benefits of good practice in this area.

5.23 Increasing Demand for Information

There is an increasing interest in the approach of individual companies to ethical matters and to corporate social responsibility in particular. Boards must therefore be concerned with the effects that the company and its activities are having on society as a whole. These can extend from the way it treats its employees, suppliers and customers to issues such as protecting the environment, child labour, health and safety, and ethical conduct. Society has generally moved from a willingness to take good corporate behaviour on trust to wanting to see it demonstrated and explained. The ASB's Reporting Statement *Operating and Financial Review* recognises that company performance is now defined in much broader terms than financial performance and, in particular, that performance reporting might incorporate non-financial measures such as those relating to corporate social responsibility issues (see PARAGRAPH 10.80).

5.24 Developing a Policy on Corporate Social Responsibility

Companies should therefore think about developing a policy on corporate social responsibility issues, as well as developing and publishing an ethical code. Points to consider include the following:

* Does the company's corporate governance framework include accountability for managing corporate social responsibility issues?
* Do the company's performance reporting processes cover corporate social responsibility issues?
* Is there a formal mechanism for identifying stakeholder concerns and for providing them with feedback on progress?
* Are the company's expectations on corporate social responsibility issues communicated to suppliers and other business partners?

Corporate Ethics

5.25   Disclosures on Business Ethics and Corporate Social Responsibility

Ethical conduct is difficult to measure and at present analysts generally look for:

- confirmation that the company has a process for establishing ethical goals;
- a statement of business conduct or a published ethical code;
- procedures to assist the achievement of ethical goals (e.g. reward systems) and
- a feedback process to measure the achievement of ethical goals and assist with the development and enhancement of the company's performance where necessary.

Recent changes to the content of the business review that forms part of the annual report to shareholders have helped to focus attention on these issues, and the reporting requirements for quoted companies in particular will be made more stringent under changes due to be introduced by CA 2006 with effect from 1 October 2007 (see **10.78**).

5.26   ABI Disclosure Guidelines

The ABI has produced disclosure guidelines to help institutional investors discuss these issues with the companies in which they invest. An updated version was published in January 2007 to take account of the requirements of the EU Modernisation Directive and CA 2006, which have introduced broader requirements on narrative reporting by companies (see **10.78**). The guidelines note that investors are anxious to avoid unnecessary prescriptive requirements or the imposition of costly measures, but hope that shareholder value will be enhanced by the early identification and management of risks arising from social, environmental and ethical matters. Shareholders with a specific interest in ethical investment may look for more extensive disclosures and some companies may wish to give additional information to attract investment from specific investors. The guidelines recommend the following disclosures:

- The annual report should include a statement on whether the board:
  - takes regular account of the significance of environmental, social and governance (ESG) matters to the business of the company;
  - has identified and assessed the significant risks to the company's short- and long-term value arising from ESG matters, as well as the opportunities to enhance value that may arise from an appropriate response;
  - has received adequate information to make this assessment and takes account of ESG matters in the training of directors and
  - has ensured that the company has in place effective systems for managing significant risks, including, where relevant, performance management systems and appropriate remuneration incentives.
- With regard to policies, procedures and verification, the annual report should:
  - include information on ESG-related risks and opportunities that may significantly affect the company's short- and long-term value, and how they might impact on the business;

- ○ describe the company's policies and procedures for managing risks and the possible impact on short- and long-term value arising from ESG matters – if the company has no such policies and procedures, the board should give reasons;
- ○ include information about the extent to which the company has complied with its policies and procedures for managing material risks arising from ESG matters and about the board's role in providing oversight – appropriate Key Performance Indicators (KPIs) should be provided where relevant;
- ○ where performance has fallen short of the objectives, describe the measures taken by board to put it back on track;
- ○ describe the procedures for verification of ESG disclosures.
- With regard to the board, the remuneration report (see **PARAGRAPH 9.20**) should state:
  - ○ whether the remuneration committee is able to consider corporate performance on ESG issues when setting the remuneration of executive directors or, where relevant, provide a reason for the absence of such discretion;
  - ○ whether the remuneration committee has ensured that the incentive structure for senior management does not raise ESG risks by inadvertently motivating irresponsible behaviour.

It is hoped that the guidelines will help to develop best practice in the area of managing and reporting on corporate social responsibility issues. They are intended to be relevant to all companies, regardless of size.

An Appendix to the guidelines sets out a number of questions on ESG issues and notes that disclosure could be addressed by considering the response to these in the annual report. The guidelines are available from the website of the Institutional Voting Information Service at http://www.ivis.co.uk.

5.27   DEFRA Guidance on Environmental Reporting

DEFRA published new guidance on environmental reporting in January 2006, in conjunction with the introduction of more specific requirements on the content of the business review that forms part of the annual directors' report. Further details can be found at **10.85**.

5.28   Global Reporting Initiative

The GRI has also developed guidance that is designed to achieve comparability in sustainability reporting. The latest version of the guidelines (G3) includes recommendations set out under the following headings:

- Principles and guidance
  - ○ defining report content by applying the principles of materiality, stakeholder inclusiveness, sustainability context and completeness;
  - ○ ensuring report quality by applying the principles of balance, comparability, accuracy, timeliness, reliability and clarity and

Corporate Ethics

○ setting the report boundary by following guidance on the range of entities that should be included in the report.
• Standards and disclosure
  ○ profile disclosures set the overall context for understanding performance;
  ○ management approach disclosures explain how specific sustainability issues are managed, including the setting of goals and targets and
  ○ performance indicators elicit comparable information on economic, environmental and social performance.

Full details are available on the GRI website at www.globalreporting.org.

5.29 Government Guidance

The Government has set up a website to support its policy of assisting the development of greater contacts between business and society. The site contains a number of case studies showing the benefits that can be obtained by adhering to good practice in the area of corporate social responsibility. There is also information on the action being taken by the Government to facilitate the development of corporate social responsibility. The site can be found at www.societyandbusiness.gov.uk.

Appendix 1

Useful Websites on Corporate Ethics

Association of British Insurers	www.abi.org.uk
National Association of Pensions Funds	www.napf.co.uk
Association of Investment Trust Companies	www.aitc.co.uk
Investment Management Association	www.investmentuk.org
Institute of Chartered Accountants in England and Wales	www.icaew.co.uk
Department for Environment, Food and Rural Affairs	www.defra.gov.uk
Global Reporting Initiative	www.globalreporting.org
Institute of Business Ethics	www.ibe.org.uk

Corporate Governance

Corporate Governance

6.1 The Evolution of Corporate Governance since 1990

At a Glance

* The first detailed guidance on corporate governance was set out in the *Cadbury Code of Best Practice* in 1992.
* Corporate governance was defined in the Cadbury Report as the system by which companies are directed and controlled.
* Good corporate governance is based on the principles of openness, integrity and accountability.
* Additional guidance was set out in the Greenbury (1995) and Hampel (1998) Codes of Best Practice and all existing guidance was then drawn together in the Combined Code.
* A major review, initiated by the Department of Trade and Industry (DTI) and the Treasury (the Higgs Review) was published in 2003.
* The recommendations of the Higgs Review included a substantial revision of the Combined Code.
* The Combined Code sets out the Principles of Good Governance and also best practice provisions for the adoption of those principles.
* Listed companies must disclose each year the extent to which they have applied the principles set out in the Combined Code, by means of a 'comply or explain' approach.
* The Financial Reporting Council (FRC) is now responsible for keeping the Combined Code up to date and made a small number of further revisions in June 2006 – companies are encouraged to adopt this version of the Code for accounting periods beginning on or after 1 November 2006.
* A consultation on further minor changes to the Code is due to commence in November 2007, with a view to the updated version of the Code coming into effect in June 2008.

6.2 The Cadbury Code of Best Practice

Corporate governance became a high profile issue in December 1992, with the publication of the *Cadbury Code of Best Practice* and the *Report of the Committee on the Financial Aspects of Corporate Governance* (the 'Cadbury Report'). This Committee, chaired by Sir Adrian Cadbury, had been formed in 1991 at a time of general concern over standards of financial reporting and accountability, particularly in the light of the BCCI and Maxwell cases, and when controversy was beginning to develop over levels of directors' remuneration. The Committee's report was based on the premise that company directors should have the freedom to develop their companies and drive them forward, but that they should do so within an effective framework of accountability. The Committee's recommendations therefore focussed primarily on the structure of the board, its control and reporting functions and the role of the external auditors, and drew on principles that were already being widely followed. Although the recommendations were aimed mainly at listed companies, the Committee's objective was to raise the overall standards of corporate governance and the general level of public confidence in financial reporting. All entities were therefore encouraged to follow the recommendations in the *Cadbury Code of Best Practice*.

6.3 *Definition of Corporate Governance*

Corporate governance was defined in the Cadbury Report as:

> 'the system by which companies are directed and controlled'.

The role of the shareholders is to appoint the directors and the external auditors, and to satisfy themselves that an appropriate governance structure is in place. The directors are responsible for setting the company's strategic aims, providing the leadership to put these into effect, supervising the management of the business and reporting to shareholders on their stewardship. The financial aspects of corporate governance are identified as the way in which the board sets financial policy and oversees its implementation (including the use of financial controls) and the process of reporting to the shareholders on the activities and development of the company.

6.4 *Openness, Integrity and Accountability*

The *Cadbury Code of Best Practice* was based on the principles of openness, integrity and accountability, which were described as follows in the Cadbury Report:

- Openness is the basis for the confidence that must exist between a business and those who have a stake in its success – an open approach to the disclosure of information contributes to the efficient working of the market economy, prompts boards to take effective action and allows shareholders and other interested parties to scrutinise companies more closely.
- Integrity means straightforward dealing and completeness – financial reporting should be honest and should present a balanced view of the company's affairs.
- The board of directors is accountable to the shareholders and effective accountability is achieved through the quality of information provided by the board to the shareholders and by the willingness of the shareholders to exercise their responsibilities as owners of the business.

6.5 Subsequent Developments

The Cadbury Committee addressed those aspects of corporate governance that it considered were most in need of immediate attention. However, they noted in their report that the situation was continually evolving, through the Accounting Standards Board's programme of new accounting standards, the development of best boardroom practice and the possibility of increased regulation through European Community initiatives. The Committee therefore emphasised the importance of keeping corporate governance guidance up to date and recommended that a further committee should be appointed within the following two to three years to examine progress on compliance with the *Cadbury Code* and consider the need to revise and update the recommendations in the light of emerging issues. The successor committee, under the chairmanship of Sir Richard Greenbury, developed new recommendations on the setting and disclosure of directors' remuneration in the *Greenbury Code of Best Practice* and a further committee, under the chairmanship of Sir Ronald Hampel, developed a new Combined Code which built on (and superseded) the recommendations set out in the Cadbury and the Greenbury Codes. The main remit of the Hampel Committee was to review the implementation of, and levels of compliance with, the two Codes that had resulted from the work of the Cadbury and Greenbury Committees. The Hampel Review resulted in the development of a new Combined Code, which drew together elements of the existing Codes and set out the broad principles of corporate governance, together with detailed guidance on the application of these principles in practice. The Hampel Report advocated a flexible approach to reporting on compliance with the Code, leaving directors free to choose how to explain their corporate governance policies in the light of the specific circumstances of the company or group. The new Combined Code was published in June 1998 and became fully effective for accounting periods ending on or after 22 December 2000 (although earlier implementation was required for aspects other than reporting on internal control).

6.6 The Higgs Review

As part of the UK Government's response to the issues raised by Enron and other high profile accounting scandals, the DTI commissioned Derek Higgs to lead a short independent review of the role and effectiveness of non-executive directors. The Higgs Report was published in January 2003 and set out recommendations to increase rigour and transparency in the appointment process for non-executive directors and to widen the spread of experience in UK boardrooms. The Report also set out the draft of a revised Combined Code, incorporating these recommendations, which was intended to become effective from 1 July 2003. A separate working group was appointed by the FRC, under the chairmanship of Sir Robert Smith, to develop further the guidance on audit committees included in the Combined Code. The resulting report 'Audit Committees: Combined Code Guidance' (commonly referred to as the Smith Report) was published in January 2003, at the same time as the Higgs Report, and included the draft of a revised section of the Combined Code on audit committees, together with supplementary guidance intended to assist boards in establishing and operating an audit committee and also directors who serve as members of an audit committee. The report identified certain essential requirements for audit committees, which were set out in bold text, and noted that compliance with these would be necessary to achieve compliance with the Combined Code. The detailed guidance in the Smith Report and the new section of the Combined Code was also intended to be effective for accounting periods beginning on or after 1 July 2003. The main points raised in the Higgs Review are summarised in **APPENDIX 3**.

6.7   Finalisation of New Combined Code

In May 2003, the FRC announced the setting up of a working group of its members to produce a revised version of the Combined Code, taking into account comments raised during the consultation period on the draft that resulted from the Higgs and Smith Reports. The new Combined Code was eventually published on 23 July 2003 and applies for accounting periods beginning on or after 1 November 2003. The document now notes that departure from the detailed Code provisions may be justified in particular circumstances, but it is still expected that listed companies will comply with them most of the time. Some specific relaxations are permitted for companies below the FTSE 350 although they are still encouraged to consider full compliance. The principles from the Higgs version were generally retained as 'main principles' (sometimes with some rewording) but some of the proposed best practice provisions became 'supporting principles' and the introduction to the Code notes that companies should report on how they have applied both the main and the supporting principles. This changed the nature and level of reporting in some areas. Changes were also made to the proposals in the Smith Report. A small number of the 'bold text' items became Combined Code provisions and must now be covered in the 'comply or explain' element of the company's reporting. Other aspects of the Smith Report previously highlighted as being essential simply became part of the supplementary guidance, which was included as an appendix to the Code along with the Turnbull Guidance (see **PARAGRAPH 6.8**) and other Higgs recommendations on good practice.

6.8   Ongoing Review of the Code

As part of the UK Post-Enron Reviews, the FRC assumed overall responsibility the Combined Code and announced its intention to keep the Code under regular review, to ensure that it is working effectively and to identify any amendments that may be needed. In January 2005, the FRC reported that its initial informal assessment of the impact of the revised Combined Code had concluded that encouraging progress had been made. In particular, the FRC found that:

- both investors and companies thought that the corporate governance climate had improved over the previous years;
- investors reported an increased dialogue with companies and greater involvement by company chairmen on corporate governance issues and

- issues such as performance evaluation and professional development are being taken more seriously.

However, the FRC also acknowledged that more time was needed for companies to plan and implement some of the new provisions, such as those relating to the number of independent non-executive directors and the balance of skills and experience within the board. The FRC began its first formal consultation on possible amendments to the Combined Code in January 2006 but proposed only two substantive amendments:

- A relaxation of the existing provisions to allow the chairman to sit on the remuneration committee under certain conditions.
- The addition of a new provision to encourage companies to include a 'vote withheld' box on AGM proxy voting forms, as recommended by the Shareholder Voting Working Group, and to publish details of proxies lodged on resolutions where votes are taken on a show of hands.

An updated version of the Combined Code, reflecting these amendments was published in June 2006 and applies for reporting years beginning on or after 1 November 2006. This version no longer includes Appendices setting out the Turnbull Guidance on internal control, the Smith Guidance and the Higgs good practice recommendations. The Turnbull Guidance was the subject of a separate review in 2006 and is available separately from the FRC's website at http://www.frc.org.uk/corporate/internalcontrol.cfm. The FRC also continues to make the Smith Guidance and the Higgs suggestions for good practice available on its website at http://www.frc.org.uk/corporate/combinedcode.cfm but emphasises that, whilst companies may find the information helpful, these guidance documents have no formal status and companies are not required to follow them when applying the Combined Code.

In April 2007, the FRC opened a further consultation to identify whether the Code is enabling companies to be led in a way that facilitates entrepreneurial success and the management of risk. There is a particular concern over the potential compliance burden for smaller listed companies, including an acknowledgement that the costs of compliance are proportionately higher for smaller companies. The FRC is therefore open to considering some modification to the requirements for smaller companies if it becomes clear that the costs of the present regulatory burden outweigh the benefits in this case. In particular, the FRC invited responses to the following questions:

- Does the Code support better board performance over time?
- Is the 'comply or explain' approach working effectively?
- What impact has the Code had on smaller companies?
- Do disclosures on the Combined Code in annual reports provide useful information to shareholders at proportionate cost to companies? If not, in what respects, and how, should they be modified?

In October 2007, the FRC reported that it had concluded that the Code is working well and that there is no need for major change at present, although there continues to be scope for improvement in the way that the Code is applied. However, it intends to begin a consultation in November 2007 on two proposed amendments to the present Code. These would:

- remove the present restriction on an individual chairing more than one FTSE 100 company and
- allow the chairman of a smaller listed company to be a member of the audit committee provided that he/she was considered to be independent on appointment.

If these changes are agreed, the amended Code is expected to come into effect from June 2008.

6.9 Structure of the Combined Code

The Combined Code was originally divided into two sections, the first setting out the principles of good governance under the key headings and the second giving the best practice provisions for each of those principles. The latest version of the Code is structured so that the main principles, supporting principles and best practice provisions are set out together under each of the following headings:

- Section 1: Companies
  - A Directors
  - B Remuneration
  - C Accountability and Audit
  - D Relations with Shareholders
- Section 2: Institutional Shareholders
  - E Institutional Shareholders

Appendices to the Code cover:

- Provisions on the design of performance-related remuneration.
- Guidance on liability of non-executive directors: care, skill and diligence.
- Disclosure of corporate governance arrangements.

This chapter provides an overview of the detailed contents of the Combined Code. Practical guidance on the application of the Code principles and the best practice provisions can be found in other chapters.

6.10 Disclosure of Compliance with the Code

The Financial Services Authority (FSA) Listing Rules require each listed company to include in its annual report:

- A narrative statement of how it has applied the principles set out in the Combined Code, with explanations to enable the shareholders to evaluate how the principles have been applied.
- A statement on whether or not it has complied throughout the accounting period with the best practice provisions set out in the Combined Code, with details of, and the reasons for, any areas or periods of non-compliance.

Other specific disclosures are required by certain sections of the Code and these are summarised in Schedule C to the June 2006 version of the Code for ease of reference. Further details on reporting under the Combined Code are given in **PARAGRAPHS 6.60–6.65**.

Recent changes to EC Company Law Directives will in future require companies whose shares are publicly traded to make a formal statement on compliance with the corporate governance code that applies or has been voluntarily adopted, and on the main features of the company's internal control and risk-management systems in relation to financial reporting. These changes are expected to be introduced from April 2008 (see **PARAGRAPH 10.95**).

6.11   Directors

At a Glance
* The revised Combined Code sets out seven main principles in respect of directors.
* The board has collective responsibility for the success of the company and for ensuring that obligations to shareholders are met.
* There should be a clear division of responsibilities between the chairman and the chief executive, and these roles should not be undertaken by the same individual.
* The board should include an appropriate balance between executive and non-executive directors and at least half of the board should comprise independent non-executives.
* There should be a formal and rigorous procedure for making board appointments and the same process should be followed for both executive and non-executive directors.
* Directors should be provided with all the information that they need to carry out their duties in an effective manner.
* All directors should receive induction training when they join the board and should keep their skills and knowledge up to date.
* The performance of the board, its committees and each individual director should be subject to formal evaluation each year.
* All directors should be subject to re-election at intervals of not more than three years.

6.12   Combined Code Principles

Section A of the Combined Code sets out the following main principles in relation to directors:

* *The board*: Every company should be headed by an effective board, which is collectively responsible for the success of the company.
* *Chairman and Chief Executive Officer (CEO)*: There should be a clear division of responsibilities at the head of the company between the running of the

board and the executive responsibility for the running of the company's business. No individual should have unfettered powers of decision.

- *Board balance and independence*: The board should include a balance of executive and non-executive directors (and in particular independent non-executive directors) such that no individual or small group of individuals can dominate the board's decision-taking.
- *Appointments to the board*: There should be a formal, rigorous and transparent procedure for the appointment of new directors to the board.
- *Information and professional development*: The board should be supplied in a timely manner with information in a form and of a quality appropriate to enable it to discharge its duties. All directors should receive induction on joining the board and should regularly update and refresh their skills and knowledge.
- *Performance evaluation*: The board should undertake a formal and rigorous annual evaluation of its own performance and that of its committees and individual directors.
- *Re-election*: All directors should be submitted to re-election at regular intervals, subject to continued satisfactory performance. The board should ensure planned and progressive refreshing of the board.

The supporting principles and best practice provisions in respect of each of the main principles are considered in more detail below.

6.13   The board

The supporting principles explain that the board's role is to provide entrepreneurial leadership of the company within a framework of prudent and effective controls which enable risk to be assessed and managed. The board should set the company's strategic aims, ensure the availability of appropriate financial and human resources and review management performance. The board is also responsible for setting the company's values and standards and ensuring that obligations to shareholders are understood and met. All directors must take decisions objectively in the interests of the company. The role of the non-executive directors is summarised as follows in the supporting principles:

- to constructively challenge and help develop proposals on strategy;
- to scrutinise the performance of management in meeting goals and objectives;
- to monitor the reporting of performance;
- to satisfy themselves on the integrity of financial information and that financial controls and systems are robust and defensible;
- to determine appropriate levels of remuneration for executive directors and
- to have a prime role in appointing (and where necessary removing) executive directors and in succession planning.

The best practice guidance highlights the following points in relation to the board:

- The board should meet sufficiently regularly to discharge its duties effectively.
- There should be a formal schedule of matters specifically reserved for board decision.

- The annual report should:
  - include a high level statement on how the board operates, identifying the types of decision that are taken by the board and those that are delegated to management;
  - identify the chairman, deputy chairman (if there is one) and senior independent director, and the chairmen and members of the audit, nomination and remuneration committees;
  - give details of the number of board and committee meetings during the year and the individual attendance by directors.
- The chairman should meet with the non-executive directors without the executives present.
- The non-executive directors, led by the senior independent director, should meet at least once a year without the chairman present to appraise his/her performance, and on other occasions where deemed appropriate.
- Where they have concerns about the way in which the company is being run or about a proposed course of action, directors should ensure that their concerns are recorded in the minutes.
- Where a non-executive director resigns, he/she should provide the chairman with a written statement setting out the reasons, for circulation to the board.
- Companies should arrange appropriate insurance cover in respect of legal action against its directors.

6.14   Board Procedures

The Cadbury Report considered in greater detail the importance of an effective system of board structures and procedures and highlighted in particular the need to:

- Appoint appropriate sub-committees of the main board (e.g. audit committee, remuneration committee, nomination committee) so that the work of the main board can be focused on key issues.
- Recognise the importance of the finance function by making it the designated responsibility of a main board director – this director should be a signatory to the annual accounts and should have a direct right of access to the audit committee.
- Maintain a formal and up to date schedule of matters to be decided collectively by the board, both to ensure that the control and direction of the company remains with the board as a whole and to safeguard against potential misjudgement or malpractice – this schedule was recommended to include as a minimum:
  - acquisition and disposal of material company assets (including subsidiaries),
  - investments,
  - capital projects,
  - authority levels,
  - treasury policies,
  - risk-management policies.
- Lay down clear rules to determine materiality for any transaction and establish which transactions require more than one board signatory.
- Agree clear procedures to be followed in exceptional circumstances where decisions need to be taken between board meetings.

It is also considered good practice for the board to establish a code of ethics or statement of business practices and to ensure that all company employees are clear about the standards of conduct that are expected of them (see **CHAPTER 5**).

6.15 *Chairman and Chief Executive*

The Cadbury Report emphasised the significance of the role of the chairman and the need for him/her to accept fully the duties and responsibilities that the role entails. In particular, the chairman needs to have the ability to stand back from the detailed day to day operation of the business and to ensure that the board as a whole exercises appropriate control and leadership and is responsive to its obligations to the shareholders. The supporting principles in the revised Code explain that the chairman is responsible for:

- leadership of the board;
- ensuring the board's effectiveness on all aspects of its role;
- setting the board's agenda;
- ensuring that the directors receive accurate, timely and clear information;
- facilitating the effective contribution of the non-executive directors;
- ensuring constructive relations between executive and non-executive directors and
- ensuring effective communication with shareholders.

The related best practice provisions emphasise that the role of chairman and chief executive should not be carried out by the same individual and that the division of responsibilities should be clearly established, set out in writing and agreed by the board. Although there was a strong encouragement in the original Code for the roles of chairman and chief executive to be separated, there was an implied acceptance that combination of these roles might have been justified in certain circumstances. The present Code sets out much more stringent requirements and provides more detailed guidance on the specific responsibilities of the chairman. The best practice provisions also note that the chairman should meet the independence criteria (see **PARAGRAPH 6.17**) at the time of appointment and that a chief executive should not go on to become chairman of the same company. However, the Code does acknowledge that the board may decide on such a progression in exceptional circumstances, provided that:

- major shareholders are consulted in advance and
- the reasons are set out to shareholders at the time of the appointment and also in the next annual report.

6.16 *Board Balance and Independence*

Legally, all directors are equally responsible for the decisions and actions of the board, regardless of whether their appointment is as an executive or non-executive. Whilst certain individuals may have particular responsibilities within the business, the board as a whole is responsible for ensuring that the company meets its obligations. The effectiveness of the board depends on how well the individual members work together as a team under the leadership of the chairman. The supporting principles in the new Combined Code note that:

- The board should not be so large as to be unwieldy but should be of sufficient sizer to achieve an appropriate balance of skills and experience and to allow changes to its composition to be managed without undue disruption.
- There should a strong element of both executive and non-executive directors to ensure that power and information are not concentrated in one or two individuals.
- When deciding the chairmanship and membership of committees, the board should pay due attention to the value of ensuring that membership is refreshed and that undue reliance is not placed on particular individuals.
- No one other than the committee chairmen and members is entitled to attend meetings of the main board committees, but others may attend at the invitation of the committee.

Under the best practice provisions on board balance and independence, the non-executive directors that are considered to be independent (see **PARAGRAPH 6.17**) should be identified in the annual report, at least half the board (excluding the chairman) should comprise independent non-executive directors and the board should appoint one of the independent non-executives to be the senior independent director, to be available to shareholders if they have concerns which contact through the normal channels (i.e. chairman, chief executive or finance director) has failed to resolve or is deemed inappropriate. Smaller companies are required to have at least two independent non-executive directors (rather than having at least half of the board represented by independent non-executives). If the board considers a director to be independent despite the existence of relationships or circumstances which might appear to impair this independence, the reasons behind the board's decision should be explained in the annual report. There is consequently a significant emphasis on the board's collective responsibility for determining which directors are considered to be independent, and for justifying their decision to the shareholders.

6.17 *Independence*

Under the present guidance, a non-executive director is considered to be independent when the board determines that he/she is independent in character and judgement and there are no relationships or circumstances which could affect, or appear to affect the director's judgement. In particular, such relationships or circumstances arise where the director:

- has been an employee of the company or group within the past five years;
- has, or has had within the last three years, a material business relationship with the company either directly or as a partner, shareholder, director or senior employee of a body that has such a relationship with the company;
- receives (or has received) additional remuneration from the company apart from a director's fee, participates in the company's share option or performance-related pay scheme, or is a member of the company's pension scheme;

- has close family ties with any of the company's advisers, directors or senior employees;
- holds cross-directorships or has significant links with other directors through involvement in other companies or bodies;
- represents a significant shareholder or
- has served on the board for more than nine years from the date of his/her first election.

6.18 *Role of Non-executives*

Executive directors are expected to have an in-depth knowledge of the business, but the independent non-executives should bring a broader perspective as a result of their experience in other fields. The particular qualities usually required of non-executive directors include:

- wide experience of business practice and boardroom procedures;
- sound judgement and principles;
- the ability to take an objective view and
- the ability to distinguish between governance and management.

Non-executive directors will usually sit on one or more of the three main board committees (audit, nomination and remuneration) and a non-executive director will chair these committees. They may also be required to take a lead where potential conflicts of interest arise – for instance, where conflict arises between the specific interests of the executive management and the company as a whole at the time of a takeover, or when considering boardroom succession. The Combined Code recommendations on the role of the non-executive director are considered in more detail in **PARAGRAPH 6.13**.

6.19 Appointments to the Board

The supporting principles in respect of appointments to the board note that appointments should be made on merit and against objective criteria, and care should be taken to ensure that appointees have enough time available for the role, especially if they are to act as chairman of one of the main board committees. The board is also required to satisfy itself that appropriate succession plans are in place for both the board and senior management to ensure a continuing balance of skills and experience. The best practice provisions recommend that:

- A nomination committee, with a majority of independent non-executive directors, should lead the process for board appointments and make recommendations to the board.
- The chairman or an independent non-executive director should chair the nomination committee (although the chairman should not chair the committee when it is dealing with the appointment of his/her successor).
- The nomination committee should make publicly available its terms of reference, explaining its role and the authority delegated to it by the board.

- The nomination committee should evaluate the balance of skills, knowledge and experience on the board and, in the light of this, prepare a description of the role and capabilities required for a particular appointment.
- For the appointment of a chairman, the nomination committee should prepare a job specification, including the time commitment expected, bearing in mind the need for availability in the event of a crisis.
- A chairman's other significant commitments should be disclosed to the board before appointment and in the annual report – any changes should be similarly reported as they arise.
- No individual should be appointed as chairman of two FTSE 100 companies (but see below).
- The terms and conditions of appointment of non-executive directors should be made available for inspection, the letter of appointment should set out the time and responsibility envisaged in the appointment and the non-executive directors should undertake that they will have sufficient time available to meet these expectations – any other significant commitments, including an indication of the time involved, should be disclosed to the board before appointment, and the board should be informed of any subsequent changes.
- The board should not agree to a full-time executive director taking on more than one non-executive directorship of a FTSE 100 company, or the chairmanship of such a company.
- The work of the nomination committee should be explained in a separate section of the annual report – this should include details of the process used in board appointments and an explanation if neither an external search consultancy nor open advertising has been used in the appointment of a chairman or non-executive director.

Although the nomination committee will deal with the detailed aspects of the selection process and then make a recommendation to the board, the actual appointment of a new director should be a matter for the board as a whole. The same appointment process should apply for both executive and non-executive directors. These provisions are aimed at ensuring that the appointment of each director is the result of an objective and transparent process.

The FRC has announced that it intends to begin a consultation in November 2007 on two proposed amendments to the present Code, one of which would remove the present restriction on an individual chairing more than one FTSE 100 company. If agreed, the change is expected to come into effect from June 2008.

6.20 *Formal Selection Process*

The main board should agree a formal selection process for new directors, together with formal terms of reference for the nomination committee. The selection process will usually involve the following steps by the nomination committee:

- identification of the need for a new director and the skills required from him/her;
- preparation of a job specification, including the time commitment expected and details of any board committees on which he/she will be expected to serve;

- preparation of a company information pack for issue to potential candidates;
- initial assessment of applicants and preparation of a short-list for interview and
- interviews and meetings with short-listed candidates and preparation of a recommendation to the main board.

The main board should then be given the opportunity to meet the recommended candidate before the matter is formally discussed by the main board and a decision on appointment is taken.

6.21   Information and Professional Development

The supporting principles in the present Code note that:

- The chairman is responsible for ensuring that directors receive accurate, timely and clear information – management has an obligation to provide such information, but directors should seek additional clarification and detail where necessary.
- The chairman should ensure that directors continually update their skills and their knowledge of the company to enable them to fulfil their role on the main board and its committees – the company should make the necessary resources available for this.
- Under the direction of the chairman, the duties of the company secretary include:
  - facilitating induction;
  - assisting with professional development;
  - ensuring good information flows within the board and its committees;
  - ensuring good information flows between non-executive directors and senior management and
  - advising the board, through the chairman, on all governance matters.

The best practice provisions recommend that the chairman should ensure that new directors receive a comprehensive, formal and tailored induction on joining the board. Major shareholders should also be offered the opportunity to meet a new non-executive director. The board should ensure that all directors, and especially non-executives, have access to independent professional advice at the company's expense and that committees are provided with sufficient resources to undertake their duties. All directors should have access to the advice and services of the company secretary who is responsible for ensuring compliance with board procedures. Both the appointment and the removal of the company secretary should be a matter for the board as a whole.

6.22   *Induction*

The Higgs suggestions for good practice (which were included include as an appendix to the July 2003 Code but are now available separately from the FRC (see **PARAGRAPH 6.8**) include an induction checklist which is intended to serve as a guideline for the development of an in-house induction programme, tailored to the needs of the company and individual non-executive directors. The checklists recommends a combination of written information, presentations, meetings with senior management, site visits and informal meetings with employees, to give the new director a balanced overview of the company and its activities. The induction process should usually include coverage of:

- the company's constitution;
- board procedures and matters reserved for the board;
- major shareholders, and the company's policy on shareholder relations;
- group structures;
- the company's products or services, and major competitors;
- major customers and suppliers, and significant contracts;
- principal assets and liabilities;
- major risks, and the company's risk-management strategy;
- key performance indicators and
- regulatory requirements.

6.23   Organisation of Board Meetings

The chairman has overall responsibility for the management of board meetings but will need to work closely with the company secretary. They should plan the agenda for each meeting well in advance, often with input from the chief executive and finance director, and ensure that the board considers all the issues that ought to come before it. Most companies prepare an annual timetable of board and related committee meetings, built around key events in the business cycle (e.g. consideration and approval of strategic plans, consideration and approval of detailed budgets, publication of half-yearly report, approval of annual report and accounts) and allowing for timely reporting from the committees to the main board. It is also important that:

- Supporting papers are set out in an appropriate level of detail and are issued well in advance of the meeting so that all directors have adequate time to prepare and can make a constructive contribution to the discussions.
- The time available is allocated in an appropriate manner between individual agenda items – it will often be helpful to indicate on the agenda the nature of each item (e.g. report only, board decision required, formal board approval required) and how much time has provisionally been allocated for the related presentation and discussion.
- Any differences of opinion that arise during meetings are dealt with in a mature, constructive and professional manner.
- The minutes provide an accurate record of the proceedings and are circulated promptly to all those entitled to receive them.

6.24   Performance Evaluation

Performance evaluation was not included in the original Combined Code. There is just one supporting principle in the present Code, which notes that:

- Individual performance evaluation should aim to show whether each director continues to contribute effectively and to demonstrate commitment to the role.

- The chairman should act on the results of this evaluation by recognising the strengths and addressing the weaknesses of the board and, where appropriate, proposing new board members of seeking the resignation of directors.

The best practice provisions recommend that the board should state in the annual report how performance evaluation of the board, its committees and individual directors has been conducted and that the non-executive directors, led by the senior independent director, should evaluate the performance of the chairman, taking into account the views of the executive directors. The Higgs suggestions for good practice (which were included include as an appendix to the July 2003 Code but are now available separately from the FRC (see **PARAGRAPH 6.8**) include a performance evaluation checklist. This notes that the process should be used constructively to improve overall board effectiveness, maximise strengths and tackle weaknesses. The results of the performance evaluation for the board as a whole should be communicated to the board, but the results of individual assessments should remain confidential to the chairman and the director concerned. The checklist includes questions that might be used to assess the effectiveness of the board, the contribution of the chairman and the performance of a non-executive director.

6.25   Re-election

There are no supporting principles in respect of re-election. The best practice provisions recommend that:

- All directors should be subject to election by the shareholders at the first Annual General Meeting (AGM) after their appointment and to re-election thereafter at intervals of no more than three years.
- The names of directors submitted for election or re-election should be accompanied by sufficient biographical details and other relevant information to enable shareholders to make an informed decision.
- Non-executive directors should be appointed for specified terms, subject to re-election and to company law provisions relating to the removal of a director.
- The board should set out in the papers accompanying the resolution to elect a non-executive director why they believe that individual should be elected.
- When a director is proposed for re-election, the chairman should confirm to shareholders that, following performance evaluation, the individual continues to make an effective contribution and to demonstrate commitment to the role.
- A proposal to re-elect a non-executive director for a term beyond six years (i.e. two terms of three years) should be subject to rigorous review and should take into account the need for progressive refreshing of the board.
- Non-executive directors may serve for more than nine years, subject to annual re-election, but this could be relevant to the assessment of the director's independence.

6.26 Directors' Remuneration and Service Contracts

At a Glance
* Remuneration levels should be sufficient to attract, motivate and retain directors of the required quality, but the company should avoid paying more than is necessary.
* Comparison with the remuneration packages and relative performance of other companies may be helpful, but should be used with caution.
* Pay and conditions elsewhere within the company or group should also be borne in mind.
* Performance-related elements should form a significant proportion of the total remuneration package for executive directors, and performance conditions should be relevant, challenging and designed to enhance the business.
* New long-term incentive schemes should be subject to shareholder approval and awards under the schemes should usually be phased.
* The pension consequences of any changes in remuneration packages should be properly considered.
* Contract or notice periods should generally be limited to one year, and appropriate attention should be paid to compensation commitments in the event of early termination.
* Company law sets out detailed requirements on the retention and inspection of directors' service contracts.
* The DTI has issued proposals for updating the present company law provisions on directors' service contracts.
* A remuneration committee of independent non-executive directors should be established to make recommendations to the board on executive remuneration packages.

6.27 Main Principles

Section B of the Combined Code sets out the following main principles in respect of remuneration:

* *Level and make-up of remuneration*: Levels of remuneration should be sufficient to attract, retain and motivate directors of the quality needed to run the company successfully, but companies should avoid paying more than is necessary for this purpose. A significant proportion of executive directors' remuneration should be structured to link rewards to corporate and individual performance.
* *Procedure*: There should be a formal and transparent procedure for developing policy on executive remuneration and for fixing the remuneration packages of individual directors. No director should be involved in setting his/her own remuneration.

The original Code also included a section on the disclosure of directors' remuneration, but this has been removed following the implementation of the Directors'

Remuneration Report Regulations 2002 which apply for accounting periods ending on or after 31 December 2002 and introduce a statutory requirement for equivalent disclosures to those previously recommended in the Code. The disclosure requirements are considered in more detail in **CHAPTER 9**.

6.28   Level and Make-up of Remuneration

The supporting principle on the level and make-up of remuneration notes that the remuneration committee should judge where to position the company relative to other companies, but should use such comparisons with caution in view of the risk of increasing remuneration levels without a corresponding improvement in performance. They should also be sensitive to pay and employment conditions elsewhere in the group, especially when determining annual salary increases. The best practice guidance is divided two sections – remuneration policy, and service contracts and compensation.

The Government is also proposing to require quoted companies to include in the directors' remuneration report an analysis of the general pattern of remuneration for the company as a whole and how this has been taken into account in setting the remuneration of the directors (see **PARAGRAPH 9.21**).

6.29   *Remuneration Policy*

The best practice provisions on remuneration policy includes the following:

- Performance-related elements should form a significant proportion of the total remuneration package for executive directors and should be designed to align their interests with those of the shareholder, and to give the directors a keen incentive to perform at the highest levels.
- In designing schemes of performance-related remuneration, the committee should follow the provisions set out in Schedule A to the Combined Code (see **PARAGRAPH 6.30**).
- Executive share options should not be issued at a discount, except as permitted by the FSA Listing Rules.
- Levels of remuneration for non-executive directors should reflect the time, commitment and responsibilities of the role and should not include share options.
- Where a company releases an executive director to serve as a non-executive director elsewhere, the remuneration report should state whether or not the director will retain earnings from the appointment and, if so, what the remuneration is.

The provisions do allow for share options to be granted to a non-executive director in exceptional circumstances, but note that shareholder approval should be sought in advance and any shares acquired through exercise of the options should be held for at least one year after the individual leaves the board. The holding of share options could also be relevant to the assessment of the director's independence (see **PARAGRAPH 6.17**).

6.30   *Performance-Related Pay*

Schedule A to the revised Combined Code comprises the guidance originally set out in the Greenbury Code of Best Practice on directors' remuneration, with a number of minor wording changes. It recommends that:

- The remuneration committee should consider whether directors should be eligible for annual bonuses and, if so, performance conditions should be relevant, stretching and designed to enhance shareholder value – upper limits should be set and disclosed and there may be a case for part payment in shares to be held for a significant period.
- The remuneration committee should consider whether the directors should be eligible for benefits under long-term incentive schemes, and in establishing such schemes should:
  - weigh traditional share option schemes against other kinds of long-term incentive schemes;
  - generally ensure that shares granted and other forms of deferred remuneration do not vest, and options are not exercisable, in less than three years;
  - encourage directors to hold their shares for a further period after vesting or exercise, subject to the need to finance any costs of acquisition or associated tax liabilities.
- Where new long-term incentive schemes are proposed, these should be approved by the shareholders and should preferably replace existing schemes, or at least form part of a well considered overall plan incorporating existing schemes – the total rewards potentially available should not be excessive.
- Payouts or grants under all incentive schemes (including new grants under existing share option schemes) should be subject to challenging performance criteria reflecting the company's objectives, and consideration should be given to criteria which reflect the company's performance relative to a group of comparator companies in certain key variables such as total shareholder return.
- Grants under executive share option and other long-term incentive schemes should normally be phased rather than awarded in one large block.
- In general, neither annual bonuses nor benefits in kind should be pensionable.
- The remuneration committee should consider the pension consequences and associated costs to the company of increases in basic salary and other changes in pensionable remuneration, especially for directors close to retirement.

6.31   Service Contracts and Compensation

The best practice guidance on directors' service contacts and compensation includes the following provisions:

- The remuneration committee should carefully consider what compensation commitments (including pension contributions and any other elements) the directors' terms of appointment would entail in the event of early termination – the aim should be to avoid rewarding poor performance and to take a robust line on reducing compensation to reflect a departing director's obligations to mitigate loss.

- Notice or contract periods should be set at one year or less – if it is necessary to offer longer notice or contract periods to new directors recruited externally, these periods should reduce to one year or less after the initial period.

The original Code included a recommendation that the remuneration committee should consider the advantages of providing explicitly in the initial contract for compensation commitments other than in the case of removal for misconduct and, where compensation was not covered in a director's contract, should tailor their approach in the case of early termination to the wide variety of circumstances. These elements have now been removed from the best practice provisions. However, the present Code is more definite that notice or contract periods should be set at one year or less, or should reduce to one year or less as soon as possible.

6.32   Service Contracts for Executive Directors

An executive director is in effect an employee of the company and it is appropriate that the terms and conditions of his/her appointment should be set out in a written contract of service between the director and the company. A comprehensive service contract can help to prevent misunderstandings and provides a useful point of reference if problems arise. Non-executive directors have a very different role to executive directors and the terms and conditions of their appointment will usually be set out in a contract for services. A service contract for an executive director should normally include:

- specific duties of the director, including the amount of time to be spent on company activities (this may be particularly important where the individual also holds posts such as non-executive directorships in other businesses);
- remuneration, including details of any arrangements involving:
  - benefits in kind (e.g. private health cover, accommodation, company car),
  - bonus schemes,
  - long-term incentive plans,
  - share options;
- holiday entitlement;
- arrangements in the case of prolonged absence through illness;
- pension arrangements;
- required notice period, and procedures in the case of dismissal;
- compensation arrangements in the event of early termination of the contract and
- confidentiality arrangements.

Other issues may need to be covered, depending on the circumstances. The Institute of Directors publishes a specimen contract of service for executive directors.

6.33 Contracts for Services of Non-executive Directors

The main role of non-executive directors is to make a positive contribution to the development of company strategy, and on matters such as company performance, standards of conduct and corporate governance issues. It is helpful to all parties for the terms of their appointment to be set out in a written contract for services. This will usually specify:

- the expected commitment, in terms of attendance at meetings of the board and its sub-committees and
- fee arrangements.

Non-executive directors will usually be paid either a fixed fee or a fixed retainer plus fees for attendance at specific meetings. The Cadbury Report emphasised the importance of striking an effective balance between recognition of the value of non-executive directors and their contribution to the company, and the need to ensure that any payments that they receive do not in effect undermine their independence. The fee arrangements should reflect the time commitment expected from the non-executive directors (which can often be quite considerable), and it can be helpful for them to take into account specific additional responsibilities, such as chairmanship of one or more of the sub-committees of the main board. It is not usually considered appropriate for non-executive directors to participate in company share option schemes, or to be provided with pension arrangements by the company.

6.34 Company Law Requirements

Company law includes specific requirements on the retention of written service contracts for directors, or written memoranda of the terms of the director's appointment if he/she does not have a written contract. Certain changes to these requirements apply with effect from 1 October 2007 as a result of the introduction of new provisions under *CA 2006*. Further details are given at **PARAGRAPHS 9.34–9.35**.

6.35 *Inspection of Contracts*

Any member of the company is entitled to inspect the copies of the directors' contracts of service (or the memoranda where there is no written service contract) without charge. If the company refuses to allow a member to inspect a contract or memorandum, the court can require immediate inspection. With effect from 1 October 2007, members also have a new right to request a copy of any director's service contract on payment of a set fee.

6.36 *Shareholder Approval for Contracts for More Than Two Years*

With effect from 1 October 2007, formal approval by the members is required for any director's service contract that extends, or is capable of extending, for more than two years. This period has been reduced from five years under the previous legislation. Further details of the legal requirements are given at **PARAGRAPHS 9.37–9.38**.

6.37 Procedure for Developing Remuneration Policy

The supporting principles on the procedure for developing remuneration policy cover the following points:

- The remuneration committee should consult the chairman and/or chief executive about the proposals on the remuneration of other executive directors, and should have access to internal and external professional advice.
- The remuneration committee should be responsible for appointing any consultants in respect of executive remuneration.
- If executive directors or senior management are involved in advising or supporting the remuneration committee, care should be taken to recognise and avoid conflicts of interest.
- The chairman of the board should ensure that the company maintains appropriate contact with its principal shareholders on remuneration issues in the same way as for other matters.

The best practice provisions include the following recommendations:

- The board should establish a remuneration committee of at least three independent non-executive directors (or two in the case of a smaller company).
- In addition, the company chairman may be a member of the remuneration committee (but should not chair it) if he/she was considered independent (see **PARAGRAPH 6.17**) on appointment as chairman.
- The committee should make available its terms of reference, explaining its role and the authority delegated to it by the board.
- Where remuneration consultants are appointed, a statement should be made on whether they have any other connection with the company.
- The remuneration committee should have delegated responsibility for setting the remuneration of all executive directors and the chairman, including pension rights and any compensation payments.
- The committee should also recommend and monitor the level and structure of remuneration for senior management – the definition of senior management for this purpose should be decided by the board but should normally include the first layer of management below board level.
- The board (or the shareholders where the company's articles require this) should determine the remuneration of the non-executive directors – where the company's articles permit, the responsibility may be delegated to a small sub-committee, which might include the chief executive.

- Shareholders should be invited to approve all new long-term incentive schemes and significant changes to existing schemes, other than in the circumstances permitted by the Listing Rules.

The relaxation of the recommendations to allow the company chairman to sit on the remuneration committee was added as part of the June 2006 revision of the Code (see **PARAGRAPH 6.8**). The principle that no director should be involved in setting his or her own remuneration continues to apply.

6.38   Accountability and Audit

At a Glance
* The board's responsibility to present a balanced and understandable assessment of the company's financial performance and financial position extends to all forms of financial reporting.
* The board should maintain a sound system of internal control.
* The board should establish an audit committee of independent non-executive directors, at least one of whom should have recent and relevant financial experience.

6.39   Main Principles

Section C of the revised Combined Code identifies three main principles on accountability and audit:

- *Financial reporting*: The board should present a balanced and understandable assessment of the company's position and prospects.
- *Internal control*: The board should maintain a sound system of internal control to safeguard the shareholders' investment and the company's assets.
- *Audit committee and auditors*: The board should establish formal and transparent arrangements for considering how they should apply the financial reporting and internal control principles mentioned above, and for maintaining an appropriate relationship with the company's auditors.

The Cadbury Report discussed the presentation of a balanced and understandable assessment of the company's position in the context of recognised accounting practice. The accounts are required by law to show a true and fair view and they should give the highest level of disclosure consonant with presenting reports that are understandable, and without causing damage to the company's competitive position. The Cadbury Report also emphasised that balance involves dealing with setbacks as well as successes and that words are as important as figures. These issues are explored in more detail in **CHAPTER 10**.

6.40 Financial Reporting

The Code includes one supporting principle in respect of financial reporting which clarifies that the board's responsibility to present balanced and understandable information extends to half-yearly reports, other price sensitive reports and reports to regulators. The related best practice provisions cover the following points:

- The directors should explain in the annual report their responsibility for preparing the accounts, and there should be a statement by the auditors about their reporting responsibilities.
- The directors should report that the business is a going concern, with supporting assumptions or qualifications as necessary.

The statement of directors' responsibilities is considered in more detail in **CHAPTER 10** and going concern is considered in **CHAPTER 12**.

6.41 Internal Control

There are no supporting principles on internal control and just one best practice provision which notes that the board should review the effectiveness of the company's (or group's) system of internal control annually at least, and should report to shareholders that they have done so. The review should cover all material controls, including financial, operational and compliance controls and risk-management systems. The Cadbury Code of Best Practice recommended that the directors should report on the effectiveness of the company's system of internal control, although the formal guidance issued subsequently required them to review and report only on internal financial control. The present requirements are considerably broader in scope and are considered in more detail in **CHAPTER 14**. The annual review of the need for an internal audit function is considered at **PARAGRAPH 2.17** above.

6.42 Audit Committee and Auditors

There are no supporting principles in respect of the audit committee and auditors, but the revised Code includes the following best practice provisions:

- The board should establish an audit committee of at least three independent non-executive directors (or two in the case of smaller companies – see also below).
- The board should satisfy itself that at least one member of the audit committee has recent and relevant financial experience.
- The main role and responsibilities of the audit committee should be set out in written terms of reference and should include:
  - monitoring the integrity of the company's financial statements and any formal announcements relating to the company's financial performance, and reviewing significant financial reporting judgements contained in them;

- reviewing the company's internal financial controls and, unless addressed by a separate risk committee of independent directors or by the board itself, the company's internal control and risk-management systems;
- monitoring and reviewing the effectiveness of the company's internal audit function;
- making recommendations to the board (for it to put to the shareholders) on the appointment, reappointment or removal of the external auditor and approving the remuneration and terms of engagement of the external auditor;
- monitoring and reviewing the external auditor's independence and objectivity and the effectiveness of the audit process, taking into account relevant UK professional and regulatory requirements and
- developing and implementing policy on the engagement of the external auditor to supply non-audit services, taking into account relevant ethical guidance on this issue, and reporting to the board on any matter where the committee considers that action or improvement is needed.

- The audit committee should make available its terms of reference, explaining its role and the authority delegated to it by the board.
- The annual report should include a separate section describing the work of the committee in discharging its responsibilities;
- The audit committee should review the arrangements by which staff may, in confidence, raise concerns about possible improprieties in matters of financial reporting or other issues, with the objective of ensuring that arrangements are in place for proportionate and independent investigation and appropriate follow-up action.
- The audit committee should monitor and review the effectiveness of internal audit activities.
- Where there is no internal audit function, should consider annually whether there is a need for one and make a recommendation of the board – the absence of an internal function should be explained in the relevant section of the annual report.
- The audit committee should have primary responsibility for making a recommendation on the appointment, reappointment or removal of the external auditors – if the board does not accept the audit committee's recommendation, the annual report and any papers recommending appointment or reappointment should include a statement from the committee explaining its recommendation and setting out the reasons why the board has taken a different position.
- if the external auditor provides non-audit services to the company, the annual report should explain to shareholders how auditor objectivity and independence is safeguarded.

All of these issues are considered in more detail in **Chapter 2**.

The FRC has announced that it intends to begin a consultation in November 2007 on two proposed amendments to the present Code, one of which would allow the chairman of a smaller listed company to be a member of the audit committee provided that he/she was considered to be independent on appointment (see **PARAGRAPH 6.17**). If agreed, the change is expected to come into effect from June 2008.

6.43   Relations with Shareholders

At a Glance
* The board should take steps to ensure that all directors develop a balanced understanding of the issues and concerns of the company's shareholders.
* All proxy votes at the AGM should be counted and the level of proxies lodged, together with the balance for and against each resolution and any abstentions, should usually be reported.
* A separate resolution should be proposed on each substantial issue.
* The chairmen of the audit, remuneration and nominations committees should be available to answer questions at the AGM and all directors should attend the meeting.
* The notice of the AGM, together with supporting papers should be issued to shareholders at least 20 working days before the meeting.

6.44   Main Principles

Section D of the revised Combined Code includes the following main principles in respect of the company's relations with its shareholders:

* *Dialogue with institutional shareholders*: There should be a dialogue with shareholders based on the mutual understanding of objectives. The board as a whole is responsible for ensuring that this dialogue takes place.
* *Constructive use of the AGM*: The board should use the AGM to communicate with private investors and encourage their participation.

6.45   Dialogue with Institutional Shareholders

The supporting principles in the revised Code note that, whilst recognising most shareholder contact will be with the chief executive and finance director, the chairman and where appropriate other directors (including the senior independent director) should maintain sufficient contact with shareholders to understand their issues and concerns, using whichever methods are most practical and efficient. The best practice provisions include the following recommendations:

* The chairman should discuss governance and strategy with major shareholders and should ensure that the views of shareholders are communicated to the board as a whole.

- Non-executive directors should be offered the opportunity to attend meetings with major shareholders and should expect to attend if requested by the shareholders.
- The senior independent director should attend sufficient meetings with a range of major shareholders to listen to their views and develop a balanced understanding of their issues and concerns.
- The board should disclose in the annual report the steps taken to ensure that the members of the board, and the non-executive directors in particular, develop an understanding of the views of major shareholders about the company (e.g. through direct face-to-face contact, analysts' or brokers' meetings, surveys of shareholder opinion, etc.).

The introduction of recommendations on meetings between the non-executive directors and major shareholders has been an interesting development. Prior to publication of the July 2003 version of the Combined Code, it was generally accepted that the chairman should be the main channel of communication with institutional investors on matters of concern and a direct approach to the senior independent director was usually seen as a last resort and an indication that something was seriously amiss. Views were initially divided on whether institutional investors should have more regular contact with the independent non-executives, but the FRC specifically noted in its initial assessment of the impact of the present Combined Code that investors were reporting improved dialogue with companies (see **PARAGRAPH 6.8**).

6.46   Constructive Use of the AGM

There are no supporting principles on constructive use of the AGM, but the June 2006 version of the Combined Code includes the following best practice provisions:

- A separate resolution should be proposed on each substantially separate issue, and in particular a resolution should be proposed on the annual report and accounts.
- For each resolution, proxy appointment forms should enable shareholders to direct their proxy to vote for or against the resolution or to withhold their vote – both the form and any announcement of the results should make it clear that a 'vote withheld' is not a vote in law and will not be counted in the calculation of votes for and against the resolution.
- The company should ensure that all valid proxy appointments received for general meetings are properly recorded and counted.
- After a vote has been taken (except where this is on a poll) the following information should be given at the meeting in respect of each resolution and should also be made available as soon as reasonably practicable on a website maintained by or on behalf of the company:
  - the number of shares in respect of which proxy appointments have been validly made;

- ○ the number of votes for the resolution;
- ○ the number of votes against the resolution and
- ○ the number of shares in respect of which the vote was directed to be withheld.
- The chairman of the board should arrange for the chairmen of the audit, remuneration and nomination committees to be available to answer questions at the AGM and for all directors to attend.
- The company should arrange for the notice of the AGM and related papers to be sent to shareholders at least 20 working days before the meeting.

These provisions were updated as part of the June 2006 revision (see **PARAGRAPH 6.8**) which applies for reporting periods beginning on or after 1 November 2006.

6.47   Accountability to Shareholders

The Cadbury Report summarised the relationship between the board and the company's shareholders as follows:

- The shareholders, as owners of the company, elect the directors to run the business on their behalf, and hold them accountable for its progress and development.
- The directors report to the shareholders on their stewardship of the company and its assets.
- The shareholders appoint external auditors to provide an independent check on the company's financial statements.

The Cadbury Committee considered suggestions on how the accountability of directors to shareholders might be strengthened but concluded that shareholders should continue to make their views known to the board through direct communication and through attendance at AGMs. The Committee also noted that shareholder organisations set up to represent shareholder interests generally might provide an opportunity for individual shareholders to act collectively if they wish. Whilst shareholders cannot be involved in the detailed direction and management of their company, they are entitled to insist on a high standard of corporate governance, evidenced by compliance with the Combined Code.

6.48   Impact of Company Law Changes

The recent company law review has resulted in a number of company law changes that are designed to improve the quality of shareholder input at the AGM. In particular, the following provisions are now included in CA 2006:

- The timing of the AGM will be linked to the company's annual reporting cycle and public companies will be required to hold an AGM within six months of the financial year end – there will no longer be a requirement for a private company to hold an AGM.
- The annual accounts and reports must be sent to shareholders:
  - ○ at least 21 days before the date of the relevant accounts meeting in the case of a public company and

- no later than the end of the period allowed for filing the accounts and reports (or no later than the date on which they are actually filed, if earlier) in the case of a private company.
- The filing periods for annual reports and accounts are reduced to:
  - six months from the end of the accounting periods in the case of a public company and
  - nine months from the end of the accounting period in the case of a private company.
- Quoted companies must publish their annual accounts and reports on a website as soon as reasonably practicable, and the information must remain on the website until the accounts and reports for the following period are similarly published – this is intended to give shareholders more opportunity to submit members' resolutions for inclusion in the notice of the AGM.
- Members will no longer be required to meet the expenses of circulating a resolution or statement in advance of a public company AGM if sufficient requests are received by the company before the end of the reporting period preceding the meeting.
- Subject to certain conditions, members of a quoted company have a new right to require the company to publish on a website a statement setting out any matter that they propose to raise at the next accounts meeting (defined as a general meeting at which annual accounts and reports are laid before the members) in relation to:
  - the audit of the company's accounts (including the auditors' report and the conduct of the audit) that are to be laid at that meeting or
  - any circumstances connected with the company's auditors ceasing to hold office since the previous accounts meeting

  and the notice of the accounts meeting must draw attention to the possibility of a statement being placed on the website under these provisions.
- Members can appoint more than one proxy, provided that each proxy is appointed to exercise the rights attaching to a different share or shares.
- The power of proxies at meetings is enhanced, enabling them to speak, vote on a show of hands as well as in a poll and join with others in demanding a poll.
- Members can demand a poll in advance of a meeting and can vote on that poll without needing to attend the meeting or appoint a proxy.
- Subject to certain conditions, members of a quoted company can require an independent scrutiny of any poll – this might be done where the poll relates to a controversial issue or there are concerns over the voting procedure adopted.
- Quoted companies must disclose on a website the results of polls at general meetings and, where relevant, specific information about the independent assessor and his report.

The changes in respect of resolutions, meetings and proxies are have been brought into effect from 1 October 2007 and those relating to the preparation, publication and audit of annual accounts and reports and audit are due to be brought into effect from 6 April 2008.

6.49   Institutional Shareholders

At a Glance
* Institutional shareholders will usually have more access to boards than individual shareholders but companies must take steps to maintain parity between shareholders.
* There is a significant degree of common interest between individual shareholders and institutional shareholders.
* Detailed guidance for institutional investors is issued by the Institutional Shareholders' Committee (ISC) and other similar organisations.
* The Combined Code now recommends that institutional shareholders should apply the principles set out in the ISC's latest Statement of Principles.
* The Combined Code also includes a number of principles on the evaluation of corporate governance disclosures and shareholder voting.

6.50   Main Principles

The Combined Code includes the following main principles in respect of institutional shareholders:

* *Dialogue with companies*: Institutional shareholders should enter into a dialogue with companies based on the mutual understanding of objectives.
* *Evaluation of governance disclosures*: When evaluating governance arrangements, particularly those relating to board structure and composition, institutional shareholders should give due weight to all relevant factors drawn to their attention.
* *Shareholder voting*: Institutional shareholders have a responsibility to make considered use of their votes.

6.51   Communication with Shareholders

The Cadbury Report raised the following issues in respect of communication with shareholders:

* Institutional shareholders will usually have more access to boards than individual shareholders, but there is still a need for companies to maintain parity between shareholders wherever possible – a board should therefore ensure that any significant statements concerning the company are made publicly so that they are equally available to all shareholders.
* In communicating with institutional shareholders, there is always a risk of the company disclosing inside information – price sensitive information should only be disclosed with the prior consent of the shareholder (who will then be unable to deal in the company's shares until the information has been made public).

- In order to develop long-term relationships, it is important for a company to communicate its strategy to the major shareholders – similarly shareholders should inform the company if they have concerns over particular aspects of the business.

6.52   Role of Institutional Shareholders

The Cadbury Report noted that institutional shareholders hold the majority of shares in listed companies, but emphasised that in many cases they hold them on behalf of individuals (e.g. as members of pension schemes or beneficiaries of insurance policies) and that there is a significant degree of common interest between individual shareholders and institutional shareholders. In particular, both have the same interest in standards of financial reporting and corporate governance. Since the publication of the Cadbury Report there has in fact been a rapid growth of active private investors. This is attributed to a variety of factors, including the interest generated by the growth of the dotcom industry (despite its subsequent problems), technological development (the Internet has made it much easier to buy and sell shares) and the substantial growth of journalism on personal financial issues. However, there is no doubt that institutional investors continue to represent a very significant proportion of shareholders and are in a unique position to develop closer links with the companies in which they invest.

The Cadbury Report drew attention to three key issues critical to the development of a constructive relationship between companies and their shareholders:

- The need for institutional investors to encourage regular contact at senior executive level to exchange views and information on strategy, performance, board membership and quality of management.
- The need for institutional investors to make positive use of their voting rights and to exercise their votes on a regular basis.
- The need for institutional investors to take a positive interest in the composition of boards and the appointment of non-executive directors with appropriate experience and independence.

These issues were developed further by the Hampel Committee in the Combined Code, although the Committee did not put forward any disclosure requirements on compliance with the principles or provisions relating to institutional shareholders. However, they indicated their hope that these shareholders would disclose to the relevant companies, and possibly also to the public as a whole, the extent to which they are following the principles and provisions set out in the Combined Code. The Higgs Review also made no significant changes to this part of the Combined Code.

6.53   Institutional Shareholders' Committee (ISC)

The ISC represents the interests and concerns of institutional investors, with representatives from the Association of British Insurers (ABI), the National Association of Pension Funds (NAPF), the Association of Investment Trust

Companies (AITC) and the Investment Management Association (IMA). The ISC has issued guidance to institutional investors covering issues such as communication with boards, the use of voting rights, board composition, directors' remuneration and takeover bids. On the subject of shareholder voting, the guidelines note that institutional investors should support boards by positive use of their voting rights unless they have good reason for doing otherwise. Where an institutional investor considers it appropriate to vote against a particular proposal, the issue should be raised with the board in good time to allow for the problem to be considered and, if possible, a satisfactory solution found. If a solution proves impossible, it may be appropriate for a spokesperson to attend the meeting to explain why the proposal is being opposed. A poll should also be demanded in such cases, to ensure that the vote is properly recorded.

6.54   Dialogue with Companies

The Combined Code includes just one supporting principle on dialogue with companies, which notes that institutional shareholders should apply the principles set out in the 'The Responsibilities of Institutional Shareholders and Agents: Statement of Principles' which is published by the ISC and should be reflected in fund manager contracts. There are no best practice provisions on this issue. The ISC guidance makes the following points in respect of communication between companies and institutional investors:

- Institutional investors have a strong obligation to exercise their influence in a responsible manner. Many already have effective channels of communication, either directly or through advisers, with the boards of companies in which they invest. The ISC recommends that such channels should be developed more widely to make the communication process more effective.
- Formal methods of communication with shareholders (for instance, through the annual reports and accounts, shareholder circulars, and the right to attend meetings) may not be sufficient to establish the type of relationship which enables directors and shareholders to obtain a deeper understanding of each other's aims and requirements.
- Institutional shareholders should take positive steps to encourage regular and systematic contact, at senior executive level on both sides, so that views and information can be exchanged on strategy, performance, board membership and quality of management. This will enable shareholders to get a better understanding of management's objectives, the problems it is facing and the quality of those involved, and also focus the attention of management on the expectations and requirements of shareholders.
- Institutional investors do not wish to become insiders and price sensitive information should generally not be transmitted during such regular contact. In exceptional circumstances, if a board needs to consult its institutional investors on issues which are price sensitive, the investors will need to accept that their ability to deal in the company's shares will be suspended. Companies must not make such disclosures inadvertently or without the consent of the institutional investor.

Corporate Governance

6.55 Evaluation of Corporate Governance Disclosures

The Combined Code includes the following supporting principles on the evaluation of corporate governance disclosures:

- Institutional shareholders should consider carefully the explanations given for departures from the Combined Code and make reasoned judgements in each case.
- If they do not accept the company's position, institutional shareholders should give an explanation to the company in writing and be prepared to enter into a dialogue.
- A box-ticking approach to assessing corporate governance should be avoided.
- When assessing corporate governance, institutional shareholders should bear in mind the size and complexity of the company and the nature of the risks and challenges that it faces.

The preamble to the Combined Code also highlights the importance of the evaluation of governance being carried out with common sense in order to promote partnership and trust, based on mutual understanding. Governance should not be evaluated in a mechanistic way and departures from the Combined Code should not automatically be treated as breaches.

6.56 Shareholder Voting

The Combined Code includes the following supporting principles on shareholder voting:

- Institutional shareholders should take steps to ensure that their voting intentions are being translated into practice.
- On request, institutional shareholders should make available to their clients information on the proportion of resolutions on which votes were cast and non-discretionary proxies lodged.
- Major shareholders should attend AGMs where appropriate and practicable, and companies and registrars should facilitate this.

The original Combined Code also included a provision that institutional shareholders should endeavour to eliminate unnecessary variations in the criteria which each applies to the corporate governance arrangements and performance of companies in which they invest, but this is no longer included in the current Code.

6.57 Voting Guidelines

Voting guidelines are regularly issued to institutional investors by organisations such as NAPF, ABI and Pensions Investment Research Consultants (PIRC), based on their assessment of the key current issues. Issues that have received most focus in recent times include directors' remuneration (including incentive schemes, service contracts and notice periods), the independence of non-executive directors and issues relating to the external audit (e.g. the level of non-audit services provided by the auditors, connections between the directors and auditors, reap-pointment or changes in the appointment of auditors, and the role and constitution of the audit committee). Directors are well advised to keep track of the current issues being raised by these organisations so that they can be forewarned of any difficulties that are likely to arise at the AGM. Relevant information can usually be found on their websites and in some cases will be circulated to larger listed companies in advance of the publication date for their annual reports and accounts.

6.58   Shareholder Voting Working Group Proposals

In February 2004, the Shareholder Voting Working Group published a report by its Chairman, Paul Myners, following a review of the problems in the current UK system for shareholder voting and in particular the fact that a number of votes seem to be regularly 'lost' in the system. The main problems appear to stem from the system under which institutional investors appoint proxies to exercise their votes in UK companies and in particular:

- a complex chain of accountability, with a variety of other parties (e.g. custodian, investment manager, voting agency, registrar) between the issuer and the beneficial owner of the shares;
- reliance on a process that is still manually intensive and largely paper based, requiring data to be printed and re-entered at various points and
- a lack of transparency in the system.

The most important step to counteract these issues was felt to be the introduction of electronic voting. The report also considered the conscious withholding of votes as a mechanism for communicating reservations about a resolution without going as far as voting against it, although this is only meaningful if the company is made aware of the reason for taking this action. The report recommended that companies should provide a 'vote withheld' box on proxy forms, in addition to the 'for' and 'against' options (which would continue to form the basis for the legal decision on whether or not the resolution is carried). A progress report on shareholder voting issues, published in March 2005, showed that 85% of FTSE 100 companies and 50% of FTSE 250 companies had voluntarily offered a 'vote withheld' box on proxy forms in 2004. The FRC also amended the Combined Code in June 2006 to incorporate additional provisions on the withholding of votes and the use of proxies (see **PARAGRAPH 6.46**) and companies are expected to adopt these for reporting periods beginning on or after 1 November 2006. Other proposals raised in the report included:

- Under electronic voting, a confirmation facility should be available to enable voters to check that their instructions have been received and their votes recorded correctly.
- As a matter of best practice, registrars should report the late receipt of instructions or explain why they have not been accepted.
- Stocklending is important in maintaining market liquidity but lenders should automatically recall the stock when contentious resolutions arise, to prevent the system being used for the express purpose of acquiring votes.

- Institutional investors should explain to the beneficial owners how a voting decision has been reached, especially where the issue is contentious.
- A poll should be called on all resolutions at company meetings.
- Company law should be amended to give more rights to proxies and to provide for the independent scrutiny of a poll if requested by shareholders – appropriate provisions have now been included in CA 2006 (see **PARAGRAPH 6.48**).

6.59　Voting Disclosure

During the company law review, the Government also considered whether institutional investors should be required to disclose publicly how they have voted. This is a complex issue and it was felt that company legislation might not be the most suitable vehicle for dealing with it. However, *Section 1277* of *CA 2006* empowers the Treasury or the Secretary of State to make regulations requiring certain institutions to provide information about the exercise of voting rights. The DTI consultation document 'Implementation of Companies Act 2006' published in February 2007 notes that the Government would still prefer an industry-led solution to this issue and indicates the intention to see how market practice evolves before considering the introduction of a mandatory regime.

6.60　Reporting Requirements

At a Glance
* Listed companies are required to make an annual statement on the extent of their compliance with the Combined Code.
* The annual report of a listed company must include a statement from the directors on going concern.
* The directors of listed companies must report to shareholders that they have reviewed the effectiveness of the company's system of internal control.
* A separate directors' remuneration report must be prepared by all quoted companies.
* The Combined Code includes recommendations on certain other disclosures which should be given in the annual report.

6.61　Statement on Compliance with the Combined Code

FSA Listing Rules currently require each listed company to include in its annual report:

- A narrative statement of how it has applied the principles (both main and supporting) set out in the Combined Code, with explanations to enable the shareholders to evaluate how the principles have been applied.

- A statement on whether or not it has complied throughout the accounting period with the best practice provisions set in the Combined Code, with details of, and the reasons for, any areas or periods of non-compliance.

The preamble to the Combined Code emphasises that neither the form nor the content of the compliance statement has been prescribed. Directors are therefore given a free hand to explain their corporate governance policies in the light of the principles set out in the Code and any special circumstances that may have led the directors to take a particular approach. Certain aspects of the company's statement on compliance with the Code must be reviewed by the auditors (see **CHAPTER 2**).

6.62 Going Concern

Under the Combined Code, the directors should report in the annual report and accounts that the business is a going concern, with supporting assumptions or qualifications as necessary. This disclosure was originally recommended by the *Cadbury Code of Best Practice* but did not become fully effective until additional guidance was issued to directors in the document *Going Concern and Financial Reporting – Guidance for Directors of Listed Companies* published in November 1994. In the case of listed companies, the inclusion of a statement on going concern is now a direct requirement of the FSA Listing Rules and the statement must also be reviewed by the auditors. This reporting requirement is considered in more detail in **CHAPTER 12**.

6.63 Internal Control

Under the Combined Code, the directors should conduct an annual review (as a minimum) of the effectiveness of the company's (or group's) system of internal control and report to shareholders that they have done so. In the case of a listed company, the FSA Listing Rules require the directors' statement on internal control to be reviewed by the auditors (see **PARAGRAPH 2.71**). The directors' review should cover all aspects of internal control, rather than just internal financial control, but there is no requirement for the directors to express an opinion on the effectiveness of the system. Guidance on reviewing internal control and reporting under the Combined Code was developed by a working party of the Institute of Chartered Accountants in England and Wales chaired by Nigel Turnbull. Their final report *Internal Control – Guidance for Directors on the Combined Code* (often referred to as the Turnbull Report) was published in September 1999.

Following a review of the recommendations, an updated version entitled *Internal Control: Revised Guidance for Directors on the Combined Code* was published by the FRC in October 2005 and applies for accounting periods beginning on or after 1 January 2006. Reporting in respect of internal control is considered in more detail in **CHAPTER 14**.

6.64 Remuneration of Directors

Company law requires all companies to disclose certain information on directors' remuneration in the annual report and accounts, but a quoted company is also required to publish details of the company's remuneration policy and extensive information on the remuneration received by each individual director in a separate directors' remuneration report. The auditors of a quoted company are required to report on certain aspects of these disclosures. These requirements are considered in more detail in CHAPTER 9, which includes a checklist of the detailed disclosures that must be given. The Combined Code no longer includes any provisions on the disclosure of directors' remuneration as this matter is now considered to be adequately covered by company law requirements.

6.65 Other Disclosures

The Combined Code also recommends that:

- certain other details are disclosed in the company's annual report each year and
- certain additional information is made generally available – the June 2006 revision to the Combined Code (see PARAGRAPH 6.8) clarifies that placing the relevant details on a website maintained by or on behalf of the company will be sufficient to satisfy this recommendation.

These additional disclosures are summarised in Schedule C to the Combined Code, together with additional disclosure requirements included in the FSA Listing Rules, so that companies can find all relevant requirements in one place. A checklist is also attached as APPENDIX 2 to this chapter.

6.66 Reporting Requirements Under EC Directives

Recent changes to EC Company Law Directives will in future require companies whose shares are publicly traded to make a formal statement on compliance with the corporate governance code that applies or has been voluntarily adopted, and on the main features of the company's internal control and risk-management systems in relation to financial reporting. These changes are expected to be introduced from April 2008. Further details are given at PARAGRAPH 10.95.

Appendix 1

Useful Websites on Corporate Governance Issues

Financial Reporting Council	www.frc.org.uk
Financial Services Authority	www.fsa.gov.uk
Institute of Directors	www.iod.com
Institute of Chartered Secretaries and Administrators	www.icsa.org.uk
Institute of Chartered Accountants in England and Wales	www.icaew.co.uk
Auditing Practices Board	www.frc.org.uk/apb

Appendix 2

Checklist of Reporting Requirements Under the Combined Code and FSA Listing Rules

In addition to the overall statement on compliance (see **PARAGRAPH 6.61**), the Combined Code requires the following specific disclosures to be given in the annual report:

- ☐ A statement on how the board operates, including a high level statement on which types of decision are taken by the board and which are delegated to management [A.1.1].
- ☐ The names of the chairman, deputy chairman (where relevant), chief executive and senior independent director [A.1.2].
- ☐ The names of chairmen and members of the main board committees (i.e. audit, nomination and remuneration) [A.1.2].
- ☐ The number of meetings of the board and its main committees, and details of individual attendance by directors [A.1.2].
- ☐ The names of the non-executive directors whom the board considers to be independent [A.3.1].
- ☐ The reasons for considering a director to be independent if there are relationships or circumstances that might be deemed to affect this [A.3.1].
- ☐ The other significant commitments of the chairman and any changes to them during the year [A.4.3].
- ☐ A description of the work of the nomination committee, in a separate section of the report, including:
  - ○ the process used in respect of board appointments;
  - ○ an explanation if neither external consultancy nor open advertising has been used in the appointment of a chairman or non-executive director [A.4.6].
- ☐ How performance evaluation of the board, its committees and the individual directors has been conducted [A.6.1].
- ☐ A description of the work of the remuneration committee as required by the Directors' Remuneration Report Regulations 2002.
- ☐ Where an executive director serves as a non-executive elsewhere, whether or not the director will retain the relevant earnings and, if so, what the remuneration is [B.1.4].
- ☐ An explanation of the directors' responsibilities for preparing the accounts and a statement on the reporting responsibilities of the auditors [C.1.1].
- ☐ A statement from the directors that the business is a going concern, with supporting assumptions or qualifications as necessary [C.1.2].

☐ A report that the board has conducted a review of the effectiveness of the company's (or group's) system of internal control [C.2.1].

☐ A description of the work of the audit committee, in a separate section of the report [C.3.3].

☐ Where relevant, the reasons for the absence of an internal audit function [C.3.5].

☐ Where relevant, a statement from the audit committee explaining its recommendation on the appointment, reappointment or removal of the external auditor and the reasons why the board has taken a different position [C.3.6]. (*Note*: This should also be included in the papers sent out to shareholders on the appointment or reappointment of an external auditor.)

☐ If the external auditor provides non-audit services, an explanation of how auditor independence and objectivity is safeguarded [C.3.7].

☐ The steps that the board has taken to ensure that members of the board, and the non-executive directors in particular, develop an understanding of the views of major shareholders about the company [D.1.2].

In addition, the following information is required to be made publicly available (e.g. by inclusion on the company's website or by making it available on request):

☐ The terms of reference of the nomination committee [A.4.1].

☐ The terms of reference of the remuneration committee [B.2.1].

☐ The terms of reference of the audit committee [C.3.3].

☐ Where remuneration consultants are appointed, a statement on whether they have any other connection with the company [B.2.1].

The Combined Code also requires the following information to be made available:

☐ The terms and conditions of appointment of non-executive directors should be made available for inspection by any person at the company's registered office during normal business hours, for 15 minutes prior to the AGM and during the AGM [A.4.4].

☐ The papers sent out to shareholders in respect of a resolution to elect or re-elect a director should include:
   ○ sufficient biographical details and any other relevant information to enable shareholders to make an informed decision [A.7.1];
   ○ why the board considers that an individual should be elected as a non-executive director [A.7.2];
   ○ in the case of re-election, confirmation from the chairman that, following formal performance evaluation, the individual continues to make an effective contribution and to demonstrate commitment to the role, including time for board and committee meetings and any other duties [A.7.2].

Appendix 3

Main Points Raised in the Higgs Review

The Higgs Report on the Role and Effectiveness of Non-Executive Directors

In April 2002 in the wake of the Enron, Marconi and other high profile corporate collapses the UK government asked Derek Higgs, chairman of Partnerships UK plc and holder of directorships in companies as diverse as Egg plc and Coventry City Football Club, to conduct a review of the role and effectiveness of non-executive directors. His report went to two cabinet ministers Patricia Hewitt (Secretary of State for Trade and Industry) and Gordon Brown (Chancellor of the Exchequer).

Whilst the review was to focus on larger corporate businesses it was to consider the implications of any proposed changes for smaller companies. The review was published on 20 January 2003. After a very positive initial reaction the review generated considerable and heated debate especially with regard to the role of the senior independent director. There was also some challenge to the principle adopted first by Cadbury, but strongly endorsed by Higgs, of 'Comply or explain'. Some felt that the conditions of capital markets and the approach of institutional shareholders and their advisers would lead to 'Comply or breach' in practice.

As things turned out the Combined Code was revised to incorporate Higgs recommendations and there has been far less consternation in the UK than in the USA where there has been considerable angst over Sarbanes Oxley and it is frequently blamed for reducing the competitive advantage of the New York capital markets relative to London.

Why Did the Review Take Place?

The government wanted to ensure that the UK system was sound and that the risk of another major corporate collapse through weak governance was minimised. They were also keen to consider the issue of the diversity of membership of public company boards.

How Did Higgs Conduct the Review?

In line with other recent government reviews no formal committee was put in place. Higgs was simply given the responsibility to get the job done. He then came up with a proposal for the way in which he was going to conduct the review which was approved. A small team from the DTI and Treasury was then formed for the duration of the review to support him.

The key stages of the review were as follows:

- extensive research;
- a formal consultation process from which 200 responses were received;
- informal consultation;
- analysis of results;
- formulation of proposals;
- testing of proposals with a small group of friends and advisers of the Review;
- presentation to the Government;
- publication and
- making change happen.

The website for the review (www.dti.gov.uk/cld/non_exec_review) contains a lot of detail including a selection of the research, the consultation document, over 200 of the formal responses to it and the report itself.

The research undertaken by the review team was impressive, consisting of a census of listed company non-executives, a MORI poll of 650 executive directors, non-executive directors and chairmen, in-depth interviews with more than 40 inputs. We have made reference to this research in several of the other chapters. The census of non-executive directors of UK listed companies was an especially welcome addition to the base of knowledge on this subject. By way of example here is the selection from this quantitative data which was contained in the published report itself.

The Current Population of Non-executive Directors

As part of the Review, research was undertaken to build a factual picture of the current population of non-executive directors. The data (1) presented below is a summary of this research. The full analysis is on the Review's website (www.dti.gov.uk/cld/non_exec_review). It should be noted that the data was drawn on 17 July 2002 and so reflects the situation at that time.

There are 5172 executive, 4610 non-executive and 1689 chairmen posts held by directors in UK listed companies (2).

Of the 3908 individuals who hold non-executive directorships in UK listed companies, 80% hold only one non-executive director post in a UK listed company, 10% hold two non-executive posts in UK listed companies and 7% also hold an executive directorship; 13% of chairmen hold more than one chairmanship; 282 individuals hold both executive and non-executive director posts in UK listed companies.

Five FTSE 100 companies and 11% of companies outside the FTSE 350 companies have a joint chairman/chief executive; 24 FTSE 100 chairmen were formerly the chief executive of the same company; 4% of executive director posts and 6% of non-executive director posts are held by women. Less than 1% of chairmen are female. In the telephone survey, which was a representative sample of directors in UK listed companies, 7% of non-executive directors were not British and 1% were from Black and ethnic minority groups.

The average age of a non-executive director in the FTSE 100 is 59, with over three quarters 55 or over. The average age of an FTSE 100 chairman is 62. Almost 40% are 65 or over.

The average remuneration of an FTSE 100 non-executive director is £44,000 pa and £23,000 pa for a non-executive director of a company outside the FTSE 350. The average remuneration of an FTSE 100 chairman is £426,000 pa (compared to an average of £78,000 pa for a chairman of a company outside the FTSE 350).

The average time in post was 4.3 years for an FTSE 100 non-executive director and 4.5 years for a non-executive director in a company outside the FTSE 350. This implies that the average tenure of non-executive directors of UK listed companies is significantly longer than four years. The average time on the board for an FTSE 100 chairman was about eight years. For a chairman of a company outside the FTSE 350, the average time was about seven years.

Most listed companies have an audit committee and a remuneration committee. One FTSE 100 company does not have an audit or a remuneration committee and 15% of companies outside the FTSE 350 do not have an audit committee.

The majority (71%) of companies outside the FTSE 350 do not have a nomination committee. Six FTSE 100 companies do not have a nomination committee.

Investment companies (3) have a different structure as their boards typically consist of a manager together with non-executive directors. On average their boards have five members. They have therefore not been included in the main analysis. Further data on them can be found on the website.

1 *The data was supplied by Hemscott and analysed by the Review Team. Further and fuller details are available on the Review website.*
2 *There are 1702 listed companies in the UK, excluding investment companies (other than 3i).*
3 *There are 480 investment companies listed in the UK (excluding 3i).*

With regard to qualitative research Higgs also sought the views of those who have been most active in this area over the last decade and also spent some time looking at the international comparisons.

The US comparison was particularly interesting as throughout the period of the Review. The USA was undergoing something of a crisis of confidence in governance and the capital markets were in turmoil. The US response was swift and legal focussing on accountability. The resulting Sarbanes Oxley legislation received a mixed reaction especially from chief executives.

The consultation process elicited over 200 formal responses. A summary of the consultation document is contained in the **APPENDICES**. As with any consultation process views provided ranged from the blatantly self-serving to the original, well balanced and helpful.

What Did He Conclude?

Essentially that the UK model of corporate governance is sound but there is an opportunity to improve through greater consistency of best practice. To quote directly:

> 'In the current global discussion about corporate governance the UK is relatively advantaged. Our approach has been evolving for more than a decade and the habits and instincts which breathe life into the system have also matured. Transparency and accountability are more developed than in some other markets.'

However he adopts a far from complacent tone in his report. For example:

> 'But there is much more that can be done. Costly boardroom failures, resulting in great loss of value and jobs, provide ready grounds for humility. Moreover whatever lead the UK may have had in this area it has not been used to full advantage.'

In his view the failures in the UK have been of a different nature to some of those in the USA:

> 'Whereas in the US most governance discussion has focussed on corporate malpractice, in the UK sharp loss of shareholder value is more common than fraud or corporate collapse.'

He therefore concludes that a different approach is required in the UK than the one taken in the USA:

> 'This review therefore focuses as much on enhancing the competence and effectiveness of boards in promoting business prosperity as on issues of accountability. My view of the role of the non-executive director in this process differs from that of US regulators who have tended to emphasise the monitoring role of the non-executive director at the possible expense of the contribution the non-executive can make to wealth creation. These two roles are complementary and should be seen as such.'

With regard to the rest of Europe:

> 'there has been much activity to strengthen corporate governance and company law standards, for example the Cromme Code in Germany and the Bouton Code in France. Their recommendations are broadly consistent with the changes I suggest be made to the Code'.

He found a high degree of consensus in the UK, especially over the principle of the unitary board. To quote:

> '... the majority view which I share sees considerable benefits continuing to flow from the unitary approach.'

and

> 'The research concludes that it is important to establish a spirit of partnership and mutual respect on the unitary board. This requires the non-executive director to build recognition by executives of their contribution in order to promote openness and trust.

Only then can non-executive directors contribute effectively. The key to non-executive effectiveness lies more in behaviours and relationships than structures and processes.'

He found the same consensus with regard to the benefit of the separation of the chairman and chief executive's roles. Interestingly a comment made elsewhere in the report states:

'At the heart of the US corporate governance is a concentration of decision-making autonomy in one individual, the chairman and CEO. Only around one fifth of US listed companies separate these roles. In contrast separation is more common practice in the UK which I believe is one of the core strengths of the UK corporate governance framework.'

Unsurprisingly Higgs found widespread recognition that the role of the non-executive had become more challenging, that in principle they should be paid more as time commitment and risk had grown, and that the expectations of investors have risen. One reason he gives for this is that institutions have found it hard to hold management to account directly themselves.

Interestingly he also found that:

'Evidence diverged on the extent to which there is a shortage of good people to take on non-executive roles. Part of the problem seems to be that the supply of talent is not being sufficiently drawn upon.'

We would agree with this but feel as he hinted at in his report that there may be a shortage of people willing and able to take on the role of chairman.

On selection he made the following point:

'People are key. Critical to improving the effectiveness of non-executive directors is raising the quality of appointees. The evidence collected for this Review shows that the current population of non-executive directors is narrowly drawn. I make recommendations to promote an open, fair and rigorous appointment process which fosters a relentless meritocracy in appointments.'

The research supporting his review found that:

'A high level of informality surrounds the process of appointing non-executive directors. Half of the non-executive directors surveyed for the review were recruited to the role through friends and personal contacts. Only four per cent had a formal interview.'

Higgs however challenged the popular perception that there are a large number of people holding multiple non-executive directorships. He found that only a quarter of non-executives in the census had more than one post in a listed company. They may of course have appointments in private companies and the public sector.

So to the no doubt disappointment of many and relief of others he concluded:

'The variety of different appointments and individual circumstances means that it is difficult and unrealistic to set a limit for the number of non-executive appointments that anyone not in full time employment should hold.'

He did, however, as noted below, make recommendations with regard to executive directors and chairman.

He also found the same degree of informality with regard to evaluating performance.

> 'Over three quarters of non-executive directors and over half of Chairmen never have a formal personal performance review.'

With regard to *diversity* his research found that:

- Non-executives are typically White males nearing retirement age with previous plc director experience.
- There are less than 20 non-executives under the age of 45 in the FTSE100.
- Of the 276 non-executive directors surveyed for this report, 7% were not British and 1% not white.
- Only 6% of non-executive posts were held by women.
- There was only one female chairman in the FTSE100 (3i Group plc).
- There was only one in the rest of the FTSE350.

He found that diversity in the public sector was much greater, with 38% of the 3856 appointments and reappointments to public bodies being female and 9% from ethnic minorities.

> 'Most FTSE one hundred companies have a nominations committee, compared to only thirty per cent of small and mid-cap companies. However interviews conducted for the review suggested that where the nominations committee does exist it is the least developed of the board's committees, usually meeting irregularly and often without a clear understanding of the extent of its role in the appointment process.'

Readers should therefore find the detail on selection processes contained in CHAPTER 1 helpful.

Higgs draws some comparisons with the public sector where much progress has been made in this area.

He found that demand for training is very low particularly in larger companies. This view was endorsed by his research which found that two-thirds of those in his telephone poll had no specific training or development. However he also states that another factor might be that current provision may not match the needs of non-executives.

Interestingly, with regard to one of the main proposals coming out of the Hampel Committee, that there should be a clearly designated senior independent non-executive (SINE):

> 'Responses to the consultation contained a range of views ... Some saw the role as unnecessary and divisive. It was pointed out that shareholders may make use of their own connections with non-executive directors, or contact the chairmen of board committees if they have concerns.'

The authors' view is that given that the SINE has most effect, or not, when there is an issue with the chairman, it is no surprise that views are divided.

There was no consensus on the need to change the name 'non-executive' and those that did suggest change had a variety of suggestions. Unsurprisingly therefore he recommends no change to the title.

Higgs recognised that remuneration has become an issue, as time commitment and risk have risen, by saying that:

'remuneration needs to be sufficient to attract and retain high calibre candidates but no more than is necessary for this purpose'

and suggesting that companies use the per diem rates of their key advisers as a way of bringing balance to the debate. In this way fees would be commensurate with the size and complexity of the company.

A great deal of thought was given to the subject of liability of non-executive directors. He sums up the dilemma well in our view.

'A concern often put to me during the course of the review was about the potential liability attaching to non-executive director roles … Some argued that consideration should be given to proportional liability and capping liability by way of contract, or some form of business judgement defence. There was however, also some very strong support for the concept of the unitary board and for the legal duties of executive and non-executive directors to be the same. Moreover, some were concerned that if liability were reduced, non-executives would not take their responsibilities so seriously, and this could undermine the unitary board.'

He didn't believe that, at this stage, concerns about potential liability were having a significant effect in deterring people from putting themselves forward but acknowledged the risk that it could. The authors' view is that he may be right with respect to the larger, more prestigious companies but that it is already having an effect below this group (see chart on **PARAGRAPH 1.3.5**).

All of his recommendations are consistent with those proposed in the company law review.

Although the review focussed on larger companies he also considered the issues with respect to smaller listed companies and concluded that:

'There should be no differentiation in the Code's provisions between larger and smaller companies.'

He did, however:

'recognise that it may take some time for smaller listed companies to comply with the new provisions and in the interim they will need to explain why they cannot do so and what steps they are taking'.

The consequence of these views is that he has taken an evolutionary rather than revolutionary approach with his recommendations:

'I do not believe that legislation is the way forward. Instead this review builds on the "comply or explain" approach established by Sir Adrian Cadbury a decade ago.'

With regard to his recommendations he concluded also that:

'I do not presume a "one size fits all" approach to governance is appropriate. There will always be exceptions, but this does not negate the need to establish the expected norm, and putting the onus on companies who consider themselves exceptions to explain why. *It is not a blue-print for box tickers, but a counsel of best practice which must be intelligently implemented with discretion.*' (italics added)

What Were His Recommendations for Change?

A summary of the recommendations is contained on pages 5–10 of the report (available on the website www.dti.gov.uk/cld/non_exec_review). They are principally under the following headings:

- Roles of the board, chairman, non-executive and SINE directors.
- The effective board.
- A definition of independence.
- Recruitment and appointment of non-executives and widening the pool.
- Induction and professional development of executive and non-executive directors and chairmen.
- Tenure and time commitment of non-executive directors.
- Remuneration of non-executive directors.
- Resignation of directors.
- Audit and remuneration committees.
- Liability of non-executive directors.
- Relationships between non-executive directors and shareholders.
- Way in which change should be made.

All of these are covered in detail below. There are however a number of overall comments to be made.

Firstly we were delighted to see that the starting point for Higgs was the role of the board itself and that it is entirely consistent with the views expressed in **Chapters 1** and **3**. The proposal to include this description of the board's role in the Combined Code we think is very helpful.

Having put the chairman's and non-executive's roles in the context of the board, Higgs also provides a description of these roles and again these are proposed to be included in the Combined Code. Happily these are also consistent with the views we have expressed elsewhere in this book.

There are a number of suggested additions for disclosure in company's annual reports (for years starting on or after 1 July 2003) again all of these are covered in detail below:

> Clearly one of the more challenging aspects of his brief related to the issue of diversity and widening the pool. Whilst not stated it seems clear that this was something that both he and the Review team and the government found easy in theory but hard in practice.

He indicates that it is hard to gain an appointment on a UK plc if you haven't had plc experience before and

> 'It has been suggested that search consultants have a tendency to identify candidates from a narrow pool of candidates.'

He suggests that one of the reasons why there might be so few female non-executive directors is that the areas where women are more strongly represented are not traditional routes to the board.

Corporate Governance

He encourages chairmen and chief executives to let their executive directors and suitable senior management just below board level take one non-executive position elsewhere.

He also says that all companies operating in international markets would benefit from having at least one international non-executive. It is hard to think of too many major companies that aren't international.

One of the areas where he does make a tangible proposal on diversity is to do with the crossover of the public and private sectors. He recommends the formation of a small group to identify the top people in the public sector who would be suitable for appointments in listed companies. Because women are represented to a much greater extent in the public sector he hopes that this will also improve the gender balance.

7

Corporate Strategy

7.1 Introduction

7 Corporate Strategy

7.1 Introduction

At a Glance
* The quality of a non-executive's strategic judgment is likely to be their most significant contribution.
* Market strategy should be decided on the basis of quality market intelligence, rather than merely statistical information.
* A company's mission statement should be clear in terms of target and aspirations.
* A board should unite behind a strategy once it has been chosen, even if the choice was not a unanimous one.

In the definition of the board's role on **PARAGRAPH 1.2** 'Right strategy' was at the top of the list and involvement in strategy is frequently described as the most enjoyable aspect of the non-executive's role. The company's strategy will have a fundamental effect on whether value is created or destroyed. What was meant by 'Right strategy' was:

> 'To ensure that the business has the right strategy, that it is being implemented and monitored and that there is a good process for formulating and adapting it.'

But what do we mean by strategy and what role should the board and a non-executive actually be performing in relation to strategy? From the board's point of view 'Strategy' should not simply include the strategy for the business but also the strategy for the company. The two are clearly linked and the linkage and impact of one on the other should be well understood. For example the board of a private company which has decided that the company should be listed or sold may elect a different strategy for the company's business than one choosing to remain in a private situation with the same owners. There are of course many definitions of strategy; the one we would like to use is:

> 'The way we are going to achieve our vision'.

Naturally this assumes that there is an agreed vision. If there isn't then any attempt at coming up with a strategy is flawed.

The executive, led by the chief executive, has responsibility for executing the agreed strategy for the business. The chairman has responsibility for executing the strategy for the ownership of the business. The board's role is to ensure that there is good process for developing strategy, choosing the strategy to be adopted and ensuring that the CEO has the best chance of leading its successful execution.

The three key elements from the board's point of view are:

- analysis – assessing the current position;
- developing options – determining a vision and strategic options;
- choice – making a judgement and
- execution – implementing, monitoring and adapting the chosen strategy.

The purpose of this chapter is not to explore the many different frameworks, tools and techniques for formulating strategy but rather to focus briefly on the non-executive's role in the process. Strategy ought to be an area where a non-executive is able to add significant value through their experience and knowledge of other markets and companies. They may also add considerable value through helping to develop the company's approach to the process of developing strategy. However it is the quality of their strategic judgement that is likely to be their most significant contribution.

7.2 Analysis: Assessing the Current Position

The chief executive must take responsibility for formulating strategy and developing a series of strategic options within the context of the board's vision for the company. Good chief executives with experienced boards are likely to draw on the experience of their board in doing this before they seek approval for their particular chosen strategy. A chief executive who presents the strategy as a *fait accompli* without proper involvement of his or her colleagues beforehand is undermining the board.

Good chairmen and chief executives will also have a finely developed understanding of different shareholder views and appetites for risk so that they avoid developing a vision or strategy which fails to get the support of the board as a whole.

The board should also be prepared to adapt the vision for the company in the light of strategic analysis. Many companies at the start of this decade had to redefine their ambitions in the light of a difficult economic environment, geopolitical tension and weak capital markets. A higher degree of external uncertainty inevitably led to more conservative and flexible strategies being adopted.

A natural starting point is an analysis of the company's position and the environment that it is operating in. Most businesses will conduct this regularly so it shouldn't be new. Richard Koch's book *The Financial Times Guide to Strategy* provides an excellent summary of the many different tools and techniques for doing this.

A non-executive will want to feel that high-quality market intelligence underpins any analysis that is undertaken and that the analysis contains a lot more than regurgitated market statistics. High-quality market intelligence is the basis for providing an in depth understanding of the strategic variables and drivers of value growth. Qualitative information is usually just as valuable as quantitative, especially with regard to customers and competitors. The non-executive will also need to understand the key assumptions being made, as well as receiving a realistic competitor analysis. There may be certain strategic parameters which have been set for some time and left unchallenged.

For example, perhaps the business is conglomerate in nature. It is important for the board to recognise these parameters and have a process for determining at suitable frequency whether they are still appropriate or need to change.

A lot of board time can be taken up discussing the minutiae of strategy when there may in fact only be a limited number of critical things to decide upon. We call these the key strategic variables.

7.3 What Are These Key Strategic Variables?

For most companies comprising a collection of activities or business units choices on the following will result in the overall strategy. A few key questions are included for each on the basis that each of these topics is worth a book in their own right.

7.3.1 *Market*

- What business activities and markets does the company choose to compete in?
- What is the basis upon which the company chooses to compete?
- Which distribution channels should the company supply its products and services through?
- What approach should the company take towards marketing alliances and partnerships?

7.3.2 *Financial*

- What level of financial risk is acceptable?
- What is the required overall return of the group?
- What is the company's strategy with regard to its investors?
- How will financial control be exercised?

7.3.3 *Operations*

- What will the company make/do itself and what will be contracted out?
- What degree of flexibility in capacity is appropriate?
- What approach should the company take towards production alliances and partnerships?
- How should operations processes be managed to maximise both financial and non-financial objectives?

7.3.4   *Human Resources*

- What kind of employer does the company want to be?
- If the company consists of several subsidiaries or divisions, does it want consistent policies and for there to be mobility across them?
- What approach is taken towards career development and succession planning?
- What remuneration policy is appropriate?

7.3.5   *Acquisition*

- What is the company's strategy with regard to organic growth and growth through acquisition?
- If there is an acquisitive strategy are there clear criteria for selection of opportunities and processes for induction and review?

7.3.6   *Forming Strategic Alliances and Partnerships*

- Should the company have alliances, joint ventures or partnerships with other companies?
- If so what form should they take?
- What criteria are there for entering into such arrangements?

However the key strategic variable is often none of the above but the 'board's ambition and appetite for risk'.

For example, a decision to be a world class business in its chosen sectors will impact on all of the above, adding cost in the short term in anticipation of gaining a sustainable advantage in the long term. A lower ambition may produce higher financial returns and lower risk in the short term.

It has not been the dominant corporate model in most of the developed economies for the last decade. The true conglomerate is in a different position to other businesses with regard to strategy, though many of the same principles hold good. For the conglomerate the strategic variables will probably relate to just three things:

- What level of return is acceptable from companies owned by the conglomerate?
- How does the conglomerate exercise financial control over those companies?
- What companies should the conglomerate own or sell?

7.4   Developing Options: Determining a Vision and Strategic Options

For some a vision for the company should be market based and realistic in the sense that it takes full account of the company's own capabilities and those of other players in its markets. Many visions centre on leadership of a particular market and a description of the core value proposition. They are then expressed as mission statement in motivational terms from a customer, staff and other key audience point of view.

If the company is expressing its vision in terms of leadership then there should be clarity over what it means by leadership and how it will be measured. Leadership could mean many things. To some it is biggest in the market, to others it means having the best performing products. To others it means most innovative or available, highest brand awareness and so on.

In his book *Hidden Champions* Helmut Simon gave an interesting analysis of a group of German *mittlestand* (mid-sized private) companies who had defined their markets very tightly in terms of product and had been able to build world leading positions in terms of quality of products, market share and profitability as a result of this focus. Their pragmatic approach to developing a vision and their absolute conviction to organising themselves to achieve it was in his view a key to their success.

Interestingly a highly successful company which has an entirely different approach to this is Microsoft, whose stated mission is far more social in nature and doesn't mention the word leadership. Their current mission is:

'To enable people and businesses throughout the world to realise their full potential'

Another highly successful business in a different sector, Southwest Airlines has the following mission statement:

'dedication to the highest quality of customer service delivered with a sense of warmth, friendliness, individual pride, and company spirit'.

Neither of these two businesses are lacking in commercial zeal and these statements should not be taken as if both organisations are charities.

A new vision statement can be used to re-energise a company and galvanise its staff if it has been through a period of difficulty or has previously had a confused direction. One of the most successful demonstrations of this was the 'World's favourite airline' vision used to re-energise British Airways in the 1980s.

With regard to developing strategic options as has been said, the chief executive and his executive colleagues are responsible for developing a recommended strategy and a small number of credible alternatives for the board to consider as a whole.

Most businesses choose the mechanism of an annual strategic plan as a way of providing a focal point for producing a comprehensive and up to date analysis and confirming or revising their vision. This process is often also intended as a way of involving and obtaining buy-in from people within the business. It is important for the non-executive to understand and feel comfortable with the key assumptions upon which the recommendations of the executive are based.

It is normal if the company hits difficulty or a new chief executive is brought in from outside that a strategic review outside the regular cycle will take place. This may be done with the assistance of a firm of strategy consultants. If this is the case the non-executive needs to be comfortable that a rigorous selection process has taken place, that there is clarity over the role of the consultants and that their work is appropriately priced and monitored. The reasons for choosing to solicit external help should also be clear. Knowledge, expertise, process skills and resource are the usual reasons for a firm being brought in to assist.

7.5 Choice: Making a Judgement

How do boards select which strategy to adopt? If they have been through the stages described above then there will have been a recommendation put forward by the chief executive which they will have had prior input.

In Gordon Donaldson's Strategic Audit article in the Harvard Business Review he put forward the idea, somewhat cynically, that boards in the USA normally only really get involved in strategy when:

> 'there is a retirement of CEO, a precipitous fall in profitability or an unsolicited takeover attempt'.

Believing that the strategy of the business is fundamental to the building or destruction of shareholder value he advocates the creation of a strategic audit committee for larger corporations. Strategic audit committees are rare even in the USA and most boards determine strategy through the conventional approach of preparing a plan and then having an away day to allow sufficient time to discuss it ahead of formal approval at a subsequent board meeting.

A traditional board meeting where there are other items on the agenda is a difficult environment for a rigorous strategic debate. It is essential if an away day approach is to be taken that its purpose is clear and that there is significant preparatory work undertaken to ensure that the board's time is used to maximum effect on the day. Tips for holding away days are contained in PARAGRAPH 3.10.

It is important that the board is united behind the strategy chosen even if there have been differences of view in developing it. Fundamental differences of view over the future strategic direction may mean that a non-executive feels they ought to resign.

In reaching the point of being able to agree to a certain strategy the board will have considered the feasibility of execution and the implications in terms of resources, financial and human in particular. Therefore at this stage in the process the non-executive just has to be satisfied that there is a good process under development for turning the strategy into action.

7.6 Execution

From the non-executive's point of view this is very straightforward as the task for executing the board's chosen strategy falls to the chief executive and the executive directors. It might be, especially in smaller businesses that he or she is asked to support certain elements. This is normally though with regard to shareholder issues or key appointments rather than operational detail.

The board's role is to ensure that there is good process for developing strategy, choosing the strategy to be adopted and ensuring that the CEO has the best chance of leading its successful execution.

A critical element of execution is the communication of the strategy internally and externally. Alignment of these is essential. The strategy should be able to be articulated in a few key bullet points and easily memorable. Leading companies will tend to test whether the strategy is well understood and agreed with when they are undertaking staff and investor surveys.

With regard to monitoring strategy there are a number of key questions for the non-executive to address and these are:

- How will the board monitor progress against the agreed strategy?
- What measures is the board using to know what effect the strategy is having on shareholder value?
- How will the board be sufficiently informed as to know when the strategy should be adapted?

Critical to this will be monitoring the key assumptions central to the strategy. In order to do this the non-executive needs to be on top of the relevant performance data. If the company has its own market intelligence capability this is an easier task. If not then published information or specific analyses will be required.

If the strategy is wrong then the sooner it is recognised and corrective action is taken the better. This does however often mean a credibility issue for the leadership of the company and this is why sometimes there is a longer gap between recognition and action than there should be. It is a very important aspect of the non-executive's role to be alive to this issue especially when they themselves have endorsed the strategy in the first place.

Directors' Duties and Liabilities

8 Directors' Duties and Liabilities

8.1 General Duties

> **At a Glance**
> * The general rules on the role and duties of a company director are set out in common law and complex case law.
> * The Companies Act 2006 introduces a new statutory statement of the general duties of directors.
> * A company director has fiduciary duties to the company (as a separate legal entity) and to its members as a whole, in addition to various legal responsibilities that apply to anyone running a business.
> * A director must act in accordance with the company's constitution and in the way most likely to promote the success of the company for the benefit of the members as a whole.
> * A director may not delegate his/her powers and must maintain independence of judgement.
> * A director must exercise reasonable care, skill and diligence.
> * A director should not enter into a transaction involving a personal interest unless he/she has disclosed that interest as required by company law.
> * A director or former director must not use company property or information for his/her own benefit unless such use has been properly authorised.
> * A director or former director must not accept any benefit conferred by a third party unless acceptance has been properly authorised, or the benefit is necessarily incidental to the proper performance of his/her role as director.
> * A company is permitted to provide certain indemnities for its directors.
> * The liability of directors in respect of statements made in the directors' report and directors' remuneration report, and any information from those reports that is included in a summary financial statement, is now set out in company law.

8.2 Statutory Position

Currently the general rules on the role and duties of a company director are laid out not in companies' legislation itself but in complex and often inaccessible case law developed over many years. This can make it difficult for directors, especially those in smaller companies, to gain a good understanding of their overall responsibilities. Consequently, the recent company law review recommended the introduction of a statutory statement of the general duties of directors and this has now been included in the Companies Act 2006 (CA 2006). The Government's stated aim in introducing these new provisions has been to create a Code of conduct for directors, based on the existing position under common law and case law. Consequently, the new provisions do not make significant changes to current requirements, although they do seek to correct certain perceived defects in respect of directors' conflicts of interest by allowing some relaxation of the strict principles that currently apply. Also, the new statutory statement does not include all the duties of a director. Some are included elsewhere in companies' legislation (for instance, the duty to prepare and file annual reports and accounts) and others are included in related legislation, such as insolvency law (for instance, the duty to consider the interests of creditors when the company's solvency is under threat). Companies House is expected to prepare more comprehensive guidance leaflets, covering all of the duties and responsibilities imposed on company directors by both company and insolvency law, for issue to all new directors. Most of the new provisions have been brought into effect from 1 October 2007. The exception is the provisions relating to directors' conflicts of interest, which are due to be brought into effect from 1 October 2008.

8.3 General Legal Responsibilities

A variety of legal responsibilities apply to the directors of a company in the same way as to anyone else involved in running a business (e.g. as a partner or sole trader) – for instance, the duty to comply with law and regulations in respect of employment, health and safety, public liability, consumer protection, VAT, excise duties and other taxes.

8.4 Fiduciary Duty

The position of a company director is, however, very different to that of someone running a business in partnership or as a sole trader, in that he/she is in a position of trust and consequently has a fiduciary duty both to the company (as a separate legal entity) and to the members who have invested in the company. This is a wide-ranging responsibility, but the main elements may be summarised as follows:

- the directors must comply with the company constitution and use their powers under it for proper purposes;
- the directors must run the company for the benefit of the members as a whole;

- the directors must always act in the interest of the company as a whole, and not for the benefit of an individual shareholder or creditor;
- the directors should act fairly as between members;
- a director should not profit personally from his/her position within the company and should avoid any conflict of interest – where a potential conflict of interest arises, the director has a duty to declare his/her personal interest to the company;
- a director has an obligation to perform his/her duties with reasonable skill and care and must maintain independence of judgement.

8.5 Statutory Statement of Directors' General Duties

The recent company law review recommended that a statement of directors' duties should be incorporated into company law, the intention being to clarify the present position by making the details more accessible and understandable, rather than to make significant changes to current law and practice.

The statutory duties are set out under the following headings in Sections 170–177 of CA 2006:

- scope and nature of general duties;
- duty to act within powers;
- duty to promote the success of the company;
- duty to exercise independent judgement;
- duty to exercise reasonable care, skill and diligence;
- duty to avoid conflicts of interest;
- duty not to accept benefits from third parties and
- duty to declare an interest in a proposed transaction or arrangement.

The duties specified in the legislation are not intended to represent an exhaustive list, but rather to highlight the main expectations of responsible business behaviour.

In practice, many of these general duties will overlap and the effect of them is to be treated as cumulative, so that directors must comply with each duty that applies in any particular case. For instance, a director cannot take an action that would constitute a breach of the duty to act within his/her powers on the basis that to do so would promote the success of the company.

The duties apply to all directors, and the following duties continue to apply to former directors after they have left office:

- the duty to avoid conflicts of interest in relation to the exploitation of property, information or opportunities of which he/she became aware whilst a director and
- the duty not to accept benefits from third parties in relation to things done or omitted during the time that he/she was a director.

The company law review also recommended the inclusion of special duties that would come into effect when a director knew, or should know, that the company was likely to be unable to meet its debts as they fall due, or that there was no reasonable prospect of the company avoiding going into insolvent liquidation. The Government concluded that this would be a very finely balanced judgement and that the fear of personal liability might lead to excessive caution. It has not, therefore, incorporated any aspects of insolvency law into the statutory statement of directors' duties, although attention will be drawn to the requirements of insolvency law in the guidance document for new directors (see **PARAGRAPH 8.2**).

8.6 *Acting Within Powers*

Directors have an obligation to act in accordance with the company's constitution and with decisions taken under that constitution, and must only exercise their powers for the purpose for which they were conferred.

8.7 *Promoting the Success of the Company*

A director must act in good faith and in the way that he/she considers will be most likely to promote the success of the company for the benefit of the members as a whole. However, in fulfilling this duty, a director must also have regard to:

- the likely long-term consequences of any decisions;
- the interests of the company's employees;
- the need to foster the company's business relationships with suppliers, customers and others;
- the impact of the company's operations on the community and the environment;
- the desirability of the company maintaining a reputation for high standards of business conduct and
- the need to act fairly between members.

The legislation notes that this duty is subject to any enactment or rule of law requiring directors to consider or act in the interests of the company's creditors in certain circumstances (for instance, the impending insolvency of the company).

In the case of an altruistic company (such as a charitable or community interest company), where the purposes of the company consist of, or include, purposes other than the benefit of its members, the directors must act in good faith in the way that they consider would be most likely to achieve those purposes.

8.8 *Exercise of Independent Judgement*

Directors must maintain their independence of judgement and should not commit themselves to act in accordance with the wishes of another party. However, this duty is not infringed by a director acting in accordance with an agreement entered into by the company that restricts the future exercise of discretion by the directors, or acting in a way authorised by the company's constitution.

8.9   *Care, Skill and Diligence*

A director must exercise the care, skill and diligence which would be exercised by a reasonably diligent person with both:

- the general knowledge, skill and experience which may reasonably be expected of a person carrying out the functions carried out by the director in relation to the company and
- the general knowledge, skill and experience that the individual director has.

8.10   *Conflicts of Interest*

Under present law, all conflicts of interest involving directors must be authorised by the members of the company, unless some alternative procedure is properly provided. By contrast, CA 2006 will allow most conflicts of interest arising from third party dealings by a director to be authorised by the board. Such authorisation will be the default position for private companies unless their constitution expressly prevents this, but public companies will need to make specific provision for this in their constitutions. However, it should be noted that the acceptance of benefits from third parties (see **Paragraph 8.11**) is dealt with in a separate section of CA 2006 and cannot be authorised by the board.

Under CA 2006, a director must avoid a situation in which he/she has, or may have, an interest that conflicts or may conflict with the interests of the company. The new legislation emphasises that this duty to avoid conflicts of interest applies in particular to the exploitation of any property, information or opportunities, regardless of whether or not the company could take advantage of them, and that a conflict of interest includes:

- a conflict of interest and duty and
- a conflict of duties.

The legislation also applies regardless of whether the interest of the director is direct or indirect. The only conflicts of interest not covered by this duty under the new legislation are those relating to transactions or arrangements with the company – these must be declared to the other directors under either Section 177 or Section 182 of CA 2006 (see **Paragraph 8.16**) unless a specific exception applies under those sections.

The duty to avoid conflicts of interest is not infringed if the matter has been authorised by the directors in accordance with company law and the company's constitution. However, such authorisation is only effective if the quorum at the relevant directors' meeting is met without counting the director in question and any other interested director, and is either agreed to without a vote, or would have been agreed without the votes of the interested director(s).

Unlike the other provisions of CA 2006 on directors' duties, which have been brought into effect from 1 October 2007, the new provisions on directors' conflicts of interest are not expected to be introduced until 1 October 2008.

Directors' Duties and Liabilities

8.11 *Benefits from Third Parties*

Directors are currently prevented from exploiting their position as a director for personal benefit. Under CA 2006, a director will be prohibited from accepting a benefit from a third party that is conferred by reason of his/her being a director or doing (or not doing) anything as director. A third party is defined as a person other than:

- the company;
- an associated body corporate or
- a person acting on behalf of the company or an associated body corporate.

The provision of a benefit that gives rise to an actual or potential conflict of interest will be caught by both this duty and the duty to avoid conflicts of interest (see **PARAGRAPH 8.10**). However, whilst it will usually be possible for the other directors to authorise a conflict of interest, the legislation makes no provision for the acceptance of a benefit from a third party to be authorised by the directors, although it will be possible for authorisation to be given by the members.

This duty is not infringed if the acceptance of the benefit cannot reasonably be regarded as likely to give rise to a conflict of interest. Once again, a conflict of interest includes a conflict of interest and duty, and a conflict of duties.

These new provisions are due to be bought into effect from 1 October 2008, together with those on conflicts of interest.

8.12 Indemnities and Insurance for Directors

Company law requirements on the provision of indemnities and insurance for directors were changed by the Companies (Audit, Investigations and Community Enterprise) Act 2004. The new provisions came into effect on 6 April 2005. A company is now permitted under Sections 309A and 309B to indemnify directors against proceedings brought by third parties. No indemnity can be provided against liabilities of the director to the company or to any associated company. The indemnity can generally cover both legal costs and the financial costs of any adverse judgement, but not:

- the legal costs of an unsuccessful defence of criminal proceedings;
- fines imposed in criminal proceedings or
- penalties imposed by regulatory bodies.

Companies who provide an indemnity under the new provisions must disclose this fact in the directors' report (see **PARAGRAPH 10.93**) and shareholders have the right to inspect any indemnification agreement. A company is also permitted to pay a director's defence costs as they are incurred. The director remains liable for the payment of any damages that are awarded to the company and, if the defence is unsuccessful, will be required to repay any costs that have been met by the company, except in the case of third party actions where the company has agreed to indemnify the director as discussed above. Companies are also permitted by Section 309A to purchase indemnity insurance for directors of the company or of an associated company.

Sections 309A and 309B of the CA 1985 are repealed with effect from 1 October 2007 and replaced by similar provisions under Sections 232 to 238 of the CA 2006.

8.13   Directors' Liability for False or Misleading Statements

CA 2006 sets out a clear statement of the liability of directors in respect of false or misleading statements made in the directors' report or the directors' remuneration report, and in any information derived from those reports that is included in a summary financial statement. A director is liable to compensate the company for any loss suffered by it as a result of any untrue or misleading statement made in such a report, or of the omission of anything which the legislation requires to be included, if:

- he knew the statement to be untrue or misleading, or was reckless as to whether it was untrue or misleading or
- he knew the omission to be a dishonest concealment of a material fact.

However, there is no liability to any person other than the company as a result of reliance on information given in the report. This section of CA 2006 came into effect on 20 January 2007 and is intended to encourage the provision of better quality forward-looking information in annual reports.

8.14   More Specific Duties

At a Glance
* A director has a duty to give the company written notification of any interests that he/she holds in shares or debentures of the company or group, and of any changes in those interests.
* Directors and other employees must ensure that they do not infringe provisions on insider dealing when entering into transactions involving the company's shares and debentures.
* A director has an obligation to disclose to the other directors any personal interest in a contract, transaction or arrangement involving the company – this requirement extends to interests held by persons connected with the director.
* Directors have a duty to provide appropriate information and explanations to the auditors.
* Where a private company intends to act by means of a written resolution, the directors have a duty to arrange for a copy of the resolution to be sent to the auditors.
* Directors have a duty to keep proper accounting records and to prepare annual accounts for the company or group.

* Under insolvency law, a liquidator can apply to the court for a director or former director to contribute personally to the company's assets if he/she knew, or should have known, that there was no prospect of the company avoiding going into insolvent liquidation.
* Any person who is knowingly a party to a company carrying on business for any fraudulent purpose, including an intent to defraud creditors, is guilty of an offence.

8.15   Disclosure of Interests in Shares and Debentures

Until 6 April 2007, each director and shadow director had a duty under CA 1985 to give written notification to the company of any interest that he/she held in the shares or debentures of the company or group and the company was obliged to record these in a register of directors' interests. The legislation also required this register to be available for public inspection. The definition of 'interests' for this purpose was very wide and specifically included interests held by the director's immediate family (i.e. spouse and children/stepchildren under the age of 18). All interests, and any subsequent changes, had to be notified to the company within five days of the interest arising or changing.

The relevant sections of CA 1985 are repealed with effect from 6 April 2007 by the Companies Act 2006 (Commencement No 1, Transitional Provisions and Savings) Order 2006 (SI 2006 No 3428). However, in the case of listed companies, similar notification and recording requirements continue to apply under the Financial Services Authority (FSA) Disclosure and Transparency Rules, as a result of the UK implementation of the requirements of the EU Market Abuse Directive. There is no longer any formal requirement for other companies to maintain equivalent records. Directors of listed must also take particular care when dealing in the company's shares and debentures that they do not infringe the rules on insider dealing set out in the Criminal Justice Act 1993. Directors and employees of listed companies should also comply with the Model Code that forms part of the FSA Listing Rules, or with any more stringent requirements adopted by the company in relation to dealing in the company's listed securities (see **PARAGRAPH 8.48**).

8.16   Disclosure of Interests in Contracts

Under Section 317 of CA 1985, a director has an obligation to disclose at a meeting of the directors any interest (whether direct or indirect) that he/she has in a contract, transaction or arrangement entered into by the company, or which the company proposes to enter into. The disclosure requirement extends to the interests of a person connected with the director, including:

* the director's spouse and children (including stepchildren);
* a body corporate with which the director is associated;

- a trustee (acting in that capacity) of any trust which includes amongst the beneficiaries:
  - the director,
  - the director's spouse, children or stepchildren,
  - any body corporate with which he is associated,
  - a partner (acting in that capacity) of the director or of any person connected with him and
  - a Scottish firm in which the director, or a person connected with him, is a partner.

The requirement to disclose specifically includes any loans, quasi-loans and credit transactions between the company and the director (see **PARAGRAPH 8.23**). The director must make the disclosure at the first meeting at which the proposed contract, transaction or arrangement is discussed, or at the first meeting after the director, or a person connected with him/her, has acquired a disclosable interest in a contract, transaction or arrangement with the company. A shadow director is required to give written notice to the directors of a disclosable interest before the meeting at which disclosure would otherwise have been required. Directors are also permitted to give general notice that they are connected with a particular company or firm and are therefore to be regarded as interested in any contract, transaction or arrangement with that entity. Whether the director can participate in any discussion or vote on the contract, transaction or arrangement will depend on the detailed provisions in the company's Articles of Association. If a director fails to disclose a notifiable interest, he/she is liable to a fine and may be prevented from retaining any private profits earned as a result of that interest. The contract, transaction or arrangement may also become voidable by the company.

Slightly different requirements will apply under CA 2006. Under Section 177 of CA 2006, a director will have a duty to disclose to the other directors any interest (direct or indirect) that he/she has in a proposed transaction or arrangement with the company. The legislation specifies that disclosure must be made to the other directors, so the duty cannot be met by making disclosure to the members, and the simple statement of an interest without details of its nature and extent will also be insufficient. The declaration can be made at a meeting of the directors, by specific notice in writing, or by general notice in writing (for instance, that the director has an interest in a specified entity and so should be regarded as having an interest in any transaction or arrangement with that entity). Similar requirements apply under Section 182 of CA 1006 in respect of an interest in an existing transaction or arrangement entered into by the company, unless it has already been declared under Section 177. In both cases, an interest does not need to be declared if it cannot reasonably be regarded as likely to give rise to a conflict of interest, or if the directors are already aware of it (or ought reasonably to be aware of it).

Similar disclosure requirements will apply to shadow directors under Section 187 of CA 2006, except that in this case the disclosure must always be made in writing (i.e. it cannot simply be made at a meeting of the directors).

The above sections of CA 2006 are due to be brought into effect from 1 October 2008.

Directors' Duties and Liabilities

8.17   Duty to Assist Auditors

Section 389A of CA 1985 grants the auditors a right of access at all times to the company's books, accounts and vouchers and entitles them to require from the directors and other officers of the company the information and explanations that they consider necessary in order to perform their duties as auditors. It is an offence for a director or other officer knowingly or recklessly to make a statement to the auditors, either orally or in writing, which conveys (or purports to convey) information or explanations which the auditors are entitled to require and which is misleading, false or deceptive. A director or officer who commits such an offence is liable to imprisonment or a fine or both. It is also an offence to delay responding to the auditors' enquiries. Further details on the duty to assist the auditors are given at **PARAGRAPH 2.50** above. For accounting periods beginning on or after 1 April 2005, directors have an additional duty to volunteer information to the auditors and the directors' report must include a confirmation that each director has made appropriate enquiries and that all information relevant to the audit has been made available to the auditors. This statement is also considered in more detail at **PARAGRAPH 2.50** above.

Similar requirements will continue to apply under CA 2006.

8.18   Use of Written Resolutions

Private companies are permitted to act by means of a written resolution rather than by a resolution of the company in general meeting or by a resolution of a meeting of any class of members of the company. Prior to 1 October 2007, under Section 381B of CA 1985, a director or secretary of the company who knows that it is proposed to seek agreement by means of a written resolution, and who knows the terms of the resolution, has a duty to arrange for a copy of the resolution to be sent to the auditors at or before the time that it is sent to the members for signature. The auditors also have the right to receive all communications relating to a written resolution that must be supplied to a member of the company. There are penalties for failure to comply although it is a defence for a director or secretary to demonstrate that it was not practicable to comply or that there were reasonable grounds to believe that the auditors had been informed of the proposed resolution. Section 502(1) of CA 2006 retains the auditor's entitlement to receive all relevant information relating to a proposed written resolution that is provided to the members, but the provisions on written resolutions under the new legislation (which replace those in CA 1985 with effect from 1 October 2007) no longer include a specific requirement to send a copy of the resolution to the auditors at or before the time that it is sent to the members.

8.19   Financial Responsibilities

The duties of the directors in respect of the maintenance of accounting records and the preparation of an annual report and accounts (including the need to make a formal statement of their responsibilities in respect of the accounts) are considered in detail in **CHAPTER 10**.

8.20   Wrongful Trading

Section 214 of the Insolvency Act 1986 deals with the issue of wrongful trading. Where a company goes into insolvent liquidation, this section enables the liquidator to apply to the court for a person who is, or has been, a director of the company to contribute personally to the company's assets if he/she knew, or ought to have concluded, before the winding up of the company commenced that the company had no reasonable prospect of avoiding going into insolvent liquidation. The legislation makes no specific reference to trading whilst insolvent, and it may therefore be acceptable for a company that is technically insolvent to continue trading if the directors consider that there is a genuine prospect of the company avoiding insolvent liquidation by doing so. In considering this issue, the facts that a director is expected to know, the conclusions that he/she is expected to reach and the steps that he/she is expected to take are those that would be known, reached or taken by a reasonably diligent person with both the general knowledge, skill and experience that may reasonably be expected of a person fulfilling that function, and the general knowledge, skill and experience that the director in question actually has. A director will not be personally liable in this way if he/she can demonstrate that, on first realising that insolvent liquidation was unavoidable, they took every step to minimise the potential loss to the company's creditors. A director is therefore advised to ensure that the minutes of board meetings include an accurate record of any concerns that he/she expresses in respect of the company's solvency.

8.21   Fraudulent Trading

Under company law, every person who is knowingly a party to a company carrying on business with the intent to defraud creditors or for any fraudulent purpose, regardless of whether the company is solvent or not, is liable to imprisonment, or a fine, or both. Fraudulent trading is also covered in Section 213 of the Insolvency Act 1986. In this case, a liquidator is able to apply to the court for a person who is, or has been, a director of the company to contribute personally to the company's assets if, in the opinion of the liquidator, the director was knowingly a party to carrying on the company's business with the intent to defraud creditors or for any fraudulent purpose. Intent to defraud can include the company incurring additional debts when the directors were aware that there was no realistic prospect of the existing creditors being paid.

8.22   Additional Obligations in the Case of Listed Companies

The directors of companies whose shares are traded on a regulated market are subject to significant additional obligations. The detailed continuing obligations of UK listed companies are set out in the FSA Listing Rules and Disclosure and Transparency Rules, all of which can be found in the FSA Handbook. The current version of the full FSA Handbook is available on the FSA website at http://fsahandbook.info/FSA/html/handbook/. The website also offers the facility for the requirements to be shown as at a specified date.

In particular, the FSA's rules include an overriding requirement for all shareholders to be treated equally and for all sensitive information to be notified to a Regulatory Information Service without delay. The directors of a listed company also have an ongoing obligation to take all reasonable care that any published statement, forecast or other information is not misleading, false or deceptive, and that it does not omit any information that is likely to affect its import.

8.23 Transactions with Directors That Require Members' Approval

---

At a Glance
* Company law requires certain transactions between a company and its directors to be formally approved by the members.
* Significant changes to the detailed requirements are made by CA 2006.
* In particular, formal approval is required for:
  ○ long-term service contracts for directors;
  ○ substantial property transactions involving directors and persons connected with them;
  ○ loans, quasi-loans and credit transactions involving directors and persons connected with them and
  ○ payments for loss of office.

8.24 Requirement for Approval by Members

Company law requires certain transactions involving a director of the company or a director of the holding company (and, in many cases, persons connected with them) to be formally approved by the members. A number of significant changes to the requirements on loans and other transactions involving directors are introduced by CA 2006. In particular, the requirements on the approval of certain transactions have been gathered together in Chapter 4 of Part 10 of CA 2006 for ease of reference and the rules have been aligned where practicable to make them more straightforward to understand and apply. The same requirements will generally apply to shadow directors, but with minor amendments in some cases. Under the legislation, members' approval is given by ordinary resolution, although a company's articles may specify a higher majority or even unanimity.

Most of Part 10 of CA 2006 has been brought into effect from 1 October 2007, the exception being the provisions on directors' conflicts of interest, which are expected to be introduced from 1 October 2008.

8.25   Long-Term Service Contracts for Directors

Under CA 1985, a service contract for a director requires formal approval by the members if it extends (or could extend) for a period of more than five years and does not allow the company to give unconditional notice at any time. Where the director is also a director of the holding company, prior approval of the contract must generally be given by the members of both the subsidiary and the holding company. The legislation also includes special provisions to prevent a company from entering into a series of shorter agreements with the same director in an attempt to create a contract that extends for more than five years without shareholder approval.

Under Section 188 of CA 2006, member approval is required for any service contract where a director is effectively guaranteed a period of employment of at least two years with the company or any of its subsidiaries. Failure to obtain the necessary approval enables the company to terminate the contract at any time by giving reasonable notice.

Further details on service contracts with directors, and the approval requirements, are given in CHAPTER 9.

8.26   Substantial Property Transactions

Substantial property transactions are those where a company buys a substantial non-cash asset from, or sells such an asset to:

- a director of the company;
- a director of the company's holding company;
- a person connected with a director of the company or
- a person connected with a director of the company's holding company.

Under Sections 320–322 of CA 1985, such transactions generally require formal approval by the members of the company (and also, where relevant, by the members of the holding company) if the value of the transaction is more than £100,000 or 10% of the company's net assets as shown in the latest accounts.

Similar approval requirements apply under Sections 190–196 of CA 2006, but with a number of changes. These include:

- providing for the aggregation of non-cash assets that form part of an arrangement (or a series of arrangements) when determining whether member approval is required;
- specifically excluding payments under directors' service contracts and payments for loss of office from the requirements of these sections;
- raising the minimum value of what may be regarded as a substantial non-cash asset from £2000 to £5000;
- expanding the exception for transactions with members to include the acquisition of assets from a person in his character as a member of the company and
- not requiring approval in the case of a company that is in administration or is being wound up (unless it is a members' voluntary winding up).

Directors' Duties and Liabilities

8.27 Loans, Quasi-loans and Credit Transactions Under CA 1985

Prior to 1 October 2007, Section 330(2) of CA 1985 generally prohibits any company from:

- making a loan to a director of the company;
- making a loan to a director of the company's holding company;
- guaranteeing a loan to a director of the company or to a director of the company's holding company;
- providing any security in connection with a loan to a director of the company or to a director of the company's holding company.

This is intended to provide a safeguard against the directors abusing their position within the company and using company assets for their personal benefit. Loans, quasi-loans and credit transactions are specifically included in the duty to disclose that is imposed on every director by Section 317 of CA 1985 (see **PARAGRAPH 8.16**).

Additional prohibitions apply in the case of a relevant company, which is defined in CA 1985 as a public company, a subsidiary of a public company, a fellow subsidiary of a public company or the holding company of a public company. In the case of relevant companies, the general prohibition on loans to directors extends to certain other transactions and arrangements. A relevant company is therefore also prohibited from:

- Making a quasi-loan to a director of the company or to a director of the company's holding company, or to a person connected with any such director.
- Guaranteeing a loan or quasi-loan, or providing any security in connection with a loan or quasi-loan to:
  ○ a director of the company, or a person connected with such a director or
  ○ a director of the company's holding company, or a person connected with such a director.
- Entering into a credit transaction as creditor for, or guaranteeing or providing security for a credit transaction made by any other person for:
  ○ a director of the company, or a person connected with such a director or
  ○ a director of the company's holding company, or a person connected with such a director.

There are a number of specific exceptions to the general prohibition on making, guaranteeing or securing loans and quasi-loans to, and credit transactions with, directors or persons connected with directors, including in particular short-term quasi-loans, small loans, certain inter-company transactions and the funding of expenditure incurred in the performance of duties as a director of the company. Special rules also apply in the case of banks and money-lending companies.

All of these requirements have been replaced by new provisions under CA 2006 with effect from 1 October 2007 (see **PARAGRAPH 8.31**).

8.28   *Quasi-loans*

A quasi-loan is a transaction between two parties (the creditor and the borrower), where the creditor pays or agrees to pay a sum on behalf of the borrower, or reimburses or agrees to reimburse expenditure incurred by the borrower, on the terms that the borrower or a person on his behalf will reimburse the creditor, or in circumstances which create a liability for the borrower or a person on his behalf to reimburse the creditor. The following are examples of quasi-loans:

- The purchase of any goods or services through the company, where the company becomes liable to pay the supplier and is subsequently reimbursed by the director.
- Personal use of a company credit card by the director, where the company settles the liability and the director subsequently reimburses the company.
- A season ticket loan, if the company buys the ticket on behalf of the director and the director makes subsequent repayments, either in cash or by deduction from his salary.
- Any personal costs paid by the company and subsequently reimbursed by the director (e.g. travel costs for a spouse who accompanies the director on a business trip).

8.29   *Credit Transactions*

A credit transaction is a transaction under which one party (the creditor):

- supplies goods under a hire purchase agreement or a conditional sale agreement;
- sells land under a hire purchase agreement or a conditional sale agreement;
- leases or hires goods in return for periodical payments;
- leases or hires land in return for periodical payments;
- otherwise supplies goods or services on the understanding that payment is to be deferred or
- otherwise disposes of land on the understanding that payment is to be deferred.

8.30   *Directors and Persons Connected with a Director*

For these purposes, a director includes a shadow director and any person occupying the position of director, regardless of his/her actual title. Under CA 1985, the following are to be treated as persons connected with a director:

- The director's spouse.
- A child or stepchild under the age of 18 (including an illegitimate child).
- A body corporate with which the director is associated, and where the director and his/her connected persons are:
  ○ interested in at least 20% of the nominal value of the equity share capital or
  ○ entitled to exercise, or control the exercise of, more than 20% of the voting power at a general meeting.

- The trustee of any trust, where the beneficiaries include:
  - the director;
  - his/her spouse;
  - his/her child (as defined above);
  - a body corporate with which he/she is associated (as defined above).
- The trustee of any trust whose terms confer on the trustees a power that may be exercised for the benefit of those noted (a person acting as trustee under an employee share scheme or a pension scheme is specifically excluded).
- A partner of the director or of any person connected with the director.
- A Scottish firm in which the director, or any person connected with him/her, is a partner or which has as a partner another Scottish firm in which the director, or a person connected with him/her, is a partner.

A person who is a director of the same company in his/her own right is not treated as a connected person of another director, even if the above criteria are met.

With effect from 1 October 2007, certain changes are made to the definition of a connected person under CA 2006. Persons connected with a director are defined in Section 252 of the CA 2006 as (and only as):

- members of the director's family, which are defined in Section 253 as:
  - the director's spouse or civil partner;
  - any person (of either sex) with whom the director lives as partner in an enduring family relationship (a grandparent, grandchild, sister, brother, aunt, uncle, nephew or niece are specifically excluded);
  - the director's children or step-children;
  - any children or step-children of a person in the second category above who also live with the director and have not yet reached the age of 18 and
  - the director's parents;
- a body corporate with whom the director is connected (as defined by Section 254, which in effect re-enacts the existing definition from CA 1985);
- a person acting in his capacity as trustee of a trust, the beneficiaries of which include the director or a person connected with him as described above, or the terms of which confer a power on the trustees that may be exercised for the benefit of the director or a person connected with him as described above – a trust for the purposes of an employees' share scheme or a pension scheme is specifically excluded from this definition;
- a person acting in his capacity as partner of the director or of a person connected with a director by virtue of any of the categories above and
- a firm that is a legal person under the law by which it is governed and in which:
  - the director is a partner;
  - a person connected with a director under one of the first three categories above is a partner; or
  - one of the partners is a firm in which the director is a partner, or in which a person connected with the director under one of the first three categories above is a partner.

A person who is himself a director of the company continues to be specifically excluded from the definition of a person connected with a director.

8.31 New Provisions Under CA 2006

New provisions on loans and other transactions with directors are brought into effect from 1 October 2007 under CA 2006. The new legislation generally relaxes the prohibitions imposed by CA 1985 and allows loans and similar transactions to take place with the approval of the members.

Under Section 197 of CA 2006, a company can only make a loan to a director of the company or of its holding company, or give a guarantee or provide a security for such a loan, if the transaction has been formally approved by the members of the company. If the director concerned is a director of the company's holding company, the transaction must also be approved by the members of the holding company. Before granting approval, the members must be provided with a memorandum setting out:

- the nature of the transaction;
- the amount of the loan and the purpose for which it is required and
- the extent of the company's liability under any transaction connected with the loan.

In addition, under Sections 198–201 of CA 2006, a public company, or a private company that is associated with a public company, must have the approval of the members of the company (and, where relevant, also of the holding company) in order to:

- make a quasi-loan to a director of the company or its holding company, or give a guarantee or provide security in connection with such a quasi-loan;
- make a quasi-loan to a person connected with a director of the company or its holding company, or give a guarantee or provide security in connection with such a quasi-loan and
- enter into a credit transaction (as creditor) for the benefit of a director of the company or its holding company, or a person connected with such a director, or give a guarantee or provide security in connection with such a credit transaction.

In all cases, the members must be provided with a memorandum setting out details of the transaction and the extent of the company's liability, as described above.

The legislation also includes provisions to ensure that similar approval requirements apply in respect of:

- any arrangement under which another person enters into a transaction that would have required approval if had been entered into by the company and, as part of the arrangement, obtains a benefit from the company or a body corporate associated with it and
- any arrangement for the assignment to the company, or the assumption by it, of any rights, obligations or liabilities under a transaction that would have required approval by the members if it had been entered into by the company.

Directors' Duties and Liabilities

There are a number of exceptions to the general rules, covering in particular:

- loans, quasi-loans, credit transactions and related guarantees or security to meet expenditure on company business, provided that the total value of transactions under this exception in respect of a director and any person connected with him does not exceed £50,000;
- money lent to fund a director's defence costs for legal proceedings in connection with any alleged negligence, default, breach of duty or breach of trust by him in relation to the company or an associated company, or in connection with regulatory action or investigation under the same circumstances;
- small loans and quasi-loans, provided that the total value of such loans and quasi-loans made in respect of a director and any person connected with him does not exceed £10,000;
- small credit transactions, provided that the total value of such credit transactions made in respect of a director and any person connected with him does not exceed £15,000;
- credit transactions made in the ordinary course of the company's business;
- intra-group transactions and
- subject to certain conditions, loans and quasi-loans made by a money-lending company in the ordinary course of the company's business.

8.32   Payments for Loss of Office

Most payments to directors for loss of office require formal approval by the members (see also **PARAGRAPH 9.19**). Depending on the particular circumstances, they may also require approval as substantial property transactions (see **PARAGRAPH 8.26**). New provisions on the circumstances in which member approval is required for payments for loss of office to a director of the company or its holding company have been introduced with effect from 1 October 2007 under Sections 215–222 of CA 2006. These replace the requirements previously set out in Sections 312–316 of CA 1985. Changes under the new provisions include:

- Extending the requirements to include:
  - payments to connected persons;
  - payments to directors in respect of the loss of any office or employment in connection with the management of the affairs of the company, and not merely loss of office as a director and
  - payments by a company to a director of its holding company.
- Extending the requirements in connection with the transfer of the undertaking or property of a company to include transfers of the undertaking or property of a subsidiary.
- Extending the requirements in connection with share transfers so as to include all transfers of shares in the company or in a subsidiary resulting from a takeover bid.
- Providing an exception for payments in discharge of certain legal obligations.
- Creating a new exception for very small payments.

8.33 Disclosure of Loans and Other Transactions with Directors

---

At a Glance

* With a small number of specific exceptions, all loans and quasi-loans to, and credit transactions with, directors are disclosable in the annual accounts, together with corresponding amounts for the previous year.
* If the required disclosures are not given, the auditors must give the information in their audit report, so far as they are reasonably able to do so.
* New disclosure requirements are due to be introduced under CA 2006.
* Annual accounts must also include details of other transactions in which a director had a material interest, either directly or indirectly.
* The board must act in good faith in deciding whether or not an interest is material for disclosure purposes.
* FRS 8 *Related Party Disclosures* also includes guidance on when a transaction should be regarded as material.
* The required details must be given individually for each director and for each relevant transaction or arrangement in the current year.
* If the required disclosures are not given, the auditors must give the information in their audit report, so far as they are reasonably able to do so.
* CA 1985 sets out a number of exceptions to the general disclosure requirements, principally in respect of transactions between group companies and those involving only small amounts.
* Additional information may need to be given in respect of some transactions with directors, under the disclosure requirements of FRS 8 *Related Party Disclosures*.
* In the case of a listed company, a transaction that involves a related party will usually require both an announcement to the market and a circular to shareholders seeking their approval.
* Loans and similar transactions involving other officers of the company must also be disclosed in the annual accounts under CA 1985.
* It can be helpful to set up standard procedures to identify any disclosable transactions each year, and to keep them to a minimum.

8.34 Disclosure of Loans, Quasi-loans and Credit Transactions Under CA 1985

With a small number of specific exceptions, all loans and quasi-loans to, and credit transactions with, directors are disclosable in the annual accounts under Section 232 of, and Schedule 6 to, CA 1985 regardless of whether or not they are permitted under the legislation. The same requirements apply to both International Accounting Standard (IAS) and Companies Act accounts. The disclosure requirements specifically include any related guarantees and securities and must cover all transactions involving anyone who was:

- a director of the company at any time during the financial year;
- a director of the company's holding company at any time during the financial year or
- a person connected with any such a director.

Under Paragraph 19 of Schedule 6 to CA 1985, the fact that a transaction may have originated before an individual became a director of the company (or before a company became a subsidiary) will not exempt it from disclosure if there was an amount outstanding under that transaction during the year. For example, if an employee receives a loan from the company at the beginning of the year and repays it when he is appointed as a director of the company later in the year, details of the loan will still be disclosable in the accounts for that year. Similar considerations apply when individuals become connected persons during the year. Under Section 237(4) of CA 1985, if the disclosure requirements have not been complied with, the auditors must include the relevant details in their audit report, so far as they are reasonably able to do so.

These disclosure requirements will be replaced in due course by new provisions under CA 2006 (see **PARAGRAPH 8.37**). In the meantime, as part of the introduction of the new approval requirements under CA 2006 which apply from 1 October 2007 (see **PARAGRAPH 8.31**), Schedule 6 to CA 1985 has been amended to ensure that all loans, quasi-loans and credit transactions involving directors and their connected persons (other than the small number of specific exceptions) continue to be disclosable, irrespective of whether they were entered into before, on or after 1 October 2007.

8.35 *Exceptions to Disclosure Requirement*

There is no requirement under company law to disclose a transaction or arrangement which was not entered into during the year and did not exist at any time during the year (i.e. transactions entered into and settled in earlier years do not continue to be disclosable – but see **PARAGRAPH 8.36** in respect of corresponding amounts). Also, credit transactions and related guarantees, securities and arrangements are not disclosable if the aggregate of the values of each transaction or arrangement for that director and his/her connected persons, after allowing for any reduction of the liabilities, does not exceed £5000. Therefore, if an individual director, together with any connected persons, does not have more than £5000 outstanding in respect of credit transactions, the details do not have to be disclosed. There is no *de minimis* disclosure exemption in respect of loans and quasi-loans to directors and connected persons.

8.36 *Comparative Information*

For accounting periods beginning before 1 January 2005, there was no requirement to provide comparative information in respect of loans to, and similar transactions with, directors in Companies Act accounts. However, the provisions of CA 1985 on the disclosure of comparatives were amended by the Companies Act 1985 (Investment Companies and Accounting and Audit Amendment) Regulations 2005 (SI 2005/2280) and the detailed requirements on the disclosure of comparatives are now set out in FRS 28 *Corresponding Amounts*. Although most of the specific exemptions previously set out in the legislation were retained, the Accounting Standards Board (ASB) took the view that comparative information on loans and similar transactions involving directors was readily available and would be useful to users of the accounts. FRS 28 therefore requires comparatives to be disclosed for accounting periods beginning on or after 1 January 2005 and ending on or after 1 October 2005. Comparatives should still be given, even if there is no amount to be disclosed for the current year. In the case of IAS accounts, the disclosure of comparative information is required by IAS 1 *Presentation of Financial Statements*.

8.37   Disclosure of Loans and Similar Transactions Under CA 2006

New disclosure requirements in respect of advances and credits granted to directors, and guarantees entered into on behalf of directors, by the company or its subsidiaries are to be introduced under CA 2006. The new disclosure requirements are set out in Section 413 of CA 2006 – this comes within Part 15 of the Act on accounts and reports, and so is due to be brought into effect from 6 April 2008.

The terminology and disclosure requirements are much more straightforward than under the present legislation. In the case of advances or credits, the disclosures cover the amount involved, the interest rate, the main conditions and any amounts repaid. In the case of guarantees, the disclosures include the main terms, the maximum potential liability for the company, and any amount paid or liability incurred. Totals must also be given for each of the monetary disclosures. There are no *de minimis* limits for the disclosure requirements.

Comparative information for these disclosures will continue to be required under FRS 28 or IAS 1 as appropriate (see **PARAGRAPH 8.36**).

8.38   Disclosure of Other Transactions with Directors

In addition to the detailed disclosures required for loans to directors, company law also requires disclosure in the annual accounts of any transaction or arrangement in which a director had a material interest, either directly or indirectly. The disclosure requirements apply to both IAS and Companies Act accounts. For these purposes, a director is treated as being interested in any transaction between:

- the company and the director, or a person connected with him/her or
- the company's holding company and the director, or a person connected with him/her.

Only those transactions in which a director has a material interest are disclosable in the accounts and the interpretation of what constitutes a material interest is one of the most difficult aspects of this legislation. The duty of each director to disclose to the other directors any interest that he has in a contract, arrangement or agreement involving the company is considered in more detail in **PARAGRAPH 8.16**. A substantial property transaction between the company and a director may also require prior shareholder approval under company law (see **PARAGRAPH 8.26**).

8.39   Materiality

Paragraph 17(2) of Schedule 6 to CA 1985 provides that an interest is not material for disclosure purposes if the board of directors of the company are of the opinion that it is not material. It is generally accepted that the board must act in good faith in reaching this decision, although the legislation makes no specific statement on this. In this context, the board is defined as 'the directors of the company preparing the accounts, or a majority of those directors, but excluding in either case the director whose interest it is.' Therefore, the director involved in the transaction must not take part in the board's decision on whether or not it is material for disclosure purposes. CA 1985 makes no mention of recording the board's decision, but it is usually advisable for the board's discussion and decision to be formally minuted. Two approaches to the interpretation of 'material' have developed:

- the relevant view – a transaction is material if knowledge of it might influence the decisions taken by the shareholders or users of the accounts, or be of specific interest to them and
- the substantive view – a transaction is material if the director's interest in it is substantial, even though the transaction itself may be small.

One of the major problems with the substantive view is that a small interest in a major contract could be considered insubstantial and therefore not material (e.g. a commission of 1% payable to a director on a company contract worth £1 million), whereas many people would consider that this is precisely the sort of arrangement that the shareholders would want to know about. The balance has tended, therefore, to favour the relevant view, but if there is any doubt over whether a transaction involving a director, or a person connected with him/her, is one in which the director has a material interest, legal advice should be taken.

Under CA 2006, the detailed disclosure requirements that are currently included in various Schedules to CA 1985 are to be included instead in regulations made under the new Act. The Department of Trade and Industry (DTI) consultation document 'Implementation of Companies Act 2006' published in February 2007 indicates an intention to retain most of the current requirements without significant change.

8.40   FRS 8/IAS 24 Approach to Materiality

The ASB also adopted the relevant view in FRS 8 *Related Party Disclosures* but preserved some element of the substantial view in respect of transactions involving directors:

> 'Transactions are material when their disclosure might reasonably be expected to influence decisions made by users of general purpose financial statements. The materiality of related party transactions is to be judged, not only in terms of their significance to the reporting entity, but also in relation to the other related party when that party is:
>
> (a) a director, key manager or other individual in a position to influence, or accountable for stewardship of, the reporting entity; or
> (b) a member of the close family of any individual mentioned above or
> (c) an entity controlled by any individual mentioned in (a) or (b) above.'

IAS 24 *Related Party Disclosures* does not include specific consideration of materiality in the context of the disclosure of related party transactions. The requirements of IAS 1 *Presentation of Financial Statements* on materiality continue to apply (see **PARAGRAPH 10.32**) but this standard considers the issue of materiality only from the perspective of the reporting entity. In practice, and especially given the level of shareholder interest in the level of remuneration and other benefits received by directors, it is usually accepted that the significance of the transaction to the individual concerned also needs to be taken into account. Consequently, compliance with IAS 24 will generally require a similar approach to that outlined in FRS 8.

8.41   Detailed Disclosures Under Company Law

Where a director has a material interest in a transaction, the following information must be given in the notes to the accounts:

- a statement that the transaction or arrangement was made or existed during the year;
- the name of the director who has a material interest in the transaction and the nature of that interest;
- where relevant the name of the connected person involved in the transaction and the name of the director with whom he/she is connected;
- the value of the transaction or arrangement and
- the principal terms of the transaction or arrangement (for instance, the rate of commission earned by the director in respect of a contract involving the company).

These details must be given individually for each relevant transaction during the year. Comparative amounts are now also required to be disclosed under FRS 28 or IAS 1 as appropriate (see **PARAGRAPH 8.36**). If the disclosure requirements have not been complied with, the auditors are required to include the relevant details in their audit report, so far as they are reasonably able to do so.

8.42 Value of a Transaction or Arrangement

The value of a transaction or arrangement is the price that could reasonably be expected to be obtained for the respective goods, services or land if they had been supplied in the ordinary course of business and on the same terms (apart from price) as they are supplied in the transaction under consideration – in other words, the price that would normally be obtained in an arm's length transaction. If the value of any transaction or arrangement cannot be expressed as a specific sum of money, for whatever reason, its value is deemed to exceed £100,000.

8.43 Exceptions to the General Disclosure Requirement

Company law provides for a number of exceptions to the general disclosure requirements including:

- a transaction between two companies does not need to be disclosed if the director's interest in the contract arises only from the fact that he is a director of both of the companies involved in the transaction;
- a contract of service between the company and a director of the company, a director of the company's holding company, or a director of any of the company's subsidiaries does not require disclosure under these provisions;
- there is no requirement to disclose a transaction or arrangement which was not entered into during the year and did not exist at any time during the year (i.e. transactions entered into and settled in earlier years do not continue to be disclosable);
- an arm's length transaction between companies in the same group does not require disclosure under these provisions;
- disclosure of a transaction between group companies should only be necessary where the company has minority interests (although the wording of this part of the legislation is ambiguous) and
- disclosure is not required where the value of disclosable transactions or arrangements involving the director, including any outstanding amounts from previous years, did not at any time during the financial year exceed in aggregate £1000 or, if more, did not exceed the lower of £5000 or 1% of the company's net assets at the end of the financial year – for this purpose, a company's net assets are the aggregate of its assets, less the aggregate of its liabilities, including any provisions for liabilities and charges.

8.44 FRS 8/IAS 24 Disclosure Requirements

FRS 8 and IAS 24 (see **PARAGRAPH 8.40**) require detailed disclosures to be given in respect of material related party transactions (which include transactions with directors). In the case of transactions with directors, some of these duplicate the disclosure requirements of company law, but others may require additional information to be given in certain cases. The ASB issued Financial Reporting Exposure Draft (FRED) 41 Related Party Disclosures in July 2007 as part of its project to achieve convergence between UK accounting standards and international accounting standards. The Exposure Draft proposes replacing FRS 8 with requirements based on the latest version of IAS 24. The main changes under the proposed new standard are that:

(i) group transactions will no longer be exempt from disclosure in the individual accounts of a parent company or of a subsidiary where 90% of more of the voting rights are controlled within the group – however, the ASB plans to include a disclosure exemption for group transactions involving wholly-owned subsidiaries, consistent with the Government's current proposals for UK implementation of recent amendments to EC Company Law Directives;

(ii) there will be a new requirement to disclose key management personnel compensation, both in total and analysed into specified categories of payment – although company law already requires detailed disclosures on directors' remuneration, the new standard is likely to increase the disclosure requirements for unquoted companies in particular; and

(iii) there will no longer be a requirement to disclose the names of transacting related parties, although the detailed disclosures will have to be given separately for each category of related party (e.g. parent, subsidiaries, key management personnel etc.).

The relevant company law changes are due to be introduced in conjunction with the detailed accounting requirements of CA 2006, with the expectation that they will apply for accounting periods beginning on or after 6 April 2008, and the ASB envisages a similar commencement date for the new standard.

8.45   Additional Requirements for Listed Companies

In the case of a listed company, a transaction that involves a related party (e.g. a transaction between the company or its subsidiary and a director or substantial shareholder or their associate) will usually require both an announcement to the market and a circular to shareholders seeking their approval. Very small transactions are generally exempt from these requirements, although details must be provided in writing to the UKLA before the transaction takes place, together with:

• confirmation from an acceptable independent adviser that the terms of the transaction are fair and reasonable and
• an undertaking to give details of the transaction in the next annual report and accounts.

The definition of a related party for these purposes is complex and companies should therefore consult their professional advisers and the UKLA to clarify the precise requirements in each case.

8.46 Loans to Other Officers of the Company

Under CA 1985, a company must also disclose in its annual accounts details of loans and similar transactions involving officers of the company other than directors. Once again, there are separate rules in respect of banks and money-lending companies. There are, however, no prohibitions on making loans to officers of the company, provided that the individuals are not also directors. The detailed disclosure requirements are set out in Part III of Schedule 6 to the CA 1985 and apply to both IAS and Companies Act accounts. All definitions are the same as those for loans to and similar transactions with directors. There is also a similar requirement for the auditors to give any missing disclosures in their audit report, so far as they are reasonably able to do so. Comparative information on loans to other officers is now also disclosable under FRS 28 or IAS 1 as appropriate (see **PARAGRAPH 8.36**).

However, loans to officers will no longer be disclosable under CA 2006. As explained in **PARAGRAPH 8.37**, the relevant changes under CA 2006 are expected to be brought into effect from 6 April 2008.

8.47 Company Procedures

Companies may find it helpful to develop a standard form for completion each year which requires every director to give formal confirmation that he/she has not been involved in any disclosable transactions or arrangements with the company, or to provide the relevant information. Such a form could include a summary of the company law requirements to remind directors of the importance of these matters. Company procedures might also include detailed guidance in the form of a directors' Code of conduct to ensure that disclosable transactions are kept to a minimum. For instance, clear rules on the way in which company credit cards are to be used and how any purchases through the company should be dealt with may help to ensure that disclosable transactions do not arise.

8.48 Share Dealings by Directors of Listed Companies

At a Glance
* A listed company must notify a Regulatory Information Service without delay of any dealings in the company's shares, or any grant of share options, involving a director or persons connected with them.
* The directors of a listed company are expected to comply with a company Code on share dealing that is no less exacting than the Model Code included in the UK Listing Rules.
* Directors and relevant employees must not deal in the company's shares without receiving clearance to do so from the chairman or another designated director.

* The company must keep a written record of all requests for clearance to deal, and of the responses given to those requests.
* Exceptions to the general rule are permitted in limited circumstances.
* Any failure to comply with the Model Code (or the company's equivalent) must be notified to the UKLA.

8.49   Notification to a Regulatory Information Service

The continuing obligations of a listed company are set out in the UK Listing Rules and the FSA's Disclosure and Transparency Rules. Both the UK Listing Rules and the Disclosure and Transparency Rules are available from the FSA website at www.fsahandbook.info/FSA/. As part of its continuing obligations, a listed company must notify a Regulatory Information Service without delay of:

* any dealings in the company's shares by directors (and persons connected with them) and
* any grant of options to a director or a person connected with him.

8.50   Compliance with the Model Code

The Model Code is appended to UK Listing Rule LR9 'Continuing Obligations' and is designed to ensure that directors and certain other relevant employees, and persons connected with them, do not deal in the company's securities when they may be in possession of unpublished price sensitive information. Listed companies must require their directors and other relevant employees to comply with a Code on share dealings that is no less exacting than the Model Code and are free to impose more stringent requirements if they wish. Both the Disclosure and Transparency Rules (DTRs) and the Model Code now reflect the requirements of the EU Market Abuse Directive and the EU Transparency Directive. Under DTR 2.8, listed companies are required to draw up a list of persons with access to inside information, whether on a regular or occasional basis. When requested, a listed company must make this list available to the FSA as soon as possible. The list must show the identity of each individual and the reason why they are included on the list, and must show the date on which the list was created or updated. The list must be updated promptly when names need to be added to or deleted from the list, or when there is a change in the reason why an individual is included in the list. The company must also take appropriate steps to ensure that those with access to inside information understand their legal and regulatory obligations, including dealing restrictions in respect of the company's shares. Generally:

* directors must not deal in any of the company's securities without obtaining advance clearance from the company chairman or another designated director;
* the chairman must not deal in any of the company's securities without obtaining advance clearance from the chief executive – if the roles of chairman and

chief executive are combined, advance clearance to deal must be obtained from the board and

- relevant individuals who are not directors must not deal in the company's securities without obtaining advance clearance from the company secretary or a designated director.

Clearance cannot be given if there is any unpublished price sensitive information, even if the individual director or employee is not aware of that information, or during close periods (i.e. specified periods before an announcement of results). The company must keep a written record of all requests for clearance to deal, and of the responses given to those requests. If permission to deal is granted, the individual concerned must deal as soon as possible and in any event within two business days of receiving clearance.

8.51 Exceptions in Limited Circumstances

Section 2 of the Model Code lists the dealings which are not subject to the Code and which can therefore take place at any time without prior clearance. In certain circumstances, grants of share options may be permitted during a prohibited period and the exercise of options during such a period may also be allowed in limited circumstances, but sale of the resulting securities will generally not be permitted. Permission to sell, but not to buy, may also be given in exceptional circumstances – the Model Code gives as an example a pressing personal financial commitment that cannot otherwise be satisfied. Directors may also be given permission to acquire qualification shares in certain circumstances.

8.52 Breaches of the Code

Any failure to comply with the Model Code (or the company's equivalent) must be notified to the UKLA as soon as possible. The UKLA will also contact the company if it becomes aware of an unnotified breach, to request an explanation. The UKLA may take disciplinary action and may require notification of the circumstances of the breach to a Regulatory Information Service.

Appendix 1

Useful Websites on Directors' Duties and Related Issues

Institute of Directors	www.iod.com
Companies House	www.companieshouse.gov.uk
BERR	www.berr.gov.uk/
DTI: Companies Act 2006	www.dti.gov.uk/bbf/co-act-2006/index.html
Financial Services Authority	www.fsa.gov.uk
Institute of Chartered Secretaries and Administrators	www.icsa.org.uk
Business Link	www.businesslink.gov.uk
Institute of Chartered Accountants in England and Wales	www.icaew.co.uk

Directors' Duties and Liabilities

9

Directors' Remuneration and Benefits

9 Directors' Remuneration and Benefits

9.1 Introduction

9.2 Directors' Remuneration

Before getting into the detail of what has become a very complex and sensitive subject, it is important from the non-executive director's point of view to consider the following, whether they are on the remuneration committee or not.

- What are the objectives?
  - there should be an overarching objective to build shareholder value;
  - there should be an alignment of the remuneration schemes and the performance objectives of the company and
  - remuneration schemes for directors should be to attract and retain relevant talent.
- What principles should the board apply in designing and implementing the directors' remuneration?
  - be market driven;
  - be commercial and fair;
  - comply with legal and accounting standards;
  - avoid unnecessary complexity and
  - be tax efficient for company and director.
- What is the process by which the board makes the key decisions with relation to directors' remuneration?

- the board process;
- a process for ensuring legal compliance;
- accounting compliance;
- investor approval and
- ensuring the engagement of the key participants.
- How will directors' remuneration issues be communicated?
  - internally and
  - externally.

Increasing complexity in the instruments used to reward directors combined with higher levels of disclosure on directors' remuneration, a perception of a widening gap between director and non-director remuneration and a greater degree of investor and media scrutiny have made this subject a considerable challenge for non-executive directors.

It is therefore very important that the non-executive keeps up to date with the latest trends, best practice and debate on the subject. A good example of the importance of this, and one covered in detail below, would be the level of knowledge required to contribute to a debate on the implications of the latest proposals on accounting for payments made in the form of shares.

The key driver of process in this area should be the remuneration committee, supported if appropriate by professional consultants. **CHAPTER 18** covers this considerably in more detail.

Disclosure appears to have become a bigger and bigger issue each year and is covered in detail below. The number of pages given over to the disclosure on directors' remuneration in many companies now exceeds that used to describe the activities of the business.

One particular aspect of directors' remuneration which was the subject of considerable debate in the early part of this decade related to the pros and cons of share options and accounting treatment.

9.3 Share Options

Share options can be a powerful mechanism for aligning the interests of management and staff with those of shareholders and most large public companies have schemes in place.

However some would argue that due to the volatility of stock markets and the good or bad fortune of the timing of grant and exercise dates, the alignment of reward and genuine performance in public companies is seldom perfect and often arbitrary.

Opponents to option schemes also argue that options are:

'A one way bet, there is no downside to an option, unlike shareholders who have actually invested hard cash to buy their shares.'

There are many issues for non-executives to consider when being asked to approve share option schemes. The following are just some of the issues to consider:

- What are the fundamental purposes of the scheme? For example, to retain key people, to focus people on maximising the value of the company, etc.

- How does the scheme fit within the overall remuneration strategy of the company?
- Is the company publicly listed or not?
- What proportion of the company's equity should be allocated to the scheme?
- Will new shares, treasury shares or market purchases be used to enable the scheme to function?
- Who will be eligible for share options? Is it for the top management only or is the scheme to be more widely spread amongst employees.
- How are options to be granted, in a one off exercise or through regular grants?
- The pricing of options.
- What performance measures will be used?
- The mechanisms for exercising and selling shares as a result of a share option scheme. Special care is obviously required if the company is private.
- Gaining the approval of shareholders.
- Is the scheme market competitive?
- The accounting treatment of share options.
- Tax. In the UK there are schemes which are approved by the Revenue and unapproved schemes. The Revenue's website www.Hmrc.gov.uk contains the criteria for approved schemes as well as other useful information relating to the taxation aspects of share option schemes. It also includes specimen scheme rules for an approved scheme.

The Combined Code has a number of provisions relating to Remuneration policy and also contains a schedule of provisions (A) which relate to the design of performance-related remuneration and refer to share-based incentives. Provision 4 in this Schedule captures the tone well

> 'Payouts or grants under all incentive schemes should be subject to challenging perform-ance criteria reflecting the company's objectives. Consideration should be given to crite-ria which reflect the company's performance relative to a group of companies in some key variables such as total shareholder return.'

This is also a complex and technical area and it is wise for any non-executive director to make sure that the board is professionally advised from a legal, accounting and human resources perspective.

With respect to accounting for share options the main international accounting standard (IAS) relating to share options and share option schemes is International Financial Reporting Standard 2 ('IFRS 2') (see **PARAGRAPH 9.12**). The International Accounting Standards board (IASB) have set up a website www.eifrs.iasb.org which contains HTML versions of the most up to date IASB information together with accompanying documents. You do however have to be subscriber to gain access to the most useful information on this site. The Finance Director or the company's auditors will probably be subscribers so it should be rel-atively straightforward to obtain the necessary documentation you require. Where relevant the Chairman of the remuneration committee will normally also be very familiar with the issues.

Directors' Remuneration and Benefits

9.4 Disclosure of Directors' Remuneration

At a Glance
* Company law requires detailed disclosures on directors' remuneration to be given in the notes to the accounts.
* Separate disclosure requirements apply for quoted and unquoted companies.
* Additional requirements also apply to listed companies under the Financial Services Authority (FSA) Listing Rules.
* Aggregate disclosures must be given in respect of emoluments, contributions to defined contribution retirement schemes, share options, amounts payable under long-term incentive schemes and the number of directors accruing benefits under defined benefit retirement schemes.
* Slightly reduced disclosure requirements apply in the case of small companies.
* Additional aggregate information must be given by quoted and Alternative Investment Market (AIM) companies.
* The auditors are required to include any missing information in their audit report.
* The money value of any benefits in kind must be included in emoluments.
* Bonus payments that require shareholder approval should normally be included in emoluments in the year in which they are approved.
* Accounting standards set out detailed requirements on the treatment of remuneration paid in the form of shares or share options.
* Awards under long-term incentive schemes are disclosable when the director becomes entitled to receive payment.
* All pension schemes must be classified as either defined contribution or defined benefit for disclosure purposes.
* Amounts paid to, or receivable by, a person connected with a director must be included in the disclosures.
* Particular difficulties can arise in groups of companies, especially if all directors' remuneration is paid by the holding company.

9.5 Disclosure Under Company Law

A company's annual accounts must include detailed information on remuneration paid to, or receivable by, anyone who was a director during the year. The disclosure requirements cover all amounts receivable by the directors in respect of their services as directors of the company (and, where relevant, of its subsidiaries), regardless of who actually makes the payment. The legislation requires basic disclosures to be given by all companies, and then makes a clear distinction between quoted and unquoted companies in requiring more detailed information to be given. The *Directors' Remuneration Report Regulations 2002 (SI 2002/1986)* introduced some significant changes to the disclosure requirements for quoted companies for accounting periods ending on or after 31 December 2002. For these purposes, a quoted company is defined as a company whose equity share capital is:

- included in the Official List of the London Stock Exchange;
- officially listed in an EEA State or
- admitted to dealing on the New York Stock Exchange or the Nasdaq exchange.

The same disclosure requirements on directors' remuneration apply, irrespective of whether the company prepares Companies Act or IAS accounts (see **PARAGRAPH 10.4**).

9.6 *Basic Accounts Disclosures for all Companies*

The basic requirement is that every company should disclose in the notes to the accounts:

- The aggregate of the emoluments paid to, or receivable by, the directors in respect of their qualifying services (which include services as director of a subsidiary or in the management of the company or group).
- The aggregate value of any contributions paid by the company in respect of directors into a pension scheme where the benefits depend on the level of contributions paid (i.e. defined contribution schemes – see **CHAPTER 17**).
- The number of directors who are accruing retirement benefits under money purchase schemes.
- The number of directors who are accruing retirement benefits under defined benefit schemes.

The contributions made during the year to define benefit retirement schemes do not have to be disclosed. Slightly reduced disclosure requirements apply in the case of small companies. Emoluments are defined in company law as including salary, bonus, fees, benefits in kind, expense allowances (if these are chargeable to UK income tax) and amounts paid on acceptance of office as director. This list is not intended to be exhaustive and any other similar amounts paid to, or receivable by, directors will therefore be disclosable. Share options, pension contributions and amounts payable under long-term incentive schemes are specifically excluded from the definition of emoluments as they are subject to separate disclosure requirements.

9.7 *Quoted and AIM Companies*

In addition to the above aggregate information, quoted companies and those whose equity share capital is listed on the AIM must disclose:

- the aggregate gains made by directors on the exercise of share options and
- the aggregate of the amounts paid to, or receivable by, directors under long-term incentive schemes in respect of qualifying services and the net value of any assets (other than cash or share options) receivable by directors under such schemes.

In the case of listed companies, certain additional disclosure requirements are imposed by the continuing obligations requirements of the FSA Listing Rules.

9.8 *Avoiding Duplication*

If any of the required details are readily ascertainable from other information included with the accounts, such as a remuneration report (see **PARAGRAPH 9.20**), they generally do not have to be disclosed again. The one exception is aggregate gains on the exercise of share options which must always be shown separately in the notes to the accounts. In practice, if the detailed information is included in a separate directors' remuneration report, it is helpful for the notes to the accounts to include a cross-reference to where it can be found.

9.9 Audit Requirements

If the accounts do not include all of the required disclosures in respect of directors' emoluments and other benefits, or transactions between the company and its directors or other officers, the auditors must include a statement of the missing details in their audit report, so far as they are reasonably able to do so. In the case of listed companies, the FSA has extended this requirement to cover disclosures required under the Listing Rules and it also applies to certain elements of the information that must be included in the directors' remuneration report (see **PARAGRAPH 9.20**).

9.10 Benefits in Kind

Emoluments specifically include the estimated money value of benefits in kind received by a director otherwise than in cash. The most common benefits in kind are as follows:

- company car;
- free or subsidised accommodation;
- insurance for the benefit of the director (e.g. private health cover, indemnity insurance, personal accident cover);
- loans at preferential interest rates and
- relocation costs (unless the relocation is clearly for business purposes).

Some of these may also be disclosable in the annual accounts as loans or transactions with directors (see **CHAPTER 8**). Share options are subject to separate disclosure requirements and are therefore specifically excluded from emoluments for disclosure purposes. The main difficulty with benefits in kind is establishing an appropriate and realistic money value for the benefit. In most cases, market value will provide the best estimate of money value.

9.11   Bonus Payments

Provision should usually be made in the accounts for bonuses in the year in which they are earned. Where a bonus payment to directors requires approval by the shareholders before the directors are entitled to receive it, it is usual to treat the bonus as being receivable by the directors (and therefore disclosable within directors' emoluments) in the year in which shareholder approval is given, even though the bonus may have been charged to the profit and loss account in an earlier period.

9.12   Shares and Share Options

In addition to the disclosures on share options referred to in **PARAGRAPH 9.7**, extensive disclosures on share options must also be given in the directors' remuneration report prepared by a quoted company (see **PARAGRAPH 9.20**). It should also be noted that detailed requirements on accounting for payments in the form of shares or share options now apply under FRS 20 *Share-based payment* or IFRS 2 *Share-based payment* as appropriate. The standards apply to all share-based payment transactions, including employee share option schemes, Save-As-You-Earn (SAYE) schemes and similar arrangements for directors and other employees, as well as any share-based transactions involving third party goods and services. The standards identify two main types of share-based payment:

- equity-settled share-based payments – where payment under the transaction is made in the form of equity instruments and
- cash-settled share-based payments – where payment is made in cash or other assets, but the amount paid is based on the value of an equity instrument of the reporting entity.

Equity-settled transactions with directors and other employees should always be measured at the fair value of the equity instrument granted. Separate requirements apply to share-based payment transactions involving third parties. Prior to the introduction of FRS 20 and IFRS 2, it was usually possible under UK accounting practice to structure employee share schemes so that there was no charge to the profit and loss account for director and employee remuneration paid in the form of shares or share options. Consequently, the new accounting requirements have had a significant impact on the accounts of companies making use of such schemes.

9.13   Long-term Incentive Schemes

Under company law, amounts payable under long-term incentive schemes are disclosable when they are paid to or receivable by the director. The director must therefore have the right to receive a sum before it becomes disclosable. Amounts should therefore normally be disclosed in the year in which the director becomes entitled to receive payment. In the case of a long-term incentive scheme, the director will not usually be entitled to receive payment until all the specified conditions have been met. Even though it will usually be necessary to accrue for the payments in each accounting year, these sums will not become disclosable until all the relevant conditions have been met and the director becomes entitled to receive payment. Complex schemes which extend over a number of years will sometimes include the provision of a guaranteed minimum payment to the directors once a specified target has been achieved. In this case, the guaranteed minimum payment will become disclosable in the year in which the target is achieved, as this is when the directors become entitled to the minimum payment. Further disclosures on long-term incentive schemes must be given in the directors' remuneration report (see **PARAGRAPH 9.20**).

9.14   Pension Arrangements

For the purposes of the company law disclosures referred to in **PARAGRAPH 9.6**, all pension schemes must be classified as either defined contribution or defined benefit schemes (see **CHAPTER 17**). Any death in service benefits are to be disregarded when classifying a pension scheme for disclosure purposes. A pension scheme under which a director will be entitled to receive both money purchase benefits and defined benefits is classified as a defined benefit scheme for disclosure purposes. Where a scheme provides for the director to receive money purchase benefits or defined benefits, whichever is the greater, the company is allowed to assume for disclosure purposes that the benefits will be whichever appears more likely at the end of the financial year in question. Listed companies must also give additional details on directors' pension arrangements in the directors' remuneration report (see **PARAGRAPH 9.20**).

9.15   Payments to and from Other Parties

Amounts paid to or receivable by a person connected with a director or a body corporate controlled by him are specifically included within the disclosure requirements. Disclosure therefore cannot be avoided by arranging for the payment to be made to a connected party. In the case of payments to a company owned by the director, the emoluments note to the accounts usually includes an explanation that some or all of the payments have been made through the company. Emoluments also include all relevant amounts in respect of a director's services paid by, or receivable from the company, the company's subsidiary undertakings and any other person, unless the director must in turn account to the company or any of its subsidiary undertakings for the amounts received.

9.16   Payments to Third Parties

The accounts must also disclose the aggregate amount paid to, or receivable by, third parties for making available the services of any person as a director of the company or otherwise in connection with the management of the affairs of the company or group. The most common example of this is an arrangement whereby a substantial investor in a company (e.g. a bank or venture capital company) has the right to appoint a director to the board of the investee company and payment for the services of this director is made to the investor rather than to the director himself.

9.17   Particular Problems in Groups of Companies

In some groups all directors' remuneration is paid by the holding company. Recharges may be made to subsidiary undertakings to reflect the cost of the services of their directors, but this will not always be done. This can cause difficulties over the disclosure of directors' remuneration in the accounts of the holding company and the subsidiaries. Directors' remuneration in the accounts of the holding company will comprise:

- remuneration paid to directors of the holding company in respect of their services to the company and management of the company and group and
- if any holding company directors are also directors of one or more of the subsidiaries, remuneration paid to them for their services in relation to these companies.

Remuneration paid to those who are directors of subsidiaries but who are not directors of the holding company is not disclosable in the accounts of the holding company. The same disclosure requirements apply in the holding company's accounts, regardless of whether some or all of the remuneration costs are recharged to the subsidiaries.

9.18   Disclosure in the Accounts of Subsidiaries

Where the holding company recharges the subsidiaries with the cost of remunerating their directors, each subsidiary should disclose as directors' remuneration the amount paid to the holding company in respect of directors' services to the company. If the holding company makes a global recharge to the subsidiaries to cover general management costs, including directors' remuneration, but the element for directors' remuneration cannot be separately identified, an appropriate apportionment should be made for disclosure purposes. Where the holding company does not recharge the subsidiaries with the costs of remunerating their directors, the costs borne by the holding company are still disclosable as directors' remuneration in the accounts of the subsidiary – it is not acceptable to simply disclose the fact that the directors have been remunerated by the holding company and not quantify the amount that they have received. However, it may be helpful to explain that this cost has been borne by the holding company and is not charged in the subsidiary's accounts.

Where directors of a subsidiary are also directors or employees of the holding company, it is sometimes argued that the holding company remunerates them only for their services to the holding company and that they receive no remuneration in respect of their services as directors of the subsidiary. The validity of this argument will usually depend on the amount of time that the director or employee devotes to the subsidiary company. If the time is relatively small it may be acceptable that he/she does not receive remuneration for services as a director of the subsidiary. In this case, a brief explanation should be included in the subsidiary's accounts.

9.19 Compensation for Loss of Office

The aggregate compensation for loss of office paid to, or receivable by, directors and former directors must also be disclosed. Compensation for loss of office constitutes a separate category of payment to directors and should not be included in the figure for directors' emoluments for the period. Where compensation payments include non-cash benefits, these should be included in the disclosures at their estimated money value and the nature of the benefit must be disclosed. Many compensation payments to directors will also require shareholder approval under company law, although this is not usually required for genuine payments in respect of damages for breach of contract or for pensions in respect of past services. If significant non-cash items are included, the compensation payments may also require approval under the provisions on substantial property transactions (see **PARAGRAPH 8.26**). Where a retired director continues to have an involvement with the company in a part-time or consultancy capacity, any payments in excess of normal market rates for the work performed may well include an element of compensation for loss of office, in which case the details should be disclosed.

9.20 Directors' Remuneration Report

At a Glance
* The directors of a quoted company are required to prepare a separate directors' remuneration report.
* Certain elements of the directors' remuneration report are subject to audit.
* The general meeting at which the annual reports and accounts are laid must include a resolution inviting the shareholders to approve the directors' remuneration report.
* The content of the directors' remuneration report is specified in the legislation and includes:
  ○ detailed information on the remuneration paid to each individual director;
  ○ a statement on the company's future remuneration policy;
  ○ an explanation of any performance-related elements of remuneration;
  ○ details of pension entitlements earned under a defined benefit retirement scheme;
  ○ details of service contracts and any related compensation commitments and

> ○ comparative information on shareholder return for the last five years.
> * The legislation also specifies which elements of the directors' remuneration report should be included in summary financial statements.

9.21   Requirements of Company Law

The directors of a quoted company are required to prepare a directors' remuneration report containing the detailed information currently specified in *Schedule 7A* to *CA 1985*. Current directors and those who have served as director in the preceding 5 years are given a specific duty to disclose relevant information to the company to enable the report to be prepared. The report must be formally approved by the directors and must be signed on behalf of the board by a director or by the company secretary. A signed copy must be delivered to the registrar as part of the company's annual reports and accounts. The auditors are required to report on the auditable part of the report (which is defined as the part covering the detailed disclosures on remuneration received by the directors) and to include any missing information in their audit report, so far as they are reasonably able to do so.

Similar requirements will continue to apply under *CA 2006*, although the detailed disclosures will be specified in new regulations to be prepared under that Act. The Department of Trade and Industry (DTI) consultation document 'Implementation of Companies Act 2006' published in February 2007 notes that most of the detailed requirements from the current Schedules to *CA 1985* will be incorporated into the new regulations without significant change. However, the DTI highlights a number of areas where changes are being considered and these include a proposal for the directors' remuneration report of a quoted company to include an analysis of the general pattern of remuneration for the company as a whole and how this has been taken into account in setting the remuneration of the directors. In a written statement in June 2007, the Minister for Industry and the Regions confirmed the intention to proceed with the introduction of this additional disclosure requirement.

9.22   Shareholder Approval

Under the legislation, the general meeting at which the annual reports and accounts are laid must include a resolution enabling the shareholders to approve the directors' remuneration report, and details of the resolution must be set out in the notice of the meeting. However, the legislation notes that this requirement does not mean that the entitlement of any individual to the remuneration shown in the report is conditional on the resolution being passed.

9.23   Contents of the Remuneration Report

The detailed contents required by company law are set out in **APPENDIX 2** to this chapter in the form of a disclosure checklist. The contents are divided into two sections in the legislation (those subject to audit and those not subject to audit) and this is reflected in the layout in **APPENDIX 2**. The legislation generally requires the detailed information to be given in tabular form and in a way that links the information to each director by name. A limited degree of aggregation is permitted in the disclosure of information on share options where the required details would otherwise result in a disclosure of excessive length. One of the potential problems here is the considerable amount of detail that may need to be given in the report. In presenting the disclosures, companies need to make a particular effort to ensure that the information that is likely to be of most interest to shareholders does not become obscured by the sheer volume of detail.

9.24   Pension Entitlements

Defined benefit retirement schemes usually link pension entitlement to final salary or average salary over a fixed period (say the last three years). The Greenbury Report suggested that, in these circumstances, the best measure of the pension entitlement earned by an individual director during the year was the present value of the additional entitlement earned as a result of the additional length of service, any increase in salary and any changes in the scheme, less any pension contributions made by the director during the period. The Report also recommended that any major changes compared with the previous year should be explained. These recommendations did not totally solve the problem, however, as there are two possible methods of calculating pension entitlement: the accrued benefit method and the transfer value method. A consultation exercise did not produce any clear consensus on which approach should be used for disclosure purposes – directors and companies were generally in favour of the accrued benefit method, whilst investors and their representatives generally preferred the transfer value method. The Faculty of Actuaries and the Institute of Actuaries therefore put forward recommendations proposing two separate disclosures for each director:

- the increase in his/her accrued pension entitlement, excluding any annual inflation adjustment made to all deferred pensions and
- the transfer value of the increased benefit, disclosed either as a figure calculated on the basis of actuarial advice, or by giving sufficient information for shareholders to make a reasonable assessment of the value.

These recommendations were accepted by the FSA and were incorporated in the Listing Rules, together with a requirement to disclose the total accrued pension entitlement of each director at the end of the financial year, and are now reflected in the detailed company law requirements on the content of the directors' remuneration report.

9.25   *Disclosure of Transfer Value*

Where a transfer value is disclosed, it should be calculated in accordance with Actuarial Guidance Note 11 (GN11) but should not include any deduction for underfunding. Companies may wish to make clear in the report that transfer values represent a liability of the company, not sums paid (or due) to the individual directors.

9.26 *Disclosure of Additional Information*

Where the company adopts the approach of providing additional information, this should normally include:

- the current age of the director;
- the normal retirement age of the director;
- any contributions paid or payable by the director during the year under the terms of the scheme;
- details of spouse and dependants' benefits;
- details of early retirement rights and options, and expectations of pension increases after retirement (whether guaranteed or not) and
- discretionary benefits for which allowance is made in transfer values on leaving, and any other relevant information which will significantly affect the value of benefits.

Voluntary contributions and benefits should not be included in any of these disclosures.

9.27 Share Performance Graph

In the case of the share performance graph, there is no requirement to disclose information for periods before the new regulations came into effect – in the early years, therefore, information will be given for one to four years as appropriate. The legislation includes detailed guidance on calculating total shareholder return for this purpose.

9.28 Impact of Company's General Remuneration Pattern

As explained at **PARAGRAPH 9.21**, the Government is planning to introduce a new requirement for the directors' remuneration report of a quoted company to include an analysis of the general pattern of remuneration for the company as a whole and how this has been taken into account in setting the remuneration of the directors. This links with the recommendation under the Combined Code that the remuneration committee should be sensitive to pay and employment conditions elsewhere in the company/group (see **PARAGRAPH 6.28**). The change is likely to be introduced in conjunction with the new accounts and audit provisions of *CA 2006*, which are generally due to be brought into effect from 6 April 2008. The current expectation is that any changes to current requirements will apply for accounting periods beginning on or after that date.

Directors' Remuneration and Benefits

9.29 Summary Financial Statements

The company law provisions on summary financial statements (see **PARAGRAPH 10.96**) require, in the case of a quoted company, the inclusion of either the whole of the directors' remuneration report or, as a minimum:

- aggregate information on directors' remuneration (see **PARAGRAPH 9.6**);
- the statement of the company's policy on directors' remuneration for future years and
- the performance graph summarising shareholder return.

9.30 Directors' Service Contracts

At a Glance
* The Combined Code includes specific provisions on the notice periods and compensation arrangements for directors.
* A comprehensive service contract for each executive director can help to prevent misunderstandings.
* Each non-executive director will usually have a contract for services.
* Company law includes provisions on the retention and location of directors' service contracts.
* Members of the company are entitled to inspect directors' service contracts.
* Shareholder approval is required for any contract giving a director a right of employment for more than two years, unless the company can give unconditional notice at any time.

9.31 Service Contracts and Compensation

The best practice guidance on directors' service contacts and compensation in the Combined Code (see **CHAPTER 6**) includes the following provisions:

- notice or contract periods should be set at one year or less;
- if it is necessary to offer longer notice or contract periods to directors recruited externally, these should reduce to one year or less after the initial period and
- the remuneration committee should consider what compensation commitments (including pension contributions) directors' terms of appointment would entail in the event of early termination – the aim should be to avoid rewarding poor performance and to take a robust line on reducing compensation to reflect a departing director's obligations to mitigate loss.

9.32 Service Contracts for Executive Directors

An executive director is in effect an employee of the company and it is appropriate that the terms and conditions of his/her appointment should be set out in a written contract of service between the director and the company. A comprehensive service contract can help to prevent misunderstandings and provides a useful point of reference if problems arise. Non-executive directors have a very different role to executive directors and the terms and conditions of their appointment will usually be set out in a contract for services. A service contract for an executive director should normally include:

- Specific duties of the director, including the amount of time to be spent on company activities (this may be particularly important where the individual also holds posts such as non-executive directorships in other businesses).
- Remuneration, including details of any arrangements involving:
  ○ benefits in kind (e.g. private health cover, accommodation, company car);
  ○ bonus schemes;
  ○ long-term incentive plans and
  ○ share options.
- Holiday entitlement
- Arrangements in the case of prolonged absence through illness
- Pension arrangements
- Required notice period, and procedures in the case of dismissal
- Compensation arrangements in the event of early termination of the contract
- Confidentiality arrangements.

Other issues may need to be covered, depending on the circumstances.

9.33   Contracts for Services of Non-executive Directors

The main role of non-executive directors is to make a positive contribution to the development of company strategy, and on matters such as company performance, standards of conduct and corporate governance issues. It is helpful to all parties for the terms of their appointment to be set out in a written contract for services. This will usually specify:

- the expected commitment, in terms of attendance at meetings of the board and its sub-committees and
- fee arrangements.

9.34   Company Law Requirements

Prior to 1 October 2007, where a director has a written contract of service with the company, *Section 318* of *CA 1985* requires the company to retain a copy of the contract at one of the following locations:

- the company's registered office;
- the place where the register of members is kept (if this is not the registered office) or

- the company's principal place of business (provided that this is in the part of Great Britain where the company is registered).

If a director does not have a written contract of service, the company must keep a written memorandum of the terms of his/her appointment. The same rules apply to a variation of a director's contract. A parent company is also required to keep copies of service contracts between its subsidiaries and their directors, or a written memorandum of the terms if these contracts are not in writing. Copies of all contracts and memoranda must be kept in the same place. If they are not kept at the registered office, the company must notify the Registrar of Companies of where they are held and of any changes in location. *Section 318(6)* of *CA 1985* emphasises that these arrangements apply equally in the case of shadow directors. However, there is no formal requirement for a company to retain a copy of a contract, variation or memorandum when the unexpired term is less than 12 months, or where the contract can be terminated by the company within the next 12 months without the payment of compensation.

With effect from 1 October 2007, similar requirements apply under Sections 227–330 of *CA 2006* but with certain notable changes. In particular:

- the definition of 'service contract' under the new legislation is expanded to include a contract for services and a letter of appointment to the office of director as well as a contract of service;
- the exemption under *Section 318* of *CA 1985* for service contracts with less than 12 months to run, or where the company can terminate the contract within the next 12 months without the payment of compensation, is not retained – all service contracts are therefore encompassed by the retention and inspection requirements of the new legislation and
- companies must continue to make every director's service contract available for inspection for at least one year from the date of termination or expiry of the contract.

9.35 Director Working Outside the UK

Prior to 1 October 2007, under *CA 1985*, where a director of the company, or of one of its subsidiaries, is required under his/her contract to work wholly or mainly outside the UK, the company is not required to keep a copy of the contract, but it must keep a memorandum giving the director's name and the provisions of the contract relating to its duration. In the case of a contract for a director of a subsidiary, the name and place of incorporation of the subsidiary must also be recorded in the memorandum. These memoranda must be kept in the same place as the contracts and memoranda relating to the other directors.

This exemption has not been carried forward into *CA 2006* and so contracts for directors working abroad are now subject to the same retention and inspection requirements are those for other directors. The relevant Part of *CA 2006* has been be brought into effect from 1 October 2007.

9.36   Inspection of Contracts

Prior to 1 October 2007, under *Section 318(7)* of *CA 1985*, any member of the company is entitled to inspect the copies of the directors' contracts of service (or the memoranda where there is no written service contract) without charge. If the company refuses to allow a member to inspect a contract or memorandum, the court can require immediate inspection.

With effect from 1 October 2007, similar inspection arrangements apply under *Section 229* of *CA 2006*, and members also have a new right to request a copy of any director's service contract on the payment of a fee to be set by regulations.

9.37   Shareholder Approval for Contracts for more than Two Years

Prior to 1 October 2007, under *Section 319* of *CA 1985*, a director cannot be given the right of employment with the company (or, where relevant, with the group) for a period of more than five years under an agreement which does not allow the company to give unconditional notice at any time, unless this term of the contract has been first approved by the company in general meeting (or, in the case of a private company, by written resolution). Employment is defined as including employment under a contract for services. Where the director is also a director of the company's holding company, prior approval to the arrangement must normally be given by the shareholders of both the subsidiary and the holding company (unless the subsidiary is wholly owned, in which case prior approval of the arrangement by the shareholders of the subsidiary is not required).

A written memorandum setting out the proposed agreement must be available for inspection by the members at the company's registered office for a period of at least 15 days before the meeting and at the meeting itself. In the case of a private company where agreement is to be by written resolution, a copy of the memorandum must be sent to each member before, or at the same time as, the resolution is provided for signature.

A term included in a director's contract in contravention of *Section 319* of *CA 1985* is void, and the agreement is deemed to include a term entitling the company to terminate the agreement at any time by the giving of reasonable notice.

With effect from 1 October 2007, similar requirements apply under *Section 188* of *CA 2006*, except that approval is now required for any contract that extends, or may extend for more than two years (rather than five years as under *CA 1985*).

9.38   Series of Agreements

Company law includes special provisions to prevent a company entering into a series of shorter agreements with the same director in an attempt to avoid the requirement for shareholder approval of a contract that in effect extends for more than five years under *CA 1985* or for more than two years under *CA 2006* (see **PARAGRAPH 9.37**).

Appendix 1

Useful Websites on Directors' Remuneration and Benefits

Institute of Directors	www.iod.com
Institute of Chartered Secretaries and Administrators	www.icsa.org.uk
Chartered Institute of Personnel and Development	www.cipd.co.uk
Business Link	www.businesslink.gov.uk
Financial Reporting Council	www.frc.org.uk
Accounting Standards Board	www.frc.org.uk/asb
Department for Work and Pensions	www.dwp.gov.uk
HM Revenue and Customs	www.hmrc.gov.uk
ICAEW Tax Faculty	www.icaew.co.uk/taxfac
Chartered Institute of Taxation	www.tax.org.uk

Directors' Remuneration and Benefits

Appendix 2

Directors' Remuneration Report Checklist

This checklist is based on the requirements of company law and current FSA Listing Rules. The second column indicates the origin of the disclosure requirement. Additional details may need to be given, depending on the specific circumstances of the company.

A Contents Subject to Audit

The following information must be disclosed and is subject to audit:

☐ For each director who served during the financial year, and in tabular form the total amount of   *Sch 7A, 6(1)–(2) & (4)*
   FSA LR 9.8.8(2)

- salary and/or fees;
- bonuses;
- expense allowances that are chargeable to UK income tax;
- any compensation for loss of office and similar payments;
- the estimated money value of any benefits in kind and
- the sum total of all these amounts, and the equivalent total for the previous financial year.

☐ The nature of any element of a remuneration package which is not cash   *Sch 7A, 6(3)*

☐ For each director who served during the financial year, and in tabular form, the number of shares subject to a share option (distinguishing between those with different terms and conditions) at: *Sch 7A, 7, 8(a)*
   FSA LR 9.8.8(2)

- the beginning of the year, or the date of appointment if later;
- the end of the year, or the date of ceasing to be a director if earlier.

☐	Information on share options awarded, exercised and lapsed during the year, and any variations to terms and conditions of a share option.	*Sch 7A, 8(b) & (d)* *FSA LR 9.8.8(2)*

☐ For each share option that was unexpired at any time during the year: *Sch 7A, 89(c)* *FSA LR 9.8.8(2)*

- the price (if any) paid for its award;
- the exercise prices;
- the date from which the option can be exercised; and
- the date on which the option expires.

☐ A summary of any performance criteria upon which the award or exercise of a share option is conditional, and any changes made in the year. *Sch 7A, 8(e)* *FSA LR 9.8.8(2)*

☐ For any share option exercised during the year, the market price at the time of exercise. *Sch 7A, 8(f)* *FSA LR 9.8.8(2)*

☐ For each share option that was unexpired at the end of the financial year: *Sch 7A, 8(g)* *FSA LR 9.8.8(2)*

- the market price at the year-end date and
- the highest and lowest market price during the year.

☐ For each director who served during the financial year, details of interests in long-term incentive schemes, showing *Sch 7A, 10, 11(a)–(c)* *FSA LR 9.8.8(3)–(6)*

- interests at the beginning of the year, or the date of appointment if later;
- awards during the year, showing whether they crystallise in the year or in subsequent years;
- the money value and number of shares, cash payments or other benefits received during the year and
- interests at the end of the year, or on ceasing to be a director if earlier.

☐ For each disclosed interest in long-term incentive schemes, the date by which the qualifying conditions have to be fulfilled *Sch 7A, 11(1)(d)*

and details of any variations in the terms
and conditions made during the year.

☐ If shares may become receivable in
respect of an interest awarded during
the year:

- the number of those shares;
- the market price of the shares at the
  time of the award and
- details of any qualifying conditions
  relating to performance.

Sch 7A, 11(2)

☐ For each scheme interest that has vested
during the year, details of any shares, the
amount of any money and the value of
any other assets that have become
receivable as a result.

Sch 7A, 11(1)(e)

☐ If shares have become receivable as a
result of an interest vesting during
the year:

- the number of those shares;
- the date on which the interest
  was awarded;
- the market price of the shares at the
  time of the award;
- the market price of the shares when
  the interest vested and
- details of any qualifying conditions
  relating to performance.

Sch 7A, 11(3)

☐ For each director who served during the
financial year and has rights under a
defined benefit retirement scheme:

- details of any changes during the
  year in their accrued benefits under
  the scheme;
- the accrued benefits at the end of the
  year;
- the transfer value of the accrued
  benefits, calculated as recommended
  by the Institute of Actuaries and Faculty
  of Actuaries (see **PARAGRAPH 9.24**);
- the equivalent transfer value at the
  end of the previous year and

Sch 7A, 12(2)
FSA LR 9.8.8(12)

- the difference between the opening transfer value and the current transfer value, after deducting any contributions made by the director in the current year.

☐ For each director who served during the financial year and has rights under a money purchase retirement scheme, details of the contributions paid or payable by the company during the year

Sch 7A, 12(3)
FSA LR 9.8.8(11)

☐ Details of certain excess retirement benefits paid to directors or former directors.

Sch 7A, 13

☐ Details of any significant awards to former directors (e.g. compensation for loss of office, pensions).

Sch 7A, 14
FSA LR 9.8.8(2)

☐ For each director who served during the financial year, the aggregate amount of any consideration (including any benefits in kind) paid to, or receivable by, a third party for making available the services of the individual as a director.

Sch 7A, 15

B   Contents Not Subject to Audit

The following information is required to be disclosed, but is not subject to audit:

☐ The names of the members of any committee that considered directors' remuneration during the year and the names of any other individuals (whether directors or not) who provided advice or services to that committee, together with details of the nature of the advice or services.

Sch 7A, 2(a)–(c)

☐ A statement of the company's policy on directors' remuneration for the forthcoming year and for subsequent financial years, drawing attention to any factors specific to the company – this must include for each individual who has served as a director between the end of the financial year

Sch 7A, 3(1) &
(2)(a)–(d)
FSA LR 9.8.8(1)

Directors' Remuneration and Benefits

under review and the date on which the annual reports and accounts are laid before the members:

- a detailed summary of any performance conditions in respect of awards under share option or long-term incentive schemes;
- an explanation of why these performance conditions were chosen;
- a summary of the methods used in assessing whether the performance conditions are met, and why those methods were chosen;
- if any performance condition involves comparison with external factors, a summary of the factors to be used and the identity of any companies or index used for comparison purposes.

☐ A description of, and explanation for, any significant changes to the terms and conditions of entitlement under share option or long-term incentive schemes.
Sch 7A, 3(2)(e)
FSA LR 9.8.8(10)

☐ An explanation of why any entitlements under share option or long-term incentive schemes are not subject to performance conditions.
Sch 7A, 3(2)(f)

☐ A statement of the company's policy on the granting of options or awards under employee share schemes and other long-term incentive schemes and an explanation and justification of any departure from, or change in, that policy during the year.
FSA LR 9.8.8(10)

☐ The relative importance of elements of remuneration that are related to performance and those that are not.
Sch 7A, 3(3)

☐ A summary of the company's policy on the duration of directors' service contracts and on notice periods and termination payments under those contracts.
Sch 7A, 3(4)

☐ The following information on the contract of service, or contract for services, of each person who served as a director during the
Sch 7A, 5(1)

financial year:

- date of the contract, the unexpired term and any notice period;
- any provision for compensation on early termination and
- sufficient information on any other provisions to enable a member to estimate the company's liability in the event of early termination of the contract.

☐ The unexpired term of any director's service contract of a director proposed for election or re-election at the forthcoming Annual General Meeting, or if any such director does not have a service contract, a statement of that fact.   *FSA LR 9.8.8(9)*

☐ Details of any service contracts which provide for, or imply, notice periods in excess of one year, or which include provisions for predetermined compensation which exceeds one year's salary and benefits, together with an explanation of the reasons.   *FSA LR 9.8.8(8)*

☐ An explanation for any significant awards during the year to former directors (e.g. compensation for loss of office, pensions).   *Sch 7A, 5(2)*

☐ An explanation of, and justification for, any elements of remuneration other than basic salary that are pensionable.   *FSA LR 9.8.8(7)*

☐ A line graph showing the total shareholder return for the last five years on: *Sch 7A, 4*

- a holding of the class of equity shares whose public trading has resulted in the company meeting the definition of a quoted company and
- a hypothetical holding of shares, based on a broad equity market index, together with the name of the index and why it was chosen.

Directors' Remuneration and Benefits

Financial Reporting

10 Financial Reporting

10.1 Accounting Standards

At a Glance

* In recent years, accounting standards in the UK have been developed by the Accounting Standards Board (ASB) under the auspices of the Financial Reporting Council (FRC), and a detailed consultation programme has been undertaken for each new standard.
* From 1 January 2005, listed groups are required to adopt international accounting standards in place of UK accounting standards, and most other companies have the option of doing this in both individual and group accounts.
* The ASB has begun a programme to converge UK accounting standards with their international equivalents and this is likely to result in significant changes to the role of the ASB.
* Accounting standards apply to all accounts that are required to show a true and fair view, although they need not be applied to immaterial items.
* Each accounting standard is effective from the date specified in the standard, although early adoption is usually encouraged.
* Accounting standards should generally be regarded as applying to all transactions, unless an individual standard requires a different approach.
* Care is required over the early adoption of accounting treatments proposed in ASB Discussion Papers or Financial Reporting Exposure Drafts (FREDs), especially where they represent the updating of an existing accounting standard.
* Directors are generally required to state whether the accounts have been prepared in accordance with applicable accounting standards.
* Additional disclosures must be given if the company departs from applicable accounting standards when preparing its annual accounts.
* The Urgent Issues Task Force (UITF) considers interpretational issues arising from existing UK accounting and company law requirements.
* The Financial Reporting Review Panel (FRRP) enquires into accounts that appear to depart from the requirements of company law, accounting standards, UITF Abstracts and similar pronouncements.

> * Certain smaller entities are permitted to adopt the Financial Reporting Standard for Smaller Entities (FRSSE) in place of other accounting standards.
> * Statements of Recommended Practice (SORPs) set out recommended accounting practice for specialised sectors or industries.

10.2   The Present Regime

Accounting standards are currently developed in the UK by the ASB under the auspices of the FRC. Both bodies were established in 1990, together with the FRRP and the UITF. The structure of these bodies can be summarised as follows:

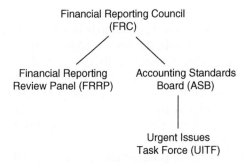

Prior to 1990, standards were developed by the Accounting Standards Committee (ASC). At its first meeting, the ASB formally adopted all existing accounting standards (22 at the time) developed by the ASC, but many of these have now been revised or superseded by new standards issued by the ASB. Standards issued by the ASC were described as Statements of Standard Accounting Practice (SSAPs) and those issued by the ASB are described as Financial Reporting Standards (FRSs). Some of the present accounting standards are therefore in the form of SSAPs whilst others are FRSs, but all have the same status for practical purposes.

The FRC's original remit has recently been widened to give it a more active role in relation to corporate governance and new responsibilities for the development of auditing standards and general oversight of the regulation of the accountancy and actuarial professions. As a result, the Auditing Practices Board (APB), the Professional Oversight Board (POB), the Accountancy and Actuarial Discipline Board (AADB) and the Board for Actuarial Standards (BAS) also come under the umbrella of the FRC in the same way as the ASB and FRRP.

10.3   Development of Accounting Standards

Historically, potential topics for accounting standards have been identified by the ASB from its own research and also from external sources, and ASB staff have then undertaken a programme of consultation and research, considering conceptual issues, existing practice in the UK, any existing pronouncements (both

in the UK and abroad) and the practical implications of introducing new requirements in the UK. A Discussion Paper has usually been prepared setting out the
main issues and inviting comments on the ASB's initial proposals. Following this
initial consultation, a FRED has been published to give those who are interested
a chance to comment on the proposals and to enable the ASB to assess the likely
level of acceptance before finalising the requirements. However, the current programme of international harmonisation means that accounting requirements are
now being developed internationally rather than at a local level, although the ASB
is generally continuing the exposure of proposed new or amended accounting
standards as FREDs before implementation in the UK.

10.4   Adoption of International Accounting Standards

For accounting periods beginning on or after 1 January 2005, listed companies
are required by an EU Regulation to prepare group accounts in accordance with
International Accounting Standards (IASs) adopted by the EU rather the UK
accounting standards. The London Stock Exchange has also announced that
companies listed on the Alternative Investment Market (AIM) must adopt IASs
for accounting periods beginning on or after 1 January 2007 and the FRC has
issued guidance for companies affected by this requirement (available from
http://www.frc.org.uk/press/pub1342.html). UK company law has been amended
to implement the EU requirement for listed groups and to give most other companies the option of preparing both individual and group accounts in accordance with IASs from 1 January 2005. The only exception is in respect of charitable
companies – these are currently excluded from the IAS regime on the basis that
IASs have been drafted with profit-making entities in mind and are therefore not
considered appropriate for the charity sector at present. The companies most
likely to take advantage of the IAS option are stand-alone listed companies, to
make them more comparable with listed groups, and subsidiaries of listed companies, to avoid having to prepare two sets of figures each year (one based on
IASs for consolidation purposes and another using UK standards for statutory
accounts purposes). Many companies are continuing to prepare their accounts in
accordance with UK accounting standards at present. A decision to adopt IASs
is generally not be reversible, although a company is permitted to revert to the
adoption of UK standards where:

- the company ceases to be listed;
- the company's parent ceases to be listed or
- the company becomes a subsidiary of a parent that does not prepare IAS
  accounts.

Where appropriate, the fact that the accounts have been prepared in accordance
with IASs must be disclosed in the notes to the accounts.

10.5   *Continuing Legal Requirements*

When a company is required or chooses to prepare IAS accounts, the detailed
provisions of UK company law on the form and content of statutory accounts

no longer apply. However, this does not mean that all accounting provisions in the legislation can be ignored. Certain provisions continue to apply even where IAS accounts are prepared, and these include:

- the requirement to prepare and file annual accounts;
- where relevant, the requirement to prepare group accounts;
- disclosure requirements in respect of directors' remuneration and employee numbers and costs;
- disclosure requirements on the remuneration received by the auditors and their associates;
- disclosure requirements in respect of subsidiaries and other undertakings in which the reporting entity holds a significant investment and
- the requirement to prepare a directors' report.

Accounts prepared in accordance with the detailed requirements of UK company law and UK accounting practice are now described as Companies Act accounts to distinguish them from IAS accounts.

10.6 *Impact for Groups*

The option of adopting IASs operates independently for group and individual accounts. There is consequently nothing to prevent a parent company from preparing group accounts on the basis of IASs and individual accounts on the basis of UK standards (or vice versa), although to do so would inevitably involve a considerable amount of additional work. Directors of parent companies are expected to ensure consistency in the adoption of IASs within the group, unless there are good reasons against this, and subsidiaries are generally be expected to prepare their accounts on the basis used by the parent for its own individual accounts, although there is a specific exception where the parent prepares both IAS group and IAS individual accounts.

10.7 UK Convergence with IASs

In March 2004, the ASB issued a Discussion Paper *UK Accounting Standards: A Strategy for Convergence with IFRS* setting out its detailed plans for achieving the convergence of UK accounting standards with international standards (IASs and IFRSs). The Discussion Paper outlined the ASB's overall strategy and also set out specific proposals on the development or revision of individual accounting standards in the next few years. Whilst many companies are continuing to adopt UK accounting standards at present, the ASB is clear in its own mind that, in the medium to long term, there can be no case for maintaining two wholly different sets of accounting standards in the UK. This would create additional burdens for those preparing accounts, undermine the credibility of financial reporting in the UK and hamper comparability. The board also takes the view that convergence in the form of broadly equivalent requirements will not be sufficient – the only way to prevent different interpretations arising in similar circumstances is for UK standards and international standards to be expressed in the same words.

The ASB initially planned to adopt a phased approach to convergence, but is now reconsidering this approach in the light of comments received from respondents and particular concerns over the latest international proposals on accounting for business combinations. These have highlighted the complexity of adopting a phased approach when there are clear inter-relationships between standards, some of which have been converged whilst others are still awaiting convergence. As a result, the ASB set out proposals for a revised convergence strategy in a short paper issued in January 2006 in advance of discussion at a public meeting later that month. This proposed a 'big bang' approach to convergence, with the ASB continuing to expose and finalise new UK accounting standards based on IFRSs but giving these new standards a common future implementation date rather than implementing them as they were finalised. The suggestion was that all of the new converged standards would come into effect for accounting periods beginning on or after 1 January 2009.

10.8   *Possibility of a Two-Tier UK Regime*

The second part of the ASB's January 2006 paper (see PARAGRAPH 10.7) considered which accounting standards should apply to which entities. This sought views on whether full IFRSs (or EU-adopted IFRSs) would be appropriate for a wider group of entities – for instance, stand-alone listed companies, those of a similar size to listed entities and those with a significant element of public interest. For companies below this level, a two-tier regime could be developed involving:

- The continuation of a specific FRRSE, based either on the IASB's SME standard or, if this is considered to be more appropriate to slightly larger entities, an updated FRSSE based on the underlying principles of IFRSs.
- A separate financial regime for the vast number of entities that are not listed (or regarded as equivalent to listed or of significant public interest) but do not qualify as small – this regime is likely to be based on full IFRSs but with appropriate exemptions or adjustments to ensure that the cost of compliance does not significantly outweigh the related benefits.

Separate consideration would need to be given to the standards that should apply to public benefit entities, balancing the need for public accountability with cost/benefit issues. The ASB also confirmed in its initial Discussion Paper (see PARAGRAPH 10.7) that it does not plan to introduce new UK standards that are more demanding or restrictive than the equivalent international standards, but where current UK requirements are already more demanding, these will generally be retained if it seems that the relevant international standard will eventually be improved.

10.9   *Latest Proposals*

In the latest consultation document on convergence, published in May 2006, the ASB suggested that:

- The scope of the FRSSE could be widened to encompass companies that qualify as medium sized to introduce simplified accounting requirements for an

additional 30,000 companies – the Government is also consulting on a further increase in the financial thresholds for small- and medium-sized companies which would increase the number of companies in these categories.
- All quoted companies and other entities with public accountability should be required to adopted IFRSs, regardless of the level of their turnover and of whether they prepare individual or group accounts.
- All subsidiaries of companies preparing IFRS group accounts should be required to adopt IFRSs, but with reduced disclosure requirements.

The ASB estimated that this would leave around 7000 companies that do not qualify as small- or medium-sized under UK company law, but do not meet the public accountability criteria and are not subsidiaries of listed or similar companies. No firm proposals were put forward for these companies at that stage, but operating a separate financial reporting regime for a relatively small number of companies may not be practicable.

The ASB published a summary of the responses to this consultation document in October 2006. There was a mixed response to all of the proposals, with none receiving overwhelming support but equally none being universally rejected. On the issue of medium-sized companies and the FRSSE, a number of respondents felt that any steps to reduce the level of administration and disclosure for medium-sized companies should be welcomed, but others raised concerns that the proposed change might result in the content of the FRSSE being driven by the needs of medium-sized companies, rather than those of the smaller entities for which it was originally designed. As a result, it may no longer be possible to keep the document simple and straightforward. There was general support for a requirement for all publicly quoted companies (including AIM and OFEX companies) to be required to adopt IFRSs, provided that a pragmatic timetable for such a move could be agreed with the relevant authorities. However, some respondents felt that the adoption of IFRSs should remain voluntary for individual companies until certain significant issues have been satisfactorily resolved. These include concerns over the impact of IFRSs on distributable reserves and the accounting treatment of group defined benefit pension schemes in individual company accounts. There was less support for the proposal to extend such a requirement to other publicly accountable entities, as this would bring organisations such as building societies, charities, housing associations and friendly, industrial and provident societies into the net. As IFRSs have not been designed with such entities in mind, accounts prepared on the basis of these standards may not meet the needs of users. The general view is that the definition of public accountability for these purposes still needs much more work. There was also considerable support for the suggestion that subsidiaries of companies preparing IFRS accounts should be required to adopt IFRSs with reduced disclosure requirements, although with the same concerns over a small number of significant accounting issues that have still to be resolved.

Overall, the responses indicated a substantial level of support for the view that there should be no more than two tiers in UK accounting practice. Entities should therefore report under IFRSs or under the FRSSE (or an equivalent based on the IASB's current SME project). Companies that do not fall into any of the categories considered in the ASB's proposals would therefore need to be incorporated into one of these regimes.

10.10   *Impact of Draft IFRS for SMEs*

In April 2007, the ASB published for UK comment the Exposure Draft of the proposed IFRS for SMEs issued by the International Accounting Standards Board (IASB). The IASB Exposure Draft identifies the scope of the proposed standard as entities that do not have public accountability but publish general purpose financial statements for external users. In particular, it should be noted that no size criteria are defined for the adoption of the standard. However, the final decision on which entities can adopt the IFRS for SMEs will rest with national regulatory authorities and standard setters, and they will be free to impose size criteria and/or financial thresholds if they consider this appropriate.

The draft IFRS omits a number of topics covered in full IFRSs on the basis that they are not generally relevant to smaller entities and incorporates simplifications in certain other areas. The ASB Consultation Paper sets out the IASB proposals in full and prefaces these with summaries of the differences between UK GAAP and the proposed IFRS, and the current FRSSE and the proposed IFRS. Also, the disclosure requirements under the draft IFRS are much more onerous than under the present FRSSE and there is no exemption from the preparation of a cash flow statement.

The ASB identified two objectives for its own consultation process:

(i) to help inform the ASB's response to the IASB and
(ii) to obtain feedback on how the draft IFRS might fit in to the ASB's project to converge UK accounting practice with international requirements.

Although no firm proposals have yet been put forward, the ASB's initial view appears to be that the IFRS for SMEs could be adopted for mid-tier companies, with smaller companies continuing to use the FRSSE, and that the FRSSE could eventually be replaced by a simplified version of the SME standard. This would achieve the ASB's objective of having all UK accounting requirements based on international standards. As previously suggested (see **Paragraph 10.9**), subsidiaries of parent companies preparing IFRS accounts would be outside the scope of both the SME standard and the FRSSE, and would be required to adopt full IFRSs but with reduced disclosure.

10.11   Changes to the Role of the ASB

In March 2005, the ASB published an Exposure Draft of a Policy Statement setting out the Board's views on its future role. With the introduction of the IAS framework in the UK and the ASB's published plans to converge UK accounting practice with international requirements (see **Paragraphs 10.7–10.10**), much of the detailed work on the development of accounting standards will in future be undertaken by the IASB and the future role of the ASB therefore needs to be reassessed. The Exposure Draft 'Accounting Standard-Setting in a Changing Environment: The Role of the Accounting Standards Board' promotes the view that the ASB will continue to have a significant role in the development of IASs through participation in debates on the key issues and by responding to IASB consultations. It will also act as a link between the IASB and interested parties in the UK by maintaining a two-way dialogue and ensuring that the views and concerns of UK parties are relayed to the IASB. The other main activities of the ASB in future are expected to include:

- implementation of the UK convergence project;
- improving communication between companies and their investors and
- influencing European policy on accounting standards.

10.12   Scope and Application of Accounting Standards

UK accounting standards apply to all accounts that are required to show a true and fair view of the profit or loss for the financial period and of the state of affairs of an entity at its balance sheet date. Consequently they apply not only to companies and groups, but also to unincorporated entities if these are required to prepare accounts that show a true and fair view. However, the requirements of accounting standards need not be applied to items that are considered immaterial in the context of the accounts as a whole. They also do not override any exemption from disclosure that is available by law. In its guidance, the ASB emphasises that, when applying accounting standards, preparers of accounts should follow the spirit and reasoning behind the requirements as explained in the standards themselves and in the ASB's *Statement of Principles for Financial Reporting*. Similarly, IASs are intended to be applied to all general purpose financial statements that are intended to present fairly the financial position, financial performance and cash flows of an entity.

The report published in 2003 by the DTI Co-ordinating Group on Audit and Accounting Issues (CGAAI) as part of the post-Enron review endorsed the need for accounting standards to be based on conceptually sound principles rather than detailed prescriptive rules, but also noted that such an approach requires companies and their auditors to be prepared to apply the standards responsibly and with integrity and not in a way that skews the underlying economic reality of the company's performance.

10.13   Effective Date of Accounting Standards

Each accounting standard is effective from a specific date set out in the standard. The date chosen will take into account the fact that companies may need time to put detailed procedures into place in order to comply with the new accounting requirements. However, in most cases the effective date set is the latest date by which compliance must be achieved, and early adoption of new accounting standards is usually encouraged. It should be noted, however, that the fact that a standard has been adopted early may need to be disclosed, and that there may be a prohibition on the early adoption of certain standards (for instance, where related company law requirements are not effective for earlier accounting periods). The question sometimes arises as to whether new requirements apply to all transactions or only to those arising after the effective date of the standard. The ASB's general view is that the requirements of UK accounting standards should be regarded as applying to all transactions, regardless of when they took place, unless a particular accounting standard specifies a different approach. Care is also required over the early adoption of accounting treatments proposed in Discussion Papers and FREDs. If the subject matter of a Discussion Paper or FRED is not covered by an existing accounting standard, the exposure document may be regarded as indicative of best practice and it may therefore be acceptable to adopt the accounting treatment proposed, bearing in mind that the final FRS may impose slightly different requirements. If the subject matter of the Discussion Paper or FRED is already covered in an accounting standard, the existing standard remains in force until it is replaced and accounts must therefore be prepared in accordance with the existing standard, even if it is expected that the standard will be superseded by new requirements. In these circumstances, it may be appropriate to explain the effect of the new proposals in a note to the accounts. Similar guidance is set out in the IASB's *Preface to international financial reporting standards* in relation to the preparation of IAS accounts.

10.14   First-Time Adoption of IFRSs

The IASB published IFRS 1 *First-time Adoption of International Financial Reporting Standards* in June 2003. With a small number of specific exceptions (which include accounting for past acquisitions), this standard requires a reporting entity to comply with all current IASB standards when it first prepares its accounts in accordance with international standards. The accounts must also explain how the transition to international standards has affected the entity's financial position, financial performance and cash flows. The stated aim is to provide investors with transparent information that is comparable over all periods presented, but in a way that keeps costs to an acceptable level. A company that is required to prepare accounts in accordance with IASs, or which chooses to do so (see **PARAGRAPH 10.4**), will therefore need to prepare comparative figures for the previous year, including an opening balance sheet for that year, on the same basis. This will be a major undertaking for any company in the year of transition to IASs. APB Bulletin 2005/3 *Guidance for Auditors on First-Time Application of IFRSs in the United Kingdom and the Republic of Ireland* also provides guidance on a number of additional issues that may arise where accounts are prepared under IFRSs for the first time. These include:

- difficulties in identifying all relevant differences between the old and new financial reporting frameworks;
- significant changes to financial reporting systems and controls, which may increase the risk of error and the possibility of fraud or aggressive earnings management;

- additional going concern issues, particularly if new accounting requirements have implications for the company's borrowing powers or cause debt covenants to be breached;
- the potential impact of changes in accounting treatments on the amount of profits that the company has available for distribution and
- the potential tax effects of the changes in accounting requirements.

10.15   Disclosure of Compliance with Accounting Standards

In the case of Companies Act accounts (see **PARAGRAPH 10.5**) *Paragraph 36A* of *Schedule 4* to *CA 1985* requires the directors to state whether the company's accounts have been prepared in accordance with applicable accounting standards. There is an exemption from the disclosure requirement (but not from the requirement to follow applicable standards) for companies that qualify as small- or medium-sized under the legislation. If there has been a departure from applicable accounting standards, particulars must be given, together with the reasons for the departure. The *Foreword to Accounting Standards* and FRS 18 *Accounting Policies* also require disclosure of the financial effect of a material departure from accounting standards. Where IAS accounts are prepared, UK company law requires this fact to be stated in the accounts and IAS 1 *Presentation of Financial Statements* requires the notes to the accounts to include a clear statement on compliance with all requirements of IASs. The financial statements cannot be described as complying with international standards unless they comply with all relevant requirements.

10.16   Applicable Accounting Standards

Section 256 of *CA 1985* defines accounting standards as 'statements of standard accounting practice issued by such body or bodies as may be prescribed by regulations'. Applicable accounting standards are those that are relevant to the company's circumstances and to the accounts. For the purposes of UK company law, FRSs and SSAPs constitute 'accounting standards'. Where IAS accounts are prepared, accounting standards are IASs that have been formally adopted by the EU.

10.17   Role of the UITF

The role of the UITF is to help the ASB to fulfil its aim of responding promptly on urgent matters as they arise. The UITF considers issues that are covered by an existing accounting standard or a provision in company law but where conflicting or unacceptable interpretations have developed, or seem likely to develop. Having considered the issue and reached a conclusion, the UITF issues its consensus in the form of an Abstract, which usually becomes effective shortly after publication. Once it is in force, a UITF Abstract has the same authority, scope and application as an accounting standard and therefore forms part of standard accounting practice. However, the role of the UITF is also expected to change as a result of the convergence of UK accounting standards with international requirements (see **PARAGRAPHS 10.7–10.10**). In future, any necessary interpretation of IASs will generally be dealt with by the International Financial Reporting Interpretations Committee (IFRIC) and will usually then be issued as a UITF Abstract for UK accounting purposes. However, where it seems that IFRIC will be unable to issue guidance in time to meet UK needs, the UITF may consider issuing its own non-mandatory guidance.

10.18   Role of the FRRP

The FRRP enquires into accounts that appear to depart from the requirements of company law, accounting standards, UITF Abstracts and similar pronouncements, including the requirement to show a true and fair view in accordance with the relevant financial framework adopted. To date, reviews have concentrated on the accounts of public companies and larger private companies, but technically all companies come within the remit of the FRRP unless they qualify as small- or medium-sized under company law. Initially, the FRRP did not review accounts on a routine basis but acted on matters drawn to its attention, either directly or indirectly. Qualified audit reports, press comment and referrals by individuals or companies could all result in an enquiry. Where revision of the accounts was considered necessary, the FRRP usually tried to reach voluntary arrangement with the directors, but could seek a Court order for revision of the accounts if it was unable to reach a satisfactory agreement with the directors.

The various post-Enron reviews undertaken in the UK resulted in recommendations that the FRRP should develop a more proactive element to its work, that the Financial Services Authority (FSA) should have a greater role in the enforcement process and that the Government should explore the scope for opening legal gateways to enable relevant information to be passed between the Inland Revenue, FSA, FRRP and DTI to help in the identification of high-risk accounts. These changes were eventually introduced by the *Companies Act (Audit, Investigations and Community Enterprise) Act 2004*. In particular, the Secretary of State is now empowered to appoint a body or bodies to keep the periodic accounts and reports of listed companies under review and, where relevant, inform the FSA of any conclusions reached. As a result, the FRRP now adopts a process of risk-based selection of accounts for review and covers all published information issued by listed companies, including half-yearly reports and, where relevant, preliminary announcements. Directors' report also come within the remit of the FRRP for accounting periods beginning on or after 1 April 2006.

Other provisions in the *Companies Act (Audit, Investigations and Community Enterprise) Act 2004* allow the Inland Revenue to disclose relevant information to facilitate the investigation of company accounts by the FRRP, enable the FRRP to require a company and any officer, employee or auditor to provide information relevant to an investigation of the company's accounts for compliance with company law requirements and establish gateways to enable the FRRP to disclose certain information to bodies such as the DTI, Treasury, Bank of England, FSA and Inland Revenue to assist them in carrying out their legal functions. These provisions came into effect on 6 April 2005. In conjunction with the recent changes, the FRRP published a revised version of its Operating Procedures in April 2005. This confirms the Panel's intention to encourage directors to make additional information available on a voluntary basis as far as possible and only to use its new powers to require the provision of information as a last resort.

In September 2007, the FRRP issued a short paper on the approach that it plans to take to the review of directors' reports and confirmed in particular that they will be examined in the context of a review of the full annual report and accounts. The paper emphasises that all of the disclosures that are required to be given in the directors' report come within the scope of the Panel's reviews, but much of its attention is likely to be focused on the enhanced business review (see **PARAGRAPH 10.78**). Factors that the FRRP particularly highlight for attention in its reviews include:

- the use of explicit cross-referencing where requirements are met by incorporating relevant material elsewhere in the annual report and accounts;
- consistency with information disclosed in the accounts and other company announcements;
- whether the report deals even-handedly with both positive and negative aspects of the development, performance and position of the business;
- the identification and description of principle risks and uncertainties and
- the use of appropriate key performance indicators (KPIs).

Most of these issues were also highlighted in 'A Review of Narrative Reporting by UK Listed Companies in 2006' published by the ASB in January 2007 (see **PARAGRAPH 10.87**).

10.19   *Recent FRRP Activity and Reports*

The Panel announced in December 2005 that its monitoring activity for 2006/07 would continue to focus on the following industry sectors identified in the risk monitoring process for the previous period, but that selection would be widened to include some companies providing services to these sectors and that its specific issues reviews would include pensions disclosures:

- automobile;
- pharmaceutical;
- retail;
- transport and
- utilities.

In December 2006, the FRRP announced that its monitoring activity for 2007/08 would focus on the following sectors:

- travel and leisure;
- retail;

- utility;
- telecommunications and
- media.

The FRRP published its third report on proactivity in September 2007, covering the period 1 April 2006 to 31 March 2007. The report deals separately with issues raised in respect of accounts prepared under IFRS and those prepared under UK accounting practice. Many of the accounts reviewed in this period had been prepared under IFRS for the first time and so the results should be of particular interest to AIM companies preparing IFRS accounts for the first time for accounting periods beginning on or after 1 January 2007. A total of 311 sets of accounts were reviewed, analysed as follows between the main categories of company:

  (i) 58 (19%) from FTSE 100 companies;
 (ii) 66 (21%) from FTSE 250 companies;
(iii) 84 (27%) from other listed companies;
 (iv) 52 (17%) from AIM companies;
  (v) 15 (5%) from third country companies and
 (vi) 36 (12%) from unlisted companies (both public & private)

The figures for listed and AIM companies include both annual and interim reports, although the emphasis is very much on annual reports. The FRRP also notes that it ensured appropriate coverage of companies that are listed in both the UK and the US.

Of the 311 annual accounts reviewed, 266 were selected under the FRRP's risk-based approach and 45 were identified as a result of complaints, referrals from other regulators and issues raised in the financial press (and the report includes a clear encouragement for professional investors and others to refer accounts to the Panel for review). The FRRP also considered all accounts brought to its attention where the audit report was qualified (see also **PARAGRAPH 2.57**). The reviews resulted in 135 requests for further information, 94 subsequent undertakings to improve financial reporting in at least one area, and 4 detailed press notices. A number of cases were still ongoing at the time of the report. However, the FRRP emphasises that it found a good overall level of compliance and that the detailed comments in the report should be seen in this context. Responses to FRRP enquiries were also felt to be well considered, with evidence of input from audit committees as well as dialogue with external auditors and industry participants over new IFRS reporting requirements.

The FRRP has also published separate reports on its reviews of the following:

  (i) the interim reports of listed companies (February 2006);
 (ii) defined benefit retirement scheme disclosures under both UK GAAP and IAS/IFRSs (August 2006 – a follow-up report on IAS/IFRS disclosure was also issued in September 2007) and
(iii) the implementation of IAS/IFRSs in the UK (December 2006).

All of these are available from the FRRP website at http://www.frc.org.uk/frrp/.

10.20   Financial Reporting Standard for Smaller Entities

An FRSSE was first published in November 1997 and came into immediate effect. A number of revised versions have been published, the latest one becoming effective in January 2007. The FRSSE may be adopted in financial statements that are intended to give a true and fair view of the financial performance and financial position of companies that qualify as small under company law and of other entities that would qualify if they were incorporated. For accounting periods beginning on or after 1 January 2005, the FRSSE is only relevant to small companies if they prepare Companies Act accounts (see **PARAGRAPH 10.5**). If the FRSSE is adopted, this fact must be stated in the accounts. The contents of the FRSSE are currently based on other UK accounting standards, but definitions and accounting requirements are set out in a more straightforward manner, and more complex issues that are not expected to arise in smaller entities are excluded. The document is reviewed on an annual basis so that its requirements are kept up to date with developments in accounting practice. Earlier versions of the FRSSE included an Appendix linking the requirements of the FRSSE with those in accounting standards and summarising the main simplifications. This has been removed from the January 2007 version to keep the document to a manageable size, but the information continues to be freely available on the ASB website at http://www.frc.org.uk/asb/technical/frsse.cfm. Where issues arise that are not specifically covered in the FRSSE, those preparing the accounts are required to have regard to other standards and UITF Abstracts as a means of establishing current practice. The FRSSE includes a specific additional requirement for the accounts to disclose any personal guarantees given by the directors in respect of company borrowings.

Also, the January 2007 version of the FRSSE amends the scope of the standard to:

(i)   reflect the fact that many small financial services companies are eligible to adopt the FRSSE for accounting periods ending on or after 31 December 2006 and

(ii) exclude small companies that choose to adopt fair value accounting so that the FRSSE does not become overcomplicated.

10.21   *'One-Stop Shop' Document*

The versions of the FRSSE published since April 2005 take the form of a 'one-stop shop' document, encompassing all of the accounting requirements that apply to small companies. Company law requirements are distinguished from other aspects of the FRSSE by being set out in small capitals in the text, and reflect the provisions that apply for accounting periods beginning on or after 1 January 2005. Only the most common balance sheet format (Format 1 from *CA 1985*) is included in the document but companies applying the FRSSE continue to have the option of adopting the alternative balance sheet format if they wish. However, in the case of the profit and loss account, only Formats 1 and 2 from *CA 1985* are now available to companies applying the FRSSE. The ASB emphasises that smaller unincorporated entities adopting the FRSSE are not bound by the company law requirements set out in the document, but notes that they should have regard to the accounting principles, presentation and disclosure requirements set out in company law (or other equivalent legislation) that are considered necessary for the presentation of a true and fair view.

10.22 *Possible Impact of IASB Proposals for SMEs*

In February 2007, the IASB published an Exposure Draft of a proposed IFRS for SMEs (see **PARAGRAPH 10.10**). Given the ASB's programme to converge UK accounting standards with international requirements (see **PARAGRAPHS 10.7–10.10**), this is likely to impact in due course on UK accounting requirements for smaller entities in the UK. However, it is clear that the ASB intends to continue with a separate UK financial reporting regime for smaller entities, based either on the proposed IFRS for SMEs or a simplified version of this.

10.23 Statement of Recommended Practice

SORPs set out recommended accounting practice for specialised sectors or industries. They are developed by bodies representing the appropriate sector or industry and are supplementary to accounting standards, legislation and other regulations affecting the business. Bodies wishing to develop a SORP are expected to meet criteria laid down by the ASB and to develop the SORP in accordance with the ASB's Code of Practice. The ASB will review the proposed SORP and, where appropriate, issue a 'negative assurance' statement for publication in the document, confirming that:

- the SORP does not appear to contain any fundamental points of principle that are unacceptable in the context of current accounting practice and
- the SORP does not conflict with an accounting standard or with the ASB's plans for future accounting standards.

The contents of a SORP do not override the requirements of accounting standards, UITF Abstracts or relevant legislation. The ASB Code of Practice specifically notes that the fact that a SORP has not been updated does not exempt relevant entities from complying with more recent accounting standards and UITF Abstracts. If new standards and Abstracts conflict with the provisions of a SORP, those provisions cease to have effect. FRS 18 *Accounting Policies* requires specific disclosures to be given in the accounts when an entity comes with the scope of a SORP.

10.24 The True and Fair View

At a Glance
- * Company law requires Companies Act accounts to show a true and fair view.
- * Different requirements apply where IAS accounts are prepared.

* The interpretation of what constitutes a true and fair view will vary over time, based largely on the requirements of the accounting standards in force at the time.
* The ASB 'Foreword to Accounting Standards' considers the status of accounting standards in the context of UK company law.
* In certain exceptional circumstances, directors preparing Companies Act accounts are required to depart from the specific accounting requirements of company law – this is commonly referred to as the use of the true and fair override.
* Specific disclosures must be given in the accounts whenever the true and fair override is used.

10.25 Requirement for Accounts to Show a True and Fair View

Where Companies Act individual accounts are prepared (see **PARAGRAPH 10.5**), company law requires a company's balance sheet to give a true and fair view of the state of affairs of the company at the end of the financial period and the profit and loss account to give a true and fair view of the profit or loss for the financial period then ended. A similar requirement applies to Companies Act group accounts. Where compliance with the provisions of the legislation is not sufficient for the accounts to give a true and fair view, the additional information necessary to achieve a true and fair view must be given in the accounts or the notes to the accounts. The true and fair view requirement applies to the accounts of all companies, regardless of their size.

10.26 Different Requirements for IAS Accounts

Similar but slightly different requirements apply where a company is required or chooses to prepare IAS individual and/or group accounts (see **PARAGRAPH 10.4**). Company law does not set out any specific requirements on the form or content of IAS accounts, although it does include a requirement for the auditors to express an opinion on whether or not the accounts show a true and fair view in accordance with the relevant financial reporting framework applied in their preparation. Two documents have been published on this issue since the IAS framework was introduced into UK company law for accounting periods beginning on or after 1 January 2005. In August 2005, the FRC published a paper 'The implications of new accounting and auditing standards for the true and fair view and auditors' responsibilities'. This sets out a detailed analysis and interpretation of the new framework of accounting and auditing standards and concludes that:

• the concept of the true and fair view remains a cornerstone of financial reporting and auditing in the UK;

- there has been no substantive change in the objectives of an audit and the nature of auditors' responsibilities and
- the need for professional judgement remains central to the work of preparers and auditors of accounts in the UK.

This paper is available from the FRC website at www.frc.org.uk/. Prior to this, in June 2005, the FRRP published an opinion by Freshfields Bruckhaus Deringer on the effect of the IAS Regulation on the requirement under *CA 1985* for accounts to show a true and fair view. The key points highlighted in this opinion are:

- the true and fair override no longer applies to companies who prepare their accounts in accordance with IASs;
- for companies preparing IAS accounts, references to the 'true and fair view' in the legislation are references to the requirement under IASs for accounts to achieve a fair presentation;
- the application of IASs, together with additional disclosure where necessary, is presumed to result in financial statements that achieve a fair presentation;
- IAS 1 *Presentation of Financial Statements* acknowledges that it may be necessary to depart from strict compliance with a requirement of a standard or related interpretation in order to achieve a fair presentation, but only in very rare circumstances, and where such a departure is required, certain additional disclosures must be given, including the nature of the departure and the reasons for it.

The opinion is available from the FRRP website at www.frc.org.uk/frrp/.

CA 2006 includes a new provision that the directors must not approve accounts unless they are satisfied that those accounts give a true and fair view of the assets, liabilities, financial position and profit or loss of the company or the group (as appropriate) and that the auditors must have regard to this duty of the directors when carrying out their functions as auditors. This is in addition to the existing requirements on the true and fair view in Companies Act accounts and applies to all accounts, irrespective of the financial framework adopted. Consequently, it should eliminate any remaining concerns over this issue. The accounts provisions of *CA 2006* are generally due to be brought into effect from 6 April 2008.

10.27   What Constitutes a True and Fair View?

Although the concept of the true and fair view lies at the heart of financial reporting in the UK, there is no clear definition, in the legislation or elsewhere, of what constitutes a true and fair view. This is essentially a question of judgement and, as a legal concept, it can only be interpreted by the Court. It is a dynamic concept and the interpretation of what constitutes a true and fair view will vary over time, based largely on the accounting standards in force at any given date. New accounting standards are developed, and existing standards revised, to take account of changes in business practice and in the general economic climate, and an accounting treatment that was accepted as giving a true and fair view 10 years ago will not necessarily achieve such a view today.

10.28 Impact of Accounting Standards

The interpretation of 'true and fair' will usually be governed by generally accepted accounting practice and, in particular, the requirements of accounting standards. Each UK accounting standard states that it applies to all financial statements that are required to show a true and fair view. The *Foreword to Accounting Standards*, issued in 1993 by the ASB, considers the status of accounting standards in the context of UK company law, and an appendix to the document sets out an opinion by Miss Mary Arden QC (now the Honourable Mrs Justice Arden) on the true and fair requirement. This includes detailed consideration of the relationship between accounting standards and the legal requirement for company accounts to show a true and fair view. The main points set out in the opinion are:

- Although the true and fair requirement is a question of law and must therefore be interpreted by the Court, this cannot be done without evidence of the practice and views of accountants – the more authoritative the practices and views, the more ready the Court will be to follow them.
- Company law gives statutory recognition to accounting standards.
- Company law requires disclosure of non-compliance with accounting standards rather than compliance with them – the Court is therefore likely to infer that accounts will usually follow accounting standards in meeting the true and fair requirement and that any departure from accounting standards needs to be explained and disclosed in the accounts.
- Once an accounting standard has been issued, the Court is likely to hold that compliance with the standard will be necessary for accounts to show a true and fair view – this view is likely to be strengthened by the extent to which the standard is subsequently accepted in practice.
- The converse will not necessarily apply, and a lack of support for an accounting standard will not automatically lead the Court to conclude that a true and fair view can be achieved without compliance with the standard.
- The fact that a departure from an accounting standard is disclosed in accordance with the requirements of company law does not necessarily mean that the departure is permitted under the legislation.

It is advisable to read the full Opinion in any case where departure from an accounting standard is being contemplated.

10.29 True and Fair Override

If, in special circumstances, compliance with the provisions in the legislation would be inconsistent with the requirement for Companies Act accounts to show a true and fair view, company law requires the directors to depart from those requirements and make specific disclosure of this in the accounts. This is commonly referred to as the use of the true and fair override. A departure from the provisions of company law might arise in one of two ways. Firstly, some accounting standards specifically require departure from the requirements of the legislation in order to achieve a true and fair view – examples include the non-depreciation of investment properties under SSAP 19 *Accounting for Investment Properties*, the treatment of certain exchange gains and losses under SSAP 20 *Foreign Currency Translation*, and the non-amortisation of certain categories of goodwill under FRS 10 *Goodwill and Intangible Assets*. Secondly, in very rare and exceptional circumstances, it may be necessary to depart from the requirements of accounting standards in order to achieve a true and fair view – the legislation requires accounts to be prepared in accordance with applicable accounting standards and a departure from these will therefore constitute a departure from the detailed provisions of company law on the form and content of Companies Act accounts.

10.30 Disclosing Use of the True and Fair Override

Where the directors depart from the detailed provisions of company law on the form and content of Companies Act accounts, the accounts must give:

- particulars of the departure;
- the reasons for the departure and
- the effect of the departure.

FRS 18 *Accounting Policies* deals with these disclosure requirements in more detail and requires the following information to be given:

- a clear and unambiguous statement that there has been a departure from the requirements of company law, accounting standards or UITF Abstracts, as appropriate, and that the departure is necessary in order to achieve a true and fair view;
- a statement of the treatment that company law, accounting standards or UITF Abstracts would normally require and a description of the treatment actually adopted and
- a description of how the position shown in the financial statements is different as a result of the departure – this should include quantification of the effect except where this is already evident in the financial statements themselves, or where the effect cannot be quantified (in which case the circumstances must be explained).

FRS 18 requires this information to be given in the note to the accounts on compliance with applicable accounting standards, or to be cross-referenced to this note. If the departure continues in future years, the disclosures must be given each year, with comparatives. If the departure applies only to the figures for previous year, the disclosures must still be given in respect of those figures.

10.31 Materiality

At a Glance
* An item is generally regarded as material to the financial statements if its misstatement or omission might reasonably be expected to influence the decisions or assessments made by a user of the financial statements.

> * The requirements of accounting standards should generally be applied to all material transactions, regardless of when they took place.
> * Key factors in assessing the materiality of an item include its size, its nature and the surrounding circumstances.
> * In making the assessment, information should be viewed from a user's perspective.
> * Both the quantative and the qualitative aspects of an item or transaction should be taken into account when assessing its materiality.

10.32   Nature of Materiality

In the case of UK accounting practice, **PARAGRAPH 3.29** of the ASB's *Statement of Principles for Financial Reporting* describes materiality as a threshold quality in that it provides a cut-off point for establishing whether an item needs to be considered in detail in relation to the accounts. The document goes on to explain that:

> 'An item of information is material to the financial statements if its misstatement or omission might reasonably be expected to influence the economic decisions of users of those financial statements, including their assessments of management's stewardship. Whether information is material or not will depend on the size and nature of the item in question judged in the particular circumstances of the case.'

The Statement also emphasises that the inclusion of immaterial information can impair the understandability of the other information provided. Immaterial information should therefore be excluded. Materiality is different to the qualitative characteristics of financial information that are discussed in the *Statement of Principles* (i.e. relevance, reliability, comparability and understandability), because these represent the characteristics that information must have if it is to be useful to a user of the accounts. The materiality of an item should be considered before its other qualities are assessed, because:

- if the information is not material, it cannot be useful to a user of the accounts and therefore does not need to be considered further;
- if the information is material, it will be useful to a user of the accounts, and its qualitative characteristics will therefore need to be assessed.

In the case of IAS accounts, a similar position is set out in the IASB's *Framework for the Preparation and Presentation of Financial Statements* and in Paragraph 11 of IAS 1 *Presentation of Financial Statements*, which states that:

> 'Omissions or misstatements of items are material if they could, individually or collectively, influence the economic decisions of users taken on the basis of the financial statements. Materiality depends on the size and nature of the omission or misstatement judged in the surrounding circumstances. The size or nature of the item, or a combination of both, could be the determining factor.'

10.33   Influence on the Decisions of Users

The main issue to be considered in establishing whether an item is material or not is whether a user of the accounts may make a different decision if the relevant detail or information is made available to him. This definition is emphasised in:

- the ASB's *Statement of Principles for Financial Reporting* [Paragraph 3.30];
- FRS 8 *Related Party Transactions* [Paragraph 20];
- the UK & Ireland version of International Standard on Auditing 320 (ISA 320) *Audit Materiality* [Paragraph 3];
- the IASB's *Framework for the Preparation and Presentation of Financial Statements* [Paragraphs 29 and 30] and
- IAS 1 *Presentation of Financial Statements* [Paragraph 11].

A similar approach is also taken in the guidance published in January 2006 by the DTI's Operating and Financial Review Working Group on Materiality (see **PARAGRAPH 10.86** below).

A wide range of users of accounts is identified in both the ASB's *Statement of Principles* and the IASB's *Framework*, including:

- existing investors, taking decisions on whether to increase, hold or sell their investments;
- potential investors, deciding whether or not to invest in the entity;
- employees and prospective employees, assessing the ability of the entity to provide secure employment opportunities, remuneration and retirement benefits;
- lenders, taking decisions on whether to maintain, increase or decrease the level of financing provided to the entity;
- suppliers and customers, taking decisions on whether to trade with the entity and
- the general public, assessing the contribution of the entity to the local economy.

10.34   Requirements of Accounting Standards

In the case of UK accounting practice, Paragraph 13 of the *Foreword to Accounting Standards* states that accounting standards need not be applied to immaterial items. The Foreword also emphasises that the requirements of accounting standards should generally be applied to all material transactions, irrespective of the date of the transaction. Many accounting standards refer to material items in one context or another. For example, accounting standards may require:

- disclosure of material items – for instance, exceptional items under the requirements of FRS 3 *Reporting financial performance*;
- disclosure of material differences where items are calculated under different methods – for instance, the disclosure of historical cost profits or losses under FRS 3 *Reporting financial performance*;

- disclosure of material events or conditions – for instance, the sale or termination of an operation under FRS 3 *Reporting financial performance*;
- the application of a specific accounting treatment to material items – for instance, adjusting the accounts for certain material post-balance sheet events under FRS 21 *Events after the Balance Sheet Date* and
- the application of a specific accounting treatment where material events or transactions occur – for instance, accounting for transactions on the basis of their economic substance under FRS 5 *Reporting the substance of transactions.*

A similar position applies under the IASB's *Framework for the Preparation and Presentation of Financial Statements* and individuals IFRSs and IASs make reference to material events, items and transactions in the same way as UK standards.

10.35   Assessing Materiality

The materiality of an item (or an error) will therefore usually need to be assessed in relation to:

- the accounts as a whole;
- the total (or totals) in which it is (or should be) included;
- the individual profit and loss account heading or balance sheet heading in which it is (or should be) included;
- other related items in the profit and loss account and balance sheet and
- the corresponding figure (or figures) for the previous year.

10.36   Key Factors to Consider

The materiality of an individual item cannot be assessed in isolation. There are three key factors, all of which are important to the assessment:

- the size of the item;
- the nature of the item and
- the surrounding circumstances.

For instance, it is not possible to say whether an item (or an error) of £35,000 is material without also knowing its nature and the reasons why it arose. Knowing the size alone is not sufficient. It is also not possible to deal with the question of materiality on a purely mathematical basis – the final assessment will often be subjective and will invariably require the exercise of judgement. Whilst percentage guidelines may be helpful as part of the assessment process (e.g. whether an item represents (say) 5% or more of the profit for the year, or (say) 10% or more of a particular balance sheet or profit and loss account heading), they should not be used as the sole means of assessing whether or not an item is material for accounting purposes.

10.37   Nature of an Item

The following points should usually be taken into account when considering the nature of an individual item or error:

- the event or transaction that gave rise to it;
- the legality of the event or transaction and its likely consequences;
- the identity of any other parties, and their relationship to the reporting entity;
- the relevant profit and loss account or balance sheet heading and
- any other related disclosure requirements, either in company law or in accounting standards.

10.38   User's Perspective

It is also important to consider both the context of the item in the accounts and the way in which the information provided may be used. A user will rarely make decisions on the basis of accounting information for one year only – he/she is more likely to:

- compare the latest information with the details for previous years, identify any trends and use this information to make projections and forecasts for future years and
- compare the latest information with equivalent information in respect of similar entities.

The impact that the information may have on decisions made by the user is of primary importance when assessing materiality. It is therefore important to view the information (or potential lack of it) from the user's perspective.

10.39   Qualitative Aspects of Transactions

The FRRP criticised the 1995 group accounts of RMC Group plc for failing to disclose an expense that the Panel considered to be material. The issue related to restrictive trade practices fines and related legal costs totalling just under £5 million which were paid by a subsidiary during 1995. The matter originally arose in 1988 and details of the legal action had been given in the group accounts each year. The 1994 accounts disclosed the matter as a contingent liability. The 1995 accounts of the subsidiary disclosed the payment of the fines, but no mention of them was made in the group accounts. The group profits for the year were £173 million, and the costs of £5 million were presumably not considered to be material in the context of the group results. The Panel took the view that the nature and circumstances of the fines were such that they should have been drawn to the attention of users of the group accounts. Their decision was based on guidance in the Institute of Chartered Accountants in England and Wales (ICAEW) statement *The Interpretation of Materiality in Financial Reporting* and the ASB *Statement of Principles* (in its draft form at that stage). The Panel has therefore emphasised that qualitative aspects of significant transactions need to be considered as well as quantitative ones.

10.40   Other Issues to Consider

Other issues that may affect the assessment of whether an item or error is material include:

- whether there is already an element of estimation or approximation in the calculation of the item – for instance, the valuation of long-term contracts will usually involve an assessment of the expected outcome, whereas the amount due to a creditor can often be calculated with a reasonable degree of precision;
- whether the inclusion or exclusion of an item, or correction or non-correction of an error, has the effect of:
  - reversing a trend;
  - turning a profit into a loss, or vice versa;
  - changing the margin of solvency shown in the balance sheet or
  - altering the degree of compliance with debt covenants;
  these are considered to be 'critical points' and may indicate that it is appropriate to use a lower materiality level than might otherwise be the case;
- an item that is small in the context of the accounts may nevertheless be material, depending on the circumstances – for instance, where a particular item of income or expenditure would normally be large, the fact that it is small in the current year may be relevant to a user of the accounts;
- as well as considering the materiality of individual items, it will usually be necessary to consider similar items in aggregate as well, as the total may be material, even if the individual components are not.

The ICAEW is also in the process of revising its guidance on materiality and published a draft version as TECH 32/96 'The Interpretation of Materiality in Financial Reporting' in July 2007. Much of the detailed guidance remains unchanged, but it has been updated to take account of changes in accounting pronouncements in the intervening years and also the fact that many companies are now required, or have the option, to prepare accounts in accordance with IASs. Consequently, the latest proposals include references to both current UK accounting practice and international requirements. Proposed changes from the previous guidance include the following:

- When assessing the materiality of errors, account should be taken of the cumulative effect of errors that were judged immaterial in previous years and so went uncorrected. The guidance notes that such unadjusted prior year items may lead to a cumulative error that is material in relation to the current year balance sheet or profit and loss account. However, this does not mean that an error that arises in, and is material to, the current year should be offset against unadjusted errors arising in earlier years. A current year error that is material in its own right should be adjusted in the current year, regardless of the impact of any unadjusted errors from earlier years. Comments were specifically invited on the appropriateness of these proposals.

- Consideration of the fact that financial statements do not comply with IASs if they contain immaterial errors made intentionally to change the presentation of an entity's financial performance or position. There is no directly equivalent provision under UK accounting standards, although the guidance notes that the creation of deliberate immaterial errors in order to influence trends is contrary to the spirit of UK financial reporting. It also refers briefly to the APB's publication *Aggressive Earnings Management* and in particular the recommendations in that document that:
  - directors and management should, as a matter of principle, correct all misstatements identified by the auditors; and
  - auditors should consider whether judgements and decisions made by directors and management could be part of a pattern of bias, even though individually they may appear reasonable.

10.41   Exclusion of Immaterial Items

The consideration of materiality is equally important in establishing whether certain details need not be shown separately in the accounts. For instance, reporting in detail on items that are not material, and which are therefore not useful to a user of the accounts, may result in information that is relevant and useful becoming obscured. However, certain information must always be disclosed to meet the requirements of company law, even though it may not appear to be material in the context of the accounts.

10.42   Statement of Directors' Responsibilities

At a Glance
- * Audited accounts that are required to show a true and fair view should include a formal statement of the directors' responsibilities in respect of the accounts.
- * If the directors do not make such a statement, the auditors must include a description of the directors' responsibilities in their audit report.
- * The statement should cover the requirements for the directors to:
  - prepare accounts that show a true and fair view;
  - select suitable accounting policies and apply them consistently;
  - make judgements and estimates that are prudent and reasonable;
  - state whether applicable accounting standards have been followed;
  - prepare accounts on a going concern basis unless this is inappropriate;
  - keep proper accounting records;
  - safeguard the assets of the company;
  - take reasonable steps to prevent fraud and other irregularities and
  - where relevant, take responsibility for the maintenance and integrity of corporate and financial information included on the company's website.

> * In the case of small- and medium-sized companies, no reference needs to be made to the adoption of applicable accounting standards.
> * A different statement of directors' responsibilities is required where the company is exempt from having its annual accounts audited.
> * The wording of the statement may need to be adapted in the case of specialised businesses and unincorporated entities.

10.43   Requirement to Include a Statement of Responsibilities in the Annual Accounts

The inclusion of a formal statement of directors' responsibilities in respect of the accounts is addressed in the UK & Ireland version of International Standard on Auditing 700 (ISA 700) *The Auditor's Report on Financial Statements*. This standard applies in all cases where audited accounts are required to show a true and fair view. Auditors are required to refer in their report to a description of the responsibilities of the directors in respect of the accounts and to distinguish the responsibilities of the auditors from those of the directors. If a statement of the directors' responsibilities is not given in the accounts, or if the statement given is not considered adequate, the auditors must include an appropriate description of the directors' responsibilities within their audit report. In the case of listed companies, the FSA requires the directors to include in the annual report a narrative statement on how it has applied the principles set out in the Combined Code, together with details of, and reasons for, any areas of non-compliance. Provision C.1.1 of the Combined Code recommends that the directors explain their responsibility for preparing the accounts and that there is also a statement by the auditors clarifying their reporting responsibilities. The purpose of both statements is to help shareholders understand the respective roles and responsibilities of the directors and the auditors.

10.44   Presentation of the Statement

It is always preferable for the directors to make a separate statement of their responsibilities for the accounts rather than leaving this to be dealt with by the auditors. The Combined Code previously recommended that the directors' statement was given 'next to' the statement of the auditors' responsibilities (which usually forms part of the audit report). The wording of the revised Combined Code is more flexible and removes any confusion over the location of the statement. It has often been given above or below the auditors' report, or on the immediately preceding page, but it is also acceptable for the statement to be given within the directors' report or in a separate corporate governance report.

10.45   Content of the Statement

The following matters should be covered in the directors' statement:

- The requirement under company law for directors to prepare annual accounts giving a true and fair view of the profit or loss for the year and of the state of affairs of the company (and, where relevant, the group) at the end of the year.
- In preparing those accounts, the requirement for the directors to:
  - ○ select suitable accounting policies;
  - ○ apply those accounting policies on a consistent basis;
  - ○ make judgements and estimates that are prudent and reasonable;
  - ○ state whether applicable accounting standards have been followed, subject to any material departures disclosed and explained in the accounts and
  - ○ prepare the accounts on a going concern basis unless it is not appropriate to presume that the company will continue in business;
- The requirement for the directors to:
  - ○ keep proper accounting records;
  - ○ safeguard the assets of the company and
  - ○ take reasonable steps to prevent and detect fraud and other irregularities.
- Where the annual accounts and reports are published on the Internet, the fact that the directors are responsible for the maintenance and integrity of any corporate and financial information included on the company's website.

The statement on compliance with applicable accounting standards need not be given where the company qualifies as small- or medium-sized under company law.

10.46   Example Wording

The latest example wording for a statement of directors' responsibilities in respect of the accounts is given in Appendix 5 to APB Bulletin 2006/6 *Auditors' Reports on Financial Statements in the United Kingdom*. This gives the following suggested wording for a non-publicly traded company:

10.47   Example: Statement of Directors' Responsibilities for the Accounts

> The directors are responsible for preparing the annual report and the financial statements in accordance with applicable law and regulations.
>
> Company law requires directors to prepare financial statements for each financial year. Under that law, the directors have elected to prepare the financial statements in accordance with United Kingdom Generally Accepted Accounting Practice (UK Accounting Standards and applicable law). The financial statements are required by law to give a true and fair view of the state of affairs of the company and of the profit or loss of the company for that period. In preparing those financial statements, the directors are required to:

- select suitable accounting policies and then apply them consistently;
- make judgments and estimates that are reasonable and prudent;
- state whether applicable UK Accounting Standards have been followed, subject to any material departures disclosed and explained in the financial statements;*
- prepare the financial statements on the going concern basis unless it is inappropriate to presume that the company will continue in business.

The directors are responsible for keeping proper accounting records which disclose with reasonable accuracy at any time the financial position of the company and to enable them to ensure that the financial statements comply with the *Companies Act 1985*. They are also responsible for safeguarding the assets of the company and hence for taking reasonable steps for the prevention and detection of fraud and other irregularities.

The directors are responsible for the maintenance and integrity of the corporate and financial information included on the company's website. Legislation in the UK governing the preparation and dissemination of financial statements may differ from legislation in other jurisdictions.[†]

* Not required for companies that qualify as small- or medium-sized under company law.
† Required only where the financial statements are published on the Internet.

The Bulletin notes that the responsibilities of the directors of a publicly traded company will be dependent in part on the particular regulatory environment in which it operates and may vary depending on the rules of the market to which the securities are admitted to trading. Directors preparing IAS accounts may also need to take legal advice on what should be included in the statement of their responsibilities.

The directors of most companies choose to make the statement in terms of their general responsibilities, as set out above. It is equally acceptable for the statement to be made in more positive terms, for instance by stating that the directors are of the opinion that appropriate accounting policies have been adopted and applied consistently.

10.48   Impact of Audit Exemption

Where a small company is exempt from an audit under company law, a different statement of directors' responsibilities is required. The legislation specifies the content of the statement and requires it to be given on the balance sheet, above the signature of director(s).

10.49   Specialised Businesses and Unincorporated Entities

ISA (UK and Ireland) 700 applies to all audit reports on accounts that are required to show a true and fair view. The wording of the statement of directors' responsibilities may need to be amended to reflect the specific requirements applying to specialised businesses (for instance banks and insurance companies). In the case of unincorporated entities (such as charities and pension funds) the responsibilities of the directors, managers or trustees may not be so clearly defined and may vary quite considerably between apparently similar entities. Care must be taken to ensure that the statement given in the annual accounts properly reflects the responsibilities actually in place under the relevant constitution or trust deed.

10.50   Form and Content of Companies Act Individual Accounts

At a Glance
* Where Companies Act accounts are prepared, company law offers a choice of four formats for the profit and loss account and two formats for the balance sheet – once a format has been chosen, it must be used consistently from year to year unless there are good reasons for making a change.
* Certain additional items must be shown in the profit and loss account and additional information or analyses must be given in the notes to the accounts.
* UK accounting standards generally require more detailed disclosures to be given in the notes to the accounts – some add new items to the standard formats or require additional statements to be included in the accounts.
* The ASB has issued proposals for replacing the profit and loss account and statement of total recognised gains and losses with a single performance statement.
* Comparative figures must be given for each item in the profit and loss account and balance sheet, and most disclosures in the notes to the accounts.
* Company law and UK accounting standards prescribe the principles to be adopted when preparing accounts.
* UK accounting standards require accounts to reflect the commercial substance of the transactions undertaken by the company.
* Fair value accounting may be adopted for certain assets and liabilities.

10.51   Preparation of Companies Act Individual Accounts

For accounting periods beginning on or after 1 January 2005, most companies have the option of preparing either Companies Act individual accounts or IAS individual accounts (see **PARAGRAPHS 10.4** and **10.5**). Where IAS accounts are prepared, the detailed provisions of company law on the form and content of accounts no longer apply and the company must comply instead with the detailed requirements of all relevant IASs. Where Companies Act accounts are prepared, the detailed company law provisions continue to apply, as do the requirements of all relevant UK accounting standards. However, in many cases, similar principles apply under both reporting frameworks. The following paragraphs summarise the main requirements in respect of Companies Act individual accounts.

10.52 Prescribed Formats

A company preparing Companies Act accounts must use one of the prescribed formats set out in the legislation for the profit and loss account and for the balance sheet. The legislation provides a choice of four formats for the profit and loss account and two formats for the balance sheet. The directors can choose which format to adopt in each case, but once a format has been selected, it must be used consistently year by year unless there are good reasons for changing to another format. If a format is changed (for instance, where a change in activity makes an alternative profit and loss account format more appropriate to the company's business), details of the change must be disclosed in the accounts and the reason for the change must be explained. The formats do not generally indicate where sub-totals should be drawn and the directors are therefore free to decide on this themselves, subject to the additional disclosure requirements of accounting standards (see **PARAGRAPH 10.53**). Small companies adopting the FRSSE are now restricted to the use of two profit and loss account formats rather than the four set out in the legislation (see **PARAGRAPH 10.20**). The profit and loss account and balance sheet formats require additional information or analyses to be given for certain items. These disclosures are usually given in the notes to the accounts, together with other detailed disclosures required by the legislation.

In addition to the details set out in the standard formats, the legislation requires every profit and loss account to show the profit or loss on ordinary activities before taxation.

10.53 Requirements of UK Accounting Standards

UK accounting standards also require additional disclosures to support figures shown in the profit and loss account and balance sheet. The additional details are usually required to be given in the notes to the accounts, except in the case of FRS 3 *Reporting Financial Performance* which requires:

- The separate disclosure of 'operating profit' on the face of the profit and loss account.
- All figures from turnover through to operating profit to be analysed into amounts relating to continuing, discontinued and newly acquired operations – as a minimum, the figures for turnover and operating profit must be analysed in this way on the face of the profit and loss account.
- Separate disclosure on the face of the profit and loss account of:
  - profits and losses on the sale or termination of operations;
  - costs of a fundamental reorganisation or restructuring that has a material effect on the nature and focus of operations and
  - profits or losses on the disposal of fixed assets (other than marginal adjustments to depreciation charged in previous years).

FRS 3 also requires annual accounts to include a statement of total recognised gains and losses, to draw together all gains and losses recognised during the financial period, and a reconciliation of movements in shareholders' funds. The same standard also deals with the definition and disclosure of exceptional items and extraordinary items (although the latter are now very rare, as a result of the stringent definitions in FRS 3). FRS 1 *Cash Flow Statements* requires the presentation of a cash flow statement in the format specified in the standard. FRS 22 *Earnings per share* sets out detailed requirements on the calculation and disclosure of earnings per share – the standard applies to all companies whose shares are publicly traded (or about to become publicly traded) and to any company which chooses to disclose earnings per share on a voluntary basis.

10.54 Expected Future Developments

In December 2000, the ASB issued FRED 22 *Revision of FRS 3: Reporting Financial Performance* which proposes some significant changes to present disclosure requirements. The proposals represent an agreed international approach to reporting financial performance and replace the present profit and loss account and statement of total recognised gains and losses with a single performance statement showing all the gains and losses recognised during a financial period. The proposed performance statement is divided into three sections:

- operating;
- financial and treasury and
- other gains and losses.

The proposals have since been taken forward as a joint ASB/IASB project and the IASB published a revised version of IAS 1 *Presentation of Financial Statements* in September 2007. This includes a requirement for companies to present income and expenses separately from changes in equity arising from transactions with owners, and the option for entities to present income and expenses in a single performance statement or in two statements (i.e. with certain income and expenses shown in a Statement of Recognised Income and Expense and all other items shown in the income statement). This approach is very similar to that already required in the UK under FRS 3 *Reporting Financial Performance*. The ASB has therefore decided not to propose amendments to UK accounting practice at present. A second stage of the project will consider the presentation and aggregation of information in the performance statement and other elements of the financial statements, and the ASB hopes that this will build on the proposals developed in FRED 22 and its subsequent joint project with the IASB.

10.55 Comparative Figures

Comparative figures must be given for each item in the profit and loss account and balance sheet and for most of the additional information that has to be disclosed in the notes to the accounts. Where any figure reported in the accounts is not directly comparable with the equivalent amount for the previous year, the comparative figure must be adjusted unless an accounting standard or UITF Abstract requires or permits an alternative treatment (e.g. on the introduction of new accounting requirements where the restatement of comparatives on a consistent basis is considered to be too onerous and would outweigh the related benefits). The notes to the accounts must give details of any adjustment made to comparative figures, together with the reason for it, and also details of any non-comparability that has not been adjusted. UK accounting standards also include detailed requirements on the use of prior period adjustments to account for changes in accounting policies and the correction of fundamental errors.

10.56   Accounting Principles

Company law requires Companies Act accounts be based on the principles of going concern, consistency, accruals and prudence. These principles apply to all companies, regardless of size, and are considered to have such general acceptance that there is no requirement to refer to the fact that they have been followed when preparing the accounts – a company is presumed to have observed them unless its accounts state otherwise. The directors are only permitted to depart from the accounting principles where there are special reasons for doing so and the accounts must disclose particulars of the departure, the reasons for it and the financial effect. Detailed guidance on the principles that should be followed when preparing annual accounts, including practical interpretation of the legal requirements, can be found in the ASB's *Statement of Principles for Financial Reporting* and in FRS 18 *Accounting Policies*. Brief details are set out below.

10.57   *Going Concern*

Company law does not provide any detailed guidance on going concern. FRS 18 describes the going concern basis as the hypothesis that the entity is to continue in operational existence for the foreseeable future. When preparing accounts, the standard requires the directors to assess whether there are any significant doubts about the entity's ability to continue as a going concern and requires financial statements to be prepared on a going concern basis unless:

* the entity is being liquidated or has ceased trading;
* the directors intend to liquidate the entity or to cease trading or
* the directors have no realistic alternative but to liquidate the entity or to cease trading.

In these circumstances the entity should prepare the financial statements on a different basis. Additional disclosures may need to be given in the notes to the accounts where uncertainties affect the assessment of going concern, and the directors of listed companies are specifically required to make a formal statement on going concern each year (see CHAPTER 12).

10.58   *Consistency*

Accounting policies provide a framework within which assets, liabilities, income and expenditure are recognised, measured and presented in financial statements, and they help to improve the comparability of financial information. Both company law and FRS 18 require accounting policies to be applied consistently within an accounting period and from one financial year to the next. However, situations will inevitably arise from time to time which make it necessary for an entity to change one or more of its accounting policies. For instance, a new accounting standard may have been introduced which requires a different accounting treatment to the one previously adopted, or the nature or scale of activities may have changed so that an existing accounting policy is no longer acceptable. FRS 18 requires accounting policies to be regularly reviewed, and sets out specific accounting and disclosure requirements that apply whenever an accounting policy is changed.

10.59   *Accruals*

Company law requires all income and charges relating to the financial year to be taken into account, regardless of the date of receipt or payment. FRS 18 also requires adoption of the accruals method of accounting, which it describes as requiring 'the non-cash effects of transactions and other events to be reflected, as far as is possible, in the financial statements for the accounting period in which they occur and not, for example, in the period in which any cash involved is received or paid'. Provision must therefore be made for all expenses and losses relating to the year in question, and for income and profits relating to that year, subject to the requirement for prudence (see **PARAGRAPH 10.60**).

10.60   *Prudence*

Company law requires the amount of any item in the accounts to be determined on a prudent basis. In particular, only profits realised at the balance sheet date should be included in the profit and loss account, and all losses or liabilities which have arisen (or are likely to arise) in respect of the current financial year or any previous financial year must be taken into account. This includes any liabilities or losses that only become apparent between the balance sheet date and the date on which the accounts are formally approved and signed by the directors. FRS 18 does not deal with prudence as such, but emphasises the need for financial information to be reliable and also the legal requirement that only realised profits are to be included in the accounts. The standard notes that profits should be treated as realised for accounting purposes only when they have been realised in the form of cash or of other assets, the ultimate cash realisation of which can be assessed with reasonable certainty. In the section on reliability, FRS 18 makes the following points:

- under conditions of uncertainty, financial information is reliable if it has been prudently prepared (i.e. a degree of caution has been applied in exercising judgement and making necessary estimates);

- it is not necessary to exercise prudence where there is no uncertainty and
- it is not appropriate to use prudence as a reason for creating hidden reserves or excessive provisions, deliberately understating assets or gains, or deliberately overstating liabilities or losses.

10.61   Substance Over Form

Under FRS 5 *Reporting the Substance of Transactions*, accounts are required to reflect the commercial substance of the transactions entered into by the reporting entity rather than their legal form (where this is different). The commercial substance of a transaction is not always easily identifiable, especially where:

- the principal benefits of an asset are in some way separated from legal ownership;
- the transaction involves options or conditions that are not commercially realistic (for instance, where the terms of an option mean that it is virtually certain not to be exercised) and
- the overall commercial effect of a series of transactions is different from the apparent effect of the individual transactions.

When assessing the substance of a transaction, the standard requires greater emphasis to be given to the aspects of the transaction that are likely to have a practical commercial effect. Where an overall commercial effect is achieved by a series of transactions, the standard requires the series to be considered as a whole rather than as individual transactions. FRS 5 is deliberately conceptual rather than factual in nature to prevent transactions being structured so as to circumvent prescribed rules.

Also, for accounting periods beginning on or after 1 January 2005, company law has been amended to require directors to have regard to the substance of the reported transaction or arrangement, in accordance with generally accepted accounting principles, when determining how items are presented in the profit and loss account and balance sheet.

10.62   Fair Value Accounting

The requirements of the EU Fair Value Directive have been introduced into UK company law for accounting periods beginning on or after 1 January 2005. Fair value accounting has been made optional rather than mandatory in the UK but can be applied to both individual and consolidated accounts. Under the new legislation, most financial instruments (including derivatives) may be included in the accounts at fair value provided that this can be determined reliably on the basis set out in the legislation. However, fair value accounting cannot currently be applied in the case of financial liabilities unless they are derivatives or are held as part of a trading portfolio. The detailed UK framework for the adoption of fair value accounting is set out in UK accounting standards (FRSs 23 to 26 and FRS 29) which apply to listed companies for accounting periods beginning on or after 1 January 2005, and to other entities for accounting periods beginning on or after 1 January 2006 (but only where they choose to adopt fair value accounting).

In March 2007, the DTI published a consultation document on the proposed UK implementation of various amendments to EC Company Law Directives, including an option for Member States to allow the adoption of fair value accounting for a slightly wider range of financial instruments by linking the legal provisions with IASs as adopted by the EU. The Government proposes to take advantage of this option in order to give companies greater flexibility, particularly in accounting for financial liabilities. The necessary changes are likely to be introduced from 6 April 2008 in conjunction with the implementation of the accounts provisions of the *CA 2006*.

10.63   Form and Content of Companies Act Group Accounts

At a Glance
* Companies Act group accounts must be prepared in the form of consolidated accounts and must generally include the accounts of the parent company and all its subsidiaries.
* Company law and FRS 2 *Accounting for Subsidiary Undertakings* set out detailed rules on what constitutes a subsidiary undertaking.
* In certain circumstances, a subsidiary undertaking is permitted or required to be excluded from the consolidated accounts.
* The assets, liabilities, profits, losses and cashflows of certain other entities ('quasi-subsidiaries') may also need to be included in the group accounts, even if these entities do not meet the legal definition of a subsidiary undertaking.
* The results of associates and joint ventures should be normally be included in group accounts using the equity method of accounting.
* Company law and accounting standards include detailed rules on the preparation of consolidated accounts and on accounting for acquisitions and mergers.
* Directors must ensure that the financial year of each subsidiary undertaking coincides with that of the parent unless there are good reasons against this.

10.64   Preparation of Companies Act Group Accounts

For accounting periods beginning on or after 1 January 2005, most parent companies have the option of preparing either Companies Act group accounts or IAS group accounts (see **PARAGRAPHS 10.4** and **10.5**). Where IAS group accounts are prepared, the detailed provisions of company law on the form and content of accounts no longer apply and the parent must comply instead with the detailed requirements of all relevant IASs. Where Companies Act group accounts are prepared, the detailed company law provisions continue to apply, as do the requirements of all relevant UK accounting standards. In particular, the requirement to prepare group accounts and the definition of a subsidiary undertaking are set out in the main legislation rather than in the detailed provisions on the form and content of accounts and so apply to all parent companies, irrespective of the financial framework adopted. The following paragraphs summarise the main requirements in respect of Companies Act group accounts. However, in many cases, similar principles also apply to IAS group accounts.

10.65 Consolidated Accounts

Companies Act group accounts must be prepared in the form of consolidated accounts and must include the accounts of the parent company and all its subsidiary undertakings. The only exception to this rule is where a subsidiary undertaking is required or permitted by the legislation, or by accounting standards, to be excluded from the consolidation. The requirements of UK accounting standards, particularly FRS 2 *Accounting for Subsidiary Undertakings*, must also be taken into account. The prescribed formats (with appropriate adaptations) and the true and fair requirement apply to Companies Act group accounts in the same way as to Companies Act individual accounts.

10.66 Definition of Subsidiary Undertaking

The detailed rules on what constitutes a subsidiary undertaking are set out in company law and in FRS 2. The focus of these definitions is the ability of the parent to control the subsidiary. Although company law uses terms such as 'exercises a dominant influence' and 'managed on a unified basis', it does not expand on these. FRS 2 gives detailed guidance on how these terms should be interpreted for practical purposes. Company law provides guidance on the interpretation of voting rights for the purpose of establishing whether an entity is a subsidiary undertaking.

10.67 Exclusion of a Subsidiary from the Group Accounts

Company law permits a subsidiary undertaking to be excluded from the consolidation if:

- severe long-term restrictions hinder the parent's ability to exercise its rights over the assets and management of the entity or
- the interest is held exclusively for resale.

FRS 2 includes detailed guidance on the conditions that should be met for exclusion to be justified on these grounds, but where the conditions are met the standard requires exclusion rather than permitting it. FRS 2 also prescribes the accounting treatment to be adopted in each case: a subsidiary excluded on the grounds of long-term restrictions should be accounted for as a fixed asset investment and an interest held exclusively for resale should be accounted for as a current asset investment. For accounting periods beginning before 1 January 2005, both company law and FRS 2 required a subsidiary to be excluded from the consolidation where its activities were so different from the rest of the group that its inclusion in the consolidation would be incompatible with the true and fair view, but both the legislation and the accounting standard have been amended so that exclusion on these grounds is no longer required or permitted for accounting periods beginning on or after 1 January 2005. Company law also permits a subsidiary to be excluded from the consolidation in two other situations:

- where inclusion would not be material for the purpose of achieving a true and fair view (if two or more subsidiaries are involved, materiality must be assessed on an aggregate basis) – FRS 2 makes no reference to this as accounting standards are only intended to apply to material items;
- where the necessary information cannot be obtained without undue expense or delay – FRS 2 does not permit exclusion on these grounds.

In any case where a subsidiary is excluded from the consolidation, both company law and FRS 2 require detailed disclosures to be given in the accounts.

10.68   Quasi-subsidiaries

An undertaking may in effect be controlled by another entity, and generate benefits for that entity, without meeting the definition of a subsidiary undertaking set out in company law or FRS 2. Such an undertaking is described as a 'quasi-subsidiary' in FRS 5 *Reporting the Substance of Transactions* and the standard generally requires the assets, liabilities, profits, losses and cash flows of the quasi-subsidiary to be included in the group accounts of the 'parent' in order to reflect the true substance of the arrangements. Consideration of whether an entity meets the definition of a 'quasi-subsidiary' must take into account:

- who gains the benefit from the entity's net assets;
- who bears the inherent risks relating to the net assets and
- who directs the operating and financial policies of the entity.

Risk is defined in the standard as including the potential to gain as well as the possible exposure to loss, and the ability to prevent others from gaining access to benefits or from directing the entity's policies are equally relevant to the assessment. As a result of changes to the company law definitions of a subsidiary for accounting periods beginning on or after 1 January 2005, certain entities that were previously included in consolidated accounts as quasi-subsidiaries are now likely to be accounted for as subsidiaries.

10.69   Associates

It has become common practice for companies and groups to carry out part of their business activities through entities that are not subsidiary undertakings but over which the investor nevertheless has a considerable degree of influence. An associate is defined as an entity, other than a subsidiary, in which the investor has a participating interest and over whose operating and financial policies the investor exercises significant influence. Company law defines a participating interest as an interest held on a long-term basis for the purpose of securing a contribution to activities through the exercise of control or influence. FRS 9 *Associates and Joint Ventures* gives detailed guidance on the practical application of this definition and of the term 'significant influence'. A shareholding of 20% or more will usually constitute a participating interest, although it is possible to rebut this presumption in certain cases. Although it would be inappropriate to consolidate fully the results, assets and liabilities of an associate into the group accounts, it is also accepted that it would be misleading to ignore the nature of the relationship and account for the associate in the same way as other investments (for instance, by simply reflecting any dividends received as income in the profit and loss account). Both company law and FRS 9 therefore require the results of associates to be included in the accounts using the equity method of accounting. Under this method, the investing group's share of the profit or loss of the associate is included in the profit and loss account, and its share of the underlying net assets of the associate is included in the group balance sheet.

10.70   Joint Ventures

FRS 9 also includes detailed guidance on the definition of a joint venture and requires such an entity to be accounted for using the gross equity method of accounting. This is broadly the same as the equity method of accounting but with two additional disclosure requirements:

- the investor's share of the turnover of the joint venture must be shown in the consolidated profit and loss account and
- the investor's share of the gross assets and liabilities of the joint venture should be shown in the consolidated balance sheet.

Care is needed in the presentation of these figures to ensure they are not confused with those of the group, or do not appear to be included as part of the totals for the group. Further disclosures must be given where a major part of the business is conducted through joint ventures.

10.71   Consolidation Rules

Both company law and FRS 2 set out detailed rules on the preparation of consolidated accounts, the main points being that:

- uniform accounting policies should be used throughout the group to determine the amounts to be included in the group accounts – where (in exceptional circumstances) this is not possible, full details of the differences must be disclosed in the accounts;
- where assets held by any group undertakings include profits or losses arising from intra-group transactions (for instance, where items in stock have been purchased from another group company at more than cost price), the full amount of the profit or loss must be eliminated when preparing the consolidated accounts;

- amounts due to and from undertakings included in the consolidation, and income and expenditure relating to transactions between them, must be eliminated from the consolidated accounts and
- the amount of capital and reserves attributable to shares held by any minority interests, and the profit or loss on ordinary activities (and any extraordinary items) attributable to them, must be shown separately in the consolidated accounts – *Schedule 4A* to *CA 1985* amends the balance sheet and profit and loss account formats to provide additional headings for these disclosures.

There are also detailed rules in the legislation, and in particular in accounting standards, on accounting for acquisitions and mergers and for any goodwill that arises on consolidation.

10.72   Acquisitions and Mergers

There are currently two permitted methods of accounting for the combination of existing businesses – acquisition accounting and merger accounting. Merger accounting can only be used when the stringent criteria set out in company law and FRS 6 *Acquisitions and Mergers* are met. Most business combinations are therefore accounted for as acquisitions. Under this method of accounting, the assets and liabilities of the acquired entity are brought into the group accounts at fair value as at the date of acquisition, and the results of the entity are included in the group accounts only from the date of acquisition. FRS 7 *Fair Values in Acquisition Accounting* sets out rules on how the fair value of each type of asset and liability should be established. Any difference between the purchase consideration and the aggregate fair value of the assets and liabilities acquired constitutes purchased goodwill.

It should be noted that this is one of the areas where there is a significant difference between UK accounting practice and the requirements of international accounting standards. Under IFRS 3, all business combinations must be accounted for as acquisitions and a number of the detailed aspects of acquisition accounting (including the accounting treatment of goodwill) vary between the two financial reporting frameworks. The ASB has published proposals to converge UK accounting practice with international requirements, but expressed certain reservations about these when publishing the relevant Exposure Drafts. The IASB is also still in the process of finalising Phase II of its business combinations project and this includes a number of controversial proposals which, if adopted, would also make significant changes to current accounting practice.

10.73   Goodwill

Goodwill is a means of recognising that the value of a business as a whole is often more than the aggregate value of the underlying assets and liabilities. Neither company law nor FRS 10 *Goodwill and Intangible Assets* permits internally generated goodwill to be recognised on the balance sheet. Goodwill is therefore only recognised for accounting purposes when it is purchased as part of a business acquisition. When a company buys an unincorporated business, any goodwill acquired will be recognised on the company's own balance sheet along with the other business assets and liabilities acquired. When a company acquires a business by buying shares in another company, any goodwill acquired is recorded only when the accounts of the company and its new subsidiary are consolidated to form group accounts. Goodwill arising in a company's own accounts and goodwill arising on consolidation must be accounted for in accordance with FRS 10. The standard requires purchased goodwill to be capitalised as an asset and amortised over its useful economic life. There is a rebuttable presumption that the useful economic life of goodwill is no more than 20 years. If it can be demonstrated that the expected life of the goodwill is indefinite, the asset should not be amortised but a detailed impairment review must be carried out each year. This treatment will require use of the true and fair override, as company law requires all goodwill to be amortised. Annual impairment reviews must also be carried if the goodwill is amortised over a period of more than 20 years. FRS 10 sets out separate requirements on accounting for negative goodwill, which arises when the purchase consideration is less than the aggregate fair value of the assets and liabilities acquired.

As noted in **PARAGRAPH 10.72**, the accounting treatment of acquisitions and the related goodwill is one area where current UK accounting practice differs significantly from international requirements.

10.74   Accounting Date of Subsidiary Undertakings

Under company law, the directors of a parent company must ensure that the financial year of each subsidiary undertaking coincides with that of the parent unless, in their opinion, there are good reasons against this. In this case, the legislation requires the group accounts to include:

- the latest accounts of the subsidiary undertaking, provided that these are for a period ending not more than three months before the financial year end of the parent company or
- interim accounts for the subsidiary made up to the financial year end of the parent company.

FRS 2 *Accounting for Subsidiary Undertakings* sets out more stringent rules, requiring the accounts of all subsidiary undertakings included in the consolidated accounts to be for the same accounting period and made up to the same accounting date as the accounts of the parent, as far as is practicable. Where a subsidiary has a different financial year end, interim accounts should therefore be prepared for consolidation purposes. Only if this is not practicable should the latest accounts of the subsidiary be used, and even then adjustments must be made to reflect any changes in the intervening period if these have a material effect on the group accounts. The standard also requires additional disclosure in the notes to the accounts when a subsidiary prepares its accounts to a different accounting date, or for a different accounting period, from that of the parent company.

10.75   Directors' Report

At a Glance
* Directors are required to prepare a formal report for each financial year – where the company is required to prepare group accounts, the directors' report must also provide information for the group as a whole.
* The detailed contents of the directors' report are prescribed in company law.
* The auditors are specifically required to consider whether the informa-tion presented in the directors' report is consistent with the annual accounts.
* The report must include a fair review of the development of the business during the year and the position at the end of the year.
* The ASB has issued a non-mandatory Reporting Statement 'Operating and Financial Review' to provide a framework for the discussion of a company's performance and financial position.
* Detailed disclosures must be given on political donations and expenditure.
* A company whose shares are publicly traded on a regulated market is required to give detailed disclosures on its capital structure and share-holdings.
* Where the company's accounts are subject to audit, the directors' report must include formal confirmation that the directors have disclosed all relevant information to the auditors.
* Certain disclosures must also be given in respect of any qualifying third party indemnity for the benefit of a director of the company or of an associated company.
* New legal requirements on corporate governance disclosures are expected to be introduced in conjunction with CA 2006.

10.76   Requirement to Prepare

Company law requires the directors to prepare a report for each financial year. The detailed contents of the report are specified in the legislation, and the detailed disclosure requirements, particularly in respect of the business review, have been made more prescriptive for accounting periods beginning on or after 1 April 2005. Further changes have been introduced for quoted companies under CA 2006. The report must be approved by the board and signed on their behalf by a director or by the company secretary. Where the company is required to prepare group accounts, the directors' report must also provide the required information for the group as whole – however, disclosure requirements in respect of the direc-tors relate only to the directors of the parent company.

10.77   Consistency with the Accounts

The information given in the directors' report must be consistent with any related information given or included in the annual accounts. The auditors are specifically required to consider whether the directors' report is consistent with the accounts and to include an opinion on this in their report on the accounts. This is a new reporting responsibility which applies for accounting periods beginning on or after 1 April 2005 – previously, auditors were only required to report on any unresolved inconsistencies identified as a result of their review of the directors' report.

10.78   Fair Review of the Business

For accounting periods beginning on or after 1 April 2005, the requirement for the directors' report to include a business review is much more prescriptive than under the previous legislation. The report must include a balanced and comprehensive review of the business and details of the principal risks and uncertainties that it faces. In particular, the review must include:

- explanations of amounts included in the financial statements for the year;
- analysis using key financial performance indicators and
- where appropriate, analysis using other key performance indicators (KPIs), particularly on environmental and employee issues.

Where a parent company prepares group accounts, the review should cover the company and the subsidiary undertakings included in the consolidation. Small companies are exempt from the requirement to include a business review in the directors' report and medium-sized companies are exempt from the requirement to disclose non-financial KPIs, although they are still expected to provide relevant financial indicators. The DTI issued additional guidance on the new requirement for an enhanced business review and in this referred specifically to the following documents as useful points of reference for directors when preparing their report:

- the ASB Reporting Statement 'Operating and Financial Review' (see PARAGRAPHS 10.80–10.84);
- guidance on reporting on employee matters published by Accounting for People;
- guidance on environmental reporting published by Department for Environment, Food and Rural Affairs (DEFRA) (see PARAGRAPH 10.85) and
- guidance published by the DTI Materiality Working Group (see PARAGRAPH 10.86).

CA 2006 imposes certain additional requirements on the content of the business review which will apply in the case of a quoted company. The new legislation provides that, to the extent necessary for an understanding of the development, performance or position of the company's business, the business review of a quoted company should include:

- the main trends and factors likely to affect the future development, performance and position of the company's business;
- information on environmental matters (including the impact of the company's business on the environment), the company's employees, and social and community issues – these disclosures should include details of the company's policies and their effectiveness and

- information about persons with whom the company has contractual or other arrangements that are essential to the company's business.

If the review does not include information on any of the matters specified in the last two points above, it must state which items have been excluded. The disclosure requirements in the last point above were added at a late stage in the Bill's progress through Parliament and gave rise to considerable debate when introduced. In particular, they are intended to highlight any ethical issues arising from the company's contractual relationships with overseas suppliers. These new provisions have been brought into effect from 1 October 2007 and apply for accounting periods beginning on or after that date.

10.79   *Disclosure Exemptions*

CA 2006 also provides that information about impending developments or matters in the course of negotiation need not be disclosed in the business review if disclosure would, in the opinion of the directors, be seriously prejudicial to the interests of the company. This applies to all companies rather just to quoted companies. Also, the disclosures on contractual business arrangements required to be given by a quoted company need not include information about a person if that disclosure would, in the opinion of the directors, be seriously prejudicial to that person and contrary to the public interest. It should be noted that this exemption makes no reference to disclosure being seriously prejudicial to the company. The relevant sections of *CA 2006* have been brought into effect from 1 October 2007 and apply for accounting periods beginning on or after that date.

10.80   ASB Reporting Statement 'Operating and Financial Review'

The ASB issued a non-mandatory Statement *Operating and Financial Review* in July 1993 to provide a framework for the discussion, within the annual report, of the main factors underlying a company's financial performance and financial position. A revised version of the Statement was published in January 2003 and provided a broader framework for the discussion of business performance than its 1993 predecessor. The document was intended primarily for listed companies and other larger organisations, but the ASB emphasised that the principles were relevant to all entities. The 2003 Statement was initially superseded by Reporting Standard 1 (RS 1) 'Operating and Financial Review' published by the ASB in May 2005 in preparation for the introduction of statutory OFRs for quoted companies, but when the statutory OFR legislation was repealed, RS 1 was replaced by a new ASB Reporting Statement 'Operating and Financial Review'. This was issued in January 2006 and sets out the latest best practice guidance on the preparation of an OFR or detailed business review. The document has two main sections – the first sets out the principles that directors should apply when preparing an OFR and the second provides a disclosure framework. Separate 'Implementation Guidance' shows how some of the recommended disclosures might be handled in practice. Although the document gives an indication of topics and issues that may need to be covered in the business review, neither the Statement nor the related 'Implementation Guidance' is intended to be exhaustive and directors may need to consider including other matters, depending on the particular circumstances of the company or group. Where relevant, companies are encouraged to disclose the fact that they have complied with the ASB Statement, but there is no requirement to do so, given its non-mandatory status.

10.81   *Presentation of an OFR Analysis*

The OFR analysis should be presented through the eyes of the directors and should focus on issues of concern to members, but recognising that the information may also be of interest to other stakeholders. The report should have a forward-looking orientation, as the objective is to help shareholders understand and assess the company's strategies and the potential for these to succeed. In particular, it should cover:

- the development and performance of the business during the year;
- the position of the business at the end of the year;
- the main trends and factors underlying the above and
- the main trends and factors likely to affect the business's future development, performance and financial position.

The directors should discuss the issues that have affected the performance of the business during the period and those that are expected to affect its future performance and financial position. In particular, the discussion should comment on the impact of any significant events occurring after the balance sheet date and on any predictive comments included in previous reviews that were not borne out by events. The ASB also notes that directors may want to include a statement that, even though it is provided in good faith, forward-looking information should be treated with caution in view of the surrounding uncertainties.

10.82   *Other Key Principles*

The OFR should:

- complement and supplement the details provided in the financial statements;
- be written in a clear and readily understandable style;
- be comprehensive and understandable;
- be balanced and neutral, dealing even-handedly with both positive and negative issues and
- be comparable over successive periods and, if appropriate, with other entities in the same industry or sector.

The ASB also emphasises that the objective of the OFR is quality rather than quantity, and that the inclusion of too much information can result in significant issues becoming obscured. As under the previous guidance, the review should highlight any adjustments that have been made to information derived from the financial statements and provide a reconciliation of the figures.

10.83   *Detailed Disclosures*

As under the previous guidance, directors are encouraged to discuss the resources available to the business, and especially any that are not reflected in the balance sheet, together with:

- the risks and uncertainties facing the business, and how these are managed;
- significant relationships likely to influence performance and business value;
- the company's capital structure, cash flows, liquidity and treasury policies and
- any receipts from, and returns to, shareholders.

The discussion should include a description of the environment in which the business operates, including its main markets, its competitive position and any significant features of the relevant regulatory, economic and social environment. The OFR should also explain the longer-term objectives of the business, including those in relevant non-financial areas, and the directors' strategies for achieving these.

10.84   *Key Performance Indicators*

There is a particular emphasis on the disclosure of the KPIs, both financial and non-financial, that the directors consider to be the most effective and critical in managing the business and measuring delivery of the company's strategies. The 'Implementation Guidance' sets out examples of KPIs that might be used and the issues that the directors need to consider in each case. DEFRA has subsequently published more detailed guidance on reporting on environmental issues (see **PARAGRAPH 10.85**). The ASB also recommends that the following details should be given for each KPI shown in the OFR, to help users understand and evaluate the information provided:

- the definition, purpose and calculation method used;
- the source of underlying data and, where relevant, an explanation of any assumptions made;
- quantification of, or commentary on, future targets and
- where available, the corresponding amount for the previous year.

Any changes to KPIs, or to the calculation methods used, from the previous year should also be highlighted and any significant changes in the underlying accounting policies adopted in the financial statements should be explained.

10.85   DEFRA Guidance on Environmental Reporting

In January 2006, the DEFRA published new guidance on environmental reporting in *Environmental Key Performance Indicators: Reporting Guidelines for UK*

Business. This defines which KPIs are likely to be most relevant to each business sector and suggests how companies can use these to manage their environmental performance. The document recommends that the directors' report discusses the impacts of the business on the environment and of the environment on the business, the policies adopted for managing these, and the company's actual performance in doing so. The report identifies 22 environmental KPIs that are considered to be significant to UK businesses, and companies are generally encouraged to report on up to five of them, concentrating on those that are most significant to their particular circumstances. The guidance looks at the underlying principles of environmental reporting, including the need for transparency, accountability and credibility, and the need for KPIs to be quantitative, relevant and comparable, so that the performance of an entity can be assessed over time and in relation to its competitors. Businesses are encouraged to present KPIs in absolute terms for the reporting period and also in relation to a normalising factor, such as turnover or production output. Each KPI reported should be accompanied by a general narrative explaining its purpose and impacts, the calculation methods used and any relevant assumptions made. Progress against targets should also be discussed, regardless of whether this reflects improvements or setbacks, with information on how any problem areas are being tackled. The guidelines also highlight the importance of reporting on any fines and associated costs incurred in respect of environmental issues, regardless of the amount and materiality of these, together with the number of any related prosecutions. The guidance can be downloaded from the DEFRA website at http://www.defra.gov.uk/environment/business/envrp/guidelines.htm.

10.86   DTI's 'Practical Guidance for Directors'

In December 2002, as part of the project to introduce a statutory OFR, the DTI established a separate working group to develop broad principles and practical guidance for directors on how to establish whether an item is sufficiently material to be included in the OFR. The group issued an initial guidance document in May 2004, in conjunction with draft regulations on the statutory OFR. An updated version of the guidance was expected to be issued once the OFR regulations had been finalised. However, following the repeal of the statutory OFR provisions before they had come fully into effect, the DTI reissued the original guidance document in January 2006 without further amendment. As a result, the document continues to refer to the draft OFR regulations, even though the guidance is now intended to assist directors in the preparation of an enhanced business review for the directors' report or a voluntary OFR.

Part I of the guidance covers the need for directors to understand the objectives of an enhanced business review or OFR and to:

- take a broad view, which includes exploring and understanding the agendas of all the stakeholders that are likely to influence the company's performance, either directly or indirectly;
- act collectively in making good faith, honest judgements on what should and need not be reported and on how the information is presented;

- identify any areas where access to additional skills and knowledge is required (e.g. environmental, social and community issues) and
- achieve an appropriate balance between historic review and the trends and factors most likely to affect future performance.

Whether an individual item is disclosed or not will depend not only on its nature and size but also on the effect that it may have in the particular circumstances of the business and on how it may be viewed in conjunction with other information about the company or group. For each area, the guidance explains the underlying principles and then illustrates them with practical examples of issues that may arise in a specific type of business and the sort of disclosure that the directors might make in these circumstances.

Part II of the guidance highlights the importance of establishing a sound process to provide evidence that the directors have taken their reporting responsibilities seriously. In particular, the process should be properly planned, recorded and communicated and should have a clear timetable which allows for appropriate consultation, both within the organisation and externally where necessary. The guidance also recommends a major internal review of the process every three to five years, linked to the company's strategic planning cycle. The process should conclude with a formal sign-off by the board as a whole, not only on the inclusion or exclusion of individual items, but also that the information given provides a thorough and balanced picture, and that nothing of significance has been overlooked.

10.87   ASB 'Review of Narrative Reporting'

In January 2007, the ASB published 'A Review of Narrative Reporting By UK Listed Companies in 2006' (available at http://www.frc.org.uk/publications/pubs.cfm), which considers separately the extent to which companies are:

- complying with company law requirements and
- adopting the best practice recommendations in the latest version of the ASB's Reporting Statement 'Operating and Financial Review' (see PARAGRAPHS 10.80–10.84).

The comments are based on the ASB's own survey of the reports prepared by 23 UK listed companies but also refer to the results of a number of other recent independent surveys.

The ASB concludes that compliance with current legal requirements is generally good but highlights scope for improvement in a number areas. The main area identified for improvement is reporting on risks and uncertainties, where there is a tendency for companies to list all risks rather than identify the principal risks and uncertainties, and where reporting currently concentrates on financial risks with little coverage of strategic, commercial and operational issues. Other areas highlighted include the disclosure of KPIs, both financial and non-financial, and the provision of forward-looking information, where companies are generally considered to be complying with the basic requirement under current company law, but will need to report in greater detail under the more stringent requirements of

CA 2006. The ASB also highlights the need for careful cross-referencing when information is included in different parts of the annual report.

As regards the adoption of best practice, the ASB notes a willingness by companies to move beyond legal compliance towards best practice although size is clearly an issue here, with FTSE 100 companies generally achieving the highest scores although even here the ASB noted a wide range of performance. The weakest areas were reporting on future development and performance and on non-financial KPIs. The ASB refers to the 'safe harbour' provisions included in CA 2006 (see **PARAGRAPH 10.89**) and hopes that these will encourage directors to be more forthcoming in reporting on future trends and developments. The ASB also found that companies are now providing considerable detail on financial KPIs but few provide a good range of non-financial KPIs, and that where KPIs are provided they are often not adequately defined and there is no explanation of why particular indicators are considered key.

Other areas identified as needing attention include information on:

- the legal, regulatory, macro economic and social environment in which the company operates;
- resources not included on the balance sheet, such as corporate reputation, brand strength and intellectual property and
- contractual arrangements and relationships (e.g. with significant customers and/or suppliers).

10.88 Forward-Looking Information

Company law has for some time required the directors' report to include an indication of the likely future developments of the company and its subsidiaries and this is also covered in the new requirements on the enhanced business review. This aspect of the directors' report can be a particular problem area for directors of listed companies, as they need to ensure that their comments cannot later be deemed to constitute a profit forecast. The DTI guidance on the preparation of an enhanced business review emphasises that directors will need to consider disclosing information on trends and factors likely to affect the future development, performance or financial position of the business where this is necessary to give the balanced and comprehensive analysis required by the legislation. The ASB recommends that an OFR or enhanced business review should have a forward-looking orientation, but notes that directors may want to include a statement that, whilst provided in good faith, forward-looking information should be treated with caution in view of the surrounding uncertainties. It is also hoped that the new provisions on directors' liability (see **PARAGRAPH 10.89**) will help to encourage this aspect of company reporting. Also, in September 2003, the ICAEW published guidance on the preparation and publication of prospective financial information (PFI). Whilst most PFI will be published in order to comply with listing and other regulatory requirements, the guidance includes a separate section on voluntary PFI, which includes relevant disclosures in an OFR or directors' report. The document *Prospective Financial Information: Guidance for UK Directors* is available from the ICAEW website at http://icaew.co.uk/pfi

10.89 Directors' Liability for False or Misleading Statements

CA 2006 also sets out a clear statement of the liability of directors in respect of false or misleading statements made in the directors' report or the directors' remuneration report (see **CHAPTER 9**), and in any information derived from those reports that is included in a summary financial statement (see **PARAGRAPH 10.96**). A director will be liable to compensate the company for any loss suffered by it as a result of any untrue or misleading statement made in such a report, or of the omission of anything which the legislation requires to be included, if:

- he knew the statement to be untrue or misleading, or was reckless as to whether it was untrue or misleading or
- he knew the omission to be a dishonest concealment of a material fact.

However, there is no liability to any person other than the company as a result of reliance on information given in the report. This section of CA 2006 has been brought into effect from 20 January 2007 by the *Companies Act 2006 (Commencement No 1, Transitional Provisions and Savings) Order 2006* (SI 2006 No 3428).

It is hoped that the inclusion of this new 'safe harbour' provision will act as an encouragement for directors to provide more meaningful forward-looking information in statutory reports, and in the business review section of the directors' report in particular.

10.90 Political Donations

Company law broadly requires:

- prior shareholder approval for political expenditure within the EU and for aggregate donations to EU political organisations of more than £5000 by a company and its subsidiaries in any 12-month period;
- disclosure of the detailed names and amounts where the aggregate amount of political expenditure and political donations in the EU by a company or group exceeds £200 and
- disclosure of the aggregate amount paid or donated to non-EU political parties (in this case there is no *de minimis* amount).

Where a payment or donation is to be made by a subsidiary, prior approval must also be obtained from the shareholders of the holding company. Wholly owned subsidiaries of UK holding companies are exempt from the disclosure requirements, on the basis that the details will be given in the holding company's accounts. If these requirements are not followed, the directors will be personally liable to make good the amount paid or donated and to pay damages for any loss suffered by the company. In the case of non-compliance by a subsidiary, the directors of the holding company will also be personally liable.

The relevant sections of *CA 1985* are repealed with effect from 1 October 2007 by the *Companies Act 2006 (Commencement No 3, Consequential Amendments, Transitional Provisions and Savings) Order 2007 (SI 2007/2194)* and replaced with similar, but slightly amended, approval requirements under Sections 362–379 of *CA 2006*. In particular, the definitions of political expenditure and political donation are extended to include those relating to independent election candidates, although these changes do not take effect until 1 October 2008. The detailed disclosure requirements are unchanged at present, but new requirements will be set out in due course in regulations made under *CA 2006*.

The DTI consultation document 'Implementation of Companies Act 2006' published in February 2007 sets out more detailed proposals for the secondary legislation required under *CA 2006* and transitional arrangements on the application of the new law to existing companies. The document highlights a number of areas where changes to current requirements are being considered and these include an increase in the disclosure threshold for both political and charitable donations from £200 to £2000. The changes are expected to be implemented with effect from 6 April 2008.

10.91   Capital Structure and Shareholdings

Section 992 of *CA 2006* introduces certain additional disclosures that must be given in the directors' reports of companies whose shares are publicly traded on a regulated market. The detailed disclosures include:

- details of the company's capital structure;
- any restrictions on the transfer of securities;
- details of significant direct or indirect holdings of the company's securities;
- details of any person who holds securities that carry special rights with regard to control of the company;
- any restrictions on voting rights;
- agreements that may result in restrictions on the transfer of securities or on voting rights;
- any rules on the appointment and replacement of directors, or on amendment of the company's articles;
- the powers of the directors, including any relating to the issuing or buying back of shares by the company;
- any significant agreements that take effect, alter or terminate on a change of control following a takeover bid and
- any agreements for compensation for loss of office or employment as a result of a takeover bid.

The report must include any necessary explanatory material on these issues, and this material must also be included in, or provided with, any summary financial statement issued by the company (see **PARAGRAPH 10.96**).

These new disclosure requirements are introduced as a result of the EC Takeovers Directive and apply to directors' reports for financial years beginning on or after 20 May 2006. As they are general disclosure requirements, designed to bring greater transparency to the market, they apply to all UK companies with voting shares traded on a regulated market, in London or elsewhere, irrespective of whether or not they are involved in a takeover. The legislation previously required detailed disclosure of the interests of the directors in the company's shares but these provisions have been repealed with effect from 6 April 2007. Consequently, companies whose shares are not publicly traded on a regulated market will no longer be required to disclose information on directors' shareholdings in the directors' report.

It should also be noted that, in the case of a listed company, FSA Listing Rule 9.8.6R continues to require certain additional disclosures in the annual report in respect of the company's shares, including:

- an analysis of each director's interests at the end of the financial year between beneficial and non-beneficial holdings;
- details of any changes in those interests between the end of the financial year and one month prior to the date of the notice of the Annual General Meeting (AGM) (or a statement that there have been no changes);
- information on major holdings of the company's shares as at a date not more than one month prior to the date of the notice of the AGM and
- certain information on the purchase of own shares by the company.

10.92   Disclosure to Auditors

Company law also requires the directors' report to include a statement to the effect that, for each person who is a director at the time that the directors' report is approved:

(i) so far as that director is aware, there is no relevant audit information of which the company's auditors are unaware and

(ii) he/she has taken all the steps that a director should have taken in order to become aware of any relevant audit information and establish that the auditors are aware of it.

Relevant audit information is defined as information needed by the auditors in connection with the preparation of their report on the annual accounts. In order to satisfy the requirement, each director should make appropriate enquiries of his/her fellow directors and of the company's auditors, and take such other steps required by the general duty of a director to exercise reasonable care, skill and diligence (see CHAPTER 8).

10.93   Qualifying Indemnities for Directors

Company law requirements on the provision of indemnities and insurance for directors were changed by the *Companies (Audit, Investigations and Community Enterprise) Act 2004*. The new provisions came into effect on 6 April 2005 and enable a company to indemnify directors against proceedings brought by third parties, although no indemnity can be provided against liabilities of the director to the company or to any associated company (see **8.12** above). If the company has provided a qualifying third party indemnity for the benefit of a director of the company or of an associated company during the year, or if such a provision is in force at the time of approval of the directors' report, the report must include a statement of that fact.

10.94   Other Disclosures

Other detailed disclosures currently required in the directors' report include:

- a statement on the company's policy on the employment, training, career development and promotion of disabled persons;
- a statement on action taken during the year to introduce, maintain or develop arrangements to provide relevant information to employees, consult them on a regular basis, encourage employee involvement in the company's performance and achieve an awareness amongst employees of financial and economic factors affecting the company's performance;
- information on the company's policy and practice on the payment of creditors;
- an indication of:
  - the company's (or group's) financial risk management objectives and policies, including the policy for hedging if hedge accounting is used and
  - the company's (or group's) exposure to price risk, credit risk, liquidity risk and cash flow risk.

Certain exemptions from these disclosures apply in specific cases (e.g. for smaller, unquoted companies).

A DTI White Paper issued in conjunction with the recent company law review included a proposal to remove the directors' report disclosure requirements in respect of employee involvement and disabled employees, on the basis that these had been superseded by more recent legislation. However, the DTI consultation document 'Implementation of Companies Act 2006' published in February 2007 notes that the DTI has now concluded that both disclosure requirements should be retained on the basis that other legislative requirements do not cover disclosure on these issues.

10.95   Corporate Governance Disclosures

In March 2007, the DTI published a consultation document on the proposed UK implementation of various amendments to existing EC Company Law Directives. These include the introduction of a legal requirement for companies whose shares are publicly traded to make a formal statement on compliance with the corporate governance code that applies or has been voluntarily adopted, and on the main features of the company's internal control and risk management systems in relation to financial reporting. Although similar disclosure requirements already apply in the UK under the FSA Listing Rules (see **PARAGRAPH 6.60**), changes will be needed to ensure that they are legally enforceable in future.

The DTI invites comments on the best option for implementation and on whether the required disclosures should be given in the directors' report or in a separate corporate governance statement. The changes are likely to be introduced in conjunction with the accounts provisions of *CA 2006* which are due to be brought into effect from 6 April 2008.

10.96   Summary Financial Statements

At a Glance

* Subject to certain conditions, companies are permitted to issue a summary financial statement to their shareholders in place of the full annual accounts and reports.
* Each shareholder retains the right to receive a copy of the full annual accounts and reports.
* The minimum content of a summary financial statement is prescribed in company law.
* A summary financial statement must also include certain statements to clarify its status, together with a special report from the auditors.
* Research has shown that companies see both advantages and disadvantages in preparing a summary financial statement, but shareholders are more likely to read a summary document than the full accounts and reports.
* There are two practical approaches to preparing a summary financial statement.
* Many companies include more than the minimum contents in a summary financial statement.

10.97   Background

Legislation permitting listed companies to issue a summary financial statement to their shareholders in place of the full annual report and accounts was first introduced in *CA 1989*. The timing of the legislation coincided with the significant increase in the number of individual shareholders as a result of the Government's privatisation programme. In 1995, a number of changes were made to the administrative process to try and encourage a greater take-up of the option, but the number of companies who issue summary financial statements remains comparatively low. For accounting periods beginning on or after 1 January 2005, the *Companies Act 1985 (International Accounting Standards and Other Accounting Amendments) Regulations 2004 (SI 2004/2947)* extend the option to prepare summary financial statements to all companies, subject to certain conditions set out in the related regulations. The detailed requirements on summary financial statements have also been updated by the *Companies (Summary Financial Statement)(Amendment) Regulations 2005 (SI 2005/2281)* to cater specifically for companies who are required or choose to prepare their annual accounts in accordance with IASs (see **PARAGRAPH 10.4**) and for the extension to all companies of the option to issue a summary financial statement. As a result, the regulations now specify that a company can only issue a summary financial statement if its full accounts have been audited.

10.98   Right to Receive Full Accounts and Reports

Even if a company decides to take advantage of the option to prepare a summary financial statement, each shareholder and other person entitled to receive the accounts retains the right to receive a copy of the full annual accounts and report in respect of any financial year. The company cannot issue summary financial statements in place of the full accounts and report without first ascertaining that the entitled individual is happy to receive them – this must be done by following one of the consultation processes set out in the legislation.

10.99   Form and Content of Summary Financial Statements

The summary financial statement must be derived from the company's annual accounts and reports. Where the underlying accounts are Companies Act accounts (see **PARAGRAPH 10.5**), the following minimum content is specified by the regulations:

- a summary profit and loss account, including:
  - turnover;
  - income from shares in group undertakings and participating interests;
  - other interest receivable and similar income, and interest payable and similar charges;
  - profit or loss on ordinary activities before taxation;
  - tax on profit or loss on ordinary activities;
  - profit or loss on ordinary activities after tax;
  - extraordinary income and charges, after tax;
  - profit or loss for the financial year;
- the following details in respect of dividends:
  - the aggregate of dividends paid in the year, other than those for which a liability existed at the previous balance sheet date;
  - the aggregate amount of dividends that the company is liable to pay at the balance sheet date and
  - the aggregate amount of dividends proposed before the date of approval of the accounts and not included in the above disclosures;
- in the case of an unquoted company, the whole of (or a summary of) the note to the accounts setting out the details of aggregate directors' remuneration required under company law;
- in the case of a quoted company, either the whole of the directors' remuneration report or, as a minimum:
  - the aggregate information on directors' remuneration required under company law;
  - the statement of the company's policy on directors' remuneration for future years;

- the performance graph summarising shareholder return;
- a summary balance sheet, showing a single amount for each item that is assigned a letter in the *CA 1985* standard formats.

Where the underlying accounts are IAS accounts (see **PARAGRAPH 10.4**), the regulations require the summary financial statement to include, as a minimum:

- the whole of (or a summary of) the note to the accounts setting out the details of aggregate directors' remuneration required under company law;
- in the case of a quoted company, a statement of the company's policy on directors' remuneration and the performance graph summarising shareholder return;
- a summary profit and loss account showing each of the headings and sub-totals required under IASs or, where the directors consider it appropriate, a combination of such headings and sub-totals where they are of similar nature;
- the information concerning dividends recognised and proposed given in the full accounts and reports;
- a summary balance sheet showing each of the headings and sub-totals required under IASs or, where the directors consider it appropriate, a combination of such headings and sub-totals where they are of similar nature.

In both cases, comparative figures must be given for each item and, where the company is required to prepare group accounts, consolidated figures must be presented. In practice, most companies who issue summary financial statements include more than the minimum information – in particular, summarised cash flow information and corporate governance reporting is usually included (see **PARAGRAPH 10.105**). Separate requirements apply for banking and insurance companies and groups.

10.100   Other Statements to be Included

The summary financial statement must be signed by a director on behalf of the board and the name of the signing director must be stated. The document must also include:

- a clear statement that it is only a summary of the information given in the company's annual accounts and (where relevant) directors' remuneration report;
- a statement on whether or not it contains additional information derived from the directors' report and, if it includes such information, the fact that it does not include the full text of the directors' report;
- a formal statement, in a prominent position, that the summary does not contain sufficient information to allow as full an understanding of the results and state of affairs of the company or group as the full documents would, and that members and other entitled persons have the right to obtain a copy of the full accounts and reports, free of charge;
- a clear statement of how members and other entitled persons can obtain the full accounts and reports for the current year, and how they can elect to receive these in future years in place of the summary financial statement;
- a report from the auditors on whether:
  - the summary financial statement is consistent with the full accounts and reports for the relevant financial year;

- ○ the summary financial complies with the requirements of company law and the related regulations;
- ○ the auditor's report on the full accounts and, where relevant, the auditable part of the directors' remuneration report was qualified or unqualified – if it was qualified, the report must be set out in full, together with any additional information needed to understand the qualification (e.g. a particular note to the accounts);
- ○ the auditors' opinion on consistency between the directors' report and the accounts was qualified or unqualified – where the opinion was qualified, the qualification must be set out in full, together with any additional material needed for the qualification to be understood and
- ○ the auditors' report on the full accounts contained a statement on inadequate accounting records or returns, accounts not in agreement with the records and returns, or a failure to obtain all the information and explanations that the auditors consider necessary – if such a statement was included, the auditors' report on the full accounts must be set out in the summary financial statements.

10.101   The Purpose of Summary Financial Statements

The provisions allowing listed companies to prepare and issue summary financial statements were introduced to recognise the fact that the needs of shareholders and other users of the accounts can vary quite significantly. The disclosures required by accounting standards and companies legislation are becoming increasingly complex, and whilst the information now required may be highly relevant to technically sophisticated users of accounts, it is evident that many private shareholders are confused by the volume of detail given in a full set of accounts. In some cases the level of detailed disclosures can actually obscure the key information that private shareholders require from the accounts. The main aims of the summary financial statement are to remove most of the more complex disclosures and concentrate on the key issues that are of relevance to individual shareholders, and to enable companies to present this key information in a user-friendly manner, for instance by making appropriate use of charts and graphs.

10.102   Perceived Advantages and Disadvantages

A working party established by the ICAEW reported in 1996 on the results of research amongst companies on why they decided to produce or not to prepare a summary financial statement, and amongst shareholders on the relative merits to them of full accounts and a summary financial statement ('Summary Financial Statements: The Way Forward' – ICAEW July 1996). The main reasons given for not making use of summary financial statements were:

- potentially higher production costs, especially in the first year, and no significant cost savings anticipated in subsequent years;
- the additional administrative burden;
- that the use of a summary financial statement would run counter to the present philosophy of providing fuller information to shareholders.

The main advantages reported by companies who had issued summary financial statements were better communication with shareholders and actual cost savings. The point on actual cost savings is particularly interesting. Whilst the majority of companies who decided to prepare summary financial statements did so primarily to improve communication with their shareholders, nearly all of them found that the exercise also achieved some cost savings. It may be that companies not currently using summary financial statements are being unnecessarily pessimistic in their assessment of the costs and the additional administrative effort required. It should be emphasised that most of the research referred to in the report was undertaken before the changes introduced by the *Companies (Summary Financial Statement) Regulations 1995 (SI 1995/2092)* which simplified the consultation process with shareholders and may already have helped to alleviate some of the concerns over costs and administration.

10.103 Views of Shareholders

The ICAEW report also summarised the results of a survey to assess the reactions of shareholders to summary financial statements. This indicated a high degree of enthusiasm for summary financial statements amongst shareholders. The key conclusions from the research were:

- shareholders were more likely to read some or all of the summary financial statement than to open and read the full accounts, and that a summarised document is therefore helpful in improving communication with shareholders;
- where a summary financial statement was made available, a very high proportion of shareholders (in the order of 90%) opted to receive the summary rather than the full annual report and accounts;
- the summarised results, chairman's statement and overall business review were the most widely read parts of the document;
- other financial information, the report by the auditors and any additional details (for instance on corporate governance issues) were generally not widely read by shareholders and
- there was a clear preference for a short document rather than a longer one.

A further point highlighted by the research was that very few companies had carried out any direct consultation with shareholders to try and identify their specific needs and ensure that these were being satisfied, despite the fact that the research amongst companies had indicated that shareholder pressure would encourage them to consider preparing a summary financial statement.

10.104 A Practical Approach to Producing Summary Financial Statements

There are essentially two approaches to the preparation of a summary financial statement:

- the production of two completely separate and free-standing documents – the summary financial statement and the full annual report and accounts and

- the production of a summary financial statement and a supplementary document containing additional information – in this case, the summary financial statement and the supplementary document together constitute the full annual report and accounts.

The second approach is by far the more common in practice. Failure to consider this method of preparation may be one of the factors that explains why companies not preparing summary financial statements quote potentially higher costs (or no anticipated cost savings) as one of the reasons against using them, whilst those preparing summary financial statements have achieved actual cost savings. A potential disadvantage of the second approach is that analysts and other technically minded users of the accounts may find it irritating to have to refer to two documents. However, this can usually be overcome by careful planning of the contents of each part of the document and clear cross-referencing.

10.105   Usual Contents of Summary Financial Statements

There is a broad consensus amongst companies who do prepare summary financial statements on the basic contents of the document. These invariably go beyond the minimum contents laid down in the regulations and usually comprise:

- financial highlights;
- chairman's statement;
- an operational review of the business, which often makes extensive use of colour photographs and other illustrations;
- the summarised profit and loss account and balance sheet;
- summarised cash flow information;
- information on directors' remuneration and
- financial calendar.

Corporate governance issues are also usually referred to in the summary financial statement, but the level of detail given varies. Despite the preference for short documents highlighted in the shareholder research, summary financial statements these days are often substantial documents, with many being between 20 and 40 pages in length.

10.106   Half-Yearly Reports

At a Glance
* The FSA Disclosure and Transparency Rules (DTRs) require listed companies to issue a half-yearly report each year, giving details of their results for the first half of the financial year.
* The DTRs require the half-yearly report to be issued within two months of the period end.

* The DTRs also require the publication of interim management statements unless the company publishes quarterly reports.
* Companies who prepare IAS accounts must comply with IAS 34 *Interim Financial Reporting* when preparing a half-yearly report.
* Companies who prepare their annual accounts under UK accounting practice should prepare their half-yearly report in accordance with ASB guidance.
* A half-yearly management report should indicate important events in the first six months of the financial year and their impact on the half-yearly results.
* Accounting policies should be consistent with those adopted in the annual accounts.
* Earnings per share should be disclosed in the same manner as in the annual accounts.
* Particular care is required over the accounting treatment of items of income and expenditure that are normally determined only once a year in conjunction with the preparation of the annual accounts.
* Corresponding amounts should be presented for the corresponding half-yearly period and the previous full year.
* A half-yearly report must now include a formal responsibility statement by the directors.
* A half-yearly report should also include the formal statements that have to be given in non-statutory accounts.
* In February 2006, the FRRP issued a short report on the results of its review of the half-yearly reports of companies affected by the transition to IASs.

10.107   Requirement to Prepare Half-Yearly Report

Listed companies have been required for many years to publish a half-yearly report, giving details of their results for the first half of the financial year. However, certain changes to the detailed requirements have been introduced for accounting periods beginning on or after 20 January 2007 as a result of UK implementation of the EU Transparency Directive. The Directive includes provisions on half-yearly reporting and has been introduced in the UK through *CA 2006* and the FSA's new DTRs. The Directive sets out detailed requirements on the content of interim and annual reports and the timing of their publication. In addition, it requires the preparation of interim management statements by companies that do not prepare quarterly reports. A half-yearly report must be issued within two months of the period end (compared with 90 days under previous UK requirements) and must include a formal responsibility statement from the directors.

In July 2007, the ASB published a new Statement 'Half-Yearly Financial Reports' which replaces the ASB Statement 'Interim Reports' for UK listed companies that continue to adopt UK accounting practice. At this stage, the ASB has made only the minimum changes necessary to the previous guidance in order to ensure that it is consistent with the DTRs and with the key aspects of related international requirements.

Listed companies preparing their annual accounts under IASs (see **PARAGRAPH 10.4**) must adopt IAS 34 *Interim Financial Reporting* when preparing a half-yearly report.

10.108   Interim Management Statements

An interim management statement must be issued between:

- 10 weeks after the beginning of the relevant six month period and
- 6 weeks before the end of that period.

The FSA has issued informal guidance on the preparation of such statements and their likely content. The statement may be based on performance reports and trading statements, but should also explain any material events and transactions in the relevant period and their impact on the company's financial position.

10.109   Review by the Auditors

There is currently no formal requirement for auditors to review or report on half-yearly reports before they are published, but the ASB recommends disclosure of the extent to which the information given in the report has been audited or reviewed. For accounting periods ending before 20 September 2007, APB Bulletin 1999/4 *Review of Interim Financial Information* sets out guidance on the procedures that should be undertaken where auditors are asked to review an interim report, although it notes that the directors (or, where relevant, the Audit Committee) may ask the auditors to carry out specific agreed procedures as an alternative to this. Where an interim report is reviewed in accordance with the APB guidance, the FSA DTRs require the auditors' review report to be published as part of the interim report. Because the recommended review work is limited in scope, and does not constitute an audit, the auditors will normally report in terms of 'negative assurance' – in other words, they report that nothing has come to their attention to indicate that material modification is required to the information presented in the report. APB Bulletin 1999/4 recommends that, where the scope of the work agreed between the directors and auditors is less than that set out in the Bulletin, the directors should describe the interim report as 'neither audited nor reviewed'.

For accounting periods ending on or after 20 September 2007, APB Bulletin 1999/4 is superseded by a UK & Ireland version of International Standard on Review Engagements 2410 (ISRE 2410) *Review of Interim Financial Information Performed by the Independent Auditor of the Entity*. Early adoption of this new standard is also permitted. ISRE (UK & Ireland) 2410 takes account of changes introduced as a result of the EC Transparency Directive (see **PARAGRAPH 10.107**) which come into effect for financial periods beginning on or after 20 January 2007. There is no change to the FSA requirements on publication of the auditor's review report, and the latest examples of such a report can be found in Appendices 4 to 8 of ISRE (UK & Ireland) 2410.

10.110   Contents of a Half-Yearly Report

For accounting periods beginning on or after 20 January 2007, when the requirements of the EU Transparency Directive apply, companies preparing their annual accounts in accordance with IASs must comply with IAS 34 *Interim Financial Reporting* in preparing their half-yearly report. Companies continuing to adopt UK accounting practice should follow the recommendations in the ASB Statement 'Half-Yearly Financial Reports' (see **PARAGRAPH 10.107**). For earlier accounting periods, the minimum contents of a half-yearly report were specified in detail the FSA Listing Rules and the ASB Statement *Interim Reports*.

The ASB Statement recommends that a half-yearly report should include:

- a half-yearly management report (as required by the DTRs);
- a condensed profit and loss account showing each of the headings and subtotals included in the most recent annual financial statements – additional line items should be included if their omission would result in a misleading view of the entity's profit or loss for the period;
- statement of total recognised gains and losses;
- condensed balance sheet and
- condensed cash flow statement.

Information should be presented in a concise manner and should be consistent and comparable with information in the most recent annual report. It should also facilitate comparison with similar companies. Sufficient supplementary information should be given to permit an understanding of the significant items within the primary statements.

IAS 34 includes similar requirements but is more prescriptive on the minimum information to be given in the notes to a half-yearly report.

10.111   Other Disclosures

The following disclosures should also be given:

- where relevant, amounts relating to associates and joint ventures should be shown separately in the summarised profit and loss account;
- turnover and operating profit in respect of any acquisitions or discontinued operations should be shown separately on the face of the summarised profit and loss account – for this purpose, operations are to be regarded as discontinued if the sale or termination was completed in the half-yearly period, or by the earlier of the date of approval of the half-yearly report or two months after the end of the half-yearly period;

- segmental analyses of turnover and profit or loss before interest should be given, using the same business and geographical classifications as in the annual accounts;
- any exceptional items occurring in the interim period should be disclosed, including where relevant items required to be shown separately in the profit and loss account under FRS 3 *Reporting financial performance* (i.e. profits and losses on the sale or termination of an operation, costs of a fundamental reorganisation or restructuring, and profits and losses on the disposal of fixed assets) and
- reconciliations of operating profit to operating cash flow and the movement of cash to the movement in net debt should be given.

The results of operations that are in the process of discontinuing, or which are expected to be classified as discontinued in the accounts for the full financial year, may be shown separately in the notes to the half-yearly report.

In addition, IAS 34 specifically requires disclosure of:

- the nature and amount of any changes in estimates of amounts reported in prior interim periods of the current financial year or in prior financial years, if these have a material effect in the current half-yearly period;
- issuances, repurchases and repayments of debts and securities;
- dividends paid, showing separately those on ordinary shares and those on other shares;
- material events subsequent to the end of the half-yearly period and
- changes in contingent liabilities or contingent assets since the last balance sheet date.

Where appropriate, IAS 34 also requires the half-yearly report to state that it complies with that standard.

The ASB Statement recommends that the half-yearly report also discloses:

- the period covered by the report;
- the date on which it was approved by the board of directors and
- the extent to which the information that it contains has been audited or reviewed.

10.112   Management Report

Because the half-yearly report is intended to update shareholders and other interested parties on the company's performance since the latest annual accounts, the management commentary should focus on recent events, activities and circumstances. The commentary should therefore discuss the financial information shown in the half-yearly profit and loss account, statement of total recognised gains and losses, balance sheet and cash flow statement in the context of events since the previous financial year end. It is important that the review does not concentrate solely on performance in the period, as shown in the profit and loss account, but also considers related issues such as working capital, liquidity and net debt. Significant trends and events mentioned in the commentary should be supported by the figures shown in the primary statements or by additional disclosures in the notes. Additional information should be given where this is necessary for an understanding of the significant items in the primary statement (for instance, additional information about company borrowings may need to be given if this is a significant issue).

The management commentary on the half-yearly figures should explain the reasons for significant movements in key indicators and give a balanced view of the trends within the business, so that readers of the report can understand the main factors influencing the company's performance during the period under review and its position at the end of that period. The report should therefore discuss both positive and negative aspects of the half-yearly period. Where the business is seasonal, it will be particularly important to provide sufficient information for readers to understand the half-yearly results in the context of the full financial year. The commentary should also draw attention to any events and changes occurring during the half-yearly period that are likely to have a significant impact in the second part of the year, even though they may not have affected the company's performance in the period under review. Where relevant it should also cover significant changes in fixed assets and investments, capital structure, financing, commitments and contingencies.

The management commentary included in a half-yearly report is not intended to be as detailed as an operating and financial review presented as part of the annual accounts and reports. However, the guidance in the ASB Reporting Statement *Operating and financial review* (see **PARAGRAPH 10.80**) may be useful in helping to identify key issues that should be discussed in the half-yearly report.

10.113   Accounting Policies

Half-yearly reports should be prepared using the company's normal accounting policies and should include a statement that the policies are the same as those disclosed in the last published accounts, or explain any differences. Where it is known that a change in accounting policy is to be made in the accounts for the full financial year, the half-yearly report should normally be prepared on the basis of the new policy, all relevant comparative figures should be restated and the cumulative effect on opening reserves should be disclosed at the foot of the statement of total recognised gains and losses. If the half-yearly figures are not presented on the basis of the new accounting policy, the estimated financial effect of the change in policy should be disclosed. Any other prior period adjustments (for instance, to correct fundamental errors) should be reflected in the half-yearly report in the same way as changes in accounting policy.

10.114   Earnings per Share

Basic earnings per share should be calculated from the half-yearly results and disclosed in the half-yearly report in the same way as in the full annual accounts. If the company adopts a policy of disclosing additional calculations of earnings per share in its annual accounts, the same details should be given in the half-yearly report.

10.115   Basis of Presentation of Financial Information

One particular issue that arises in the case of a half-yearly report is whether the half-yearly period is treated as part of an annual reporting cycle or as a discrete accounting period, distinct from the annual cycle. IAS 34 requires measurements for a half-yearly reporting period to be made on a year-to-date basis, rather than as if the half-yearly period is an independent reporting period, and requires the same principles for the recognition of assets, liabilities, income and expenditure as in the preparation of the annual accounts. Both IAS 34 and the ASB Statement give guidance on the practicalities of implementing this requirement. For items of income or expenditure that are normally determined only at the end of the financial period (e.g. bonuses, volume discounts, sales commissions), the accounting treatment in the half-yearly report will depend on whether there is an obligation at the end of the half-yearly period to transfer economic benefits as a result of past events. For instance, if a profit-related bonus is to be paid at the end of the year, it will be appropriate to recognise a proportion of this in the interim period, based on the profit earned to date, if past practice shows that the company has a constructive obligation to make the payment. A genuinely discretionary bonus paid at the end of the year would not be recognised in the interim figures. However, it will sometimes be necessary to look at the expected income or expense for the full year in order to calculate the amount to be recognised in the half-yearly period. The most obvious example here is taxation and considerable guidance is given on this in both IAS 34 and the ASB Statement. The likely effective tax rate for the full year should be calculated, expressed as a percentage of the expected results for the full year, and this percentage should be applied to the interim profit or loss to calculate the interim tax charge. More detailed calculations may be needed where different tax jurisdictions are involved or where different tax rates apply to material categories of income. Other points to note in relation to the presentation of financial information in half-yearly reports are:

- the results of foreign group entities should be translated in line with the company's usual accounting policy;
- asset revaluations will not usually be required for half-yearly report purposes, although certain disclosures are recommended and
- materiality should be assessed in relation to the half-yearly period rather than the expected results and financial position at the end of the financial year.

10.116   Corresponding Amounts

Corresponding amounts for the summarised profit and loss account, statement of total recognised gains and losses and summarised cash flow statement should cover the corresponding half-yearly period in the previous year and also the last full financial year. This is to help provide a meaningful view of the company's performance to date, especially where the business is seasonal. In the case of the balance sheet, the critical comparative figures are those for the last full financial year, although those for the corresponding half-yearly period may also be given.

10.117   Directors' Responsibility Statement

For accounting periods beginning on or after 20 January 2007, the EU Transparency Directive requires a half-yearly report to include a responsibility statement by the directors confirming that, to the best of their knowledge:

- the condensed financial statements give a true and fair view; and
- their management report includes a fair review of the business and the principal risks and uncertainties that it faces.

The 'true and fair' requirement in particular has given rise to considerable concern, given that this term has until now been reserved for full financial statements, including detailed notes to the accounts. Consequently, in developing its new DTRs, the FSA has agreed that the first of these requirements can be satisfied by a statement that the interim report has been prepared in accordance with IAS 34 (where international accounting standards have been adopted) or with relevant ASB guidance (where UK accounting practice has been adopted), subject to the need to confirm that a report prepared on this basis is not misleading.

Similarly, in ISRE (UK and Ireland) 2410 (see **PARAGRAPH 10.109**), the APB does not require the auditor to provide a 'true and fair' opinion but continues a form of negative assurance reporting, as under previous APB guidance, but with a much more detailed conclusion that refers specifically to the reporting framework adopted.

10.118   Statutory Disclosure

Where a half-yearly report contains information for a full financial year of the company or information as at the company's normal financial year (for instance, comparative profit and loss account information for the previous financial year, and comparative balance sheet information as at the end of the last financial year), the half-yearly report will constitute 'non-statutory accounts' under company law and must include the formal statements required by the legislation.

10.119   FRRP Review of Half-Yearly Reports

The remit of the FRRP (see **PARAGRAPH 10.18**) has been widened to include reviews of all financial information published by companies that come within the scope of its activities, including half-yearly reports and preliminary announcements. The Panel announced in December 2004 that one of the key elements of its pro-activity work programme for 2005/06 would be a review of half-yearly reports prepared by listed groups who would be adopting IASs for the first time, and in February 2006 it published a short report on its work to date in this area. UK listed companies were not required to comply with IAS 34 *Interim Financial Reporting* in the period under review and the report notes that few opted to do so voluntarily. The FRRP review therefore concentrated on compliance with the requirements of the UK Listing Rules on the form and content of a half-yearly report. A total of 70 reports were reviewed and that Panel raised issues on 16 of these. Three of these cases were still ongoing at the time that the report was published. Two cases involved complex or controversial issues and so required the appointment of Panel groups, but the other 14 were dealt with by written requests to the companies concerned to provide additional information. No formal press announcements had been made by the FRRP as a result of the reviews completed by the time of the report, and there had been no requirement for companies to restate their published results, although the Panel notes that a number had agreed to make improved disclosures in the future. Issues highlighted in the reviews have included the following:

- *Income statement*: The format of this part of the report is less prescriptive under IASs and the FRRP noted that some companies were using sub-totals such as 'trading profit' or 'operating profit' but were excluding certain items that the Panel expected to be included. In some cases, companies also failed to provide separate details of material amounts of overseas tax and tax relating to associates, and gave a net figure for finance income and costs rather than the separate amounts.
- *Cash flow statement*: Certain items in the cash flow statement were misclassified between investing and financing activities and the definition of cash equivalents was not always sufficiently precise, leading to uncertainty over which items had been included.
- *Statement of Changes in Equity*: This should have two separate elements – a Statement of Recognised Income and Expense and a Statement of Changes in Equity – and the Panel noted some confusion over the allocation of items between the two. Particular problems were identified with the treatment of actuarial gains and losses on defined benefit retirement schemes and credits relating to share options.
- *Accounting policies*: The Panel noted that most new accounting policies arising from the adoption of IASs were described clearly and comprehensively, but there were cases where an accounting policy was not clear or did not appear to cover all aspects of the business or where inappropriate wordings from UK GAAP had been retained. However, the Panel was satisfied that the main problem was over the description of the policies actually adopted rather than over the policies themselves.
- *True and fair override*: The true and fair override now applies only where Companies Act accounts are prepared (see **PARAGRAPHS 10.4** and **10.5**). The Panel emphasised that, in the rare circumstances where a departure from a standard was considered necessary in IAS accounts, the accounts should make clear that this was a departure under the provisions of IAS 1 *Presentation of Financial Information* rather than a true and fair override under company law.

The Panel also noted the omission in some cases of certain aspects of the statement in respect of the auditors' report on the last financial statements and emphasised that a half-yearly report prepared under IASs continues to constitute non-statutory accounts (see **PARAGRAPH 10.118**).

10.120   Preliminary Announcements

At a Glance

* The FSA Listing Rules previously required listed companies to make a preliminary announcement of their annual results and dividends within 120 days of the year end, but this has become voluntary for accounting periods beginning on or after 20 January 2007.
* Where a preliminary announcement is prepared, existing FSA and ASB guidance will continue to apply.
* The ASB Statement *Preliminary announcements* encourages companies to make their preliminary announcement within 60 days of the year end and to issue their accounts and reports as soon as practicable thereafter.
* The audit of the underlying accounts should be substantially complete before the preliminary announcement is issued.
* The FSA requires directors to obtain agreement from the auditors before the preliminary announcement is issued and to give details in the announcement of any qualification of the auditors' report.
* Companies are encouraged to make their preliminary announcement widely available in order to maintain parity between shareholders.
* FSA requirements on the minimum contents of a preliminary announcement are broadly consistent with the recommendations set out in the ASB Statement.
* The management commentary should discuss the results for the second half of the year as well as the company's overall performance and financial position.
* The preliminary announcement should be prepared on the basis of the company's normal accounting policies – any changes in accounting policy should be explained and the financial effect should be disclosed.
* Earnings per share should be calculated and disclosed in the same way as in the annual accounts.
* Comparative figures should cover the last full financial year – companies are also encouraged to disclose the figures for the second half of the year, with comparatives.
* A preliminary announcement must include the formal statements that have to be given in non-statutory accounts.

10.121   Requirement to Prepare a Preliminary Announcement

For accounting periods beginning before 20 January 2007, the FSA Listing Rules required listed companies to notify a preliminary statement of annual results and dividends immediately after it had been approved by the board. The preliminary announcement had to be notified within 120 days of the end of the accounting period, although an extension of this deadline could be granted in exceptional circumstances. The minimum contents required by the Listing Rules were broadly in line with those set out in the ASB Statement *Preliminary Announcements*. Technically, this document is non-mandatory but it sets out best practice on the form and content of preliminary announcements and listed companies were therefore encouraged to follow its recommendations. In many ways, half-yearly reports and preliminary announcements are very similar in nature. Both communicate new information on the company's performance and financial position and, in each case, the reaction of the financial markets to the information given can be significant.

For accounting periods beginning on or after 20 January 2007, when the EU Transparency Directive comes into effect, the publication of a preliminary announcement becomes voluntary rather than mandatory. Where such an announcement is prepared, the FSA has emphasised that the existing requirements on content and auditor approval will continue to apply.

10.122   Impact of IAS Accounts

The ASB Statement 'Preliminary Announcements' was developed in the context of accounts and reports prepared under the detailed form and content requirements of company law and so does not take account of the requirement for listed groups to adopt international accounting standards (IASs) from 1 January 2005 (see **PARAGRAPH 10.4**). Where such companies continue to prepare a preliminary announcement on a voluntary basis, the recommendations set out in the ASB Statement continue to represent best practice and are consistent with previous FSA requirements on preliminary announcements. No international accounting standards or other pronouncements deal specifically with the preparation and content of a preliminary announcement.

10.123   Timing of Preliminary Announcement

The ASB Statement encourages companies to issue their preliminary announcement within 60 days of the financial year end, and to issue the full report and accounts (and, where relevant, the summary financial statement) as soon as practicable thereafter, although it acknowledges that individual circumstances may make it impractical for some companies to achieve this target. When the preparation of a preliminary announcement was mandatory the FSA set a longer deadline of 120 days from the end of the accounting period. The Listing Rules now simply specify that, where a preliminary announcement is prepared, it must be published as soon as possible after it has been approved by the board. The ASB Statement also considers the need for the figures in the preliminary announcement to be reliable and the impact that this might have on the timing of publication. It recommends that:

- the audit of the draft financial statements should be substantially complete at the date of the announcement;
- all the figures in the preliminary announcement should agree with the draft financial statements on which the audit is substantially complete and
- any non-financial information or commentary included in the preliminary announcement should be consistent with the draft financial statements and with the figures set out in the preliminary announcement.

Companies are encouraged to make their preliminary announcement as soon as the main figures have been agreed by the auditors, rather than waiting for the audit to be fully completed. This recognises that, in practice, it will usually take time to finalise the detailed notes to the financial statements and the other reports published with them, but this will not affect the reliability of the principal figures. APB Bulletin 2004/1 *The Auditors' Association with Preliminary Announcements* provides guidance on when the audit should be regarded as being substantially complete. To prevent any misunderstanding, the ASB Statement recommends that the preliminary announcement should state that the audit report on the full financial statements has not yet been signed, if that is the case.

10.124 Need to Obtain Auditors' Agreement

It is important that the information released in a preliminary announcement is reliable and the FSA therefore requires the directors to obtain agreement from the auditors before a preliminary announcement is approved for issue. APB Bulletin 2004/1 recommends that the role of the auditors in respect of the preliminary announcement is set out in writing (this is usually dealt with by including an appropriate paragraph in the audit engagement letter) and that the auditors issue a formal letter to the directors confirming their agreement to publication of a preliminary announcement. If the audit report on the financial statements is likely to be qualified, the FSA requires the preliminary announcement to include details of the nature of the qualification.

In February 2003, the APB wrote to the auditors of listed companies to alert them to the fact that shareholders can sometimes be misled by the way in which pro forma information is included in unaudited announcements of half-yearly and annual results in addition to the statutory figures. In the APB's view, pro forma information is most likely to misinform when it is given greater prominence than statutory information, where its purpose is not explained and when it is not reconciled to the statutory information. Before agreeing to the release of a preliminary announcement, auditors are therefore recommended to consider whether:

- appropriate prominence has been given to the statutory figures;
- any pro forma information states clearly why it has been prepared;
- any pro forma information is reconciled to the statutory figures and
- any pro forma information is not misleading in the form or context in which it is presented.

This guidance has now been incorporated in APB Bulletin 2004/1.

10.125   Distribution of Preliminary Announcement

Half-yearly reports are issued to all shareholders, but preliminary announcements tend to be issued only to financial analysts and institutional shareholders. The ASB Statement emphasises that all shareholders should be treated equally and encourages companies to make better use of technology (for instance, by making preliminary announcements available on the Internet) and to give all shareholders the option of receiving a copy of the preliminary announcement as soon as it is issued (for instance, by establishing a pre-registration scheme or publishing an address or telephone number from which copies can be obtained).

10.126   Contents of a Preliminary Announcement

Where a preliminary announcement is prepared, the FSA specifies that it must contain, in the form of a table, the figures required to be given in a half-yearly report (i.e. a summarised profit and loss account, balance sheet, statement of total recognised gains and losses, and cash flow statement), together with any significant information to enable the company's results and financial position to be properly assessed. The ASB Statement sets out more detailed recommendations although, as explained in **PARAGRAPH 10.122**, the Statement was prepared in the context of Companies Act accounts and so the detailed recommendations are not entirely appropriate for a company that prepares IAS accounts and so should be adapted accordingly.

The ASB recommends the following contents for a preliminary announcement:

- A balanced narrative commentary on the main factors influencing performance during the period and the financial position at the period end.
- A summarised profit and loss account, showing:
  - turnover;
  - operating profit or loss;
  - net interest payable/receivable;
  - profit or loss on ordinary activities before tax;
  - tax on profit or loss on ordinary activities;
  - profit or loss on ordinary activities after tax;
  - minority interests;
  - profit or loss for the period.
- Details of dividends paid and proposed.
- A statement of total recognised gains and losses.
- A summarised balance sheet, showing:
  - fixed assets;
  - current assets:
    - stocks;
    - debtors;
    - cash at bank and in hand;
    - other;

- ○ creditors: amounts falling due within one year;
- ○ net current assets/liabilities;
- ○ total assets less current liabilities;
- ○ creditors: amounts falling due after more than one year;
- ○ provisions for liabilities and charges;
- ○ capital and reserves;
- ○ minority interests.
- A summarised cash flow statement, showing:
  - ○ net cash inflow/outflow from operating activities;
  - ○ returns on investments and servicing of finance;
  - ○ taxation;
  - ○ capital expenditure and financial investment;
  - ○ acquisitions and disposals;
  - ○ equity dividends paid;
  - ○ management of liquid resources;
  - ○ financing;
  - ○ increase/decrease in cash.

A reconciliation of movements in shareholders' funds only needs to be included when there are additional movements to be explained (i.e. movements other than those shown in the statement of total recognised gains and losses).

10.127   Other Disclosures

The ASB Statement also recommends the following additional disclosures:

- where significant, amounts relating to associates and joint ventures should be shown separately in the summarised profit and loss account;
- turnover and operating profit in respect of any acquisitions or discontinued operations should be shown separately on the face of the summarised profit and loss account;
- where significant, the segmental analyses of turnover and profit or loss before interest to be given in the full report and accounts should also be disclosed in the preliminary announcement;
- sufficient information should be given for readers to understand any significant changes in the effective tax rate from the previous year – in some cases, the tax charge may need to be analysed into its main components;
- any exceptional items should be disclosed, either or the face of the profit and loss account or in the notes;
- reconciliations of operating profit to operating cash flow and the movement of cash to the movement in net debt should be given and
- the preliminary announcement should state the period covered and the date on which it was formally approved by the board of directors.

10.128   Management Commentary

The aim of the management commentary in a preliminary announcement is to enable shareholders and other interested parties to understand the main factors that have influenced the company's performance during the financial year and its financial position at the year end. As well as commenting on the year as a whole, the ASB Statement recommends that management discuss and explain in particular the salient features of the second half of the year (i.e. the period not covered by the half-yearly report). These represent new information for shareholders, but are often subsumed into the details of the full year without specific comment. It is also important that the review does not concentrate solely on performance in the period, as shown in the profit and loss account, but also considers related issues such as working capital, liquidity and net debt. Significant trends and events mentioned in the commentary should be supported by the figures shown in the primary statements or by additional disclosures in the notes. Additional information should be given where this is necessary for an understanding of the significant items in the primary statements. The information given in the preliminary announcement should be succinct, consistent with the details to be given in the full report and accounts, and comparable with reports previously published.

The report should discuss both positive and negative aspects of the financial year and should include adequate information on any seasonal activity, so that the impact of this can be fully appreciated. The commentary should also draw attention to any events and changes occurring during the current financial year that are likely to have a significant impact in the following year, even though they may not have affected the company's performance in the period under review. Where relevant it should also cover significant changes in fixed assets and investments, capital structure, financing, commitments and contingencies.

The management commentary included in a preliminary announcement is not intended to be as detailed as an operating and financial review presented as part of the annual accounts and reports. However, the guidance in the ASB Statement *Operating and financial review* (see **PARAGRAPH 10.80**) may be useful in helping to identify key issues that should be discussed in the preliminary announcement.

10.129   Accounting Policies

The accounting policies used in preparing the preliminary announcement should be consistent with those in the full accounts, and the preliminary announcement should include a statement that the policies are the same as those disclosed in the last published accounts, or explain any differences. If there has been a change in accounting policy, the preliminary announcement should be prepared on the new accounting policy, all relevant comparative figures should be restated on the basis of the new policy and the cumulative effect on opening reserves should be disclosed. If any other prior period adjustments are necessary (for instance, to correct fundamental errors) these should be reflected in the preliminary announcement in the same way as changes in accounting policy.

10.130 Earnings per Share

Basic earnings per share should be calculated and disclosed in the preliminary announcement in the same way as in the full annual accounts. If the company adopts a policy of disclosing additional calculations of earnings per share in its annual accounts, the same details should be given in the preliminary announcement.

10.131 Corresponding Amounts

Corresponding amounts for the summarised profit and loss account, statement of total recognised gains and losses, summarised balance sheet and summarised cash flow statement should cover the last full financial year. The ASB Statement also recommends that the preliminary announcement should set out information on the second half of the year, together with comparatives for the equivalent period in the previous year, to support the management commentary and facilitate an understanding of the company's current performance.

10.132 Statutory Disclosure

A preliminary announcement contains information for the current and previous financial years of the company and also information as at the company's current and previous financial year end. It therefore constitutes 'non-statutory accounts' under company law and must include the statements required by the legislation.

10.133 Reporting on the Internet

> **At a Glance**
> * Many companies now use a website to disseminate financial information, but concern has been expressed over the lack of any formal requirements or guidance on this form of financial reporting.
> * Under *CA 2006*, quoted companies will be required to publish their annual accounts and reports on a website maintained by or on behalf of the company.
> * A Discussion Paper published by the International Accounting Standards Committee (IASC) in 1999 set out suggested contents for a Code of Conduct on Internet reporting.
> * Further guidance was issued in August 2002 by the International Federation of Accountants (IFAC).
> * Company law now permits companies to distribute their annual accounts and reports electronically.
> * Auditing Standards specify the steps that auditors should take when accounts are to be made available on a website or distributed electronically.
> * The Institute of Chartered Secretaries and Administrators (ICSA) has issued guidance on communicating electronically with shareholders.

10.134   Impact of the Internet

Research has shown that at least 80% of listed companies with websites make use of them to disseminate financial information. In due course, under the requirements of *CA 2006*, all quoted companies will be required to publish their annual accounts and reports on a website maintained by or on behalf of the company, and to retain them on the website (as a minimum) until the accounts and the reports for the following financial year have been similarly published. These changes are due to be brought into effect from 6 April 2008 and it is expected that they will apply for accounting periods beginning on or after that date. However, this form of reporting goes beyond the traditional reporting boundaries and there is concern that regulators and accounting standard setters are not keeping pace with the technological changes. There is a consequent lack of any formal guidance on this form of reporting and users have no guarantee on the quality of the information presented or on its comparability with the information published by other businesses. There is particular concern that companies often fail to distinguish information that has been audited from that which is unaudited.

There is also a wide variety in the level of information provided. Some websites include only brief summary reports, some allow downloading of electronic versions of the printed financial statements and others present the full financial statements for on-screen viewing. Where the website includes only extracts of the full financial report, there is concern that users may be given a misleading impression. Many sites simply present financial information as if it were in printed form, which can make it cumbersome and inflexible. More advanced sites allow users to manipulate the underlying data to suit their own purposes, and this is expected to become more widespread as technology continues to develop.

10.135   Suggested Code of Conduct

A discussion paper published in November 1999 by the IASC, which has now been superseded by the IASB, concluded that a Code of Conduct for Internet reporting should be developed to deal with issues of immediate concern, and that in the longer-term standards should be established to deal with reporting by means of developing technologies. The paper set out the recommended content of a Code of Conduct and, although this is not a formal document, companies which are already making use of the Internet for financial reporting may find it helpful to bear in mind the points raised. The recommendations include the following:

- *Consistency*. Financial information published on the Internet should be consistent with similar information published in another medium (e.g. in printed form). If documents provided online do not include the full information from the original format, this fact should be stated and a point of contact provided for obtaining the missing information. If any information provided on the Internet is additional to that provided in another form, this fact should also be stated.
- *Multiple online files*. Where financial reports are divided into separate documents for online presentation, the complete set should be listed together on the website and there should be appropriate cross-referencing between documents.

- *Boundaries of financial statements.* The boundaries of the complete set of financial statements should be clearly recognisable so that a user knows when he/she has moved out of this area.
- *Other financial information.* Where an entity includes on its website financial information or similar data that is not derived from its financial statements (e.g. forecasts, environmental information, social responsibility information), this information should not be presented in a manner which suggests that it conforms to an international or similar reporting standard.
- *Excerpts.* If a website includes only excerpts from a complete set of financial statements (e.g. just an income statement or a balance sheet, without the related notes), it should be clearly identified as an excerpt and details should be provided of how the full copy can be obtained.
- *Historical summaries.* If a historical financial summary is published on the website, the underlying accounting principles should be clearly identified. In particular, it should be clear whether the figures are those originally reported or whether they have been restated to be consistent with the requirements of new reporting standards.
- *Supplementary information.* Supplementary information that would not otherwise be widely available (e.g. data for analysts' briefings, press releases, other investor relations material) should be provided online for the benefit of all shareholders.
- *Auditors' report.* It should be clear which information is subject to an audit opinion, and any qualification in the auditors' report should be clearly noted. If information is provided in more than one language, but only the primary language financial statements were audited, this fact should be stated in the translated versions.
- *Stability.* All pages should be identifiable and re-creatable to enable users to bookmark them and return to the data in future.
- *Archiving.* Once financial information has been made available online, it should be archived and should not be removed from the site. Archived information should be clearly identified as such to avoid confusion with more recent material.
- *Dating.* All pages should show clearly the date of origin and the date of the last amendment.
- *Downloads.* Key data should be provided in a format that can be downloaded for off-line analysis. As a minimum, the statutory filings made by the entity in its primary jurisdictions should be downloadable.
- *Notification of updates.* Users should be informed of significant changes to the website, either through an e-mail notification service or by providing a date order listing of changes.
- *Currency conversions.* If the website offers a facility for changing the reporting currency on the basis of period end or average exchange rates, this 'convenience translation' should be clearly identified for what it is and should state that it does not conform to the translation requirements of accounting standards.
- *Responsibility.* Users have a right to presume that the entity is taking legal responsibility for the accuracy and completeness of the financial information

provided on its website. If this is not the case, this fact should be clearly stated. Any data on the site that was created outside the company should be clearly identified and its source noted.

- *Security*. All reasonable precautions should be taken to prevent unauthorised alteration of the data. The discussion paper proposes that, once a Code of Conduct is developed, websites providing financial information should be required to state their compliance with the Code, or specify any departures.
- *Other recommendations*. Other recommendations in the discussion paper include the following:
  - listed companies should prepare their websites in such a way that business reporting information for investors is clearly distinguished from promotional and other material;
  - auditors of listed companies should be responsible for ensuring that audited and unaudited information on the website is clearly distinguished and
  - auditors of listed companies should ensure that the company conforms fully to the Code of Conduct where it claims to do so, or that any deviations are noted in the audit report.

10.136 Subsequent Guidance from IFAC

In August 2002, the IFAC published *Financial Reporting on the Internet*. This has been developed by IFAC staff in the course of work on other projects and builds on the IASC discussion paper. The paper has not been formally approved by IFAC and consequently does not have the status of a formal IFAC document. It is intended to stimulate discussion and provide guidance to companies currently using the Internet to report financial information. It considers issues under the following headings:

- *Internet Reporting Policy – Matters of principle*: This summarises management's responsibility for considering:
  - the type of information to be provided;
  - the involvement of the auditor;
  - the format in which the information will be provided and
  - when the information will be provided.
- *Internet Reporting Policy – Practical Issues: This covers:*
  - the need to distinguish clearly between audited and unaudited information;
  - the need to distinguish between information intended to supplement the financial information (e.g. press and analysts briefings) and promotional or marketing information;
  - the use and maintenance of hyperlinks to third party Internet sites (e.g. financial analysts);
  - the inclusion of third party analyses and information on a company website;
  - the frequency of changes to financial information provided on a website.
- *Internet Reporting Policy – Control Issues: This covers:*
  - controls over the approval of information provided on a website;
  - the security of financial information provided on a website;

○ the need to state clearly how users can obtain further information in either electronic or written form.
- *Management's Responsibilities for Content: This includes guidance on:*
  ○ ensuring the consistency of financial information to be provided on a website;
  ○ the need to establish retention policies for website material;
  ○ dealing with changes in accounting policy.
- *Timeliness*: This discusses the need for website information to be clearly dated and the need to ensure that any requirements on the release of price sensitive information are complied with.
- *Content – Financial Information*: This deals with publication of the auditors' report, interim financial reporting, and the disclosure of aggregated, disaggregated or additional financial information on a website.
- *Security:* This emphasises management's responsibility for preventing the corruption or distortion of financial information on a website by employees (either accidentally or intentionally) or by third parties. As well as ensuring that changes are properly authorised, the controls and procedures should enable all changes to be detected and monitored.
- *Other Issues*: Other issues covered in the paper include the translation of financial information into other languages, the provision of information in a format that can be downloaded and procedures to inform interested parties of changes to the website.

The paper can be downloaded free of charge from the Bookstore (under the 'Other' category) on the IFAC website at http://www.ifac.org/Store/

10.137 Satisfying Legal Requirements by Electronic Means

For some time, company law has allowed companies to make use of electronic communication to satisfy the legal requirements on the provision of annual accounts and reports to shareholders and other persons entitled to receive them. In particular a company may:

- send accounts and reports electronically to an e-mail address notified to the company for that purpose by the person entitled to receive the documents; or
- where both the company and the person entitled to receive the annual accounts and reports so agree, publish the documents on a website and notify the entitled person in the manner agreed that they have been published in this way – in particular, the company must provide the recipient with both the website address and details of how to access the documents within the website.

New provisions on electronic communication have recently been introduced by the *Companies Act 2006 (Commencement No 1, Transitional Provisions and Savings) Order 2006* (SI 2006 No 3428). With effect from 1 January 2007, this implements new provisions on electronic communication with and by the registrar and with effect from 20 January 2007, it implements new provisions on electronic communication by and with shareholders. These are designed to encourage more shareholders to make use of electronic communication and so reduce the need for companies to prepare large quantities of hard copy documents, many of which may not be read in detail.

10.138   Audit Considerations

Initial guidance on the additional audit considerations that arise when financial information is made available electronically is set out in APB Bulletin 2001/1 *The Electronic Publication of Auditors' Reports*. This emphasises that the directors are responsible for ensuring that financial information made available on a website is not tampered with or amended. APB Bulletin 2006/6 *Auditors' Reports on Financial Statements in the United Kingdom* now recommends that an additional paragraph is included at the end of the statement of directors' responsibilities where the company's financial statements are published on a website (see **PARAGRAPH 10.42**). Bulletin 2001/1 also provides guidance on the work that auditors should do when financial statements are published on a website or distributed to shareholders by electronic means, and on the adjustments that should be made to the wording of the auditors' report when published electronically. Appendix 1 to the UK & Ireland version of ISA 720 *Other information in documents also containing audited financial statements* also covers:

- the work that auditors should carry out to check information that is presented electronically;
- issues relating to the wording of the audit report in order to identify which information has been audited, reviewed or read (as appropriate);
- the need to identify the accounting and auditing standards that have been applied and
- the need to limit the auditors' association with any other information distributed with the annual report.

10.139   ICSA Guidance on Electronic Communications

The ICSA has issued detailed guidance on the new provisions on electronic communication with shareholders introduced by *CA 2006* with effect from 20 January 2007. *ICSA Guidance on Electronic Communications with Shareholders 2007* (available at http://www.icsa.org.uk/) replaces a similar document published by ICSA in December 2000 and includes a summary of the various provisions of *CA 2006* which deal with electronic communication with and by shareholders and the definitions that apply for these purposes. A separate section summarises the additional requirements applying to listed companies under the new FSA Disclosure and Transparency Rules (DTRs).

The main part of the document sets out practical guidance on the impact of the changes and ICSA's best practice recommendations. Significant issues covered in the practical guidance include:

- Giving notice of a meeting by means of a website.
- Using electronic communication to send documents relating to meetings.
- When information and documents sent electronically are deemed to have been delivered.
- Notifying shareholders about the publication of new material on the website.
- Management of the website, including:
  - the need to consider the varying levels of technology available to shareholders;
  - the need to distinguish clearly between audited and unaudited information; and
  - the potential impact of the requirement that shareholders must be able to retain or save a copy of documents or information provided through the website.
- The internal records that the company should keep.

Appendix 1

Useful Websites on Financial Reporting Issues

Financial Reporting Council	www.frc.org.uk
Accounting Standards Board	www.frc.org.uk/asb
International Accounting Standards Board	www.iasb.org
Financial Reporting Review Panel	www.frc.org.uk/frrp
Auditing Practices Board	www.frc.org.uk/apb
Institute of Chartered Accountants in England and Wales	www.icaew.co.uk
Institute of Chartered Accountants of Scotland	www.icas.org.uk
Institute of Chartered Accountants in Ireland	www.icai.ie
Association of Chartered Certified Accountants	www.acca.co.uk
Chartered Institute of Public Finance and Accountancy	www.cipfa.org.uk
International Federation of Accountants	www.ifac.org
Institute of Chartered Secretaries and Administrators	www.icsa.org.uk

Fraud and Illegal Acts

Fraud and Illegal Acts

11.1 Understanding Fraud

At a Glance

* Fraud encompasses the use of deception to obtain unjust or illegal financial gain, and intentional misrepresentations affecting the financial statements.
* The nature of fraud usually depends on the type of business, the reason for the fraud and who is perpetrating it.
* The view that fraud is a victimless crime is rapidly losing ground.
* Recent terrorist attacks and accounting scandals have heightened the general awareness of fraud and the damage that it can cause to the economy.
* A principal theme is the need for a major change in business culture and attitudes.
* Fraud may involve an individual or a group of people, and may involve management, employees or third parties (or a combination of these).
* The two key factors that encourage fraud are motive and opportunity.
* Accounting manipulation is usually driven by business pressures, whereas other forms of fraud are usually driven by personal pressures.
* Unidentified or temporary weaknesses in systems and controls can increase the inherent risk of fraud.
* The Internet creates increasing opportunities for high speed and high frequency fraud.
* Increased regulation has been imposed as a result of recent accounting scandals.
* The primary role of the Fraud Advisory Panel is to raise awareness of the social and economic damage caused by fraud.
* Useful information can be found on websites dedicated to the issue of fraud.

11.2 What Is Fraud?

There is no single definition of fraud. Auditing Standards describe fraud as comprising:

* the use of deception to obtain unjust or illegal financial advantage and
* intentional misrepresentations affecting the financial statements.

Fraud may involve physical theft or misappropriation of cash or goods, recording transactions with no substance (such as payments to fictitious employees or suppliers) and falsifying or altering accounting and other records to cover up theft or misappropriation. It also includes the manipulation or distortion of data, either for tangible gain (for instance to increase the payments under bonus or commission schemes) or simply to present the details in a more favourable light (for instance, to meet targets, show improved results or enhance share performance). The nature of fraud often depends on the type of business, the reason for the fraud and who is perpetrating it. Certain businesses, particularly those involving access to high levels of cash or movable goods, are particularly vulnerable to fraud involving personal gain for the fraudster. In this context, the more common types of fraud include the theft of cash or stock, the submission of false expense claims and purchasing frauds involving false invoices or fictitious suppliers. Financial information will usually be misstated in these cases, but primarily to cover up the fraudulent activity rather than as an end in itself. Fraud involving the intentional misrepresentation of financial information is more likely to be driven by the need to meet or exceed performance targets, either for a business segment or for the business as a whole, and is much more likely to involve those in more senior positions within the business.

The Fraud Act 2006, which received Royal Assent in November 2006 and generally came into effect on 15 January 2007, creates a statutory offence of fraud which is committed when a person dishonestly carries out one of the following acts with the intent of making a gain, causing loss or exposing another person to the risk of loss:

- makes a false representation;
- wrongfully fails to disclose information or
- secretly abuses a position of trust.

11.3   New and Emerging Areas of Fraud

The growth of e-commerce and the wide availability of the Internet has created a number of new avenues for fraudsters to explore. Recent years have seen a worrying growth in cybercrime, including activities such as cyberlaundering, cyberextortion, advanced fee frauds, the sale of stolen or counterfeit goods through the Internet, credit card fraud, computer hacking, phishing, cybersquatting, and other e-mail and Internet scams. Many e-commerce transactions proceed without human intervention by the service provider and automated transactions should therefore be subject to particularly careful scrutiny. Identity theft, where the fraudster uses the identity of an individual or a company to open bank accounts and/or obtain payments, credit or goods and services, is also facilitated by use of the Internet. The Fraud Advisory Panel has published a number of useful guides and reports on these and other issues, all of which are available free of charge from its website (see **11.11**).

11.4   A Low Profile Issue?

Fraud has tended to be given a relatively low profile within the business community. Concerns over the impact of adverse publicity have resulted in many companies being reluctant to report and follow up any frauds that are identified and it is therefore difficult to estimate the true cost of fraud, although the report *The Economic Cost of Fraud* produced for the Home Office by National Economic Research Associates (NERA) towards the end of 2000 suggested that it could be in the order of £14 billion pa. However, the view that fraud is a victim-less crime is rapidly losing ground as everyone becomes more aware of the impact that serious fraud can have on the general public in terms of business fail-ures (and thus reduced employment opportunities), loss of (or reductions in) pensions and savings, higher insurance premiums, higher banking costs and, potentially, higher taxes.

11.5 Impact of Recent Events

The terrorist attacks in New York and Washington in September 2001 and var-ious accounting scandals that have come to light in recent months, especially those at Enron and Worldcom, have all served to heightened the general aware-ness of fraud and the damage that it can cause to the business economy. There has been an increased focus on the use of fraud and money laundering to secure funds to support terrorist activity, and on the need for tighter legislation and controls to prevent this. Similarly, the various accounting scandals have high-lighted how quickly share prices and the investment markets can collapse when business confidence is destroyed. Whilst these are large, high profile businesses, the issue of fraud, the damage it can cause and the need to prevent it, are equally relevant in a smaller, owner-managed company.

11.6 Need for Culture Change

One of the principal themes emerging from recent events is the need for a major change in business culture and attitudes. Various initiatives have been developed in recent years, including the Combined Code (and its predecessor Codes), to try and create a business culture of transparency, integrity and accountability. This is something that must come from the top of an organisation – it will only happen if the board is prepared to recognise the issue and take appropriate action, setting a strong example at board level. In particular, it is important to encourage a climate of openness and trust, where all employees accept the responsibility for uphold-ing high standards and feel confident in reporting any concerns to management. The Government has also expressed concern that awards of large share options packages to senior executives might be creating 'perverse incentives' rather than encouraging the achievement of performance targets. Both the Combined Code and the regulations for quoted companies on the Directors' Remuneration Report require the disclosure of detailed information on the use of share options and other long-term incentive schemes (see CHAPTERS 6 and 9), and the Government has instigated further examination of the use of such schemes.

11.7 Who Perpetrates Fraud?

Fraud on a company may involve a single individual or a group of individuals, and may be committed by management, employees or third parties. In many cases, a degree of collusion will be needed in order to perpetrate the fraud. Employee or management fraud intended to achieve personal gain will often be committed with third party help, and those committing fraud from outside the organisation will often need internal assistance. For instance, many purchasing frauds require collusion between a supplier and an employee involved with purchases transactions. The two key factors that encourage fraud are motive and opportunity. The motive for fraud can be very wide ranging. Accounting manipulation is usually driven by business pressures, such as:

- the need to achieve or exceed budgets and targets;
- the need to maintain or improve the share price;
- the need to secure additional funding and
- the need to support weak or failing ventures.

The demands on senior management are not only internal and there is particular concern that the attitude of financial analysts and commentators is fuelling the development of an aggressive attitude to earnings management within the business community. Unrealistic reporting deadlines can also put undue pressure on senior management. Other types of fraud are more likely to be driven by personal pressures, such as those arising from excessive greed, an attempt to resolve personal financial difficulties, general career dissatisfaction or a desire for revenge. Businesses can also become the victims of various types of cyber-crime, usually perpetrated by third parties who have no direct connection with the company (see **PARAGRAPH 11.3**).

11.8   Nature of Fraud

Accounting manipulations that amount to fraud include:

- the creation of false sales;
- the deliberate overstatement of assets;
- the deliberate suppression of liabilities;
- failure to take account of the substance of all elements of a transaction (i.e. recognising only those elements that help to achieve the required overstatement or understatement of income, expenses, assets or liabilities);
- delaying or advancing income or expenditure;
- manipulation of pricing agreements and
- inappropriate use of reserves.

In the case of other types of fraud, the opportunity is usually greatest where there are limited deterrents or little chance of the fraud being discovered. Many of those who commit this type of fraud are opportunists, and unidentified, or even temporary, weaknesses in systems and controls can make the company especially vulnerable. New business activities, changes to management information systems, changes in management, the prolonged absence of key individuals and weakened controls as a result of reduced staffing levels can all increase the inherent risk of fraud. There can also be particular problems in areas where management are heavily reliant on specialist expertise. For instance, if the management team has only limited computer expertise, they may in effect place heavy reliance on relatively junior employees in areas where there is enormous scope for manipulation. It is usually inevitable that what begins as a small fraud will grow, particularly where accounts manipulation is involved, either as an end in itself or to cover up a fraud of a different type. If income for the current year has been inflated in order to show the required level of performance, further inflation is going to be needed in the next accounting period in order to maintain the 'growth'.

11.9   Internet Fraud

Fraud is now more organised than ever before and the Internet has opened up increasing opportunities for high speed and high frequency frauds. Relatively common Internet frauds include identity fraud, credit card fraud and the theft of confidential data. Particular care is needed when developing websites, as poor programming and website design can result in relatively easy but unauthorised access being given to data, which can then be corrupted or used for fraudulent purposes. Also, encryption techniques will sometimes not be as sound as they appear and may therefore not give the required degree of physical security over data.

11.10   Reaction to Accounting Scandals

The UK reaction to recent accounting scandals is likely to result in an increased regulatory cost for business generally, although there is a strong awareness of the need to avoid creating regulatory overload and to weigh the perceived advantages of certain measures against the potential adverse consequences. Reviews of financial reporting, auditing and the role of non-executive directors commissioned by the UK Government resulted in the introduction of a revised Combined Code (see **CHAPTER 6**) and certain changes to the regulation of the audit and accountancy profession.

In particular, this included the introduction of:

- a considerably more demanding role for audit committees in ensuring proper protection of shareholder interests in relation to financial reporting and internal control and a requirement for audit committees to report in detail on their activities each year;
- a specific requirement for audit committees to carry out an annual assessment of the qualifications, expertise, resources, effectiveness and independence of the external auditors;
- a recommendation that auditors of listed companies and other public interest entities should publish detailed information, covering whole firm financial information, organisational structure and reward systems, how quality is achieved and monitored, and the policies and procedures used to manage threats to independence;
- the development of more detailed guidance on auditor independence, and in particular on the provision of non-audit services to audit clients, and an enhanced role for the audit committee in developing company policy on this;
- new measures for regulating the accountancy profession and for monitoring the performance of audit firms with listed and other public interest clients and

- an enhanced role for the Financial Reporting Review Panel (FRRP) in monitoring and enforcing compliance with accounting standards.

The reviews decided against the mandatory rotation of auditors on the grounds that there are sensible and effective alternatives to this. The above issues are considered in more detail in **CHAPTERS 2** and **10**.

11.11   The Fraud Advisory Panel

The Fraud Advisory Panel was established in 1996, on the initiative of the Institute of Chartered Accountants in England and Wales (ICAEW), and it acts as a focal point for the generation and exchange of ideas and information aimed at fighting fraud in its various forms. The members of the Panel are drawn from the legal and accountancy professions, industry and commerce, the academic world, the police and a range of government and quasi-governmental bodies. The work of the Panel is directed by a Steering Group and is carried out by a series of working parties. The Panel's primary role is to raise awareness of the social and economic damage caused by fraud, and in particular to:

- develop proposals to reform the law and public policy on fraud;
- develop proposals to enhance the investigation and prosecution of fraud;
- advise business on fraud prevention, detection and reporting;
- assist in improving fraud-related education and training in business and the professions and
- establish a more accurate picture of the extent, causes and nature of fraud.

The reports and guidance material produced by the Panel to date include:

- Cybercrime: Protecting your Mobile Device (July 2006)
- Fraud Bill: Guidance for Industry (April 2006)
- Fighting Fraud: A Guide for SMEs (2nd Edition – February 2006)
- Sample Fraud Policy Statements (February 2006)
- Protecting Your IT Systems: A Guide for SMEs (September 2005)
- Have You Been Scammed? Identifying Internet and E-mail Scams (July 2004)
- Cybercrime & the Proceeds of Crime Act (March 2004)
- Identity Theft: Do You Know the Signs? (July 2003)
- Cybercrime: What Every SME Should Know (2002)

These are all available free of charge from the Panel's website at www.fraudadvisorypanel.org. Membership of the Panel is open to individuals and corporate bodies that share its values. Further information can be obtained from the Fraud Advisory Panel, Chartered Accountants' Hall, P.O. Box 433, Moorgate Place, London, EC2P 2BJ (telephone 020 7920 8721; fax 020 7920 8545).

11.12   Other Information

The Fraud Advisory Panel's website (www.fraudadvisorypanel.org) includes a useful list of other websites providing information on fraud and related issues.

The Treasury also published *Managing the Risk of Fraud* in May 2003 and this can be downloaded from www.hm-treasury.gov.uk (under Public spending and reporting – Governance risk management).

11.13 Responsibility for Fraud Prevention and Detection

> **At a Glance**
> * Company directors have a collective responsibility for taking reasonable steps to prevent and detect fraud and other irregularities.
> * An internal audit function can help management to identify and assess fraud risk and develop appropriate systems and controls.
> * External auditors are required to plan their work so that they have a reasonable expectation of detecting material errors and misstatements arising from fraud, but do not have a responsibility to detect all fraud or error that may exist within a business.
> * The role of the audit committee is to provide assurance that the board's collective responsibility for financial matters and internal control is being properly discharged.

11.14 Collective Responsibility of Directors

The directors have joint and several responsibilities for safeguarding the assets of the company, and must therefore take reasonable steps to prevent and detect fraud and other irregularities. This is specifically referred to in the statement of the directors' responsibilities that must be published as part of the annual accounts (see **CHAPTER 10**). Although it may be helpful for management purposes to allocate the management of security issues to a specific director or other senior individual within the organisation, the directors always retain collective responsibility for the prevention and detection of fraud.

11.15 Role of Internal Audit

Internal auditors are not responsible for designing and implementing systems, nor for the prevention and detection of fraud. However, the work of an internal audit function can help management to identify and assess potential risks within the business, and to develop appropriate systems and controls to reduce these risks to an acceptable level. This includes the inherent risk of fraud. The internal audit function provides a useful source of information for management on what is actually happening within the organisation. Its remit is generally much wider than the prevention and detection of fraud, and includes providing assurance on issues such as the completeness and accuracy of the company's accounting and other records, and the overall efficiency of the operations. However, by focussing its efforts on the effectiveness of the company's system of internal control, reporting any weaknesses and concerns and recommending appropriate changes to policies, procedures and controls, an internal audit function can help the directors to demonstrate that they are paying due attention to their responsibility for safeguarding the company's assets. Internal auditors can also be commissioned to undertake special assignments to assist management in the development of the business. These might include occasional more detailed forensic checks on accounting and other operational controls designed to limit the opportunity for fraud. Further information on establishing and operating an internal audit function is given in CHAPTER 2.

11.16   Role of External Auditors

For many years there has been a commonly held, and misconceived, view that the detection of fraud is an important aspect of the role of the external auditors. The auditing profession has made considerable efforts in recent years to explain the role and responsibilities of external auditors, and the nature of an audit, in an attempt to eliminate this 'expectation gap'. External auditors are appointed to express an independent opinion on the annual financial statements. Their work is therefore directed towards identifying any potentially material misstatements in the accounts, including any that arise as a result of fraud and other irregularities. Auditors are required to plan their work so that they have a reasonable expectation of detecting material errors and misstatements arising from fraud. In carrying out their work, the external auditors will review the company's systems and controls, carry out certain test checks, and report to management any weaknesses and concerns that they identify, but the external audit should not be relied upon to detect all fraud and irregularities that may exist within the organisation. The auditors will usually emphasise this in their report to management on significant issues that have come to their attention during the audit (see CHAPTER 2). If the company does not have an internal audit function, the directors might consider arranging for the external auditors to carry out more detailed forensic checks on the systems and controls as a separate exercise from time to time. If the external auditors do detect, or have reason to suspect, fraud during the course of their work, they will normally report this to the directors. However, separate arrangements may apply where the auditors suspect that directors are involved in the fraud, or in the case of regulated businesses. If the company has an audit committee, the auditors may report through that committee if they have reason to believe that executive directors may be involved in the fraud.

11.17   Role of the Audit Committee

The precise role of the audit committee must be tailored to the needs of the individual company, but broadly the role of an audit committee is to provide assurance that the board's collective responsibility for financial matters and internal control is being properly discharged. The audit committee's responsibilities will usually include reviewing the results of the work of the external auditors and, where relevant, the internal auditors, and ensuring that points brought to the attention of management are being properly followed up and actioned. Under the present Combined Code, the specific responsibilities of the audit committee include:

- reviewing the company's internal financial controls and, unless addressed by a separate risk committee of independent directors or by the board itself, the company's internal control and risk management systems and
- reviewing the arrangements by which staff may, in confidence, raise concerns about possible improprieties in matters of financial reporting or other issues, with the objective of ensuring that arrangements are in place for proportionate and independent investigation and appropriate follow-up action.

The existence of an audit committee can also help to demonstrate a climate of discipline and control within the business and can provide a useful forum, independent of the executive management team, for the finance director, external auditors and head of internal audit to raise issues of concern where necessary. Further information is given in CHAPTER 2.

11.18   Minimising the Risk of Fraud

At a Glance
* Fraud risk should be managed in a way that reduces it to an acceptable level.
* Rigorous personnel procedures, for both permanent and temporary staff, can help to reduce the risk of fraud.
* The likelihood of fraud arising should be assessed for each area of the company's activities (including those that are peripheral to the main business), and the controls to prevent each fraud risk should be identified.
* Steps should be taken to correct any missing or weak controls.
* The importance of management attitude and the general ethos of the organisation cannot be overemphasised.
* Biometrics can now be used to improve the security of access controls.
* All businesses should be aware of the risks of becoming inadvertently involved in money laundering.

11.19   Managing the Risk

Fraud is one of the many inevitable risks that any business faces. The risk of fraud arising can never be wholly eliminated, but it can be managed and reduced to an acceptable level by taking practical, common sense precautions and making use of cost-effective accounting and operational controls. Careful planning should enable appropriate controls to be introduced without disrupting the efficient operation of the business. However, the potential benefit of reducing risk to an acceptable level must always be balanced against the cost of doing so. If the directors decide not to take steps to reduce a potential risk, on the basis that the ongoing cost of doing so is too great, it is important that they do so with a clear understanding of the possible consequences.

11.20   Personnel Procedures

Rigorous personnel procedures can help to reduce the risk of fraud. It is particularly important to take up references for all potential new employees and to follow these up thoroughly. Organisations frequently fail to confirm the qualifications and experience of prospective employees, follow up any apparent gaps in the previous employment record or investigate further any issues that may be referred to, however obliquely, in references from former employers. Consideration should also be given to introducing the same procedures for temporary staff, particularly where they are to work in areas of the business that could be particularly susceptible to fraud. If temporary staff will have the same access to company records and assets as permanent employees, there is little justification for less rigorous personnel checks. Where the business makes regular use of temporary staff through employment agencies, it will usually be appropriate to check that the agency has adequate procedures in place on this. If certain services are contracted out to other organisations (for instance, cleaning or maintenance services) it will usually be sensible to confirm that the main contractor carries out thorough checks on his employees and that proper records are maintained of who is working at each location at any given time. This is especially important when the individuals have regular access to the company's premises at times when management and staff are not usually present. Contracts of service for employees should normally provide for immediate suspension on the suspicion of fraud, to help prevent further loss and to preserve security over company records and assets. Similar arrangements may be appropriate for temporary staff and for contracted services.

11.21   Review and Assessment of Activities

The initial step in minimising the risk of fraud is to identify all the company's activities and assess the likelihood of fraud arising in each area. This review should encompass all those activities that are peripheral to the main business but which may nevertheless provide scope for material fraud. In many ways these activities often represent a higher risk as they can easily be overlooked and are frequently not subjected to the same degree of scrutiny as the key aspects of the business. For instance, peripheral activities might include the disposal of fixed assets, or the management of the company's car fleet. It is important to recognise that giving one person access both to company assets and to the related accounting or operational records significantly increases the opportunity for fraud. Hence the frequent emphasis by auditors on the need for segregation of duties wherever practicable. If at all possible, the following five aspects of a transaction should be fully segregated:

- initiation;
- authorisation;

- execution;
- custody of any related assets and
- recording in the accounting records.

If segregation is not possible (e.g. due to the small size of the organisation and the limited number of staff available) compensating checks and controls should be introduced. Business operations in remote locations will also usually present a higher risk of fraud – a higher degree of autonomy may be necessary for a remote operation to function efficiently, but this will usually bring with it an increased risk of abuse.

11.22   E-commerce and IT Issues

Businesses should also undertake a careful review and assessment of the potential exposure to the additional risks arising from cybercrime and other e-commerce and IT issues. Both internal and external risks should be considered, including those arising from:

- the actions of management and employees;
- viruses, bots and other malware;
- computer hacking;
- extortion and denial of service attacks and
- the use of unprotected wireless networks.

Businesses should also consider the need to ensure compliance with any relevant legal and other requirements – for instance, security standards set out in the Payment Card Industry (PCI) rules and the obligation under the Data Protection Act 1998 to protect any personal information entrusted to them.

11.23   Assessment of Controls

Having identified the fraud risks, the next step is to identify the controls that are already in place to prevent fraud wherever a potential risk arises. This should highlight any areas where:

- there is an absence of appropriate controls;
- controls are weak or
- there is a lack of appropriate management information.

Steps can then be taken to introduce new or enhanced controls and to improve the flow of information. In some cases, the analysis may reveal an excess of controls in a particular area, which might enable some rationalisation and provide scope for additional controls in weaker areas. It is important to remember that a control that is effective in preventing errors will not necessarily be effective in preventing fraud (e.g. a determined fraudster can easily forge an authorisation signature). It is also essential to confirm that the controls identified do actually operate in practice.

11.24   Management Attitude

The importance of management attitude and the general ethos of the organisation cannot be overemphasised. Fraud is much less likely to be perpetrated in a culture that is honest and open. It is essential that the directors make their views on the unacceptability of fraud and dishonesty explicit and that they lead by example, by setting out clear rules (and not bending them) and ensuring that all business practices are honest and above board. Employees should be left in no doubt as to the consequences of involvement in fraud. Management can impress this on their staff by:

- having a clear company policy on fraud, publicising this within the organisation and drawing it to the attention of third parties, such as customers and suppliers;
- including fraud awareness in staff induction programmes;
- incorporating ongoing fraud awareness training into staff development programmes and emphasising that all employees have a responsibility for the prevention and detection of fraud;
- having a confidential 'whistle-blowing' procedure (see **PARAGRAPH 11.29**);
- developing a fraud response plan, to make it clear that action will be taken promptly and effectively if fraud is identified (see **PARAGRAPH 11.35**);
- following up all allegations of fraud sensitively but thoroughly, and being prepared to take action against any perpetrators of fraud who are identified.

Implementing an effective system of internal control, and monitoring it regularly, helps to ensure that transactions are recorded accurately and that company assets are safeguarded. It also demonstrates to the employees that the directors take their responsibilities in this area seriously. A relaxed management attitude towards procedures and controls sends the opposite message. Rewarding staff for appropriate attention to control and compliance issues, as well as for financial performance, can also help to highlight the importance of these issues to the business as a whole.

11.25   Biometrics

A relatively recent development is the increasing use of biometrics to help protect a business against fraud – for instance, the use of techniques such as facial recognition, finger print recognition and iris recognition gives a much higher level of access security than a system of passwords.

11.26   Money Laundering

Certain businesses, in particular those in the financial services sector, are subject to stringent legal requirements in respect of the identification and reporting of money laundering and it is essential that such businesses have procedures and controls in place to ensure that they fulfil their duties in this area. However, any business could potentially be an unwitting party to money laundering and it is therefore advisable to ensure that management and staff are aware of the need to question unusual and potentially dubious transactions and know who to inform in such circumstances. Cash-oriented businesses are particularly attractive to money launderers. New regulations on money laundering were introduced in 2003 under the Proceeds of Crime Act 2002 in an attempt to make criminal activity less profitable. The definition of money laundering under the new legislation is much broader and encompasses acquiring, possessing, dealing with or concealing the proceeds of any activity that constitutes a criminal offence in the UK. Certain professionals, including accountants and solicitors, now have a duty to report any knowledge or suspicions of money laundering by their clients to the Serious and Organised Crime Agency (SOCA). Specific rules also apply to any business that deals in goods and accepts in cash the equivalent of 15,000 euros (approximately £10,000) or more for any single transaction. Such businesses must register with HM Customs and Excise and put anti-money laundering systems in place or stop accepting large payments in cash and insist on payment by methods such as credit card or cheque.

11.27   Detection of Fraud

At a Glance
* All managers and staff should be aware of the potential warning signs of fraud.
* A clear, straightforward procedure for 'whistle-blowing' by employees can be of significant help in the detection of fraud.
* Any business areas performing differently from expectations should be investigated.
* The use of management override of internal controls should be carefully monitored.
* Any seemingly unusual behaviour by employees should be investigated.
* Any apparently unusual transactions should always be investigated.
* The company should maintain its own fraud record and analyse the information for any particular patterns.

11.28   Awareness of Warning Signs

Many frauds come to light by accident or as a the result of a tip-off, but putting procedures in place to detect fraud can help to ensure that any irregularities come to light at an early stage and that any loss is minimised. They can also act as a useful deterrent. It may be helpful to allocate the management of security issues, including the prevention and detection of fraud, to a specific individual within the organisation. However, all members of the management team, and preferably all employees, need to be aware of the potential warning signs of fraud and to be constantly alert for them. Experience has shown that when fraud is detected, the warning signs have often been apparent for sometime but have either not been noticed by management or have been noted but not acted upon. A strong system of internal controls should help to ensure that any irregularities are highlighted.

However, regular monitoring is important, both to check that the controls are actually operating as intended (for instance, staff may be tempted to take short cuts to save time) and to ensure that controls are kept up to date as the business develops (for instance, new activities may not be adequately covered by existing controls, or organisational changes may have inadvertently resulted in a control lapsing). It is also important to consider whether management can override the controls and, if so, how often this is done in practice. An internal audit function can provide valuable assistance on these points. Taking prompt and appropriate action on weaknesses in systems and controls highlighted by the auditors (both external and internal) helps to demonstrate management's commitment to operating an effective system of internal control.

11.29   Whistle-Blowing Procedures

The company should develop and publicise a clear, straightforward system for 'whistle-blowing' by employees. This will only operate satisfactorily if there is a climate of openness, honesty and trust and if employees feel confident that they will not suffer personally as a result of raising their concerns. Options to consider include reporting:

- through the line manager – although such a system will need to provide for cases where the employee suspects the line manager of being implicated in the fraud;
- directly to an identified member of senior management;
- directly to an identified member of the audit committee or
- through a confidential fraud telephone hotline (which may be either internal or external).

It is generally inadvisable to use e-mail for this purpose. Whatever method best suits the company's circumstances, it is important that employees see that their concerns are taken seriously and are properly followed up, and that confidentiality is maintained. Where suspected fraud is reported in good faith, the employee will usually be protected under the *Public Interest Disclosure Act 1998*. The effective operation of the 'whistle-blowing' procedures should be regularly reviewed. In particular, under the best practice provisions set out in the Combined Code, the audit committee should assume responsibility for carrying out a review of the company's arrangements to enable staff to raise concerns in confidence (see PARAGRAPHS 2.16 and 6.42).

11.30   Business Areas Performing Unexpectedly

Directors should ensure that regular checks are carried out, using performance indicators relevant to the business, to identify any areas that are performing differently from expectations. For example, where a business area regularly performs better than expected, it is possible that the results are being manipulated, whilst a business that is consistently falling below expectations could potentially be the subject of cash or purchasing frauds. Wherever possible, financial information should be reviewed in conjunction with non-financial data as this may help to highlight any inconsistencies (for instance, it should be possible to review payroll totals in conjunction with independently prepared details of employee numbers). The most useful performance indicators will depend on the nature of the business, but those in common use include the following:

- Gross margin – significant fluctuations could indicate manipulation of sales figures, purchasing fraud or theft of stock.
- Stock turnover – significant fluctuations could indicate theft of stock, or purchasing fraud.
- Debtors:sales ratio (average debtor days) – significant fluctuations could indicate manipulation of sales figures, or teeming and lading of cash received.
- Age analysis of debtors – increase in old balances could indicate cash fraud.
- Creditors:purchases ratio (average creditor days) – significant fluctuations could indicate purchasing fraud.
- Average pay per employee – significant increase could indicate payments to fictitious employees.

Unusual trends or fluctuations should be thoroughly investigated, and apparently plausible explanations should always be corroborated. It is also worth remembering that too much consistency might in itself be suspicious. It has been known for a business unit to perform exactly in line with budget each year – on further investigation, it transpired that the unit had in fact performed consistently above budget and that management and staff had colluded to divide the excess profits between them.

11.31   Opportunity for Management Override

Directors should be constantly aware of situations where line managers and senior employees may have the opportunity to override internal controls, or to arrange for figures to be presented in a more positive light. This can be a particular problem where an autocratic individual occupies a senior post, or in the case of remote operations, where local management may need a higher level of autonomy for the operation to function efficiently. These situations should be subject to careful monitoring and, in the case of other locations, regular visits should be made to check on what is actually happening in practice. An internal audit function can be very useful in this situation. The setting of performance targets and the operation of incentive schemes are well accepted methods of managing businesses. However, both require careful monitoring and review on a regular basis. The setting of over-ambitious targets can encourage manipulation of the figures to show the desired result, and this can be a particular problem where employee earnings are directly affected by the financial performance of the business (for instance, through bonus schemes, profit sharing schemes, sales commission or earn out arrangements).

11.32   Staff Issues

Low staff morale can generate a higher risk of fraud, and a high level of staff turnover could be indicative of general management problems and potential fraud. Disaffected staff may be tempted to cut corners or not operate controls properly, or may be tempted to take advantage of systems weaknesses as revenge for lack of job satisfaction or to redress the feeling that they are not being adequately rewarded for their efforts. Independent debriefing of leavers can sometimes highlight the existence of fraudulent activity or concerns over dishonest business practices that would not otherwise have come to light. Any seemingly unusual behaviour by employees should be investigated. For example:

- A reluctance to take regular holidays may be due to the need to conceal an ongoing fraud. Fraud can often come to light during a sudden and unexpected absence of the person perpetrating it. Some organisations have a rule that staff must take at least two consecutive weeks' holiday each year – both for the physical well-being of the employee and to reduce the opportunity for long-term fraud to go undetected.
- Regular late-working by individual employees, whether paid or unpaid, should always be investigated and monitored – it may result from a need to cover up fraudulent activities in the absence of other members of staff. There are numerous examples of apparently diligent, long-standing employees working long hours, seemingly for the benefit of the company, but in fact to conceal their fraudulent activity. A trusted employee can be in a powerful position, especially if management have become relaxed about monitoring his/her activities.
- A refusal to change jobs or accept a promotion, or the consistent failure by a manager to delegate certain activities, may all be due to the need to conceal an ongoing fraud.
- An apparent discrepancy between an employee's earnings and his/her lifestyle is a common indicator of fraud.

11.33   Unusual Transactions

Management should always investigate apparently unusual transactions – for instance, an individual transaction that cannot immediately be explained or which seems to lack commercial substance or sense, or an unexpected quantity of a particular type of transaction, such as an abnormally high level of sales credit notes or an unusually large number of outstanding items on the bank reconciliation (especially if they seem to have been outstanding for sometime). Frequent or regular systems breakdowns may also be a warning signal – they can provide a useful opportunity to conceal transactions or manipulate financial information. Businesses undertaking automated e-commerce transactions should also ensure that these are subject to careful scrutiny, with particular attention to the following issues:

- Is the transaction or activity normal for this customer?
- Does the transaction make sense from a commercial/personal point of view?
- Has the pattern of transactions changed?
- If the transaction is with an overseas entity, is there a good business reason for this?

11.34   Collating Information on Fraud

An issue that is often overlooked is the potential benefit of a company maintaining its own record of suspected and actual fraud, and analysing this to see
if any particular patterns emerge. This may be helpful in the ongoing development and monitoring the company's response to fraud.

11.35   Developing a Fraud Response Plan

> **At a Glance**
> * A fraud response plan sets out company policy on fraud and the action
>   to be taken when fraud is suspected.
> * The plan should explain who will lead the investigation and the
>   detailed procedures that will be followed.
> * The fraud response plan should be regularly reviewed to ensure that it
>   is kept up to date.

11.36   Benefits of a Fraud Response Plan

A fraud response plan should include the general company policy on fraud and
should also set out the action to be taken when fraud is suspected. Having a
detailed fraud response plan in place helps to ensure that everyone is clear about
the action that needs to be taken if and when fraud is identified or suspected.
Thinking about the issues in advance helps management to ensure that all the relevant aspects are covered. It is much more difficult to react promptly and effectively without a plan to follow. In particular, a detailed document setting out the
policies and procedures to be followed in the case of fraud has the following
benefits:

* it demonstrates that management is in control of the situation;
* it can help to minimise the risk of further loss once the fraud has been
  detected;
* it should improve the chance of recovering the loss already incurred, or of
  maximising the amount recovered and
* it can help the company to minimise the potential adverse commercial effect
  (for instance, where supplier or customer accounts are affected).

It also provides a clear statement to employees that the directors are not prepared to condone fraud and will take appropriate action against anyone found
to be involved in fraudulent activity.

11.37   Contents of the Plan

The plan should include the following:

* A clear statement of company policy on fraud, and in particular who should
  be contacted when there is any suspicion of fraud.

- Who will take responsibility for leading any investigation of suspected fraud.
- Relevant legal and personnel procedures. As noted above, it will usually be helpful to ensure that employment contracts provide for any employee suspected of fraud to be suspended immediately and either isolated or removed from the premises. The company should adopt a consistent policy for staff throughout the organisation – employees can be given the wrong message if (say) management are treated more leniently than other members of staff.
- Specific procedures for securing the company's assets and records when fraud is suspected, both to prevent further loss and to ensure that potential evidence is not destroyed – for instance, the procedures might include changing locks, security passes and computer passwords. Particular care is needed in these days of advanced computer technology – it has been known for a suspended employee to delete vital information by accessing the company's records from a remote computer terminal.
- Procedures for carrying out a detailed investigation into the suspected fraud – this may be done internally or may require specialist assistance. In particular, the gathering of supporting evidence will usually require expert knowledge to ensure that it is sufficiently reliable for use in a prosecution.
- Procedures for making contact with the police, the company's insurers and the business regulators (where relevant).
- Procedures for making internal reports on the issue (e.g. to the audit committee or main board).
- The company's policy on seeking the recovery of funds.
- Procedures for dealing with any publicity issues that might arise from the fraud.

It is also important that the directors should be seen to act immediately to enhance controls over the business area that was the subject of the fraudulent activity.

11.38   Regular Review

The fraud response plan should be subject to regular review to ensure that it takes account of any recent changes – for instance, new developments within the business, changes resulting from the development of new technologies and any new external reporting requirements.

Appendix 1

Useful Websites on Fraud and Related Issues

Fraud Advisory Panel	www.fraudadvisorypanel.org
ICAEW Audit and Assurance Faculty	www.icaew.co.uk/aafac
Institute of Internal Auditors (UK and Ireland)	www.iia.org.uk
Institute of Directors	www.iod.com
Business Link	www.businesslink.gov.uk
Department for Business, Enterprise and Regulatory Reform	www.berr.gov.uk
European Anti-Fraud Office	http://europa.eu.int/comm/dgs/olaf/
ACPO Fraud Prevention	www.uk-fraud.info/
Crimestoppers	www.crimestoppers.org.uk
National Criminal Intelligence Service	www.ncis.gov.uk
National Hi-Tech Crime Unit	www.nhtcu.org/
Serious Fraud Office	www.sfo.gov.uk
Serious and Organised Crime Agency	www.soca.gov.uk

Appendix 2

Checklist: Prevention and Detection of Fraud

This checklist summarises some of the key issues that need to be considered when dealing with the prevention and detection of fraud. It should not be regarded as comprehensive – other issues may need to be taken into account, depending on the particular circumstances of the business.

☐ Are all directors made fully aware of their collective responsibility for the prevention and detection of fraud?

☐ Do the directors encourage a business culture that is open and honest, and lead by example?

☐ Has the company developed a clear policy on fraud and is this:
- widely publicised amongst employees?
- drawn to the attention of third parties (e.g. customers and suppliers)?

☐ Do the company's personnel procedures ensure that:
- the stated qualifications and experience of new employees are verified?
- Any apparent gaps in the employment record of new employees are investigated?
- References are taken up for all new employees?
- Any points raised in employee references are followed up?
- The same procedures are applied for temporary as well as permanent staff?
- Where agency staff are used, the company understands the level of checking that has been carried out by the agency?
- Where a service is contracted out to a third party, the company understands the level of checking carried out by the contractor, especially where individuals will be given access to the company's premises outside normal working hours?
- All employment contracts and other service contracts provide for immediate suspension on the suspicion of fraud?
- All employees are required to take at least two consecutive weeks' holiday each year?
- Regular late-working by employees is monitored and investigated?
- An independent debriefing interview is held with all leavers?

☐ Is fraud awareness included in staff induction programmes?

☐ Is ongoing fraud awareness training incorporated into staff development programmes?

☐ Does the company have a confidential 'whistle-blowing' procedure?

☐ Is the effectiveness of the 'whistle-blowing' procedure subject to regular review?

☐ Are staff rewarded for appropriate attention to compliance and control issues as well as for financial performance?

☐ Has the company assessed the likelihood of fraud arising:
- in each principal area of the business?
- in each peripheral area of the business (e.g. disposal of fixed assets, management of company car scheme)?

☐ Has the company identified and assessed the controls that operate to prevent fraud in each case where a potential risk arises and taken steps to:
- introduce new controls where gaps are evident?
- strengthen potentially weak controls?
- ensure the proper flow of relevant management information?
- rationalise any areas where excessive bureaucracy has been identified?

☐ Has the company confirmed that the identified controls are actually operating in practice?

☐ Do the company's procedures ensure that, as far as practicable, the following aspects of each business transaction are segregated:
- initiation;
- authorisation;
- execution;
- custody of related assets and
- recording in the accounting records?

☐ Are procedures and controls regularly reviewed and updated to take account of developments in the business?

☐ Are procedures and controls regularly reviewed and updated to take account of technological developments and the potential impact on the business of cybercrime and related fraud issues?

☐ If the company is subject to legal requirements in respect of money laundering, have appropriate procedures and controls been put in place?

☐ Are all directors and staff aware of the issues relating to money laundering, and the risk of the company becoming inadvertently involved?

☐ Have procedures been put into place to detect and prevent inadvertent involvement in money laundering activities?

☐ Are all directors and staff made aware of the potential warning signs of fraud?

- ☐ Is the use of management override of controls monitored and reviewed?

- ☐ Have appropriate performance indicators been identified for each aspect of the business?

- ☐ Are all variations from expected performance, and any unusual trends, thoroughly investigated and explanations corroborated?

- ☐ Is the use of incentive schemes and performance targets monitored and reviewed, to confirm that it is not encouraging manipulation of the underlying figures?

- ☐ Are regular control visits made to remote business locations?

- ☐ Do the company's procedures ensure that all unusual transactions are investigated?

- ☐ Do the directors collate information on actual and suspected fraud within the business and review this for any particular patterns?

- ☐ Does the company have an up to date fraud response plan setting out:
  - the company policy on fraud?
  - who will lead any investigation into suspected fraud?
  - the detailed procedures that will be followed, covering in particular:
    - ○ suspension and isolation/removal of relevant individuals;
    - ○ protection of the company's records and assets;
    - ○ gathering of reliable evidence;
    - ○ contact with relevant third parties (e.g. police, insurers, regulators) and
    - ○ internal reporting?
  - the company's policy on seeking recovery of funds?
  - procedures for dealing with any related publicity issues?

Going Concern

12 Going Concern

12.1 Background and Current Guidance

At a Glance

* Company law and accounting standards generally require annual accounts to be prepared on a going concern basis.
* Under the Combined Code, directors should report in the annual report and accounts that the business is a going concern, with supporting assumptions or qualifications where necessary.
* The document 'Going Concern and Financial Reporting – Guidance for Directors of Listed Companies' sets out the principles that directors should follow in relation to going concern.
* Additional guidance on the subject of going concern can be found in the UK & Ireland version of International Standard on Auditing 570 (ISA 570) *Going concern.*

12.2 Accounting Requirements

The *Companies Act 1985* (*CA 1985*) specifies that, for accounts purposes, a company is presumed to be carrying on business as a going concern, but gives no further guidance on this issue. Detailed guidance on the use of the going concern basis when preparing accounts is provided in:

- International Accounting Standard 1 (IAS 1) *Presentation of Financial Statements* where accounts are prepared in accordance with IASs.
- Financial Reporting Standard 18 (FRS 18) *Accounting Policies* where accounts are prepared in accordance with UK accounting practice.

UK Auditing Standards also require the annual report of each company to include a statement of the directors' responsibilities for the preparation of the accounts and this should also refer to the use of the going concern basis (see CHAPTER 10).

12.3 Significance of the Going Concern Assumption

The use of the going concern basis for the preparation of accounts is of particular significance when assessing the appropriateness of the accounting policies adopted. Some items in the accounts would be unchanged if the entity was not considered to be a going concern, but others might be significantly affected by this. For instance, fixed assets are usually included in the accounts at cost or valuation, depreciated to reflect the proportion of the life of the asset that has been used up in the business to date. The balance sheet value of the assets essentially represents their value to the business as a going concern, but will not necessarily represent the amount that would be realised if the individual assets had to be sold. If an entity is being liquidated or has ceased trading, a different accounting treatment may therefore need to be adopted for these assets. Other costs and liabilities may also need to be included in the accounts – for instance, penalties for the breach or early termination of contracts such as leases and other rental agreements.

12.4 Combined Code Recommendations

The Combined Code recommends that the directors should report in the annual report and accounts that the business is a going concern, with supporting assumptions or qualifications as necessary. This disclosure was originally recommended by the *Cadbury Code of Best Practice* but did not become fully effective until additional guidance was issued to directors in the document *Going Concern and Financial Reporting – Guidance for Directors of Listed Companies* published in November 1994. In the case of listed companies, the inclusion of a statement on going concern is now a direct requirement of the Financial Services Authority (FSA) Listing Rules and the statement must also be reviewed by the auditors.

12.5 Joint Working Group Guidance

The guidance set out in *Going Concern and Financial Reporting – Guidance for Directors of Listed Companies* was developed by a Joint Working Group (JWG) and sets out the governance principles that directors should adopt in relation to going concern. The guidance is addressed primarily to listed companies, but it was hoped that the clarification of the concept of going concern would be of general benefit to all entities and would assist directors in meeting their obligations under company law. The document has three main objectives:

- to explain the significance of going concern in relation to financial statements;
- to describe the procedures that an explicit statement on going concern may entail and
- to recommend appropriate disclosures.

12.6 Other Guidance

Additional guidance on the subject of going concern can be found in the UK & Ireland version of ISA 570 *Going concern* (available from the Auditing Practices

Board's website at http://www.frc.org.uk/apb/publications/isa.cfm). Although the primary objective of this document is to assist auditors when considering going concern, some of the issues raised may also be of help to directors when making their annual assessment of whether the company is a going concern. In particular ISA (UK and Ireland) 570 sets out illustrative summaries of financial, operational and other indicators of potential going concern difficulties, including:

Financial indicators of potential going concern difficulties

- a net liability or net current liability position;
- necessary borrowing facilities not yet agreed;
- fixed-term borrowings approaching maturity without realistic prospects of renewal or repayment;
- excessive reliance on short-term borrowing to finance long-term assets;
- major debt repayment falling due where refinancing is necessary to the entity's continued existence;
- major restructuring of debt;
- indications of withdrawal of support by lenders and other creditors;
- negative operating cash flows indicated by historical or prospective financial statements;
- adverse key financial ratios;
- substantial operating losses or significant deterioration in the value of assets used to generate cash flows;
- major losses or cash flow problems since the balance sheet date;
- arrears or discontinuance of dividends;
- inability to pay creditors on due dates;
- inability to comply with terms of loan agreements;
- reduction in normal terms of trade credit by suppliers;
- change from credit to cash-on-delivery transactions with suppliers;
- inability to obtain financing for essential new product development or other essential investments and
- substantial sales of fixed assets not intended to be replaced.

Operational and other indicators of potential going concern difficulties

- loss of key management or staff without replacement;
- loss of a major market, franchise, licence or principal supplier;
- labour difficulties or shortages of important supplies;
- fundamental changes in the market or technology to which the entity is unable to adapt adequately;
- excessive dependence on a few product lines where the market is depressed;
- technical developments which render a key product obsolete;
- non-compliance with capital or other statutory requirements;
- pending legal or regulatory proceedings against the entity that may, if successful, result in claims that are unlikely to be satisfied;
- changes in legislation or government policy expected to adversely affect the entity and
- issues which involve a range of possible outcomes so wide that an unfavourable result could affect the appropriateness of the going concern basis.

The guidance emphasises that the above lists are not exhaustive, nor does the existence of one or more of these issues always signify a material uncertainty over the entity's ability to continue as a going concern. Consideration should also be given to any related mitigating factors, such as management's plans to raise finance from other sources, or to seek alternative sources of supply, and the extent to which these are likely to be successful (see also **PARAGRAPH 12.20**).

12.7   Directors' Assessment of Going Concern

At a Glance
* Going concern is defined as the hypothesis that the entity is to continue in operational existence for the foreseeable future.
* The term 'foreseeable future' is not defined, but additional disclosures should be given when the period considered by the directors is less than 12 months from the date on which the accounts are approved.
* When preparing the company's annual accounts, the directors should give formal consideration to the issue of going concern each year and should assess in particular whether there are any factors which cast doubt on the entity's ability to continue in operational existence.
* Factors to take into account include forecasts and budgets, cash flow and borrowing requirements, contingent liabilities, market develop-ments and financial adaptability.
* The directors' consideration of going concern should normally be updated when the half-yearly report is formally reviewed by the board.

12.8   Basis of Preparation of Accounts

FRS 18 generally requires financial statements to be prepared on a going con-cern basis unless:

(i)   the entity is being liquidated or has ceased trading; or
(ii) the directors intend to liquidate the entity or to cease trading; or
(iii) the directors have no realistic alternative but to liquidate the entity or to cease trading.

In these circumstances the entity should prepare its financial statements on a different basis. Similarly, Paragraph 23 of the International Accounting Standards Board's (IASB's) *Framework for the Preparation and Presentation of Financial Statements* states that:

(i)   financial statements will normally be prepared on the assumption that an entity is a going concern and will continue in operation for the foreseeable future and
(ii) if there is an intention or need to liquidate or curtail materially the scale of the entity's operations, the financial statements may need to be prepared on a different basis – if so, the basis used must be disclosed.

IAS 1 *Presentation of Financial Statements* requires financial statements to be prepared on a going concern basis unless management either intends to liquidate the entity, or to cease trading, or has no realistic alternative but to do so. The JWG guidance emphasises that it will not usually be appropriate to adopt the going concern basis for the accounts if there is any intention or need to enter into a scheme of arrangement with the company's creditors, make an application for an administration order or put the company into administrative receivership or liquidation. However, the restructuring of a business, even on a major scale, is a relatively common practice these days and will not usually result in the going concern basis being an inappropriate basis for the preparation of the accounts.

12.9　Definition of Going Concern

FRS 18 *Accounting Policies* describes the going concern basis as the hypothesis that the entity is to continue in operational existence for the foreseeable future and notes that this basis will usually provide the most relevant information to users of the accounts. The standard therefore requires directors to assess, when preparing accounts, whether there are any significant doubts about the entity's ability to continue as a going concern. In making this assessment, the directors must take into account all available information about the foreseeable future. The guidance in the standard emphasises that the degree of consideration needed in order to make this assessment will vary depending on the circumstances of the entity. If there is a history of profitable operations with ready access to financial resources when required, and this situation is expected to continue, the consideration of going concern may be less detailed than when there are concerns over issues such as expected profitability, the ability to meet debt repayment schedules and the availability of alternative sources of finance.

A similar definition of going concern is given in the IASB's *Framework for the Preparation and Presentation of Financial Statements* and IAS 1 *Presentation of Financial Statements* requires management to make an assessment of the entity's ability to continue as a going concern and to take account of all available information about the future. The standard also includes similar guidance on the degree of consideration required and the fact that this depends on the circumstances of each case.

12.10　What Is the Foreseeable Future?

Neither accounting standards nor company law explain the term 'foreseeable future' and the JWG guidance emphasises that it is not appropriate to set a minimum period to which the directors should pay particular attention when considering the issue of going concern. However, the guidance does make the following points:

- any consideration involving the foreseeable future involves making judgements about future events which are inherently uncertain;
- in general terms, the degree of uncertainty increases significantly the further into the future the consideration is taken;
- the judgement is valid only at the point in time at which it is made.

- in assessing going concern, the directors should take into account all the information of which they are aware at the time the judgement is made, and their statement on going concern should be made on the basis of the information that is known to them at the date on which they approve the financial statements.

Although no minimum review period is specified, the guidance does note that where the period considered by the directors has been limited, for example, to a period of less than one year from the date of approval of the financial statements, the directors should consider whether additional disclosure should be made to explain the assumptions underlying the adoption of the going concern basis. FRS 18 now requires additional disclosures to be given in the accounts in these circumstances. IAS 1 requires management to consider a period that is at least, but is not limited to, 12 months from the balance sheet date.

12.11 Procedures to Be Carried Out

In order to be able to make the required statement on going concern each year, the directors will need to:

- give formal consideration to the issue of going concern;
- consider whether there are any factors which cast doubt on the entity's ability to continue in operational existence for the foreseeable future, and whether the going concern basis is appropriate for the financial statements and
- consider whether additional disclosure is necessary in the annual report and accounts.

It is not acceptable for directors to simply assume that the business can be treated as a going concern without carrying out any procedures to confirm this. However, many of the recommended procedures will already be carried out by directors and senior management for other purposes, such as the development of strategic plans, the preparation of budgets and forecasts, and risk management. All that may be necessary in these circumstances is to summarise the procedures already carried out, and the issues arising from them, and for the directors to consider whether any additional procedures need to be undertaken to cover any aspects that have not already been adequately dealt with. In practice, much of the work will be done prior to the approval of the accounts, but because the directors are required to make their assessment on the basis of the information known to them on the date on which the accounts are approved, they will need to update their review to take account of any changes in circumstances that have arisen since the detailed procedures were carried out.

12.12 Factors to Consider

Many different factors will be relevant to a consideration of whether a company is a going concern, and these will vary with the nature of the business under review. Some factors will be within the control of the directors, others may be external and therefore outside their direct control. Similar factors will need to be taken into account in preparing budgets and forecasts and the directors should therefore have a good understanding of the most significant issues for their company. The JWG guidance sets out examples of major areas that directors will usually need to consider in order to identify whether they are, or could become, significant in relation to going concern – the list is not intended to be exhaustive but rather to indicate the sort of factors that should be taken into account when considering going concern. The areas identified in the guidance are:

- forecasts and budgets;
- borrowing requirements;
- liability management;
- contingent liabilities;
- products and markets;
- financial risk management and
- financial adaptability.

An appendix to the document sets out detailed procedures that may be followed, although the guidance emphasises that these should not be regarded as checklists, partly because not all of the procedures will be relevant in every case, and also because procedures which are not listed may be appropriate in certain circumstances. Each of the main areas is considered briefly below.

12.13   Forecasts and Budgets

Budgets and cash flow forecasts should be prepared for at least the period to the next balance sheet date. Alternatively, they may be prepared on a rolling basis covering a 12-month period. Subsequent periods will usually be covered by medium- or long-term plans, giving a general indication of how the business is expected to perform. Directors should bear in mind the need to consider a period of at least 12 months from the date on which they formally approve the accounts (see **PARAGRAPH 12.10**). Budgets and forecasts will usually be supported by a detailed summary of the underlying assumptions and the directors will need to confirm that these are reasonable. Directors may also wish to carry out sensitivity analyses on the figures, particularly where the timing of cash receipts may be uncertain or the level of activity may vary significantly. Other factors that may need to be considered include:

- whether the budgets and forecasts need to be updated for changes in the assumptions or actual results to date;
- the interaction between assumptions;
- whether the budgets and forecasts provide adequately for rising costs;
- whether the budgets and forecasts take appropriate account of seasonal fluctuations and
- the accuracy of budgets and forecasts in previous years – it may be appropriate to document and analyse significant variances and consider whether these are likely to arise again in the current year.

12.14   Borrowing Requirements

The facilities available to the company should be reviewed and compared in detail to cash flow forecasts for at least the period to the next balance sheet date. It will often be appropriate to carry out sensitivity analyses on the critical assumptions when making this comparison, to identify whether facilities would be adequate even in a worst case scenario or whether covenants would be likely to be breached in these circumstances. The directors should seek to ensure that there are no anticipated shortfalls in facilities against requirements, no arrears of interest and no other breaches of covenants. There may be mitigating factors which would enable the directors to cope with any potential problems, for instance where they have scope to alter the amount or timing of significant cash flows. Any potential deficits, arrears or breaches that cannot be covered should be discussed with the company's bankers at an early stage to determine any action that needs to be taken and to prevent problems crystallising if possible. The onus is on the directors to be satisfied that appropriate and committed financing arrangements are in place.

12.15   Liability Management

The directors should ensure that the company's financial plans indicate appropriate matching of cash outflows with cash inflows. It is particularly important to ensure that cash outflows include all known liabilities, such as loan repayments, payments of tax and VAT, and any commitments which may be off-balance sheet (for instance, certain leasing commitments or forward exchange contracts). It may also be appropriate to consider whether the company is particularly dependent on individual suppliers, and the impact that a failure in supply might have on the company's ability to meet its cash outflows.

12.16   Contingent Liabilities

The directors should review the company's exposure to contingent liabilities, including:

- liabilities experienced in the past and which might recur, such as legal proceedings, and those arising from guarantees, warranties and product liability claims not covered by insurance and
- new contingencies that may arise in the future, such as environmental clean-up costs or future decommissioning costs.

12.17   Products and Markets

The directors should consider the size and strength of the market, the company's market share and whether the market may change as a result of economic, political or other factors. In more complex businesses, this will usually need to be done by major product line. Depending on the nature of the business, this review may also need to take into account technical research and development, to confirm that this is adequate and can be maintained at an appropriate level for the foreseeable future. Other factors that may need to be considered include:

- product quality and expected life;
- the adequacy of the company's marketing strategy;
- the adequacy of the company's costing system, and in particular whether costs are updated on a regular basis;
- the customer mix, and in particular whether the business is dependent on a small number of significant customers – if so, the risk of losing one or more of them and the likelihood of finding alternative sales markets may also need to be assessed and
- the level of dependence on inter-group trading and the financial implications of this.

12.18   Financial Risk Management

Directors should identify which financial risks are most significant for their company and their current approach to managing these. For instance, financial risks might include exposure to fixed price contracts or to significant fluctuations in foreign currency exchange rates. Sensitivity analyses may need to be performed if assumptions on factors such as interest rates and foreign currency are particularly critical to the cash flow forecasts.

12.19   Other Factors

The JWG identifies a number of other factors that may need to be taken into account in particular circumstances, including:

- recurring operating losses or fluctuating profits and losses;
- the impact of dividend arrears;
- non-compliance with statutory capital requirements;
- the impact of labour difficulties;
- the potential impact of the loss of key management and staff, and the likelihood of finding suitable replacements quickly;
- the potential impact of the loss of a key patent or franchise;
- the impact of long-overdue debtors, or high stock levels;
- the impact of potential losses on long-term contracts and
- the potential impact of the company's fixed asset replacement policy (e.g. if funds are not available to replace assets regularly, there is the potential for increased maintenance costs, higher levels of down-time or quality control problems).

12.20   Financial Adaptability

Financial adaptability is the ability of the company to take effective action to alter the amounts and timings of cash flows to respond to unexpected needs or opportunities. Financial adaptability can help to mitigate any of the factors discussed above in relation to going concern. Consideration of financial adaptability might include reviewing:

- the ability to dispose of assets or postpone the replacement of assets, or to finance assets from other sources (e.g. leasing rather than outright purchase);
- the potential for obtaining new sources of finance;
- the possibility of extending or renewing loans, or restructuring debt and
- the possibility of raising additional share capital.

12.21   Overall Assessment and Conclusion

Once they have carried out all the individual procedures that they consider appropriate, the directors should determine the likely outcome by considering the range of potential outcomes and the probability of their occurrence and taking into account the implications of any interaction between the various factors. In practice, this will usually be evidenced by the board:

- considering a paper summarising the going concern position of the company;
- discussing the implications of the issues and
- reaching a formal conclusion on going concern.

If the directors become aware of any factors that cast doubt on the ability of the entity to continue in operational existence for the foreseeable future, they will need to carry out additional detailed investigations to determine the extent of the problem and to decide how the company can best respond to it. They will also usually need to make additional disclosure in the annual report and accounts.

12.22   Half-Yearly Reporting

Going concern will not usually be considered in the same level of detail in the context of a half-yearly report as in the case of the annual report and accounts. However, the JWG guidance notes that at the time that the half-yearly report is approved, the directors should review their previous work on going concern and see whether any of the significant factors identified at that time have changed in the intervening period to such an extent as to affect the appropriateness of the going concern presumption. More information on the preparation of half-yearly reports is given in CHAPTER 10.

12.23   Application of the Guidance to Groups

In the case of a group, the JWG guidance notes that the directors of the parent company should make a going concern statement in relation to both the parent company and the group as a whole. However, the statement in respect of the group should not be taken as implying that each of the individual companies within the group is considered to be a going concern.

12.24   Disclosures in Respect of Going Concern

At a Glance

* The JWG guidance includes illustrative wording for the directors' statement, depending on the company's circumstances.
* Some companies give additional details on the steps that the directors have taken in reaching their conclusions.
* Where the directors conclude that the company is unlikely to continue in operational existence for the foreseeable future, they will usually need to take legal advice on the wording of their statement.
* In some situations it is good practice to confirm in the notes to the accounts that the going concern basis has been adopted and why this is considered appropriate.
* Where the period considered by the directors has been limited to a period of less than 12 months from the date on which the accounts are formally approved by the directors, this fact must be disclosed in the notes to the accounts.
* The statement can be presented in a separate section of the annual report and accounts dealing with corporate governance issues or within the Operating and Financial Review.

12.25   Making a Formal Statement on Going Concern

Having carried out appropriate procedures, the directors should be able to reach one of three possible conclusions:

(i) there is a reasonable expectation that the company will continue in operational existence for the foreseeable future, and the going concern basis is therefore appropriate for the financial statements;

(ii) there are factors that cast doubt on the ability of the company to continue in operational existence for the foreseeable future, but the directors consider that it is still appropriate to use the going concern basis in preparing the financial statements or

(iii) it is unlikely that the company will continue in operational existence for the foreseeable future and it may therefore not be appropriate to use the going concern basis in preparing the financial statements.

In the case of listed companies, the JWG guidance sets out recommendations on the disclosures that should be given in each of these circumstances in order to comply with the Combined Code. It is important to remember that FRS 18 and IAS 1 also require certain disclosures to be given in the annual accounts in the situations (ii) and (iii) above, and that these apply to all companies, not just those whose shares are listed.

12.26   Going Concern Presumption Appropriate

Where the directors conclude that there are no indications to suggest that the company will be unable to continue in operational existence for the foreseeable future, and that the going concern presumption is therefore an appropriate basis for the preparation of the accounts, the JWG guidance suggests the following basic disclosure:

> 'After making enquiries, the directors have a reasonable expectation that the company has adequate resources to continue in operational existence for the foreseeable future. For this reason, they continue to adopt the going concern basis in preparing the accounts.'

The implication of this recommendation is that details of the 'supporting assumptions or qualifications as necessary' specifically required by the Combined Code only need to be given where there are some doubts or uncertainties over the continuation of the business. A number of companies have gone beyond the basic disclosure suggested in the guidance, and have given details of the steps that the directors have taken in reaching their conclusions, along the following lines:

> 'The directors have reviewed the company's budget for 200X and outline plans for the following two years. After taking into account the cash flow implications of the plans, including proposed capital expenditure and reorganisation costs, and after comparing these to the company's committed borrowing facilities, the directors are satisfied that it is appropriate to prepare the accounts on a going concern basis.'

12.27   Going Concern Basis Used Despite Certain Doubts

If there are some doubts or uncertainties over the appropriateness of the going concern basis for the accounts, the directors should explain the circumstances by giving details of:

- the factors that give rise to the problems (including any external factors that are beyond their control) and
- the action being taken to deal with the problem.

For instance, such a situation might arise where loan covenants have been breached so that the loan has technically become repayable on demand, and the facility is in the course of being renegotiated. The JWG guidance sets out the following example of how the disclosure requirements might be met in these circumstances:

> 'The company is in breach of certain loan covenants at its balance sheet date and so the company's bankers could recall their loans at any time. The directors continue to be involved in negotiations with the company's bankers and as yet no demands for repayments have been received. The negotiations are at an early stage and, although the directors are optimistic about the outcome, it is as yet too early to make predictions with any certainty. In the light of the actions described ... the directors consider it appropriate to adopt the going concern basis in preparing the accounts.'

12.28   Going Concern Basis Not Appropriate

Where the directors conclude that the company is unlikely to continue in operational existence for the foreseeable future, they may need to prepare accounts on an alternative basis, such as a break-up basis. Where UK accounting practice is adopted, it should be noted that the requirements of FRS 18 have been made more stringent for accounting periods beginning on or after 1 January 2005, so that the going concern basis can no longer be adopted in this situation (see **PARAGRAPH 12.8**). By contrast, international accounting practice continues to state that the accounts may need to be prepared on a different basis in these circumstances. In any case where the use of the going concern basis is not considered appropriate, the accounts must disclose the basis on which they have been prepared and the reason why the entity is no longer considered to be a going concern. This applies under both UK and international accounting practice. This situation is expected to arise only rarely in practice, but in these circumstances the directors will have to state that, in their opinion, the company is no longer a going concern. They will usually need to take legal advice on the wording of such a statement. The fact that the company is not considered to be a going concern does not necessarily mean that it is insolvent, but the directors will need to give appropriate consideration to this and in particular to the wrongful trading provisions of the *Insolvency Act 1986*.

12.29   Other Situations Where Disclosure May Be Appropriate

Unless a formal statement on going concern is needed in order to comply with the Combined Code, it is not usually considered necessary to disclose the use of the going concern basis in the accounts – users are entitled to assume that has been adopted in the absence of any information to the contrary. However, where it is not apparent from the accounts themselves that the entity is a going concern (e.g. where the entity has made a loss during the year and the balance sheet shows net liabilities), it is good practice to confirm that the accounts have been prepared on the going concern basis and to explain why the directors consider this to be appropriate. For instance, it may be that a parent undertaking has formally agreed to make ongoing financial support available to the reporting entity and that the directors have taken this into account in their going concern assessment. The following disclosures illustrate how this situation might be explained:

Example 1 – Going Concern Disclosure: Subordination of Balance Due to Parent Undertaking

The company's parent undertaking has confirmed that it will not seek repayment of the amount owed to it until the company's other liabilities have been met in full. Having considered this and all other information available to them up to the date on which the financial statements were approved, the directors consider that it is appropriate to prepare the financial statements on a going concern basis.

(Going Concern)

> ***Example 2 – Going Concern Disclosure: Ongoing Financial Support from Parent Undertaking***
>
> The company's parent company has confirmed that it will continue to make available such financial support as is required to enable the company to continue to trade for the foreseeable future. Having considered this and all other information available to them up to the date on which the financial statements were approved, the directors consider that it is appropriate to prepare the financial statements on a going concern basis.

12.30   Period Considered Less than One Year

Under UK accounting practice, where the period considered by the directors has been limited to a period of less than 12 months from the date on which the accounts are formally approved by the directors, FRS 18 requires this fact to be disclosed in the notes to the accounts and it may also be advisable to refer to this in the Combined Code statement on going concern (see **PARAGRAPH 12.10**).

12.31   Location of the Directors' Statement

The JWG guidance suggests that the directors' statement on going concern should be given in the Operating and Financial Review, as the detailed discussion and analysis given in this review will usually help to put the going concern statement into context. However, given that the review is a historical statement, the directors may need to incorporate additional information for going concern purposes (e.g. new factors that have arisen, or that are expected to arise). In practice, many companies present the going concern statement as part of a separate section of the annual report and accounts dealing with corporate governance issues rather than as part of the Operating and Financial Review. However, where FRS 18 or IAS 1 require disclosures to be given in respect of going concern issues, these details must be given in the accounts themselves and it will usually be advisable to cross-reference the directors' statement to the disclosures.

Appendix 1

Useful Websites on Going Concern Issues

Financial Reporting Council	www.frc.org.uk
Financial Services Authority	www.fsa.gov.uk
Institute of Directors	www.iod.com
Institute of Chartered Accountants in England and Wales	www.icaew.co.uk
Accounting Standards Board	www.frc.org.uk/asb
International Accounting Standards Board	www.iasb.org
Auditing Practices Board	www.frc.org.uk/apb

Going Concern

Appendix 2

Checklist: Assessment of Going Concern

This checklist summarises some of the issues that directors may need to consider when assessing whether the company is a going concern. Not every item will be relevant to every company. Similarly, the checklist should not be regarded as comprehensive – other factors may need to be taken into account, depending on the specific circumstances of the company.

A Financial indicators of potential going concern problems

☐ Is the company in a net liability or net current liability position?

☐ Have necessary borrowing facilities still to be agreed?

☐ Are fixed-term borrowings approaching maturity without realistic prospects of renewal or repayment?

☐ Is the company placing excessive reliance on short-term borrowing to finance long-term assets?

☐ Does the company have major debt repayment falling due without adequate facilities to cover this?

☐ Does the company need to undertake a major restructuring of debt?

☐ Are there any indications of a withdrawal of support by lenders and other creditors?

☐ Has the company experienced negative operating cash flows in recent years?

☐ Do forecasts indicate future negative operating cash flows?

☐ Is the company experiencing adverse key financial ratios?

☐ Has the company suffered substantial operating losses in recent periods?

☐ Has the company suffered a significant deterioration in the value of assets used to generate cash flows?

☐ Have significant losses arisen since the balance sheet date?

☐ Have major cash flow problems arisen since the balance sheet date?

☐ Is the company experiencing problems in paying or maintaining dividends?

☐ Is the company having difficulty paying its creditors (including tax, VAT and any off-balance sheet commitments) on the due dates?

☐ Has the company defaulted on, or otherwise breached, the terms of existing loan agreements?

☐ Is the company experiencing difficulty in meeting the interest cost on borrowings?

☐ Has there been a reduction in the normal terms of trade credit by suppliers?

☐ Has the company been forced to change from credit to cash-on-delivery transactions with suppliers?

☐ Is the company experiencing difficulty in obtaining financing for essential new product development or other essential investments?

☐ Has the company been forced to sell substantial fixed assets without appropriate replacement?

☐ Does the company have significant exposure to fluctuations in exchange rates?

☐ Does the company have significant exposure to losses arising on fixed price contracts?

B   Operational and other indicators of potential going concern difficulties

☐ Is the company having difficulty in adapting to fundamental changes in the market?

☐ Is the company having difficulty adapting to fundamental technological change?

☐ Is the company heavily dependent on a limited range of products or services for which the market is depressed?

☐ Have recent technical developments rendered a key product obsolete?

☐ Has the company been forced to reduce the level of its operations (e.g. as a result of new legislation, environmental issues, etc.)?

☐ Has the company lost key customers?

☐ Has the company lost a significant market, franchise, patent or licence?

☐ Has the company lost one or more principal suppliers?

☐ Has the company lost key members of management or staff without suitable replacement?

☐ Is the company experiencing difficulty in recruiting the appropriate calibre and number of staff?

☐ Is the company encountering problems with labour organisations (e.g. trade unions)?

Going Concern

- ☐ Is the company experiencing serious quality control problems?
- ☐ Is the company experiencing significant uninsured warranty or product liability claims?
- ☐ Is the company incurring increased maintenance costs and down-time as a result of an inability to fund the replacement of fixed assets?
- ☐ Is the company involved in major litigation, where an adverse judgement may threaten the continuation of the business?
- ☐ Are there pending legal or regulatory proceedings against the entity that may, if successful, result in claims that are unlikely to be satisfied?
- ☐ Has the company given significant guarantees that are likely to be called upon?
- ☐ Are significant commitments likely to arise from environmental issues or new legislation?
- ☐ Are changes in legislation or government policy likely to have an adverse impact on the entity?
- ☐ Is the company encountering difficult in complying with capital or other statutory requirements?

Appendix 3

Checklist: Going Concern Review

This checklist summarises the main steps that directors should take when carrying out an annual review of going concern. The checklist should not be regarded as comprehensive – other steps may need to be taken, depending on the specific circumstances of the company.

☐ Review the company's budgeting process and consider whether the resulting budget is appropriate for going concern review purposes – for instance, does the budget represent the best estimate of the results for the review period or has it been prepared with additional objectives in mind (e.g. to set performance targets) which might result in it being over-optimistic?

☐ Review the assumptions made during the budgeting process – for instance, those on:
  - general issues such as inflation, interest rates and the economy;
  - individual items of income and expenditure;
  - customer demand;
  - the availability of supplies and labour;
  - the availability of finance;
  - the incidence of product and warranty claims and
  - the outcome and impact of contingent liabilities and guarantees.

☐ Are the assumptions:
  - realistic?
  - consistent with each other?
  - still valid at the time of the going concern review?

☐ Review the impact on the budget of changes in critical assumptions.

☐ Review the company's cash flow forecast and consider:
  - whether adequate financing is already available or whether additional facilities need to be negotiated;
  - if the term of any of the facilities is due to end within the period reviewed, whether confirmation should be sought of the likely continuation of that facility and
  - the impact of any changes in critical assumptions.

☐ Consider whether any other factors cast doubt on the company's ability to continue operations for the foreseeable future (see Going Concern Checklist).

Going Concern

☐ Consider whether the going concern assumption is appropriate and whether any additional disclosures need to be given in the accounts.

☐ Prepare a memorandum on going concern for formal consideration by the main board.

☐ Prepare a statement on going concern for inclusion in the annual report (listed companies only).

13

Insurance

Insurance

13 Insurance

13.1 Introduction

> **At a Glance**
> * All directors are advised to carry Directors' and Officers' liability insurance.

This chapter concerns insurance for the directors themselves as opposed to insurance for the company. This is known commonly as 'Directors and Officers liability insurance' or 'D&O cover'. It is of course one of the duties of a non-executive to ensure that the company is appropriately insured for the relevant risks it faces. The insurance of directors has become a highly technical area and it is important to take relevant professional technical and legal advice before entering into any such arrangements. For the avoidance of doubt the authors assume the reader will seek such advice and we therefore accept no responsibility.

In the 2007 Independent Remuneration Solutions survey 93% of the independent chairman and non-executive directors polled said that their companies offered them Director's indemnity insurance.

Following the collapse of Enron, the seventh biggest business by market capitalisation in the USA, in 2001 most insurers across the world reviewed the cover that they were prepared to provide. They also reviewed the rates for which they were prepared to provide that cover as well as the conditions and exclusions contained in their policies.

It is possible to design a policy to suit the specific requirements of any company, but as most companies now have these polices for their directors the major insurers have designed template policies. One decision a director has to take is whether they want to take out an individual policy or whether they are comfortable with the policies provided by the companies on whose boards they serve.

Members of The Institute of Directors can take advantage of the personal indemnity policy it has arranged with Chubb Insurance Company of Europe.

13.2 What Are You Insuring Against?

In our research we reviewed policies from a range of insurers. What was striking was that many of these policies were much clearer about what cover they were not providing than that which they were.

The purpose of a D&O policy is to provide cover for loss, including defence expenses, arising from claims made by third parties against the directors personally for wrongful acts.

A wrongful act is typically described as:

'any actual or alleged act, error, omission, misstatement, misleading statement or breach of duty by the director in their capacity as a director or officer of the company'.

Policies from the leading insurers will normally include provisions for advance payment of legal expenses.

What they will not cover is described in detail under 'Exclusions' below but here are a few of the highlights:

- Any litigation or actions which commenced before the inception of the policy.
- Situations where the director has been acting fraudulently or dishonestly.
- Actions brought outside the specified jurisdictions stated in the policy.
- Physical damage to humans or tangible property.
- Not always but usually, directorships in companies with negative net worth.

13.3   How Are Most Policies Structured?

Each insurer will have their own preferred presentational style but most policies contain the following elements:

- a schedule for the insurance certificate;
- the insuring agreement;
- definitions;
- exclusions;
- conditions;
- discovery period and
- extensions.

A brief description of each of these elements and points to consider is provided below.

13.4   *A Schedule for the Insurance Certificate*

This will normally list the following details:

- company or companies to which the policy refers;
- principal address of the company;
- policy period;
- limit of liability in the aggregate and specifically for individual directors if relevant;
- retention;
- retroactive period;
- acquisition limit and
- premium.

If the company has or intends to have subsidiaries then it is important for the directors of the holding company to understand the extent of their liability for actions arising from the activities of these subsidiaries. Policies should contain an automatic cover for subsidiaries clause for subsidiaries below a specified percentage of the assets of the group. The same will be the case for future acquisitions.

Policy periods tend to be very precise, for example, stating the hour that the cover commences and ceases.

The limit of liability in aggregate means the limit for all of the directors, executive and non-executive. Some policies also include specific amounts for individual directors, for example the chairman or chief executive. The limit will generally include:

- retention relates usually to an amount held back by the insurer. This is common in the USA and Canada and
- retroactive period.

13.5   *The Insuring Agreement*

This will simply state that the insurer will pay on behalf of the insured all loss which the insurer is legally liable to pay to the extent that they are not indemnified by the company. Most will specify that this includes defence expenses. If the one you are considering doesn't then it is of questionable value!

13.6   *Exclusions*

In the UK these will typically be the following:

- for death, bodily injury, sickness or disease;
- acts which are found by a court to be fraudulent or dishonest;
- any personal profit or gain for which the insured was not legally entitled;
- any circumstances where there is collusion between the person bringing the action and the insured;
- actions brought in certain jurisdictions (these may be insurer specific) and
- no payment for the directors' own time spent in defending claims.

13.7   *Conditions*

These relate to:

- the manner in which claims are made;
- the process for making claims and paying advances and
- the arrangements for retention;

as well as any conditions the insurer may determine because of the nature of business or the history of individual directors.

13.8   *Some Other Practical Issues to Consider*

In UK if the policy premium is paid for by the company it is deemed to be a taxable benefit.

You are only covered if the premium has been paid.

How do you know that the premium has been paid if it is a company rather than individual policy? The simplest way is to have your interest in the policy noted with the insurer and diarise when the premium falls due to be paid.

14

Internal Control

Internal Control

14 Internal Control

14.1 Requirements on Internal Control

> **At a Glance**
> * Under the Combined Code, directors should review the effectiveness of the company's system of internal control at least annually and report to shareholders that they have done so.
> * Guidance on reviewing and reporting on internal control is set out in 'Internal Control – Guidance for Directors on the Combined Code' (often referred to as the 'Turnbull Report').
> * The form or content of the directors' statement on internal control is not prescribed in detail by the Combined Code or the related guidance.

14.2 The Combined Code

Provision C.2.1 of the Combined Code requires the directors to conduct an annual review (as a minimum) of the effectiveness of the company's (or group's) system of internal control and to report to shareholders that they have done so. Their review should cover all aspects of internal control, rather than just internal financial control. However, there is no longer a requirement for them to express an opinion on the effectiveness of the system.

14.3 Turnbull Guidance

Guidance on reviewing internal control and reporting under the Combined Code was developed by a working party of the Institute of Chartered Accountants in England and Wales (ICAEW) chaired by Nigel Turnbull. Their final report *Internal Control – Guidance for Directors on the Combined Code* (often referred to as the Turnbull Report) was published in September 1999. Following a review of the recommendations, an updated version entitled *Internal Control: Revised Guidance for Directors on the Combined Code* was published by the Financial Reporting Council (FRC) in October 2005 and applies for accounting periods beginning on or after 1 January 2006. The guidance clarifies what is expected of the board of a listed company in terms of:

- applying Principle C.2 of the Combined Code (maintaining a sound system of internal control to safeguard the shareholders' investment and the company's assets) and
- determining the extent of their compliance with the best practice guidance set out in Provision C.2.1 of the Combined Code (review of the effectiveness of the system of internal controls).

The original document also included detailed guidance on dealing with Provision C.3.5 in respect of the annual review of the need for an internal audit function (if the company does not have one) but this has been removed from the revised guidance on the basis that responsibility for this review now rests with the audit committee (see **PARAGRAPH 2.17**).

14.4   Aims of the Working Party

The objective of the Internal Control Working Party was to develop guidance that:

- can be tailored to the circumstances of an individual company;
- identifies sound business practice, by linking internal control with risk management and placing emphasis on the key controls that a company should maintain;
- provides meaningful high-level information and avoids extensive disclosure that does not add to a user's understanding and
- will remain relevant and be capable of evolving with the business environment.

This approach is in line with the Preamble to the Combined Code, which emphasises that there is no intention to prescribe the form or content of the various reporting statements required by the Code, but rather that companies should be free to explain their governance policies in the light of the principles set out in the Code and in the context of any special circumstances specific to the company. At the end the 2005 review of the Turnbull Guidance, the FRC reported the review group's conclusion that the guidance had helped to improve internal control in UK listed companies and that only limited changes were required to bring it up to date. In particular, the following changes were subsequently incorporated into the revised version of the guidance document:

- Boards should review their application of the guidance on a continuing basis.
- Boards should not be required to make a statement in the annual report and accounts on the effectiveness of the company's internal control system, but they should confirm that necessary action has been or is being taken to remedy any significant failings or weaknesses identified from the reviews of the effectiveness of the internal control system.
- Boards should look on the internal control statement in the annual report and accounts as an opportunity to explain to shareholders how they manage risk.

- In reaching their decisions on internal control issues, directors should apply the same standard of care as in the exercise of their other general duties as directors.

The review also concluded that there should be no extension of the external auditors' responsibilities in relation to the company's internal control statement.

14.5   Risk Management and Internal Control

At a Glance
* The Turnbull guidance is based on the principle that companies will adopt a risk-based approach to establishing a system of internal control, and that the review of its effectiveness will be part of the normal process of managing the business.
* The directors of a parent company are responsible for reviewing and reporting on internal control for the group as a whole.
* An effective system of internal control should provide reasonable assurance against business failure, material error, fraud or breaches of regulations.
* A sound system of internal control includes policies and processes to safeguard company assets, identify and manage liabilities, maintain proper records and generate information that is timely, relevant and reliable.

14.6   Importance of Risk Management and Internal Control

Internal control is one of the main elements in the management of risk, along with the transfer of risk to third parties (e.g. through insurance arrangements), the sharing of risk (e.g. through participation in joint ventures) and contingency planning. The risks that any entity faces will inevitably change as the business develops and the environment in which it operates evolves. Companies must therefore regularly review and evaluate the risks to which they are exposed. The aim will usually be to manage and control business risk rather than to attempt to eliminate it completely. The Turnbull guidance is based on the principle that companies will adopt a risk-based approach to establishing of a system of internal control and to the regular review of its effectiveness. The review of the effectiveness of the internal control system should therefore be part of the normal process of managing the business rather than a specific exercise carried out only in order to comply with the recommendations of the Combined Code.

In August 2007, the International Federation of Accountants (IFAC) released a new publication *Internal Control from a Risk-Based Perspective*, which features interviews conducted with 10 senior professional accountants in business on their experiences and views on establishing effective internal control systems. The interviews help to demonstrate the importance of a risk-based approach to internal control in the management of overall risk. They also consider the nature of risk and how to establish an internal control system that helps to drive performance and support strategic objectives. The paper is part of a wider IFAC project on internal control which is intended to result in the development of principles-based good practice guidance. This is scheduled for publication in 2008. The August 2007 paper can be downloaded free of charge from http://www.ifac.org/store.

14.7   Group Perspective

The guidance notes specifically that references to a company should be taken, where relevant, to refer to a group. The directors of a parent company are therefore responsible for reviewing the effectiveness of internal control from the perspective of the group as a whole and for reporting to the shareholders on this. Where the board's report does not cover any joint ventures or associates of the group, this fact should be disclosed.

14.8   Responsibility for the System of Internal Control

The detailed work involved in establishing, operating and monitoring a system of internal control should be carried out by individuals with the necessary skills, technical knowledge, objectivity and understanding of the business, its objectives, the industries and markets in which it operates and the risks that it faces. The detailed work will usually be delegated by the board to management and all employees are likely to have some responsibility for internal control as part of their accountability for achieving objectives. However, the board as a whole retains ultimate responsibility for the company's system of internal control. It must therefore set appropriate policies on internal control and satisfy itself on a regular basis that the system is functioning well in practice and that it is effective in managing the risks that the business faces.

14.9   Factors to Consider

A system of internal control can never provide absolute protection against business failure, material error, fraud or breaches of regulations, but it should be able to provide reasonable assurance against these problems. In determining policies on internal control and assessing what constitutes a good system of internal control in the particular circumstances of the company, the board should consider:

- the nature and extent of the risks that the company faces;
- the extent and categories of risk that it regards as acceptable for the company to bear;
- the likelihood of the risks crystallising;
- the company's ability to reduce the incidence, and impact on the business, of risks that do crystallise and
- the costs and benefits of operating relevant controls.

The limitations on any system of internal control include human fallibility, management override of controls and the risk of unforeseen events and circumstances arising.

14.10 Definition of Internal Control

A system of internal control is defined in the guidance as encompassing the policies, processes, tasks, behaviours and other aspects of the company that, taken together:

- facilitate its effective and efficient operation by enabling it to respond appropriately to significant risks (including business, operational, financial and compliance risks);
- help to ensure the quality of internal and external reporting and
- help to ensure compliance with applicable laws and regulations.

They include policies and processes to safeguard company assets from loss, fraud or inappropriate use, identify and manage liabilities, maintain proper records and generate information that is timely, relevant and reliable.

14.11 Elements of a Sound System of Internal Control

A sound system of internal control should reflect the company's control environment (see **PARAGRAPH 14.12**) and organisational structure, and should include:

- control activities;
- information and communication processes and
- processes for monitoring the continuing effectiveness of the system.

The internal control system should be embedded in the company's operations and should form part of its culture. It must be capable of responding promptly to new risks as the business develops and should include procedures for reporting immediately to management when significant control weaknesses or failures are identified. The information provided to management might include regular reports on progress against the company's business objectives (e.g. by using agreed performance indicators) together with information on issues such as customer satisfaction and employee attitudes.

14.12 Control Environment

A company's control environment is usually considered to include:

- a commitment by directors, management and employees to competence, integrity and a climate of trust (e.g. leadership by example, development of an appropriate culture within the business);
- the communication to all managers and employees of agreed standards of behaviour and control consciousness, which support the business objectives and risk management and internal control systems (e.g. written Codes of conduct, formal disciplinary procedures, formal procedures for the appraisal of performance);
- clear organisational structures, which help to ensure that authority, responsibility and accountability are clearly defined and that decisions and actions are taken by the appropriate individuals;

Internal Control

- clear communication to employees of what is expected of them, and of their freedom to act (e.g. in respect of customer relations, service levels, health and safety issues, environmental matters, financial and other reporting issues);
- allocation of sufficient time and resources to risk management and internal control and
- provision of relevant training on risk and control issues, so that management and employees develop the necessary knowledge, skills and tools to support achievement of the company's objectives and the effective management of risk.

14.13   Reviewing the Effectiveness of Internal Control

> **At a Glance**
> * The board as a whole must form its own view on the adequacy of the review of internal control.
> * The precise role of the audit committee will vary between companies.
> * There should be a defined process for the board's review of the effectiveness of the internal control system each year, to provide adequate support for the directors' statement in the annual report.
> * Where a company does not have an internal audit function, the audit committee should consider annually whether there is a need to establish one.

14.14   Role of the Audit Committee

The board may delegate to the audit committee or other board committees certain aspects of the review of the effectiveness of the system of internal control (for instance, those aspects that are particularly relevant to their activities), but the board as a whole should form its own view on the adequacy of the review after due and careful enquiry. In other words, it will not be sufficient for the audit committee alone to review the effectiveness of the system of internal control. The audit committee should report formally to the board, who should then take a collective decision on the adequacy of the review. The October 2005 version of the Turnbull guidance emphasises that, in reaching their decisions on internal control issues, directors should apply the same standard of care as in the exercise of their other general duties as directors. The precise role of the audit committee will vary between companies and will depend on factors such as the size, style and composition of the board and the nature of the principal risks that the business faces. The audit committee will usually consider financial controls, but may also be asked by the board to act as the focal point for reviews of the wider aspects of internal control. These issues should be considered by the board when the terms of reference for the audit committee are established and reviewed (see CHAPTER 2).

14.15   The Process of the Review

There should be a defined process for the board's review of the effectiveness of the company's system of internal control, to provide adequate support for the statement made by the directors in the annual report. The board should take account of all the information available to it up to the date on which the annual report is approved and signed. The board should not rely solely on the monitoring processes that form part of the business operations, but should receive and review regular reports on internal control, and should also carry out a specific annual exercise to support the statement in the annual report and to ensure that all significant aspects of internal control have been covered.

14.16   Suggested Approach

The Turnbull guidance suggests the following approach:

- There should be an agreed procedure for the board (or relevant committee) to receive and review regular reports on internal control from management or others qualified to prepare them (e.g. internal audit).
- The reports should provide a balanced assessment of the areas covered and should identify both the significant risks involved and the effectiveness of the internal control system in managing those risks.
- The board (or relevant committee) should:
  - consider the key risks and assess how they have been identified, evaluated and managed;
  - assess the effectiveness of the internal control system in managing those risks, taking into account the impact of any weaknesses or control failings that have been reported;
  - consider whether appropriate and prompt action is being taken to remedy weaknesses or failings;
  - consider whether the findings indicate a need for more extensive monitoring of the internal control system.
- The board should carry out a specific annual assessment to support the statement in the annual report – this assessment should cover:
  - changes since the last review in the nature and extent of significant risks;
  - the company's ability to respond effectively to change (both internal and external);
  - the scope and quality of the ongoing monitoring of the system of internal control, including where appropriate the internal audit function;
  - the extent and frequency of reporting to the board (or relevant committee) of the results of the monitoring process, enabling it to build up a cumulative assessment of the state of internal control and the effectiveness with which risk is managed;
  - the incidence of major control weaknesses or failings identified during the period and the extent to which they have resulted in unforeseen outcomes

Internal Control

or contingencies that have had, could have had, or may in future have, a material impact on results;
○ the effectiveness of the year-end financial reporting process.

Where significant control weaknesses or failings are identified, the board should determine how these arose and should reassess the effectiveness of management's ongoing processes for designing, operating and monitoring the system of internal control.

14.17   Review of the Need for an Internal Audit Function

Provision C.3.5 of the Combined Code states that the audit committee of a company without an internal audit function should consider annually whether there is a need to establish one and make an appropriate recommendation to the board. The original Code included a more general recommendation on the need for a regular review of this issue and this issue was therefore covered in the original version of the Turnbull Guidance, but has been removed from the revised version. The audit committee's review is considered in more detail in **PARAGRAPH 2.17**. Where there is an internal audit function, Provision C.3.5 of the Combined Code states that the audit committee should review the effectiveness of its activities. This is also considered in **PARAGRAPH 2.17**.

14.18   The Annual Statement on Internal Control

At a Glance
* The annual statement should summarise the process that the board has applied, including where relevant the role of the audit committee, and acknowledge the board's responsibility for the system of internal control.
* In the case of listed companies, the auditors are required to review the directors' statement on internal control and to report any concerns in their report on the annual accounts.

14.19   Minimum Disclosure

The board's annual statement on internal control should provide users of the annual report and accounts with meaningful, high-level information. Particular care should be taken to ensure that the statement does not give a misleading impression. As a minimum, the board should disclose where applicable that:

• there is an ongoing process for identifying, evaluating and managing key risks;
• this has been in place for the year under review and up to the date of approval of the annual report and accounts and
• this process accords with the relevant guidance on internal control and is regularly reviewed by the board.

The statement should also summarise the process that the board has applied in reviewing the effectiveness of the system of internal control, including where relevant the role of the audit committee or other committees, and confirm that necessary actions have been (or are being) taken to remedy any significant weaknesses or failings identified in the review. The board may also want to provide additional information to help users of the report and accounts understand the company's risk management processes and the internal control system.

14.20 Where One or More of the Statements Cannot Be Made

If the board is unable to make any of these disclosures, this fact should be stated and the board should explain what action is being taken to rectify the situation. Where relevant, the board will also have to disclose that they have failed to conduct a review of the effectiveness of the company's system of internal control, or that they have not considered the need for an internal audit function if they do not already have one (see **PARAGRAPH 14.17**). Where weaknesses in internal control have resulted in significant problems which have been disclosed in the annual accounts, the board should describe the processes that it has applied to deal with the internal control aspects of the problems.

14.21 Acknowledgement of Responsibility

The statement should also include an acknowledgement that the board is responsible for the company's system of internal control and for reviewing its effectiveness, together with an explanation that such a system can only provide reasonable and not absolute assurance against material misstatement or loss.

14.22 Reporting by Auditors

Where directors are required by the Financial Services Authority (FSA) Listing Rules to include in the annual report and accounts a statement on compliance with the Combined Code and ongoing concern, the Listing Rules also require these statements to be reviewed by the auditors. In the case of the compliance statement, the auditors' review is only required to cover certain aspects, but these specifically include the directors' statement on internal control. Under the latest professional guidance, the auditors are required to explain this reporting requirement in the section of their report that sets out their responsibilities as auditors. If the auditors are not satisfied with the adequacy of the corporate governance disclosures and cannot resolve the problems through discussion with the directors, they are required to report their concerns in a separate paragraph as part of their opinion on the financial statements, but this will not constitute a qualification of their report on the annual accounts.

Internal Control

14.23   Additional Company Reporting Under SEC Requirements

Non-US companies registered with the US Securities and Exchange Commission (SEC) are required by the Sarbanes-Oxley Act 2002 and related SEC rules apply to comply with certain additional reporting requirements in respect of internal control. Section 404(a) of the Act requires judgements on the effectiveness of material controls over financial reporting to be made in the context of a suitable framework and the SEC has confirmed that the Turnbull guidance is considered to provide such a framework. In December 2004, the FRC issued an additional guide for companies registered with the SEC on how the Turnbull Guidance should be used in complying with the US reporting requirement. The guide can be downloaded from the FRC website at http://www.frc.org.uk/corporate.

Appendix 1

Useful Websites on Internal Control

Financial Reporting Council	www.frc.org.uk
Financial Services Authority	www.fsa.gov.uk
Institute of Directors	www.iod.com
Institute of Internal Auditors (UK and Ireland)	www.iia.org.uk
Institute of Chartered Secretaries and Administrators	www.icsa.org.uk
Institute of Chartered Accountants in England and Wales	www.icaew.co.uk
Auditing Practices Board	www.frc.org.uk/apb
Internal Controls Design	www.internalcontrolsdesign.co.uk/

Appendix 2

Checklist: Internal Control

This checklist summarises the issues that directors may need to consider in relation to internal control and is based on the ICAEW guidance document *Internal Control – Guidance for Directors on the Combined Code*. The checklist should not be regarded as comprehensive – directors may need to consider other issues, depending on the specific circumstances of the company.

☐ Does the company have clear business objectives and have these been communicated to all management and staff?

☐ Do the directors and senior management demonstrate an appropriate commitment to competence, integrity and the development of a climate of trust?

☐ Does the board adopt a professional approach to financial reporting?

☐ Has the company developed agreed standards of behaviour to support business objectives and risk management?

☐ Has it communicated these standards to all management and staff, for instance by means of:
- written codes of conduct;
- formal appraisal procedures;
- formal disciplinary procedures and
- performance reward schemes?

☐ Does the company have a clear organisational structure, with clearly defined lines of authority, responsibility and accountability?

☐ Are decisions and actions throughout the company properly co-ordinated?

☐ Does the organisational structure ensure that decisions are taken at an appropriate level and by appropriate individuals?

☐ Are sufficient time and resources allocated to risk management and internal control?

☐ Are management and staff provided with relevant training on business risk and internal control issues?

☐ Has the company developed a formal analysis of key risks, covering:
- operational risk (both internal and external);
- financial risk;
- compliance risk and
- other risks?

- [ ] Is business risk assessed on an ongoing basis and is the analysis of key risks regularly updated to take account of new developments, both within the business and externally?
- [ ] Have clear policies and strategies been developed to deal with significant risks identified in the assessment?
- [ ] Does management have a clear understanding of the level of risk that is regarded as acceptable to the board?
- [ ] Have appropriate communication channels been put into place to enable individuals to report suspected fraud, breaches of law or regulations, or other irregularities?
- [ ] Does the board receive regular reports on progress against business objectives and the related risk factors – for instance:
  - performance reports;
  - relevant performance indicators;
  - customer service levels;
  - quality control;
  - customer satisfaction and
  - employee attitudes?
- [ ] Does the board, or an appropriate committee, receive and review regular reports on internal control and:
  - consider how the key risks have been identified, evaluated and managed;
  - assess the effectiveness of the internal control system in managing those risks;
  - consider whether the company's financial and other information systems capture relevant, reliable and up-to-date information;
  - consider whether the company's financial and other information systems deliver appropriate information to the right individuals at the right time?
- [ ] Has the potential impact of identified internal control weaknesses or failures been properly established and considered?
- [ ] Has prompt and effective action been taken to deal with any internal control weaknesses or failures that have been identified?
- [ ] Are there appropriate procedures to confirm that agreed action is actually taken in practice?
- [ ] Has the board carried out a specific annual assessment to support the internal control statement in the annual report (see **PARAGRAPH 14.15**)?
- [ ] If the company has an internal audit function, has the board (or an appropriate committee) reviewed its remit, authority, resources and scope of work?
- [ ] If the company does not have an internal audit function, has the need to establish one been formally considered?

Investor Relations

15.1   Introduction

15 Investor Relations

15.1 Introduction

> **At a Glance**
> * Investor relations are vital for a company to build the investor base it wants.
> * A prospective non-executive should carry out due diligence on the company's shareholders before agreeing to join.
> * A non-executive can find a public-to-private transaction challenging, especially where protecting shareholders' interests are concerned.
> * The increasing sophistication of media relations, and the growth of the Internet, have increased the scope of investor relations.

An 'investor relations' strategy is predicated on an 'investor' strategy. Inevitably the current shareholder base will have been shaped by the history of the company. This may or may not be the ideal mix for the company. If not ideal then the board clearly needs to decide what investors it requires before it develops and executes a strategy for managing communications with them. Moving from a current mix to an ideal one is much easier if the company's performance is strong and the general investment climate is healthy.

As we write this second edition of this Non-Executive Director's Handbook the Capital markets have been under severe pressure following issues in the United States with sub prime mortgage lending and a subsequent run on Northern Rock in the UK. The rise of Hedge funds combined with more fragile markets makes it more difficult for public companies to achieve the shareholder base that they desire. Good investor relations are therefore critical. 'Whatever the state of capital markets of how well the company is performing achieving the desired shareholding base will be easier if there is an effective investor relations strategy in place and the execution capability to match. For public companies the quality of the investor relations website and the annual report are obvious indicators of the company's approach to investor relations.

Many large public companies also now do shareholder opinion surveys. These surveys undertaken by specialist consultants can provide some interesting insights into not just the views of the shareholders on the company and its management but also the effectiveness of its communications'.

15.2 Objectives of a Typical Investor Relations Strategy

The objectives of a typical investor relations strategy are for the company to have:

- the investors it wants;
- a good understanding of what those investors require;
- a group of shareholders who support the company's vision and strategy and
- cost effective communications;

and for shareholders to have:

- an accurate understanding of the company's vision, strategy and performance;
- the feeling that the objectives that they have for their shareholding are being met and
- confidence in the board and the governance of the company.

If these objectives are met then the company will have a strong, well informed and supportive shareholder base to assist its development in a cost effective way.

The strategy must also recognise the importance of representing the company in a balanced way, being positive yet minimising the chances of disappointing investors. The board also needs to be conscious of any divergence in messages being given to any of the business's key audience groups.

Many companies, public and private, have widespread employee share ownership so it is therefore important that there is also good internal communication on shareholder issues and that these are consistent with external messages.

15.3 Who Takes Part in Investor Relations?

There are several important groups of people who take part in and influence investor relations for companies. The key groups are the shareholders, the board and its principal advisers. The exact mix and the relative importance of each group naturally depend upon the specific company.

- Shareholders who may be from several categories (institutional, venture capital or private equity, private, family, trade, current and former employees).
- Executive directors, most notably the chief executive and finance director.
- Investor relations director (if public and relevant).
- The chairman.
- The senior independent non-executive (SINE) director (or deputy chairman).
- Non-executive directors.
- Brokers who oversee the relationship with institutional investors.
- Market makers.
- Financial PR advisers.
- Bankers or other providers of finance to the company.
- Financial journalists.
- Equities analysts (the house analyst employed by the broker and others who follow the company).

15.4 What Should the Non-executive Director's Role be in Investor Relations?

At a minimum it should be to ensure that there is an appropriate investor relations strategy, that the right resources are in place to achieve the agreed strategy and that there is good visibility of the performance of investor relations. The non-executive must also possess a good understanding of what the company's investors expect from the non-executive directors of the company. Whether public or private there will be certain key dates and documents that the non-executive will need to be available for or to approve. They therefore need to be aware of these and make themselves available as appropriate.

For public companies the finance director will typically have the primary responsibility for developing and implementing the investor relations strategy. The degree of sophistication varies. Larger public companies will have dedicated investor relations teams, regularly survey investor views, have the benefit of comprehensive investor information on their website and so on. In smaller public companies the finance director will be able to delegate less.

No matter what the size or nature of ownership of the company the balance between making investors keen to keep or increase their investment and reflecting a fair perspective on the outlook for the company is a critical one to achieve.

The principal points of contact between investors and the company will tend to be the chief executive, finance director and chairman. Indeed in the Higgs report, which focussed on larger listed companies, the section on 'Relationships with shareholders' contains the following remarks:

> '... only rarely do non-executive directors hear at first hand the views of major shareholders. The majority of non-executive directors (52%) surveyed for the review never discuss company business with their investors. Within the FTSE 100, contact is rarer still: only about one in five FTSE 100 non-executive directors discuss company business with investors once a year or more often'.

and

> 'Qualitative research undertaken for the review showed that in normal circumstances non-executive directors and shareholders have only minimal direct contact. Interviews with investors revealed that rarely do they speak directly with non-executive directors, and only then where there is a serious problem. Even in these circumstances, discussion often centred on director remuneration rather than on wider strategy or governance issues.'

So it is likely to be the case that many private company non-executives have greater contact with investors than their public counterparts. In venture capital backed situations where often the investing institution has introduced the non-executive this will certainly be the case.

Whether there is a high level of contact or not, the non-executive's reputation and standing with investors is important. Non-executives with high-investor credibility, whether that is with a small group of family investors or Wall Street, can add considerable value to the company.

15.5 Understanding the Shareholder

Understanding who the shareholders are and what their objectives might be is an important part of the due diligence a non-executive will undertake before agreeing to accept the appointment (see **PARAGRAPH 1.18** for due diligence checklist). The context is important and if shareholders do for whatever reason have differing objectives the non-executive needs to understand what they are and how he or she is going to deal with them.

It is sometimes hard in practice to achieve the ideal level of knowledge, either because of the company's situation, the circumstances of the appointment, or the logistical challenge involved, especially if there are large numbers of shareholders of different types. It is also sometimes the case that investors aren't clear themselves about what they want from their investment.

Achieving the desired level of understanding may be easier in private companies than in listed ones. The number of shareholders is usually smaller, the executive management are frequently the major shareholders, and if there are venture capitalists involved they will have clearly stated intentions. However in family companies with diverse groups of shareholders it can be just as difficult as for a listed company.

The new or prospective non-executive needs to go about the process of understanding shareholder views sensitively, especially in circumstances where shareholders are not used to being asked or there are obvious differences. So the first thing they need to do is to agree with the chairman how they will do this. He will also need to be careful when gathering views from shareholders to recognise the risks of expressing any views which diverge from those given by the chairman, chief executive or finance director.

15.6 What Do the Company's Brokers Do?

The broker may be part of an integrated investment banking house which is providing a range of other services to the company. The non-executive director needs as part of his due diligence to understand who is providing key advisory services to the company as well as the links between the company's various advisers.

In summary the broker's job is to supply institutional investors with the information that they need on the company and give the company honest feedback on how investors view the company and the stock.

The brokers will generally oversee, co-ordinate or manage the company's contacts with institutional shareholders. This is especially the case at or around the time of the announcement of key results or significant events (e.g. major acquisition or fund raising).

They will employ what is known as an analyst, typically known as the 'House analyst' who essentially acts as the 'expert' on the company. The London Stock Exchange's excellent guide to investor relations *A Practical Guide to Investor Relations* sums up their position as follows:

> 'While the house analyst's research must be objective to be credible, and is intended to form the basis of commercial investment decisions by institutions and other investors, it

is widely accepted by the market that the house analyst will generally be unable to take a highly critical position on the company or its stock.'

In 2002 in the wake of the Enron, Worldcom and Global Crossing scandals in the USA there was increased focus on the role of brokers and house analysts in particular.

It is important that the management, usually the finance director and, if relevant, the investor relations director, put sufficient time and effort into ensuring that the house analyst and the broker have an appropriate depth of understanding of the company and the markets in which it operates.

For even large businesses there will be a limited number of other analysts who cover the company in any depth. In the UK this tends to be 15–20 depending upon the size and importance of the sector the company is operating in. This is a highly competitive job and the nature of the people who do it is that they are very bright and aggressive.

Brokers should also monitor activity in the shares of the company and produce accurate summaries of the shareholder register. Many larger listed companies circulate as part of their regular board reports a summary from the brokers of key movements since the last report. This monitoring is valuable input to the investor relations strategy and to determining communications priorities. It is important for the company to learn whether the sale of entire holding is a vote of no confidence in the business or simply a programmed reduction as part of a wider strategy to reduce holdings of a particular profile.

As with any of the key advisers to the company the non-executive will want to ensure that they are happy with the selection. It is, however, unusual for them to be too actively involved in the process. Contact is normally limited to the presentations that the brokers may make to the board, usually at the time of results or significant events.

15.7 Market Makers

Every company quoted on SEAQ, the London Stock Exchange's quote driven system, must have at least two market makers quoting two-way process in its shares. The house broker will normally want to be one of these.

Non-executive directors have little if any contact with market makers.

15.8 Special Issues for Smaller Quoted Companies

It is often argued that investor relations has become particularly challenging for smaller quoted companies (SQCs). Several reasons are given for this including:

- Consolidation of the fund management industry. The impact of which means there are few analysts following the company or even the sector.
- Indexation – The consequence of which is that analysts are focussed on analysing indices rather than companies.
- Low liquidity which undermines the economics of doing the analysis.
- The difficulties of raising capital.

As a consequence the non-executive often has a greater role to play in support-ing the chairman, chief executive and finance director in SQCs.

The Waterstone report for the UK's Department of Trade and Industry (DTI) in 1999 highlighted the challenges. In our view the situation has become worse rather than better, despite the success of AIM. A survey undertaken by BDO pub-lished in 2003 of over 100 directors of listed companies capitalised between £10 and £200 million showed that:

- 66% felt that the stock market didn't fairly value their company;
- 48% of them felt constrained by lack of access to equity funds;
- 51% said that they would consider a public-to-private transaction within the next year or two and
- 54% of them wouldn't consider a flotation if they were a private company.

Interestingly, as part of the same survey, 83 institutional fund managers were also interviewed with the following results:

- 64% felt that the stock market failed to value fairly companies with a sub-£250 million capitalisation;
- 41% felt that the growth potential of profitable smaller companies was being constrained by lack of access to new equity funds and
- 58% felt that there wasn't enough analyst coverage of SQCs.

15.9 Public-to-Private Transactions: Issues for the Non-executive Director

The authors feel that the level of disenchantment described above is unhealthy and probably unsustainable. One solution for those companies who don't feel that they are receiving sufficient benefit from being a public company is to go private.

Venture capital and private equity funds have significant capital to fuel the growth in public-to-privates. However the process of going private is not straightforward. The lack of concentrated shareholding blocks in many smaller quoted businesses often means that it is difficult to make a transaction happen in practice. Other barriers to public-to-private transactions have been the costs, regulatory compliance issues and the perceived risk by the initial bidder that the company is put into play and they might lose.

A non-executive can be placed in an awkward situation in a public-to-private. Achieving fairness for existing shareholders whilst meeting the legiti-mate needs of management and their backers, as well as competing offerors for the company, is inherently difficult. Non-executive directors therefore need to be aware of the process and the issues involved. In particular they should be aware of the specific provisions in the Takeover Code which relate to their role.

The first thing to be clear about is whether they are acting as an independent non-executive director. **PARAGRAPH 1.3.3** contains the description of independ-ence used by Sir Derek Higgs in his review and substantially adopted in Section A.3.1 of the Combined Code. It is wise for any director in such a situation to take relevant advice and check the latest version of the Combined Code and the

Takeover Code. These can be found on the websites of the Financial Reporting Council (www.frc.org.uk) and the Takeover Panel (thetakeoverpanel.org.uk).

The easiest circumstance is where the non-executive has no ongoing role on the board post-transaction. In this circumstance as a director the non-executive will want to ensure that a proper process is being followed and that the conflicts of interest which arise are managed properly. An important part of any public-to-private process is the flow of information to the various interested parties. The non-executive will want to be assured that these are conducted in the right way.

Any non-executive who becomes involved in a potential public-to-private must obtain good advice and should learn from the experience of others who have gone through the process before.

Clarity over each director's position is essential from the outset whether they are executive of non-executive. The target's board should constitute an 'Independent committee'. This is an express requirement of the Code. The committee should comprise only those directors of the target who are not in the buyout team. One of the first roles of that independent committee will be to consider whether it is appropriate for confidential information to be disclosed to the buyout backers. The release of the information should only then occur if an appropriate confidentiality agreement is executed beforehand.

The non-executive has to be aware of the duties of the management team in the process. The buyout team should declare their conflict and cannot and should not join in with the recommendation of the independent members of the board in an expression of views on the offer. However, they will still need to take responsibility for other information contained in any circular or advertisement issued by the target and in particular the responsibility statement that is part and parcel of any document issued by the bidder on behalf of the buyout team.

The executive directors and any non-executive directors who are making the bid owe fiduciary duties to the company and must observe the necessary due process that is established by the Takeover Code and company law. So they must act in the interests of the company and should not put themselves in a position where their duty to the company may conflict with their own personal interests. Accordingly they should not withhold information from the company's shareholders, that if provided to them, would enable the shareholder to negotiate a better price.

However there are practical issues to overcome if they are to achieve this. Firstly, the duty of confidentiality as well as insider dealing laws precludes the management from disclosing either unpublished price sensitive information (PSI) or other confidential information in breach of their contractual and fiduciary duties to their backers. The challenge is that they will need to do this before they can make an offer and the venture capitalist will need access to financial information that is available to the management but not to the public generally.

This type of information belongs to the company and cannot be made available to the financial backers without the prior consent of the independent directors who must authorise its release. Failure to comply could result in the management team losing their jobs and facing a claim for damages if the release of the information caused financial loss to the business.

Investor Relations

The Code expressly requires any information given by the buyout team to their backers to be given equally and promptly to any other competing bidders or potential bidders. It is one of the jobs of the independent committee to monitor the information given by the target company (including members of the buyout team acting in their role as employees or directors of the target) to the buyout team's backers.

The Code further provides that the board of the target must appoint competent independent financial advisers. If the existing financial advisers to the company are particularly closely connected with the buyout team, the independent committee must consider appointing new financial advisers to advice on the merits of the proposal. The Code stipulates that whenever requested, the buyout team must promptly furnish to the independent directors or their advisers all information which has been furnished by the buyout team to its external financial backers (venture capitalists and bankers).

As can be seen there are several different information flows and the disclosure obligations differ on the important distinction of who has generated the information and in what capacity and to whom it is given. Information generated by the management of the target company in their capacity as members of the buyout team does not need to be supplied to a competing bidder. However, that same information has to be supplied to the independent directors.

An express requirement of the Code is that absolute secrecy be maintained right from the preliminary stages of the proposed buyout. This is to guard against rumour or speculation which may cause an untoward movement in the share price causing a need for an announcement. A crucial aspect in this regard is the obligation on the buyout team or its advisers to consult with the Takeover Panel if negotiations or discussions concerning the potential offer are about to be extended to include more than a very restricted number of people.

The board as a whole will also need to consider, as early as possible, the remuneration arrangements for independent directors in the course of the offer period and whether any termination payment is to be made to those directors.

This is important for a number of reasons. At the conclusion of the offer, whether successful or unsuccessful, there will need to be a clear understanding of what is owed to the directors by the target company. Proper consideration needs to be given to existing letters of appointment so as to ensure that no breach of *Section 312* of the *Companies Act 1985* occurs. Moreover, it helps to avoid any subsequent allegations that the independence of the directors has been impaired.

In addition to all of the above, the Institutional Shareholders' Committee has issued practice guidelines for buyouts of public companies. They are entirely consistent with the Takeover Code as should be expected but the following are worthy or particular note:

- No buyout proposal is likely to be favourably received unless there has been a strong independent non-executive presence on the board of the target for some time.
- It is unlikely that any buyout is going to be treated seriously without a sympathetic initial response and final recommendation by the independent non-executive directors of the target.

- It is not appropriate for the bidders to deploy as advisers those who had previously been employed by the target unless the independent non-executives clear that proposal or the independents feel that they would be better protected by appointment of new advisers.

One other area for non-executive input relates to the approval of documents. The main document is the offer document itself. This should be prepared in accordance with the provisions of the Takeover Code and the listing rules. The Code requires that any document issued to the shareholders by the buyout bidder must include a statement accepting responsibility for the information contained and this is not a task to be undertaken lightly. It requires absolutely accuracy as to the form and content of the offer document.

There will then be documentation relating to the financial backers of the buyout. This will be reflected in a shareholders' agreement. This is effectively the agreement between the venture capitalists and the management team and any other shareholders of the new company.

The venture capitalist will appreciate that warranties from the shareholders in the public offer is not feasible, but will want to obtain warranties and disclosures from any director that it can get them from. This approach is designed as much to flush out any issues as shift financial risk.

When it comes to the financing of the bid the Code requires that there be certainty of funds to prevent bids being made flippantly without financial backing. So the buyout team will have to have certainty of funding. In a private buyout funding is usually signed up at the same time as all the other documents are signed. In a public-to-private buyout the funding needs to be signed up prior to the announcement of a firm intention to make the offer even though it won't complete until some time later.

Another aspect the non-executive needs to be aware of is 'Financial Assistance'. In most cases the buyout will involve a leveraged financial structure and the providers of the debt will be looking to the assets of the target company as security. The rules prohibiting the giving of financial assistance in connection with the purchase of shares in the target company absolutely preclude those assets being secured until the company is a private company. Conversion to private status will not take place until after the compulsory acquisition of dissenting shareholders is completed so the funding structure of a buyout invariably consists of a staged process.

In conclusion these transactions are highly complex, uncertain and require a great deal of planning from the outset. It is critical for the non-executive to understand the process and be clear on what their own role in the process is.

15.10   Media Relations

The financial media in most developed markets are sophisticated and need to be dealt with in a highly professional manner. In the UK there are a limited number of key titles and journalists who will be relevant to a particular company, unless the company is a retail or consumer branded business. The company also needs to consider electronic media in addition to print and broadcast.

The key role for non-executives in media relations is to ensure that the company has an appropriate strategy, to be aware of how successful that strategy is and support it as relevant. This support is unlikely to include representing the company in the media and more likely to include support with the selection process of advisers and the introduction of useful contacts.

Larger businesses may have more than one adviser and may have specialists for their product and corporate public relations activities.

A non-executive who is experienced in this area may be able to add considerable value simply by imparting this experience through advice to the key spokesmen (i.e. the chief executive, chairman and finance director). These are the people that investors and the press really want to see. An experienced non-executive may also help in other ways, for example, helping the company to avoid the dangers of publicity stunts borne out of exuberance. If the media lose trust or confidence their audiences are likely to do the same shortly afterwards.

Active non-executives will want to be aware of the company's key media spokesmen and messages and be assured that there is integration and consistency with marketing communications to other audiences.

15.11   Investor Relations with Private Investors

For public companies with large numbers of retail investors, communications can be a challenge for the following reasons:

- The cost of communications materials.
- Handling queries and questions from shareholders.
- The nature of Annual General Meetings in the UK.
- The regulatory requirements relating to the provision of information to shareholders.

The channels of communication are straightforward:

- personal contact;
- mail;
- shareholder meetings (e.g. Annual General Meeting);
- Internet;
- regional/retail brokers.

For public companies, personal contact other than at the AGM or through enquiry handling is uneconomic. The main channels used are mail, Internet and through using the increasingly sophisticated regional and retail brokers.

In private companies where the number of shareholders is far smaller, personal contact is the main method.

15.12   The Impact of the Internet on Investor Relations

The development of the Internet has driven several changes to the nature of investor relations, especially with retail investors. The Internet boom of the late

1990s expanded the numbers of people buying shares in most of the developed economies, particularly in the US. Trading through the Internet also expanded and changed the economics of share buying. However, probably the most fundamental and long lasting change from the retail shareholder's point of view has been in relation to the provision and speed of communication of information.

From the company's point of view the main benefits arise from the greater efficiency and reduced cost of providing information direct to the shareholder. Some argue that the greatest benefit of all has been the development of the FAQ ('Frequently Asked Questions') sections on company websites.

15.13   Share Dealing and PSI

Non-executive directors are bound by the same rules as any other director when it comes to dealing in shares (see **PARAGRAPH 6.47**).

15.14   What Did the Higgs Report Say about the Non-executive Director's Relationships with Shareholders?

There was a whole section devoted to it in the report. This is covered in **CHAPTER 13**. There was particular sensitivity over the role of SINEs in investor relations in the published reactions to the report. Most adverse comment centred on the dangers of the senior independent director usurping the chairman's role.

The report clearly states that the primary channel of communication between the company and investors should be the CEO, FD and chairman. The senior independent director should be a safety valve when this isn't working. The suggested increase in contact between SINEs and institutions was to ensure that SINEs have earlier awareness of an issue and a mechanism for institutions to express it.

15.15   Useful Reference Points

The following organisations websites contain a wealth of information and best practice advice on a wide range of topics relating to investor relations:

- London Stock Exchange   www.londonstockexchange.com
- The National Association of Pension funds   www.napf.co.uk
- The Association of British Insurers   www.abi.org.uk
- The Investor Relations Society   www.ir-soc.org.uk
- The Institute of Chartered Secretaries and Administrators   www.icsa.org.uk

Investor Relations

Nominations Committees

16.1 Introduction
Appendix 1 Terms of Reference for a Nominations Committee

16   Nominations Committees

16.1   Introduction

> **At a Glance**
> * It is best practice for all board appointments to be made through a formal and transparent process involving a nominations committee.
> * The nominations committee will normally also ensure that there is a robust succession plan in place for all key board roles (e.g. chairman, chief executive, finance director and senior independent director).
> * Since the Higgs Review some nominations committees have also taken on the role of supporting the chairman in organising the board performance review process.

For most listed companies the purpose of a nominations committee is straightforward and that is to 'ensure that there is a formal and transparent procedure for appointing new directors to the board and to make recommendations to the board on *all* new board appointments'.

'All' means executive, non-executive and of course the chairman.

We have included the sample terms of reference for a nominations committee in the **APPENDICES**. Institute of Company Secretaries and Administrators (ICSA) have also produced a very helpful guidance note (020321) which is available on their website.

In Derek Higgs Review of the role and effectiveness of non-executives, which was focussed on listed companies, he says that:

> 'Almost all FTSE100 companies have a nominations committee, compared to only 30% of companies outside the FTSE350. However, interviews conducted for the review suggested that where the nominations committee does exist, it is the least developed of the board's committees, usually meeting irregularly and often without a clear understanding of the extent of its role in the appointment process.'

As expected following the publication of the Higgs Review in 2003, greater focus has been placed by public companies on the role of the nominations committee. The authors believe that the incorporation of its recommendations in to the Combined Code and the Code's 'comply or explain' approach has led to not just an increase in the use of nominations committees but also greater effectiveness. A sign of this is the fact that in the 2007 Independent Remuneration Solutions survey of independent chairman and non-executive directors the proportion of appointments made using a professional search firm had risen in larger quoted companies from 40–50% to 90–95% since 2002.

Contrast this with the following quotes from the Higgs Review:

> 'A high level of informality surrounds the process of appointing non-executive directors. Almost half of the non-executive directors surveyed for the review were recruited to their role through personal contacts or friendships. Only 4% had a formal interview, and 1% had obtained their job through answering an advertisement. This situation has been widely criticised in responses to consultation.'

and

> 'I believe that a rigorous, fair and open appointments process is essential to promote meritocracy in the boardroom and that existing best practice for nominating and appointing directors should be universally adopted.'

The relevant section of the Combined Code is A.4 where it starts by stating that:

> 'There should be a formal, rigorous and transparent procedure for the appointment of new directors to the board.'

Then through a series of supporting principles and provisions states that there should be a nominations committee, sets out its role in summary and also ends by stating in A.4.6 that:

> 'A separate section of the annual report should describe the work of the nomination committee, including the process it has used in relation to board appointments. An explanation should be given if neither an external search consultancy nor open advertising has been used in the appointment of a chairman or non-executive director.'

And finally

> 'I therefore recommend that, when an appointment of a non-executive director is put forward for approval to shareholders, the board should explain why they believe the individual should be appointed and how they meet the requirements of the role.'

All of which appears straightforward. However there are some issues for non-executives on nominations committees.

16.2   The Existence of a Committee

If the company is listed then there needs to be a standing committee of the board comprised of a majority of independent non-executives. In practice this will mean committees of five or more.

For non-listed companies it is more normal for the chairman and a non-executive to lead the process with active involvement of the chief executive. This may or may not be a formal committee. The board may just approve the delegation of the election process to a couple of its members and then approve, or not the recommendations that they make.

16.3   Executive and Non-executive Appointments

As the Combined Code states that: 'There should be a formal, rigorous and transparent procedure for the appointment of new directors to the board'. It is assumed that this applies as much to executive directors as non-executive directors or the chairman. The authors feel that non-executives can add considerable value especially in smaller or private companies in supporting the process of senior executive appointments. This is especially true with respect to the appointment of a new finance director.

16.4   The Use of Search Firms

This is covered in detail in CHAPTER 1. We would simply reiterate that if a search firm is to be used then as with any other supplier there should be an objective selection process and they should be appropriately managed.

16.5   Succession Planning

Derek Higgs stated in his review that:

> 'The committee should satisfy itself that processes and plans are in place for orderly succession for appointments to the board and to senior management to maintain an appropriate balance of skills on the board. I recommend that the Combined Code include reference to this important role for the nominations committee.'

Many boards have what is sometimes described as the 'falling under a bus list'. This is a simple list of the current board and who in the event of a tragic accident, physical or commercial, would replace them. These generally work on the assumption that a direct replacement is made.

Succession planning for the key roles of chief executive and chairman is covered in PARAGRAPH 3.4.2.

16.6   Linkage with the Remuneration Committee

An important part of any appointment process will be the determination of the terms and conditions of the appointment. Consequently there needs to be strong linkage between the nominations and remuneration committees. Most nominations committees will receive guidance from the remuneration committee at an early stage in a recruitment process as to what terms should be offered for the process. This tends to be more straightforward for non-executive appointments, where it is common for all non-executives to be paid fees on the same basis, than for executive appointments.

16.7   Interaction with the Chairman

One controversial aspect of the Higgs Review was the suggestion that the nominations committee could include the chairman but that it should be chaired by an independent non-executive, ideally the senior independent director. This evoked a strong reaction from some chairman who felt that as leaders of the boardroom team they ought to be the ones driving 'team selection' for all but their own positions.

Sir Adrian Cadbury in his excellent book *Corporate governance and Chairmanship* has a different view to Higgs:

> 'I believe that the chairman of the board should wherever possible chair this committee, since it is chairmen who are responsible for the working of their boards and who should therefore play a leading part in selecting their team.'

The sensitive area is obviously to do with the succession of the chairman himself. If the nominations committee has done its job with regard to planning then the candidate will be an existing non-executive director. For example it may have been a selection requirement of one of the existing non-executives that they be capable of becoming chairman.

The Financial Reporting Council came down on the side of the chairman and provision A.4.1 clearly states that:

> 'The chairman or an independent non-executive director should chair the committee, but the chairman should not chair the nomination committee when it is dealing with the appointment of a successor to the chairmanship.'

According to the Higgs Report the new chairman should be deemed to be independent (definition in the **APPENDICES**) at the time of his or her appointment.

The more challenging situation is where there is no internal candidate and the nominations committee needs to look outside. What role should the existing chairman play here? Clearly this depends upon the circumstances of his retirement. If he is being removed for underperformance then his role is obviously limited. If on the other hand he is retiring positively then he may have a lot to offer the process. This is definitely a situation where judgement is required and where, if there is a strong non-executive supporting the chairman, it is far easier to manage whether they are formally described as the senior independent non-executive or not.

Given the critical importance of the relationship between the chairman and chief executive it is essential that the chief executive is appropriately involved in the selection of any new chairman.

16.8   Interaction with the Chief Executive

Any board appointment will be a significant matter for the chief executive and the best CEOs will be actively engaged in the process. For example in recruiting top executive talent they will be the key salesman in the process as well as the key decision maker on who should be selected.

When it comes to non-executive appointments no decent potential non-executive would consider taking an appointment without meeting the chief executive and vice versa. If the chief executive is uncomfortable with a prospective non-executive then normally it is harder for the non-executive to be appointed even if there are issues with the chief executive and the non-executive is the ideal candidate.

The degree of influence a CEO has over board appointments is the cause of much debate especially in the US and in France where power has tended to be concentrated to a greater degree in the hands of one person than in the UK. One of the roles of the nominations committee is to ensure that there is the right level of engagement of the chief executive so that they are brought into the process but do not dominate the process to the extent that the board ends up being 'a bunch of the CEO's poodles'.

16.9   Interaction with the Company's Human Resources Director

If the company has a human resources director then he or she should be a key person in any recruitment or selection process. Views differ as to whether the HR director should be on the nominations committee. Technically if the nominations committee is a true sub-committee of the board then they cannot be unless they are also on the board. What typically happens therefore is that the HR director is an adviser to the committee and will attend most meetings.

The reality is that in situations where the HR director is effective they have an important and active role to play. Where they are less effective they tend to simply carry out the instructions of the nominations committee.

16.10   What Skills and Experience Are Needed to Be a Member of Nominations Committee

The nominations committee as a whole needs to be excellent at judging people, rigorous in their selection process and good at communicating with the rest of the board. It is easier to achieve this if the members of the committee have had considerable experience of board appointments and at least one is a current or former chairman or chief executive. Good process won't in itself ensure success and often it is the most intuitive member of the nominations committee who adds the most value when it comes to key appointments. The chairman of the committee therefore needs to be a good chairman.

Appendix 1

Terms of Reference for a Nominations Committee

You will want to word this in the style of the company's other communications. What is presented below is a slightly more formal version than is necessary but easily adaptable. We have drawn heavily on the ICSA template.

1. Name
    The committee shall be a standing committee of the board known as the 'Nominations Committee'.
2. Purpose
    To ensure that there is a formal and transparent process for the appointment of new directors to the board and to make recommendations to the board on all new board appointments.
3. Members and chairman
    (a) The committee shall comprise any three or more non-executive directors of the company, considered by the board to be independent for this purpose, appointed from time to time by Resolution of the board of whom one shall from time to time be appointed by the board to act as chairman.
    (b) Notwithstanding **PARAGRAPH 3(a)** where a quorum would not otherwise be available for a meeting of the committee to take place the chairman and the senior non-executive director (or deputy chairman) shall have the power to co-opt any appropriate non-executive director (including themselves) as an additional member of the committee.
4. Quorum
    The quorum for the transaction of business by the committee shall be the chairman of the committee together with any one other member of the committee.
    In the absence of the chairman of the committee the senior independent non-executive director or, in his absence the chairman of the board or any other non-executive director they co-opt to the committee in accordance with Paragraph 3(a) can take his place.
5. Fees
    Additional remuneration at such a rate as the board may determine shall be payable to each member of the remuneration committee other than the chairman of the board or any other director co-opted to the committee in accordance with **PARAGRAPH 3(b)**.
6. Conduct of business
    (a) Meetings
        The committee shall meet not less than once a year and at such other times as the chairman of the committee shall require. All meetings of the committee shall be convened by the company secretary on the

instructions of the chairman of the committee or, in his absence, the member of the committee in accordance with **PARAGRAPH 4**.

(b) Consultation

The committee shall consult with the chairman of the board (if not a member of the committee) and/or the chief executive and may consult with the human resources director, and shall have the power to employ the services of any external search consultant or other professional adviser as it thinks fit, and may invite any of such persons to attend such meetings of the committee as it considers appropriate. The budget for fees payable by the committee to external advisers is to be agreed with the board at the beginning of each year.

(c) Support

The company secretary shall be the Secretary to the committee and shall provide the committee such support and advice as it may require and shall be entitled to independent access to the chairman of the committee at all times.

(d) Voting

Each member of the committee shall have one vote. Note: there are three members of the committee.

(e) Written resolution

A resolution in writing signed by all members of the committee entitled to receive notice of a meeting of the committee shall be as valid and effective as if the same had been passed at a meeting of the committee duly convened and held.

7. Duties of the committee

The committee shall:

(a) regularly review the structure, size and composition of the board and make recommendations to the board with regard to any adjustments that are deemed necessary;

(b) be responsible for identifying and nominating for the approval of the board, candidates to fill board vacancies as and when they arise;

(c) keep under review the leadership needs of the organisation with a view to ensuring the continued ability to compete effectively in the organisation's market place;

(d) keep up to date and fully *au fait* with strategic issues and commercial changes affecting the company and the market in which it operates.

It shall also make recommendations to the board on:

(e) plans for succession, in particular, of the chairman and the chief executive;

(f) the re-appointment of any non-executive director at the conclusion of his or her specified term of office;

(g) for the continuation (or not) in service of any director who has reached the age of (specify);

(h) the re-election by shareholders of any director under the 'retirement by rotation' provisions in the company's Articles of Association;

(j) any matters relating to the continuation in office as a director of any director at any time;

(k) the appointment of any director to executive or other office other than to the positions of chairman and chief executive, the recommendation for which would be considered at a meeting of all the non-executive directors regarding the position of chief executive and all the directors regarding the position of chairman.

8. Powers of the committee

The committee is authorised to seek any information it requires from any employee of the company in order to perform its duties.

The committee is authorised to obtain, at the company's expense, outside legal or other professional advice on any matters within its terms of reference.

9. Additional duties of chairman

The chairman of the committee is authorised and requested to attend (or to arrange for another member of the committee to attend each Annual General Meeting of the company to deal with shareholders' questions about directors' remuneration.

Pension Arrangements for Employees

17 Pension Arrangements for Employees

17.1 Types of Pension Scheme

> **At a Glance**
> * The provision of good retirement benefits is often seen as an important element of the remuneration package offered to employees and the action of a responsible employer.
> * Employees are increasingly being encouraged to contract out of the secondary State pension scheme and to make their own alternative provision.
> * Under a defined benefit scheme, the benefits payable on retirement are fixed, either as an amount or as a proportion of salary – this is advantageous for the scheme member but the cost to the employer can fluctuate significantly over time.
> * Under a defined contribution scheme, the benefits payable on retirement depend on the amount accumulated in respect of each scheme member – the employer has the benefit of a fixed cost but the employee bears the risk of the fund being insufficient to provide the level of retirement benefits hoped for.
> * Employers may wish to consider alternative options to share the risks of pension provision more equitably between employers and employees.
> * Any individual (and their employer) can contribute to a personal pension, provided that he/she is not already a member of an occupational pension scheme.
> * Certain individuals who are members of an occupational pension scheme can also contribute to a personal or stakeholder pension.
> * All employers with five or more employees must generally give them access to a stakeholder pension scheme, unless they have made alternative pension provision.

17.2 Introduction

The issue of employee pensions has become a hot political, economic and social topic. This is due to several factors including the following.

- A demographic shift in most developed nations to an older population.
- The social shift to earlier effective retirement ages.
- Significant weak performance of pension funds arising out of the collapse in stock markets in the early 2000s.
- Structural issues with state pension funding and a political desire to move responsibility from the state to individuals.
- The failure of Equitable Life and the reduction in payouts from with-profits endowment policies.

The whole atmosphere around pensions has changed considerably from one where most employees thought that there was no risk to their pension to one where there is significant anxiety. It is therefore critical that non-executive directors, especially those that sit or intend sitting on remuneration committees, have a good understanding of the pensions position of the companies on whose boards they serve.

17.3   Retirement Provisions for Employees

Although most employees will qualify for State pension benefits on retirement, many people will want to make additional provision to ensure that they can maintain their lifestyle after retirement and perhaps to give themselves the option of retiring before the normal retirement age. The provision of good retirement benefits is therefore often seen as an important element of the remuneration package offered to employees and potential employees and the action of a responsible employer. Generous tax benefits are also available on contributions by employers and employees to pension schemes approved by the HM Revenue and Customs.

17.4   State Pensions

Most employees will qualify for basic State pension on retirement, although the amount that they receive will depend on whether they have a full National Insurance Contributions record, the details for which are very complex. In addition to basic pension, the State Second Pension (previously the State Earnings Related Pension Scheme or SERPS) enables employees to build up a pension entitlement related to their earnings. Employees can choose to remain within the State Second Scheme, or to contract out of this and participate instead in an occupational pension scheme offered by their employer or make other personal pension arrangements. There is a continuing encouragement for employees to contract out of the additional State Scheme and make alternative pension provision in order to reduce the potential burden on government resources of present demographic trends (i.e. reducing birth rates and longer life expectancy). Consequently, many employers already offer their employees access to an occupational pension scheme, which may operate on the basis of defined benefits or defined contributions (or a combination of these), or to some form of group personal pension plan.

State pension arrangements have also recently been the subject of a major review. A Government White Paper 'Security in retirement: towards a new pensions system' published in May 2006 set out a number of proposals for significant changes to the State Pension system which will affect those reaching State

Pension age on or after 6 April 2010, and a related Pensions Bill was introduced into Parliament in November 2006. In particular, the proposed changes include:

- the introduction of new system of personal accounts (see below);
- increasing the State Pension age from 65 to 68 between 2024 and 2046 and
- abolishing contracting out for defined contribution occupational pension schemes and personal pension schemes.

The proposed system of personal accounts represents a new national pensions savings scheme based on an employee contribution of 4% of salary, a Government contribution of 1% in the form of tax relief and an employer contribution of 3% of salary. Involvement in this scheme would be automatic, with each employee having the option of opting out if they wish. This contrasts with the present approach where employees are generally given the opportunity to opt in to pension arrangements if they wish. This change could result in a significant increase in employer costs in respect of pensions, given that many employees currently choose not to take advantage of some of the pension benefits offered to them through defined contribution or stakeholder schemes.

17.5   Defined Benefit Schemes

A defined benefit retirement scheme is one under which the benefits payable on retirement are fixed, either as an amount or as a proportion of salary. Where benefits are defined in relation to salary they are usually based on the individual's final salary or his/her average salary for (say) the last three years before retirement. This is advantageous for the member, as he/she is assured of receiving a pension of a known amount. However, the employer has a commitment to ensure that sufficient funds are invested to enable the scheme to meet the guaranteed pension payments. The cost to the employer is consequently very dependent on a variety of factors and can fluctuate significantly over time. The cost of operating a defined benefit scheme has generally increased in recent years as a result of high salary levels, changes in life expectancy and the poor performance of the underlying investment markets. The current problems may be even more significant where past surpluses in the scheme have been used to fund improved benefits or contribution holidays. The nature of defined benefit schemes also means that they are more tightly regulated than defined contribution schemes and the accounting implications are much more complex. Defined benefit schemes are therefore generally becoming less popular with employers and many companies have opted to close their defined benefit schemes, either completely or at least to new members. Contributions to the scheme will often be paid by both the employer and the employee, but the level of the employee's contribution will usually be fixed and it is therefore the employer contribution that varies to make good any deficit in funding or, where permitted, to absorb any surplus that arises.

17.6   *Accounting for Defined Benefit Schemes*

Financial Reporting Standard 17 (FRS 17) *Retirement Benefits* was published in November 2000 and became fully effective for accounting periods beginning

Pension Arrangements
for Employees

on or after 1 January 2005 for companies continuing to adopt UK accounting practice. FRS 17 introduced significant changes to the way in which defined benefit retirement schemes are accounted for and has had a significant impact on the profit and loss accounts and balance sheets of many companies. The standard specifies how scheme assets and scheme liabilities should be measured and generally requires the surplus or deficit in the scheme to be recognised as an asset or liability on the balance sheet. The depressed state of the equity market in recent years has resulted in many pension schemes showing a deficit in funding and the new accounting requirements have introduced the related liabilities onto company balance sheets. In some cases, there have been consequences for the company's ability to comply with existing loan covenants or the availability of sufficient distributable reserves to maintain dividend payments. Companies preparing International Accounting Standard (IAS) accounts have faced similar issues in complying the requirements of IAS 19 *Employee Benefits* which is in fact much wider in scope than the UK standard. FRS 17 in particular received a certain degree of criticism and was in some cases quoted as the cause of companies deciding to close their defined benefit schemes and replace them with defined contribution schemes. However, the accounting standard is not the root cause of the problem – the new accounting requirements are simply forcing directors to recognise that defined benefit retirement schemes can leave a business exposed to significant risks which need to be managed in the same way as other business risks. Further information on accounting for retirement benefits is given in **PARAGRAPHS 17.30–17.46**.

17.7 Defined Contribution Schemes

In the case of a defined contribution scheme (sometimes referred to as a 'money purchase scheme'), a fixed amount is contributed each year in respect of each member of the scheme, usually divided between the employer and employee and set as a proportion of the employee's salary. The amount contributed in respect of each individual member is accumulated in a separate account, and the pension payable to that employee will depend on the value of that fund at the date of his/her retirement. The employer therefore has the benefit of a fixed cost, but the employee bears the risk of the fund being insufficient to provide the level of pension that he/she hoped for at the time of retirement. The scheme funds may be invested in a variety of ways – in some schemes, the individual members may participate in decisions on how their particular fund is dealt with, in others this will be entirely at the discretion of the pension scheme trustees. A defined contribution scheme may be established as:

- an employer-sponsored occupational pension scheme approved by the Inland Revenue or
- a group personal pension arrangement, under which an individual pension plan is arranged for each employee.

In the case of a group personal pension arrangement, it is not compulsory for the employer to make contributions to the scheme.

17.8　Other Options

The two basic forms of pension scheme discussed above leave the risks associated with the provision of retirement benefits primarily with the employer (in the case of defined benefit schemes) or with the employee (in the case of defined contribution schemes). Some companies may feel that neither of these is entirely appropriate for them and may therefore wish to explore other options that share the risks and costs of pension provision more equitably between employer and employee. Other options that may be worth considering are considered briefly below, in a broadly reducing order of risk to the employer.

17.9　*Shared Risk Final Salary Scheme*

A shared risk final salary scheme preserves the advantages of a defined benefit scheme in that the retirement benefits continue to be based on the employee's final salary, but there is a greater sharing of the associated risk between the employer and the employee. This sharing can be achieved by one or more of the following:

- making both the employer and employee contributions variable, depending on the results of the regular actuarial valuation;
- giving scheme members the option of paying a higher contribution in order to maintain benefits at the current level, or continuing at the current contribution level and accepting the resulting reduction in benefits or
- providing guaranteed benefits at a relatively low level, with additional benefits granted on a discretionary basis if funding levels, or company performance, permit.

17.10　*Career Average Salary Scheme*

Under a career average salary scheme, retirement benefits are accrued each year in relation to the employee's salary for that year and the annual benefit is then revalued each year, up to retirement, in line with an appropriate index. Breaking the link between retirement benefits and the employee's final salary removes the impact of salary inflation during the employment period. The employee's pension on retirement is the aggregate of the revalued benefit calculated for each year of employment.

17.11　*Hybrid Schemes*

Hybrid schemes usually provide the employee with a mixture of defined benefit and money purchase benefits. For instance, a hybrid scheme might provide money purchase benefits up to a certain age (say 40) and then defined benefits for subsequent years of employment. This type of scheme can be advantageous to younger employees, who may want to transfer the money purchase benefits if their employment changes, but also gives older employees the security of defined benefits as they approach retirement age. Alternatively, a hybrid scheme may provide defined benefits on salary up to a specified level, and then money purchase benefits in respect of any salary above this. This can be particularly helpful in giving lower-paid employees the security of fixed retirement benefits whilst transferring some of the associated risk to those on higher salaries.

17.12 *Cash Schemes*

An employer can commit to providing a guaranteed lump sum to the employee at retirement, usually based on a proportion of final salary for each year of service, as in the case of a standard defined benefit scheme. The risk up to the date of retirement therefore continues to be borne by the employer, but the risk after retirement is transferred to the employee, who can retain part of the lump sum and use the balance to purchase an annuity.

17.13 *Insured Schemes*

An insured pension scheme is one under which the scheme trustees enter into an agreement with a life assurance company and pay appropriate premiums to secure the required benefits for the members and meet the costs of administering the scheme. This approach is more straightforward administratively and is therefore often favoured by smaller companies. In the case of a defined contribution scheme, a series of insurance policies may be needed to match the separate funds for the individual members.

17.14 Personal Pensions

Any individual can contribute to a personal pension, provided that he/she is not already a member of an occupational pension scheme. The individual makes contributions into an account with a personal pension provider, who invests the money on their behalf. Employers can also contribute to the personal pension plan of an employee. There are limits on the amount that an individual can contribute to a personal pension in each tax year, based on their earnings in that period and on their age. The percentage of earnings that can be contributed increases as the individual gets closer to retirement. From April 2001, members of an occupational pension scheme who earn less than £30,000 pa, and who are not controlling directors, are allowed to contribute up to £3600 each year to an additional personal or stakeholder pension.

17.15 Stakeholder Pensions

A stakeholder pension is a particular type of personal pension which became available from 6 April 2001 to encourage more people, especially those who are not high earners, to plan for their retirement. With effect from October 2001, the *Welfare Reform and Pensions Act 1999* and the *Stakeholder Pension Schemes Regulations 2000 (SI 2000/1403)* require all employers with five or more employees to give their employees access to a stakeholder pension scheme, although there is no requirement for an employer to offer such access to employees earning less than the lower earnings limit. However, an employer who operates an occupational pension scheme is exempt from the stakeholder requirement if the current scheme is open to all employees who:

- are aged over 18 and are more than five years younger than the normal retirement age under the scheme and
- have completed one year's service with the company.

Where an existing scheme does not meet the requirements for exemption, it may be possible to make some modifications so that the employer qualifies for exemption, although the full cost of doing so will need to be carefully considered. The only commitment required from the employer is to provide the required level of access to the pension scheme – individual employees remain free to decide whether or not to join and the employer is not currently required to make any contributions to the scheme (although this may be introduced at some point in the future).

17.16   *Group Personal Pension Arrangement*

An employer is also exempt from the requirement to provide access to a stakeholder pension where a group personal pension arrangement is in place and:

- it is a term of the employment contract that all employees aged 18 or over who have completed three months' service and whose earnings are at least equivalent to the lower earnings limit have a right to join the scheme;
- the employer will pay contributions of at least 3% of the employee's basic pay (or a lower amount equivalent to the contributions that the employee is willing to make);
- the employer offers a payroll deduction facility to members of the scheme;
- the scheme does not impose any penalties on members who transfer out or stop making contributions.

17.17   *Checklist of Stakeholder Pension Requirements*

Any employer with five or more employees who is not covered by one of the above exemptions must:

- consult with employees or their representative organisations about the choice of stakeholder scheme;
- nominate a stakeholder scheme;
- provide employees or their representative organisations with contact details for the nominated scheme;
- allow representatives of the nominated scheme reasonable access to the employees and
- enable the employees to make contributions to the nominated scheme by deduction from their pay, and forward these contributions to the scheme within 19 days of the end of the month in which they were deducted.

17.18   Pension Scheme Administration

At a Glance

* The *Pensions Act 2004* is now the main legislation governing the control and management of occupational pension schemes.
* The Pensions Regulator supervises the regulation of all occupational pension schemes.
* Most pension schemes are set up as trusts and established under a formal trust deed – the trustees must therefore comply with trust law as well as the more specific requirements of pensions legislation.
* Pensions legislation also gives the sponsoring employer certain duties and responsibilities.
* Most defined benefit schemes are subject to a minimum funding requirement.
* Pension scheme trustees generally have a duty to obtain audited financial statements within seven months of the end of the scheme financial year.
* The form and content of pension scheme accounts is specified in various regulations under the *Pensions Act 1995* and also in the Statement of Recommended Practice ('SORP') *Financial Reports of Pension Schemes.*
* Preliminary proposals have been issued for changes to the form and content of pension scheme reports and accounts.
* Certain schemes are exempt from the requirement to appoint scheme auditors, although some of them may still require an audit under the terms of their trust deed.
* Regulations under the *Pensions Act 1995* set out the procedures that must be followed when appointing auditors and when there is a change of auditor.
* The HM Revenue and Customs Pension Schemes Office ('PSO') is responsible for approving pension schemes for tax purposes, and for withdrawing approval where necessary.

17.19   Pension Act 2004

The Pensions Act 2004 is now the main legislation governing the management and control of occupational pension schemes. The Act is primarily enabling legislation and detailed requirements are set out in related regulations and Codes of Practice developed under the Act. Certain regulations established under the Pensions Act 1995 also remain in force, including in particular the following regulations governing financial reporting and auditing requirements:

* the *Occupational Pension Schemes (Disclosure of Information) Regulations 1996 (SI 1996/1655 as amended by subsequent SIs)*;
* the *Occupational Pension Schemes (Scheme Administration) Regulations 1996 (SI 1996/1715 as amended by subsequent SIs)* and

- the *Occupational Pension Schemes (Requirement to Obtain Audited Accounts and a Statement from the Auditor) Regulations 1996 (SI 1996/1975 as amended by subsequent SIs).*

17.20   The Pensions Regulator

The Pensions Act 2004 also established the position of the Pensions Regulator, to take on the functions previously carried out by the Occupational Pensions Regulatory Authority (OPRA), but with considerably wider powers and responsibilities. The main objectives of the Regulator are to protect the interests of occupational pension scheme members, limit the situations in which compensation from the Pension Protection Fund might be required and improve the administration of pension schemes. The Regulator's powers include:

- Collecting data on individual schemes through regular returns, reports of breaches and other notifiable events – the Regulator also has the power to demand certain documents or information relevant to its work.
- Taking action to protect the security of members' benefits where necessary – this might include:
  - issuing improvement notices to individuals or companies, requiring action to be taken within a specific time limit;
  - taking steps to recover unpaid contributions from employers;
  - issuing a freezing order to temporarily halt the winding-up of a scheme, so that any concerns can be investigated;
  - the disqualification of trustees;
  - the imposition of fines for breaches of the requirements and prosecution in the courts in the case of certain offences;
- where there is reason to believe that an employer is deliberately trying to avoid its pension obligation and relying on the Pension Protection Fund to meet the liabilities, issuing contribution notices, financial support directions and/or restoration orders.

17.21   Pension Scheme Trustees

Most pension schemes are set up as trusts and are established under a formal trust deed, which gives the scheme trustees responsibility for stewardship and custody of the scheme assets. Most pension schemes must therefore comply with general trust law as well as with the more specific requirements of pensions legislation, and the duties of the pension scheme trustees will usually include:

- observing the terms of the trust;
- acting at all times in the best interests of the beneficiaries of the trust;
- acting impartially between any different classes of beneficiary;
- acting prudently and making appropriate use of any particular skills and experience that they have;
- not profiting from the trust (other than as members of the scheme);

- exercising investment powers in accordance with the legislation;
- appointing professional advisers;
- maintaining specified bank accounts, books and records; and
- obtaining audited financial statements and appropriate reports from the actuary.

A trustee of the pension scheme who is also a director of the sponsoring company must take particular care not be influenced by his dual capacity. The legislation also includes specific provisions on the appointment of member-nominated trustees. Certain individuals are disqualified from acting as a trustee, including individuals with a conviction for an offence involving dishonesty or deception, undischarged bankrupts and those disqualified from appointment as a company director. The Pensions Act 2004 also introduces new requirements on the knowledge and understanding that trustees are expected to have in order to fulfil their role effectively, although there is a special dispensation for new trustees to give them a period of six months in which to undertake appropriate training. It is also important for such knowledge and skills to be kept up to date and both individual trustees and the board as a whole are recommended to keep appropriate records of the training undertaken. The Pensions Regulator (see PARAGRAPH 17.20) provides a number of guidance documents for pension scheme trustees to help them to understand their duties and responsibilities. These are available from the Pension Regulator's website at www.thepensionsregulator.gov.uk. A free online training resource for pension scheme trustees is also available at www.trusteetoolkit.com.

17.22 Sponsoring Employer

The sponsoring employer is also given a number of duties and responsibilities under the legislation, including:

- paying employer contributions in accordance with a defined schedule;
- paying employee contributions over to the scheme within 19 days of the end of the month in which they are deducted from employees' pay;
- where the employer operates the pensions payroll on behalf of the scheme, paying into a separate bank account any benefits which have not been paid to members within two days;
- a duty to disclose to the trustees or managers the occurrence of any event relating to the employer which could reasonably be considered to be of material significance to the exercise of their functions and
- a duty to disclose to the trustees or managers any information reasonably required for the proper performance of their duties or those of the professional advisers to the scheme.

Under the regulations, the power to make payments to employers may only be exercised by the trustees.

17.23 Statutory Funding Objective

Under the Pensions Act 2004, a new Statutory Funding Objective has been introduced to replace the previous Minimum Funding Requirement, which gave rise to a number of concerns when it was initially implemented and which the Government now considers has not fulfilled its purpose. The new objective is that a defined benefit scheme has sufficient assets to meets its current and future liabilities, calculated on an actuarial basis. The calculation of scheme liabilities must be based on prudent economic and actuarial assumptions and carried out with actuarial advice, using an accrued benefits funding method. Any change from the method or assumptions used in the previous calculation must be justified by a change of legal, demographic or economic circumstances. Each scheme must prepare a Statement of Funding Principles setting out how the Statutory Funding Objective will be met. Detailed requirements are set out Code of Practice 3, which also emphasises the need for trustees to have a proper understanding of the funding decisions they make and the implications for the scheme. The *Occupational Pension Schemes (Scheme Funding) Regulations 2005* set out the information that should be covered in the Statement of Funding. This includes information on:

- any funding objectives provided in the scheme rules, or which the trustees have adopted, in addition to the statutory funding objective;
- any arrangements for a person other than the employer or a member to contribute;
- any power to make payments to the employer out of the scheme and when such power may be exercised;
- any discretionary power to provide benefits for any members and the extent to which this is taken into account in funding;
- how often the trustees obtain actuarial valuations.

If an actuarial valuation shows that a scheme is not in a position to meet its liabilities, the trustees must put a recovery plan into place and send a copy to the Pensions Regulator. The recovery plan must specify the period over which the shortfall in funding is to be eliminated so that the Statutory Funding Objective can be met. The Code of Practice notes that the aim should be for the shortfall to be eliminated as quickly as the employer can reasonably afford.

17.24   Financial Reporting

Under current legislation, pension scheme trustees have a duty to obtain audited financial statements within seven months of the end of the scheme financial year. Auditors have a duty to report to the Pensions Regulator (see **PARAGRAPH 17.20**) any breach of this provision by the trustees.

17.25   Checklist for Annual Pension Scheme Report

The annual report should comprise the following:

- a trustees' report, providing information on the management of the scheme and developments during the scheme year;

- an investment report, reviewing investment policy and the performance of the scheme during the year;
- a compliance statement, giving additional disclosures about the scheme required by the legislation and any other voluntary disclosures which are not sufficiently material to require inclusion in the trustees' report;
- financial statements giving a true and fair view of the financial transactions of the scheme during the year and of the disposition of its net assets at the end of the year and
- actuarial statements – these vary depending on the nature of the scheme but will usually include an opinion from the actuary on the security of accrued rights and prospective rights, and on compliance with the minimum funding requirement.

The form and content of the financial statements are specified in various regulations under the *Pensions Act 1995* and the trustees are also required to state whether they have been prepared in accordance with the SORP 'Financial Reports of Pension Schemes', issued by the Pensions Research Accountants Group ('PRAG') under the Accounting Standards Board ('ASB') Code of Practice for the development of SORPs (see **PARAGRAPH 10.23**).

17.26   Proposals for Changes

The Pensions Regulator issued a consultation document on possible changes to the form and content of pension scheme annual reports and accounts in June 2006 and published a summary of the responses in December 2006. In particular, there appears to be a strong view that a clear distinction should be drawn between disclosure to members of the scheme and the stewardship role of the trustees as set out in the annual accounts and reports of the scheme. It is generally felt that the disclosure needs of members are better met through the Summary Funding Statement (SFS), the Statutory Money Purchase Illustration (SMPI) and abbreviated reports and accounts, and that the content of the detailed accounts and reports should be restricted to matters relevant to the accountability of the trustees. There is also a strongly held view that including actuarial liabilities in pension scheme accounts could be a complex and costly exercise and would not add significantly to their value. In the case of defined benefit schemes, the funding position of the scheme is likely to be the main concern for scheme members and this information is best disclosed through the SFS. In the case of defined contribution schemes, the key issue for members is investment performance and greater attention should therefore be given to the adequacy of the SMPI. The inclusion of a number of variables in this statement appears to cause confusion and more consideration should be given to improving the content, for instance by requiring investment performance to be benchmarked against the top five performing funds and including better sensitivity analysis of estimated future investment returns and the expected size of the retirement fund.

Many respondents were not in favour of sending out the full accounts and reports to members, and felt that better use could be made of summary financial statements. However, governance of the scheme is seen as a key issue of concern to members, and there was strong support for improved communication through a governance statement. In future, summary financial statements could form the principal means of communicating with scheme member and there is scope for drawing together summary financial information and appropriate funding and governance disclosures in a single document, which could either be subject to audit or to a consistency check with the detailed accounts.

The ASB's wide-ranging review of pensions accounting (see **PARAGRAPH 17.47**) also covers pension scheme accounts. The Discussion Summary 'Pension Scheme Reporting' (which sets out only tentative views at this stage) considers the main objectives of pension scheme accounts and reports and concludes that the primary users of the information are the scheme members, on the basis that other interested parties will generally use the information provided to protect the interests of the members. The document also considers the disclosure principles that should apply to pension scheme reports and concludes that the report should include:

(i)   information on the trustees' stewardship, presented briefly, concisely and in a way that it is readily understandable to members and other users;
(ii) a corporate governance statement;
(iii) transparent and clear information about investment performance, with a realistic view of how the fund is performing at a given moment in time, and putting this into context; and
(iv) information on the investment policies adopted and the risks and rewards relevant to the assets held by the fund.

The document notes in particular that there is a need for greater clarity in reporting on investment performance and for information to be provided in a comprehensible format to enable scheme members to understand the risks that the fund is undertaking on their behalf and to be aware of the risk profile of the assets that are being managed by the scheme.

In a further major change, the document suggests that where a pension fund assumes the obligation to pay retirement benefits, it should recognise a liability for those benefits in its accounts. This is despite a general view in the UK that the costs of recognising such liabilities would outweigh the resulting benefits – the document emphasises that in many other countries the recognition of such liabilities in the scheme balance sheet has been achieved smoothly and without undue cost.

17.27   Audit

Section 47 of the *Pensions Act 1995* requires the trustees or managers of every occupational pension scheme to appoint suitably qualified auditors. The scope of the auditors' work and the format and content of their report varies depending on the nature of the scheme. Certain changes to the requirements were made by the *Occupational Pension Schemes (Administration and Audit)*

(Amendment) Regulations 2005 (SI 2005/2426) for accounting periods beginning on or after 22 September 2005. As a result, the following are now generally exempt from the requirement to appoint scheme auditors:

- Superannuation funds and unfunded schemes.
- Schemes with less than two members.
- A scheme with fewer than 12 members where all of the members are trustees, and either:
  - all trustee decisions must be made by the unanimous agreement of the trustees who are members of the scheme or
  - the scheme has an independent trustee, who is registered in accordance with regulations made under Section 23(4) of the *Pensions Act 1995*.
- A scheme with fewer than 12 members where all of the members are directors of a company which is the sole trustee of the scheme and either:
  - all decisions made by the company in its capacity as trustee must be made by the unanimous agreement of the directors who are members of the scheme or
  - one of the company directors is independent of the scheme and is registered in accordance with regulations made under Section 23(4) of the *Pensions Act 1995*.
- A scheme providing relevant benefits which, on or after 6 April 2006, is not a registered scheme and
- Certain specifically named schemes and public service schemes.

However, the trust deed for such schemes may still require an audit, even though the scheme is exempt from this requirement under the regulations. Audited accounts may also be required in certain specific circumstances, such as where an emergency scheme funding valuation or Pension Protection Fund valuation is required. Also, certain earmarked schemes that are exempt from the full audit requirement must still appoint auditors under the legislation to report on the contributions made to the scheme.

17.28   *Process for Appointing Auditors*

Where the appointment of auditors is required by law, the regulations lay down specific appointment procedures that must be followed. The trustees are required to send a Notice of Appointment to the auditors specifying:

- the date on which the appointment is to take effect;
- to whom the auditors are to report and
- from whom the auditors will take instructions.

Guidance issued by the Auditing Practices Board ('APB') recommends that the Notice should also:

- state the date of the scheme year end and specify which scheme years are to be subject to audit and
- be clear as to the name of the scheme to which the auditor is being appointed – where the appointment covers a number of schemes, there should be a separate letter for each scheme or a schedule detailing all the schemes covered.

The appointment does not become effective until the auditors have formally acknowledged receipt of the Notice of Appointment, which they are required to do within one month. They should also formally document the terms of their engagement in a letter to the trustees, to help prevent any misunderstandings over the scope of their work and the respective responsibilities of the scheme auditors, trustees and managers. If an auditor ceases to hold office for any reason, the trustees are required to make a new appointment within three months. Auditors who are invited to accept appointment after this deadline may need to report to the Pensions Regulator (see **PARAGRAPH 17.20**) the breach of duty by the trustees. Auditors who resign or are removed are required to make a statement of any circumstances connected with their resignation or removal which, in their opinion, significantly affect the interests of the members, prospective members or beneficiaries of the scheme, or to state that there are no such circumstances. A copy of the statement must be included in the annual report, except where it is simply a declaration that there are no circumstances to report.

17.29 Taxation

The HM Revenue and Customs PSO is responsible for approving and registering pension schemes for tax purposes, and for withdrawing that approval where necessary. Almost all schemes are approved under the Inland Revenue's discretionary powers rather than under the restricted conditions set out in the *Income and Corporation Taxes Act 1988*. Approval of a scheme means that employer and employee contributions to that scheme are deductible for tax purposes. Changes to an approved scheme must be notified to the PSO and approval of the scheme will automatically lapse if the alteration is not considered to be acceptable. An exempt approved scheme is exempt from UK income tax on investment income and capital gains arising on its investments.

17.30 Accounting for Pensions and Other Retirement Benefits

At a Glance
* Companies continuing to adopt UK accounting practice must comply with FRS 17 *Retirement Benefits* in accounting for pension and similar costs.
* Companies preparing IAS accounts must comply with the requirements of IAS 19 *Employee Benefits*, rather than those of FRS 17.
* In the case of a defined contribution scheme, the contributions payable by the employer for each accounting period are charged to the profit and loss account.
* In the case of a defined benefit scheme, the annual cost to the employer is more difficult to quantify and requires regular actuarial calculations to be carried out.

* Scheme assets must be measured at fair value and scheme liabilities must be measured on an actuarial basis, using the projected unit method of valuation.
* Actuarial assumptions should be mutually compatible and should achieve the best estimate of the future cash flows that will arise.
* Scheme liabilities should be discounted at the current rate of return on a high quality bond of equivalent currency and term.
* The surplus or deficit in the scheme should generally be recognised as a separate item on the face of the balance sheet.
* Accounting standards specify how the change in the net defined asset or liability each year should be reflected in the profit and loss account and statement of total recognised gains and losses.
* Detailed disclosures must be given in the notes to the accounts.
* Special requirements may apply where more than one employer participates in a defined benefit scheme (e.g. where a single scheme operates for a group of companies).

17.31   Requirements of Accounting Standards

Companies continuing to adopt UK accounting practice must comply with FRS 17 *Retirement Benefits*. The standard deals with how an employer should account for the costs and liabilities arising from the provision of retirement benefits for employees, and its requirements cover all forms of retirement benefits that an employer is committed to making, regardless of whether that commitment is statutory, contractual or implicit, and irrespective of whether the commitment arises in the UK or abroad.

Companies preparing IAS accounts must comply with IAS 19 *Employee Benefits* rather than FRS 17. The international standard is wider in scope than FRS 17, but generally imposes similar requirements on accounting for retirement benefits. The main differences are as follows:

• There is more flexibility in the accounting treatment of actuarial gains and losses under IAS 19.
• Different requirements apply to group pension schemes under IAS 19.
• IAS 19 does not allow defined benefit pension assets and liabilities to be shown net of any related deferred tax.

The requirements of both standards are complex and only an outline of the key issues is given here.

17.32   Accounting for a Defined Contribution Scheme

Accounting for a defined contribution scheme is relatively straightforward. The cost to the employer is equal to the contributions payable to the scheme for the accounting period and the charge to the profit and loss account each year will therefore represent the contributions payable by the employer in respect of that accounting period. This figure must be calculated on an accruals basis and the amount charged may therefore not be the same as the amount actually paid over to the scheme during the period. The standard specifies that the cost must be recognised in arriving at operating profit in the profit and loss account and the notes to the accounts must include the following disclosures:

- the nature of the scheme (i.e. the fact that it is a defined contribution scheme);
- the cost for the period and
- any outstanding or prepaid contributions at the balance sheet date.

17.33   Difficulties with Defined Benefit Schemes

Under a defined benefit scheme, the employer will usually have a commitment to ensure that there are sufficient funds in the scheme to pay the appropriate benefits and may be required to make good any potential deficit in the funding of the scheme. In the case of a defined benefit scheme, therefore, the full extent of the employer's commitment is more difficult to quantify and to account for. Actuarial calculations must be carried out on a regular basis to establish the overall funding level of the scheme and to assess the level of contributions required to maintain adequate funding of the scheme. One of the particular problems is the very long-term nature of such schemes and the fact that a number of assumptions about future events will need to be made in order to carry out the calculations. Most of the detailed requirements of FRS 17 and IAS 19 therefore deal with accounting for defined benefit retirement schemes.

17.34   Actuarial Valuations

Actuarial valuations provide the actuary's best estimate of the cost to the employer of providing the promised retirement benefits to employees. In carrying out a valuation, a number of assumptions about future events will need to be made and the decisions taken here can have a very significant effect on the level of contributions required. The main assumptions will cover issues such as:

- future pay increases;
- future rates of inflation;
- increases in pension payments;
- changes to the number of employees in the scheme;
- the age profile of employees and
- expected earnings from scheme investments.

Once decisions have been reached on these factors, the actuary will assess how the scheme should be funded to ensure that adequate resources are available to meet the pension commitments as they fall due. The aim is to ensure that present and future contributions to the scheme will be sufficient to secure payment of the agreed benefits to employees as they retire.

17.35   Valuation Methods

Various actuarial methods can be used to determine the liabilities of a defined benefit scheme and thus the level of contributions needed to achieve and maintain adequate funding. The two principal categories of actuarial valuation methods are:

- *Accrued benefits methods*: These are based on the principle that the obligation to provide retirement benefits to an employee will be greater as that employee gets closer to retirement.
- *Prospective benefits methods*: These are based on the principle that the obligation to provide retirement benefits to an employee accumulates evenly throughout the period of that individual's employment.

Accounting standards currently require scheme liabilities to be measured using the projected unit method. This is an accrued benefits valuation method under which allowance is made for projected earnings. Further guidance on this method is given in Guidance Note 26 (GN26) *Pension Fund Terminology* issued by the Faculty and Institute of Actuaries (for information on obtaining copies, see the Faculty and Institute of Actuaries website at www.actuaries.org.uk).

17.36   Measurement of Scheme Assets and Liabilities

Scheme assets should be measured at their fair value at the company's balance sheet date. Scheme assets include current assets as well as investments, and any current liabilities (such as accrued expenses) should be deducted. Accounting standards include specific guidance on establishing fair value for each category of pension scheme asset. Scheme liabilities comprise liabilities in respect of:

- benefits promised under the formal terms of the scheme and
- any constructive obligations for further benefits where a public statement or past practice by the employer has created a valid expectation in the employees that these benefits will be granted.

These liabilities should be measured on an actuarial basis using the projected unit method (see PARAGRAPH 17.35).

17.37   Actuarial Assumptions

Actuarial assumptions underlying the valuation of scheme liabilities should be mutually compatible (i.e. they must reflect the underlying economic factors on a consistent basis), and they should lead to the best estimate of the future cash flows that will arise. The directors (or equivalent) have ultimate responsibility for the assumptions, but they should be set on advice given by an actuary. Any assumptions that are affected by economic conditions should reflect market expectations at the balance sheet date. The assumptions should also reflect expected future events that will affect the cost of the benefits to which the employer is committed (either legally or constructively) at the balance sheet date. Depending on the nature of the scheme these will usually include:

- expected cost of living increases;
- salary increases (where the pension is to be based on final salary) and
- expected early retirement (where the scheme gives this right to employees).

Expected future redundancies should not be reflected in the assumptions as the employer is not committed to making them. When the employer does become committed to making redundancies, the impact on the scheme should be treated as a settlement or curtailment. Also, it should not be assumed that benefits will be reduced below those currently promised (e.g. on the grounds that the employer will curtail the scheme at some point in the future).

17.38   Discounting of Scheme Liabilities

Scheme liabilities should be discounted at a rate reflecting the time value of money and the characteristics of the liability. This should be assumed to be the current rate of return on a high quality (AA) corporate bond of equivalent currency and term to the scheme liabilities. If no suitable corporate bond can be identified, the rate of return on appropriate government bonds, together with a margin for assumed credit risk spreads (from the global bond markets) may provide an acceptable alternative.

17.39   Frequency of Valuations

Full actuarial valuations by a professionally qualified actuary should be obtained at intervals not exceeding three years. The actuary should review the valuation at each balance sheet date and update it to reflect current conditions – for instance, the fair values of scheme assets and financial assumptions such as the discount rate may need to be adjusted each year.

17.40   Balance Sheet Recognition of Surplus or Deficit

The surplus or deficit in a defined benefit scheme is the excess or shortfall of the value of the scheme assets over or below the present value of the scheme liabilities. The employer should recognise:

- a liability to the extent that it reflects a legal or constructive obligation to make good the deficit and
- an asset to the extent that this can be recovered through reduced contributions or through refunds from the scheme.

A legal obligation to make good a deficit in the scheme may arise under the terms of the trust deed. A constructive obligation may arise if the employer has in the past acted to make good similar deficits. A scheme surplus will give rise to an asset for the employer to the extent that the employer has control over its use as a result of past events. Under most schemes, the employer's obligation will be to pay contributions at the level recommended by the actuary to keep the scheme fully funded. There will not usually be any requirement to generate a surplus in the scheme. Where a surplus does arise, it is therefore unlikely that the employer could be required to continue to make contributions to maintain the surplus. Also, the decision on whether the surplus should be used to improve scheme benefits will usually rest with the employer. In most cases, therefore, control over the use of a surplus will rest with the employer. FRS 17 gives detailed guidance on determining the amount that can be recovered from reduced contributions, reflecting refunds from the scheme in the accounts of the employer and accounting for a surplus that is used to improve benefits.

17.41   Balance Sheet Presentation

Where Companies Act accounts are prepared (see **PARAGRAPH 10.5**) any unpaid pension contributions at the balance sheet date should be shown within creditors due within one year. The defined benefit asset or liability, net of any related deferred tax, should be shown separately on the face of the balance sheet as follows:

- In a balance sheet prepared under Format 1 of *Schedule 4* to the *Companies Act 1985*, after item J (Accruals and deferred income) but before item K (Capital and reserves).
- In a balance sheet prepared under Format 2 of *Schedule 4* to the *Companies Act 1985*, an asset should be shown after item D (Prepayments and accrued income) in the 'Assets' section and a liability should be shown after item D (Accruals and deferred income) in the 'Liabilities' section.

Appendix I to FRS 17 gives an example layout for this disclosure. Where an employer has more than one scheme, the total of any defined benefit assets and the total of any defined benefit liabilities should be shown separately on the face of the balance sheet.

17.42   Performance Statements

FRS 17 requires the change in the net defined benefit asset or liability (other than changes arising from contributions to the scheme) to be analysed into its detailed components and prescribes how each component should be reflected in the performance statements (i.e. the profit and loss account and statement of total recognised gains and losses).
   Broadly:

- current service cost should be taken into account in arriving at operating profit;
- the net of interest cost and the expected return on assets should be shown as other finance costs, adjacent to interest on the profit and loss account; and
- actuarial gains and losses should be recognised in the statement of total recognised gains and losses.

The standard also includes detailed requirements on accounting for past service costs (which arise when an employer commits to providing a higher level of benefit than previously promised), settlements, curtailments, and death in service and incapacity benefits. It also deals with accounting for any tax effects arising from pension costs and commitments.

IAS 19 analyses the changes in scheme assets and liabilities into the same components as FRS 17, but only requires recognition of the net total in the income statement.

17.43   Disclosure

The disclosure requirements of FRS 17 have been aligned with those required under IAS 19 for accounting periods beginning on or after 6 April 2007. The principal disclosures now required for defined benefit schemes include:

- Information that enables users of the financial statements to evaluate the nature of the entity's defined benefit schemes and the financial effects of changes in those schemes during the accounting period.
- A general description of the type of scheme.
- A detailed reconciliation of opening and closing balances of the present value of scheme liabilities.
- An analysis of scheme liabilities into amounts arising from schemes that are wholly unfunded and those that are wholly or partly funded.
- A detailed reconciliation of the opening and closing balance of the fair value of scheme assets.
- A reconciliation of the present value of scheme liabilities and the fair value of scheme assets to the assets and liabilities recognised in the balance sheet.
- A detailed analysis of the total expense or income recognised in the performance statement(s).
- For each major category of scheme assets, the percentage or amount that each constitutes of the fair value of total scheme assets.
- The amounts included in the fair value of scheme assets for:
  ○ each category of the entity's own financial instruments;
  ○ any property occupied by, or other assets use by, the entity.
- A narrative description of the basis used to determine the overall expected rate of return on assets, including the effect of the major categories of scheme assets.
- The actual return on scheme assets.
- The principal actuarial assumptions used as at the balance sheet date.
- The effect of a one percentage point increase and decrease in the assumed retirement healthcare cost trend rates on:
  ○ the aggregate of the current service cost and interest cost components of net periodic retirement healthcare costs;
  ○ the accumulated retirement healthcare obligation for healthcare costs.
- The employer's best estimate of contributions expected to be paid to the scheme during the accounting period beginning after the balance sheet date.

- The amounts for the current accounting period and the previous four accounting periods of:
  - the present value of scheme liabilities, the fair value of scheme assets and the surplus or deficit in the scheme; and
  - the experience adjustments arising on scheme liabilities and scheme assets, expressed either as an amount or as a percentage of scheme liabilities or scheme assets, respectively, at the balance sheet date.

17.44   ASB Reporting Statement 'Retirement Benefits: Disclosures'

The ASB also published a Reporting Statement 'Retirement Benefits: Disclosures' in January 2007. This is non-mandatory, but sets out best practice guidance with the aim of promoting greater transparency in reporting on defined benefit retirement schemes. The guidance has been prepared in the context of current UK accounting practice but the underlying principles of the recommendations may also be relevant to those preparing IAS accounts.

The Statement identifies six principles that should be considered when reporting on defined benefit schemes:

- the relationship between the reporting entity and the trustees (or managers) of the defined benefit scheme;
- the principal assumptions used to measure scheme liabilities;
- the sensitivity of the principal assumptions used to measure scheme liabilities;
- how liabilities arising from the defined benefit scheme are measured;
- future funding obligations in respect of the defined benefit scheme and
- the nature and extent of the risks arising from financial instruments held by the defined benefit scheme.

The Statement recommends that directors provide certain additional disclosures in the notes to the accounts to complement those required by FRS 17 *Retirement Benefits*. These are intended to help accounts users to assess the risks and rewards arising from such a scheme, but provide companies with a degree of flexibility in how they present the relevant information, depending on the significance of the issues in their particular circumstances. The recommended additional disclosures include:

- Information to enable users to understand the relationship between the reporting entity and the trustees of the scheme.
- Sufficient information about the principal assumptions used to measure scheme liabilities (including mortality rates) to enable users to understand the inherent uncertainties.
- A sensitivity analysis for the principal assumptions used to measure scheme liabilities.
- Information to enable users to understand the method of measuring scheme liabilities, including the cost of buying out benefits where this information is made available to trustees or members of the scheme.

- Information to allow users to assess the entity's funding obligations in respect of the scheme, including:
  - any funding principles that the entity has agreed or chosen to operate in respect of the scheme;
  - where relevant, any additional contributions and the number of years over which the entity has agreed to make these in order to reduce or recover a deficit in the scheme;
  - the duration of scheme liabilities;
  - information to allow users to assess the projected cash flows of the scheme – the guidance notes that this might usefully be provided in graphical form.
- Information to enable users to evaluate the entity's exposure to the risks and rewards of financial instruments held by the scheme, including:
  - the exposures to risk and how they arise;
  - the methods used to measure risk;
  - the approach to managing risk and
  - any changes in these issues from the previous period.

The Statement includes illustrative examples for each of these recommendations.

17.45 Entities with More than One Defined Benefit Scheme

Where an employer has more than one defined benefit scheme, the required disclosures may be given in total, separately or in such groupings as are felt to be most useful (for instance, by geographical location, or where schemes are subject to significantly different risks). Where the disclosures are given in total, the assumptions should be given in the form of weighted averages or relatively narrow ranges, with separate disclosure of any items outside the range.

17.46 Multi-employer Schemes

In some cases, more than one employer may participate in the same retirement scheme. For instance, this situation is relatively common in groups of companies, where a single retirement scheme is operated for the whole group and each subsidiary participates in the scheme in respect of its own employees. If the scheme is a defined contribution scheme, the multi-employer aspect does not give rise to any particular accounting issues. Where more than one employer participates in a defined benefit scheme, the general requirement under FRS 17 is that each employer should account for the scheme as a defined benefit scheme. However, the standard recognises that this may not be appropriate or practical in every case and two specific exceptions to this general rule are therefore permitted.

- Where the employer's contributions are set in relation to the current service period only (i.e. they are not affected by any surplus or deficit in the scheme relating to the past service of its own employees or any other members of the scheme), the scheme should be accounted for as a defined contribution scheme – this treatment should only be adopted where there is clear evidence

Pension Arrangements for Employees

that the employer cannot be required to pay additional contributions relating to past service, including the existence of a third party which accepts the obligation to fund the pension payments if the scheme's assets should prove to be insufficient.

- Where the employer's contributions are affected by a surplus or deficit in the scheme but the employer is unable to identify its share of the underlying assets and liabilities in the scheme on a consistent and reasonable basis, the employer should account for the scheme as a defined contribution scheme but should disclose:
  - the fact that the scheme is a defined benefit scheme but the employer is unable to identify its share of the underlying assets and liabilities; and
  - any available information on the surplus or deficit in the scheme and the implications for the employer.

In the case of a group scheme, the second exception only enables the individual subsidiaries (and, where appropriate, the parent company in its own individual accounts) to account for the scheme as a defined contribution scheme. The scheme must still be accounted for as defined benefit scheme in the group accounts, as it does not constitute a multi-employer scheme at this level and the impracticality of identifying individual shares of the underlying assets and liabilities is no longer relevant.

Although IAS 19 includes similar requirements to FRS 17 in respect of multi-employer plans, it also includes separate requirements on accounting for group pension plans and specifically excludes from the definition of multi-employer plans any defined benefit plans that share risks between various entities under common control, for example a parent and its subsidiaries. In the case of group pension plan, information on the plan as a whole should be obtained in accordance with IAS 19 and the net cost should then be apportioned between the entities participating in the plan as follows:

- where there is a contractual agreement or stated group policy for sharing the costs of the plan, the costs should be recognised in the accounts of the individual group entities in line with that agreement or policy; or
- where there is no contractual agreement or stated group policy for sharing the costs of the plan, the full cost of the plan should be recognised in the accounts of the entity that is the sponsoring employer under law, and the other group entities should recognise in their individual accounts a cost equal to their contribution payable for the reporting period.

17.47 Possible Changes to Accounting Requirements

In October 2005, the ASB announced that it was undertaking a research project into accounting for pension costs. The implementation of FRS 17 has given rise to comments on a number of issues and the UK legal and regulatory environment for company pension schemes has changed significantly since the standard was originally published. In particular, a number of the changes introduced by the Pensions Act 2004 may have an impact on relevant financial reporting issues. There are also certain differences between FRS 17 and IAS 19, and the international standard is also likely to be reviewed in the relatively near future. The ASB's project is therefore intended to assist the future development of both UK standards and IASs and is intended to consider the fundamental principles of pensions accounting, as well as financial reporting by pension schemes. Particular issues identified for consideration include:

- How the relationship between an employer and a pension scheme can best be reflected in the employer's financial statements.
- How an employer's liability in respect of pensions should be quantified, including:
  ○ the most appropriate actuarial method to use;
  ○ whether the employer's liability should reflect future salary increases;
  ○ what discount rate should be used to translate future cash flows into a realistic present value.
- Whether (and, if so, how) the expected return on assets should be reflected in the employer's financial statements.
- The impact on financial reporting of recent regulatory developments and
- Whether the disclosures currently required are still appropriate.

17.48   *Preliminary Views*

In April 2007, the ASB published five Discussion Summaries as an update on the progress of the review but emphasised that:

- these were being issued to provide up to date information on the status of the project;
- each summary represented work-in-progress towards a formal discussion paper and
- only tentative preliminary views were being expressed at this stage – the preliminary conclusions did not represent official ASB opinions, and may change as the project progresses.

The Discussion Summary on pension scheme reporting is considered at **PARAGRAPH 17.26**, in conjunction with earlier proposals put forward by the Pensions Regulator. The contents of the other four Discussion Summaries are summarised below. All of the documents are available from the ASB website at http://www.frc.org.uk/asb/technical/projects/project0065.html.

17.49   *Asset Measurement*

The first Discussion Summary considers the options for measuring assets used to fund an entity's retirement benefit obligations. It notes that such assets are closely linked to scheme liabilities because they ultimately provide the cash to settle the liabilities when they fall due. Accounts users therefore need to understand how the assets and liabilities interrelate. The paper considers the type of asset commonly held to fund retirement benefit obligations and reviews the various measurement methods required for such assets by current accounting standards. The preliminary conclusion is that:

- the measurement of scheme assets should be based on current (rather than historical) information;
- market-based measures (such as market value) are more appropriate than entity-specific measures (such as value in use), and that exit price is a more appropriate measure than entry price and
- where there is no active market for an asset, a market-based value should be estimated using valuation techniques set out in other accounting standards, with supporting disclosures on the techniques used and the nature and extent of risks arising.

17.50   *Retirement Benefit Liabilities*

The second Discussion Summary considers the measurement of retirement benefit liabilities and is the longest and most complex of the five documents. It considers the measurement principles used in accounting for liabilities in general, but notes that the significant differences in respect of pension liabilities include the complexity of the arrangements, the length of time between liabilities being incurred and settled, and the range of factors that can create uncertainty over the eventual outcome. The preliminary views expressed in the paper include:

- a current value approach to measurement is the most appropriate;
- measurement should generally be based on the 'settlement amount', reflecting the cash outflows needed to settle the liability, now or in the future;
- in the absence of an active transfer market, fair value is not an adequate or appropriate measurement objective for retirement benefit liabilities;
- where alternative means of settling a liability are available and within the employer's control, the liability should be reported at the lowest amount and
- measurement of the liability should include any settlement expenses.

17.51   *Recognition and Presentation*

The third Discussion Summary considers how the cost of retirement benefits should be recognised and presented in the employer's accounts and what should be recognised in the balance sheet in respect of retirement benefit funds. The total cost for retirement benefits comprises a number of different components and the paper concludes that each of these should be presented separately in the profit and loss account line item to which it relates. In particular, this will enable an appropriate distinction to be made between operating and financing items.

Three options are considered for the treatment of actuarial gains and losses:

- recognition in the profit and loss account;
- immediate recognition in a statement of other recognised income and expense and

- immediate recognition in a statement of other recognised income and expense, but with eventual recycling to the profit and loss account.

The preliminary view is that actuarial gains and losses are in effect changes in the estimate of the liability for retirement benefits from one accounting period to another and that the first option is the only justifiable accounting treatment. The main advantages are that it is easy to understand and consistent with the treatment of other estimated provisions. The main disadvantages are increased volatility in the profit and loss account and an inability to distinguish changes that are outside management's control.

This Discussion Summary also concludes that:

- where material, actuarial gains and losses should be presented as a single line item in the profit and loss account on the basis that this makes it easier for users to understand the remeasurement that has taken place and to appreciate the inherent uncertainty in the measurement of liabilities and
- the actual return on assets should be reported in the profit and loss account – accounting standards currently require the expected return to be included in the profit and loss account, with any difference between this and the actual return treated as an actuarial gain or loss.

17.52 Consolidation

The fourth Discussion Summary considers whether retirement benefit funds should be included in the consolidated accounts of the employer. The paper notes that this needs to be considered in the context of providing useful information to users of the employer's financial statements and that, where the entity holds sufficient rights in relation to scheme assets and liabilities for the fund to be considered part of the entity, consolidation provides more useful information about the resources available to the entity. Present UK accounting is based on the premise that trustees control the retirement benefits fund, so that it is not generally regarded as a subsidiary or quasi-subsidiary of the employer, but the Discussion Summary questions whether this presumption is correct. It notes that the relationship between the sponsoring entity and the trustees, and in particular the power of the trustees, is fundamental in establishing who controls the retirement benefits fund. Whether the trustees are independent of the employer will generally be evident from the actions of the trustees, and the ability to control the investment and funding policies of the fund is a critical issue.

Pension Arrangements
for Employees

Appendix 1

Useful Websites on Pensions Issues

The Pensions Regulator	www.thepensionsregulator.gov.uk
The Trustee Toolkit	www.trusteetoolkit.com
The Pension Service	www.thepensionservice.gov.uk
Department of Work and Pensions	www.dwp.gov.uk
Pension Advisory Service	www.stakeholderhelpline.org.uk
The Pension Trust	www.thepensiontrust.org.uk
Occupational Pensioners Alliance	www.opalliance.org.uk
Business Link	www.businesslink.gov.uk
Institute of Directors	www.iod.com
Faculty and Institute of Actuaries	www.actuaries.org.uk
Accounting Standards Board	www.frc.org.uk/asb
Pension Research Accountants Group	www.prag.org.uk
HM Revenue and Customs	www.hmrc.gov.uk
Chartered Institute of Management Accountants	www.cimaglobal.com

Remuneration Committee

Remuneration Committee

Remuneration Committee

18 Remuneration Committee

18.1 Establishing a Remuneration Committee

At a Glance
* The Combined Code sets out two main principles and three supporting principles on the setting and make-up of directors' remuneration.
* A remuneration committee should be established to make recommendations to the main board on remuneration policy and to determine the remuneration package of each individual director.
* The remuneration committee should have at least three members, all of whom are independent non-executive directors of the company.
* Subject to certain conditions, the company chairman may be an additional member of the remuneration committee, but should not chair it.
* The chairman and the chief executive may attend meetings of the remuneration committee by invitation.
* It is normal practice for the committee to take external advice.

18.2 Combined Code Principles

Section B of the Combined Code includes the following main principles in respect of remuneration:

* levels of remuneration should be sufficient to attract and retain the directors needed to run the company successfully, although companies should avoid paying more than is necessary for this purpose, and a significant proportion of executive directors' remuneration should be structured to link rewards to corporate and individual performance and
* there should be a formal and transparent procedure for developing policy on executive remuneration and for fixing the remuneration packages of individual directors, and no director should be involved in setting his/her own remuneration.

The supporting principles in this section of the Code emphasise that:

* the remuneration committee should judge where to position the company relative to other companies, but should use such comparisons with caution in

view of the risk of increasing remuneration levels without a corresponding improvement in performance;

- the remuneration committee should also be sensitive to pay and employment conditions elsewhere in the group, especially when determining annual salary increases;
- the remuneration committee should consult the chairman and/or chief executive about proposals on the remuneration of other executive directors;
- the remuneration committee should be responsible for appointing any consultants in respect of the remuneration of executive directors;
- if executive directors or senior management are involved in advising or supporting the remuneration committee, care should be taken to recognise and avoid conflicts of interest and
- the chairman of the board should ensure that the company maintains appropriate contact with its principal shareholders on remuneration issues in the same way as for other matters.

18.3   Membership of the Remuneration Committee

The best practice provisions in the Combined Code recommend that the board establishes a remuneration committee of at least three non-executive directors (or two in the case of a smaller company) all of whom are independent of management and free from any business or other relationship which could materially affect their independent judgement (see **PARAGRAPH 6.17**). As a result of a change made to the Code in June 2006, the company chairman may be an additional member of the remuneration committee (but should not chair it) if he/she was considered to be independent at the time of his/her appointment as chairman (see **PARAGRAPH 6.17**). The committee should make available its terms of reference (for instance, by publication on a website maintained by or on behalf of the company) to explain its role and the authority delegated to it by the board. If remuneration consultants are appointed, a statement should also be made on whether they have any other connection with the company – once again, this could be dealt with by publication on the relevant website.

The remuneration committee should have delegated responsibility for setting the remuneration of all executive directors and the company chairman, including pension rights and any compensation payments. Where the company chairman is a member of the committee, it should be remembered that the principle that no director should be involved in setting his or her own remuneration (see **PARAGRAPH 18.2**) continues to apply.

The committee should also recommend and monitor the level and structure of remuneration for senior management. The definition of senior management for this purpose should be decided by the board but should normally include the first layer of management below board level. The board (or the shareholders where the company's articles require this) should determine the remuneration of the non-executive directors but, where the company's articles permit, responsibility for this may be delegated to a small sub-committee, which may include the chief executive.

Shareholders should be specifically invited to approve all new long-term incentive schemes and significant changes to existing schemes, other than in the circumstances permitted by the Listing Rules.

The IRS/3i 2003 survey contained a special analysis of the workings on remuneration committees. The information below is based on the responses of 283 members of remuneration committees. The size of the committee inevitably relates to the size of the company but this is how they responded with regard to size of the committee when asked to think about their most and least effective remuneration committees.

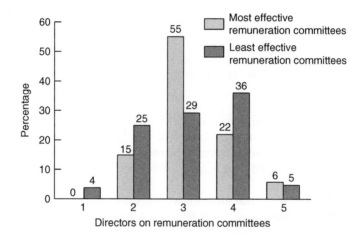

So the conclusion appears to be that effective remuneration committees tend to have three or four members.

In the most effective committees 80% of the membership were non-executive directors compared with only 58% in the least effective. Given Higgs recommendations it would have been interesting to see whether there was any difference in performance between those with only independent non-executives.

With regard to selecting a chairman for the remuneration committee there was an interesting difference in approach between the most and least effective remuneration committees.

How is the chairman of the remuneration committee chosen?

So unsurprisingly chairmen chosen on the basis of their skills, knowledge or relevant experience seem to be more prevalent in the most effective and those chosen ritualistically more prevalent in the weaker committees. Chairing this committee has become an increasingly important and complex job so it is important that the chairman is chosen professionally.

There is surprisingly little training available on this subject thoughmost of the major consultancies operating in this area provide regular update briefings.

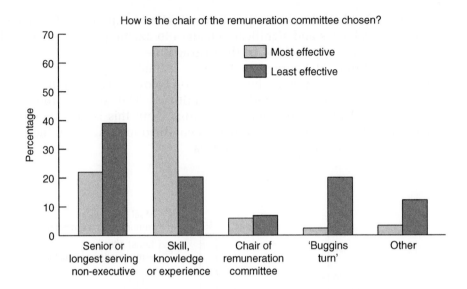

The tenure of members was something also looked at in the IRS/3i survey. A surprisingly high number, some two-thirds, had no fixed term, and there was little variation between chairman or member of the committee. This was not a topic that the sample had strong views on, believing that best practice was developing.

One observation the authors would make with regard to composition has to do with communication. It is important that at least one of the members is knowledgeable and skilled in the communication aspects of remuneration. Many highly successful companies have had issues in this area through weak communication and it is a subject the press especially in the UK are both vigilant and expert in.

18.4   Attendance at Meetings

Independence is considered a critical issue in this sensitive area, in which there is plenty of scope for conflicts of interest. Although membership of the committee should be restricted to independent non-executive directors, the company chairman and chief executive may attend meetings when invited to do so. In this context, it should be noted that the best practice provisions state that the remuneration committee should consult the chairman and/or chief executive about the proposals on the remuneration of other executive directors.

Membership of the remuneration committee requires a significant time commitment as the chart on page 24 shows with c three days per year of formal time. In order to keep up to date with best practice members of remuneration committees might also commit further time in addition to preparing for meetings in attending conferences and seminars on the subject.

	Days	Chairman (%)	Member (%)
Formal meetings	1	5	23
	2	41	27
	3	17	13
	4	17	19
	5+	20	18
Informal	1	16	40
	2	33	22
	3	18	14
	4+	33	24
Preparation	1	36	50
	2	31	35
	3	13	7
	4+	20	8

18.5   The Use of Remuneration Consultants

Given the complexity of remuneration issues and the need to consider remuneration policy and quantum in relation to the market as a whole it is normal for remuneration consultants to be employed to assist the work of the committee.

We would suggest that the same principles be adopted as those used in choosing other professional advisers. There should be a clear role, there should be a competitive pitch and they should be managed tightly.

Where consultants are to be appointment to assist with the setting of executive remuneration, the remuneration committee should be responsible for the appointment and a formal statement should be published on whether they have any other connection with the company (see PARAGRAPHS **18.2** and **18.3**).

The use of independent remuneration consultants has become the norm where there is a formal remuneration committee in place. The 2007 Independent Remuneration Solutions Independent Chairman and Non-Executive director survey to which 256 directors who sat on 442 remuneration committees showed that 89% of companies with formal remuneration committees used one or more advisers.

18.6   Duties of the Remuneration Committee

At a Glance
* The responsibilities of the remuneration committee should be set out in formal terms of reference, which should be made publicly available.
* These responsibilities normally include determining the following:
  ○ remuneration policy;
  ○ targets for performance-related pay;
  ○ pension arrangements;
  ○ termination payments;

Remuneration Committee

> ○ the individual remuneration package for each director;
> ○ where relevant, the selection and appointment of external consultants;
> ○ ensuring that the company complies with all relevant reporting requirements in respect of directors' remuneration.
> * Performance-related elements should normally form a significant part of the total remuneration package for executive directors.
> * The remuneration committee is responsible for setting the level and structure of any compensation payments to directors.

18.7   Terms of Reference

The terms of reference of the remuneration committee should set out the committee's delegated responsibilities and should be subject to annual review. They should also be made publicly available, usually by publication on a website maintained by or on behalf of the company. The main duties of the remuneration committee will normally include:

- *Remuneration policy*: The remuneration committee should determine and agree with the board the framework or broad policy for the remuneration of the chairman and other executives, and of senior management as designated by the board. The committee may be asked to consider the remuneration packages of all executives at or above a specified management level, or to deal with all packages above a certain figure. In particular, the Higgs suggestions for good practice (see **PARAGRAPH 6.8**) recommend that:
  - ○ as a minimum, the remuneration committee should have delegated responsibility for setting the remuneration for all executive directors, the chairman and the company secretary;
  - ○ the remuneration of the non-executive directors should be considered by the chairman and the executive directors and
  - ○ no director or manager should be involved in setting his/her own remuneration.
- *Performance-related pay*: The remuneration committee should determine the targets for any performance-related pay schemes operated by the company.
- *Pension arrangements*: The remuneration committee should determine the policy for, and scope of, the pension arrangements for each executive director.
- *Termination payments*: The remuneration committee should ensure that contractual terms in respect of termination payments, and any payments actually made, are fair to both the individual and the company. In particular, the committee has a responsibility to ensure that failure is not rewarded and that the duty to mitigate loss is fully recognised.
- *Individual remuneration packages*: The remuneration committee should determine the remuneration of each executive director, within the terms of the agreed policy, including where appropriate the award of bonuses, incentive payments and share options. In doing so, the committee should give due regard to the

recommendations in the Combined Code and related guidance and, where appropriate, any requirements of the Financial Services Authority (FSA).

- *Expenses*: The remuneration committee should agree the policy for authorising claims for expenses by the chairman and the chief executive.
- *Employee benefits*: The remuneration committee should be aware of, and advise on, any major changes in employee benefit structures within the company or group.
- *External advice*: Where remuneration consultants are to be appointed in an advisory capacity, the remuneration committee should have exclusive responsibility for establishing the selection criteria and for selecting, appointing and setting their terms of reference.
- *Disclosure*: The remuneration committee is responsible for ensuring that:
  - the company complies with the disclosure requirements of the *Directors' Remuneration Report Regulations 2002 (SI 2002/1986)* and of the Combined Code (see CHAPTER 9);
  - the frequency of, and attendance levels at, meetings of the remuneration committee are disclosed in the company's annual report and
  - the committee's terms of reference are made publicly available.

The Institute of Chartered Secretaries and Administrators (ICSA) produces a useful specimen terms of reference for a remuneration committee. A further example is set out in APPENDIX 2 to this chapter.

18.8 Developing Remuneration Policy

Judgements on remuneration require sensitivity, both to the expectations of the individual directors concerned and to the concerns and perceptions of investors and other stakeholders, such as employees. The Combined Code emphasises that the remuneration committee should:

- provide the packages necessary to attract, retain and motivate executive directors of the required quality, but should avoid paying more than is necessary;
- judge where to position the company relative to other companies, and be aware of the remuneration packages and relative performance of other companies, but use such comparisons with caution in view of the risk of increasing remuneration levels without a corresponding improvement in performance and
- be sensitive to the wider scene, including pay and conditions elsewhere in the group, especially when determining annual salary increases.

There is particular concern that external remuneration consultants may be currently perceived as being too close to executive management and too willing to encourage companies to position themselves in the top quartile of their peer group. Hence the Combined Code recommendation that, where consultants are to be appointed, their selection and terms of reference should be controlled by the remuneration committee and not by the executive directors.

The Government has also indicated its intention to require the annual directors' remuneration report prepared by quoted companies (see PARAGRAPH 9.20) to include an analysis of the general pattern of remuneration for the company as a whole and how this has been taken into account in setting the remuneration of the directors. This change is expected to be included in regulations under the *Companies Act 2006* and to apply for accounting periods beginning on or after 6 April 2008.

18.9   Make-Up of Remuneration

The best practice provisions in the Combined Code include the following points:

- performance-related elements should form a significant proportion of the total remuneration package for executive directors and should be designed to align their interests with those of the shareholder, and to give the directors a keen incentive to perform at the highest levels;
- executive share options should not be issued at a discount, except as permitted by the FSA Listing Rules;
- in designing schemes of performance-related remuneration, the committee should follow the provisions set out in Schedule A to the Combined Code (see **PARAGRAPH 18.10**) and
- the levels of remuneration for non-executive directors should reflect the time, commitment and responsibilities of the role and should not include share options.

Also, where a company releases an executive director to serve as a non-executive director elsewhere, the Combined Code recommends that the remuneration report should state whether or not the director will retain earnings from the appointment and, if so, what the remuneration is.

18.10   Performance-Related Pay

Schedule A to the Combined Code comprises the guidance originally set out in the Greenbury Code of Best Practice on directors' remuneration, with a number of minor wording changes. It recommends that:

- the remuneration committee should consider whether directors should be eligible for annual bonuses and, if so, performance conditions should be relevant, stretching and designed to enhance the business – upper limits should always be considered and there may be a case for part payment in shares to be held for a significant period;
- the remuneration committee should consider whether the directors should be eligible for benefits under long-term incentive schemes, and in establishing such schemes should:
  - weigh traditional share option schemes against other kinds of long-term incentive schemes;
  - generally ensure that shares granted and other forms of deferred remuneration do not vest, and options are not exercisable, in less than three years;
  - encourage directors to hold their shares for a further period after vesting or exercise, subject to the need to finance any costs of acquisition or associated tax liabilities;

- where new long-term incentive schemes are proposed, these should be approved by the shareholders and should generally replace existing schemes, or at least form part of a well-considered overall plan incorporating existing schemes – the total rewards potentially available should not be excessive;
- payouts or grants under all incentive schemes (including new grants under existing share option schemes) should be subject to challenging performance criteria reflecting the company's objectives, and consideration should be given to criteria which reflect the company's performance relative to a group of comparator companies in certain key variables such as total shareholder return;
- grants under executive share option and other long-term incentive schemes should normally be phased rather than awarded in one large block;
- the remuneration committee should consider the pension consequences and associated costs to the company of increases in basic salary and other changes in remuneration, especially for directors close to retirement and
- in general, neither annual bonuses nor benefits in kind should be pensionable.

18.11   Compensation Payments

The remuneration committee should also be responsible for setting the level and structure of compensation payments for senior executives. The best practice provisions of the Combined Code recommend that:

- the remuneration committee should carefully consider what compensation commitments (including pension contributions and any other elements) the directors' terms of appointment would entail in the event of early termination – the aim should be to avoid rewarding poor performance and to take a robust line on reducing compensation to reflect a departing director's obligations to mitigate loss and
- notice or contract periods should be set at one year or less – if it is necessary to offer longer notice or contract periods to new directors recruited externally, these periods should reduce to one year or less after the initial period.

The original Combined Code included a recommendation that the remuneration committee should consider the advantages of providing explicitly in the initial contract for compensation commitments other than in the case of removal for misconduct and, where compensation was not covered in a director's contract, should tailor their approach in the case of early termination to the wide variety of circumstances. These elements have now been removed from the best practice provisions.

18.12   Issues of Concern to Shareholders

The Institutional Shareholders' Committee (ISC) represents the interests and concerns of institutional investors, with representatives from the Association of British Insurers (ABI), the National Association of Pension Funds (NAPF), the Association of Investment Trust Companies (AITC) and the Investment Management Association (IMA). The ISC issues guidance to institutional investors covering issues such as communication with boards, the use of voting rights, board composition, directors' remuneration and takeover bids. Voting guidelines are also issued regularly to institutional investors by organisations such as NAPF, ABI and PIRC (Pensions Investment Research Consultants), based on their assessment of the key current issues. Issues that have received most focus include directors' remuneration (including incentive schemes, service contracts and notice periods), the independence of non-executive directors and issues relating to the external audit (e.g. the level of non-audit services provided by the auditors, connections between the directors and auditors, reappointment or changes in the appointment of auditors, and the role and constitution of the audit committee). Members of the remuneration committee are therefore advised to keep track of the issues being raised by these organisations in the area of directors' remuneration. Relevant information can usually be found on their websites and in some cases will be circulated to larger listed companies in advance of the publication date for their annual reports and accounts.

18.13 Meetings and Agendas

At a Glance
* The number and frequency of meetings will vary, depending on the circumstances of the company, but the remuneration committee should meet at least once each year.
* The company secretary should act as secretary to the committee.
* Minutes of remuneration committee meetings should be circulated to all main board directors.
* The annual report should list the members of the remuneration committee and give details of the number of meetings held and the attendance levels.
* The effectiveness of the remuneration committee should be reviewed each year.

18.14 Meetings of the Remuneration Committee

The number and frequency of remuneration committee meetings will vary depending on the specific circumstances of the company and the precise remit of the committee, as set out in its terms of reference. The committee must meet at least once a year to prepare the company's annual remuneration report. This meeting will need to be scheduled close to the year-end to ensure the availability of the relevant information for the financial year. Further information on this report, and a checklist of the required contents, can be found in CHAPTER 9.

18.15 Secretary

It is recommended that the company secretary acts as secretary to the remuneration committee. This should ensure that the committee has access to appropriate advice on procedural or constitutional issues and should facilitate appropriate liaison and co-ordination with the other main board committees.

18.16   Minutes

The proceedings and decisions taken at meetings of the remuneration committee should be formally recorded and copies of the minutes should be circulated to all members of the main board for information. It is also good practice to keep detailed attendance records for remuneration committee meetings and for the board of directors to review these on an annual basis to confirm that each member is making an appropriate contribution to the work of the committee. Attendance information will also need to be retained for inclusion in the annual report on the committee's activities (see PARAGRAPH 18.17).

18.17   Reporting to Shareholders

The Combined Code recommends that the annual report should include:

- the names of all members of the remuneration committee during the period;
- the number of remuneration committee meetings and the attendance by each member and
- a description of the work of the remuneration committee, as required by the *Directors' Remuneration Report Regulations 2002 (SI 2002/1986)*.

As explained above, the remuneration committee is also responsible for ensuring that the company complies with all of the necessary disclosure requirements in respect of directors' remuneration. Where relevant, this includes the requirement for a formal statement on whether external consultants appointed to assist with executive remuneration have any other connection with the company (see PARAGRAPH 18.5).

18.18   Self-assessment and Appraisal

The Combined Code recommends that the effectiveness of the board and each of its main committees should be reviewed and evaluated annually by the board (see PARAGRAPH 6.24). This might be done by considering developments generally in the role and activities of remuneration committees and discussing the extent to which the remuneration committee is considered to have fulfilled the various aspects of its terms of reference. Specific issues to consider might include:

- Are there appropriate procedures for appointing committee members?
- Does the committee have the appropriate mix of knowledge and skills?
- Is the amount and nature of training and administrative support appropriate?
- Are the committee's terms of reference appropriate?
- Does the committee adequately fulfil its role?
- Is the frequency and timing of committee meetings appropriate?
- Are agendas and appropriate supporting information circulated to committee members in good time?

Remuneration Committee

- Does the committee's workload require a change of emphasis?
- What significant issues does the committee need to address in the coming year?

It is also best practice for the chairman of the main board, together with the executive directors, to review the contribution of individual non-executives to the work of the board, including where appropriate their activities as members of the remuneration committee.

Appendix 1

Useful Websites on Issues Relating to Remuneration Committees

Financial Reporting Council	www.frc.org.uk
Financial Services Authority	www.fsa.gov.uk
Institute of Directors	www.iod.com
Institute of Chartered Secretaries and Administrators	www.icsa.org.uk
Institute of Chartered Accountants in England and Wales	www.icaew.co.uk

Remuneration Committee

Appendix 2

Specimen Terms of Reference for a Remuneration Committee

These specimen terms of reference are for guidance only and should be developed and adapted as necessary to suit the specific circumstances of the company or group.

1   Constitution

1.1   The Board hereby resolves to establish a committee of the board, to be known as the Remuneration Committee ('the committee').

2   Membership

2.1   The committee shall be appointed by the board on the recommendation of the Nomination Committee in consultation with the chairman of the Remuneration Committee. All members of the committee shall be non-executive directors of the company who are independent of management and free from any business or other relationship which could interfere with the exercise of their independent judgement. The committee shall consist of not less than three members. Two members shall comprise a quorum at any meeting of the committee.

2.2   In addition, the Company Chairman may be a member of the Remuneration Committee provided that he was independent at the time of his appointment as Company Chairman.

2.3   The chairman of the committee shall be appointed by the Board from amongst the independent non-executive directors. The Company Chairman shall not chair the Remuneration Committee.

2.4   Appointments to the Remuneration Committee shall be for a period of up to three years, which may be extended for two further three-year periods, provided the director remains independent.

3   Secretary

3.1   The Company Secretary or their nominee shall act as the Secretary of the committee.

4   Meetings

4.1   The committee shall meet (not less than once a year) (quarterly) and at such other times as the chairman of the committee shall require.

4.2   Meetings shall be convened by the Secretary of the committee at the request of any committee member.

4.3   Unless otherwise agreed, notice of each meeting confirming the venue, time and date together with an agenda of items to be discussed, shall be forwarded to each member of the committee, any other person required to attend and all other non-executive directors, no fewer than … working days prior to the date of the meeting.

4.4   Only members of the Remuneration Committee have the right to attend committee meetings, but the Chief Executive, Company Chairman (if not a member of the committee) and Director of Human Resources may attend meetings at the invitation of the committee.

5   Minutes of Meetings

5.1   The Secretary shall minute the proceedings and resolutions of all committee meetings, including the names of those present and in attendance.

5.2   Minutes of committee meetings shall be circulated promptly to all members of the Remuneration Committee and, once agreed, to all members of the board, unless a conflict of interest exists.

6   Authority

6.1   The Remuneration Committee is authorised by the board to seek any information it requires from any employee of the company in order to perform its duties.

6.2   In connection with its duties, the Remuneration Committee is authorised by the board to obtain, at the company's expense, any necessary external legal or other professional advice.

6.3   The Remuneration Committee shall be exclusively responsible for establishing the selection criteria, selecting, appointing and setting the terms of reference for any remuneration consultants who advise the committee and assist in the provision of reliable, up to date information about remuneration in other companies. The Committee shall have full authority to commission any reports or surveys which it deems necessary to help it fulfil its obligations.

6.4   Although the Committee can seek the advice and assistance of any of the company's executives, it must ensure that this role is clearly separated from their role within the business.

7   Responsibilities

7.1   The responsibilities of the committee shall be as follows:

(i) To determine and agree with the board the framework or broad policy for the remuneration of the Chief Executive, the Chairman of the company and such other members of the executive management as it is designated to consider. The remuneration of non-executive directors shall be a matter for the executive members of the board. No director or manager shall be involved in any decisions as to his or her own remuneration. In order to assure his/her independence, the committee will also review and recommend to the Board the remuneration of the Company Secretary.

(ii) In determining the company's remuneration policy, to take into account all factors which the committee deems necessary. The objective of the company's remuneration policy shall be to ensure that members of the executive management of the company are provided with appropriate incentives to encourage enhanced performance and are, in a fair and responsible manner, rewarded for their individual contributions to the success of the company.

(iii) To liaise with the Nomination Committee to ensure that the remuneration of newly appointed executives is within the company's overall policy.

(iv) To determine targets for any performance-related pay schemes operated by the company and ask the board, when appropriate, to seek shareholder approval for any long-term incentive arrangements.

(v) Within the terms of the agreed policy, to determine the total individual remuneration package of each executive director including, where appropriate, bonuses, incentive payments and share options or other share awards.

(vi) To determine the policy for and scope of pension arrangements, service agreements, termination payments and compensation commitments in respect of the executive directors.

(vii) In determining such packages and arrangements, to give due regard to the comments and recommendations of the Combined Code as well as the UK Listing Authority's Listing Rules and associated guidance.

(viii) To review the remuneration policies of competitor companies and their relative performance, but ensure that such information is not used to create an upward ratchet of remuneration levels without a corresponding improvement in performance.

(ix) To be aware of, and oversee, any major changes in employee benefit structures throughout the company or group.

(x) To agree the policy for authorising the reimbursement of any claims for expenses from the Chief Executive and Chairman of the company.

(xi) To ensure that the company complies with all relevant provisions on the disclosure of the company's remuneration policy and practice, and remuneration payments (including pensions), as set out in the *Directors' Remuneration Report Regulations 2002* and the Combined Code.

8   Reporting

8.1   The Committee Chairman shall report formally to the board after each meeting on all matters within its duties and responsibilities.

8.2 The Remuneration Committee shall make appropriate recommendations to the board on any area within its remit where it considers that action or improvement is required.

8.3 The responsibilities and activities of the Remuneration Committee shall be disclosed in the annual report to shareholders.

8.4 The Committee Chairman shall attend the Annual General Meeting to respond to any shareholder questions on the activities of the Remuneration Committee.

9 Other

9.1 The Committee shall, at least once a year, review its own performance, constitution and terms of reference to ensure that it is operating at maximum effectiveness and, where necessary, recommend any changes to the board for approval.

Remuneration Committee

19

Risk Management

19 Risk Management

19.1 The Importance of Risk Management

> **At a Glance**
> * The management of business risk has become a significant main board responsibility.
> * Each business must decide on the most appropriate organisational risk management structure.
> * Where an executive risk management committee is appointed, its role should be set out in written terms of reference.
> * If there is no risk management committee, the audit committee should be responsible for reviewing the company's risk management systems.
> * Strategic and operational risks have now become the most significant issues for many companies.
> * The directors should begin by identifying the company's appetite for risk.
> * Companies may wish to make use of specialist resources in dealing with certain aspects of risk management.
> * Risk management is not an annual compliance issue, but an ongoing exercise that should be integral to the business.

19.2 Main Board Responsibility

There is much greater awareness today of the significance of business risk than was the case even 10 or 15 years ago. Business risk now has a very wide definition, encompassing both strategic and operational issues as well as financial risk, and the management of business risk has become a significant main board responsibility. Good risk management needs strong leadership from the top of the organisation, and a sound system of monitoring and reporting. Many aspects of business risk are now regulated by the Government (e.g. health and safety, employment, product liability, environmental issues) but they nevertheless remain a compliance risk for each company, as failure to comply with the relevant requirements may itself have a significant impact on the business. There is now a general consensus that risk management is not simply a matter of compliance but a process that can facilitate the growth and development of thecompany, by creating real and sustainable value as well as helping to protect investors. Good risk management also involves the management of both upside and downside risk. The focus is often on identifying and managing downside risk, but risk strategies to ensure that business opportunities are not missed are equally important.

19.3 Organisational Structure

Each business must decide on the most appropriate organisational risk management structure to suit its own specific circumstances. Options to consider include:

- appointing an executive risk management committee – this will usually include the CEO, finance director and the heads of the business operating units;
- appointing a head of risk management (usually at board level);
- developing an internal risk management function;
- appointing individual employees to deal with specialist issues (e.g. health and safety).

Businesses in the same industry or sector, facing similar risks, will often choose different risk management strategies, reflecting their differing individual circumstances. The internal audit function will also have an important role to play in the monitoring of systems and reporting of risk (see **CHAPTER 2**). Whatever organisational structure is chosen, risk management should be seen as an intrinsic element of the company's procedures and should involve all managers and employees to some degree.

19.4 Risk Management Committee

Where the company chooses to appoint an executive risk management committee, its role should be clearly distinguished from that of the audit committee. As with any board committee, it is advisable to develop written terms of reference, which might encompass the following remit:

- To approve the company's risk management strategy and risk management policy.
- To review reports on key risks prepared by business operating units, management and the board.
- To monitor the company's (or group's) overall exposure to risk and ensure that it remains within the limits set by the board.
- To assess the effectiveness of the company's (or group's) risk management systems.
- To provide early warning to the board on emerging risk issues and/or significant changes in the company's (or group's) exposure to risk.
- In conjunction with audit committee, to review the company's statement on internal control with reference to risk management, prior to endorsement by the board.

If an executive risk management committee is not appointed, the Combined Code specifically brings the review of the company's risk management systems within the remit of the audit committee (see **CHAPTER 2**). Whichever approach is adopted, companies may find it helpful to develop a responsibility checklist summarising the key areas of risk and who is responsible for monitoring the relevant issues.

19.5   Main Risks

Whilst the finance director will usually need to be involved in the company's risk management processes, it is important that risk management is not considered from a solely financial perspective, as this may lead to critical strategic or operating risks being underestimated or overlooked. Strategic and operational risks have now become the most significant issues for many companies. For instance, a survey by Deloitte and Touche in 1999 highlighted the following risks, in order of precedence, as being of most concern to directors:

- failure to manage major projects effectively;
- failure of corporate strategy;
- a failure to innovate;
- poor reputation and/or brand management and
- a lack of employee motivation and poor performance.

A particular difficulty here is that traditional risk management techniques tend to focus on risks where there is relatively strong historical data, and where the potential impact and likelihood of occurrence can therefore be identified with a degree of statistical probability. Such data is rarely available to support decisions on strategic and operational issues. For instance, there is currently concern that businesses may not be taking adequate measures to deal with risks arising from emerging issues, such as e-commerce, because of a failure to understand, identify and assess the underlying risks.

19.6   Appetite for Risk

Regardless of which organisational structure is adopted to deal with business risk, the first step must always be for the directors to identify the company's appetite for risk – in other words, the extent to which it is willing to accept a degree of risk. Some businesses by their very nature need to accept a certain level of risk in order to be able to operate. An important factor here is for the directors to develop an awareness of the relative risks of others in the same industry or sector, highlight any differences and understand why they are willing to take an alternative approach.

19.7   Using External Resources

Depending on the nature of the business and the potential risk areas, directors may wish to make use of specialist resources outside the company in approaching certain aspects of risk management. Areas where external consultants may be able to provide useful assistance include:

- risk assessment and risk modelling methodologies – these can be used to help identify the exposure of the business to different types of risk;
- business continuity planning, disaster recovery and crisis management, including personal safety issues (e.g. in hostage or similar situations);
- change/project management services and
- specialised advice on specific areas of risk (reputation, environmental issues).

Risk Management

19.8   Key Points on Risk Management

The key points to remember in relation to risk management are:

- risk management is not an annual compliance issue, but an ongoing exercise that should be integral to the business;
- the risk management process should be led at board level but should involve everyone in the organisation;
- the main focus should be on risks which are significant to the company as a whole;
- risk management procedures should be kept as simple and straightforward as possible;
- effective reporting mechanisms and early warning indicators should be developed as part of the risk management process.

19.9   The Risk Management Process

> **At a Glance**
> * Management needs to understand why, how and where business risks originate.
> * Each identified risk should be evaluated by assessing the likelihood of its occurrence and the potential impact on the company.
> * The most appropriate approach for dealing with each identified risk should be chosen.
> * Appropriate monitoring and reporting arrangements should also be put into place.
> * Management must be alert to the possibility of new risks arising and take prompt action to assess and deal with these.

19.10   Principal Elements of the Process

Risk management is an ongoing process that will usually involve the following steps:

- Identify the risks that are inherent in the company's strategy.
- Rank risks by likelihood and severity (see **PARAGRAPH 19.12**).
- Agree on the appropriate approach for dealing with each risk (see **PARAGRAPH 19.13**).
- Where appropriate, take action to eliminate or transfer risks.
- Implement controls to manage the remaining risks.
- Monitor the effectiveness of risk management actions and controls.
- Continuously improve the system, based on past experience.

19.11   Analysing Business Risk

Management needs to understand why, how and where business risks originate, both inside the organisation and as a result of external factors. A variety of techniques can be used to help managers assess the likelihood of risks crystallising and quantify the potential impact on the business, both financially and in operational terms. The Turnbull guidance (see **CHAPTER 14**) uses four categories to analyse and define risk:

- business or strategic risk;
- financial risk;
- operational risk and
- compliance risk.

An illustrative analysis of risks within these categories is given in **APPENDIX 2** to this chapter. Environmental risk may be included within compliance risk, or may need to be considered as a separate risk category, depending on its significance to the business. Other classifications of risk have been developed (e.g. hazard, market and enterprise) and may be found to be more helpful, depending on the nature of the company and its activities. In its briefing document 'No surprises: Working for better risk reporting' published in June 2002, the Institute of Chartered Accountants in England and Wales (ICAEW) concludes that some degree of commonality should be developed in the classification of risk in order to improve the comparability of risk reporting, but at present there is no overall consensus and each business is free to choose the analysis that best suits its own situation.

19.12 Ranking Risks by Likelihood and Severity

Each identified risk needs to be evaluated by assessing the likelihood of its occurrence and the potential impact on the company if the risk does crystallise. For instance, this can be done by using a risk matrix or diagram, plotting likelihood on one axis and severity of impact on the other:

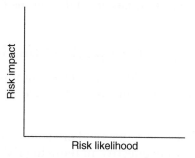

This should highlight the most significant risks, so that the initial effort can be concentrated in these areas, and then move on to lower category risks. The following diagram shows the order of priority in tackling identified risks:

High impact Low likelihood 2	High impact High likelihood 1
Low impact Low likelihood 4	Low impact High likelihood 3

Measuring the potential impact of risk may be difficult, especially where risks are interlinked. The financial impact of each identified risk needs to be taken into account but this will not always be the only consideration and non-financial data such as staff retention and satisfaction, trend analysis, benchmarking and segmental information may also need to be considered.

19.13   Dealing with Risk

Once identified, each risk can be handled in one of four ways:

- *Accept*: Accepting the risk without any further action is usually only practical if it is unlikely to crystallise in practice and/or the impact on the organisation is likely to be minimal. Very few risks will come into this category.
- *Transfer*: Transferring some or all of the risk to another party might involve:
  - taking out insurance, which involves weighing the cost of the insurance against the potential impact of the risk, should it occur;
  - the use of financial market instruments (e.g. hedges, futures and options) to limit the company's exposure;
  - outsourcing certain activities, although this will usually involve sharing the risk rather than transferring it or
  - including indemnities and similar risk-sharing provisions in contracts with suppliers and customers.
- *Reduce and manage*: Most risks are dealt with by reducing them as far as possible and then managing any residual risk by developing contingency plans which help to control or limit the impact if the risk crystallises.
- *Eliminate*: Where the potential impact of a risk is particularly significant, a business may have no alternative but to eliminate all possibility that the risk could crystallise (e.g. by ceasing a dangerous production process).

19.14   Monitoring and Reporting on Risk

Once appropriate actions have been taken, or procedures agreed, to reduce risk to an acceptable level, monitoring and reporting arrangements must be put into place to:

- confirm that the agreed actions and procedures are implemented in practice and
- confirm that they are effective in reducing risk to the required level or
- identify any further action that needs to be taken as a result of issues identified during the monitoring process.

The company's internal audit function will usually have a significant role to play here, and the external auditors will also provide feedback on any issues identified during their work (see CHAPTER 2). The monitoring and reporting process should enable directors and managers, and subsequently the company's shareholders, to see that business risks are being properly considered and addressed on a continuous basis.

19.15　Continuous Process

Risk management is not a one-off exercise. The business and economic environment is changing constantly, and sometimes rapidly, and it is important for management to be alert to new risks arising from developments in business activities and from changes in legislation and the general economic climate. Methods of assessing and managing risk also change over time and directors need to keep up with developments here as well.

19.16　Additional Guidance

There are numerous sources of additional guidance on risk management. In particular, the ICAEW publication 'Implementing Turnbull: A Boardroom Briefing' provides a useful overview of the risk management process in the context of corporate governance. It was issued in September 1999 to help directors with the implementation of the recommendations in the Turnbull Report (see **CHAPTER 14**) but many of the issues raised are still relevant. The document can be downloaded from the ICAEW website at http://www.icaew.co.uk/risk, which also provides access to other detailed guidance on risk management and links to other website with articles, news items and details of training events on risk management issues.

19.17　Reporting on Risk

At a Glance
* Both the Accounting Standards Board (ASB) Reporting Statement 'Operating and Financial Review' and the Combined Code recommend, and company law now requires, that directors discuss in the annual report the principal risks facing the business and how these are managed.
* Disclosures should be specific to the business and should concentrate on the most significant areas of risk.
* FRS 29 requires detailed disclosures on how financial instruments affect the company's risk profile and how risks arising from them are managed.

19.18　Investor Requirements

Investors need to have a proper understanding of the risks that a business faces, the measures used to evaluate those risks and the action taken to manage the company's exposure to risk. The ASB Reporting Statement 'Operating and Financial Review' (see **PARAGRAPH 10.80**) recommends that directors discuss in the annual report the main factors underlying the company's performance and the principal risks that the business faces. The Combined Code requirements on internal control reporting cover internal control in its widest sense and specifically include risk management (see **CHAPTER 14**).

Risk Management

For accounting periods beginning on or after 1 April 2005, the Companies Act 1985 specifies in greater detail the required content of the business review in the directors' report, and more stringent requirements still have been introduced for quoted companies with effect from 1 October 2007 under the Companies Act 2006 (see **PARAGRAPH 10.78**). The required disclosures now include a balanced and comprehensive review of the business and details of the principal risks and uncertainties that it faces.

The report 'A Review of Narrative Reporting By UK Listed Companies in 2006' published by the ASB in January 2006 (available at http://www.frc.org.uk/publications/pubs.cfm) considered the extent to which companies were complying with company law requirements on business reviews and adopting the more extensive best practice recommendations in the ASB Reporting Statement 'Operating and Financial Review'. One of the main areas identified for improvement was reporting on risks and uncertainties, where the ASB identified a tendency for companies to list all risks rather than identify the principal risks and uncertainties, and where reporting often concentrated on financial risks with little coverage of strategic, commercial and operational issues.

19.19   Relevant Disclosure

The present disclosure requirements are expressed in broad terms only and give directors a free hand to present the relevant issues in the specific context and circumstances of the business. An integrated risk management process should facilitate risk reporting that is relevant and concentrates on the risks that are most significant to the business. Providing a detailed listing of all the risks that the business might potentially face is more likely to mask the information that investors and other users of the report need to be able to identify. Reporting should also be balanced and should cover both 'downside risk' (i.e. the risk that something will go wrong) and 'volatility risk' (i.e. the uncertainty that gives the potential for gain as well as the risk of loss).

19.20   Risks Associated with Financial Instruments

Both UK and international accounting standards require the disclosure of detailed information in respect of financial instruments, although these apply primarily to listed companies at present. The detailed disclosures required by accounting standards are intended to help users of the accounts to understand and evaluate:

- the significance of financial instruments to the company's financial performance and financial position;
- the amount, timing and certainty of future cash flows relating to financial instruments and
- the nature and extent of the risks arising from the financial instruments to which the company is exposed at the reporting date.

The disclosures therefore focus on market risk, credit risk, liquidity risk and cash flow interest rate risk to which the company is exposed, and the policies and procedures used to manage these risks.

The standards do not prescribe the format, location or level of detail of the required disclosures, although guidance is provided on the issues that directors should take into account when making judgements on these. Given the wide variety of financial instruments available these days, the standards set out only minimum disclosure requirements, with the implication that these may need to be expanded on, depending on the particular circumstances of the business. The minimum disclosures include:

- Information on the extent and nature of the financial instruments, including significant terms and conditions that may affect the amount, timing and certainty of future cash flows.
- The accounting policies adopted, including the criteria for recognition and the basis of measurement adopted.
- Information about the entity's exposure to interest rate risk, including contractual repricing or maturity dates, and effective interest rates.
- Information about the entity's exposure to credit risk, including its maximum exposure to credit risk at the balance sheet date, without taking account of the fair value of any collateral, in the event of other parties failing to perform their obligations under financial instruments and any significant concentrations of credit risk.
- The fair value of each class of financial assets and financial liabilities in a way that allows this to be compared with the corresponding carrying amount in the balance sheet.
- Details of financial assets pledged as collateral for liabilities and contingent liabilities, together with any material terms and conditions relating to them.
- Details of any multiple embedded derivative features in compound financial instruments issued by the entity.
- For any defaults or breaches in the period in respect of loans payable at the balance sheet date, and any other breaches of loan agreements which permit the lender to demand repayment (unless the breach has been remedied, or the loan renegotiated, before the balance sheet date):
  - details of the default or breach;
  - the amount recognised at the balance sheet date in respect of the relevant loan;
  - whether the default has been remedied or the loan renegotiated before the date on which the financial statements were authorised for issue and
- detailed information in respect of any instruments that create a potentially significant exposure to risk, either individually or as a class.

A number of other detailed disclosure requirements apply in relation to the adoption of fair value accounting for financial assets and financial liabilities and also where hedge accounting has been applied.

Risk Management

19.21 Disclosures on Capital Structure

For accounting periods beginning on or after 1 January 2007, the UK and international accounting standards on financial instrument disclosures also encompass detailed disclosure requirements in respect of the company's capital. The aim is for companies to provide information that enables users of the financial statements to understand and evaluate the company's objectives, policies and processes for managing capital. The minimum disclosures include:

- qualitative information about the company's objectives, policies and processes for managing capital, including (but not limited to):
  - a description of what is managed as capital,
  - if the company is subject to externally imposed capital requirements, the nature of the requirements and how they are incorporated into the management of capital and
  - how the company is meeting its objectives for managing capital.
- summary quantitative data on what is managed as capital – for instance, some forms of subordinated debt may be regarded as capital, whilst certain components of equity may not be regarded as capital;
- any changes in the above details from the previous accounting period;
- whether the company has complied during the period with any externally imposed capital requirements and
- if it has not complied with such requirements, the consequences of the non-compliance.

The disclosures should be based on information provided internally to the company's key management personnel. Also, aggregate disclosure may not be sufficient to provide users with useful information or may distort a user's understanding of the entity's capital resources. For instance, where capital is managed in a number of different ways or the entity is subject to a number of different capital requirements, due to the nature of its activities or to the different jurisdictions in which it operates, separate information may need to be provided.

Appendix 1

Useful Websites on Risk Management Issues

Financial Reporting Council	www.frc.org.uk
Institute of Directors	www.iod.com
Institute of Chartered Secretaries and Administrators	www.icsa.org.uk
Institute of Chartered Accountants in England and Wales	www.icaew.co.uk
Institute of Internal Auditors (UK and Ireland)	www.iia.org.uk
Health and Safety Executive	www.hse.gov.uk/risk/
Department for Business, Enterprise and Regulatory Reform	www.berr.gov.uk
Business Link	www.businesslink.gov.uk
Association of Corporate Treasurers	www.treasurers.org

Risk Management

Appendix 2

Analysis of Risks

The following summary provides an analysis of the more common risks faced by a business. It should not be regarded as a comprehensive listing:

Financial risks
Credit risk
Market risk
Liquidity risk
Interest rate risk
Currency risk
Treasury risk
Going concern difficulties
Overtrading
Unidentified liabilities
Fraud
Misuse of resources
Misstatement of financial information
Accounting system breakdown
Unreliable management information

Operational risks
Reliance on key customers
Reliance on key suppliers
Loss of key management and staff
Lack of business continuity
Lack of succession planning
Skills shortage
Materials shortage
Loss of significant assets
Failure of new product or service
Poor customer satisfaction levels
Quality problems
Lack of employee motivation
Product liability problems
Loss of key contracts
Failure of major project
Failure to implement change
Industrial action
Breach of confidentiality

Strategic risks
Inappropriate business strategy
Failure to keep up with technological change
Failure to innovate
Competitive pressure on market share
Competitive pressure on prices
Poor brand management
Loss of reputation
Economic difficulties:
   Specific to the industry/sector
   General
Adverse Government policy
Inability to raise sufficient capital
Significant ethical problems
Missed business opportunities

Compliance risks
Breach of law, regulations or rules – e.g.
   Companies Act 1985/2006
   FSA Listing Rules
   Employment law
   Health and safety law
   Environmental regulations
   Competition law
Significant tax errors or problems
Significant VAT errors or problems

Training and Development

20 Training and Development

20.1 Introduction

The Combined Code states that:

> 'All directors should receive induction on joining the board and should regularly update and refresh their skills and knowledge.'
>
> For any non-executive, it is important to be clear about your current knowledge, skills and behaviours and to regularly review what additional training and development you need. The form of that training and development should be a healthy mix of the formal and the experiential.

The authors argue that this is a bit weak and that board training should commence much earlier on in the careers of people in business. They should possess the knowledge, skills and experience to perform these roles well.

One inhibitor to this has been the availability of suitable training courses. For example few MBA programmes have contained modules on board skills despite the fact that the ambition of most MBAs is to be on a board as soon as they can following graduation.

There are however now a number of training and development opportunities for non-executives in the UK. We have grouped these below under four headings: The Institute of Directors ('the IoD') (www.iod.com), the business schools, events run by professional intermediaries and finally those organised by member organisations other than the IoD.

20.2 The Institute of Directors

The IoD's philosophy statement includes the following:

> 'Directors realise that high standards of excellence and professionalism in the boardroom are essential for business success. The IOD has been supporting directors in their professional development for many years.'

The IoD's website contains a list of over 20 courses under the headings of the following:

- Strategy and leadership
- Finance

- Directors skills and
- Effective board

The IoD also has created the Chartered director qualification and runs a series of courses and examinations for those interested in achieving this qualification. At the time of writing the eligibility criteria were that:

- You must be a full Member or Fellow of the Institute and be registered for or have passed the Diploma examination in Company Direction.
- Your length of experience in a director role or equivalent should be either three full years' experience in a director level role for holders of a recognised degree or professional qualification or seven full years' experience in a director level role, for those who do not hold a recognised degree or professional qualification.

20.3   Business Schools

Most of the leading business schools now have a short course available on the subject. The most developed of the UK ones is the two-day Cranfield Non-Executive Directors Seminar. Details can be found on their website link at http://www.som.cranfield.ac.uk/som/executive/execcourse.asp?page=85

These courses typically involve sessions on the legal and technical aspects of the role together with case study-based role-plays on the practical aspects.

In the USA, the flagship course is Harvard Business School's Executive Education run by Professor Jay Lorsch, Harvard's guru on board effectiveness. The course normally attracts participants from all around the world. The material is naturally focussed on the USA.

20.4   Professional Intermediaries

Most of the larger firms of accountants and lawyers run excellent technical briefing meetings for non-executives. KPMG and Ernst and Young also run a series of highly selective events for their larger corporate contacts. These and those of the search firms usually take the form of expert speakers giving short addresses aimed at stimulating debate.

20.5   Training and Development Provided by Member Organisations

A number of member organisations for independent directors have developed over the last 20 years. Some of these are very international in their focus including 3i's people programmes and others more local or sector or interest based.

The philosophy of 3i's people programmes is very much geared to peer learning on an international basis and focussed on the added value aspects of the roles of chairman and independent directors as well as how they interface with executive management and shareholders in a private equity context.

Appendices

* Acknowledgements
* Bibliography
* Draft Letter from a Chairman to a Remuneration Consultant
* Draft Letter from Search Firm to Chairman with Regard to Appointing Them to Recruit a Non-executive Director
* Guidance Note on the Subject of Independent Professional Advice
* ICSA Guidance Note on Matters Reserved for the Board
* Terms of Reference for Higgs Review of Role and Effectiveness of Non-executives
* Appointment Letter for Non-executive Director
* Performance Evaluation Guidance
* Useful Websites

Acknowledgements

Baroness Hogg, Oliver Stocken, Tony Brierley, 3i group plc
Sir George Russell
Sir Derek Higgs
Sir Adrian Cadbury
Murray Steele Cranfield School of Management
Ian Barlow, David Bishop KPMG
Harvard Business School
Henley Management College
ICSA
Peter Brown Independent Remuneration Solutions
INSEAD
Institute of Directors
Kogan Page
Sean O'Hare Price Waterhouse Coopers
Virginia Bottomley Odgers

Bibliography

* Committee on Corporate governance Final report
  Sir Ronald Hampel
* Corporate Governance and Chairmanship Sir Adrian Cadbury 2002
  Oxford University Press ISBN 0-19-925200-9
* Directors Dilemmas: Patrick Dunne
  Kogan Page ISBN 0-7494-4345-6

- Directors remuneration: A report of the study Group: Sir Richard Greenbury
  Gee publishing ISBN 1-86089-012-1
- Final report committee on corporate governance 1998
  Gee Publishing ISBN 1-86089-034-2
- Harvard Business Review on Corporate Governance
  Harvard Business School Press ISBN 1-57851-237-9
- Harvard Business review on negotiation and conflict resolution
  ISBN-13: 978-1-57851-236-2
- Keeping Good company Jonathan Charkham: 1994 Oxford University Press
  Pawns or Potentates: Professor Jay Lorsch
  Harvard Business School Press
  ISBN 0-87584-216-X
- Report of the committee on the financial aspects of corporate governance 1992
  Gee Publishing ISBN 0-85258-915-8
  Running Board Meetings: Patrick Dunne
  ISBN 0-7494-4347-2
- The Company Chairman: Sir Adrian Cadbury
  Director Books Fitzwilliam Publishing Cambridge
  ISBN-10: 1-87055-526-0
  The Effective Director: Chris Pierce
- Kogan Page
  ISBN 0-7494-3551-8
- The Financial Times Guide to Strategy: Richard Koch
  Financial Times/Prentice Hall
  ISBN 0-273-65022-X
- The ICSA Remuneration committee guide Sean O'Hare
  ISBN 1-86072-333-0
- Tolleys Finance Directors Handbook
- Tolleys Company Meetings
- Tolleys Company Secretaries Handbook
- Tottel Publishing Company Acquisitions Handbook
  ISBN 978-1-84592-457-7
- The Pocket Director B Tricker
  Economist Books
  ISBN-10: 1-861-97000-5
- Winning Decisions, J. Edward Russo and Paul J. Schoemaker
  ISBN 0-385-50225-7
- Wharton on Making Decisions Stephen J. Hoch, Howard C. Kunreuther; The
  Wharton Scholl with Robert E. Gunther

Draft Letter from the Chairman of the Remuneration Committee to a Potential Remuneration Consultant

This letter should be sent by the chairman of the remuneration committee or signed on his behalf and not sent by the chief executive, finance director, company secretary or human resources director.

Dear Consultant

EITHER:

Further to our meeting this morning it gives me great pleasure to invite you to attend the next meeting of the remuneration committee of ABC plc at **[TIME]** on **[DATE]** dd/mm/yy. As chairman of the remuneration committee I am inviting you to attend to present your credentials and to quote for an assignment to help the committee review the following.

OR:

Further to your presentation to the remuneration committee of ABC plc this morning I am delighted to confirm that we would like you to undertake an assignment to help the committee review the following.

- The salaries and benefits packages of the chairman, senior independent director and non-executive directors.
- The short-term cash bonus schemes for the executive directors and the chief executives of the operating divisions.
- The current long-term incentive schemes which consist of a combination of share option schemes and long-term incentive plans.

Our primary objective is to build shareholder value by being competitive in the remuneration marketplace without overcompensating our executive team. Your report needs to be specific to us at this stage in our growth and not simply a generalised statistical study.

As chairman of the remuneration committee, I will be your client for this assignment but the chief executive, finance director, company secretary and human resources director, know it (has been/will be) commissioned and you can ask them for any additional information you need.

We can arrange for you to meet individual executives if you need to.

Your draft report should be delivered to me and not discussed with others in advance and the final report needs to be ready for the remuneration committee meeting on 10th August.

I enclose the following information:

1. Job specifications, employment contracts and CVs for the directors to be included in the review.

2. Information on the make up of the current executive directors' packages which is of course published in our annual accounts.
3. Copies of the last five years' accounts with the full remuneration committee report.
4. The legal documents setting up our share option and LTIP schemes.

We would like your review to include full details of other companies whose remuneration you consider to be relevant to ourselves, together with a recommendation on whether comparator group performance should become the criterion for full or partial encashment of our long-term incentive schemes. If you consider this a suitable mechanism would you please suggest what comparator companies should be included. If you need to check these with our principal institutional investors please give me a ring and I will arrange access for you.

We are naturally concerned to ensure that all parts of the remuneration package are as tax efficient for the company and the individuals as possible. We accept that you are not tax specialists but do expect that you have weighed up the issues of income and capital gains tax as well as national insurance in your recommendations.

If you need more information on executive directors' pension arrangements I am sure our company secretary XX would be delighted to provide you with it.

I look forward to receiving confirmation of your willingness to present on the dd/mm/yy.

OR:

I look forward to receiving confirmation of your willingness to accept this assignment on the following terms.

Terms as negotiated and we look forward to receiving your draft report on dd/mm/yy.

Yours sincerely
Mr John Brown
Chairman of remuneration committee
ABC plc

Draft Letter from Search Firm to Chairman with Regard to Appointing Them to Recruit a Non-executive Director

This letter is typically sent by the search firm to the chairman, who is typically also the chairman of the Nominations Committee. It is normally a summary of a meeting held to agree the points contained within and the chairman by signing his acceptance to it at the foot of the letter thereby appoints the search firm.

Dear Chairman

EITHER:

Thank you very much for giving us the opportunity to assist the selection process for your new non-executive director. X and I very much enjoyed our meeting with the nominations committee yesterday and delighted that you have chosen us for this very important assignment. Naturally we are disappointed that you have taken the decision not to use our comprehensive board audit process before proceeding with the search. However if you change your mind on this please just let us know.

As promised I am writing to summarise our discussions and cover the following:

- The background to the search.
- The specification and competencies we agreed that the ideal candidate should possess.
- Logistical considerations for candidates.
- Our process for conducting the search.
- Proposed remuneration for the new non-executive.
- Our fees, terms and conditions.

It is very important with regard to our description on the background to the company, the description of the role and the candidate specification, that you alert us to anything that you feel needs amendment. These will form the basis of the briefing notes to our researchers and when making our initial approaches to candidates.

The Background to the Search

This part of the letter will cover around a page of description of the company, its products, markets, geographical spread, headline financial performance and so on. It will also contain a section on the situation of the company and a statement of the company's strategy.

It will then provide a brief profile of the current board and describe why a new non-executive is being sought. For example:

> 'The recent acquisition by the company of XYZ Inc in the United States has significantly increased the scale and geographical spread of the business and the board feels it is important to strengthen the board as a result.'

or

> 'The company's core institutional shareholders have expressed a desire to see someone on the board with a financial background.'

or

> 'Following the announcement of the proposed retirement of X you are looking to succeed him with someone with similar experience but additionally the capability of becoming chairman of the Audit committee.'

The Specification and Competencies Required of the Ideal Candidate

We will be expecting all potential candidates to possess the generic characteristics and competencies of a good non-executive director for a company of your standing. At XYZ firm we believe these are the following:

(select from the list contained in 1.3.3, 1.3.4 and 1.3.5)

However given the specific circumstances of the company at this stage in its development we would emphasise the following:

- strategic ability;
- city credibility and
- international and organisational capability.

Before you see candidates, we will therefore have considered the following:

- Their track record of developing and implementing successful strategies relevant to the company and an appreciation of the key strategic variables facing you.
- Their track record and reputation with key institutional shareholders and advisers.
- Their appreciation of the issues currently facing the company with regard to investor relations.
- Their record in developing successful international operations and success in leading transformational acquisition integration.
- Their appreciation of the international challenges facing the company at the moment.

There then would be some additional specificity, for example:

'Given the background we will aim if possible to find someone who has lived and worked in Germany and built a successful German operation.'

or

'The acquisition in the US brings with it not just a US business but a collection of businesses in South America. We will therefore look for candidates with proven experience of successfully integrating acquisitions and operating experience of the US and Brazil etc.'

We understand that it is policy for all non-executives post their induction period to become members of either the Audit, remuneration or nominations committees. At this point you would like any candidates chosen for interview to be capable of serving on the X committee.

Logistical Considerations for Candidates

We understand the following will need to be taken into account:

Formal board meetings are held nine times pa. The locations and dates are set out in the attached appendix. There are also two additional board away days, one focussed on strategy, the other succession planning. The dates and locations for these are also in **APPENDIX X**.

Meetings of the X committee are held in the late afternoon preceding the board dinner on the day before the board meeting.

Because of the rotation of board meetings around the company's key operating subsidiary locations there is typically a dinner held the night before the board. It is expected that the non-executive will attend these dinners.

The company believes that physical presence is very important and so attendance of meetings by video or telephone is not acceptable.

You recognise that this is a significant time commitment and envisage it totalling 30 days pa.

Our Process for Conducting the Search

The key stages in the process and likely time frames once you have formally agreed the contents of this letter are as follows.

- Interviews with current board to give us a deeper understanding of the board and the special requirements of your situation (three weeks).
- Sourcing of potential candidates (four weeks).
- Presentation to the nominations committee of a shortlist of potential candidates (five or six) that we would like to approach (one week later).
- Approaching candidates and initial interviews conducted by ourselves (four weeks).
- Interviews with the chosen panel (four weeks).
- Agreement of terms in principle.
- Referencing and candidates' own due diligence.

Naturally some of these activities will run in parallel so we would expect that you should be able to have someone on board in time for your [Month] board meeting.

We would suggest that the presentation to the nominations committee takes place by conference call with a detailed report on each candidate supplied in advance.

Given our considerable experience of these selection processes we have produced several guidance notes for interviewing prospective non-executives. I have included these.

With regard to referencing we will provide a substantive referencing report to you and in addition provide you with contact details for you to make your own enquiries. If you would like and candidates are in agreement we can also undertake psychometric testing. We can also suggest methods for successful induction if this would be helpful. The additional fees for these extra services and our complete board audit product are detailed below.

I will be taking personal responsibility for this assignment myself and will be supported by X and Y. In addition given our global reach and superb pool of talent in the USA I will be involving Z from our New York office.

Remuneration for the Chosen Candidate

The basic components of remuneration will be the following:

- A fee of £35,000 pa based on an assumed time commitment of 30 days.
- An additional fee of £5000 pa payable for membership of board committees.
- An agreed basis of payment for circumstances where the director's time commitment is significantly greater than originally envisaged (e.g. during a major transaction).
- A description of allowable expenses.

- Clarity over Directors and Officers liability insurance, that is whether it is paid for by the company or the individual and the details of the cover provided (see **CHAPTER 13** for more information relating to Directors and Officers liability insurance).
- A proposal regarding obtaining equity in the company where relevant, for example in venture capital or private equity backed businesses.
- Services provided by the company to enable the director to carry out his duties (e.g. access to legal advice).

Our Fees, Terms and Conditions

Our professional fees for this assignment will be £50,000, payable in four equal instalments. The first will be upon acceptance of this letter, the second upon offer of the position, the third upon appointment of the successful candidate and the fourth three months after appointment. We will also make an additional charge of 10% of the fee to cover other expenses excluding any international travel. VAT of course is chargeable on both on fees and expenses and invoices are payable within 14 days.

Should acceptable candidates not have been found within the next three months we will continue to search on your behalf for no additional cost.

If for any reason the search should be cancelled our fees will be adjusted to reflect the time commitment and expenses incurred up to that point.

In the event of potential candidates being hired by the company for positions other than the specific non-executive director appointment described above we would make an additional charge of £30,000.

A detailed copy of our firm's approach to doing business is attached.

I have to say I am very much looking forward to starting work and consider this a great assignment for our business. We are impressed with the thoroughness with which you have conducted the tendering process.

Kind regards
Yours sincerely
Joe Smooth

Our Approach to Doing Business

Our General Approach

Getting the right person is our mission. A rigorous approach to selection is therefore critical in achieving this aim. We believe that the track record of a candidate should be the starting point for understanding their capability in the proposed role, so place a great deal of emphasis on thorough research into candidates' backgrounds.

Confidentiality and Data Protection

It is our policy not to divulge our client's identity without prior approval. We would not normally inform candidates of the client's identity in any event until we had established that they might be suitably qualified and interested in the role. We will do everything we can to avoid any speculation in the industry recognising that given the specification this may not be achievable in practice.

The client will also undertake to use material provided by our firm in connection with this search strictly for the purposes of assessing and selecting a candidate. The client will not disclose any material to anyone other than those in the client's organisation who are involved in the selection process. Any materials provided remain the property of our firm and should be returned if requested.

The client will not attempt to contact any candidate directly without our firm's prior knowledge and agreement.

The client undertakes to indemnify our firm against all losses, expenses and liabilities incurred by our firm and its directors or employees arising directly or indirectly as a result of the loss of unauthorised use or disclosure of any part of the material, or from breach of the terms of this engagement.

Exclusivity

By accepting this assignment we undertake not to undertake non-executive assignments for any of the specified competitors in the list below.

Sourcing Candidates

We will develop through a combination of systematic research and the extensive database that we have, a comprehensive list of potential candidates. We always welcome suggestions from the board and will ask for them as part of our initial interviews. In addition we will need to know those individuals who may appear to be suitably qualified but who you deem not to be suitable candidates. It would also be helpful for you to provide us with candidates you have considered for non-executive positions with the company before.

Reference Information

Referencing information will contain third party opinion (as opposed to factual information) in relation to a candidate. The client should understand that such opinion is of the third party, and our firm makes no guarantee or endorsement as to its accuracy or reasonableness. Naturally all materials are supplied in good faith, however we will not accept any responsibility for any errors or omissions in the material or for any loss or damage arising out of any reliance on the material.

Client Referrals

Given the impressive networks of current board members we would expect that the board may already have in mind suitable candidates to nominate for entry into the selection process. These candidates should be referred to us as soon as possible so we can add them to the pool generated by our systematic research. It is critical that they are treated on the same basis as other candidates are evaluated to the same high standards. For the sake of clarity there is no reduction in fee if the candidate chosen was originally suggested by the client.

Negotiating Packages

Our approach is to agree with the client the parameters of the package to be offered to the chosen candidate and then for us to agree this with the candidate in question. It is our policy for non-executive appointments to make this clear at earliest possible stage to avoid any embarrassment later.

Ensuring a Successful Appointment

It is our policy to follow up all assignments 90 days following the appointment with a call to the chairman and to the new non-executive to evaluate the effectiveness of the appointment. We will then feed back to the nominations committee the results of this.

ICSA Guidance Note 011102 Model Board Resolution on Independent Professional Advice

The London Stock Exchange's principles of good Governance and Code of Best Practice (The Combined Code) states in article A.1.3:

> 'There should be a procedure agreed by the board for directors, in the furtherance of their duties, to take independent professional advice if necessary, at the company's expense.'

The following is suggested wording for a resolution of the board to give effect to the above principle.

> 'It was resolved THAT
> Subject to the following procedures and limitations, the directors of the company shall, both individually and collectively, have the right to consult the company's professional advisers [and, if necessary,] [or] [and if they are not satisfied with the advice received,] see independent professional advice at the company's expense in the furtherance of their duties as directors of the company.

1. A director shall give prior notice to [the chairman, the company secretary of the senior non-executive director] [the company secretary] [the chairman] of his or her intention to seek independent professional advice under this procedure and shall provide the name(s) of any professional advisers he proposes to instruct together with a brief summary of the subject matter.
2. [the company secretary shall provide written acknowledgement of receipt of the notification which shall state whether the fees for the professional advice sought are payable by the company under these procedures.] A director shall obtain the prior approval of [the chairman or in his absence the Deputy chairman] [senior independent non-executive] [where the fees of the independent professional adviser are likely to exceed a certain amount].

For the avoidance of doubt, the above restrictions shall not apply to executive directors acting in the furtherance of their executive responsibilities and within their delegated powers.

Independent professional advice for the purposes of this resolution shall include legal advice and the advice of accountants and other professional advisers on matters of law, accounting and other regulatory matters but shall exclude advice concerning the personal interests of the director concerned (such as his service contract with the company or his dealings in the company's securities or disputes with the company).

[Any advice obtained under this procedure shall be made available to the other members of the board, if the board so requests.]'

Paragraph 1 is intended to ensure that the company is aware that a director intends to take independent advice.

Paragraph 2 is suggested for those companies who seek to place restrictions on directors' freedom to consult professional advisers and who require prior notification to be given. The company secretary's statement as to whether the company would be liable to pay the fees could be guidance only.

An Alternative

A much neater solution would be to authorise a member of the board (preferably the senior non-executive director) to commit the company to pay or contribute (up to a fixed amount) to the costs of independent advice. Whenever the director commits the company, he could be required to notify the chairman or other director.

ICSA Guidance Note 011104 Matters Reserved for the Board

For latest updates visit Institute of Chartered Secretaries and Administrators (ICSA) website (www.icsa.org.uk) Guidance notes section.

No matter how effective a board of directors may be it is not possible for the directors to have hands on involvement in every area of the company's business. An effective board controls the business but delegates day to day responsibility to the executive management. That said there are a number of matters which are required, or that should be in the interests of the company, only to be decided by the board of directors as a whole. It is incumbent upon the board to make it clear what these Matters reserved for the Board are.

The relative importance of some matters included in this Guidance note will vary according to the size and nature of the company's business. For example all companies will have a different view on the establishment of financial limits for transactions which should be referred to the board. Equally, there may well be items not mentioned in the Guidance note which some companies (e.g. those subject to additional forms of external regulation) would wish to include in their own schedule.

Multiple Signatures

In drawing up a schedule of Matters reserved for the Board, companies should clarify which transactions require multiple board signatures on the relevant documentation.

Delegation

Certain of the matters included in this Guidance note should, under the recommendations of the Cadbury Committee and/or the Combined Code, be the responsibility of the audit, nomination or remuneration committee. However, full delegation is not permitted in these cases as the final decision on the matter is required to be taken by the whole board.

Urgent Matters

In drawing up this schedule of Matters reserved for the Board it is important to establish procedures for dealing with matters that have to be dealt with urgently, often between board meetings. It is recommended that, where practical, the approval of all of the directors should be obtained by means of written resolution. In all cases however the procedures should balance the need for urgency with the overriding principle that each director should be given as much information as possible and have an opportunity to requisition an emergency meeting of the board to discuss the matter prior to commitment of the company.

The following schedule has been produced to assist boards of directors and company secretaries in preparing a schedule of Matters reserved for the Board in accordance with good corporate governance.

Items marked * are not considered suitable for delegation to a committee of the board, for example because of Companies Act requirements or because, under the recommendations of the Cadbury Report or Combined Code, they are the responsibility of an audit, nomination or remuneration committee, with final decision required to be taken by the board as a whole.

Companies Act Requirements

1.* Approval of interim and final financial statements.
2.* Approval of the interim and final dividend and recommendation of the final dividend.
3.* Approval of any significant changes in accounting policies or practices.
4.* Appointment or removal of the company secretary.
5.* Remuneration of the auditors [where, as is usual, shareholders have delegated this power to the board] and recommendations for the appointment or removal of auditors [possibly following recommendations of the audit committee].
6. Resolutions and corresponding documentation to be put forward to the shareholders at a General Meeting.

Stock Exchange/Financial Services Authority

7.* Approval of all circulars and listing particulars [approval of routine documents such as periodic circulars re scrip dividend procedures or exercise of conversion rights could be delegated to a committee].

8.* Approval of press releases concerning matters decided by the board.

Board Membership and Board Committees

9. *Board appointments and removals and any special terms and conditions attached to the appointment [subject to recommendations of the remuneration committee].

10. *Terms of reference of chairman, chief executive and other executive directors.

11. *Terms of reference and membership of board committees.

Management

12. *Approval of the Group's long-term objectives and commercial strategy.

13. *Approval of the annual operating and capital expenditure budgets.

14. *Changes relating to the Group's capital structure or its status as a plc.

15. *Appointments to the boards of subsidiaries.

16. *Terms and conditions of directors and senior executives.

17. *Changes to the Group's management and control structure.

Cadbury/Combined Code Recommendations

18. Major capital projects.

19. Material, either by reason of size or strategically, contracts of the company [or any subsidiary] in the ordinary course of business, e.g. bank borrowings [above a certain amount] and acquisition or disposal of fixed assets [above a certain amount].

20. Contracts of the company [or any subsidiary] not in the ordinary course of business, e.g. loans and repayments [above a certain amount]; foreign currency transactions [above a certain amount]; major acquisitions or disposals [above a certain amount].

21. Major investments [including the acquisition or disposal of interests of more than [5] per cent in the voting shares of any company or the making of any takeover bid].

22. Risk management strategy.

23. Treasury policies [including foreign currency exposure].

Miscellaneous

24. Review of the company's overall corporate governance arrangements.

25. Major changes in the rules of the company's pension scheme, or changes of trustees or [when this subject is subject to the approval of the company] changes in the fund management arrangements.

26. Major changes in employee share schemes and the allocation of share options.
27. Formulation of policy regarding charitable donations.
28. Political donations.
29. Approval of the company's principal professional advisers.
30. Prosecution, defence or settlement of litigation [involving above [a certain amount] or being otherwise material to the interests of the company].
31. Internal control arrangements.
32. Health and Safety policy.
33. Environmental policy.
34. Directors and Officers liability insurance.
35. This schedule of matters reserved for board decisions.

Terms of Reference for the Higgs Review of the Role and Effectiveness of Non-executive Directors

Objective

Building on the work of the Company Law review and the Myners review, the Government has commissioned Derek Higgs to lead a short independent review of the role and effectiveness of non-executive directors in the UK.

Background

Non-executive directors play a central role in UK corporate governance. The Company Law review noted 'a growing body of evidence from the USA suggesting that companies with a strong contingent of non-executives produce superior performance'.

In the decade since the introduction of the Cadbury Code, the role of non-executives has undoubtedly strengthened.

From the point of view of UK productivity, performance, progressive strengthening of the quality and role of non-executives is strongly desirable.

Proposal

Though the Government has an open mind, its preferred starting point in this area is, if possible, an approach based on best practice, not regulation or legislation.

The Government believes it would be valuable for a senior figure from the business world, building on the work of the Company Law review, of Myners, and of the Institute of Directors and others, to undertake a review to assess:

- the population of non-executive directors in the UK – who are they, how are they appointed, how the pool might be widened, etc.;
- their 'independence';
- their effectiveness;

- accountability: their relationship – actual and potential – with institutional investors;
- issues relating to non-executive directors' remuneration;
- the role of the Combined Code;
- what, if anything, could be done – by individual boards, by institutional investors, by Government or otherwise – to strengthen the quality, independence and effectiveness of non-executive directors.

This review will look at this in an international context.

The aim of the review is:

- to build and publish an accurate picture of the status quo;
- to lead a debate on these issues, especially in the business and financial worlds;
- to make any recommendations – to Government and to others – which the reviewer thinks appropriate.

Sample Letter of Non-executive Director Appointment

On [date], upon the recommendation of the nomination committee, the board of [company] ('the Company') has appointed you as non-executive director. I am writing to set out the terms of your appointment. It is agreed that this is a contract for services and is not a contract of employment.

Appointment

Your appointment will be for an initial term of three years commencing on [date], unless otherwise terminated earlier by and at the discretion of either party upon [one month's] written notice. Continuation of your contract of appointment is contingent on satisfactory performance and re-election at forthcoming Annual General Meetings (AGMs). Non-executive directors are typically expected to serve two three-year terms, although the board may invite you to serve for an additional period.

Time Commitment

Overall we anticipate a time commitment of [number] days per month after the induction phase. This will include attendance at [monthly] board meetings, the AGM, [one] annual board away day, and [at least one] site visit per year. In addition, you will be expected to devote appropriate preparation time ahead of each meeting.

By accepting this appointment, you have confirmed that you are able to allocate sufficient time to meet the expectations of your role. The agreement of the chairman should be sought before accepting additional commitments that might affect the time you are able to devote to your role as a non-executive director of the company.

Role

Non-executive directors have the same general legal responsibilities to the company as any other director. The board as a whole is collectively responsible for promoting the success of the company by directing and supervising the company's affairs. The board:

- provides entrepreneurial leadership of the company within a framework of prudent and effective controls which enable risk to be assessed and managed;
- sets the company's strategic aims, ensures that the necessary financial and human resources are in place for the company to meet its objectives and reviews management performance; and
- sets the company's values and standards and ensures that its obligations to its shareholders and others are understood and met.

In addition to these requirements of all directors, the role of the non-executive has the following key elements:

- *Strategy*: Non-executive directors should constructively challenge and contribute to the development of strategy.
- *Performance*: Non-executive directors should scrutinise the performance of management in meeting agreed goals and objectives and monitor the reporting of performance.
- *Risk*: Non-executive directors should satisfy themselves that financial information is accurate and that financial controls and systems of risk management are robust and defensible.
- *People*: Non-executive directors are responsible for determining appropriate levels of remuneration of executive directors and have a prime role in appointing, and where necessary removing, senior management and in succession planning.

Fees

You will be paid a fee of £ [amount] gross pa which will be paid monthly in arrears, [plus [number] ordinary shares of the company pa, both of] which will be subject to an annual review by the board. The company will reimburse you for all reasonable and properly documented expenses you incur in performing the duties of your office.

Outside Interests

It is accepted and acknowledged that you have business interests other than those of the company and have declared any conflicts that are apparent at present. In the event that you become aware of any potential conflicts of interest, these should be disclosed to the chairman and company secretary as soon as apparent.

[The board of the company have determined you to be independent according to the provision of the Combined Code.]

Confidentiality

All information acquired during your appointment is confidential to the company and should not be released, either during your appointment or following termination (by whatever means), to third parties without prior clearance from the chairman.

Your attention is also drawn to the requirements under both legislation and regulation as to the disclosure of price sensitive information. Consequently you should avoid making any statements that might risk a breach of these requirements without prior clearance from the chairman or company secretary.

Induction

Immediately after appointment, the Company will provide a comprehensive, formal and tailored induction. This will include the information pack recommended by the ICSA, available at www.icsa.org.uk. We will also arrange for site visits and meetings with senior and middle management and the company's auditors. We will also arrange for you to meet major investors in the first 12 months of your appointment.

Review Process

The performance of individual directors and the whole board and its committees is evaluated annually. If, in the interim, there are any matters which cause you concern about your role you should discuss them with the chairman as soon as is appropriate.

Insurance

The Company has directors' and officers' liability insurance and it is intended to maintain such cover for the full term of your appointment. The current indemnity limit is £ [amount]; a copy of the policy document is attached.

Independent Professional Advice

Occasions may arise when you consider that you need professional advice in the furtherance of your duties as a director. Circumstances may occur when it will be appropriate for you to seek advice from independent advisers at the company's expense. A copy of the board's agreed procedure under which directors may obtain such independent advice is attached. The Company will reimburse the full cost of expenditure incurred in accordance with the attached policy.

Committees

This letter refers to your appointment as a non-executive director of the Company. In the event that you are also asked to serve on one or more of the board committees this will be covered in a separate communication setting out the committee(s)'s terms of reference, any specific responsibilities and any additional fees that may be involved.

Guidance on Performance Evaluation

The Combined Code reflects that is to say that the performance of the board as a whole, of its committees and of its members, is evaluated at least once a year. Companies should disclose in their annual report whether such performance evaluation is taking place.

It is the responsibility of the chairman to select an effective process and to act on its outcome. The use of an external third party to conduct the evaluation will bring objectivity to the process.

The evaluation process will be used constructively as a mechanism to improve board effectiveness, maximise strengths and tackle weaknesses. The results of board evaluation should be shared with the board as a whole, while the results of individual assessments should remain confidential between the chairman and the non-executive director concerned.

The following are some of the questions that should be considered in a performance evaluation. They are, however, by no means definitive or exhaustive and companies will wish to tailor the questions to suit their own needs and circumstances.

The responses to these questions and others should enable boards to assess how they are performing and to identify how certain elements of their performance areas might be improved.

Performance Evaluation of the Board

- How well has the board performed against any performance objectives that have been set?
- What has been the board's contribution to the testing and development of strategy?
- What has been the board's contribution to ensuring robust and effective risk management?
- Is the composition of the board and its committees appropriate, with the right mix of knowledge and skills to maximise performance in the light of future strategy? Are inside and outside the board relationships working effectively?
- How has the board responded to any problems or crises that have emerged and could or should these have been foreseen?
- Are the matters specifically reserved for the board the right ones?
- How well does the board communicate with the management team, company employees and others? How effectively does it use mechanisms such as the AGM and the annual report?
- Is the board as a whole up to date with latest developments in the regulatory environment and the market?

- How effective are the board's committees? (Specific questions on the performance of each committee should be included such as, for example, their role, their composition and their interaction with the board.)

The processes that help underpin the board's effectiveness should also be evaluated. For example:

- Is appropriate, timely information of the right length and quality provided to the board and is management responsive to requests for clarification or amplification? Does the board provide helpful feedback to management on its requirements?
- Are sufficient board and committee meetings of appropriate length held to enable proper consideration of issues? Is time used effectively?
- Are board procedures conducive to effective performance and flexible enough to deal with all eventualities?

In addition, there are some specific issues relating to the chairman which should be included as part of an evaluation of the board's performance. For example:

- Is the chairman demonstrating effective leadership of the board?
- Are relationships and communications with shareholders well managed?
- Are relationships and communications within the board constructive?
- Are the processes for setting the agenda working? Do they enable board members to raise issues and concerns?
- Is the company secretary being used appropriately and to maximum value?

Performance Evaluation of the Non-executive Director

The chairman and other board members should consider the following issues and the individual concerned should also be asked to assess themselves. For each non-executive director:

- How well prepared and informed are they for board meetings and is their meeting attendance satisfactory?
- Do they demonstrate a willingness to devote time and effort to understand the company and its business and a readiness to participate in events outside the boardroom, such as site visits?
- What has been the quality and value of their contributions at board meetings?
- What has been their contribution to development of strategy and to risk management?
- How successfully have they brought their knowledge and experience to bear in the consideration of strategy?
- How effectively have they probed to test information and assumptions? Where necessary, how resolute are they in maintaining their own views and resisting pressure from others?
- How effectively and proactively have they followed up their areas of concern?
- How effective and successful are their relationships with fellow board members, the company secretary and senior management? Does their performance and behaviour engender mutual trust and respect within the board?

- How actively and successfully do they refresh their knowledge and skills and are they up to date with:
  - the latest developments in areas such as corporate governance framework and financial reporting?
  - the industry and market conditions?
- How well do they communicate with fellow board members, senior management and others, for example shareholders. Are they able to present their views convincingly yet diplomatically and do they listen and take on board the views of others?

Useful Websites

- www.icsa.org.uk
- www.dti.gov.uk/cld/non_exec_review/
- http://www.idpmultimedia.com.au
- www.iod.co.uk
- www.3i.com
- www.boardseat.com
- http://www.boardex.com/
- http://www.conference-board.org/
- http://www.calpers-governance.org/principles/international/ceogo.com
- http://www.dti.gov.uk/cld/non_exec_review/

Table of Statutes

Table of Statutory Instruments

Index

Printed and bound by CPI Group (UK) Ltd, Croydon, CR0 4YY

08/05/2025

01864864-0001